New Perspectives on

MICROSOFT®
FRONTPAGE® 2002

Comprehensive

Handwritten notes:
Info folknow
— Practic ?
Shift enter
Blockbild st 1000
mimic 91

**COURSE
TECHNOLOGY**

THOMSON LEARNING

New Perspectives on Microsoft® FrontPage® 2002—Comprehensive
is published by Course Technology.

Managing Editor:
Greg Donald

Senior Editor:
Donna Gridley

Senior Product Manager:
Kathy Finnegan

Product Manager:
Melissa Hathaway

Technology Product Manager:
Amanda Young

Editorial Assistant:
Jessica Engstrom

Marketing Manager:
Sean Teare

Developmental Editor:
Judy Adamski

Production Editor:
Daphne Barbas

Composition:
GEX Publishing Services

Text Designer:
Meral Dabcovich

Cover Designer:
Efrat Reis

New Perspectives on

MICROSOFT®
FRONTPAGE® 2002

Comprehensive

JESSICA EVANS

COURSE
TECHNOLOGY

THOMSON LEARNING

Australia • Canada • Mexico • Singapore • Spain • United Kingdom • United States

APPROVED COURSEWARE

What does this logo mean?

It means this courseware has been approved by the Microsoft® Office User Specialist Program to be among the finest available for learning Microsoft FrontPage® 2002. It also means that upon completion of this courseware, you may be prepared to become a Microsoft Office User Specialist.

What is a Microsoft Office User Specialist?

A Microsoft Office User Specialist is an individual who has certified his or her skills in one or more of the Microsoft Office desktop applications of Microsoft Word, Microsoft Excel, Microsoft PowerPoint®, Microsoft Outlook® or Microsoft Access, or in Microsoft Project. The Microsoft Office User Specialist Program typically offers certification exams at the "Core" and "Expert" skill levels.* The Microsoft Office User Specialist Program is the only Microsoft approved program in the world for certifying proficiency in Microsoft Office desktop applications and Microsoft Project. This certification can be a valuable asset in any job search or career advancement.

More Information:

To learn more about becoming a Microsoft Office User Specialist, visit www.mous.net

To purchase a Microsoft Office User Specialist certification exam, visit www.DesktopIQ.com

To learn about other Microsoft Office User Specialist approved courseware from Course Technology, visit www.course.com/NewPerspectives/TeachersLounge/mous.cfm

* The availability of Microsoft Office User Specialist certification exams varies by application, application version and language. Visit www.mous.net for exam availability.

Microsoft, the Microsoft Office User Specialist Logo, PowerPoint and Outlook are either registered trademarks or trademarks of Microsoft Corporation in the United States and/or other countries.

Preface

New Perspectives

Course Technology is the world leader in information technology education. The New Perspectives Series is an integral part of Course Technology's success. Visit our Web site to see a whole new perspective on teaching and learning solutions.

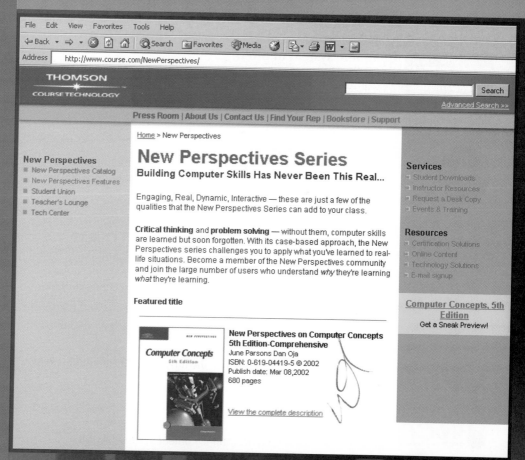

New Perspectives — Building Computer Skills Has Never Been This Real

Why *New Perspectives will work for you.*

Critical thinking and **problem solving**—without them, computer skills are learned but soon forgotten. With its **case-based** approach, the New Perspectives Series challenges students to apply what they've learned to real-life situations. Become a member of the New Perspectives community and watch your students not only **master** computer skills, but also **retain** and carry this **knowledge** into the world.

New Perspectives catalog
Our online catalog is never out of date! Go to the Catalog link on our Web site to check out our available titles, request a desk copy, download a book preview, or locate online files.

Complete system of offerings
Whether you're looking for a Brief book, an Advanced book, or something in between, we've got you covered. Go to the Catalog link on our Web site to find the level of coverage that's right for you.

Instructor materials
We have all the tools you need—data files, solution files, figure files, a sample syllabus, and ExamView, our powerful testing software package.

How well do your students know Microsoft Office?
Experience the power, ease, and flexibility of SAM XP and TOM. These innovative software tools provide the first truly integrated technology-based training and assessment solution for your applications course. Click the Tech Center link to learn more.

Get certified
If you want to get certified, we have the titles for you. Find out more by clicking the Teacher's Lounge link.

Interested in online learning?
Enhance your course with rich online content for use through MyCourse 2.0, WebCT, and Blackboard. Go to the Teacher's Lounge to find the platform that's right for you.

Your link to the future is at www.course.com/NewPerspectives

What you need to know about this book.

- Student Online Companion takes students to the Web for additional work.

- ExamView testing software gives you the option of generating a printed test, LAN-based test, or test over the Internet.

- New Perspectives Labs provide students with self-paced practice on computer-related topics.

- Students will appreciate the tour of an existing Web site in Tutorial 1, where they view and use Web pages that they will develop over the course of the book. This approach ensures that students will have a solid foundation on which to build as they progress through the tutorials.

- Each tutorial emphasizes planning as a part of Web site development, so students are always focused on creating a single part of a larger site in the context of an overall site plan.

- The book emphasizes and integrates Web site design principles throughout the hands-on coverage to ensure that students are learning about overall site design and other important information they'll need to know as they develop their own Web sites.

- Upon completing this book, students will be able to plan, create, develop, publish, and maintain a Web site that includes shared borders, link bars, form components, search components, hit counters, banner ad managers, data access pages, and Office XP components.

- The scenarios in our end-of-tutorial exercises will hold students' interest, and the number of exploratory exercises will challenge students and give them a sense of accomplishment.

- This book is certified at the MOUS Expert level for FrontPage 2002!

CASE	TROUBLE?	SESSION 1.1	QUICK CHECK	RW
Tutorial Case Each tutorial begins with a problem presented in a case that is meaningful to students. The case sets the scene to help students understand what they will do in the tutorial.	**TROUBLE? Paragraphs** These paragraphs anticipate the mistakes or problems that students may have and help them continue with the tutorial.	**Sessions** Each tutorial is divided into sessions designed to be completed in about 45 minutes each. Students should take as much time as they need and take a break between sessions.	**Quick Check Questions** Each session concludes with conceptual Quick Check questions that test students' understanding of what they learned in the session.	**Reference Windows** Reference Windows are succinct summaries of the most important tasks covered in a tutorial. They preview actions students will perform in the steps to follow.

BRIEF CONTENTS

TABLE OF CONTENTS

Tutorial 3   FP 3.01

Using Lists, Hyperlinks, Pictures, and the Tasks List

Tutorial 6   FP 6.01

Publishing a Web Site

Preparing the Search and Feedback Web Pages FP 6.01

Additional Case 1   ADD 1

*Creating a Web Site for Security
Shredding, Inc.*

Additional Case 2   ADD 6

*Creating a Web Site for Pet Adoption
Services, Inc.*

Additional Case 3   ADD 11

*Creating a Web Site for Marty Sharik,
Realtor*

Acknowledgments

I would like to thank reviewers Rebekah Tidwell of Carson Newman College and Lee University, and Sandy Weber of Gateway Technical College, for their excellent comments and suggestions. This book is a better product because of your efforts.

I have always been blessed to be a part of the best publishing team in the business. I would like to thank all of the people at Course Technology who have made this book a success. I am grateful to Donna Gridley, Senior Editor, for the opportunities she has given me, and to Kathy Finnegan, Senior Product Manager, who has endured many long, complicated conversations about FrontPage Server Extensions without abandoning ship. I would also like to thank my Developmental Editor, Judy Adamski, for her constant support and wisdom, and her willingness to experiment endlessly on THE COMPUTER to figure out why our Web pages sometimes looked different. And a final note of thanks goes to Daphne Barbas, one of the best production editors with whom I have ever worked, for making sure that this book was published quickly and accurately.

It's always the case that I can write an entire book, but when it comes time to thank people who mean a great deal to me, I don't know where to start. I have been fortunate to be surrounded by people who support me in my endeavors. At the very top of that list is my husband, Richard. Our daughter Hannah is a great source of happiness in our lives. You are the best family in the whole world.

And finally, to our friend Herman Gotcher, who provided love, strength, and comic relief in good times and bad, and many, many, happy memories that will last a lifetime…we miss you already.

Jessica Evans

New Perspectives on

MICROSOFT®

FRONTPAGE® 2002

Read **This Before You Begin**

To the Student

Data Disks

To complete the Level I tutorials, Review Assignments, and Case Problems, you will need either one or six Data Disks. Your instructor will either provide you with these Data Disk(s) or ask you to make your own.

If you are making your own Data Disk(s), you will need to copy a set of folders from a file server, standalone computer, or the Web onto your disk(s). Your instructor will tell you which computer, drive letter, and folders contain the files you need. You could also download the folders by going to **www.course.com** and following the instructions on the screen.

Before creating your Data Disk(s), check with your instructor to find out where you will be storing your Web sites. If you will store your Web sites on a hard or network drive, you can put all of the Data Files on **one** floppy disk. In that case, you will copy the My Webs, Tutorial.02, Tutorial.03, Tutorial.04, Tutorial.05, and Tutorial.06 folders onto one blank, formatted high-density disk and label it Data Disk 1: Tutorials 1-6.

If you will store your Web sites on drive A, you will need **six** blank, formatted high-density disks. The information below shows you which folders go on each of your disks, so that you will have enough disk space to complete all the tutorials, Review Assignments, and Case Problems.

Data Disk 1

Write this on the disk label:
Data Disk 1: Tutorial 1
Put these folders on the disk:
My Webs\SunnyMorningProducts
My Webs\Carpenter

Data Disks 2-6

Label these five disks as follows:
Data Disk 2: Tutorials 2-6 and Review Assignments
Data Disk 3: Case Problem 1 (Tutorials 2-6)
Data Disk 4: Case Problem 2 (Tutorials 2-6)
Data Disk 5: Case Problem 3 (Tutorials 2-6)
Data Disk 6: Case Problem 4 (Tutorials 2-6)
Put these five folders on **each** of the five disks:
Tutorial.02
Tutorial.03
Tutorial.04
Tutorial.05
Tutorial.06

When you begin each tutorial, be sure you are using the correct Data Disk. Refer to the "File Finder" chart at the back of this text for more detailed information on which files are used in which tutorials. See the inside front or inside back cover of this book for more information on Data Disk files, or ask your instructor or technical support person for assistance.

Course Labs

The FrontPage Level I tutorials feature three interactive Course Labs to help you understand hypermedia, the Internet and World Wide Web, and HTML concepts. There are Lab Assignments at the end of Tutorials 1 and 3 that relate to these Labs.

To start a Lab, click the **Start** button on the Windows taskbar, point to **Programs**, point to **Course Labs**, point to **New Perspectives Course Labs**, and then click the name of the Lab you want to use.

Using Your Own Computer

If you are going to work through this book using your own computer, you need:

- ■ **Computer System** Microsoft Windows NT, 2000 Professional, or higher must be installed on your computer. This book assumes a typical installation of Microsoft FrontPage 2002. You also must have Internet Information Server version 5.0 or higher and the Microsoft FrontPage 2002 Server Extensions installed and configured to be able to publish Web sites in Tutorial 6. The recommended browser for viewing Web pages is Internet Explorer 5.0 or higher.

- ■ **Data Disk(s)** You will not be able to complete the tutorials or exercises in this book using your own computer until you have your Data Disk(s).

- ■ **Course Labs** See your instructor or technical support person to obtain the Course Lab software for use on your own computer.

Visit Our World Wide Web Site

Additional materials designed especially for you are available on the World Wide Web.
Go to **www.course.com/NewPerspectives**.

To the Instructor

The Data Disk Files and Course Labs are available on the Instructor's Resource Kit for this title. Follow the instructions in the Help file on the CD-ROM to install the programs to your network or standalone computer. For information on creating Data Disks or the Course Labs, see the "To the Student" section above.

You are granted a license to copy the Data Files and Course Labs to any computer or computer network used by students who have purchased this book.

INTRODUCING FRONTPAGE 2002

Exploring the Web Site for Sunny Morning Products

Sunny Morning Products

Sunny Morning Products is an international bottler and distributor of the Olympic Gold brand of fresh orange juice and thirst-quencher sports drinks. Olympic Gold products are sold in grocery stores, convenience stores, and many other outlets. Located in Garden Grove, California, the company was established in 1909 by Edwin Towle. Edwin's great-grandson, Jacob Towle, now serves as the company's president. To better accommodate the many customers and visitors who wanted to tour the citrus groves owned by Sunny Morning Products, Edwin opened the Sunshine Country Store in 1951. In addition to selling Olympic Gold juice products, the Country Store also sells fresh produce, such as oranges and grapefruits. In 1987, Jacob expanded the Sunshine Country Store's operations to include mail-order sales of citrus products.

Amanda Bay has been working for Sunny Morning Products for two years as a marketing manager. Her main duty is to assist Jacob in promoting and marketing Sunny Morning Products. One of Amanda's latest projects was to create a Web site for Sunny Morning Products so as to reach both new and existing customers online. Because of the overwhelming success of this initial Web site, Jacob decided to expand the company's Web activities into other areas of the business. He assigned Amanda the task of training employees in Web site development so that each department will have at least one employee who can plan, develop, create, and manage Web pages for that department.

In response, Amanda prepared a Web site development training program that uses Microsoft FrontPage 2002. During the first part of the training program, participants explore the current Web site for Sunny Morning Products to build their Web development skills. Then participants use FrontPage to create a new Web site and Web pages. Upon completing the training program, trainees are ready to work on new Web development projects in their own departments.

As a management intern in the marketing department, you will participate in Amanda's training program. Once you've completed the program, you will have the skills needed to plan, develop, create, and manage Web pages for your department.

SESSION 1.1

In this session, you will learn about the Internet and the World Wide Web. You will use a browser to open and explore a Web site, and you will access different kinds of Web pages. Finally, you will use the browser to print a Web page.

The Internet

The **Internet** is a large, worldwide collection of computer networks that are connected to one another. In a **network**, two or more computers are connected together for purposes of sharing resources and communication. Within a network, one computer is designated as the server, which functions as the network's central computer. The **network server**, or **host**, is a powerful computer that stores and distributes information and resources across the network to individual computers. The Internet is not a single, massive computer, but rather a collection of millions of connected computers through which users exchange information. The Internet allows you to communicate and share data with people in the next office, across the street, or around the world.

The Internet's resources are organized in a **client/server architecture**. The server runs computer software that coordinates and communicates with the other computers connected to it. These other computers are called **clients**; a personal computer that is connected to the Internet is one example of a client. The server to which the client is connected stores information and processes the client's requests for that information. When a client requests information from a server, that request is transferred in the form of a file. The server then finds the information and returns it to the client, also in the form of a file. This file travels over the Internet from one server to another until it eventually reaches the client that requested it. Sometimes the file travels through many different servers before finally reaching this client.

To access the Internet, you need an account with a commercial information service provider, commonly called an Internet service provider. An **Internet service provider (ISP)** is a business that provides a connection to the Internet for individuals, businesses, and organizations for a fee. An ISP might be a small, local business or a large, national provider, such as the Microsoft Network or America Online. Many colleges, universities, and large businesses have their own direct connections to the Internet and, in effect, act as their own ISPs.

The World Wide Web

The **World Wide Web** (or simply the **Web**) is a part of the Internet that provides information stored on servers that are connected to the Internet around the world. The Web organizes its resources in a standardized way so that information is easily stored, transferred, and displayed among the various types of computers connected to it. Millions of businesses regularly use the Web for activities ranging from advertising to retailing.

An electronic document of information on the Web is called a **Web page**. Each page includes information ranging from simple text to complex multimedia. A **Web site** is a set of related Web pages available from the Web server on which they are stored. A **Web server** is an Internet server that stores Web pages. Each Web server can have multiple Web sites. For example, a college or university might maintain a single Web server on which each faculty member or student could maintain a separate Web site with his or her collection of

Computer
History
Hypermedia

related Web pages. When a single Web site contains different, smaller Web sites, the smaller sites are called **subwebs**.

Most Web sites consist not of a single Web page, but rather of a series of Web pages that are linked together. **Hyperlinks**, or **links**, are keywords, phrases, or pictures in a Web page that, when clicked using a mouse, will connect you to related information located in the same Web page, in the same Web site, or in another Web site. A hyperlink might open another Web page or play a video clip or a sound file. The process of using a hyperlink to connect to another location on the Web is called **linking**. When you click a hyperlink with your mouse, you retrieve the hyperlink's file from the Web server on which it resides. Your Web browser then opens or plays this file on your computer. A **Web browser** is the software program that requests, retrieves, interprets, and displays the content of a Web page on a client. A Web browser can locate a Web page on a server anywhere in the world. **Microsoft Internet Explorer**, or **Internet Explorer**, is a powerful and easy-to-use Web browser. You will learn more about Internet Explorer later in this session.

Figure 1-1 shows a simplified version of how a client computer in Texas might receive a file from a university library's Web server in England. The entire transfer might take anywhere from a few seconds to several minutes, depending on factors such as the page's content and the speed of your Internet connection.

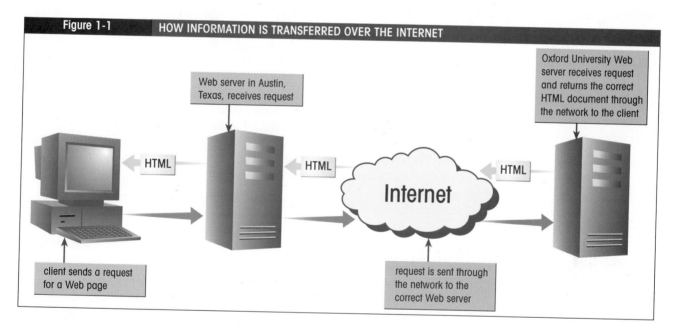

Figure 1-1   HOW INFORMATION IS TRANSFERRED OVER THE INTERNET

Web server in Austin, Texas, receives request

Oxford University Web server receives request and returns the correct HTML document through the network to the client

HTML   HTML   Internet   HTML

client sends a request for a Web page

request is sent through the network to the correct Web server

Hypertext **Markup Language Documents**

The Internet connects many types of computers through servers located around the world. Computers connected to the Internet vary in terms of which file formats they can display, so the client's Web browser must determine how to best display information on the client. This **portability**, or the ability of software to run on many computers, means that the software does not depend on a particular type of hardware to run. As a result, Web page developers are freed from the burden of making their Web pages compatible with every type of computer and many different operating systems.

The device most commonly used for storing information for transfer and display on the various computers that are connected to the Internet is the **hypertext document**. Hypertext documents are written in a programming language called **Hypertext Markup Language** (**HTML**). For this reason, hypertext documents are also called **HTML documents**. HTML documents use a standard group of characters, called a **character set**, which all computers recognize. In addition, each HTML document contains special codes that a Web browser interprets to display data in the desired format on a client. A Web page is, in fact, an HTML document that is stored on a Web server. You will learn more about HTML in Session 1.3.

Web Servers

To function as a Web server, a server connected to the Internet must run special software that enables it to receive and execute clients' requests for Web pages. Microsoft provides three versions of Web server software: the FrontPage Personal Web Server, the Microsoft Personal Web Server, and Internet Information Services. The FrontPage Personal Web Server is used with either Windows 95/98 or Windows NT, the Microsoft Personal Web Server is used only with Windows 95/98, and Internet Information Services is used with Windows NT and Windows 2000. In this book, you will use Internet Information Services for Windows 2000 to develop and test a Web site.

Many Web pages can be developed and tested using a **disk-based Web**, which lets you store and retrieve Web pages on a computer's disk drive. To access a disk-based Web, you use a drive letter and the page's pathname with backslashes—for example, A:\My Webs\SunnyMorningProducts\index.htm. The testing of more advanced features of a Web site, such as the ability to process forms or conduct searches, requires a server. A **server-based Web** uses Web server software that is installed on either a client or a server. A server-based Web is accessed by using the prefix "http:" and the file's pathname with forward slashes—for example, http://localhost/SunnyMorningProducts/index.htm.

If you are storing the Data Files for this book on your computer's floppy, hard, or network drive (the steps in this tutorial assume that your Data Files are stored on drive A), you will examine the Web site for Sunny Morning Products as a disk-based Web. If your Data Files for this book are loaded on a Web server, then you will examine the same Web site as a server-based Web. You will work with both types of Web sites in this book. (You will use a server-based Web and learn more about Web servers in Tutorial 6.) Your instructor or technical support person will advise you of any differences that you might encounter while working through the tutorials in this book.

Getting Started with Internet Explorer

As noted earlier, Internet Explorer is a Web browser that displays HTML documents on a client. Internet Explorer 5.0 is installed automatically when you install FrontPage 2002 using the Microsoft Office XP CD, or you can download and install it from the Microsoft Web site (www.microsoft.com). This book uses Internet Explorer as the default Web browser. If you are using a different version of Internet Explorer or a different Web browser, such as Netscape Navigator, your instructor will provide you with specific instructions for its use. In these cases, the appearance of your screens might differ somewhat from the figures in these tutorials, but these variations should not affect your work in FrontPage.

Unlike some software programs, Internet Explorer does not always open with a standard start-up screen, or start page. A **start page** is the first page that opens when you start your Web browser. The address for your start page is called a **Uniform Resource Locator** (**URL**), and every resource on the Internet has its own URL. If no start page has been defined for your browser, then a blank or default Web page opens from your computer's hard drive. If the start page contains a URL for a Web site, then the home page for that Web site opens. A **home page** is the first page that opens for a Web site. It often contains information about the host computer or sponsoring organization or individual, hyperlinks to other Web sites, and associated pictures and sounds. Figure 1-2 shows an example of a home page and identifies some key components of the Internet Explorer window.

Figure 1-2   SAMPLE HOME PAGE FOR THE AMERICAN CARPENTERS SOCIETY

Figure 1-3 describes some of the components of the Internet Explorer window in more detail.

Figure 1-3   COMPONENTS OF THE INTERNET EXPLORER WINDOW

COMPONENT	DESCRIPTION
Address bar	Located below the Standard Buttons toolbar; displays the URL of the currently displayed Web page
Menu bar	Located below the title bar; provides access to all commands available in Internet Explorer
Scroll bar	Located at the right and bottom of the window; moves the window's contents vertically or horizontally when the Web page exceeds the window's size
Standard Buttons toolbar	Located below the menu bar; includes icons that represent shortcuts to commonly used commands
Status bar	Located at the bottom of the window; shows messages related to the status of the current Web page or browser action
Title bar	Located at the top of the screen; indicates the title of the current Web page and the name of the browser program

Starting Internet Explorer

You start Internet Explorer just like any other program. When Internet Explorer starts, you might see any one of the following pages:

- The Microsoft home page
- Your educational institution's or employer's home page
- A home page that you or your technical support person set as the default
- A blank page
- A page indicating that no start page is available

You can customize Internet Explorer to open almost any Web page as its start page. For example, when Amanda starts Internet Explorer from her office computer, the home page for Sunny Morning Products opens as her start page because she often uses this Web site during the day.

You are ready to begin exploring the Web site for Sunny Morning Products as the first phase of your training. After you have a better understanding of the different Web pages that you can create in a Web site, you will learn how to create similar Web pages using FrontPage. First, you need to start Internet Explorer.

To start Internet Explorer:

1. Make sure that your computer is on and that the Windows desktop appears. See Figure 1-4.

Figure 1-4	WINDOWS 2000 DESKTOP

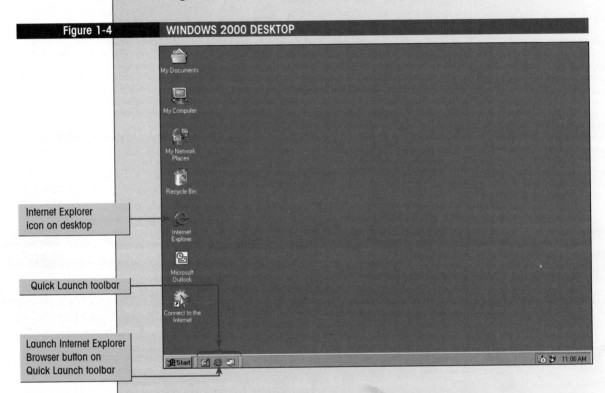

Internet Explorer icon on desktop

Quick Launch toolbar

Launch Internet Explorer Browser button on Quick Launch toolbar

TROUBLE? If you do not see the Quick Launch toolbar on your taskbar, this is not a problem. Continue with Step 2.

TROUBLE? Your desktop might look different from the one shown in Figure 1-4 and contain different icons; this is not a problem.

2. Click the **Launch Internet Explorer Browser** button on the Quick Launch toolbar to start the program. If you do not see the Quick Launch toolbar on your taskbar, double-click the **Internet Explorer** icon on the desktop.

The start page for your copy of Internet Explorer opens in the browser. Figure 1-5 shows the home page for Sunny Morning Products. Depending on your system configuration, your start page might be different, but this is not a problem. Figure 1-5 identifies the key components of a home page.

| Figure 1-5 | HOME PAGE FOR SUNNY MORNING PRODUCTS |

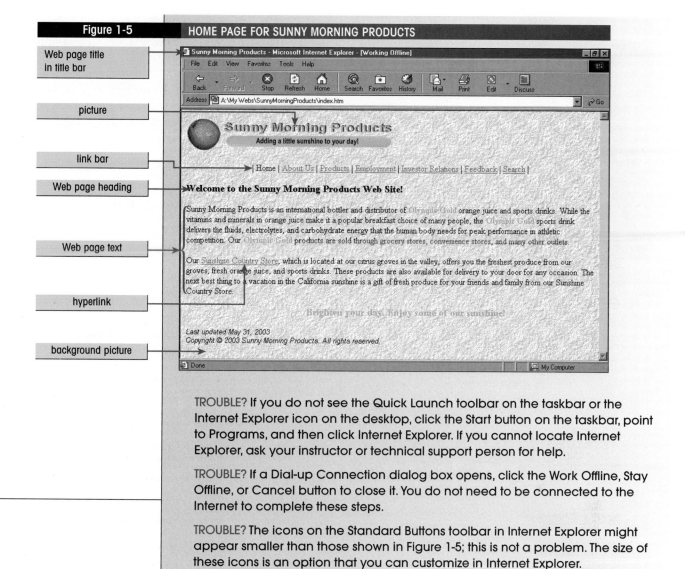

Web page title in title bar

picture

link bar

Web page heading

Web page text

hyperlink

background picture

TROUBLE? If you do not see the Quick Launch toolbar on the taskbar or the Internet Explorer icon on the desktop, click the Start button on the taskbar, point to Programs, and then click Internet Explorer. If you cannot locate Internet Explorer, ask your instructor or technical support person for help.

TROUBLE? If a Dial-up Connection dialog box opens, click the Work Offline, Stay Offline, or Cancel button to close it. You do not need to be connected to the Internet to complete these steps.

TROUBLE? The icons on the Standard Buttons toolbar in Internet Explorer might appear smaller than those shown in Figure 1-5; this is not a problem. The size of these icons is an option that you can customize in Internet Explorer.

3. If necessary, click the **Maximize** button ▢ on the Internet Explorer title bar to maximize the window.

Figure 1-6 describes some common elements in a home page that are identified in Figure 1-5.

Figure 1-6	COMMON ELEMENTS IN A HOME PAGE
ELEMENT	**DESCRIPTION**
Background	Enhances the appearance of a Web page by using a color or picture. Text and pictures appear on top of the Web page's background if one is used.
Heading	Provides a formatted heading in the Web page to differentiate Web page sections.
Hyperlink	When clicked, opens another Web page or scrolls to a new location in the current Web page. Hyperlink text usually appears in a different color and is underlined to distinguish it from other Web page text.
Link bar	Contains hyperlinks to other Web pages. The link bar can be located anywhere on the Web page and can include text, buttons, or pictures that contain hyperlinks.
Picture	An image on a Web page that might contain a hyperlink.
Text	The content of the Web page.
Title	Located in the browser's title bar, identifies the title of the open Web page.

Opening a Web Page with a URL

Recall that each Web page is identified by a URL. A URL contains the address for the Web server or computer that stores the Web site, plus an optional pathname to a specific Web page at that site. The most common method of identifying individual servers or computers on a network is to use an Internet Protocol address. An **Internet Protocol (IP) address** is a unique number consisting of four sets of numbers separated by periods (such as 141.209.151.119) that identifies a specific server or computer. IP addresses are difficult to remember, so most users rely on domain names to find Web sites. A **domain name** is an IP address that consists of letters instead of numbers, such as www.whitehouse.gov. Whether you use an IP address or a domain name, a URL identifies a Web page's location on the Web so that client computers can find and retrieve it. A URL can be broken down as follows:

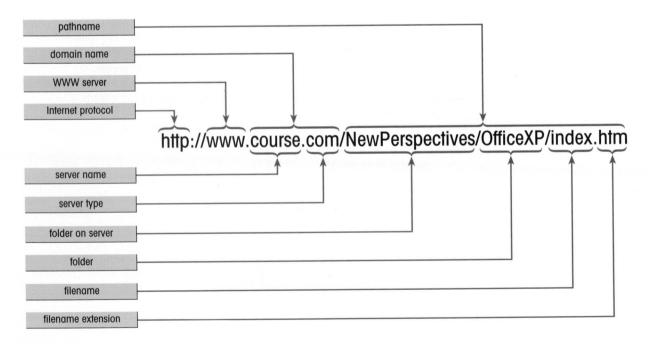

This URL identifies the exact address of the server or computer on which the page resides, and the type of organization that owns and operates it. In the URL, *http* represents the Internet communications protocol for accessing a page on the Web; *www* specifies that the server is a Web server; *course* specifies the name of the organization that owns the server; and *.com* indicates that the server is owned by a commercial entity. Other common types of servers in the United States are education (.edu), organization (.org), and governmental (.gov).

In addition, all files stored on a Web server must have a unique pathname, just like files stored on a disk. The pathname that follows the domain name *www.course.com* specifies the file named index.htm, which is stored in the OfficeXP folder, which is in turn stored in the NewPerspectives folder. The **pathname** in a URL includes the folder name(s), filename, and filename extension for locating the Web page. The extension for all Web pages is either *.html* or *.htm*, both of which indicate an HTML document. (The .html extension is generally reserved for computers that run the UNIX operating system, whereas the .htm extension is used most often with personal computers that run Windows or Macintosh operating systems.) Internet Explorer processes files with either of these extensions as HTML documents.

The Internet: World Wide Web

To access a particular Web site or to open a location, type its URL in the Address bar, and then press the Enter key. Internet Explorer connects to the server specified by that address, sends a request for information, opens the home page or a specific file identified in the URL, and then displays the information.

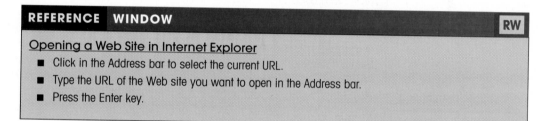

REFERENCE WINDOW   RW

Opening a Web Site in Internet Explorer
- Click in the Address bar to select the current URL.
- Type the URL of the Web site you want to open in the Address bar.
- Press the Enter key.

Amanda wants you to examine the Web site for Sunny Morning Products to familiarize yourself with its features. As you work through the tutorials in this book, you will use FrontPage to create a similar Web site and Web pages. Don't be concerned if you can't remember all of the details of this Web site. You will learn about each element described in this overview in more detail as you progress through Amanda's training course. Because you are using a disk-based Web, your URL will include the pathname to the Web site that is stored on your Data Disk, instead of a URL to a Web page stored on a Web server.

To open a Web site in Internet Explorer:

1. Make sure that Internet Explorer is open and that your Data Disk is in the appropriate disk drive.

TROUBLE? You must have a Data Disk to complete the tutorials in this book. If you do not have a Data Disk, ask your instructor or technical support person for help.

2. Click in the **Address bar** to select the entire URL that currently appears there.

TROUBLE? If the URL is not selected, then you double-clicked the insertion point in the Address bar and changed to editing mode. Select the URL in the Address bar, and then continue with Step 3.

3. Type **A:\My Webs\SunnyMorningProducts\index.htm** in the Address bar. This URL identifies the location of the home page of the disk-based Web that is stored on your Data Disk. In this book, you will store all Web sites in the My Webs folder on your Data Disk.

   As you type the Web address, Internet Explorer's AutoComplete feature might complete the address for you, or it might open a drop-down menu of previously opened URLs that are similar to or match the one that you are typing. The suggested match is highlighted in the Address bar. You can press the Enter key to open the selected URL, click another URL in the list, or just continue typing.

   TROUBLE? If your instructor provides you with a different access method than the one described in Step 3, use that method.

4. Press the **Enter** key. The home page for Sunny Morning Products opens. See Figure 1-7. If your computer can play sound and your speakers are turned on, you will hear a background sound.

Figure 1-7   OPENING A WEB PAGE WITH A URL

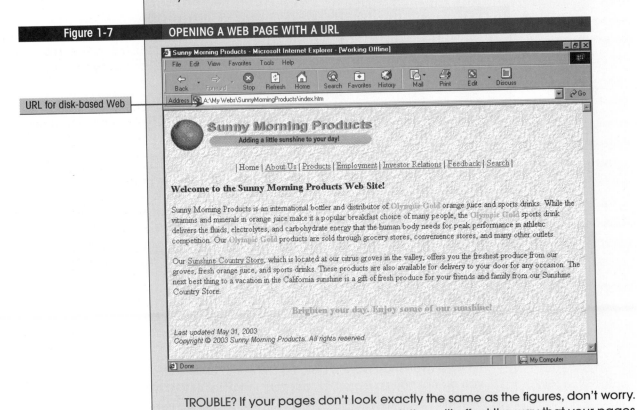

URL for disk-based Web

TROUBLE? If your pages don't look exactly the same as the figures, don't worry. Factors such as monitor size and resolution will affect the way that your pages are displayed.

5. If desired, click the **Stop** button on the Standard Buttons toolbar to stop the music.

Next, you will examine the various hyperlinks in the home page.

Linking **to and within Web Pages**

A hyperlink on the Internet, like a link in a chain, connects two end points. The home page for Sunny Morning Products contains several text hyperlinks, all of which appear as underlined text. Clicking a hyperlink opens the linked Web page in the browser. As noted earlier, a hyperlink can connect you to another location within the current Web page or to an entirely different Web page or Web site.

Because you will create and test Web page hyperlinks while learning how to develop a Web site, Amanda wants you to practice using hyperlinks to move from one Web page to another.

To link to a new Web page:

1. Point to (but don't click) the **Products** hyperlink in the link bar at the top of the page. Most Web pages include a **link bar** containing hyperlinks that open other pages in the Web site. Notice that the pointer changes from a ⌖ shape to a 🖑 shape to indicate that you are pointing to a hyperlink. In addition, the pathname for the linked page (products.htm) appears in the lower-left corner on the status bar.

2. Point to (but don't click) the **Sunshine Country Store** hyperlink in the second paragraph in the Web page. The status bar indicates that this hyperlink also points to the products.htm page. You can create more than one hyperlink to the same Web page.

3. Click the **Employment** hyperlink in the link bar. The Employment Web page, which contains a bulleted list of hyperlinks, opens in the browser and replaces the home page. See Figure 1-8.

| Figure 1-8 | EMPLOYMENT WEB PAGE |

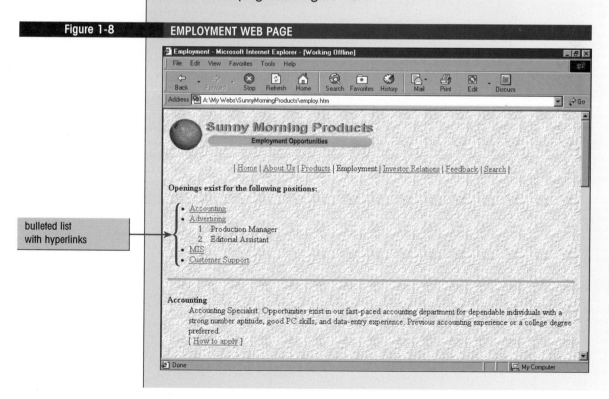

bulleted list
with hyperlinks

TROUBLE? If the color of your hyperlinks does not match the figure, don't worry. Your browser might be configured to display hyperlinks using a different color. In addition, hyperlinks that have been clicked will usually appear in a different color.

Next, Amanda wants you to examine an **internal hyperlink**, or a **bookmark**, which is a hyperlink that connects to another location within the same Web page. An internal hyperlink in a Web page is often used to let the user return to the top of the page as an alternative to using the vertical scroll bar to scroll up the page. A "top of page" hyperlink is particularly useful in long Web pages, such as the Employment Web page that currently appears in your browser.

To link to a location within a Web page:

1. Point to the **MIS** text in the bulleted list. Notice that the pathname on the status bar displays the text #MIS, which identifies the location of the hyperlink. The pound sign (#) indicates that this text serves as an internal hyperlink to a location within the same document. See Figure 1-9.

Figure 1-9	EXAMINING AN INTERNAL HYPERLINK IN A WEB PAGE

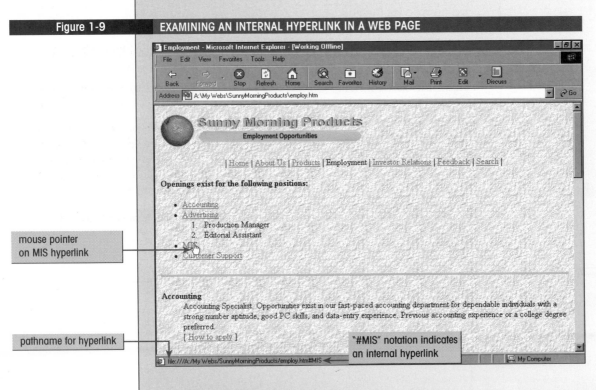

mouse pointer on MIS hyperlink

pathname for hyperlink

"#MIS" notation indicates an internal hyperlink

2. Click the **MIS** hyperlink. The Employment Web page automatically scrolls to the MIS section. See Figure 1-10.

Figure 1-10   MIS SECTION IN THE EMPLOYMENT WEB PAGE

MIS section

hyperlink to the
"How to apply" section

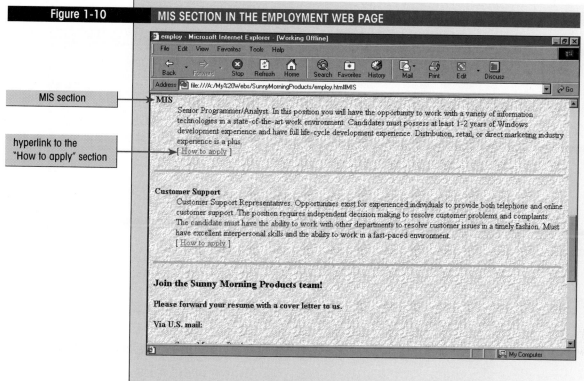

3. Click the **How to apply** hyperlink at the end of the MIS job description. The Employment Web page automatically moves to the "How to apply" section.

   Clicking any of the "How to apply" hyperlinks in this Web page will move you to this location. In addition to creating a hyperlink to another location in the same Web page, you can create a hyperlink for sending e-mail messages. For example, the Employment Web page contains the e-mail address of the Human Resources manager.

4. Press **Ctrl + End** to move to the bottom of the Web page. See Figure 1-11.

| Figure 1-11 | BOTTOM OF THE EMPLOYMENT WEB PAGE |

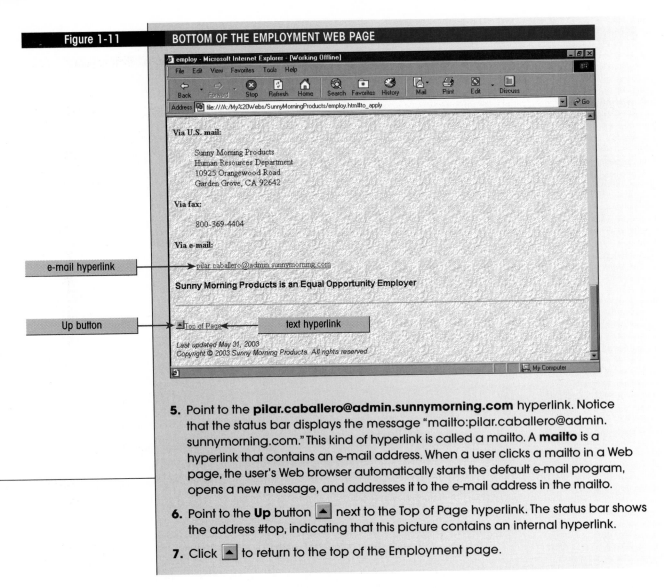

5. Point to the **pilar.caballero@admin.sunnymorning.com** hyperlink. Notice that the status bar displays the message "mailto:pilar.caballero@admin.sunnymorning.com." This kind of hyperlink is called a mailto. A **mailto** is a hyperlink that contains an e-mail address. When a user clicks a mailto in a Web page, the user's Web browser automatically starts the default e-mail program, opens a new message, and addresses it to the e-mail address in the mailto.

6. Point to the **Up** button ⏶ next to the Top of Page hyperlink. The status bar shows the address #top, indicating that this picture contains an internal hyperlink.

7. Click ⏶ to return to the top of the Employment page.

So far, you have reviewed only single pages in the SunnyMorningProducts Web site. Now Amanda wants you to use a different kind of Web page that enables you to display multiple pages on your screen simultaneously.

Examining a Frames Page

You can divide one Web page into several different windows, called **frames**, and display a different Web page in each frame. For example, one frame can continuously display a table of contents, while a second frame displays a page selected from that table of contents. With this organization, you can easily select pages from the table of contents because it remains displayed. A Web page that is divided into several frames that display other Web pages is called a **frames page** (or a **frameset**). You can scroll the contents of a frame if the Web page displayed in that frame is larger than the frame's size. Clicking a hyperlink in one frame might change the Web page displayed in another frame.

Amanda used a frames page to create the Products Web page that you will examine next.

To examine a frames page:

1. Click the **Products** hyperlink in the link bar at the top of the Employment Web page. The Products Web page opens. See Figure 1-12.

Figure 1-12	PRODUCTS FRAMES PAGE

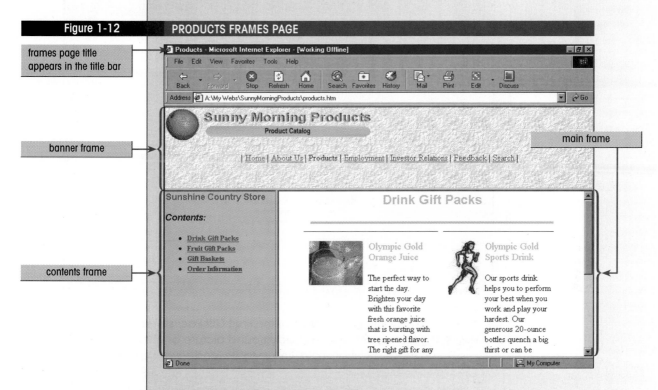

frames page title appears in the title bar

banner frame

main frame

contents frame

TROUBLE? Depending on your monitor's resolution, your frames page might display pages with sizes different from those shown in Figure 1-12, and you might see scroll bars in all of the frames. This is not a problem.

The Products Web page is a frames page that is divided into three frames; you can also use FrontPage to create frames pages with two, four, or more frames. In this frames page, the top frame, called the **banner frame**, contains the Sunny Morning Products logo and a link bar with hyperlinks that open other Web pages in the SunnyMorningProducts Web site. Clicking a hyperlink in the link bar opens the linked page and replaces the frames page. The left frame, called the **contents frame**, contains a bulleted list of hyperlinks that opens pages in the main frame. The right frame, called the **main frame**, contains a scrollable Web page that opens after you click a hyperlink in the contents frame. The Drink Gift Packs Web page currently appears in the main frame.

2. Click the **Fruit Gift Packs** hyperlink in the contents frame to open this Web page in the main frame. The pictures in this page are part of a **Photo Gallery**, which is a special feature in FrontPage that lets you add images, captions, and descriptions to create a group of photos in a Web page. See Figure 1-13.

| Figure 1-13 | FRUIT GIFT PACKS WEB PAGE IN MAIN FRAME |

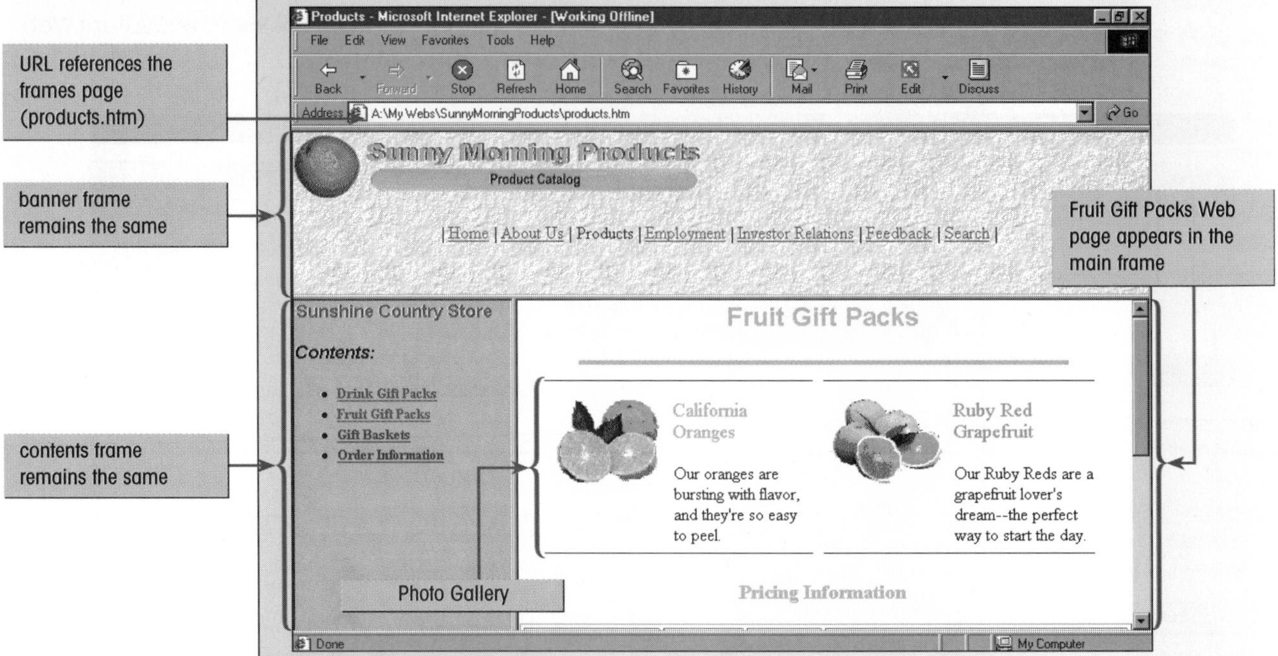

URL references the
frames page
(products.htm)

banner frame
remains the same

Fruit Gift Packs Web
page appears in the
main frame

contents frame
remains the same

Photo Gallery

3. Scroll down to view the contents of the Fruit Gift Packs Web page. Notice that this Web page does not use a background picture or color, but does include a centered heading, a horizontal line, a table, and several pictures.

4. Scroll up the page (if necessary) until you see the California Oranges picture, and then place your mouse pointer on it. The text "California Oranges" appears in a box for a moment and then disappears; this is **alternative text**. If your Web browser could not display or find the file for this picture, then the alternative text "California Oranges" would appear in its place. The picture's filename appears on the status bar when the pointer is positioned on the picture, which indicates that this picture contains a hyperlink.

5. Click the **Gift Baskets** hyperlink in the contents frame to open this Web page in the main frame. Scroll down until you see a table listing available products and their prices. See Figure 1-14. Many Web developers use tables in their Web pages to control the arrangement of information on a page. You will learn more about tables in Tutorial 4.

Figure 1-14 | **GIFT BASKETS WEB PAGE IN MAIN FRAME**

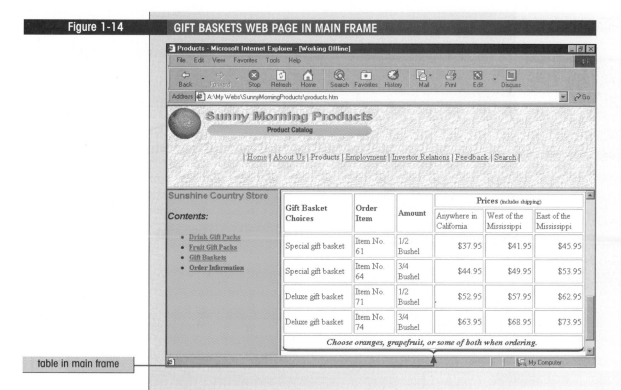

table in main frame

6. Click the **Order Information** hyperlink in the contents frame to open the Order Information page. Notice that this Web page uses a picture as its background.

Using **FrontPage Web Components**

So far, you have viewed only static Web pages. A **static Web page** is a Web page that you request from the server and that opens in a browser. Web pages also can be interactive. An **interactive**, or **dynamic**, **Web page** doesn't already exist as a file on the server, but rather is created based on data entered by the user. For example, to complete a survey on the Web, you could use a Web page to enter your responses to the various questions, and then use your browser to send your responses to the server for processing. The server would process the data and return a response in the form of a Web page whose content would be based in whole or in part on the data you entered. If you use FrontPage to create an online survey, the browser might also display a graph of the survey results collected from all forms submitted to the server for processing.

In a FrontPage Web site, a feature called a FrontPage Web component handles the processing of this type of user input on the server. A **FrontPage Web component** is a prewritten program that carries out a particular processing function. FrontPage offers many components that you can include in Web pages for implementing various server processing activities. For example, the **Search component** is used to create a Search Web page that accepts a user's search request and then searches the pages in a Web site to find matching Web pages. You can also use FrontPage to accept a user's search request and search the Internet to find matching Web pages.

REFERENCE **WINDOW**   **RW**

Using a Search Web Page
- Type the text you want to find in the Search for text box.
- Click the Start Search button (or the Search button).

The SunnyMorningProducts Web site contains a Search Web page that enables users to locate matching keywords in any Web page in the Web site and to perform Internet searches. Amanda wants you to use the Search page so that you will recognize the effectiveness of this type of component in designing a Web site. Keep in mind, however, that a Web component requires the processing capabilities of a server to generate a response. Because you are using a disk-based Web in this tutorial, you won't receive a response to your search request. (Your Web browser would display a search results page if it were stored on a Web server.)

To use the Search Web page:

1. Click the **Search** hyperlink in the banner frame at the top of the Products page. The Search page opens, replacing the entire frames page in the browser. See Figure 1-15.

Figure 1-15   SEARCH WEB PAGE

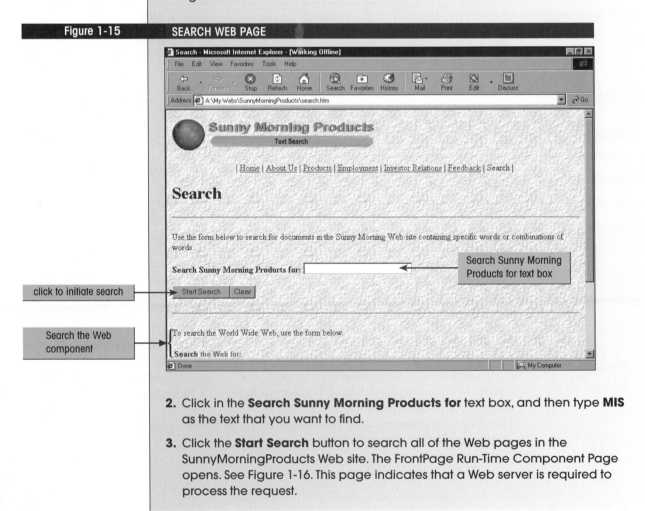

click to initiate search

Search the Web component

Search Sunny Morning Products for text box

2. Click in the **Search Sunny Morning Products for** text box, and then type **MIS** as the text that you want to find.

3. Click the **Start Search** button to search all of the Web pages in the SunnyMorningProducts Web site. The FrontPage Run-Time Component Page opens. See Figure 1-16. This page indicates that a Web server is required to process the request.

Figure 1-16   FRONTPAGE RUN-TIME COMPONENT PAGE

message indicating that
a server is required

message suggesting
an appropriate action
to take

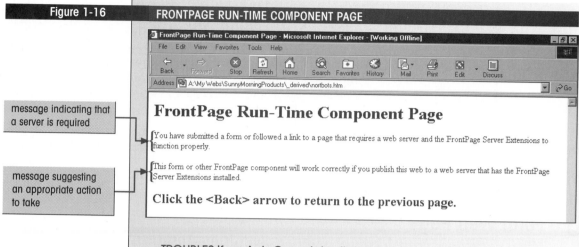

FrontPage Run-Time Component Page

You have submitted a form or followed a link to a page that requires a web server and the FrontPage Server Extensions to function properly.

This form or other FrontPage component will work correctly if you publish this web to a web server that has the FrontPage Server Extensions installed.

Click the <Back> arrow to return to the previous page.

TROUBLE? If an AutoComplete dialog box opens and asks whether you want to turn on this feature, click the No button.

If you performed your search using a server-based Web, instead of a disk-based Web, a search confirmation page would open. This page would list all Web pages that contain a match for the text that you entered in the text box. Clicking a Web page in this list would open that page in the browser.

4. Click the **Back** button ⇦ on the Standard Buttons toolbar to return to the Search page, and then press **Ctrl + End** to scroll to the bottom of the page. See Figure 1-17.

Figure 1-17   SEARCH THE WEB COMPONENT

enter keywords here

link to advanced
search directions

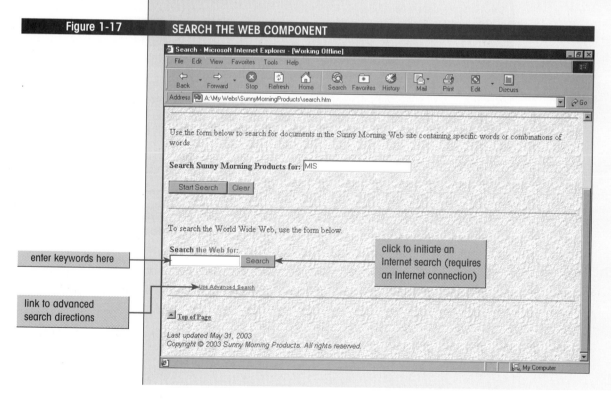

click to initiate an
Internet search (requires
an Internet connection)

> Notice that the page contains a second text box that lets users search the Web using keywords. If you enter text into this text box and have an Internet connection, a search page at MSN would open and provide a list of hyperlinks to sites that match your keywords. This feature, which is implemented using a FrontPage Web component, requires no additional programming knowledge on the part of the Web site developer.

You will perform these types of searches using a server-based Web in Tutorial 6. At that time, you will see how the Search Web page returns a page of hyperlinks to Web pages in the SunnyMorningProducts Web site that contain your search text.

Using a Form Web Page

Often, Web pages are forms that a user completes and submits to a Web server for processing. A Web page that contains a form allows you to gather input from users. This information is then sent to the Web server for processing, with the results being saved to a text file or to a Web page on the server. A **form** contains form objects, such as text boxes and check boxes, into which users input the requested information.

REFERENCE WINDOW   **RW**

Using a Web Page That Contains a Form
- Enter the data for each field in the form.
- Click the Submit Comments button (or the Submit button) to send the form's contents to the server.

The SunnyMorningProducts Web site includes two Web pages that contain forms: the customer order form, which processes customer orders, and the feedback form, which gathers customer feedback. A FrontPage Web component processes these forms on the server. Amanda wants you to practice using a form Web page, as it will be an important feature in Web sites that you will later develop for your department.

To use a Web page that contains a form:

1. With the Search Web page displayed in the browser window, press **Ctrl + Home** to scroll to the top of the page, and then click the **Feedback** hyperlink to open this Web page.

2. Scroll down the Feedback Web page until you see several form objects, including option buttons, a drop-down menu, and a scrolling text box. See Figure 1-18.

Figure 1-18	FORM OBJECTS IN THE FEEDBACK WEB PAGE

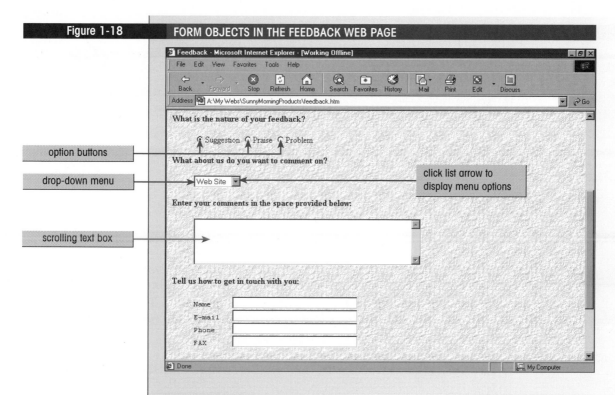

3. Click the **Praise** option button under "What is the nature of your feedback?" to select it.

4. Click the **list arrow** under "What about us do you want to comment on?" to display the menu options, and then click **Products**.

5. Click in the **scrolling text box**, and then type the following message: **Your Olympic Gold sports drink is great stuff. It really gives us the extra energy we need to keep going during our slow-pitch softball games. Without it, we wouldn't have won the company trophy. The new lemon-mango-strawberry flavor is super.**

6. Scroll down (if necessary) until you see additional form objects at the bottom of the page. See Figure 1-19. This part of the form uses several text boxes, a check box, and two buttons.

| Figure 1-19 | ADDITIONAL FORM OBJECTS IN THE FEEDBACK WEB PAGE |

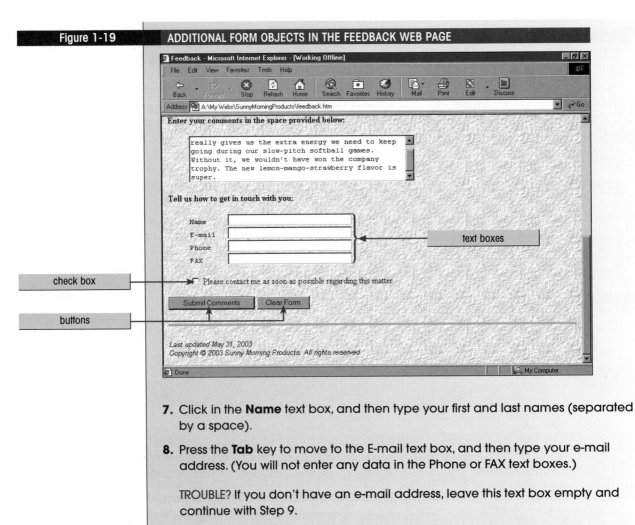

7. Click in the **Name** text box, and then type your first and last names (separated by a space).

8. Press the **Tab** key to move to the E-mail text box, and then type your e-mail address. (You will not enter any data in the Phone or FAX text boxes.)

   TROUBLE? If you don't have an e-mail address, leave this text box empty and continue with Step 9.

9. Click the **Please contact me as soon as possible regarding this matter** check box to select it. The data entry for this form is now complete.

10. Click the **Submit Comments** button to submit the form to the server. The FrontPage Run-Time Component Page opens. Because you are using a disk-based Web, no server is available to process your submission.

11. Click the **Back** button ⇐ on the Standard Buttons toolbar to return to the Feedback Web page.

12. Click the **Clear Form** button. This button clears all form fields, resetting the form to its original state.

When you submit a form using a server-based Web, a default confirmation Web page opens in the browser and the form's results are stored in a file on the server. You will learn about creating and processing forms in Tutorial 6.

Printing a Web Page

Sometimes you might want to print a Web page, such as when you need a paper copy of the information you have viewed or when you plan to give the information to someone who doesn't have Internet access. Also, if you visit other Web sites and find an interesting page, you might want to keep a printout to use as a reference while designing your own Web pages. In general, you can print any Web page that you can open. You continue your training by printing the Investor Relations Web page.

To print a Web page and close Internet Explorer:

1. Scroll up to the top of the Feedback Web page, and then click the **Investor Relations** hyperlink in the link bar. The Investor Relations Web page contains two tables: a summary of the company's financial performance and current stock information.

2. Click the **Print** button 🖨 on the Standard Buttons toolbar to print the current Web page.

   You have successfully examined several Web pages and printed the Investor Relations page. Next, you will close Internet Explorer.

3. Click the **Close** button ☒ on the Internet Explorer title bar to close the browser.

You have completed the first part of your training by examining the main features of the SunnyMorningProducts Web site. In the next session, you will explore this Web site using FrontPage.

Session 1.1 QUICK CHECK

1. The _____ is a worldwide collection of computer networks that are connected to one another.

2. How do a Web browser and a Web server work together to provide you with information?

3. A(n) _____ page is the first page that a browser opens when it starts.

4. The address of a specific file on the Web is called its _____.

5. A keyword, phrase, or picture in a Web page that you click to open another Web page or a different location in the same Web page is called a(n) _____.

6. What is the main difference between a disk-based Web and a server-based Web?

7. True or False: The address that identifies a specific computer on the Internet is called an Internet Protocol address.

8. True or False: A Web site is a set of related Web pages that are available from a Web server.

SESSION 1.2

In this session, you will learn how to use FrontPage to create and maintain a Web site. You will open a Web site in different views to see its contents, navigation structure, available reports, and hyperlinks.

What Is FrontPage?

Microsoft FrontPage simplifies the development, maintenance, and publication of a Web site. Using this program, you can create, view, edit, and publish your Web site; insert and edit text, pictures, and photo galleries in your Web pages; import and export files; add, test, and repair hyperlinks to and within your pages; and generate a variety of reports about your Web site's function and usage. Thus FrontPage lets you create, view, and manage your entire Web site. It includes features that facilitate Web site creation, such as templates for creating Web pages and built-in functions for processing Web pages.

To create professional-looking Web pages, you don't need to know HTML. Instead, you can use FrontPage's graphical interface to create Web pages and to develop and publish Web sites. When you **publish** a Web site, you store the Web site's files and folders on a Web server, which makes the Web site available to people using the Internet. FrontPage creates the HTML code for you automatically; a Web browser then interprets this code to display the data in your Web pages correctly.

A **FrontPage Web site**, or more simply a **Web site**, consists of the Web pages, files, and folders that make up the content of your Web site. It also includes the specific FrontPage Server Extension support files that allow your Web site to function correctly when it is accessed by Internet visitors. **FrontPage Server Extensions** are a set of programs and scripts that support FrontPage and allow a Web browser to send and receive Web pages that are processed by a Web server. When you create a Web site using FrontPage, these Server Extensions are created and included in the Web site automatically. You will learn more about the FrontPage Server Extensions in Tutorial 6.

You can create and publish a FrontPage Web site on your computer, on a local area network, or on the Internet so that people can access it using a Web browser. A **local area network (LAN)**, is a group of computers that are located near one another and connected so as to share data, files, software, and hardware. The computers in the offices of Sunny Morning Products are configured in a LAN.

Starting FrontPage and Opening a Web Site

You are now ready to begin your training by starting FrontPage and using it to examine the Web site for Sunny Morning Products. You start FrontPage in the same manner as you start other Windows programs. After examining Amanda's existing Web site, you will use FrontPage to create and manage a similar site as you complete the tutorials in this book.

REFERENCE WINDOW   **RW**

Opening a Web Site
- Click the list arrow for the Open button on the Standard toolbar.
- Click Open Web in the list.
- Click the folder that contains your Web site.
- Click the Open button.

To start FrontPage and open the SunnyMorningProducts Web site:

1. Click the **Start** button on the taskbar, point to **Programs**, and then click **Microsoft FrontPage** to open FrontPage. A blank page opens in the FrontPage program window. See Figure 1-20.

Figure 1-20   FRONTPAGE PROGRAM WINDOW

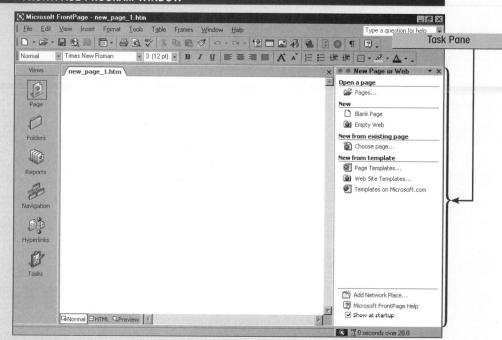

TROUBLE? If a dialog box opens and asks if you want to make FrontPage your default HTML editor, click the No button.

TROUBLE? FrontPage might open the previously used Web site, instead of the blank page shown in Figure 1-20. If a Web site name is listed in the title bar instead of "Microsoft FrontPage – new_page_1.htm," click File on the menu bar, click Close Web, and then continue with Step 2.

TROUBLE? FrontPage might open in a different view than the one shown in Figure 1-20, in which case your desktop might have a different appearance. This is not a problem; continue with Step 2.

TROUBLE? If necessary, click the Maximize button ▣ on the title bar to maximize the FrontPage program window.

FrontPage provides two options for opening items. First, you can open a single file, regardless of whether it is part of a Web site. Second, you can open an entire Web site, which gives you access to all of that Web site's files. The **Task Pane** allows you to open an existing page either by clicking a page name in the "Open a page" section or by clicking the "Pages" option to open a file not listed in the "Open a page" list. Because Amanda wants you to examine all of the files for the SunnyMorningProducts Web site, you will choose the option to open a Web site.

2. Click the **list arrow** for the Open button 📂 on the Standard toolbar. The Open button allows you to open either a single Web page or an entire Web site. You will open a Web site next.

3. Click **Open Web** in the list. The Open Web dialog box opens.

   TROUBLE? If the Open File dialog box opens, then either you clicked the Open button instead of its list arrow or you clicked Open in the list instead of Open Web. Click the Cancel button, and then repeat Steps 2 and 3.

   You need to change to the drive or folder that contains your Data Disk to open the SunnyMorningProducts Web site.

4. Click the **Look in** list arrow, and then click the drive or folder that contains your Data Disk.

5. Double-click the **My Webs** folder, and then click the **SunnyMorningProducts** folder to select it. This folder contains the files for the Web site for Sunny Morning Products. Notice that this folder contains a blue dot, which indicates that FrontPage has configured this folder to store a Web site. A Windows folder would appear without the blue dot.

6. Click the **Open** button in the dialog box to open the Web site in FrontPage.

7. If necessary, click the **Folders** button 📁 on the Views bar to change to Folders view. See Figure 1-21. Notice that the Task Pane has closed, providing more room to view the contents of the Web site. To turn the Task Pane back on, you could click View on the menu bar, and then click Task Pane. Because the Task Pane occupies a lot of room on the screen, this book generally directs you to use the menu commands and toolbars to perform tasks, instead of the equivalent items on the Task Pane.

Figure 1-21	SUNNYMORNINGPRODUCTS WEB SITE IN FOLDERS VIEW

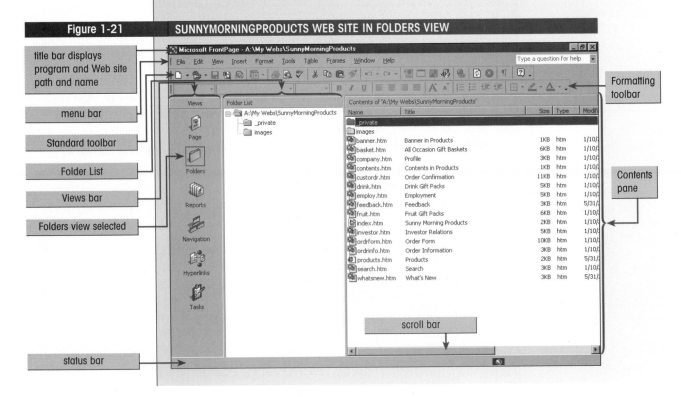

TROUBLE? The names of the files and folders in your Contents pane might appear in uppercase letters, lowercase letters, or mixed-case letters. Each file and folder is uniquely identified by its name, regardless of the case of the letters.

In Figure 1-21, a different icon appears to the left of the index.htm page's name. The 🏠 icon indicates that this page is the Web site's home page. If you open the SunnyMorningProducts Web site in a browser and do not request a specific file, index.htm will open automatically. The other files in the Web site use icons to indicate that they are HTML documents.

Figure 1-22 describes the various components of the FrontPage window that appear in Figure 1-21 in more detail.

Figure 1-22	COMPONENTS OF THE FRONTPAGE WINDOW
COMPONENT	**DESCRIPTION**
Contents pane	Contains the open Web page or Web site
Folder List	Contains the folders and files that make up the open Web site
Menu bar	Located below the title bar; provides access to all options available in the current FrontPage view
Scroll bars	Located at the right and bottom of the window (as necessary); scrolls the window vertically and horizontally
Status bar	Located at the bottom of the window; displays messages about the current Web page or FrontPage action as well as the name of a toolbar button when you position the pointer over the button
Title bar	Located at the top of the window; displays the program's name and the path and name of the open Web site
Toolbars	Located below the menu bar; contains different icons that represent shortcuts to commonly used commands
Views bar	Provides the list of available views for your Web site

Using Views

FrontPage **views** provide different ways of looking at the information in your Web site so that you can create and manage it more effectively. Clicking the buttons on the Views bar allows you to switch among the different views, such as Folders or Page view. Six views are available, as described in Figure 1-23 and in the following sections.

Figure 1-23		FRONTPAGE VIEWS
VIEW	**BUTTON**	**DESCRIPTION**
Page	📄	Use to create, edit, and format the content of a Web page
Folders	📁	Use to view, create, delete, copy, and move folders in the open Web site
Reports	📑	Use to analyze, summarize, and produce various types of reports about a Web site
Navigation	🗂	Use to create or display a Web site's navigation structure, which identifies the relationships among pages
Hyperlinks	🔗	Use to examine graphically the hyperlinks between Web pages in a Web site
Tasks	📋	Use to maintain a list of the tasks required to complete a Web site

Page View

You use **Page view** to create, edit, and format the content of a Web page. The filename of an open Web page in Page view appears as a tab at the top of the Contents pane. You can customize Page view in many ways:

- To see more of the open Web page in the Contents pane, close the Views bar and/or the Folder List by clicking View on the menu bar, and then clicking Views Bar and/or Folder List as needed. To open these items again, repeat the process.
- To show or hide the formatting symbols in your document, click the Show All button ¶ on the Standard toolbar.
- To see more of the open Web page in Page view, display the Standard and Formatting toolbars on one row by clicking View on the menu bar, pointing to Toolbars, and then clicking Customize. On the Options tab, click the Show Standard and Formatting toolbars on two rows check box. The disadvantage of having the toolbars share one row is that some buttons located at the end of the toolbar do not appear on the screen. To see them, click the More Buttons button on the right side of the toolbar. The figures in these tutorials assume that your toolbars appear on two rows so that you can readily locate and click all of the toolbar buttons.

Next, Amanda asks you to open the home page of the SunnyMorningProducts Web site in Page view.

To open and preview a page in Page view:

1. Double-click **index.htm** in the Contents pane to open the home page in Page view. See Figure 1-24. Notice how the toolbars change to display options that you can use to edit this page. The filename for the current page, index.htm, appears both in the title bar and as a page tab at the top of the Contents pane.

   TROUBLE? If your Folder List does not close automatically, click the Toggle Pane button on the Standard toolbar so your screen matches Figure 1-24.

| Figure 1-24 | PAGE VIEW OF THE SUNNY MORNING PRODUCTS HOME PAGE |

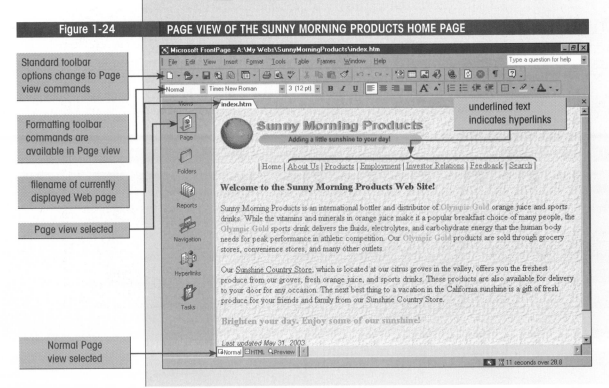

Standard toolbar options change to Page view commands

Formatting toolbar commands are available in Page view

filename of currently displayed Web page

Page view selected

underlined text indicates hyperlinks

Normal Page view selected

You can use three Page views to examine your Web page: Normal, HTML, and Preview. To switch among these views, click the buttons in the lower-left corner of the Contents pane, as shown in Figure 1-24, to switch among these views. Most of the time, you will work in **Normal Page view**, in which you can add to, revise, and format the content of your Web page. When you open a Web page in Page view, it usually opens in Normal Page view. **HTML Page view** lets you view and edit the HTML code for your Web page. **Preview Page view** allows you to quickly see your page as it will appear in a Web browser, without actually starting a browser.

By default, the Views bar is open so that you can easily switch among the different FrontPage views. When you are working in a view, you can close the Views bar to ensure that more of the view appears on the screen.

2. Click **View** on the menu bar, and then click **Views Bar**. The Views bar closes and the home page fills the screen. You can turn the Views bar back on by repeating Step 2. For now, however, you will leave the Views bar hidden so that you can see more of the Web page. (Showing or hiding the Views bar is a matter of personal preference.)

3. Point to the **Products** hyperlink at the top of the page. When you point to this hyperlink, the name of the linked file (products.htm) appears in the lower-left corner on the status bar. Also, a ScreenTip indicates that you can press the Ctrl key and click the hyperlink (Ctrl + Click) to follow the hyperlink. When you **follow** a hyperlink, you open the linked page.

4. Click the **Preview** button at the bottom of the window. The view changes to show how your Web page will look when viewed by a Web browser connected to the Internet. See Figure 1-25.

| Figure 1-25 | PREVIEW OF THE HOME PAGE |

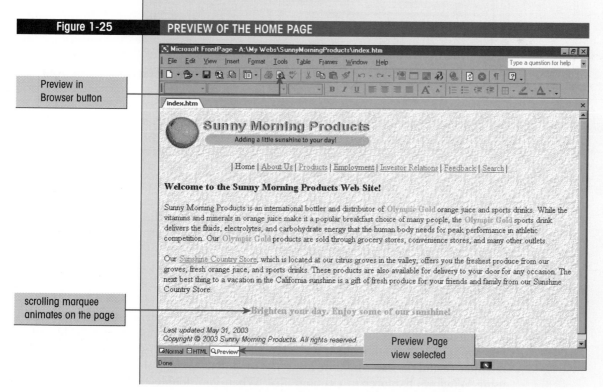

Preview in Browser button

scrolling marquee animates on the page

Preview Page view selected

This page contains an active element, called a marquee, which causes the text "Brighten your day. Enjoy some of our sunshine!" to scroll across the bottom of the screen.

5. Click the **Preview in Browser** button [icon] on the Standard toolbar to open the Web page in a browser. If necessary, maximize the browser window by clicking the **Maximize** button [icon] on the title bar. See Figure 1-26.

| Figure 1-26 | HOME PAGE IN INTERNET EXPLORER |

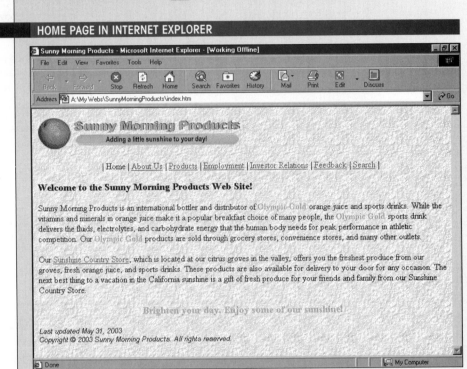

TROUBLE? This book assumes that you are using Internet Explorer 5.x as your Web browser. If you are using an earlier version of Internet Explorer or Netscape Navigator version 4.5 or lower, then your Web page might not animate the text on the page. Your instructor might direct you to perform different steps so that you can use your Web browser correctly.

Notice that the page looks approximately the same in the browser as when you viewed it using the Preview button in FrontPage. The Preview button does not always provide an accurate rendering of the page as it will ultimately appear in the browser, however, so it is important to open a Web page in the browser periodically as you are developing it to ensure that your design will be displayed correctly.

Folders View

You use **Folders view** to view and navigate the folders in your FrontPage Web site. Clicking a folder in Folders view shows the folder's contents, along with valuable information about each file in the folder, such as its size, type, title, the name of the person who last modified it, and the date and time it was last modified. Using Folders view is very similar to using Windows Explorer to examine files. When you double-click a filename in Folders view, that file opens in Page view.

Amanda wants you to examine the files and folders that make up the Web site, so you will change to Folders view.

To change to Folders view:

1. Click the **Close** button ☒ on the browser title bar to close it.

2. Click the **Microsoft FrontPage** program button on the taskbar to return to FrontPage (if necessary), and then click the **Normal** button to return to Normal Page view.

3. Click **View** on the menu bar, and then click **Views Bar** to show the Views bar.

4. Click the **Folders** button 📁 on the Views bar to change to Folders view. The Web site is stored in the SunnyMorningProducts folder, which contains two sub-folders (_private and images) and 16 files. The **_private folder** stores the hidden files that make up a Web site. **Hidden files** are not accessible to users of your Web site after it is published. You will learn more about hidden files in Tutorial 6. The **images folder** stores all of the picture and multimedia files that are included in the pages of a Web site.

TROUBLE? If you see more files and folders in the Web site, don't worry. FrontPage might be configured to display hidden files and folders.

Reports View

Reports view lets you analyze and summarize your Web site and generate reports about your Web site. The different types of reports identify the names of and important information about all of the site's files; pages that contain problems, such as broken hyperlinks; workflow information describing the development status of each page in the site and the person assigned to complete it; and usage information about Web sites that are stored on a server, such as the number of site users, the browsers used to access the site, and the keywords used to search the site for information.

The **Site Summary report** includes statistical information to help you to manage your Web site, such as data about the total number and size of the site's files, the number of pictures in the site, and the names of Web pages in the site that download slowly (pages that take longer than a set number of seconds using a 28.8 bps modem; the default setting is 30 seconds). FrontPage automatically generates a Site Summary report when you change to Reports view. You will use Reports view frequently as you develop your own site, so Amanda wants you to examine this general report in some detail.

To change to Reports view:

1. Click the **Reports** button 🗔 on the Views bar. Figure 1-27 shows a Site Summary report for the SunnyMorningProducts Web site. It is a good idea to run a Site Summary report periodically as you develop a Web site so that you can locate and correct problems as you work. You can also use the Reports button on the Reporting toolbar to display different reports.

| Figure 1-27 | SITE SUMMARY REPORT IN REPORTS VIEW |

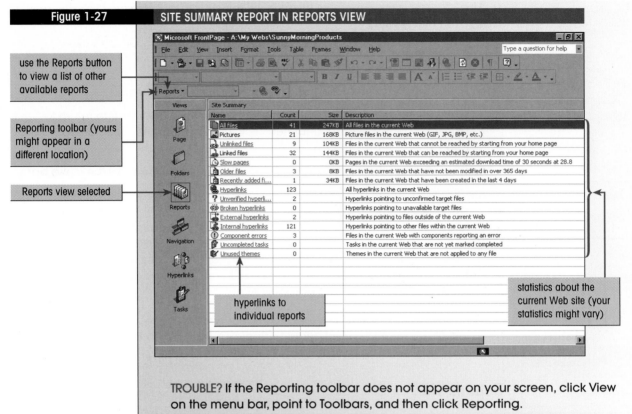

use the Reports button to view a list of other available reports

Reporting toolbar (yours might appear in a different location)

Reports view selected

hyperlinks to individual reports

statistics about the current Web site (your statistics might vary)

TROUBLE? If the Reporting toolbar does not appear on your screen, click View on the menu bar, point to Toolbars, and then click Reporting.

TROUBLE? If the Reporting toolbar blocks part of the Site Summary report, drag it to an open area of your screen so that you can see the entire report.

TROUBLE? If the Site Summary report does not appear, click the Reports button on the Reporting toolbar, and then click Site Summary in the list.

Navigation View

Navigation view displays your Web site as a diagram that shows its navigation structure as a folder-like hierarchy resembling an organization chart. This hierarchy allows you to drag and drop pages into your site structure to show how pages are related to one another. If necessary, you can resize Navigation view to better fit the Contents pane, thereby making it easier to examine this diagram. In addition, you can rearrange the view to rotate the objects, and you can print Navigation view.

Amanda asks you to open the SunnyMorningProducts Web site in Navigation view so that you can examine its structure.

To explore a Web site in Navigation view:

1. Click the **Navigation** button on the Views bar to change to Navigation view for the SunnyMorningProducts Web site.

2. If necessary, click the **Zoom** list arrow on the Navigation toolbar, and then click **Size To Fit** to resize Navigation view to fit the Contents pane. See Figure 1-28. When Amanda created the SunnyMorningProducts Web site, she added the pages shown in the navigation diagram to the Web site's navigation structure.

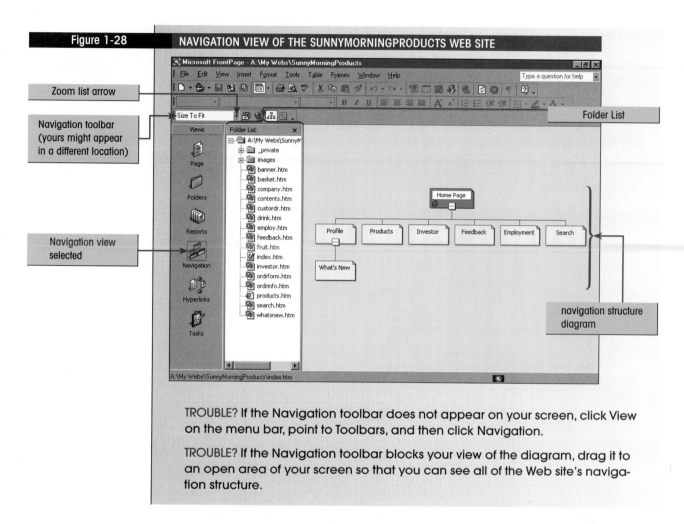

Figure 1-28 NAVIGATION VIEW OF THE SUNNYMORNINGPRODUCTS WEB SITE

Zoom list arrow

Navigation toolbar (yours might appear in a different location)

Navigation view selected

Folder List

navigation structure diagram

TROUBLE? If the Navigation toolbar does not appear on your screen, click View on the menu bar, point to Toolbars, and then click Navigation.

TROUBLE? If the Navigation toolbar blocks your view of the diagram, drag it to an open area of your screen so that you can see all of the Web site's navigation structure.

Navigation view shows that the home page is the top-level page in the Web site. The top-level page in a Web site is called the **parent page**; normally, a Web site's home page is its parent page. A page that appears below the parent page or any other page in a Web site's structure is called a **child page**. Seven child pages appear below the home page. The What's New Web page is a child page of the Profile Web page, which is itself a child page of the home page. When you create a new Web site, only the home page is displayed in Navigation view. To add a page to Navigation view, drag its filename from the Folder List and then drop it into the correct position in the navigation structure. You use Navigation view when creating a **FrontPage link bar** (also known as a **FrontPage navigation bar**), which is a group of hyperlinks that connect the pages in the Web site; FrontPage creates and updates this type of link bar automatically. You will learn more about Navigation view and link bars in Tutorial 5.

Hyperlinks View

In **Hyperlinks view**, your Web site appears graphically as a hierarchical picture of the hyperlinks that connect its files, including multimedia files.

Amanda wants you to know how to view a Web site in Hyperlinks view so you will understand how the Web pages that make up the Web site are linked together. Hyperlinks view shows only part of the entire Web site at one time, so you must adjust the page to view all of its areas.

To view a Web site in Hyperlinks view:

1. Click the **Hyperlinks** button 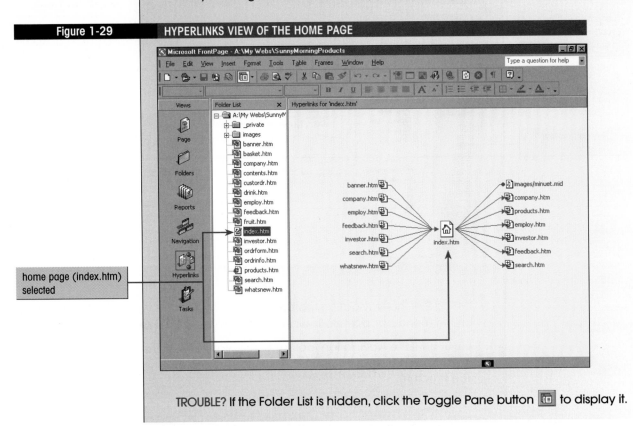 on the Views bar, and then click **index.htm** in the Folder List. Hyperlinks view of the home page (index.htm) for the SunnyMorningProducts Web site appears. See Figure 1-29.

Figure 1-29	HYPERLINKS VIEW OF THE HOME PAGE

home page (index.htm) selected

TROUBLE? If the Folder List is hidden, click the Toggle Pane button to display it.

You can customize Hyperlinks view to display page titles instead of page filenames, so your Hyperlinks view might include different names from those shown in Figure 1-29. To display the page titles or filenames, right-click an empty area in the Contents pane in Hyperlinks view, and then click Show Page Titles on the shortcut menu to turn this feature on or off.

In Figure 1-29, most of the hyperlinks end with an arrow, but one ends with a bullet. An arrow indicates a hyperlink to another Web page in your Web site; a bullet indicates a hyperlink to a sound or other type of file.

Switching Between Pages

Although the default Web page in Hyperlinks view is the home page (as displayed in the Contents pane), you can easily switch to another page in the Web site. The selected page then becomes the focus of Hyperlinks view. When you create and maintain a Web site, you should use Hyperlinks view to examine the various pages that make up the Web site to ensure that they are linked correctly. FrontPage makes it easy for you to follow the hyperlinks from one page to the next.

Amanda asks you to change the focus of Hyperlinks view to the Products page, so you can examine its hyperlinks.

To switch between pages:

1. Click **products.htm** in the Folder List. The Products page becomes the focus, and its hyperlinks are displayed in the Contents pane so that you can readily see the origin and destination of each hyperlink to and from the Products Web page.

2. Click **index.htm** in the Folder List to redisplay this page with the focus in the Contents pane.

Following a Hyperlink

You can follow the hyperlinks from one document to another by expanding (showing) or contracting (hiding) the hyperlinks displayed in Hyperlinks view. Expanding the hyperlinks enables you to see how the pages in a Web site are interconnected.

Amanda asks you to follow the hyperlinks from the Products page.

To follow a hyperlink:

1. Click the **Toggle Pane** button on the Standard toolbar to close the Folder List.

2. Click the **plus (+)** symbol in the products.htm icon to expand this hyperlink and display the pages used with the Products frames page.

3. Click the **plus (+)** symbol in the contents.htm icon to expand this hyperlink. The diagram includes the pages referenced by all of the hyperlinks in the content frame.

4. Click the **plus (+)** symbol in the ordrinfo.htm icon to expand this hyperlink. See Figure 1-30. Now you can see how the hyperlinks extend from the home page to the ordrinfo.htm page, and beyond.

| Figure 1-30 | EXPANDED HYPERLINKS IN HYPERLINKS VIEW |

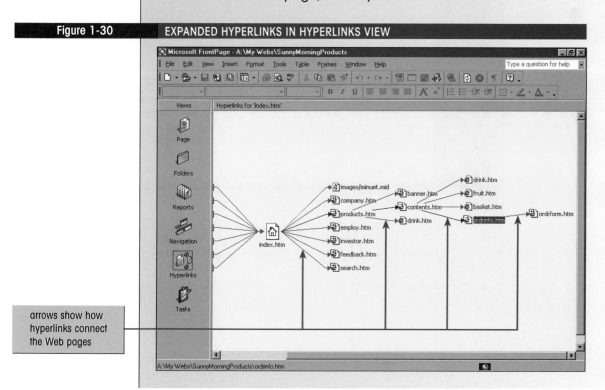

arrows show how hyperlinks connect the Web pages

To contract the hyperlinks, you would click the minus (-) symbol for the desired page.

Displaying a Repeated Hyperlink

As you saw in Session 1.1, a Web page can contain multiple hyperlinks to the same location in a page or in a Web site. A hyperlink to a location that already is the target of another hyperlink is called a **repeated hyperlink**. You can examine the repeated hyperlinks in a Web site in Hyperlinks view to determine whether you have defined all of the necessary hyperlinks among the pages in your Web site. The home page contains two hyperlinks to the Products page: one in the link bar and another in the text in the page, as you will see next.

To display the repeated hyperlinks in the home page:

1. Right-click any empty area in the Contents pane, and then click **Repeated Hyperlinks** on the shortcut menu. Hyperlinks view changes to show the repeated hyperlinks for the home page. See Figure 1-31. As you learned in Session 1.1, the home page contains two links to the products.htm page: one in the link bar at the top of the page, and another with the text "Sunshine Country Store," which appears in the second paragraph.

| Figure 1-31 | REPEATED HYPERLINKS FOR THE HOME PAGE |

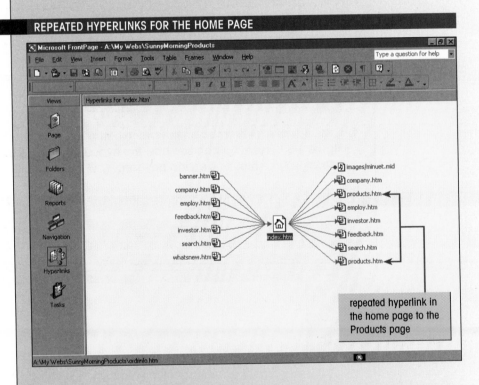

repeated hyperlink in the home page to the Products page

TROUBLE? If you see a check mark in front of the Repeated Hyperlinks command on the shortcut menu, then this feature is already turned on; clicking it will turn off the display of the repeated hyperlinks.

2. Repeat Step 1 to turn off the display of the repeated hyperlinks.

Tasks View

To manage the development of a Web site by one or more people, you can use a **Tasks list**, which provides a detailed listing of the necessary activities or items required to complete a Web site. The Tasks list describes each task, indicates the person assigned to complete it, and specifies the task's priority. Once you have completed the initial design of your Web site, you can create a Tasks list that describes all of the pages you need to develop. You can then add activities to it, modify the task names, assign developers, and include descriptions as desired. When a task is finished, you can mark it as completed and then archive or delete it from the Tasks list. To open the Tasks list, click the Tasks button 🗊 on the Views bar. When many people are collaborating to develop a new Web site, they can use Tasks view to manage the Web site's overall development. You will learn more about Tasks view in Tutorial 3.

Closing a Web Site and Exiting FrontPage

Because you can configure FrontPage to open the previously used Web site when it starts, it is a good idea to close the open Web before closing FrontPage. This approach ensures that another user won't receive an error message when trying to start FrontPage.

Amanda asks you to close the SunnyMorningProducts Web site and then exit FrontPage.

To close a Web site and exit FrontPage:

1. Click **File** on the menu bar, and then click **Close Web**. FrontPage closes the SunnyMorningProducts Web site. You can tell that the Web site was closed because the title bar now says "Microsoft FrontPage." When a Web site is open, the Web site's path and name also appear in the title bar.

   TROUBLE? If you do not see the Close Web command on the File menu, click the double-arrow that appears at the bottom of the menu.

2. Click the **Close** button ☒ on the FrontPage title bar to close the program.

In the next session, Amanda will review some basic HTML concepts with you. Although you will use FrontPage to create and edit your Web pages, it is important for you to understand the HTML code that FrontPage uses to create those pages.

Session 1.2 QUICK CHECK

1. What is the main advantage of using FrontPage to create and maintain a Web site?

2. You create, edit, and format the content of a Web page in _____ view.

3. The FrontPage view that lets you analyze and summarize your Web site is _____ view.

4. The FrontPage view that shows your Web site's hierarchy of parent and child pages is _____ view.

5. What is a repeated hyperlink?

6. You can use a(n) _____ to manage the development of a Web site and to coordinate the efforts of many people.

7. True or False: You can use Page view to see the HTML code that FrontPage used to create a Web page.

8. True or False: It is a good idea to close the open Web site before exiting FrontPage.

SESSION 1.3

In this session, you will learn how to use HTML to create a Web page. You will use FrontPage and Internet Explorer to view the HTML code for a Web page. Finally, you will use the FrontPage Help system.

How HTML Works

HTML is used to describe the appearance of a Web page that you create with FrontPage. The code in an HTML document specifies the appearance of text in terms of its font (such as Arial or Times Roman), its attributes (such as bold or italic), or its placement (such as a heading or a bulleted list). An HTML document also specifies the playing of sound files, the placement of pictures, and the appearance of the page's background, if these elements are used. A Web browser interprets the HTML codes in a Web page to determine how to display and use these elements on the page when a client views the page.

Even though HTML uses a standard character set to ensure that documents can be easily transferred and viewed by many different types of computers, not all Web browsers will interpret these codes and display the requested HTML document in exactly the same way. For example, text that is formatted as bold might be displayed as bold text by one browser and as blue text by another browser. Even with this limitation, the use of HTML in storing, transferring, and viewing HTML documents among the many different computers that are connected to the Internet is the key element in providing a standard method for displaying information.

Understanding HTML Tags

The HTML document that creates a Web page contains codes, called **tags**, which the browser interprets when displaying the page. The name of an HTML tag is enclosed in angle brackets (< >). Most tags are **two-sided**; that is, they are used in pairs that consist of an opening tag and a closing tag. The **opening tag** tells the browser to turn on a particular feature and apply it to the document content that follows this tag. The browser continues applying the feature until it encounters the **closing tag**, which tells the browser to stop applying the feature. The forward slash character identifies a closing tag (/) in the tag name. For example, the tags <BODY> and </BODY> specify the beginning and end of the body of an HTML document, respectively, and the tags <B> and </B> indicate the beginning and end of bold text, respectively.

Some tags are **one-sided**, requiring only an opening tag. With this type of tag, the browser stops applying the formatting indicated by the one-sided tag when it encounters a new line.

Figure 1-32 lists some common tags. The ellipsis (...) in the tags indicates the content that is entered by the Web page creator, either between two-sided tags or within a one-sided tag.

Figure 1-32	SELECTED HTML TAG DESCRIPTIONS	
HTML TAG	**DESCRIPTION**	**USE**
<! ... >	Creates a comment, which is not displayed in the Web page. A comment might identify the page's developer or document the code.	To document HTML code and to insert comments. For example, a comment might indicate that a frames page may not be recognized by all Web browsers.
<A> ... </A>	Defines a hyperlink or an anchor.	Indicates an internal or external hyperlink and the file or location that will open.
<B> ... </B>	Changes text to bold.	
<BGSOUND SRC=...>	Specifies a background sound.	Indicates the filename containing the sound.
<BLOCKQUOTE> ... </BLOCKQUOTE>	Indents text.	Sets off long quotations or other text indention.
<BODY> ... </BODY>	Encloses the body of the HTML document.	
 	Forces a new line break on a page.	
<DD> ... </DD>	Specifies a definition within a glossary list.	Provides a heading line for a defined term.
<DL> ... </DL>	Specifies a definition or glossary list.	
<DT> ... </DT>	Specifies a definition term within a glossary list.	Provides the font size and indentation information for a defined term.
<EM> ... </EM>	Emphasizes text, usually with italic.	
<H1> ... </H1> <H2> ... </H2> <H3> ... </H3> <H4> ... </H4> <H5> ... </H5> <H6> ... </H6>	Specifies a heading and its level.	Indicates the font size of a heading. H1 has the largest size; H6 has the smallest size.
<HR>	Draws a horizontal line across the page.	Provides a visual break for sections of a page.
<HTML> ... </HTML>	Encloses the entire HTML document.	Identifies the file as one that contains HTML codes.
<I> ... </I>	Changes text to italic.	
<IMG> ... </IMG>	Specifies the appearance of a picture in a page.	Inserts a picture file into the HTML document.
<LI> ... </LI>	Specifies an individual element in a bulleted or numbered list.	
<OL> ... </OL>	Specifies an ordered list of elements.	Creates numbered elements in a list.
<P> ... </P>	Divides text into paragraphs separated by blank lines.	
<PRE> ... </PRE>	Specifies preformatted text.	Keeps the spacing arrangement of text as entered in the document. Use for text that needs special indentations or column layouts.
<STRONG> ... </STRONG>	Strongly emphasizes text, usually with bold.	
<TABLE> ... </TABLE>	Specifies a table.	Organizes data in a row-and-column table arrangement.
<TD> ... </TD>	Defines the data contained in a table's cells.	
<TH> ... </TH>	Creates a row of headings in a table.	
<TITLE> ... </TITLE>	Defines the text that appears in the Web browser's title bar.	Creates the Web page's title.
<TR> ... </TR>	Indicates a row in a table.	Provides rows that hold the data for each cell.
<TT> ... </TT>	Formats text in a typewriter font, usually Courier.	Applies a monospace font; used with the <PRE> tag.
<UL> ... </UL>	Specifies an unordered list of elements.	Creates bulleted elements in a list.

Just as important as the tags themselves is the order of their placement. Tags often appear within each other, as **nested tags**. The browser first processes the tag on the outside, called the **outside tag**; it then processes the tag on the inside, called the **inside tag**. When nesting tags, you must close the inside tag before closing the outside tag. When you create a nested list—for example, a bulleted list within a numbered list—FrontPage handles the opening and closing of each pair of tags automatically. You need to be concerned with nesting the tags only if you decide to make changes directly to your HTML code, which is not the recommended approach when using FrontPage. However, it is helpful to understand how a browser applies different formats to a single code segment.

Many HTML tags require one or more **attributes**, or **properties**, which specify additional information about the tag. For example, an attribute might supply a sound's filename to an HTML tag that plays a sound when the Web page is loaded. Attributes appear within the brackets that enclose the tag.

Figure 1-33 shows some HTML tags for the Sunny Morning Products home page. (*Note*: For clarity, tag names are set in all capital letters in the text, even though they appear in lowercase letters in FrontPage.) The <BODY> tag specifies the beginning of the body of the HTML document. Included within this tag is the BACKGROUND attribute, which specifies the filename of the page's background picture. The <BGSOUND> tag indicates that a background sound is included. The source of this sound, which is a sound file, is specified by the SRC (for "source") attribute. The LOOP attribute specifies how many times the browser should play the sound.

Figure 1-33	HTML CODE IN PAGE VIEW

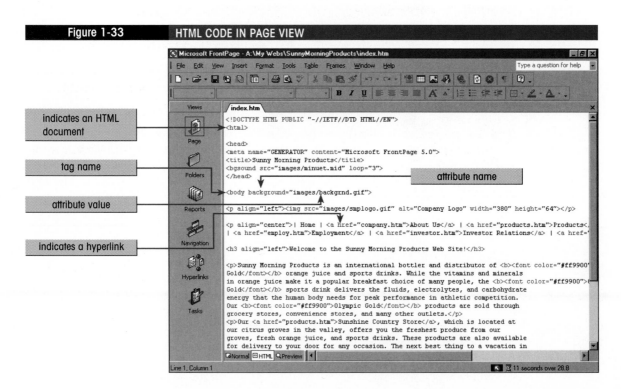

You can create an HTML document using a program other than FrontPage; for example, you can use a text editor, such as Notepad, or an HTML authoring program. Notepad does not insert any HTML codes into its document file. Instead, you must write and edit the codes yourself, and, therefore, you need to know each tag's name and its attributes. Writing HTML code can prove tedious when you are creating a complex Web page. By contrast, FrontPage's ability to enter HTML codes automatically lets you create an HTML document without learning HTML. Regardless of which method you used to create a Web page, you can work with FrontPage to open and revise the Web page.

Viewing **HTML Code**

By viewing the HTML code for a Web page, you can see how a particular feature has been implemented using HTML tags. In this book, you will create and edit Web pages using FrontPage. You will also study the HTML code that FrontPage used to create the Web page so as to gain a better understanding of how HTML works. Some Web page developers find it easier to make changes directly to the HTML code, even when they are working in FrontPage. You can examine a Web page's HTML code by using FrontPage, a Web browser, or any text editor.

Viewing HTML Code Using FrontPage

When you view HTML code in FrontPage, the HTML codes appear in a different color (usually blue) to distinguish between your page's content and the HTML tags that FrontPage created automatically. Amanda asks you to examine the HTML code for the Sunny Morning Products home page.

To view HTML code using FrontPage:

1. If necessary, start FrontPage, open the **SunnyMorningProducts** Web site in Folders view, and then open the home page (**index.htm**) in Page view.

2. Click the **HTML** button at the bottom of the Contents pane to display the page's HTML code. Notice that the HTML tags appear in blue, and the content of the Web page (as entered by the page's creator) appears in black.

   TROUBLE? If your HTML tags appear in a different color, don't worry. You can change the settings in FrontPage to customize the appearance of HTML Page view.

3. Inspect the HTML code and try to identify which tags provide the formatting instructions that create the home page. As you work through the tutorials in this book, you will learn about the various HTML tags that specify the appearance of the Web pages for Sunny Morning Products.

4. Click the **Normal** button to return to Normal Page view.

Viewing HTML Code Using Internet Explorer

You can also view HTML code through your Web browser. This option is convenient when you want to inspect the HTML code for a Web page that was created by someone else and that you opened on the Web. Next, you will view the HTML code for the Sunny Morning Products home page using Internet Explorer.

To view HTML code using Internet Explorer:

1. Click the **Preview in Browser** button [image] on the Standard toolbar. If necessary, maximize the Internet Explorer window. (You can click the Stop button [image] to stop the music, if desired.) The home page opens in the browser.

---

2. Click **View** on the menu bar, click **Source**, and then maximize the Notepad window, if necessary. Notepad starts automatically and displays the HTML document used to create this Web page. When you view the HTML code in Notepad, it's a good idea to turn on the Word Wrap feature so that all of the HTML code will fit inside the window.

3. Click **Format** on the Notepad menu bar, and then click **Word Wrap**. Now all of the HTML code fits within the Notepad window. The HTML code matches that displayed in HTML Page view, except the HTML tags do not appear in a different color.

   TROUBLE? If the Word Wrap command has a check mark in front of it, then the Word Wrap feature is already on. If you accidentally turned off the Word Wrap feature, repeat Step 3 to turn it back on.

4. Click the **Close** button ☒ on the Notepad program window.

5. If necessary, click the **No** button to close the dialog box and Notepad.

6. Click ☒ on the Internet Explorer program window to close Internet Explorer.

Getting Help in FrontPage

The FrontPage Help system provides the same options as the Help systems found in other Windows and Office programs, including the Contents, Answer Wizard, and Index tabs. There are several different ways to use the Help system, so you can choose the one that you like the best. The different ways of accessing Help are as follows:

- Type a question in the Ask a Question box, which appears on the menu bar. After you enter your question, press the Enter key. A list box opens and displays a selection of topics that might answer your question. Clicking a topic opens the Microsoft FrontPage Help window and displays the specified Help topic.

- Click Help on the menu bar, and then click Microsoft FrontPage Help. The Office Assistant opens, providing a text box in which you can ask a question. After typing your question, click the Search button to start the search. The Office Assistant will display a list of topics that might answer your question. Clicking a topic opens the Microsoft FrontPage Help window and displays your requested topic.

- Click Help on the menu bar, and then click What's This. The pointer changes to a ⟨?⟩ shape. Clicking an item in the window will display a ScreenTip with a short description of that item. Not all screen objects have Help items associated with them; in this case, the ScreenTip will inform you that no Help item exists for the screen object. In many dialog boxes, you can click the question mark button on the title bar to activate this type of Help for the objects in the dialog box.

Using the Ask a Question box is an easy way to get Help. Amanda wants you to try this method to obtain more information about printing the HTML code for a Web page, so you'll both gain experience with the Help system and learn how to perform this task.

To use the Ask a Question box to get Help:

1. Click in the **Ask a Question** box on the menu bar. An insertion point replaces the "Type a question for help" text.

2. Type **How do I print the HTML code for a Web page?** in the box, and then press the **Enter** key. See Figure 1-34. Help lists several topics; "Print a web page" might answer your question. The last option, "None of the above, search for more on the Web," is a hyperlink that opens a page at the Microsoft Web site, where you can search for additional topics related to your question.

Figure 1-34	USING THE ASK A QUESTION BOX

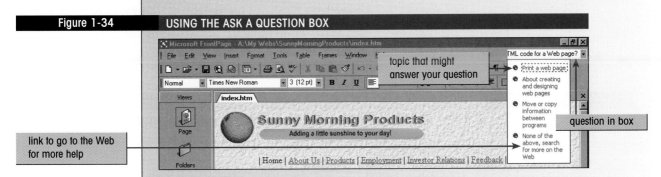

3. Click **Print a web page**. The Microsoft FrontPage Help window opens. If necessary, click the **Maximize** button 🔲 on the Help window title bar to maximize the Help window. See Figure 1-35.

Figure 1-35	MICROSOFT FRONTPAGE HELP WINDOW

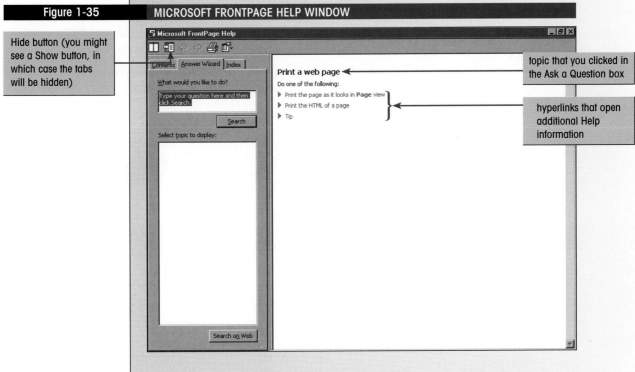

TROUBLE? If the Contents, Answer Wizard, and Index tabs are hidden, click the Show button 🔳.

You can manipulate the Help window just like any other window so as to make it easier to use. For example, you might want to create more room for the Help page. After you click the Show button, it changes to the Hide button, which you can click to hide the Contents, Answer Wizard, and Index tabs. The **Contents tab** allows you to search for information that is organized into groups by subject, such as "Designing Webs" or "Authoring HTML." The **Answer Wizard tab** lets you find Help by asking a question; this Wizard provides hyperlinks to information that might answer your question. You can enter a specific term or phrase on the **Index tab**; Help then displays a list of hyperlinks that contain that term or phrase.

You can also restore the Help window and resize it so that you can see the FrontPage and Help windows at the same time.

4. Click the **Print the HTML of a page** link in the main window. Help displays a page with the steps for printing the HTML code for a Web page. See Figure 1-36.

Figure 1-36	HELP DISPLAYED USING A HYPERLINK

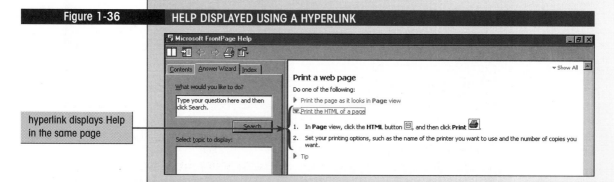

hyperlink displays Help in the same page

Amanda wants you to learn how to display HTML tags in Normal Page view. She suggests that you use the Answer Wizard to find Help on this subject.

5. If necessary, click the **Answer Wizard** tab to select it. The "Type your question here and then click Search" phrase is selected in the What would you like to do? text box.

6. Type **How do I display the HTML code for a Web page?** and then click the **Search** button. The Select a topic to display box lists several topics that might answer your question. Notice that one of the items starts with "WEB:". If you click this item, Help will connect to the Internet and display additional information about this topic.

7. Click **Show or hide HTML tags in the Normal pane**, and then click the **To show HTML tags** link in the main window. Clicking the link displays the Help information on the selected topic. See Figure 1-37.

| Figure 1-37 | USING THE ANSWER WIZARD TAB |

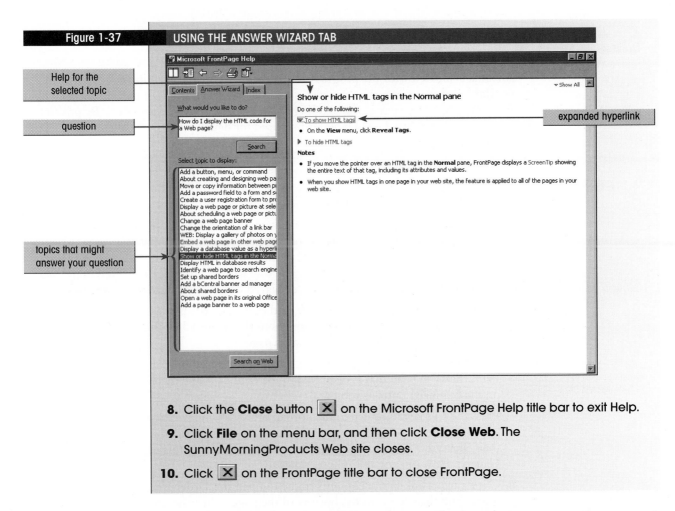

8. Click the **Close** button ☒ on the Microsoft FrontPage Help title bar to exit Help.

9. Click **File** on the menu bar, and then click **Close Web**. The SunnyMorningProducts Web site closes.

10. Click ☒ on the FrontPage title bar to close FrontPage.

Now that you have a better understanding of Microsoft FrontPage and are familiar with the Web site that Amanda created for Sunny Morning Products, you can proceed with the next part of your training. In Tutorial 2, you will learn the five-part process for developing a Web site.

Session 1.3 QUICK CHECK

1. Some HTML tags require _____ that contain additional information about an HTML document's appearance.

2. What are two methods for viewing the HTML code of a Web page?

3. Write a line of HTML code to italicize the words "home page" in a Web page.

4. The _____ tab in the Microsoft FrontPage Help window lets you find information that is organized into groups by subject.

5. True or False: You can use HTML to create a nested list in a Web page.

6. True or False: When HTML code is displayed in Internet Explorer, the HTML tags and properties appear in different colors.

REVIEW ASSIGNMENTS

Amanda is pleased with the progress you are making in your training course. Before you continue with your training, however, she wants you to examine some additional Web page features to increase your understanding of Web pages and Web browsers. By practicing these related skills, you will be better prepared for developing future Web pages.

If necessary, start Internet Explorer, insert your Data Disk in the appropriate drive, and then do the following:

Explore
1. Type A:\My Webs\SunnyMorningProducts\index.htm in the Address bar, and then press the Enter key to open the home page for Sunny Morning Products.

2. Click View on the menu bar, and then click Full Screen to increase the size of the Internet Explorer window. Next, click the Products hyperlink to open that Web page. Examine each of the four alternatives available in the contents frame in turn by selecting each hyperlink to open the linked Web page. Note whether the page displayed in the main frame changes while the other pages displayed in the other frames remain the same.

3. Click the Fruit Gift Packs hyperlink, and then click the picture to the left of the "Ruby Red Grapefruit" heading. What happens to the page? Click the Back button on the toolbar to return to the Fruit Gift Packs page.

4. Click anywhere in the banner frame, except on a hyperlink, to give this frame the focus. Print the Web page that is displayed in the banner frame by clicking the Print button on the Standard Buttons toolbar.

5. Press the F11 key to return to the normal browser window. Right-click the page (but not a hyperlink or picture) that appears in the main frame to open the shortcut menu, and then click View Source to display the HTML code. Does this page contain a Photo Gallery? How can you tell? Close Notepad.

6. Click a hyperlink in the contents frame to open the Order Information page in the main frame, and then scroll to the bottom of the page. Click the order form hyperlink to open the Order Form page in the main frame.

Explore
7. Fill out the order form using your name and other data that you make up, and then print the Order Form Web page.

Explore
8. Click the Send Order button to simulate the action of submitting a completed order form. What happens after you submit the form, and why?

Explore
9. Return to the Order Form page, and click the Clear Order button to remove the data that you entered from the order form. Right-click a blank area in the Order Form page, and then click View Source on the shortcut menu to open the Notepad window and display the HTML code used to create this page. Type your first and last names on the first line of the document, click File on the menu bar, click Print to print the code, and then close the Notepad program window without saving your changes.

Explore
10. Review the printout of the Order Form Web page, and then circle the HTML code that creates the Send Order button. Close Internet Explorer.

11. Start FrontPage and open the **SunnyMorningProducts** Web site in Navigation view. Click the Print button on the Standard toolbar to print the view.

Explore
12. In the Ask a Question box, ask "How do I specify settings for a slow page?" Review the information that you find, and then print it using the appropriate toolbar button. Close Help.

Explore
13. Switch to Reports view. Run a Slow Pages report and find all pages that take longer than 15 seconds to download with an Internet connection speed of 28.8 bps. Which page(s), if any, did your report identify?

Explore

14. Change to Hyperlinks view, set the **contents.htm** page as the focus, and then print Hyperlinks view. (*Hint*: FrontPage does not have a feature to print Hyperlinks view, so you must print the screen. In Hyperlinks view, press the Print Screen key on the keyboard. Click the Start button on the taskbar, point to Programs, point to Accessories, and then click WordPad. Click the Paste button on the WordPad Standard toolbar to paste the image into the blank WordPad document. Click File on the menu bar, click Page Setup, click the Landscape option button in the Orientation section, and then click the OK button. Click the Print button on the Standard toolbar to print the image. Close WordPad without saving your changes.)

15. Close the **SunnyMorningProducts** Web site, and then close FrontPage.

CASE PROBLEMS

Case 1. Exploring the Web Site for the American Carpenters Society   The American Carpenters Society (ACS) is a not-for-profit organization that enhances the skills of professional carpenters. ACS has a small staff of 15 people at its headquarters that supports its entire membership. Recently, Kevin Mortillaro, ACS president, hired you to support all of the group's end-user computing activities. Kevin wants you to maintain the daily operations of the organization's computers and the ACS Web site. He had previously contracted EarthShare, its current ISP, to create and maintain the ACS Web site. Now he prefers to have the ongoing development of the Web site managed in-house so that you can easily adapt it.

If necessary, start Internet Explorer, insert your Data Disk in the appropriate drive, and then do the following:

1. Open the home page for the **Carpenter** Web site on your Data Disk. (*Hint*: Type the following text into the appropriate location in Internet Explorer: A:\My Webs\Carpenter\index.htm, and then press the Enter key.)

2. Click the Membership Benefits hyperlink at the top of the Web page to open the Membership Benefits Web page. Examine each of the four alternatives available in the Table of Contents by clicking a hyperlink and opening the linked Web page. Note whether the page that opens in the main frame changes while the pages in the other frames remain the same.

3. Click anywhere in the banner frame (but not a hyperlink) to select the banner frame.

4. Print the page that appears in the banner frame, and then print the page that appears in the main frame.

Explore

5. Use Internet Explorer to display the HTML code for the Membership Benefits Web page. Type your name on the first line of the document, and then print it. What does the HTML code for this page describe? Close Notepad without saving your changes.

6. Right-click the main frame to open the shortcut menu, and then click View Source to display the HTML code for the page. Does this code describe the main frame or is it the same code that you saw in Step 5? Type your name on the first line of the document, print the HTML code, and then close Notepad without saving your changes.

7. Click the Become A Member hyperlink in the banner frame to open that page. Does the Become A Member page replace the frames page, or does it appear in the main frame?

Explore

8. Complete the Become A Member form with your name and other data that you make up, and then print the completed form.

9. Click the Submit Form button to simulate the action of submitting a completed Become A Member form to the server. What happens after you submit the form, and why?

Explore 10. In Internet Explorer, click the Back button on the Standard Buttons toolbar, click the Reset Form button to remove the data you entered in the Become A Member form, and then display the HTML code for the form. Type your name on the first line of the document, and then print the HTML code. Close Notepad without saving your changes. Review the HTML code, and circle the HTML code for the Submit Form button on the printout.

11. Click the Who's Who hyperlink to open the Who's Who Web page. Does this page contain a table?

Explore 12. Display the HTML code for the Who's Who Web page. Type your name on the first line of the document, and then print the HTML code. Close Notepad without saving your changes, and then close Internet Explorer. Review the printout of the HTML code, and locate and circle the tags that create the table in the Web page.

Explore 13. Start FrontPage and open the **Carpenter** Web site from the My Webs folder on your Data Disk. Change to Hyperlinks view for the home page, and then print it. (*Hint*: FrontPage does not have a feature to print Hyperlinks view, so you must print the screen. In Hyperlinks view, press the Print Screen key on the keyboard. Click the Start button on the taskbar, point to Programs, point to Accessories, and then click WordPad. Click the Paste button on the WordPad Standard toolbar to paste the image into the blank WordPad document. Click File on the menu bar, click Page Setup, click the Landscape option button in the Orientation section, and then click the OK button. Click the Print button on the Standard toolbar to print the image. Close WordPad without saving your changes.)

14. Close the **Carpenter** Web site, and then close FrontPage.

Case 2. Examining Web Sites for Guardian Mutual Insurance Guardian Mutual Insurance (GMI) is a large, national insurance company, which sells insurance to both individuals and businesses. GMI employs a staff of nearly 100 computer programmers and analysts who maintain and build its management information systems. Marcella Riley is the Human Resources manager at GMI. She recently hired Ollie Sherman as a systems analyst and assigned him to GMI's Web development team. Marcella wants you to help Ollie review some competitors' Web sites to gather some ideas for developing GMI's Web site. (*Note*: You must have an Internet connection to complete this Case Problem.)

If necessary, start your Web browser, and then do the following:

Explore 1. Use your Web browser to connect to the Internet and then visit at least five business-oriented Web sites. Examine Web sites that provide corporate information as well as sites designed for doing business on the Internet.

2. While studying each site, analyze the amount and type of information provided, and note the site's overall appearance and ease of use.

3. Based on the standards described in the case introduction, identify the three Web sites that you feel are the best. Print the pages for each (a maximum of 10 pages for any one site).

4. For each Web site, choose one Web page and print its HTML code. Note which pages contain at least one <TABLE> tag.

Explore 5. Draw a diagram similar to what might appear in Navigation view for one of the sites.

Explore 6. For each Web site, write a one-page report that describes its key features. Your report should include the following information: best and worst features, features that need improvement, suggestions for improvement, and commentary about ease of use and overall style.

7. Based on the reports you completed in Step 6, identify which sites you rated as the best and the worst. Defend your selections.

8. Close your Web browser and your Internet connection, if necessary.

LAB ASSIGNMENTS

These Lab Assignments are designed to accompany the interactive Course Labs called Computer History Hypermedia and The Internet: World Wide Web. To start a Lab, click the Start button on the Windows taskbar, point to Programs, point to Course Labs, point to New Perspectives Applications, and then click Computer History Hypermedia or The Internet: World Wide Web. If you do not see Course Labs on your Programs menu, see your instructor or technical support person.

Computer History Hypermedia The Computer History Hypermedia Lab is an example of a multimedia hypertext, or hypermedia, that contains text, pictures, and recordings which trace the origins of computers. This Lab provides you with two benefits: first, you learn how to use hypermedia links, and second, you learn about some of the events that took place as the computer age dawned.

1. Click the Steps button to learn how to use the Computer History Hypermedia Lab. As you proceed through the Steps, answer all the Quick Check questions that appear. After you complete the Steps, you will see a Quick Check Summary Report. Follow the instructions on the screen to print this report.

   Click the Explore button. Find the name and date for each of the following:
   a. First automatic adding machine
   b. First electronic computer
   c. First fully electronic stored-program computer
   d. First widely used high-level programming language
   e. First microprocessor
   f. First microcomputer
   g. First word-processing program
   h. First spreadsheet program

2. Select one of the following computer pioneers and write a one-page paper about that person's contribution to the computer industry: Grace Hopper, Charles Babbage, Augusta Ada, Jack Kilby, Thomas Watson, or J. Presper Eckert.

3. Use this Lab to research the history of the computer. Based on your research, write a paper explaining how you would respond to the question, "Who invented the computer?"

The Internet: World Wide Web One of the most popular services on the Internet is the World Wide Web. This Lab is a Web simulator that teaches you how to use Web browser software to find information. You can use this Lab whether or not your school provides you with Internet access.

1. Click the Steps button to learn how to use Web browser software. As you proceed through the Steps, answer all of the Quick Check questions that appear. After you complete the Steps, you will see a Quick Check Summary Report. Follow the instructions on the screen to print this report.

2. Click the Explore button on the Welcome screen. Use the Web browser to locate a weather map of the Caribbean Virgin Islands. What is its URL?

3. A SCUBA diver named Wadson Lachouffe has been searching for the fabled treasure of Greybeard the pirate. A link from the Adventure Travel Web site www.atour.com leads to Wadson's Web page called "Hidden Treasure." In Explore, locate the Hidden Treasure page and answer the following questions:
   a. What was the name of Greybeard's ship?
   b. What was Greybeard's favorite food?
   c. What does Wadson think happened to Greybeard's ship?

4. In the Steps, you found a graphic of Jupiter from the photo archives of the Jet Propulsion Laboratory. In the Explore section of the Lab, you can also find a graphic of Saturn. Suppose one of your friends wanted a picture of Saturn for an astronomy report. Make a list of the blue, underlined links your friend must click in the correct order to find the Saturn graphic. Assume that your friend will begin at the Web Trainer home page.

5. Enter the URL http://www.atour.com to jump to the Adventure Travel Web site. Write a one-page description of this site. In your paper, include a description of the information at the site, the number of pages the site contains, and a diagram of the links it contains.

6. Chris Thomson is a student at UVI and has his own Web pages. In Explore, look at the information Chris has included on his pages. Suppose you could create your own Web page. What would you include? Use word-processing software to design your own Web pages. Make sure you indicate the graphics and links you would use.

QUICK | CHECK ANSWERS

Session 1.1

1. Internet
2. The Web browser requests and receives information that is stored on the Web server for the client.
3. start
4. Uniform Resource Locator (URL)
5. hyperlink (link)
6. disk-based Web files are obtained from a disk without the use of a server program; server-based Web files require a server for processing
7. True
8. True

Session 1.2

1. It creates all of the HTML code for you.
2. Page
3. Reports
4. Navigation
5. A hyperlink to a location that already has a hyperlink to it in that same page.
6. Tasks list
7. True
8. True

Session 1.3

1. attributes (or properties)
2. Use the HTML button in Page view, or use the Source command on the View menu in Internet Explorer.
3. <I>home page</I>
4. Contents
5. True
6. False

OBJECTIVES

In this tutorial you will:

- Study the five-part process for developing a Web site

- Use FrontPage to create a Web site and a Web page

- Enter and spell check text in a Web page

- Save a Web page

- Format a Web page

- View a Web page in a browser

- Print a Web page

- Add a background picture and sound to a Web page

- Insert a picture, horizontal line, and marquee in a Web page

- Promote a Web site using META tags

CREATING
A WEB SITE AND
A WEB PAGE

Developing the Home Page for
Sunny Morning Products

CASE

Sunny Morning Products

Before Amanda Bay began developing the Web site for Sunny Morning Products, she visited the Web sites of many of the company's competitors. She compiled a list of six sites that had Web presences similar to the one she envisioned for her company. Amanda then met with Jacob Towle and the Web site development team to review these sites and to clarify the requirements for the Web site for Sunny Morning Products. They discussed the Web site's overall design as well as the specific design and content of its home page. In addition, they agreed that Amanda would develop the home page and Jacob would review it. Amanda then would incorporate Jacob's input into the development of the pages in the rest of the Web site.

In this tutorial, you continue your Web training course by studying Amanda's five-part process for developing and creating the Web site for Sunny Morning Products. You will create the company's home page and apply different formatting techniques to organize the information in this page. You will also add a picture and a sound to the home page.

SESSION 2.1

In this session, you will study the five-part process for creating and developing a Web site. You will create a Web site, enter text, check spelling, and create a link bar. Finally, you will close a Web page, a Web site, and FrontPage.

Developing a Web Site

A commercial Web site often results from the efforts of a development team consisting of a copy writer, an editor, a graphic designer, a programmer, a systems administrator, and a marketing representative, with a Web design director as the team's coordinator. Figure 2-1 shows the organization of this type of team and lists some of the general responsibilities of each member. Often, a single employee, called the **webmaster**, is assigned these responsibilities. Individuals who own small businesses or who just have information to put on the Web may also create and develop their own Web sites. Regardless of who is responsible for developing a Web site, FrontPage makes it easy to perform the various activities required to create and administer it.

Figure 2-1	WEB DEVELOPMENT TEAM

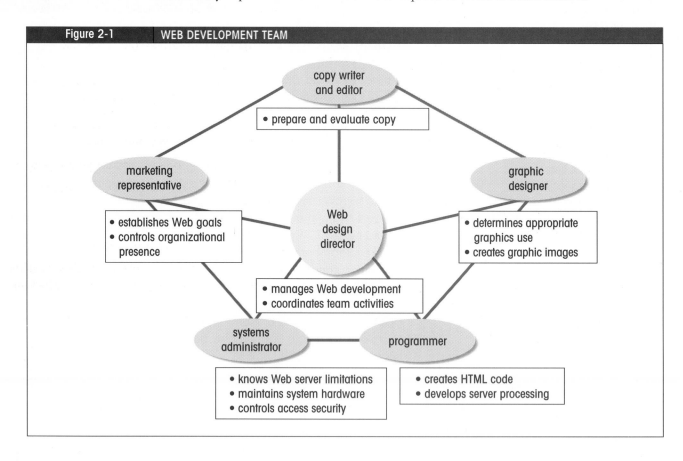

Developing a Web site is a multitask process that includes the following activities:

- Define the goal and purpose of the Web site
- Determine and prepare the Web site's contents
- Design the Web site
- Build the Web site
- Test the Web site

Amanda is ready to explain the first step in this process—defining the site's goal and purpose.

Defining the Web Site's Goal and Purpose

As the first step in creating a professional-looking Web site, the Web site development team defines the site's goal and purpose. What do you want to achieve with your site? What will a Web site help you accomplish that other marketing media cannot? Who is your target audience? After all members of the Web site development team met together, they decided that Sunny Morning Products wants to develop a Web site that establishes a corporate Web presence and markets the items sold through the Sunshine Country Store.

After agreeing on the Web site's goal and purpose, the team discussed the Web site's requirements. Amanda then met with each of the company's department heads to obtain the preliminary information necessary to begin developing the site. Specific factors to consider when planning a Web site include the following:

- **Primary intent:** What is the purpose of the Web site?
- **Short- and long-term goals:** What specific goals should the Web site meet? For example, do you want to market your company's products to boost sales or to increase the company's visibility?
- **Intended audience:** Who do you want or expect to visit your Web site? The quality and level of the design and the information must meet the expectations of the intended audience.

Using this preliminary information, Amanda created a planning analysis sheet. A **planning analysis sheet** is a document that answers the following questions:

1. What are the objectives of the Web site? For example, you might be taking advantage of an opportunity or responding to specific customer needs.

2. What data do you need to create your Web pages? This information is your **input**.

3. What specific results are you seeking? This information describes your **output**, or the information that your Web site should provide.

4. How will you connect the Web pages in your Web site? Hyperlinks connect the Web pages to give users access to the information in your Web site.

Figure 2-2 shows Amanda's completed planning analysis sheet for the Web site. This document contains all the information you need to begin working on the Sunny Morning Products Web site.

Figure 2-2   **AMANDA'S PLANNING ANALYSIS SHEET FOR THE WEB SITE**

Planning Analysis Sheet

Objective

Develop a marketing and corporate Web site that provides relevant company information and allows users to place orders from the Sunshine Country Store.

Requirements

Company description

Mission statement

List of product groups and individual product descriptions and prices

List of available positions and their job descriptions

Financial performance and stock information

Results

Web pages with the following information:

> Company description
>
> Current press releases
>
> Product descriptions and ordering information
>
> Employment information
>
> Investor information
>
> Customer feedback form
>
> Search capability for Web content

Determining and Preparing the Web Site's Contents

After preparing a planning analysis sheet, you are ready to begin developing the Web site's content. You should gather relevant documents, workbooks, presentations, and other data that you might use or adapt for use in the Web site. As part of this step, you might need to revisit people who were involved in planning the Web site to see if they have material that you can use in your Web pages.

Content is the most fundamental aspect of Web design because the success of any Web site ultimately depends on the quality of its information. Streamlined, appropriate language is an essential part of any well-designed site.

Designing the Web Site

Your next step in developing a Web site is to design the site. In the commercial and competitive realm of the Web, good graphic design is crucial. The overall layout and quality of the pictures and graphics in a Web page should enhance the page's contents and make it interesting to view for its users.

During this stage, you should ask and answer questions related to your company's organizational image. What message is your company trying to convey? What distinguishes your organization from its competitors? Should the Web site be classic, stylish, or contemporary?

Armed with the answers to these questions, you can sketch a design of the site, including its individual pages. In this way, you can plan the relationships among Web pages before creating them and connecting them using hyperlinks. Figure 2-3 shows Amanda's plan for linking the pages in the Web site. The plan specifies which Web pages must be created and the likely hyperlinks that will connect the Web pages.

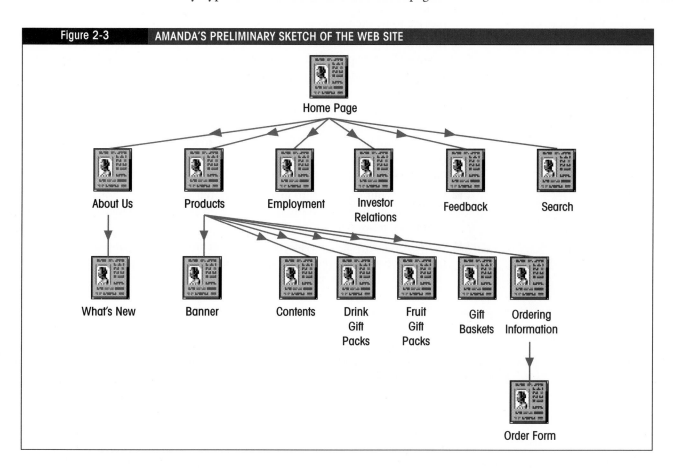

Figure 2-3   AMANDA'S PRELIMINARY SKETCH OF THE WEB SITE

With your Web design plan in place, you can begin building the site. You will create all of the pages for the Web site as you work through the tutorials in this book.

Building the Web Site

As you transform your Web site's plan into a FrontPage Web site, it is important to recognize that Internet Explorer and other popular Web browsers, such as Netscape Navigator, might display your pages in slightly different ways. When creating a Web site, you should always test your pages in different browsers to ensure that your pages will be displayed correctly.

Fortunately, FrontPage includes an option that you can set before developing any Web pages to ensure compatibility with certain browsers, servers, and Internet technologies. For example, if your Web site will be viewed using both Internet Explorer and Netscape Navigator, you might choose to develop it with the settings enabled for creating pages that are supported by both browsers. When you set this option, FrontPage dims commands that are not supported by both browsers. To enable these settings, click Tools on the menu bar, click Page Options, and then click the Compatibility tab. This book uses the default setting for FrontPage, which is to create a Web site supported by Internet Explorer 5.0.

Another important consideration during this phase is that the best Web sites are visually appealing, convey information correctly and succinctly, and download quickly. Keep the following guidelines in mind while you are building a Web site:

- Know and adhere to the stated goals for the site as you decide how to present its information.

- Consider your audience's reaction to every piece of information and every picture to be included.

- Include components that download quickly. People often leave a site if downloading its pages takes too long. Large pictures can download slowly; if you must include them, provide an option to download them as separate Web pages.

- Make the site visually appealing. Strike a balance between a site design that is too simple and one that is chaotic. Make the text large enough for easy viewing, and use color and font variations to add interest and to draw attention to items. However, don't use so many different fonts, colors, or features on a page that the excessive formatting becomes distracting.

- Organize your content into groups of related information. For example, if you are designing a Web site for a bookstore, arrange the material according to subject areas.

- Include appropriate navigation options, including a hyperlink in every page in the Web site that returns to the home page. Make it easy for users to move around in your site.

Testing the Web Site

The final step in developing a Web site is to test it. This step includes verifying that all hyperlinks work correctly and that all multimedia files are available. You should thoroughly test a Web site before publishing it to a Web server. In these tutorials, you will test Web pages using Preview Page view and also in a browser. It is also important to test your Web site using different browsers, and different versions of those browsers, to ensure that all pages function and appear correctly.

Creating the Sunny Web Site

Through the five-part Web development process, Amanda identified a clear vision of the Web site needed by Sunny Morning Products. After reviewing her planning analysis sheet for the Web site and its preliminary design, you are ready to begin creating the Web site.

When building a new Web site, you must first create the FrontPage Web that will contain the individual Web pages in the site. A **FrontPage Web** is a Windows folder, similar to a file folder that you might use in other programs. The additional files and folders used by FrontPage—the FrontPage Server Extensions—are saved in the FrontPage Web folder. You always use FrontPage to create the folder for your Web site.

Note: The Web site that you will create and use in these tutorials is named "Sunny." This Web site differs from the SunnyMorningProducts Web site that you explored in Tutorial 1. Always make sure that you are working in the correct Web site.

To create the Sunny Web site:

1. Make sure that your Data Disk is in the appropriate drive.

2. Start **Microsoft FrontPage**, make sure that you are in Page view, and verify that the Views bar and Task Pane are open. (To turn on the Views bar, click View on the menu bar, and then click Views Bar. To open the Task Pane, click View on the menu bar, and then click Task Pane.)

TROUBLE? If a dialog box opens and asks whether you would like to make FrontPage your default editor, click the No button.

TROUBLE? If FrontPage automatically opens a Web site, click File on the menu bar, and then click Close Web to close it. If you want to set FrontPage so that it doesn't automatically open the Web site that was open the last time FrontPage was used, click Tools on the menu bar, click Options, click the General tab, and then click the "Open last Web automatically when FrontPage starts" check box to clear it. Click the OK button to close the Options dialog box.

FrontPage includes a variety of templates and Wizards that you can use to create a new Web site. To access these options, you open the Web Site Templates dialog box.

3. In the "New" section of the Task Pane, click **Empty Web**. The Web Site Templates dialog box opens. See Figure 2-4.

Figure 2-4	WEB SITE TEMPLATES DIALOG BOX

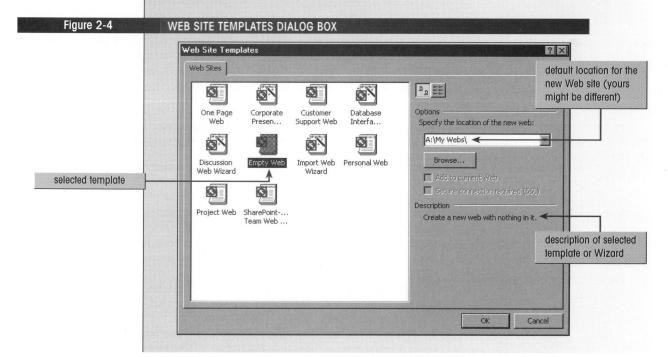

The options in this dialog box allow you to create a new FrontPage Web using one of six templates (see Figure 2-4). Alternatively, you can use one of four Wizards to answer questions about the FrontPage Web that you want to create, and then FrontPage will create it for you. When you click an icon in the Web Sites Templates dialog box, its description appears in the Description section. Figure 2-5 describes the various templates and Wizards that you can use to create a new Web site.

Figure 2-5	OPTIONS FOR CREATING A NEW FRONTPAGE WEB SITE
WEB SITE NAME	**DESCRIPTION**
One Page Web	Creates a Web site that contains one blank page, index.htm, which becomes the site's home page
Corporate Presence Wizard	Creates a Web site with pages that a corporation might use
Customer Support Web	Creates a Web site that contains pages useful for companies providing customer support, particularly software companies
Database Interface Wizard	Creates a Web site that you can connect to a database in which you can add, view, update, and delete records
Discussion Web Wizard	Creates a Web site that contains a table of contents, full-text searching capability, and threads organized around a specific discussion topic
Empty Web	Creates a Web site that contains no pages
Import Web Wizard	Creates a Web site that contains pages imported from another location, such as another Web site or a hard drive
Personal Web	Creates a Web site that an individual might use to publish pages about his or her interests and favorite Web sites
Project Web	Creates a Web site that contains a list of members, a schedule, status information, and a discussion archive related to a specific project
SharePoint-based Team Web Site	Creates a Web site with tools that group members can use to collaborate on a project, including a calendar, a library for storing shared documents, a tasks list, and a contacts list

When you create a new Web site, you must select a template or Wizard on which to base your new site. Next, you must specify the location in which to store the Web site's files and folders. In these tutorials, you will store your Web sites in a My Webs folder on your Data Disk.

4. Click the **One Page Web** icon. Notice that the Description box changes to show that you will create a new Web site that contains one page.

5. Select the text in the Specify the location of the new web text box, and then type **A:\My Webs\Sunny** in the text box.

   TROUBLE? If you are storing your Data Files on a different drive or in a different folder, your instructor might provide you with a location different from that given in Step 5. Ask your instructor or technical support person for help if you are unsure of the location in which to create your FrontPage Webs.

6. Click the **OK** button to create a new FrontPage Web using the One Page Web template.

   TROUBLE? If a dialog box opens and indicates that FrontPage must convert this folder to a FrontPage Web, click the Yes button to continue.

> After a few moments, FrontPage creates the new Sunny Web site, creates and saves the Web site's home page, and closes the Task Pane. You must change to Folders view to view the files and folders in the Sunny Web site.
>
> 7. Click the **Folders** button 🗂 on the Views bar to change to Folders view. Folders view shows that your new Web site contains two folders (_private and images) and one file (index.htm).

When you used the One Page Web template to create the Sunny Web site, FrontPage created and saved the Sunny Web site's home page as **index.htm**. If you are creating your Web site on a Web server rather than on disk, then the home page is named **default.htm**. A Web browser will recognize either of these files—index.htm or default.htm—as a Web site's home page.

Creating a Web Page

After creating a Web site, you create its individual Web pages. FrontPage automatically created and saved the index.htm (or default.htm) home page when you used the One Page Web template to create the new FrontPage Web.

Entering Text in a Web Page

The home page doesn't contain any content yet, so your first task is to add content to it. As part of Amanda's Web development training program, you will prepare a home page for Sunny Morning Products that is similar to the one that you examined in Tutorial 1.

> ### To enter text in a Web page:
>
> 1. Open the Sunny Web site's home page by double-clicking **index.htm** in the Contents pane in Folders view. The blank home page, which FrontPage saved automatically when you created the Web site, opens in Page view. Notice that the name of the home page—index.htm—appears both as a page tab at the top of the Contents pane and in the FrontPage title bar.
>
>   TROUBLE? If you are using a server-based Web, double-click default.htm in the Contents pane in Folders view to open the home page in Page view.
>
> 2. Type **Sunny Morning Products is an international bottler and distributor of Olympic Gold orange juice and sports drink.** and then press the **spacebar**. As in any word-processing program, you do not need to press the Enter key at the end of each line. You press the Enter key only once when advancing to a new paragraph.
>
>   Amanda has stored the rest of the content for the home page in a Word document. She suggests that you copy the text from this Word document and paste it into your Web page, to save yourself some typing.
>
> 3. Start **Microsoft Word** and open the **Home** file from the Tutorial.02 folder on your Data Disk. This document contains text that you will copy and then paste into the home page.
>
> 4. Click **Edit** on the menu bar, and then click **Select All**. The text in the document is selected.

5. Click the **Copy** button 🖺 on the Standard toolbar to copy the selected text to the Windows Clipboard.

6. Click the **Close** button ✖ on the Word title bar to close Word. If necessary, click the **Microsoft FrontPage** program button on the taskbar to return to FrontPage.

   The insertion point appears after the space that you typed at the end of the sentence. You can paste the text into this location.

7. Click the **Paste** button 🖺 on the Standard toolbar. The text that you copied from the Word document appears in the Web page. See Figure 2-6.

| Figure 2-6 | WEB PAGE AFTER PASTING TEXT FROM A WORD DOCUMENT |

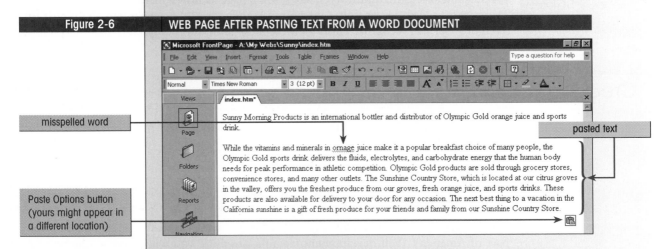

Notice that a Paste Options button appears below the pasted text. The Paste Options button is an example of a **smart tag**, which provides choices for establishing the layout and content of pasted text in a Web page. When you paste text into a Web page, FrontPage provides three options related to the format of the pasted text. The first option, Use Destination Styles, removes any styles in the original document in which the text appeared and uses any defined styles in the Web page in their place. The second option, Keep Source Formatting, ensures that any formatting applied to the original text is retained in the Web page. For example, if the pasted text uses specific fonts or colors, choosing this option would ensure that these characteristics carry over to the Web page. The third option, Keep Text Only, pastes just the text, without retaining any formatting. Depending on the format of the pasted text, some of these options may not appear in the list. Working with plain text gives you greater flexibility as you work in FrontPage, so Amanda asks you to choose this option.

8. Click the **Paste Options** button 🖺 that appears below the pasted text, and then click the **Keep Text Only** option button. Now you have plain text, without any formatting.

   Amanda tells you that a break should appear before the sentence that begins "The Sunshine Country Store."

9. Click to the left of the letter **T** in The Sunshine Country Store, and then press the **Enter** key. See Figure 2-7. You press the Enter key only once when advancing to a new paragraph. You do not need to press the Enter key twice, as you would in Word, because FrontPage automatically inserts blank space above a new paragraph. Also, notice that the Paste Options button has disappeared. This button is visible only when you first paste text from another location.

Figure 2-7   HOME PAGE WITH TWO PARAGRAPHS

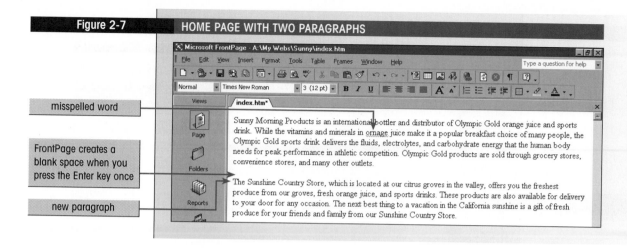

misspelled word

FrontPage creates a
blank space when you
press the Enter key once

new paragraph

Now the text of the home page appears in the document. Amanda notices an error in the first paragraph. She suggests that you check the spelling in the home page to catch any other problems.

Spell Checking a Web Page

Notice that a red, wavy underline appears under the word "ornage" in the first paragraph. Like Microsoft Word, FrontPage highlights misspelled words. You should always check the spelling in your Web pages as part of the development process.

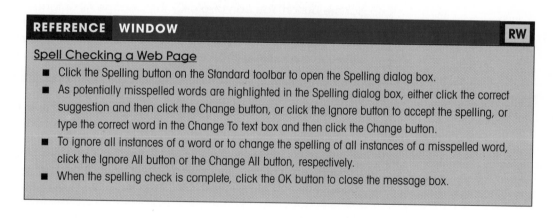

REFERENCE WINDOW   RW

Spell Checking a Web Page
- Click the Spelling button on the Standard toolbar to open the Spelling dialog box.
- As potentially misspelled words are highlighted in the Spelling dialog box, either click the correct suggestion and then click the Change button, or click the Ignore button to accept the spelling, or type the correct word in the Change To text box and then click the Change button.
- To ignore all instances of a word or to change the spelling of all instances of a misspelled word, click the Ignore All button or the Change All button, respectively.
- When the spelling check is complete, click the OK button to close the message box.

To check the spelling in a Web page:

1. Click the **Spelling** button 🗹 on the Standard toolbar. The Spelling dialog box opens with the word "ornage" displayed in the Not in Dictionary text box. See Figure 2-8.

| Figure 2-8 | SPELLING DIALOG BOX |

misspelled word

suggested corrections for the misspelled word

options for ignoring, changing, or adding words

TROUBLE? If a different word appears in the Not in Dictionary text box, you may have typed a word in the first sentence incorrectly. Use the information in the following paragraph to ignore or change the word as appropriate.

You can click one of the suggested corrections in the Suggestions list box to change the spelling of the selected word, and then click the Change button. Alternatively, you can type a new spelling in the Change To text box, and then click the Change button. If the selected word is spelled correctly, click the Ignore button. You can also click the Change All or Ignore All button to avoid checking the spelling of the same word again. If you want to add a word to FrontPage's dictionary, click the Add button; normally, you should add only those words to the dictionary that you will type often, such as your name.

2. Click **orange** in the Suggestions list box, and then click the **Change** button.

   TROUBLE? If you do not encounter any misspelled words in your Web page, then the word "ornage" is in your dictionary. Click the OK button to close the Spelling dialog box and, if necessary, edit the word to change it to "orange."

3. If necessary, correct any other misspellings that appear in the Spelling dialog box. When you are finished, click the **OK** button to continue.

Adding a Link Bar

Next, you will add the link bar, which will contain hyperlinks that open other Web pages, to the home page. Although you can add a link bar before including any text information, you will often find it helpful to see how the main body of your text appears in the page before creating a link bar.

With FrontPage, you can create a link bar in two ways. First, you can enter text, format it, and then create hyperlinks to create a **user-defined link bar**. Second, you can create a **FrontPage link bar**, which is a group of hyperlinks created and managed by FrontPage. In this tutorial, you will implement a user-defined link bar. You will learn more about creating FrontPage link bars in Tutorial 5 and about hyperlinks in Tutorial 3.

You create a user-defined link bar from text that you type just like any other text in your Web page. You separate the entries in your link bar using one of several options. One popular way to separate entries is to use special characters, such as a vertical bar (|) or square brackets ([ ]), as the separators. A single vertical bar is typically placed between entries, whereas square brackets surround each entry.

For the home page of the Sunny Web site, you decide to place the link bar at the top of the page and use the vertical bar character (|) as the separator. With Amanda's assistance, you are ready to create the link bar at the top of the home page.

To create a link bar:

1. Click before the word **Sunny** at the beginning of the first line of the home page.

2. Press the **Enter** key to insert a line before the first paragraph, and then press the **up arrow** key ↑. The insertion point moves to the beginning of the new line, where you will type the text for the link bar.

3. Type the following link bar text exactly as it appears. Be sure to type the vertical bar and spacebar characters before the first entry. After each subsequent entry, press the spacebar, type the vertical bar, and then press the spacebar again. The text for the link bar should fit on one line.

   | Home | About Us | Products | Employment | Investor Relations | Feedback | Search |

   TROUBLE? The key for typing the vertical bar character (|) is located below or to the left of the Backspace key. You must press and hold down the Shift key to type it.

   Your completed link bar should match the one shown in Figure 2-9.

| Figure 2-9 | LINK BAR FOR THE HOME PAGE |

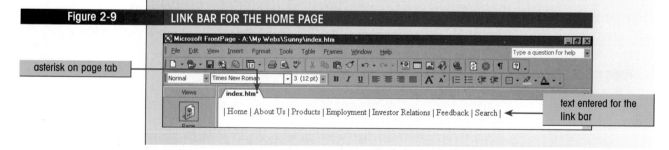

You may have noticed that the index.htm page tab at the top of the Contents pane includes an asterisk (*). The asterisk reminds you that the page contains unsaved changes. You are finished with your work on the home page for now, so you will save it.

Saving a Web Page

Saving your work on a regular basis is important. You use the Save command on the File menu or the Save button on the Standard toolbar to save a Web page. Keep in mind that using the Save command or Save button does not create a separate version of your old Web page; instead, it replaces the old version with the new version. To retain the original file and create a new file, you must save the Web page with a different filename by using the Save As command on the File menu.

REFERENCE WINDOW   **RW**

<u>Saving a Web Page</u>
- Click the Save button on the Standard toolbar.
  or
- Click File on the menu bar, and then click Save.

Amanda asks you to save the Sunny Web site's home page.

To save the home page:

1. Click the **Save** button 🖫 on the Standard toolbar to save the home page. Because the home page was automatically assigned the filename index.htm when FrontPage created it, the page is saved immediately without requesting a filename. Notice that the asterisk following the index.htm text on the page tab disappears.

Your work on the home page is finished, so Amanda asks you to close the page, the Sunny Web site, and FrontPage.

Closing **a Web Page, a Web Site, and FrontPage**

You can close a single Web page, a Web site, or FrontPage by choosing the appropriate Close command. When you close FrontPage, it automatically closes any open page or site. If you did not save your changes to an open Web page, FrontPage will prompt you to do so before closing the page. Next, you will close the home page, the Sunny Web site, and FrontPage.

To close a Web page, a Web site, and FrontPage:

1. Click the **Close** button ☒ on the Contents pane to close the home page. You have not made any changes since the last time you saved the page, so the home page closes and the Contents pane no longer displays a Web page.

   TROUBLE? If you changed the Web page since you last saved it, a FrontPage message box opens and asks whether you want to save the file. Click the Yes button to save your changes and to close the home page.

2. Click **File** on the menu bar, and then click **Close Web**. The Sunny Web site closes, but FrontPage remains open.

   TROUBLE? If you do not see the Close Web command on the File menu, click the double-arrow that appears at the bottom of the File menu. The rest of the menu will open and display the Close Web command.

3. Click ☒ on the FrontPage title bar to close FrontPage.

Amanda is pleased with your progress in creating the home page. In the next session, you will format the home page to make it more visually interesting.

Session 2.1 QUICK CHECK

1. List the five major tasks involved in developing a Web site.

2. When you create a new Web site on a server, FrontPage automatically creates a home page named _____.

3. Describe the two ways to create a link bar in a Web page.

4. True or False: You should test your Web pages in different browsers to ensure that your pages are displayed correctly.

5. True or False: FrontPage automatically saves your Web pages while you are working on them, so you do not need to periodically save them.

6. To close a FrontPage Web site, click File on the menu bar, and then click _____.

SESSION 2.2

In this session, you will format a Web page by changing the style, color, and alignment of text and by inserting special characters. You will test the appearance of your Web page by viewing it in a browser. Finally, you will use FrontPage to print a Web page.

Formatting a Web Page

You can make your Web pages more interesting and visually appealing by formatting them to draw attention to important content. **Formatting** is the process of changing the appearance of text in a Web page; it does not alter the Web page's content. You must be in Page view to apply formatting. You can access the FrontPage formatting options in three ways:

- Use the Format menu command, which provides access to all formatting commands, ranging from revising paragraph organization to creating numbered lists.

- Right-click the text or an object in a Web page to open the shortcut menu, which provides quick access to many formatting commands, such as those for fonts, numbered lists, or special effects. You can use the shortcut menu commands to apply formatting to specific characters, words, text, or pictures.

- Click the buttons on the Formatting toolbar. Figure 2-10 describes the Formatting toolbar buttons and their uses in more detail.

Figure 2-10	FORMATTING TOOLBAR BUTTONS	
BUTTON NAME	**BUTTON**	**FUNCTION**
Style list box	Normal	Lets you apply different styles, such as headings, to paragraphs in your document; contains styles compatible with HTML
Font list box	Times New Roman	Lets you apply a font to a selection; contains fonts that are available on your system
Font Size list box	3 (12 pt)	Lets you apply different font sizes to a selection; contains sizes compatible with HTML, where 1 is the smallest and 7 is the largest
Bold	B	Changes selected text to bold
Italic	I	Changes selected text to italic
Underline	U	Changes selected text to underlined
Align Left		Changes the alignment of the selected paragraph or object to left
Center		Changes the alignment of the selected paragraph or object to centered
Align Right		Changes the alignment of the selected paragraph or object to right
Justify		Changes the alignment of the selected paragraph to justified
Increase Font Size	A	Increases the font size of the selected text to the next higher HTML level
Decrease Font Size	A	Decreases the font size of the selected text to the next lower HTML level
Numbering		Changes a list of selected items to a numbered list
Bullets		Changes a list of selected items to a bulleted list
Decrease Indent		Moves the indentation of a selected line or paragraph left by one tab stop (0.5 inch)
Increase Indent		Moves the indentation of a selected line or paragraph right by one tab stop (0.5 inch)
Borders		Adds a border to the selected text; use the list arrow to select a border option other than the one displayed on the button
Highlight		Highlights the selected text; click the list arrow to choose a highlight color other than the one displayed on the button or to choose None to remove highlighting from the selected text
Font Color	A	Changes the color of the selected text; click the list arrow to choose a text color other than the one displayed on the button

Now that the home page of the Sunny Web site contains text and a link bar, Amanda asks you to continue developing it by adding headings, aligning text, and changing fonts.

Creating Headings

Headings in a Web page function like headings in other documents. The heading options available for your Web page are limited to those defined by HTML tags. HTML provides six levels of headings, identified as H1, H2, and so on. H1 uses the largest font; H6 uses the smallest font. You can change the alignment of a heading before or after you enter its text.

REFERENCE   WINDOW   RW

Creating a Heading in a Web Page
- Click anywhere in the paragraph that will serve as the heading.
- Click the Style list arrow on the Formatting toolbar to display a list of available paragraph format styles, and then click the desired heading style.

You will create two headings in the home page: one at the top of the page that welcomes visitors to the site, and another at the bottom of the page that contains a slogan.

To open the Sunny Web site and create the headings:

1. Make sure that your Data Disk is in the appropriate drive, and then start **FrontPage**.

2. Click the list arrow for the **Open** button on the Standard toolbar, click **Open Web**, change to the drive or folder that contains your Data Disk, double-click the **My Webs** folder on your Data Disk, click the **Sunny** folder (if necessary), and then click the **Open** button.

3. Click the **Folders** button on the Views bar to change to Folders view, and then double-click **index.htm** in the Contents pane to open the home page in Page view.

4. Click anywhere in the link bar, press the **End** key to move the insertion point to the end of the link bar, and then press the **Enter** key to insert a new line below the link bar.

5. Type **Welcome to the Sunny Morning Products Web Site!** on the new line as the text for your heading.

   You will apply a heading style to distinguish this text from the rest of the Web page.

6. Click the **Style** list arrow on the Formatting toolbar to display the list of available paragraph styles. These styles correspond to the HTML tags that you can use to define the various paragraphs in your Web page.

7. Click **Heading 3** to apply this style to the heading.

   Next, you will add another heading at the bottom of the home page.

8. Press **Ctrl + End** to insert a new line below the last paragraph of the Web page, and then type **Brighten your day. Enjoy some of our sunshine!** as the heading.

9. Repeat Steps 6 and 7 to apply the **Heading 3** style to the heading you created in Step 8. The home page now contains two headings. See Figure 2-11.

| Figure 2-11 | HOME PAGE WITH NEW HEADINGS |

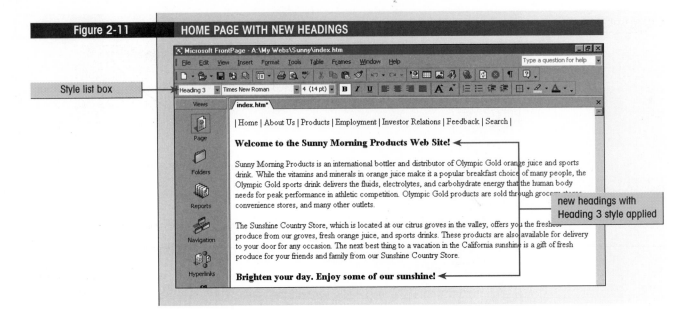

Style list box

new headings with Heading 3 style applied

Aligning Text

Like a word-processing program, FrontPage allows you to justify, left-align, center, or right-align text in a Web page. The Web browser interprets the alignment tags based on the formatting you apply and displays the text accordingly.

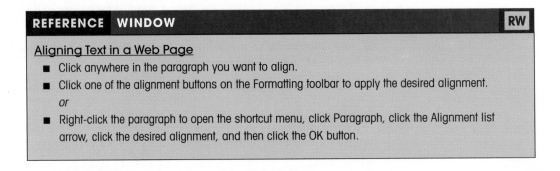

REFERENCE WINDOW   RW

Aligning Text in a Web Page

- Click anywhere in the paragraph you want to align.
- Click one of the alignment buttons on the Formatting toolbar to apply the desired alignment.

  or
- Right-click the paragraph to open the shortcut menu, click Paragraph, click the Alignment list arrow, click the desired alignment, and then click the OK button.

Next, you'll center the heading you just created at the bottom of the home page. Then, to balance the Web page, you will center the link bar.

To center text in a Web page:

1. With the insertion point positioned at the end of the heading at the bottom of the page, click the **Center** button on the Formatting toolbar to center the heading.

2. Click anywhere in the link bar at the top of the page.

3. Click to center the link bar. See Figure 2-12.

Figure 2-12   **CENTERING TEXT IN THE HOME PAGE**

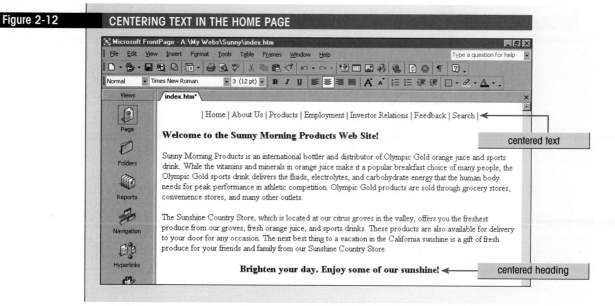

Using Fonts

A **font** is a set of letters, numbers, and symbols distinguished by their typeface, point size, and style. You can apply any of the following font styles to the text in your Web pages: regular, italic, bold, and bold italic. In addition, you can apply underlining to any of these font styles. Note that you can **toggle** the application of these styles to selected text. That is, if the style is not applied, then selecting the style applies it; if the style is applied, then selecting the style removes it.

In addition to including headings, Amanda asks you to insert a footer at the bottom of the home page that contains the company's copyright notice and the date that the page was last revised. You will apply italics to the footer to distinguish it from other text in the page.

To enter and format the footer text:

1. Press **Ctrl + End** to move to the bottom of the home page and to insert a new line after the last paragraph.

2. Type **Last updated May 31, 2003** as the first line of the footer.

3. Press **Shift + Enter** to advance to a new line without starting a new paragraph and without inserting a blank line between paragraphs.

4. Type **Copyright 2003 Sunny Morning Products. All rights reserved.** as the second line of the footer.

   Now that you've entered the footer information, you will format it by applying italics.

5. Use the mouse to select both lines of the footer, click the **Italic** button ☐ on the Formatting toolbar, and then click anywhere in the selected text to deselect it. The completed footer information now appears italicized. See Figure 2-13.

Figure 2-13   **FORMATTED FOOTER**

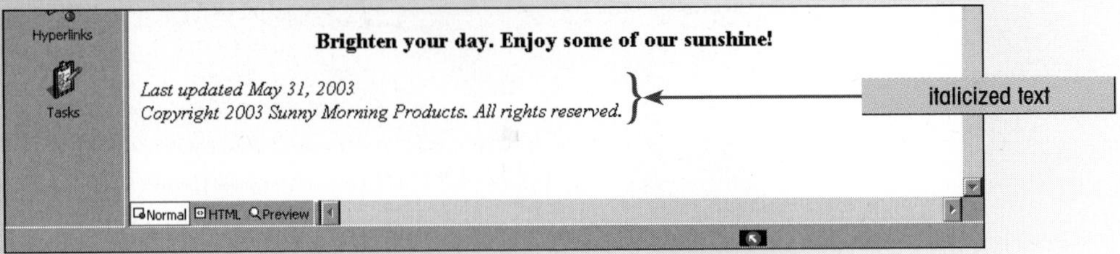

Brighten your day. Enjoy some of our sunshine!

Last updated May 31, 2003
Copyright 2003 Sunny Morning Products. All rights reserved.

italicized text

Inserting Special Characters

You can insert special characters, such as the copyright symbol (©), in the text of a Web page just as you can in other types of documents. In FrontPage, you insert special characters using the Symbol dialog box. Amanda asks you to add a copyright symbol after the word "Copyright" in the footer.

To insert a special character:

1. Click to the right of the letter **t** in the word "Copyright" in the footer, and then press the **spacebar**. You will place the copyright symbol here.

2. Click **Insert** on the menu bar, and then click **Symbol** to open the Symbol dialog box.

3. Scroll down to the seventh row of symbols, click the © symbol (ninth character from the left), click the **Insert** button, and then click the **Close** button. The Symbol dialog box closes and the copyright symbol appears in the footer.

Changing Font Size

You can change the size of text that appears in a Web page by selecting the desired text and then using the Font Size list arrow or the Increase Font Size and Decrease Font Size buttons on the Formatting toolbar. Just like headings, font sizes are limited to ones supported by HTML. Font size 1 is the smallest, and font size 7 is the largest. When designing a Web page, you often will need to experiment with these font sizes to find the best one for your purposes.

Amanda instructs you to change the size of the footer text so that it is smaller than other text in the page.

To change text size:

1. Use the mouse to select both lines of the footer, and then click the **Decrease Font Size** button on the Formatting toolbar. The font size is reduced to 10 points, which is the HTML equivalent of font size 2. See Figure 2-14. Notice that the Font Size list box on the Formatting toolbar now displays "2 (10 pt)" to reflect the new size.

Figure 2-14   **CHANGING THE FONT SIZE**

Font Size list box shows
the HTML font size 2

selected text in the
Web page

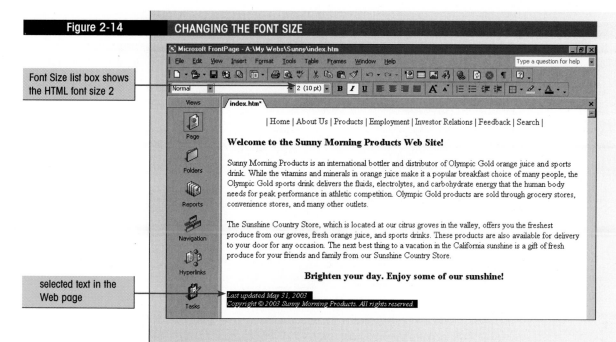

2. Click anywhere in the footer to deselect it.

3. Click the **Save** button 🖫 on the Standard toolbar to save the home page.

Changing Text Color

As part of the Web page design, Amanda wants the "Olympic Gold" text to have a more prominent appearance so as to distinguish this brand name from other text. She thinks that the brand name will stand out more if it is formatted as bold, orange text.

To change text color:

1. Press **Ctrl + Home** to return to the top of the home page.

2. Select **Olympic Gold** in the first sentence of the first paragraph.

3. Click the **Bold** button 🅱 on the Formatting toolbar to change this text to bold.

4. Click the **list arrow** for the Font Color button 🔠 on the Formatting toolbar to open the color palette, and then click **More Colors** to open the More Colors dialog box. See Figure 2-15.

Figure 2-15   MORE COLORS DIALOG BOX

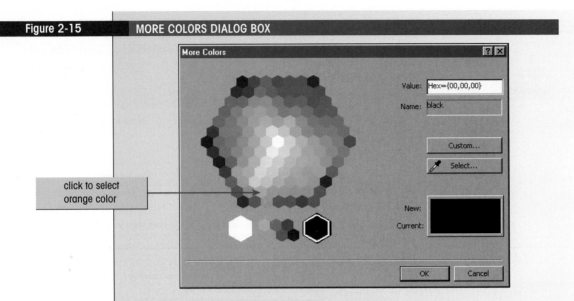

click to select
orange color

In the More Colors dialog box, you select an existing color by clicking it in the color palette. Alternatively, you can create a custom color by clicking the Custom button. You need an orange color, which you can select from the palette.

5. Click the **orange** color (second to last row, third color from the left) to select it, and then click the **OK** button to close the More Colors dialog box and apply the orange color to the selected text.

6. Click anywhere in the first paragraph to deselect the Olympic Gold text.

Using the Format Painter

Amanda wants you to apply the bold, orange formatting to the other occurrences of the "Olympic Gold" text in the home page. You could select each occurrence of this text and apply the desired formatting changes to it. An easier way to achieve this goal, however, is to use the Format Painter. The **Format Painter** lets you copy the format from existing formatted text and apply it to new text.

To use the Format Painter:

1. Click anywhere in the orange **Olympic Gold** text in the first sentence of the first paragraph.

   If you click the Format Painter button once, you can copy the format of the selected text and apply it once to any other text. If you double-click the Format Painter button, you can continue to apply the format to additional locations until you click the button again to turn it off. You need to copy the format and apply it to the two other occurrences of the Olympic Gold text, so you will double-click the Format Painter button.

2. Double-click the **Format Painter** button ![icon] on the Standard toolbar to set the button to apply the format more than once.

3. Use the pointer, which changes to a 🖌️I shape, to select the **Olympic Gold** text in the second sentence of the first paragraph. The text is selected and changes to bold, orange text.

4. Repeat Step 3 to change the **Olympic Gold** text in the next sentence to bold, orange text.

5. Click 🖌️ to turn off the Format Painter, and then click the selected text to deselect it. See Figure 2-16. Now the Olympic Gold brand name stands out clearly in the home page.

Figure 2-16	CHANGING TEXT COLOR

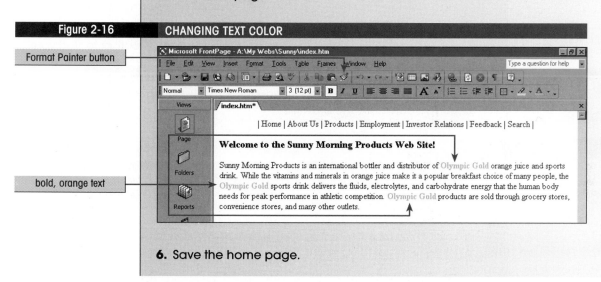

6. Save the home page.

Amanda is ready for you to complete the final step in the process of developing a Web page—testing it.

Testing a Web Page

For now, your testing will be limited primarily to verifying that the appearance of the home page is correct when it is displayed in a browser. Using the Preview button to test the page lets you look at the Web page without actually opening it in a browser. When you use the Preview in Browser button on the Standard toolbar to test a page, Internet Explorer (or your default Web browser) starts and opens the page. You should check the page in a Web browser periodically to verify that the colors, fonts, and other elements are being applied and positioned correctly. As you add other features (such as hyperlinks) to your Web pages, you should confirm that they work correctly by testing them in the browser.

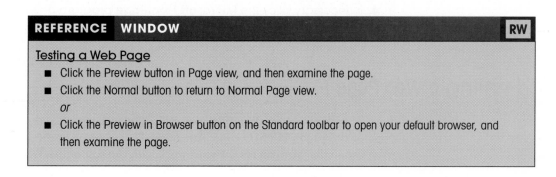

REFERENCE WINDOW   **RW**

Testing a Web Page
- Click the Preview button in Page view, and then examine the page.
- Click the Normal button to return to Normal Page view.
  or
- Click the Preview in Browser button on the Standard toolbar to open your default browser, and then examine the page.

Now that you have completed your work on the home page for Amanda, you need to test it. First, you will view the page in Preview Page view. Then you will view the Web page in the browser window.

> ## To test the Web page and close the browser:
>
> **1.** Click the **Preview** button at the bottom of the Contents pane. The home page for the Sunny Web site is displayed as it will appear when viewed using a Web browser. Note that the "Olympic Gold" text occurrences appear as bold, orange text. The Web page has the desired appearance, so you are ready to test it in the browser.
>
> **2.** Click the **Preview in Browser** button on the Standard toolbar to start your browser and open the home page. If necessary, maximize the browser program window. See Figure 2-17. The home page should look approximately the same as when you previewed it using the Preview button. Your test was successful, so you can close the browser.

Figure 2-17	HOME PAGE DISPLAYED IN THE BROWSER

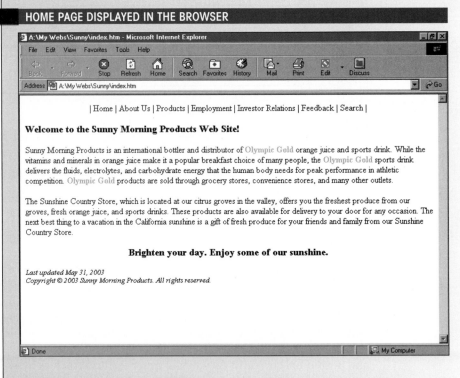

> **3.** Click the **Close** button ☒ on the browser title bar to close it.
>
> **4.** If necessary, click the **Microsoft FrontPage** program button on the taskbar to return to FrontPage.

Printing a Web Page

Printing a Web page is helpful when you want to keep a paper copy to review later or a copy of the page's HTML code. Amanda asks you to print the home page for the Sunny Web site so that you can review your work with the rest of the Web site development team.

You will print it in Normal Page view. To print a page's HTML code, you would change to HTML Page view before clicking the Print button. You cannot print a Web page from Preview Page view, so you'll need to switch to Normal Page view. After printing the page, you will close FrontPage.

To print a Web page and exit FrontPage:

1. Click the **Normal** button to display the home page in Normal Page view, and then click the **Print** button 🖨 on the Standard toolbar to print the home page.

   With the printed page in hand, you are ready to review your work with the Web site development team. Now that you have successfully created and printed the home page for Sunny Morning Products, you are ready to close the Web and exit FrontPage.

2. Click **File** on the menu bar, and then click **Close Web**. The Sunny Web closes.

3. Click the **Close** button ☒ on the FrontPage title bar to exit FrontPage.

In the next session, you will add a picture, a sound, and an active element to the home page. You will also learn how to make your Web site available to Web search engines.

Session 2.2 QUICK CHECK

1. Describe the three methods that you can use to access the formatting commands in Page view.

2. Which HTML heading style identifies the largest font size available for use in headings?

3. Which HTML font size produces the largest font?

4. A set of letters, numbers, and symbols that are distinguished by their typeface, point size, and style is called a(n) _____.

5. How would you use the Format Painter to apply the formatting of selected text to one other location in a Web page?

6. True or False: You can print a Web page in Preview Page view.

7. True or False: It is important to test the appearance of a Web page periodically in the browser to make sure that it is being displayed correctly.

SESSION 2.3

In this session, you will revise a Web page by changing its background color and inserting a background picture and sound. You will save a Web page with embedded files. In addition, you will add a picture, a horizontal line, and a marquee to the home page. Finally, you will learn the significance of including META tags in a Web page so that Web search engines can index your Web site.

Revising a Web Page

After creating a Web page, you can add to, delete, or change its contents using the same text-editing features that you used to create the page. In Sessions 2.1 and 2.2, you entered and formatted the basic content of the home page for Sunny Morning Products. The Web site development team is pleased with your progress, and now the team asks you to revise the home page by including picture and sound files to give it a more professional presentation. Figure 2-18 shows Amanda's planning analysis sheet with the team's recommendations for revising the home page.

Figure 2-18	AMANDA'S REVISED PLANNING ANALYSIS SHEET FOR THE HOME PAGE

Planning Analysis Sheet

Objective

Modify the home page to include the Sunny Morning Products logo, a background picture and sound, a marquee, and META tags.

Requirements

Picture file for the logo

File for background picture

File for background sound

Results

Home page with the following enhancements:

       Background picture applied to it

       Logo that displays alternative text added at the top of the page

       Background sound that plays once

       Scrolling marquee

       META tags that identify the Web site's contents

With these suggestions in mind, you are ready to continue working on the home page.

Changing the Background Color of a Web Page

Like the other features of a Web page, the background color can make the Web page more attractive and easier to read. If you don't specify a background color, the default background color is white. You can change the background color to any available color. When choosing a background color for a Web page, make sure that it coordinates with the color of the page's text. You might need to try several colors before you find one that provides the desired appearance for your Web page.

FrontPage automatically applied the default background color of white to the home page. Although a white background usually provides a good contrast, changing it to another color is easy.

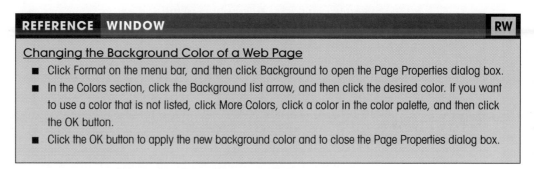

REFERENCE   WINDOW   **RW**

__Changing the Background Color of a Web Page__
- Click Format on the menu bar, and then click Background to open the Page Properties dialog box.
- In the Colors section, click the Background list arrow, and then click the desired color. If you want to use a color that is not listed, click More Colors, click a color in the color palette, and then click the OK button.
- Click the OK button to apply the new background color and to close the Page Properties dialog box.

Although Amanda feels that white is a good background color, she asks you to try another color to see whether it might be more attractive for the home page.

To change the background color of the home page:

1. Start **FrontPage**, open the **Sunny** Web site from your Data Disk, change to Folders view, and then open the home page in Page view.

2. Click **Format** on the menu bar, and then click **Background** to open the Page Properties dialog box with the Background tab selected. See Figure 2-19. In the Colors section, the background color is currently set to Automatic, which produces the default color, white.

Figure 2-19   **BACKGROUND SETTINGS FOR THE HOME PAGE**

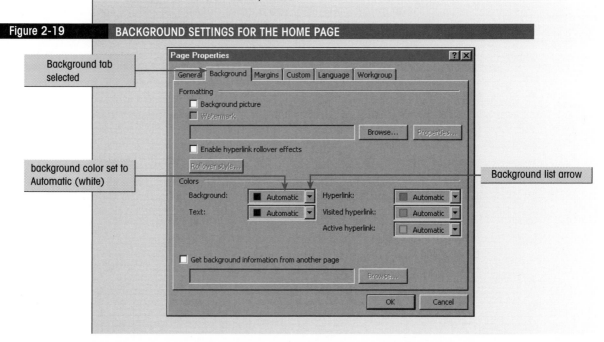

TROUBLE? If you do not see the Background command on the Format menu, click the double-arrow that appears at the bottom of the Format menu.

3. In the Colors section, click the **Background** list arrow to display the list of available standard colors as well as the colors that are currently used in your Web page.

TROUBLE? If you don't see the same colors given in the steps, use a similar color. Your color selections might differ, depending on your system's settings.

4. Point to the **blue** color in the Standard colors section. After a few seconds, a ScreenTip identifies the color as "Blue." See Figure 2-20.

Figure 2-20	BACKGROUND COLOR OPTIONS FOR THE HOME PAGE

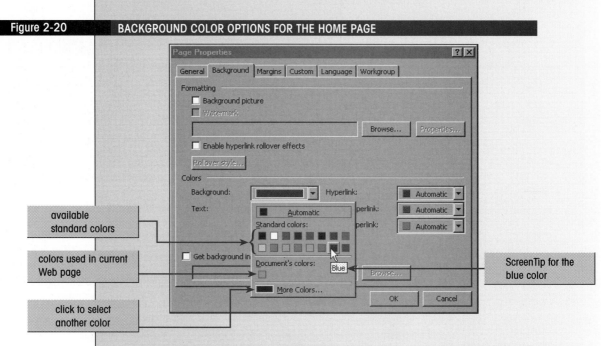

available standard colors

colors used in current Web page

click to select another color

ScreenTip for the blue color

Sometimes FrontPage will use a word such as "Blue" to describe a color. At other times, you might see a color defined by values such as "RR,00,99." These values specify the amounts of red, green, and blue that are combined to create the selected color.

5. Click the **blue** color to select it, and then click the **OK** button to close the Page Properties dialog box. The home page is displayed with the blue background color. See Figure 2-21.

Figure 2-21	WEB PAGE WITH BLUE BACKGROUND COLOR

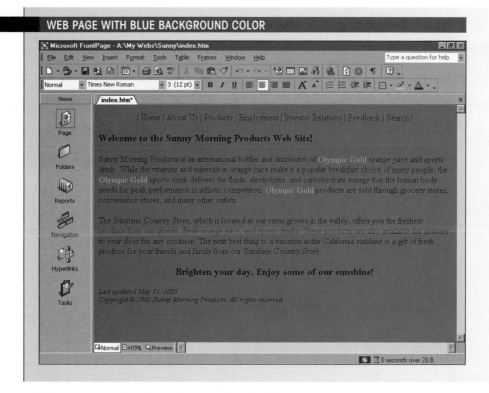

Although the blue background looks nice, it doesn't provide enough contrast with the black text. You could change the page's text to a lighter color to create a better contrast, or you could choose a more appropriate background color. Another option is to restore the default color. After discussing several other potential background colors with Amanda, you decide to reset the background color to the default (white).

To reset the default background color:

1. Click **Format** on the menu bar, and then click **Background**.

2. Click the **Background** list arrow, and then click **Automatic**. Selecting the Automatic option is the same as selecting the default color (white).

3. Click the **OK** button. The home page appears again with the default background color of white.

Although the text in the Web page is much easier to read against the default background color, the page is not visually appealing. Amanda explains that there is another way to improve the appearance of a Web page—by inserting a background picture.

Inserting a Background Picture

A **picture** is any file that contains a graphic image, such as a logo, photograph, or computer-generated image. A **background picture**, which appears behind the Web page text, can be almost any picture file. Note, however, that some pictures work better than others to provide a background against which to read the Web page text. FrontPage provides many files that you can use to create a background picture. You can use a photo or other picture as a background picture, as well.

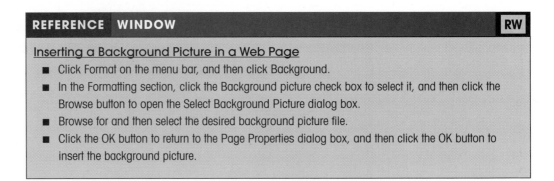

REFERENCE WINDOW   **RW**

Inserting a Background Picture in a Web Page

- Click Format on the menu bar, and then click Background.
- In the Formatting section, click the Background picture check box to select it, and then click the Browse button to open the Select Background Picture dialog box.
- Browse for and then select the desired background picture file.
- Click the OK button to return to the Page Properties dialog box, and then click the OK button to insert the background picture.

Amanda asks you to insert the background picture that she saved in the Tutorial.02 folder on your Data Disk to enhance the appearance of the home page.

To insert the background picture:

1. Click **Format** on the menu bar, and then click **Background** to open the Page Properties dialog box with the Background tab selected.

2. In the Formatting section, click the **Background picture** check box to select it, and then click the **Browse** button. The Select Background Picture dialog box opens. You will use a file on your Data Disk.

3. Click the **Look in** list arrow, select the drive or folder that contains your Data Disk, and then double-click the **Tutorial.02** folder to display its contents.

4. Double-click **WP53196** in the list box. The Page Properties dialog box reappears, and shows that you are inserting a file from the Tutorial.02 folder as a background picture. See Figure 2-22.

Figure 2-22	BACKGROUND PICTURE SETTINGS

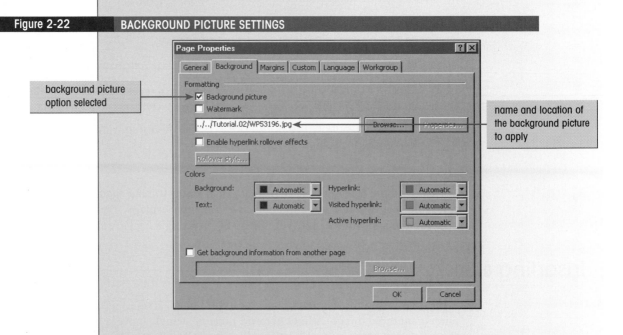

background picture option selected

name and location of the background picture to apply

5. Click the **OK** button to close the Page Properties dialog box. The background picture now appears in the home page for Sunny Morning Products.

Saving an Embedded File in a Web Site

The new background picture is attractive, and the text in the home page remains easy to read. Before testing the home page in the browser, however, you need to save the home page. When you inserted the background picture in the Web page, you **embedded** it into your Web site. This embedded file does not become part of your Web site until you save it in the Web site's images folder, which contains the picture and other multimedia files that are used in your Web site. Saving the embedded background picture file in your Web site ensures that all of your Web site's files are saved within the Web site itself and that they will be accessible to all users.

REFERENCE WINDOW   **RW**

Saving a Web Page That Contains an Embedded File
- Click the Save button on the Standard toolbar. The Save Embedded Files dialog box opens.
- If necessary, click the Change Folder button, select the images folder for the current Web site, and then click the OK button.
- Click the OK button to save the Web page and the embedded file.

To save the home page and the embedded picture file:

1. Click the **Save** button on the Standard toolbar. The Save Embedded Files dialog box opens. You need to save the background picture file, WP53196.jpg, in the Sunny Web site's images folder.

   TROUBLE? If the images folder already appears in the Folder column in the Save Embedded Files dialog box, skip to Step 4.

2. Click the **Change Folder** button to open the Change Folder dialog box. Notice that the path in the Look in list box shows the Sunny Web on your Data Disk. The folders contained in the Sunny Web appear in the dialog box. You will store all of the Web's picture and multimedia files in the Web's images folder.

   TROUBLE? If the Sunny Web on your Data Disk does not appear in the Look in list box, use the Look in list arrow to browse to the Sunny Web.

3. Click the **images** folder to select it, and then click the **OK** button to return to the Save Embedded Files dialog box. See Figure 2-23.

Figure 2-23   SAVE EMBEDDED FILES DIALOG BOX

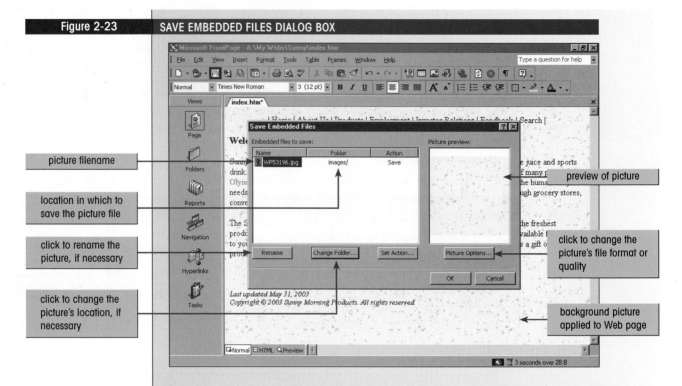

picture filename

location in which to
save the picture file

click to rename the
picture, if necessary

click to change the
picture's location, if
necessary

preview of picture

click to change the
picture's file format or
quality

background picture
applied to Web page

Notice that the Save Embedded Files dialog box shows the name of the embedded file (WP53196.jpg), the folder in which to save the file (images/), the action to perform (Save), and a preview of the picture. If you make a mistake, you can use this dialog box to rename the picture, to change the folder in which to save it, or to change the action as necessary. In addition, clicking the Picture Options button lets you change the picture's properties. For example, you might change the file from one format to another or change the quality of the image.

4. Click the **OK** button to save this file in the images folder and to save the home page. After a few seconds, the file is saved and your Web site is updated.

Now that you have saved the home page, you need to test it using the browser.

To test a background picture using a browser:

1. Click the **Preview in Browser** button 🔍 on the Standard toolbar to start the browser and open the home page. Notice how the background picture adds visual interest to the page while maintaining the readability of the Web page's content. Your test is successful, so you can close the browser.

2. Click the **Close** button ☒ on the browser's title bar to close it.

3. If necessary, click the **Microsoft FrontPage** program button on the taskbar to return to FrontPage.

Your test of the background picture was a success—adding the image improved the appearance of the home page. Now Amanda wants you to add the Sunny Morning Products logo to the page.

Adding a Picture to a Web Page

You can also use a picture to add visual interest to a Web page or to serve as a hyperlink that opens another Web page. Two of the most popular formats for picture files are the following:

- **GIF**, pronounced "jiff" or "giff" (with a hard "g"), stands for **Graphics Interchange Format**. This format supports color and different screen resolutions, making it suitable for scanned photos and pictures with smaller file sizes.
- **JPG** (or **JPEG**), pronounced "jay-peg," stands for **Joint Photographic Experts Group**. This format is suitable for large pictures because it converts them to a format with smaller file sizes.

Most Web browsers will display pictures that are created using either of these picture file formats.

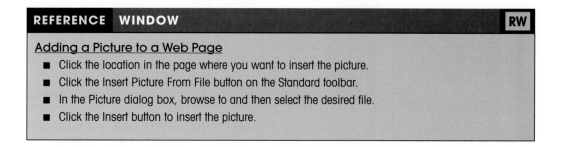

REFERENCE   WINDOW   **RW**

Adding a Picture to a Web Page
- Click the location in the page where you want to insert the picture.
- Click the Insert Picture From File button on the Standard toolbar.
- In the Picture dialog box, browse to and then select the desired file.
- Click the Insert button to insert the picture.

Amanda has already created the Sunny Morning Products logo, which she saved in the Tutorial.02 folder on your Data Disk. She asks you to add this picture at the top of the home page.

To add a picture to a Web page:

1. Click anywhere in the link bar at the top of the page, press the **Home** key, press the **Enter** key to create a new line, and then press the **up arrow** key ↑ to move the insertion point to the new line. The insertion point now appears in the location where you want to add the picture. Notice that the Center button on the Formatting toolbar is selected, indicating that the new line is centered.

2. Click the **Insert Picture From File** button 🖼 on the Standard toolbar. The Picture dialog box opens.

3. If necessary, click the **Look in** list arrow, change to the drive or folder that contains your Data Disk, and then double-click the **Tutorial.02** folder to display its contents.

4. Double-click **SMPLogo** to insert the logo in the Web page, and then click the **logo** in the Web page to select it. See Figure 2-24.

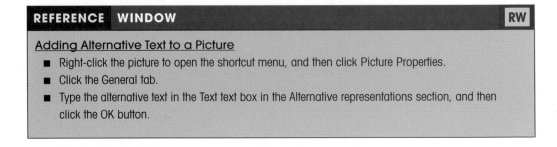

Figure 2-24   PICTURE INSERTED IN THE HOME PAGE

Pictures toolbar appears when a picture is selected (your toolbar might appear in a different location)

selection handles indicate that the picture is selected

centered picture

time to download this page using a 28.8 bps modem

TROUBLE? If the Pictures toolbar does not appear automatically when you select the logo, click View on the menu bar, point to Toolbars, and then click Pictures.

Notice that the current paragraph alignment—centered—is applied to the logo. Notice also the **selection handles**—eight small squares around the logo—that you can use to resize the selected picture. The Pictures toolbar appears as either a floating or docked toolbar, depending on your system configuration. Finally, the status bar indicates that the page with this picture inserted will take approximately six seconds to download using a 28.8 bps modem.

A picture might take some time to appear in a Web page. The length of the delay depends on the transmission speed from the Web server to the client's browser. Often, while a picture is being transferred from the server to the client's browser, an alternative text message appears. **Alternative text** is a descriptive message that identifies a picture in a Web page. You can use this optional feature to inform the user that a picture file is being transmitted to the browser but has not yet arrived. In addition, the message appears when you point to the picture in the browser. Alternative text that you add to a picture in a Web page consists of HTML code.

REFERENCE WINDOW   **RW**

Adding Alternative Text to a Picture
- Right-click the picture to open the shortcut menu, and then click Picture Properties.
- Click the General tab.
- Type the alternative text in the Text text box in the Alternative representations section, and then click the OK button.

FrontPage estimated that it would take approximately six seconds to download the logo (see Figure 2-24). Although this time is acceptable, Amanda explains that adding alternative text to the picture is good design practice. She asks you to include alternative text for the Sunny Morning Products logo.

To add alternative text to a picture and test it:

1. Right-click the **logo** to open the shortcut menu, and then click **Picture Properties** to open the Picture Properties dialog box.

2. Click the **General** tab. See Figure 2-25. Notice that the GIF option button is selected in the Type section, indicating the selected picture's file format.

| Figure 2-25 | GENERAL SETTINGS FOR THE SELECTED PICTURE |

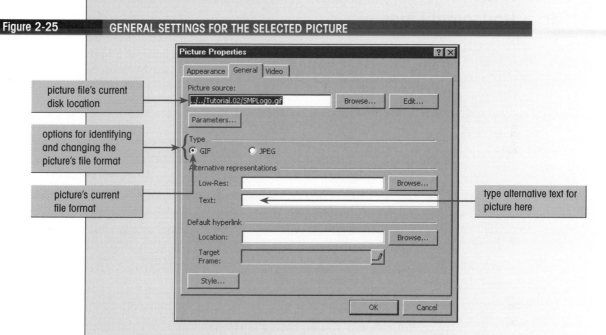

3. Click in the **Text** text box in the Alternative representations section, type **Sunny Morning Products Logo**, and then click the **OK** button. The Picture Properties dialog box closes.

   You can see the alternative text that you added by using either Preview Page view or the browser. You will test the alternative text using Preview Page view.

4. Click the **Preview** button. Point to the **logo** until the ScreenTip displays the alternative text that you added in Step 3. After a few seconds, the alternative text will disappear.

5. Click the **Normal** button to return to Normal Page view.

Now if the picture fails to download from the server or downloads slowly, the alternative text will be displayed in place of the picture or during the download. You added another picture to your Web site, so you need to save its file in the Sunny Web site's images folder.

To save the home page with the logo file:

1. Click the **Save** button 🖫 on the Standard toolbar. The Save Embedded Files dialog box opens and displays the name of the new embedded file (SMPLogo.gif), the folder in which it will be saved (images/), and the action to perform (Save). Notice that the Picture preview box shows a preview of the picture.

2. Click the **OK** button to save the embedded file in the Sunny Web site and your changes to the home page. After a few seconds, the file is saved and your Web site is updated.

Using **Horizontal Lines**

Sometimes you might want to emphasize specific parts of a Web page. One way to do this is to provide a visual break between sections of text by inserting a horizontal line. After inserting a horizontal line, you can change its characteristics by adjusting its length, width, and color.

REFERENCE WINDOW   **RW**

Inserting a Horizontal Line and Changing Its Properties
- Click at the beginning of the line directly below the location in which to insert the horizontal line.
- Click Insert on the menu bar, and then click Horizontal Line to insert a horizontal line.
- If necessary, double-click the horizontal line in the Web page, and then use the Horizontal Line Properties dialog box to change its characteristics.

To provide a visual break between the main body of the text and the footer in the home page, Amanda asks you to insert a horizontal line above the footer.

To insert a horizontal line in the home page:

1. Press **Ctrl + End** to scroll to the bottom of the Sunny Morning Products home page.

2. Click to the left of the word **Last** at the beginning of the first line of the footer. The insertion point is now positioned directly below the location in which to insert the horizontal line.

3. Click **Insert** on the menu bar, and then click **Horizontal Line**. A horizontal line is inserted above the footer.

Next, Amanda asks you to make the line more prominent by making it shorter and wider and by changing its color.

To change horizontal line settings:

1. Double-click the **horizontal line** to select it and open the Horizontal Line Properties dialog box. See Figure 2-26.

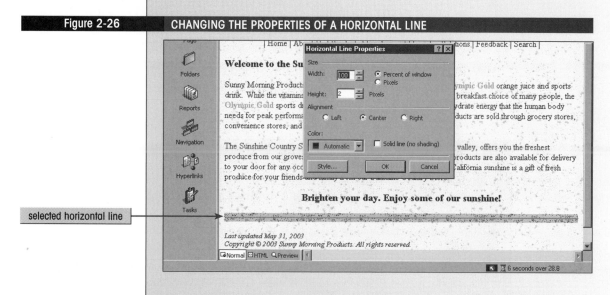

2. In the Size section, replace the selected text in the Width text box by typing **90**. The line's width will now be 90% of the screen's width.

3. Click the **Height** up arrow until the value is set to **5**. The height of the line will now be 5 pixels.

4. Click the **Color** list arrow, and then click the **orange** color in the Document's colors section. You applied the same orange color to the Olympic Gold text in the home page in Session 2.2.

5. Click the **OK** button, and then click below the horizontal line to deselect it. The horizontal line appears as a centered, thicker, shorter, orange line. See Figure 2-27.

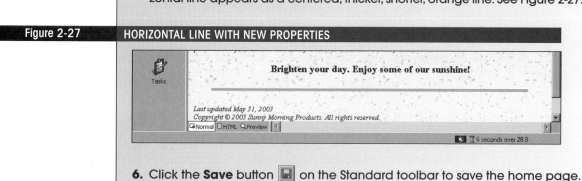

6. Click the **Save** button 🖫 on the Standard toolbar to save the home page.

Adding a Background Sound to a Web Page

The Sunny Morning Products logo that you added to the home page is an example of a multimedia file. You can add a variety of multimedia files to your Web site, including picture, video, and sound files. Sound files add interest to a page, but they also have a disadvantage: They are often very large and thus can take a long time to download. Two of the most popular sound file types for Web pages are the following:

- **WAV** (*.WAV), which is the standard file format for sound on personal computers.
- **MIDI** (*.MID), which stands for **Musical Instrument Digital Interface**. The electronic music industry uses this format for controlling devices that emit music, such as synthesizers and sound cards.

WAV files usually produce better-quality sound than do MIDI files. On the other hand, MIDI files are usually smaller than WAV files and therefore download from the Web server more quickly.

REFERENCE WINDOW   **RW**

Adding a Background Sound to a Web Page
- Click File on the menu bar, click Properties, and make sure that the General tab is selected in the Page Properties dialog box.
- Click the Browse button in the Background sound section.
- Use the Look in list arrow to browse for the desired file, and then double-click the sound filename.
- Select the Forever check box to play the sound continuously, or clear the Forever check box and then use the Loop text box to specify how many times to play the sound.
- Click the OK button.

Amanda asks you to add a sound file that will play once when the home page is opened or refreshed in the browser. She has already saved a MIDI sound file, which plays a minuet, in the Tutorial.02 folder on your Data Disk.

To add a background sound to a Web page:

1. Click **File** on the menu bar, click **Properties** to open the Page Properties dialog box, and then make sure that the **General** tab is selected.

2. Click the **Browse** button in the Background sound section to open the Background Sound dialog box.

3. Use the **Look in** list arrow to browse to the drive or folder that contains your Data Disk, and then double-click the **Tutorial.02** folder to open it. The file list shows the sound (audio) files found in the Tutorial.02 folder.

4. Double-click **Minuet** to select it as the background sound and return to the Page Properties dialog box. Notice that the Minuet.mid file is now listed in the Location text box in the Background sound section.

   TROUBLE? If you do not see the Minuet file in the Select File dialog box, verify that the Look in folder displays the Tutorial.02 folder on your Data Disk and that the Files of type list box is set to display "All Audio Files." If you still do not see the Minuet file, ask your instructor or technical support person for help.

When you add a background sound to a Web page, the default is for the sound to play forever (that is, continuously) while the page that contains it remains open in the browser. You can change this setting to specify a particular number of times that the sound should play. Now that you've added the background sound to the home page, you will set it to play only once.

To adjust the loop setting for a background sound, and then save and test it:

1. In the Background sound section, click the **Forever** check box to deselect the continuous loop and to enable the Loop text box.

2. Click the **Loop** up arrow once to change the value to **1**, and then click the **OK** button to close the Page Properties dialog box.

   Now you can save the Minuet file in the Sunny Web site.

3. Click the **Save** button [icon] on the Standard toolbar to open the Save Embedded Files dialog box. If necessary, click the **Change Folder** button, click the **images** folder in the Sunny Web site, and then click the **OK** button.

4. Click the **OK** button to save the file.

   Next, you will test the page in a browser.

5. Click the **Preview in Browser** button [icon] on the Standard toolbar to open the home page in the browser. The background sound will play once and then stop.

   TROUBLE? If you do not hear the background sound, make sure that your computer is equipped with a sound card and that the speakers are turned on. If you still do not hear the sound, ask your instructor or technical support person for help.

   TROUBLE? If the music sounds like it is playing too slowly, don't worry. This performance reflects your computer's hardware and software setups.

6. Click the **Refresh** button [icon] on the toolbar. When you refresh a Web page, it is reloaded in the browser. In this example, the background sound starts to play again.

   TROUBLE? If you are using Netscape Navigator, click the Reload button [icon] on the toolbar.

7. Click the **Stop** button [icon] on the toolbar to stop the music.

8. Click the **Close** button [icon] on the browser title bar to close it.

9. If necessary, click the **Microsoft FrontPage** program button on the taskbar to return to FrontPage.

Amanda is pleased with the enhancements you have made to the home page. She asks you to add one more feature to make the page more interesting: a marquee.

Using a Marquee

Another way to draw attention to information in a Web page is to scroll text across the page. A **marquee** is a text box that displays a scrolling message in a Web page. You can create a marquee by using existing text or by entering new text. You should use marquees sparingly, however, because they can easily overpower a Web page and distract users.

REFERENCE   WINDOW   RW

Creating a Marquee in a Web Page

- Select the text in the Web page that will appear in the marquee.
- Click the Web Component button on the Standard toolbar to open the Insert Web Component dialog box.
- If necessary, click Dynamic Effects in the Component type list, and then click Marquee in the Choose an effect list.
- Click the Finish button. The Marquee Properties dialog box opens.
- If necessary, edit the text for the marquee in the Text text box.
- In the Behavior section, click the option button to implement the desired behavior for the marquee's text.
- Specify any other desired characteristics of the marquee, such as the direction, speed, size, and/or background color of its text, or accept the default settings for these characteristics.
- If necessary, click the Style button, click the Format button in the Modify Style dialog box, and then click an option in the list that opens to change the settings for the marquee's font, paragraph, border, bullets, and position.
- Click the OK button.

Amanda wants you to create a marquee that draws more attention to the sentences, "Brighten your day. Enjoy some of our sunshine!" Placing this text in a marquee will animate it when the user views the home page in a browser. When creating a marquee, keep in mind that the text in a marquee should fit on one line, and that shorter phrases or sentences work better than longer ones.

To create and test the marquee:

1. Scroll down the home page, and then select the text **Brighten your day. Enjoy some of our sunshine!** in the home page. This text will appear in your marquee.

2. Click the **Web Component** button 🖼 on the Standard toolbar. The Insert Web Component dialog box opens.

3. Click **Dynamic Effects** in the Component type list (if necessary), and then click **Marquee** in the Choose an effect list. A description of the Marquee Web component appears in the dialog box.

4. Click the **Finish** button. The Marquee Properties dialog box opens. See Figure 2-28. Notice that the text you selected appears in the Text text box automatically.

Figure 2-28 MARQUEE PROPERTIES DIALOG BOX

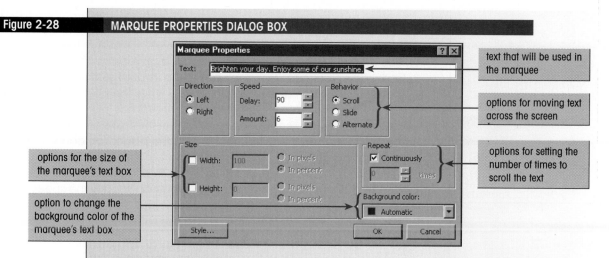

text that will be used in the marquee

options for moving text across the screen

options for setting the number of times to scroll the text

options for the size of the marquee's text box

option to change the background color of the marquee's text box

TROUBLE? If a space appears after the exclamation point in the Text text box, you selected the hard return at the end of the paragraph in the Web page. Click the Cancel button, and then repeat Steps 1–4, making sure to select only the text.

5. Click the **Alternate** option button in the Behavior section. Selecting this setting causes the marquee's text to move back and forth across the screen. The Scroll setting causes the text to move across the screen in only one direction, and the Slide setting causes the text to scroll across the screen and then stop.

6. In the Size section, click the **Width** check box to select it, select the value in the Width text box and type **90**, and then (if necessary) click the **In percent** option button to select that option. These settings limit the width of the marquee to 90% of the screen's width. Notice that you can set similar limits on the marquee's height or use pixels as the unit of measurement.

TROUBLE? If you accidentally close the Marquee Properties dialog box, double-click the marquee text in the Web page to reopen it.

Amanda suggests that you use a different background color for the marquee's text box so that it will stand out in the page.

7. Click the **Background color** list arrow to open the list of available colors. See Figure 2-29.

Figure 2-29 CHANGING THE MARQUEE'S BACKGROUND COLOR

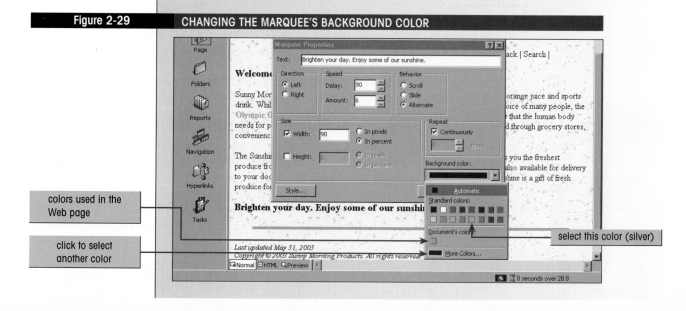

colors used in the Web page

click to select another color

select this color (silver)

8. Click the **silver** color in the Standard colors section (see Figure 2-29). This color has the ScreenTip "Silver."

Notice that you can change other marquee options as well. For example, selecting the Continuously check box in the Repeat section causes the marquee's text to remain animated indefinitely while the page is open. If you clear this check box, you can specify the number of times that the marquee's text will move across the screen. You can also set the text's direction of movement so that it scrolls from the left or right side of the page. You can specify delay and speed parameters in the Speed section. In the Delay text box, you can specify the amount of time, in milliseconds, that the text should wait before it begins to move. In the Amount text box, you can specify the speed at which the text should move in the marquee. The default settings for these options are acceptable, so you will close the dialog box.

9. Click the **OK** button. The Marquee Properties dialog box closes and a marquee with a silver background surrounds the heading in the Web page. No movement is shown, however. To test this feature, you must save the page and then change to Preview Page view.

10. Click the **Save** button 🖫 on the Standard toolbar, and then click the **Preview** button to preview the page. If necessary, scroll down the page to see the marquee. The text moves back and forth in the silver marquee.

11. Click the **Normal** button to return to Normal Page view.

Amanda is pleased with the revised content and appearance of the home page. Next, she asks you to include information in the home page that will help Web search engines locate the Sunny Morning Products Web site.

Using META Tags

A Web site can be an effective marketing tool for a company—but only if people are aware that the site exists. One way to promote a Web site to potential users relies on indexing. **Indexing** is the process of listing a Web site in Web search engines. An **index** is a database that Web users search to find specific Web sites. Normally, you conduct searches using a **Web search engine**, which is a Web site that automatically gathers and maintains information about all of the Web sites on the Web. Each Web search engine uses a different method to index the Web, so your search results using different search engines might vary. In addition to using indexing, some search engines, such as Yahoo!, list Web sites by category. Other search engines, such as AltaVista, Excite, and HotBot, search the Web for new sites and compile data about the information contained within each site.

Most search engines gather information about Web sites by collecting data based on META tags entered into the HTML document by the Web page's developer. A **META tag** is an HTML tag including text that identifies how the Web page's developer wants to add the Web site to a search engine's index. For example, if a user enters the search term "orange juice" in a Web search engine, Amanda wants the search engine to find the Sunny Morning Products home page. To accomplish this objective, you will add a keywords META tag with the phrase "orange juice" to the home page.

A META tag can include different attributes that specify a site's subject, author, keywords, or description. FrontPage automatically creates four META tags in all FrontPage-created documents to indicate the page's default character set and language, identify the

Web page as being created with FrontPage, and specify that the Web page is an "http" page. FrontPage places all META tags at the beginning of the HTML document. META tags do not change the appearance of the Web page; only search engines use them for the purpose of updating their search indexes.

REFERENCE WINDOW **RW**

Inserting META Tags in a Web Page

- Right-click anywhere in the Web page to open the shortcut menu, click Page Properties, and then click the Custom tab.
- Click the Add button in the User variables section.
- Type the META tag name in the Name text box, and then press the Tab key.
- Type the desired text for the META tag in the Value text box.
- Click the OK button.
- Click the Add button, and then repeat the process to add additional META tags as necessary.
- Click the OK button.

To promote the Web site for Sunny Morning Products, Amanda asks you to include indexing information in the home page so that the site will be added automatically to the indexes of various Web search engines. You will add two META tags—description and keywords—to the home page.

To insert META tags in the home page:

1. Right-click anywhere in the Web page to open the shortcut menu, click **Page Properties** to open the Page Properties dialog box, and then click the **Custom** tab.

2. In the User variables section, click the **Add** button to open the User Meta Variable dialog box.

   TROUBLE? If you accidentally click the Add button in the System variables section, the System META Variable (HTTP-EQUIV) dialog box opens rather than the User Meta Variable dialog box. Click the Cancel button, and then repeat Step 2. (Creating system variables is beyond the scope of this tutorial.)

3. Type **description** in the Name text box, and then press the **Tab** key to move the insertion point to the Value text box. You will use the description META tag to summarize the Web site's contents.

4. With the insertion point in the Value text box, type **Sunny Morning Products produces Olympic Gold brand orange juice and sports drink. Check out our Sunshine Country Store.** as the description. As you type, the text automatically scrolls across the text box. See Figure 2-30.

Figure 2-30   DEFINING META TAGS FOR THE HOME PAGE

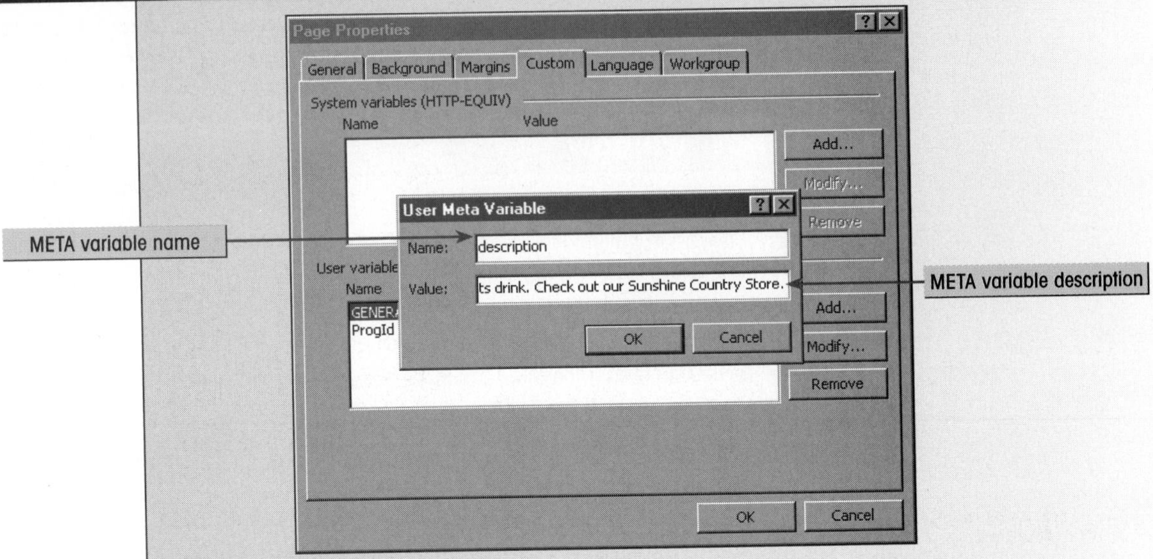

META variable name

META variable description

5. Click the **OK** button to return to the Page Properties dialog box. Notice that the text you just typed in the Name and Value text boxes now appears in the Name and Value columns in the User variables section.

6. Click the **Add** button in the User variables section again, type **keywords** in the Name text box, and then press the **Tab** key to advance to the Value text box. Web search engines use the keywords META tag to catalog your Web site.

7. Type **orange juice, sports drink, citrus products, gifts, holiday gifts, oranges, grapefruit** in the Value text box as the desired keywords.

8. Click the **OK** button in the User Meta Variable dialog box to return to the Page Properties dialog box, and then click the **OK** button to close the Page Properties dialog box.

9. Click the **Save** button 🖫 on the Standard toolbar to save the home page.

META tags do not appear in the Web page when it is viewed either in FrontPage or in a browser. Amanda wants you to view the META tags in the HTML code to better understand the exact information that search engines will add to their indexes. Viewing the tags also allows you to confirm that the entries were correctly inserted in the HTML code.

Viewing **HTML Code**

Recall from Tutorial 1 that FrontPage produces the HTML code for your Web page automatically and that a Web browser interprets this code to display the page. In creating the home page for Sunny Morning Products, you used FrontPage to include many features that are represented by HTML tags, including paragraph styles, multimedia files, and a marquee. For example, the BGSOUND tag specifies the background sound you inserted, and the ALIGN property of the P (paragraph) tag specifies a paragraph's alignment. The H3 tag specifies a heading and its style, and the MARQUEE tag specifies the use of a marquee in the page. FrontPage created each of these tags and their related properties as you created the home page. Even though FrontPage creates HTML code automatically, it is important for Web site developers to understand HTML code because it serves as the foundation of any Web page.

Amanda wants you to examine the HTML code for the home page to gain a better understanding of the code created by FrontPage. As you learn more about HTML, you will gain confidence and become more comfortable making changes to the Web page by editing the HTML code itself.

To view the HTML code for the home page and close FrontPage:

1. Press **Ctrl + Home** to scroll to the top of the home page.

2. Click the **HTML** button to switch to that view and to display the HTML code for the home page. See Figure 2-31. Examine the HTML code that FrontPage created to insert the META tags, the background sound, and other features of the home page.

Figure 2-31	VIEWING THE FIRST PAGE OF HTML CODE FOR THE HOME PAGE

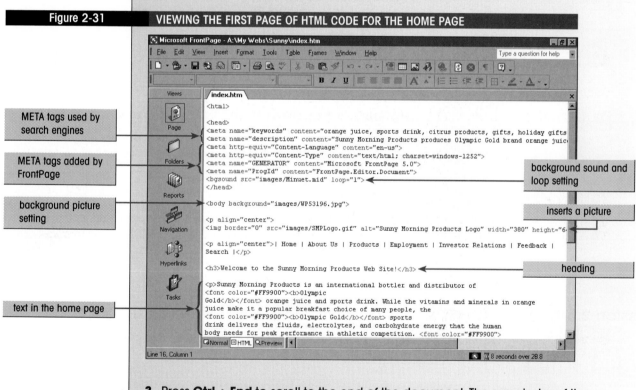

META tags used by search engines

META tags added by FrontPage

background picture setting

text in the home page

background sound and loop setting

inserts a picture

heading

3. Press **Ctrl + End** to scroll to the end of the document. The remainder of the HTML code appears in your window. See Figure 2-32. Examine the HTML code that created the marquee, the footer, and other features of the home page.

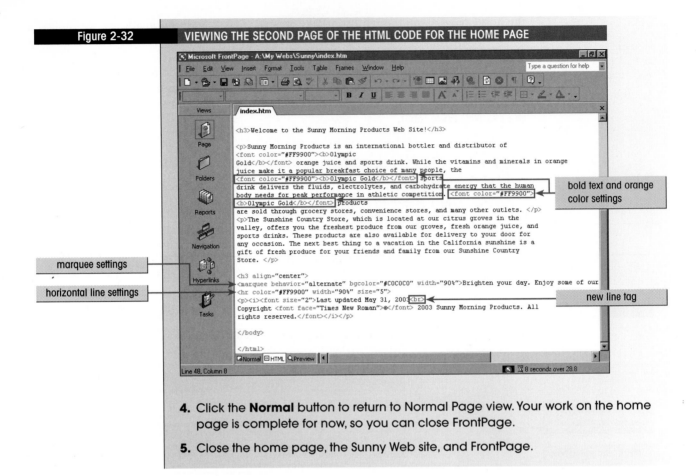

Figure 2-32 — VIEWING THE SECOND PAGE OF THE HTML CODE FOR THE HOME PAGE

4. Click the **Normal** button to return to Normal Page view. Your work on the home page is complete for now, so you can close FrontPage.

5. Close the home page, the Sunny Web site, and FrontPage.

After creating the home page and revising its contents and features, you are well on your way to implementing the Web site design for Sunny Morning Products. You are confident that the home page design meets the requirements of the Web site development team. In Tutorial 3, you will create additional pages and link them to each other by using hyperlinks.

Session 2.3 QUICK CHECK

1. The default background color of a Web page when you first create it is _____.

2. Which two common picture file formats are used in Web pages?

3. In addition to being a good design practice, why should you add alternative text to a picture that you use in your Web page?

4. A good way to separate sections in a Web page is to insert a(n) _____.

5. Describe two popular sound file formats that you can use in a Web page.

6. Text that is formatted to become animated in a Web page when it is displayed in the browser appears in a(n) _____.

7. What is the purpose of the images folder that is automatically created when you create a FrontPage Web?

8. To supply information that is used by a search engine to make your Web site available to Internet users, use a(n) _____.

REVIEW ASSIGNMENTS

Amanda is pleased with the progress you are making in her training course. She asks you to finish formatting the home page by inserting another horizontal line and changing the HTML code.

If necessary, start FrontPage and insert your Data Disk in the appropriate disk drive, and then do the following:

1. Open the **Sunny** Web site (which you created in the tutorial) from the My Webs folder on your Data Disk, change to Folders view, and then open the home page (**index.htm** or **default.htm**) in Page view.

2. Add a horizontal line between the "Welcome" heading and the first paragraph of the narrative text. If necessary, change the line to make it the same size and color as the line you added at the bottom of the page in the tutorial. (*Hint:* If you can't remember the set-tings you applied to the other horizontal line, double-click it to examine its properties.)

3. Center the "Welcome" heading in the home page.

Explore 4. Use the Page Properties dialog box to add the title "Home Page" to the **index.htm** page. (*Hint:* Type the title in the Title text box.)

Explore 5. Change to HTML Page view, and then locate the HTML tags that apply the Heading 3 style to the "Welcome" heading. Change the HTML code so that the "Welcome" head-ing uses the Heading 1 style. (*Hint:* Change the opening and closing tags to use the Heading 1 style.) Save your changes to the home page, and then preview the page in the browser. Describe what happened to the "Welcome" heading.

6. Use the browser to print the HTML code for the home page.

7. Use the Source command on the View menu in Internet Explorer to examine the HTML code for the home page. Next, change the "Welcome" heading's style back to Heading 3. Save your changes, and then refresh the page in the browser.

8. Close the browser, and then close the **Sunny** Web site and FrontPage.

CASE PROBLEMS

Case 1. Preparing a Web Presence for Royal Hair Care Products Royal Hair Care Products, established in 1984, is a leader in hair care products for women, men, and chil-dren. Its current product line includes shampoos, conditioners, hair sprays, and styling gels. All products carry a satisfaction guarantee. The company's newest product is Quick Dry Solution, which when applied to wet hair, dries it quickly without the need for a hair dryer. Quick Dry Solution is available in either a gel form or a liquid spray. The easy-to-use product leaves hair feeling natural and manageable.

Recently, Valerie Suarez, the president of Royal Hair Care Products, hired Nathan Dubois as an information systems specialist and assigned him to Royal's Web site development team. Valerie wants Nathan to design Royal's Web site and then create a home page for the company. Valerie and Nathan met with the rest of the Web site development team members. In the meeting, all agreed that, in addition to the home page, the company needs six pages with the following titles: (1) About Us, (2) News, (3) Employment, (4) Financial Info, (5) Feedback, and (6) Search. Valerie has asked you to assist Nathan in developing the site and the home page.

If necessary, start FrontPage, insert your Data Disk in the appropriate disk drive, and then do the following:

1. Prepare a planning analysis sheet for the **Royal** Web site.

2. Prepare a Web site plan that shows the desired Web pages and the expected hyperlinks from the home page.

3. Use the One Page Web template to create the **Royal** Web site in the My Webs folder on your Data Disk. (*Hint:* Specify the location as My Webs\Royal to create the **Royal** Web site and the My Webs folder.)

4. Open the home page in Normal Page view. Start Word and open the **Royal.doc** file from the Tutorial.02 folder on your Data Disk. Select all of the text in the document, and then copy it to the Windows Clipboard. Close Word and paste the text into the home page. Choose the option to keep the text only, and use the Spelling button to correct any misspelled words. Change the paragraph so that the sentence beginning "Our newest product is Quick Dry Solution" and the sentence following it appear in a separate paragraph. Save the home page.

5. Create the heading "Welcome to the Royal Web Site." on a new line at the top of the home page. Change the style of this line to Heading 3, and then center it.

6. Create a link bar for the home page based on your design for the Web site. Limit the link bar to a single line, and center it in the home page. Change the text in the link bar to bold and the Normal style, and then change its color to blue.

Explore ▶ 7. Add a footer at the bottom of the page that includes a copyright symbol and the company name on the first line. On the next line, type "Last updated," and then add a field that automatically updates the date and time since you last changed the Web page. (*Hint:* To add the date and time field, click Insert on the menu bar, and then click Date and Time.) Format the date using the format month day, year—for example, "September 22, 2003." Do not specify a time. Change the footer text to bold, its color to blue, and then reduce its font size by one HTML level.

8. Add a horizontal line to the Web page between the "Welcome" heading and the first paragraph. Change the line's color to blue.

9. On a new line at the top of the home page, insert the logo file for the company, **Royal.gif**, from the Tutorial.02 folder.

Explore ▶ 10. On a new, centered line above the footer, place the text "Exceeding all of your styling needs since 1984." in a marquee. Change the marquee's default settings to an alternate marquee that uses 90% of the page's width. Select coordinating colors for the marquee's text and background to match the logo's colors. (*Hint:* Click the Style button in the Marquee Properties dialog box, and then click the Format button in the Modify Style dialog box to change the format of the text in the marquee.)

11. To the home page, add the **Quantum.mid** file from the Tutorial.02 folder as a background sound that plays once.

Explore ▶ 12. Create appropriate META description and keywords tags for the home page, and then save the home page. Save all multimedia files in the Web site's images folder.

Explore ▶ 13. Use the Page Properties dialog box to add the title "Home Page" to the **index.htm** page. (*Hint:* Type the title in the Title text box.)

14. In FrontPage, print the HTML code for the home page. On the printout, circle the META tags for the description and keywords that you added and the tags for the background picture and sound.

15. Preview the home page in a browser. If necessary, return to FrontPage and make any corrections. When you are finished, close the browser, the **Royal** Web site, and FrontPage.

Case 2. Developing a Web Site for Buffalo Trading Post   Buffalo Trading Post (BTP) is a regional retail clothing business that specializes in buying, selling, and trading used clothing. The company buys all of its merchandise from people who bring the items to one of its trading post stores. Employees then sort these items based on style, size, fabric, and garment condition. Although BTP specializes in natural-fabric clothing items, it also carries a limited inventory of polyester, acetate, Lycra, and other manufactured fibers to capitalize on current styles and trends. BTP accepts only clothing in good condition for resale and attracts a loyal following of fashion enthusiasts and bargain hunters.

Karla Perez was recently hired by the president of the company, Donna Vargas, as a systems analyst and was assigned to BTP's Web site development team. Donna wants Karla to prepare a plan for BTP's Web site and then create its home page. Karla and Donna met with the rest of the Web site development team. They agreed that, in addition to the home page, the site should include five pages with the following titles: (1) Who, (2) How, (3) What, (4) Where, and (5) Contact. Donna has asked you to help Karla with the development of the site and its home page.

If necessary, start FrontPage and insert your Data Disk in the appropriate disk drive, and then do the following:

1. Prepare a planning analysis sheet for BTP's Web site.

2. Prepare a Web site plan that shows the desired Web pages and the expected hyperlinks from the home page.

3. Use the One Page Web template to create the **Buffalo** Web site in the My Webs folder on your Data Disk. (*Hint:* Specify the location as My Webs\Buffalo to create the **Buffalo** Web site and the My Webs folder.)

4. Open the home page in Normal Page view. Start Word and open the **Buffalo.doc** file from the Tutorial.02 folder on your Data Disk. Select all of the text in the document, and then copy it to the Windows Clipboard. Close Word and paste the text into the home page. Choose the option to keep the text only, and use the Spelling button to correct any misspelled words. Change the paragraph so that the sentence beginning "We also carry a limited inventory" and the sentences following it appear in a separate paragraph. Save the home page.

5. Create a heading, determine the most appropriate style and alignment for it, and place it above the text you entered in Step 4.

6. Create a link bar for the home page, and then center it. Change the color of the link bar to a color of your choice and the style of the link bar to bold.

Explore ▷ 7. Add a footer that consists of the copyright symbol and the company name on the first line. On the next line, add the following text: BTP™ is a registered trademark of Buffalo Trading Post. (*Hint:* Use the symbol set to insert the trademark character.) Change the footer text to bold, 10-point, Arial font.

8. Add a horizontal line between the link bar and the heading that you created in Step 5. Change the line's color to match the one that you used for the link bar. Change the line's height to 4 pixels and its width to 90% of the window's width.

9. Format the first instance of the text "Buffalo Trading Post" in the page's narrative so that it is easily distinguished. Use the Format Painter to change other text occurrences of "Buffalo Trading Post" to match the first instance.

10. Change the background color of the home page to one that complements the text that you entered in Step 6.

Explore ▷ 11. Use the Page Properties dialog box to add the title "Home Page" to the **index.htm** page. (*Hint:* Type the title in the Title text box.)

12. Insert the **Buffalo.gif** picture from the Tutorial.02 folder on a new, centered line below the heading at the top of the Web page. Add the alternative text "Buffalo Trading Post Logo" to the picture.

Explore ➤ 13. Create a slogan for BTP and place it in a marquee on a new centered line above the footer. Select appropriate colors for the marquee's text and background. Format the text as normal, 12-point, Comic Sans MS font. (*Hint:* Click the Style button in the Marquee Properties dialog box, click the Format button in the Modify Style dialog box, and then click Font to change the marquee text color and style.)

14. Add the **Cheers.mid** file from the Tutorial.02 folder as a background sound that plays once.

Explore ➤ 15. Create appropriate META description and keywords tags in the home page.

16. Save all multimedia files for the home page in the Web site's images folder.

17. Use FrontPage to print the HTML code for the home page. On the printout, circle the META tags for the description and keywords and the tags for the horizontal line and link bar.

18. Preview the home page in a browser. If necessary, return to FrontPage and make any needed corrections. When you are finished, close the browser, the **Buffalo** Web site, and FrontPage.

Case 3. Creating a Web Site for Garden Grill Garden Grill is a growing chain of casual, full-service restaurants. Its moderately priced menu features delicious dishes taken from various locations around the world. Garden Grill uses sophisticated consumer marketing research techniques to monitor customer satisfaction and evolving customer expectations. It strives to be a market leader in its segment by utilizing technology as a competitive advantage. Since 1976, management has used in-store computers to assist in the operation of the restaurants. The corporate office provides support 7 days a week, 24 hours a day. Management believes that its information systems have positioned the chain to handle both its current needs and its future growth.

The corporate office has prepared a long-range information systems plan, which it reviews annually with all levels of management. The plan for the coming year includes the development of a Web site. Shannon Taylor just completed her management orientation at the corporate offices of Garden Grill and was assigned to work with Nolan Simmons, who manages the information systems department. Last week, Nolan's job responsibilities were increased to include managing the company's Web site development team. Nolan wants Shannon to help him prepare the Web design plan and create a home page for Garden Grill.

Nolan and Shannon just met with the rest of the Web site development team. All agreed that, in addition to the home page, the company's Web site should include six pages with the following titles: (1) Company Profile, (2) Menu, (3) Franchise Info, (4) Employment Opportunities, (5) Feedback, and (6) Search. Nolan has asked you to assist Shannon with the design and development activities.

If necessary, start FrontPage and insert your Data Disk in the appropriate disk drive, and then do the following:

1. Prepare a planning analysis sheet for Garden Grill's Web site.

2. Prepare a Web site plan that shows the desired Web pages and the expected hyperlinks from the home page.

3. Use the One Page Web template to create the **Garden** Web site in the My Webs folder on your Data Disk. (*Hint:* Specify the location as My Webs\Garden to create the **Garden** Web site and the My Webs folder.)

4. Open the home page in Normal Page view. Start Word and open the **Garden.doc** file from the Tutorial.02 folder on your Data Disk. Select all of the text in the document, and then copy it to the Windows Clipboard. Close Word and paste the text into the home page. Choose the option to keep the text only, and use the Spelling button to correct any misspelled words. Change the paragraph so that the sentence beginning "Garden Grill is a premier" and the sentences following it appear in a separate paragraph. Save the home page.

5. Create the heading "Welcome to Garden Grill. Join us for food and fun!" and place it above the text you entered in Step 4. Change the heading's style to Heading 3 and its font style to Arial. (*Hint:* Use the Font list arrow on the Formatting toolbar.) Center the heading, and change its color to red.

6. Create a link bar for the home page below the heading that you created in Step 5. Follow your Web site design plan, and limit the bar to a single line in the Web page. (*Hint:* You might need to reduce the font size of the link bar to make it fit on one line.) Use square brackets ([ ]) to enclose the navigation items. Change the color of the text in the link bar to purple, its style to bold, and its font to Century Gothic. Center the link bar.

7. Insert the **Garden.gif** picture from the Tutorial.02 folder on a new line below the link bar, and then center it.

Explore 8. Add a footer that consists of the copyright symbol and the company name on the first line. On the second line, add the text "Last updated" and a date field that indicates when the page was last edited. (*Hint:* To add the date field, click Insert on the menu bar, and then click Date and Time.) Format the date with the day of the week and the full date with the month spelled out.

9. Change the style of the footer you created in Step 8 to italic, 10-point, Arial font. Change the footer's color to match the color that you used for the link bar.

10. To the home page, apply the background picture file named **WB02245.gif** that is saved in the Tutorial.02 folder.

11. Add at least one horizontal line to the Web page; its length should be half the width of the page and its color should complement the rest of the Web page.

Explore 12. Enter "Come to Garden Grill for food and fun!" as the slogan for Garden Grill on a new line above the footer and place it in a centered, sliding marquee that is 85% of the page's width. Change the marquee's text to white, 14-point, bold, Century Gothic font. (*Hint:* Click the Style button in the Marquee Properties dialog box, click the Format button, and then click Font to change the marquee text font color and style.) In the Marquee Properties dialog box, use the Background color list arrow to change the background color of the marquee to match the color of the link bar.

13. Add the **Casper.mid** file from the Tutorial.02 folder as a background sound that plays once.

Explore 14. Create appropriate META description and keywords tags and include them in the home page.

Explore 15. Use the Page Properties dialog box to add the title "Home Page" to the **index.htm** page. (*Hint:* Type the title in the Title text box.)

16. Save all multimedia files for the home page in the Web site's images folder.

17. Test the home page using a browser. If necessary, return to FrontPage and correct any errors. Print the page using a browser, and then close the browser.

18. Use FrontPage to print the HTML code for the home page. Circle the META tags and the tags that created the marquee.

19. Close the **Garden** Web site and FrontPage.

Explore   *Case 4. Producing a Web Site for Replay Music Factory* Replay Music Factory (RMF) is a regional music store that specializes in buying, selling, and trading used compact discs (CDs). As the sale of new CDs expands, phenomenal growth is expected in the market for used CDs. Unlike records and tapes, used CDs offer quality that is comparable to that of new CDs, along with substantial savings. RMF buys used CDs from three sources: the Internet, customers, and brokers. This strategy allows the store to offer a wide variety of music to the most discriminating listener. The company's quality control division has found the defect rate for the used CDs to be less than 1%, so all of its products are 100% guaranteed.

Alec Johnston was recently hired by RMF president, Charlene Fields, as a systems analyst and was assigned to RMF's Web site development team. Charlene wants you to help Alec design the Web site and create a home page for it.

If necessary, start FrontPage and insert your Data Disk in the appropriate disk drive, and then do the following:

1. Prepare a planning analysis sheet for RMF's Web site. Determine which features and functions should be included in this Web site. If you have access to the Internet, visit three to five other Web sites that offer services similar to RMF. If you do not have Internet access, use information that you have learned from other sources, such as magazine or newspaper articles, or televised news reports.

2. Prepare a Web site plan that shows the desired Web pages and the expected hyperlinks from the home page.

3. Use the One Page Web template to create the **Replay** Web site in the My Webs folder on your Data Disk. (*Hint:* Specify the location as My Webs\Replay to create the Replay Web site and the My Webs folder.)

4. Use FrontPage to write, enter, edit, and spell check at least two paragraphs of content for the home page. Use any available reference sources to help develop your content, including other commercial Web sites.

5. Create a heading and place it above the text that you entered in Step 4. Apply an appropriate style, alignment, and color to the heading.

6. Create a link bar above the heading that you created in Step 5. Separate the link bar entries with a tilde (~). Change the text color in the link bar to match that of the heading, and apply an appropriate alignment to it.

7. Add a footer that includes the current date (in any format you choose), the copyright symbol, and the company name. (*Hint:* To add the date field, click Insert on the menu bar, and then click Date and Time.)

8. Use formatting and color to improve the appearance of your Web page. Save your changes to the home page.

9. Create a slogan for RMF and place it in a scrolling marquee on a new centered line above the footer. Select appropriate colors for the marquee text and background. (*Hint:* Click the Style button in the Marquee Properties dialog box, click the Format button in the Modify Style dialog box, and then click Font to change the font style and color of the marquee text.)

10. Locate a MIDI or WAV file on your computer and include it as a background sound that plays twice. (*Hint:* Sound files are usually saved in the Windows\Media folder on your computer. If you cannot find a MIDI or WAV file on your system, use any MIDI file in the Tutorial.02 folder on your Data Disk.)

11. Apply the background picture saved as **WB61689.jpg** in the Tutorial.02 folder to the home page.

12. Insert the **CD.gif** picture from the Tutorial.02 folder on a new line between the link bar and the heading. Apply an appropriate alignment to the picture.

13. Add at least one horizontal line to the Web page; the line should be 5 pixels in height and an appropriate color.

14. Create appropriate META description and keywords tags and include them in the home page.

15. Use the Page Properties dialog box to add the title "Home Page" to the **index.htm** page. (*Hint:* Type the title in the Title text box.)

16. Save all multimedia files for the home page in the Web site's images folder.

17. Test the Web page using a browser. If necessary, return to FrontPage and correct any errors. Print the page using the browser, and then close the browser.

18. Use FrontPage to print the HTML code for the home page. On the printout, circle the HTML tags that define the date field that you added in Step 7 and the logo that you added in Step 12.

19. Close the browser, the **Replay** Web site, and FrontPage.

QUICK CHECK ANSWERS

Session 2.1

1. Define the site's goal and purpose, determine and prepare the site's contents, design the site, build the site, test the site
2. default.htm
3. Enter text, separated by special characters such as a vertical bar or brackets, or use FrontPage to generate a link bar
4. True
5. False
6. Close Web

Session 2.2

1. Format menu, shortcut menu, or Formatting toolbar buttons
2. H1
3. 7
4. font
5. Select the text whose format you want to copy, click the Format Painter button on the Standard toolbar once, and then select the text to which you want to copy the format with the Format Painter pointer.
6. False
7. True

Session 2.3

1. white
2. GIF and JPEG (JPG)
3. Alternative text identifies the name of the file that is being downloaded so that the user knows that it is being transmitted to the browser but has not yet arrived.
4. horizontal line
5. WAV (*.WAV) is the standard for sound on personal computers; MIDI (*.MID) is used by the electronic music industry for controlling devices that emit music, such as synthesizers and sound cards.
6. marquee
7. The images folder stores all of the multimedia files used in the pages of the Web site.
8. META tag

OBJECTIVES

In this tutorial you will:

- Import an existing Web page into a Web site

- Insert a file created in another program in a Web page

- Create definition, bulleted, numbered, and nested lists

- Create bookmarks and hyperlinks to them

- Create and test hyperlinks

- Create a hyperlink to an e-mail address

- Convert a JPEG picture to GIF format with a transparent background

- Create a hyperlink hotspot in a picture

- View and print Hyperlinks view for a Web site

- Use the Tasks list to view, add, reassign, complete, and delete tasks

LAB

Web Pages & HTML

USING LISTS,
HYPERLINKS,
PICTURES, AND
THE TASKS LIST

Creating the Employment Web Page

CASE

Sunny Morning Products

Amanda Bay created the design for the Sunny Morning Products Web site and for several Web pages, for which she received approval from the Web site development team. The link bar entries in the home page include hyperlinks that open six other pages: About Us, Products, Employment, Investor Relations, Feedback, and Search. In addition to completing each of these pages, Amanda needs to create hyperlinks that link each page to the home page.

At the request of Pilar Caballero, Human Resources manager at Sunny Morning Products, Amanda focused first on developing the Employment Web page, which provides information about current employment opportunities at Sunny Morning Products. She created a draft of this Web page and then met with Pilar to review the page's proposed design and content. For organizational purposes, Amanda captured the meeting results in a planning analysis sheet.

In this tutorial, you will continue developing the Sunny Web site by creating the Employment Web page. You will use lists, hyperlinks, pictures, and a Tasks list to turn a partially completed Web page into a finished one.

SESSION 3.1

In this session, you will import an existing Web page into a Web site and insert the contents of an Office document in a Web page. In addition, you will create definition, bulleted, numbered, and nested lists.

Importing a Web Page into a Web Site

You can easily import an existing Web page into your current Web site. Importing allows you to incorporate Web pages—even those created with programs other than FrontPage—into a Web site. In addition, you can import different types of files, such as Word documents and Excel workbooks, into a Web site and automatically convert them to HTML. Importing content into a Web site saves you the trouble of retyping the material.

Amanda has already started developing the Employment Web page and now asks that you import her partially completed Web page into the Sunny Web site. Figure 3-1 shows Amanda's planning analysis sheet for the revisions to the Employment Web page.

Figure 3-1	AMANDA'S PLANNING ANALYSIS SHEET FOR THE EMPLOYMENT WEB PAGE

Planning Analysis Sheet

Objective

Create an Employment Web page that includes a table of contents and descriptions for the position openings.

Requirements

Partially completed Employment Web page

Job descriptions for the MIS and Customer Support positions

Picture file for the page's logo

Results

Employment Web page with the following information:

Table of contents

Complete job descriptions

Links from the table of contents to each job description

E-mail hyperlink for contacting the Human Resources manager

Logo that provides a corporate identity for the page

The Employment Web page that Amanda started is not saved in the Sunny Web site, so you must import it. First you will open the Sunny Web site, and then you will import Amanda's partially completed Employment Web page into it.

<u>Importing an Existing Web Page into a Web Site</u>
- In Folders view, open the Web site into which you will import the existing Web page.
- Click File on the menu bar, click Import, and then click the Add File button in the Import dialog box to display a list of files.
- Browse to the desired file, and then double-click it.
- Click the OK button to import the page.

After importing Amanda's Web page, you can modify it just like any other Web page.

To open the Sunny Web site and import an existing Web page into it:

1. Make sure your Data Disk is in the appropriate disk drive, start **FrontPage**, and then open the **Sunny** Web site from your Data Disk in Folders view.

2. Click **File** on the menu bar, and then click **Import** to open the Import dialog box.

3. Click the **Add File** button to open the Add File to Import List dialog box.

4. Click the **Look in** list arrow, change to the drive or folder that contains your Data Disk, and then double-click the **Tutorial.03** folder to display its contents.

5. Double-click **EmpPage** to select it and return to the Import dialog box. The full path of the EmpPage.htm file appears in the Import dialog box. If you wanted to import another page at this time, you could click the Add File button and select another file. Clicking the Add Folder button lets you import a folder and all of its files into the Web site. Clicking the From Web button starts the Import Web Wizard, which you can use to import Web pages from a disk or network location or a URL.

   TROUBLE? If you selected the wrong file to import, make sure that the file you imported by mistake is selected, click the Remove button in the Import dialog box, and then repeat Steps 3 through 5 to select the correct file.

6. Click the **OK** button. The Employment Web page, EmpPage.htm, is now in the Sunny Web site. See Figure 3-2.

Figure 3-2	EMPLOYMENT WEB PAGE IMPORTED INTO THE SUNNY WEB SITE

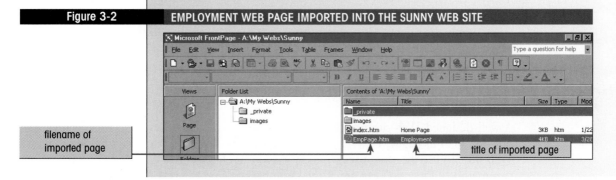

Now that you've imported the Employment Web page into the Sunny Web site, you can open it just like any other Web page.

To open the imported Web page:

1. Double-click **EmpPage.htm** in the Contents pane to open the partially completed Web page in Page view. Notice that the Employment Web page appears with the default white background. See Figure 3-3.

| Figure 3-3 | PARTIALLY COMPLETED EMPLOYMENT WEB PAGE IN PAGE VIEW |

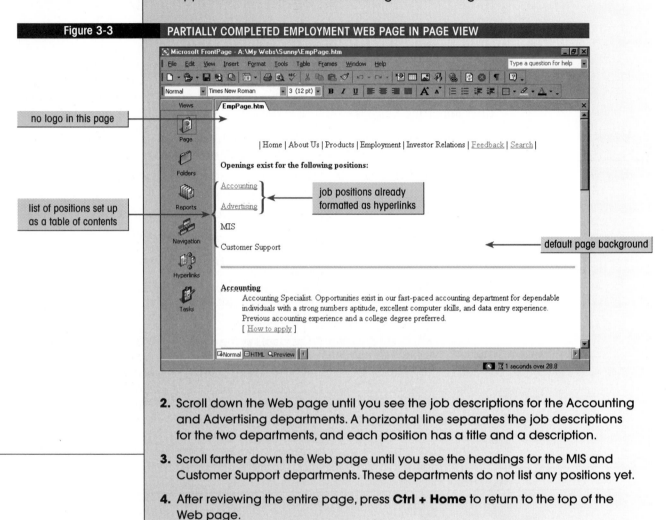

no logo in this page

list of positions set up as a table of contents

job positions already formatted as hyperlinks

default page background

2. Scroll down the Web page until you see the job descriptions for the Accounting and Advertising departments. A horizontal line separates the job descriptions for the two departments, and each position has a title and a description.

3. Scroll farther down the Web page until you see the headings for the MIS and Customer Support departments. These departments do not list any positions yet.

4. After reviewing the entire page, press **Ctrl + Home** to return to the top of the Web page.

Before you add any new features or text to the Employment Web page, Amanda wants you to apply the same background to this page that you applied to the home page so the two pages will have the same appearance.

Specifying a Common Background

A well-designed Web site usually uses the same design features—color, background, and so on—for all of its pages. This similarity provides a visual cue that the pages belong to the same Web site. To use the same background for every Web page in a Web site, you can use one of two methods. First, you can apply the same background to every Web page in the Web site. Second, you can specify that a page use the same background as another Web page, such as the home page. With the second method, changing the background of the home page, for example, also changes the backgrounds of all pages that use the same background as the home page.

To specify a background from an existing Web page:

1. Click **Format** on the menu bar, and then click **Background** to display the background settings in the Page Properties dialog box.

2. Click the **Get background information from another page** check box, and then click the **Browse** button to open the Current Web dialog box.

   You'll apply the same background as the home page.

3. Click **index.htm** to select the home page, and then click the **OK** button to return to the Page Properties dialog box. See Figure 3-4. Notice that index.htm now appears in the Get background information from another page text box.

Figure 3-4 SPECIFYING A COMMON BACKGROUND

background for the Employment Web page is now linked to the home page

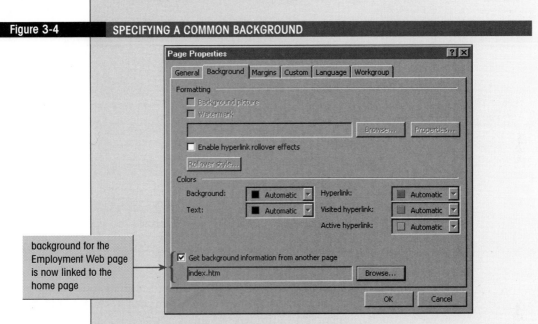

TROUBLE? If default.htm, rather than index.htm, appears in the file list, click default.htm.

4. Click the **OK** button. The Page Properties dialog box closes, and the Employment page is displayed with the new background. See Figure 3-5.

Figure 3-5   EMPLOYMENT WEB PAGE WITH THE NEW BACKGROUND

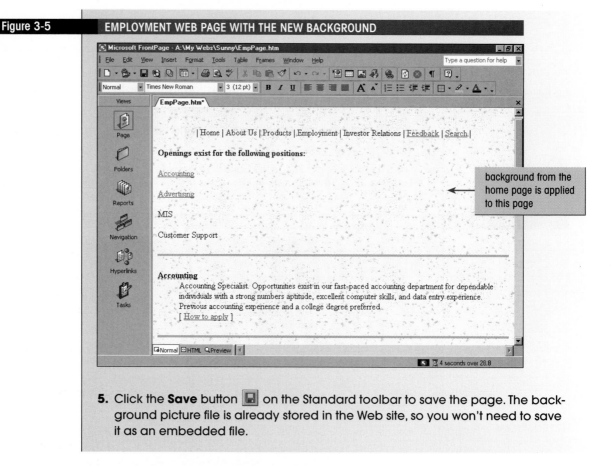

5. Click the **Save** button 💾 on the Standard toolbar to save the page. The background picture file is already stored in the Web site, so you won't need to save it as an embedded file.

Now that you have successfully updated the design of the Employment page by linking its background to the home page, you are ready to add the information for the new positions in the Customer Support and MIS departments.

Inserting a File in a Web Page

You can enter new content for a Web page by typing all of the necessary text in the Web page in Page view. If the content already exists in another text-based file format or in a Word, Excel, or PowerPoint file, however, you can insert it directly into the page instead of retyping it. When you include content from another file in a Web page, FrontPage automatically converts the new content to HTML code. Being able to insert the contents of a file in a Web page allows members of a Web site development team to divide the tasks required to complete a Web page and to exchange information.

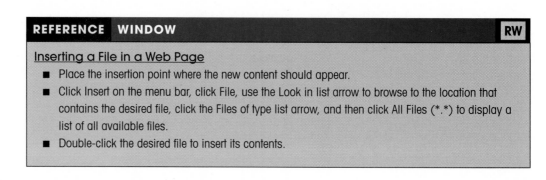

REFERENCE WINDOW   RW

Inserting a File in a Web Page
■ Place the insertion point where the new content should appear.
■ Click Insert on the menu bar, click File, use the Look in list arrow to browse to the location that contains the desired file, click the Files of type list arrow, and then click All Files (*.*) to display a list of all available files.
■ Double-click the desired file to insert its contents.

Pilar prepared a job description for the Customer Support position and saved it as a Word document, so you won't need to retype this information. She asks you to follow the design used for the Accounting and Advertising departments by placing the new job description below the Customer Support heading.

To include a Word file in a Web page:

1. Scroll down the Web page until you see the Customer Support heading that appears between two horizontal lines, and then click the blank line below the heading.

   TROUBLE? If the Customer Support heading does not have a horizontal line immediately above and below it, you are not in the job description area of the Web page. Repeat Step 1.

2. Click **Insert** on the menu bar, and then click **File**. The Select File dialog box opens.

3. If necessary, click the **Look in** list arrow, change to the drive or folder that contains your Data Disk, and then double-click the **Tutorial.03** folder to display its contents.

   By default, FrontPage displays only HTML files. You need to display Word files, however, to find Pilar's document.

4. Click the **Files of type** list arrow to display a list of available file types, and then click **Word 97-2002 (*.doc)** to display a list of Word files.

5. Double-click **Customer** to open the file and convert its content to HTML code. The Customer Support Representatives job title and description appear in the Web page below the Customer Support heading. See Figure 3-6.

Figure 3-6	NEW CUSTOMER SUPPORT POSITION ADDED TO THE WEB PAGE

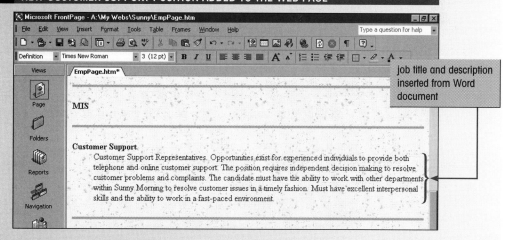

TROUBLE? If a Microsoft FrontPage dialog box opens and informs you that it can't import the specified format because it is not currently installed, insert your Microsoft Office XP CD or your Microsoft FrontPage 2002 CD into the correct drive, and then click the Yes button. If you do not have this CD, ask your instructor or technical support person for help.

Now that you have included the Customer Support position in the Employment Web page, Amanda asks you to add the MIS position as well.

Creating Lists

A list offers a convenient way to display a series of text items in a Web page. You can use FrontPage to create bulleted, numbered, and definition lists, as well as **nested lists**, which are lists within lists. You will use all of these list types to complete the Employment Web page.

Creating a Definition List

A **definition list** contains defined terms and their definitions. A **defined term** is a term that is being explained. In most cases, you will left-align a defined term with the page margin and indent its **definition**, or description, below it. The list of jobs and their job descriptions in the Employment Web page is organized as a definition list. As shown in Figure 3-6, the definition (the job description) is indented under the defined term (the Customer Support heading). When creating a definition list, you apply the Defined Term and the Definition styles to the items in the list. When you added the job description below the Customer Support heading, the text was formatted automatically using the Definition style because Amanda already applied that style to the line where you inserted the contents of the Word document.

REFERENCE WINDOW   **RW**

Creating a Definition List
- Select the line that will contain the first item in the definition list, and then type the term you want to define.

  or
- Click an existing line that you want to use for the defined term.
- Click the Style list arrow on the Formatting toolbar, and then click Defined Term.
- Press the Enter key, and then type the definition for the term.
- If necessary, press the Enter key twice to end the definition list.

When Amanda created the plan for the Employment Web page, Pilar had not yet provided the MIS position description. Amanda formatted the MIS heading as a normal paragraph. She now asks you to change the current line style to Defined Term and then to enter the MIS job title and description (the definition) to complete the definition list.

To add a defined term and definition to the list:

1. If necessary, scroll up the Employment Web page until you see the MIS heading that appears between two horizontal lines. Amanda already added horizontal lines above and below the MIS heading to set it off from the other positions.

2. Click immediately to the right of **MIS** to place the insertion point there. See Figure 3-7.

Figure 3-7 | ADDING THE MIS JOB DESCRIPTION

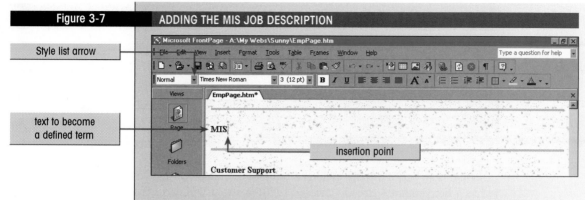

Style list arrow

text to become
a defined term

insertion point

Customer Support

TROUBLE? If the MIS heading does not have a horizontal line immediately above and below it, you are not in the job description area of the Web page. Scroll to the MIS heading, and then repeat Step 2.

3. Click the **Style** list arrow on the Formatting toolbar to display the list of available formats, and then click **Defined Term** as the desired paragraph format. Defined Term now appears in the Style list box, and the MIS heading changes to the Defined Term style.

4. Press the **Enter** key to create a new indented line below the MIS heading with the Definition style applied to it. When you press the Enter key on a line that has the Defined Term style applied to it, FrontPage automatically formats the next line with the Definition style.

5. Type the MIS job description exactly as it appears in Figure 3-8.

Figure 3-8 | MIS JOB TITLE AND DESCRIPTION

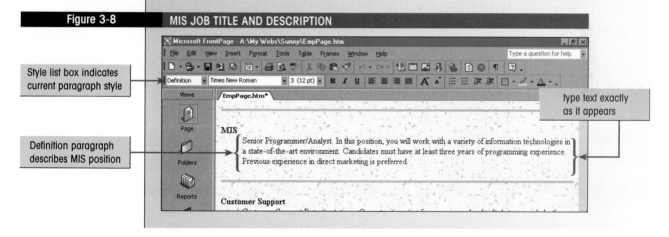

Style list box indicates
current paragraph style

type text exactly
as it appears

MIS

Definition paragraph
describes MIS position

Senior Programmer/Analyst. In this position, you will work with a variety of information technologies in a state-of-the-art environment. Candidates must have at least three years of programming experience. Previous experience in direct marketing is preferred.

Customer Support

Now that you added the two new job titles and descriptions to the Employment Web page, Amanda asks you to create the table of contents using a bulleted list.

Creating a Bulleted List

A **bulleted list**, or an **unordered list**, contains items that are not sequentially organized. Each item in the list begins with a bullet character. You can create a bulleted list either by clicking the Bullets button on the Formatting toolbar before typing the items in the list, or by selecting existing text and then clicking the Bullets button.

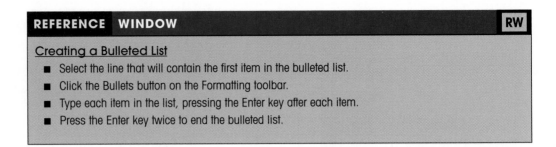

> **REFERENCE WINDOW**   **RW**
>
> <u>Creating a Bulleted List</u>
> - Select the line that will contain the first item in the bulleted list.
> - Click the Bullets button on the Formatting toolbar.
> - Type each item in the list, pressing the Enter key after each item.
> - Press the Enter key twice to end the bulleted list.

Long Web pages usually include a table of contents at the top of the page that is formatted as a list. Amanda already entered the items that will form the table of contents for the page, as shown in Figure 3-9. Amanda asks you to format the list of department names as a bulleted list.

To create a bulleted list:

1. Press **Ctrl + Home** to scroll to the top of the Web page, and then select the **Accounting**, **Advertising**, **MIS**, and **Customer Support** department names that form the table of contents. See Figure 3-9.

Figure 3-9	CREATING THE TABLE OF CONTENTS

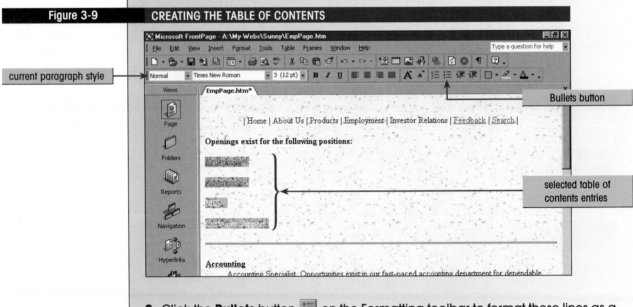

2. Click the **Bullets** button 📇 on the Formatting toolbar to format these lines as a bulleted list, and then click the first item in the list to deselect the bulleted list. See Figure 3-10.

Figure 3-10

TABLE OF CONTENTS FORMATTED AS A BULLETED LIST

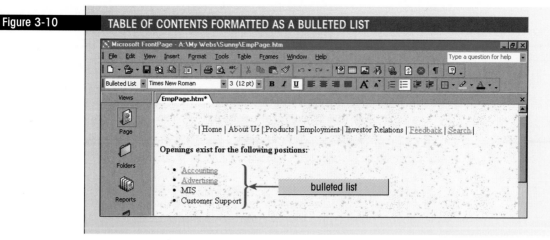

Next, Amanda asks you to format the two job openings in the Advertising department to be more prominent in the Web page.

Creating a Numbered, Nested List

A **numbered list**, or an **ordered list**, contains sequentially numbered or alphabetical items. It is the same as a bulleted list, except that each item begins with a number or letter instead of a bullet. Amanda wants you to organize the Advertising department's job openings for a Production Manager and an Editorial Assistant as a numbered list. This structure will better differentiate between the two available positions in the Advertising department.

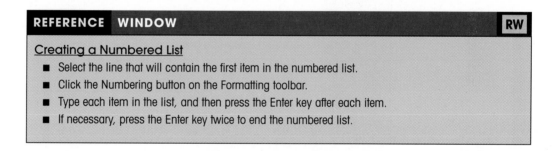

REFERENCE WINDOW   **RW**

Creating a Numbered List
- Select the line that will contain the first item in the numbered list.
- Click the Numbering button on the Formatting toolbar.
- Type each item in the list, and then press the Enter key after each item.
- If necessary, press the Enter key twice to end the numbered list.

Amanda wants you to insert the numbered list as a nested list within the existing bulleted list of position openings.

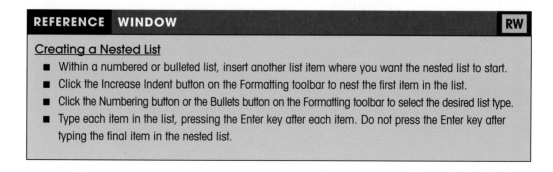

REFERENCE WINDOW   **RW**

Creating a Nested List
- Within a numbered or bulleted list, insert another list item where you want the nested list to start.
- Click the Increase Indent button on the Formatting toolbar to nest the first item in the list.
- Click the Numbering button or the Bullets button on the Formatting toolbar to select the desired list type.
- Type each item in the list, pressing the Enter key after each item. Do not press the Enter key after typing the final item in the nested list.

To create a nested, numbered list:

1. Click to the right of the **Advertising** item in the bulleted list, and then press the **Enter** key to insert a new line with a bullet.

2. Click the **Increase Indent** button [icon] on the Formatting toolbar to indent this paragraph and change its style to Normal. Notice that additional space now separates the first two bulleted items from the last two items.

3. Click the **Numbering** button [icon] on the Formatting toolbar *twice*. The additional space is deleted and the number 1 appears.

   TROUBLE? If all of the items change to a numbered list, then you did not click the Increase Indent button before you clicked the Numbering button. Click the Bullets button, and then repeat Steps 2 and 3.

4. Type **Production Manager** as the first numbered list item, and then press the **Enter** key. FrontPage continues the nested list on the second line by inserting the number 2.

5. Type **Editorial Assistant** as the second numbered list item to complete the numbered list. See Figure 3-11.

| Figure 3-11 | TABLE OF CONTENTS WITH A NESTED NUMBERED LIST |

6. Click the **Save** button [icon] on the Standard toolbar to save your changes.

You've now formatted the table of contents as a bulleted list and organized the two advertising positions as a numbered, nested list. In the next session, you'll format the MIS and Customer Support items in the table of contents as hyperlinks so that users can link directly to the correct job descriptions.

Session 3.1 Quick Check

1. True or False: The content of a Word document is converted to HTML when the file is inserted in a Web page.

2. True or False: You cannot import Web pages created by programs other than FrontPage into a FrontPage Web site.

3. A(n) _____ list is one that is not sequentially organized.

4. What is a nested list?

5. True or False: You press the Enter key twice to end a bulleted or numbered list.

6. To start a nested list, click the _____ button on the Formatting toolbar to create the first item in the list.

SESSION 3.2

In this session, you will create a bookmark, specify a hyperlink to a bookmark, and use several methods to create hyperlinks to other Web pages. You also will create a hyperlink that contains an e-mail address. Then you will convert a picture saved in JPEG format to GIF format, make a GIF picture transparent, and create a hotspot in a picture. Then you will test the hyperlinks within a Web page, between Web pages, and to an e-mail hyperlink. Finally, you will view a Web site in Hyperlinks view and print it.

Creating Bookmarks and Hyperlinks to Bookmarks

A **bookmark** is a named location in a Web page that is the target of a hyperlink. A bookmark often consists of text as the location. For example, the table of contents at the top of the Employment Web page is organized so that users can scroll to each department's job listings by clicking the department name in the list. You can also create a bookmark to a location that is not based on text. For example, clicking a "Top of Page" hyperlink in a Web page automatically scrolls to the top of the Web page; in this case, the hyperlink is to a bookmark that was created at the top of the Web page. You can place bookmarks anywhere in a Web page to make it easier for users to navigate the page.

When viewed in Page view, text in a bookmark appears as dashed, underlined text. When a bookmark is not based on text, the bookmark appears as an icon when viewed in Page view. When you view a page with bookmarks using your browser, no underlining or other identification of the bookmark appears.

Each bookmark within a Web page must have a unique name. You can use the suggested name of the bookmark—which is taken from the text that you selected when you created it—or you can assign a new name. The bookmark's name serves to identify its location in the Web page.

Creating a Text-Based Bookmark

Amanda designed the Employment Web page so that each department listed in the table of contents is associated with a bookmark in the Web page. She already created two text-based bookmarks—one each for the Accounting and Advertising departments.

Creating a Text-Based Bookmark in a Web Page
- Select the text for the bookmark.
- Click Insert on the menu bar, and then click Bookmark.
- Type the bookmark name in the Bookmark name text box, or accept the suggested name.
- Click the OK button to create the bookmark.

Next, you will create bookmarks for the MIS and Customer Support departments.

To create a text-based bookmark:

1. If you took a break after the last session, make sure that FrontPage is running, that your Data Disk is in the correct drive, that the **Sunny** Web site is open, and that the Employment Web page (**EmpPage.htm**) is open in Page view.

2. Scroll down the Employment Web page so you can see the MIS heading that appears between two horizontal lines.

3. Double-click the **MIS** heading, which will become the location of the new bookmark, to select it.

4. Click **Insert** on the menu bar, and then click **Bookmark** to open the Bookmark dialog box. See Figure 3-12.

Figure 3-12	BOOKMARK DIALOG BOX

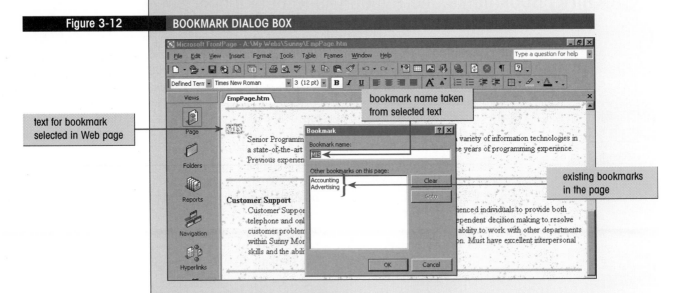

Notice that "MIS" appears in the Bookmark name text box as the suggested name for this bookmark. This name was taken from the selected text—MIS—in the Employment Web page. Also notice that the Other bookmarks on this page list box shows the two bookmarks that Amanda already created. You can use MIS as the new bookmark's name.

5. Click the **OK** button to accept the suggested name for the bookmark, and then click the **MIS** heading in the Web page to deselect it. MIS now appears with a dashed underline, which indicates that it is a bookmark.

Next, you will create the bookmark for the Customer Support heading. You can use the word "Customer" as the bookmark, instead of using the entire heading.

6. Scroll down the Web page as necessary until you see the Customer Support heading, double-click **Customer** in the heading, click **Insert** on the menu bar, click **Bookmark**, click the **OK** button to create the bookmark for this location, and then click **Customer** to deselect it. See Figure 3-13.

| Figure 3-13 | EMPLOYMENT WEB PAGE WITH NEW BOOKMARKS |

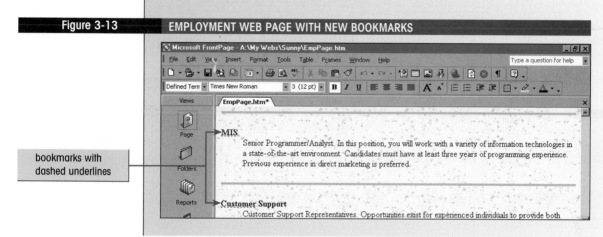

bookmarks with
dashed underlines

Amanda explains that the next step is to link the bookmarks to their associated text by creating hyperlinks.

Creating a Hyperlink to a Bookmark

Amanda asks you to create hyperlinks from the MIS and Customer Support entries in the table of contents to their corresponding bookmarks. When a user clicks a hyperlink to a bookmark, the Web page scrolls automatically to the bookmark's location in the Web page. Figure 3-14 illustrates how these bookmarks will work.

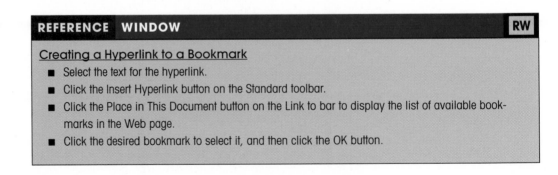

Figure 3-14   **EMPLOYMENT WEB PAGE WITH BOOKMARKS**

hyperlink reference to bookmark

hyperlinks

bookmarks

Creating a Hyperlink to a Bookmark

- Select the text for the hyperlink.
- Click the Insert Hyperlink button on the Standard toolbar.
- Click the Place in This Document button on the Link to bar to display the list of available bookmarks in the Web page.
- Click the desired bookmark to select it, and then click the OK button.

Next, you will create the hyperlinks from the MIS and Customer Support entries in the table of contents near the top of the page to the appropriate bookmarks in the body of the Web page.

To create the hyperlinks to the bookmarks:

1. Press **Ctrl + Home** to scroll to the top of the Web page.

   You begin by creating a hyperlink to the MIS bookmark.

2. Double-click **MIS** in the table of contents (the bulleted list) to select the text for the hyperlink.

3. Click the **Insert Hyperlink** button 🖺 on the Standard toolbar to open the Insert Hyperlink dialog box.

4. Click the **Place in This Document** button 🖼 on the Link to bar to display a list of bookmarks in the Employment Web page. See Figure 3-15.

Figure 3-15	BOOKMARKS IN THE EMPLOYMENT WEB PAGE

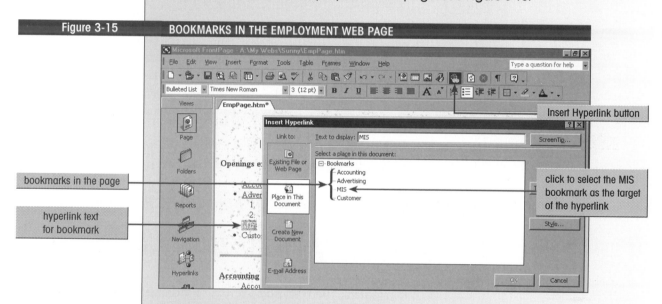

TROUBLE? If you do not see the bookmarks in the page, click the plus box to the left of the Bookmarks heading to display the list.

5. Click **MIS** to select it, and then click the **OK** button. The Insert Hyperlink dialog box closes.

6. Click the **MIS** text to deselect it. "MIS" now appears as blue text with a solid underline, indicating that it is a hyperlink.

7. Point to the **MIS** hyperlink. When you point to the hyperlink, the status bar displays the text #MIS, which identifies the bookmark's location in the Web page. The pound sign (#) indicates that the hyperlink is located in the same Web page. This type of hyperlink is called an **internal hyperlink**.

8. Select **Customer Support** in the table of contents as the next hyperlink, and then repeat Steps 3 through 6 using the Customer bookmark.

9. Point to the **Customer Support** hyperlink. Notice that the name of the hyperlink—#Customer—appears on the status bar and confirms the existence of an internal hyperlink to the bookmark that you created. See Figure 3-16.

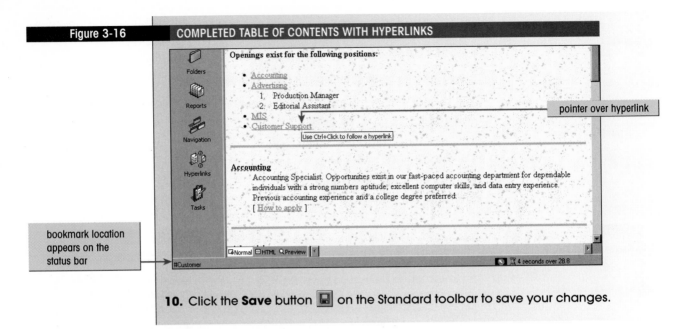

Figure 3-16   COMPLETED TABLE OF CONTENTS WITH HYPERLINKS

10. Click the **Save** button 🖫 on the Standard toolbar to save your changes.

Before continuing, you need to verify that the hyperlinks to the bookmarks work correctly. You will test the hyperlinks using the Preview Page view.

To test an internal hyperlink using Preview Page view:

1. Click the **Preview** button.

2. Point to the **MIS** hyperlink in the table of contents. The pointer changes to a 🖑 shape.

3. Click the **MIS** hyperlink. The Web page scrolls so that the MIS bookmark's location is at the top of the window. Notice that the MIS bookmark does not have a dashed underline.

Your test was successful so you can return to Normal Page view.

4. Click the **Normal** button.

You have now completed the internal hyperlinks from the entries in the table of contents to their respective departments in the Employment Web page. Amanda now explains that job applicants need to be able to contact Sunny Morning Products. Regardless of the position in which applicants are interested, they need to access the same contact information to apply for the job. You can identify the location of this contact information with a single bookmark; in this case, you will create a bookmark that is not based on text. You will create hyperlinks to that bookmark that will let applicants contact Sunny Morning Products.

Creating Nontext-Based Bookmarks

All of the bookmarks that you have created so far used text in the Web page to identify their locations. You can, however, create a bookmark that is based not on text, but rather on a specific location in the page. In this case, an icon appears in Page view to show the bookmark's location. When you view the Web page in a browser, the icon is not visible.

Next, you will insert a nontext-based bookmark to the Sunny Morning Products contact information.

To create a nontext-based bookmark:

1. Scroll down the Web page until you see the phrase, "Join the Sunny Morning Products team!" This text is the first line of the contact information.

2. Click to the left of the **J** in "Join" (but do not select the word "Join") to place the insertion point at the location of the new bookmark.

   TROUBLE? If you selected the "J" in "Join" or the entire word "Join," repeat Step 2.

3. Click **Insert** on the menu bar, and then click **Bookmark** to open the Bookmark dialog box.

   Because you did not select any text, FrontPage does not suggest a name for the bookmark. When you create bookmark names, it is a good idea to select ones that describe the location in which the bookmark appears, so it is easy to recognize a bookmark in the page. When you click the "How to apply" hyperlink in this page, the page will scroll to the bookmark. For this reason, "To Apply" is a good bookmark name in this case.

4. Type **To Apply** in the Bookmark name text box as the name for this new bookmark, click the **OK** button, and then press the **End** key to deselect the icon. A bookmark icon that has a dashed underline appears to the left of the word "Join." See Figure 3-17.

Figure 3-17	CREATING A BOOKMARK THAT IS NOT BASED ON TEXT

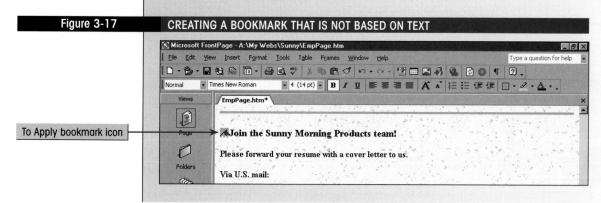

To Apply bookmark icon

Next, you will create the hyperlinks from the job descriptions to this new bookmark, following the same process you used when creating hyperlinks earlier in this session.

Creating Multiple Hyperlinks to a Bookmark

A bookmark can have many hyperlinks to it from different locations within a Web page. For example, regardless of the positions in which they are interested, all applicants need to access the same contact information. You can create a single bookmark in the Web page and then set a hyperlink from each job description to that bookmark. When multiple hyperlinks reference a single bookmark, the bookmark has **multiple hyperlinks**, or **multiple references**, to it.

Amanda designed the Employment Web page to include a hyperlink from each job description to the nontext-based bookmark for the Sunny Morning Products contact information. She already created the hyperlinks from the Accounting and Advertising departments to the "To Apply" bookmark. You will create the hyperlinks from the other two departments—MIS and Customer Support—to the same "To Apply" bookmark.

To create multiple hyperlinks to the same bookmark:

1. Scroll up the Web page until you see the MIS heading.

2. Click to the right of the last line in the job description to position the insertion point there.

3. Press **Shift + Enter** to create a new line within the same paragraph.

   Next, add the text for the new hyperlink.

4. Type [**How to apply**] (including the space after the opening bracket and before the closing bracket), and then select the text **How to apply** as the hyperlink text.

5. Click the **Insert Hyperlink** button 🔗 on the Standard toolbar to open the Insert Hyperlink dialog box, and then if necessary, click the **Place in This Document** button 🔲 to display the list of available bookmarks.

6. Click **To Apply**, click the **OK** button to return to the Web page, and then click **How to apply** to deselect the text. The text is now blue and underlined, which indicates that you created a hyperlink.

7. If necessary, scroll down the Web page until you see the Customer Support heading, and then repeat Steps 2 through 6 to create a second How to apply hyperlink below the Customer Support Representatives job description to the To Apply bookmark.

8. Save the Employment Web page.

You have now created several hyperlinks to the bookmarks in the Employment Web page. Next, Amanda asks you to create hyperlinks to other Web pages. When you are finished, you will test all of these hyperlinks in the browser to verify that they work correctly.

Linking **to Other Web Pages**

You can create hyperlinks that open other Web pages, rather than just accessing other locations in the same Web page. These hyperlinks can connect to another page within the same Web site or to a page at a different Web site. To create a hyperlink to another Web page, you select the location in the page where the link should appear and then specify the hyperlink's target. The **target** of a hyperlink is the page that opens when a user clicks the hyperlink. Usually, hyperlinks that open other Web pages within the same Web site appear in the link bar.

REFERENCE   WINDOW   **RW**

Creating a Hyperlink to an Existing Web Page
- Select the text or picture to use as the hyperlink.
- Click the Insert Hyperlink button on the Standard toolbar. If necessary, click the Existing File or Web Page button on the Link to bar.
- Browse to and then click the filename of the Web page that the hyperlink should open.
- Click the OK button.

Amanda wants you to create one hyperlink from the Employment Web page to the home page and another hyperlink from the home page to the Employment Web page. These hyperlinks will allow users to easily navigate between these Web pages. Amanda has already included the various Web page names in the link bar of the Employment Web page, but she did not create the hyperlinks to the pages.

To create a hyperlink to another Web page:

1. Press **Ctrl + Home** to scroll to the top of the Employment Web page.

2. Double-click the word **Home** in the link bar to select it. This text will become a hyperlink that opens the home page when clicked.

3. Click the **Insert Hyperlink** button 🔗 on the Standard toolbar to open the Insert Hyperlink dialog box, and then click the **Existing File or Web Page** button 🔲 on the Link to bar. See Figure 3-18.

| Figure 3-18 | INSERT HYPERLINK DIALOG BOX |

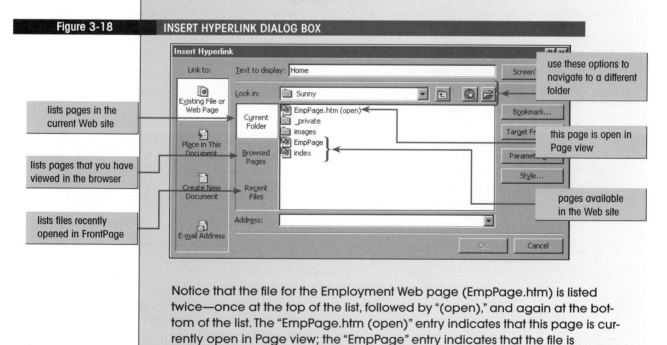

Notice that the file for the Employment Web page (EmpPage.htm) is listed twice—once at the top of the list, followed by "(open)," and again at the bottom of the list. The "EmpPage.htm (open)" entry indicates that this page is currently open in Page view; the "EmpPage" entry indicates that the file is available in the Web site. The file for the home page (index) is not open, so it is listed only once, as an available page.

Also notice that you can link to existing files in the current folder (in this case, the Sunny Web site), to browsed pages (pages you have opened in the Web browser), and to recent files (files that you have recently opened in FrontPage).

4. Click **index** to select it as the target Web page for the hyperlink. Notice that the Address list box now displays the filename for the selected page, index.htm.

   TROUBLE? If your Web site contains the file default.htm rather than index.htm, click default.htm to select the home page.

5. Click the **OK** button to close the Insert Hyperlink dialog box and return to the Web page.

6. Click **Home** in the link bar to deselect the new hyperlink. "Home" is now formatted as underlined, blue text.

7. Point to the **Home** hyperlink. See Figure 3-19. Notice that index.htm appears on the status bar to identify the page targeted by the hyperlink.

Figure 3-19	HYPERLINK TO HOME PAGE IN THE EMPLOYMENT WEB PAGE

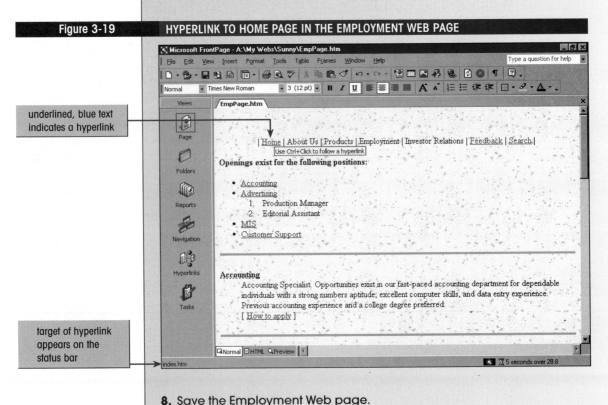

underlined, blue text indicates a hyperlink

target of hyperlink appears on the status bar

8. Save the Employment Web page.

Now that you have successfully established the hyperlink from the Employment Web page to the home page, you must create the hyperlink from the home page to the Employment Web page. Although you could use the same method to create the return hyperlink, Amanda wants to show you another method.

Creating a Hyperlink Using Drag and Drop

Drag and drop is another method by which you can create a hyperlink between pages in a Web site. By default, the title of the linked page (the **target page**) becomes the text for the hyperlink in the Web page that contains the hyperlink (the **source page**). Therefore, you might want to consider a title for a Web page that you can use later as the text for its hyperlink.

To use drag and drop to create a hyperlink, open the source page in Page view and then open the Folder List. Select the filename of the target page in the Folder List and position the pointer in the location where you want to insert the hyperlink. When you release the mouse button, FrontPage creates a hyperlink using the target page's title. You can change the hyperlink's name by editing it after placing the hyperlink in the Web page.

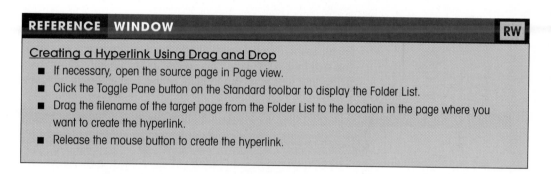

REFERENCE WINDOW   RW

Creating a Hyperlink Using Drag and Drop
- If necessary, open the source page in Page view.
- Click the Toggle Pane button on the Standard toolbar to display the Folder List.
- Drag the filename of the target page from the Folder List to the location in the page where you want to create the hyperlink.
- Release the mouse button to create the hyperlink.

Amanda asks you to use drag and drop to create a hyperlink from the home page to the Employment page. After you create this second hyperlink, you will test both hyperlinks in the browser.

To create a hyperlink using drag and drop:

1. In the Employment Web page, point to the **Home** hyperlink in the link bar, press and hold down the **Ctrl** key, and then click the **Home** hyperlink and release the **Ctrl** key. The home page opens in Page view.

2. Click the **Toggle Pane** button 🖼 on the Standard toolbar. The Folder List opens to the right of the Views bar and displays the files and folders in the Sunny Web site.

3. Click **EmpPage.htm** (the target page) in the Folder List to select it, and then hold down the left mouse button as you drag the pointer from the Folder List to the home page. The pointer changes to a ⊘ shape while you are moving the file out of the Folder List; it changes to a ⊵ when it is in Page view. Do *not* release the mouse button yet.

4. While still holding down the mouse button, move the pointer to the left of the **E** in "Employment" in the link bar in the home page. See Figure 3-20.

Figure 3-20   CREATING THE HYPERLINK TO THE EMPLOYMENT WEB PAGE

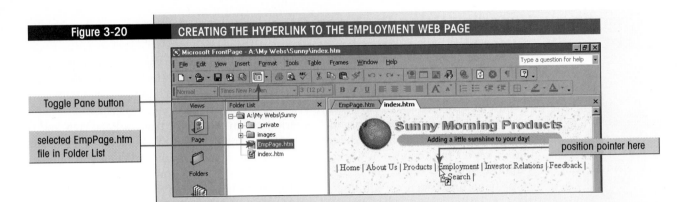

- Toggle Pane button
- selected EmpPage.htm file in Folder List
- position pointer here

5. Release the mouse button to create the hyperlink, and then click **Employment** to deselect it. An Employment hyperlink is inserted in the link bar in the home page, using the page title from the Employment Web page. See Figure 3-21. The text in the link bar now appears as "EmploymentEmployment" because the page title was inserted in front of the text already present in the link bar.

Figure 3-21   HYPERLINK ADDED TO THE LINK BAR

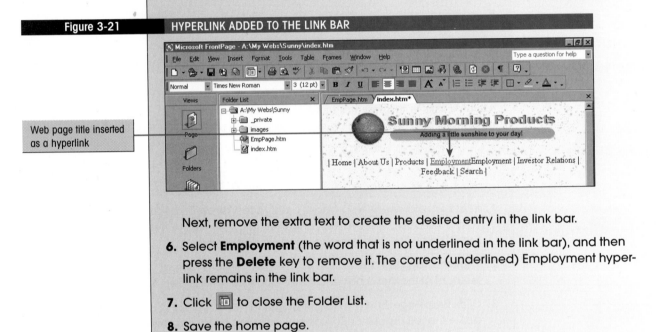

- Web page title inserted as a hyperlink

Next, remove the extra text to create the desired entry in the link bar.

6. Select **Employment** (the word that is not underlined in the link bar), and then press the **Delete** key to remove it. The correct (underlined) Employment hyperlink remains in the link bar.

7. Click 🔲 to close the Folder List.

8. Save the home page.

Now you can test the hyperlinks between the home page and the Employment Web page in a browser.

To test hyperlinks between Web pages in a browser:

1. Click the **Preview in Browser** button 🔍 on the Standard toolbar to open the home page in a browser. Notice that the Employment entry in the link bar is underlined, indicating that it is a hyperlink.

2. Point to the **Employment** hyperlink. Notice that "file:///A:/My Webs/Sunny/EmpPage.htm" appears on the status bar to confirm that this hyperlink connects to a different Web page.

> TROUBLE? If your files are stored in a different location or on a different drive, then your path will be different.
>
> **3.** Click the **Employment** hyperlink in the link bar. The Employment Web page opens.
>
> **4.** Click the **Home** hyperlink in the link bar of the Employment Web page to reopen the home page.
>
> **5.** Close the browser window and return to FrontPage.

You have successfully completed the hyperlink test. You will create the remaining hyperlinks and their Web pages as you complete the tutorials in this book. To finish the Employment Web page, you need to establish a way for applicants to send an e-mail message to the Human Resources manager when they are interested in applying for a position listed in this page.

Creating a Hyperlink to an E-mail Address

A **mailto** is a special hyperlink that contains an e-mail address. When a user clicks a mailto in a Web page, the mailto automatically starts the browser's default e-mail program and addresses a message to the address contained in the mailto. The user then can type the message and send it as usual.

When you type an e-mail address in a Web page in Page view, FrontPage automatically recognizes it as a mailto, creates the necessary hyperlink, and changes the appearance of the address to that of a hyperlink.

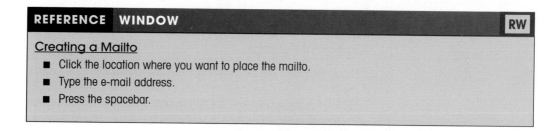

REFERENCE WINDOW   **RW**

Creating a Mailto
- Click the location where you want to place the mailto.
- Type the e-mail address.
- Press the spacebar.

Amanda wants to include Pilar's e-mail address in the Employment Web page so that applicants can send their resumes to her via e-mail.

To create a mailto:

1. Click the **EmpPage.htm** tab at the top of the Contents pane in Page view to open the Employment Web page.

2. Press **Ctrl + End** to scroll to the bottom of the Employment Web page.

3. Click at the end of the **Via e-mail:** heading to place the insertion point there.

4. Press the **Enter** key to insert a new line for the mailto, and then click the **Increase Indent** button [⊞] on the Formatting toolbar to indent the line. Because the "Via e-mail:" text is bold, the new line will also use bold formatting.

5. Type **pilar.caballero@admin.sunnymorning.com** and then press the **spacebar**. When you press the spacebar, FrontPage automatically recognizes the e-mail address as a mailto, creates a hyperlink for it, and changes it to underlined, blue text to indicate that it is a hyperlink. The red, wavy line under part of the mailto indicates a word that was not found in the FrontPage dictionary.

6. Point to the **pilar.caballero@admin.sunnymorning.com** mailto. The description of the mailto appears on the status bar. See Figure 3-22.

| Figure 3-22 | MAILTO IN THE EMPLOYMENT WEB PAGE |

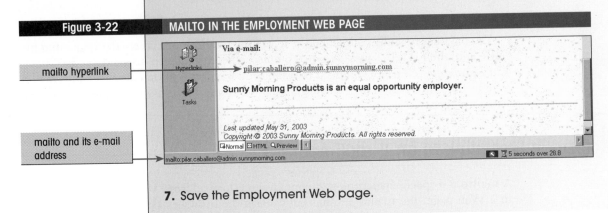

7. Save the Employment Web page.

Pilar's e-mail address is now included in the Employment Web page. Next, you can test this feature in a browser.

To test a mailto:

1. Click the **Preview in Browser** button [img] on the Standard toolbar to open the Employment Web page in the browser, and then press **Ctrl + End** to scroll to the bottom of the page.

2. Click the **pilar.caballero@admin.sunnymorning.com** mailto to start your default e-mail program and to open a new message. Figure 3-23 shows the New Message window for Microsoft Outlook Express (the default mail program for Internet Explorer 5.0). If your computer uses an e-mail program other than Microsoft Outlook Express, then your e-mail window will look different.

| Figure 3-23 | MICROSOFT OUTLOOK EXPRESS NEW MESSAGE WINDOW |

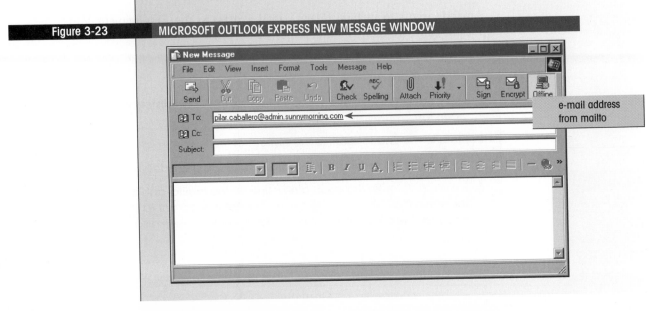

TROUBLE? If an Outlook Express dialog box opens and asks whether you want to specify a default e-mail program, click the No button.

TROUBLE? If an Internet Connection Wizard dialog box opens, click the Cancel button, and then click the Yes button to close the dialog box.

TROUBLE? If a Microsoft Outlook dialog box opens and indicates that no e-mail client is specified for your computer, click the OK button to continue.

Because the Outlook Express mail program started when you clicked the mailto in the Web page, your test is complete. An applicant who wants to send a message to Pilar regarding any of the open positions would type a subject and a message and attach his or her resume to it, if necessary. Because you are just testing the mailto to see whether it links to your Internet e-mail program, rather than actually sending a message to Pilar, you can close the New Message window.

3. Click the **Close** button ⊠ on the New Message window to return to the Employment Web page.

4. Click ⊠ on the browser title bar to close it.

Your successful test of the Employment Web page confirms that an applicant can examine the job descriptions and send a message to Pilar.

According to Amanda's plan for the Sunny Web site, each page will eventually include the Sunny Morning Products logo at the top of the page. The logo for each page is slightly different, however, and the logos are stored in different file formats. Although the graphics designer who created the logos saved the one for the Employment Web page as a JPEG file, Amanda wants you to use a GIF file instead. She asks you to use FrontPage to convert the logo to another format, instead of asking the graphics designer to perform the conversion.

Converting a Picture to a Different Format

In Tutorial 2, you learned about two popular file formats for pictures that are used in Web pages: GIF and JPEG. FrontPage lets you convert a picture saved in one format to another without using a graphics program.

If you are working in a graphics program, such as Adobe Illustrator or PhotoShop, you can usually edit the characteristics of any picture file—for example, by changing the background color or adding special effects to the picture's edges. In FrontPage, however, pictures must be in the GIF format to add these types of effects. For instance, if you try to change the background of a JPEG file, FrontPage will open a message box indicating that you must convert the picture to GIF format before you can change it.

As noted earlier, the logo for the Employment Web page is saved as a JPEG file. Amanda wants you to convert the logo to GIF format to minimize the file's size and download time. She also wants you to change the picture's appearance. For these reasons, you need to convert the JPEG picture to GIF format. Before you can change the file's format, however, you must insert it in the Employment Web page.

To insert a picture in a Web page:

1. Press **Ctrl + Home** to move the insertion point to the top of the Employment Web page. You will insert the logo in this location.

2. Click the **Insert Picture From File** button 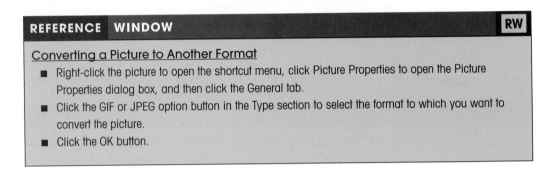 on the Standard toolbar to open the Picture dialog box.

3. Make sure that the drive or folder that contains your Data Disk appears in the Look in text box, double-click the **Tutorial.03** folder, and then double-click **Employ**. The JPEG picture is inserted at the top of the page. The subtitle for the picture is Employment Opportunities, which identifies the content of this Web page.

Next, you will convert the logo from the JPEG format to the space-saving GIF format, which will decrease the picture's file size and prepare it for editing. You will then save the picture file in the Sunny Web site.

REFERENCE WINDOW   **RW**

Converting a Picture to Another Format

■ Right-click the picture to open the shortcut menu, click Picture Properties to open the Picture Properties dialog box, and then click the General tab.
■ Click the GIF or JPEG option button in the Type section to select the format to which you want to convert the picture.
■ Click the OK button.

To convert a picture from JPEG to GIF format and then save it:

1. Click the **logo** to select it. Eight small squares appear as selection handles at the edges of the picture to indicate that it is selected, and the Pictures toolbar appears. See Figure 3-24.

   TROUBLE? If the Pictures toolbar does not appear automatically, click View on the menu bar, point to Toolbars, and then click Pictures.

Figure 3-24	JPEG PICTURE INSERTED IN THE EMPLOYMENT WEB PAGE

Pictures toolbar (yours might appear in a different location)

selection handles

selected JPEG picture

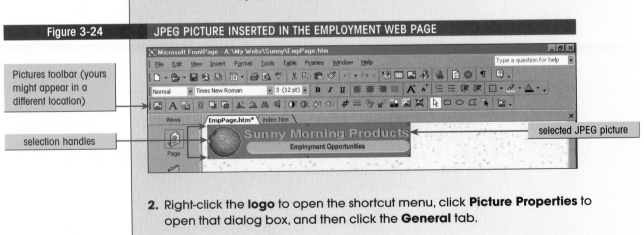

2. Right-click the **logo** to open the shortcut menu, click **Picture Properties** to open that dialog box, and then click the **General** tab.

3. In the Type section, click the **GIF** option button to select it.

The Picture Properties dialog box is already open, so Amanda asks you to add the alternative text for the logo before closing the dialog box.

4. In the Alternative representations section, type **Employment Opportunities Logo** in the Text text box, and then click the **OK** button to return to the Employment Web page.

5. Click the **Save** button 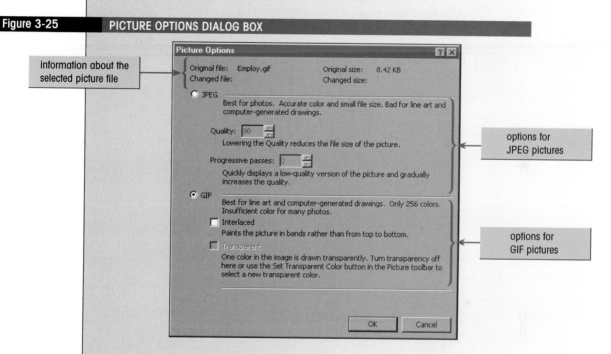 on the Standard toolbar. The Save Embedded Files dialog box opens, with the Employ.gif file in the Embedded files to save list box. The GIF file extension confirms that you converted the picture to GIF format.

6. Click the **Picture Options** button. See Figure 3-25.

Figure 3-25	PICTURE OPTIONS DIALOG BOX

information about the selected picture file

Picture Options

Original file: Employ.gif   Original size: 8.42 KB
Changed file: Changed size:

○ JPEG
Best for photos. Accurate color and small file size. Bad for line art and computer-generated drawings.

Quality: 90

Lowering the Quality reduces the file size of the picture.

Progressive passes: 0

Quickly displays a low-quality version of the picture and gradually increases the quality.

options for JPEG pictures

● GIF
Best for line art and computer-generated drawings. Only 256 colors. Insufficient color for many photos.

☐ Interlaced
Paints the picture in bands rather than from top to bottom.

☐ Transparent
One color in the image is drawn transparently. Turn transparency off here or use the Set Transparent Color button in the Picture toolbar to select a new transparent color.

options for GIF pictures

OK   Cancel

When you save a picture as an embedded file in a Web site, you can use the Picture Options dialog box to specify the quality and download method for the file. For example, clicking the Interlaced check box causes a GIF picture to be displayed with increasing detail as it is being downloaded from the server. You also can make the background of a picture transparent, so that the background of the Web page will show through the picture, by checking the Transparent check box (when this option is enabled). Because the JPEG format does not support transparency or interlacing, these options are not available for this format. For a JPEG picture, you can set the desired quality as a number from 1 to 100, with 100 being the best. In addition, you can set the number of progressive passes as a number from 0 to 100, with 100 being the most passes; the browser will then make this number of passes to display the picture before it is completely downloaded from the server. For more information about editing pictures and setting their characteristics, consult FrontPage Help.

You will accept the default GIF settings.

7. Click the **OK** button to close the Picture Options dialog box, make sure that the picture will be saved in the Web site's images folder, and then click the **OK** button to save the Employ.gif file and the Employment Web page.

TROUBLE? If images/ is not selected as the destination folder in which to save the Employ.gif file, click the Change Folder button, click the images folder to select it, click the OK button to return to the Save Embedded Files dialog box, and then click the OK button to save the file.

Notice that the background of the logo is blue. This logo's color doesn't match the one in the home page, so Amanda asks you to change the blue background to transparent.

Changing a Color in a Picture to Transparent

One way to enhance the appearance of a picture in a Web page is to change one of the picture's colors to transparent. A transparent color will not be visible in the picture, thereby allowing the page's background to show through.

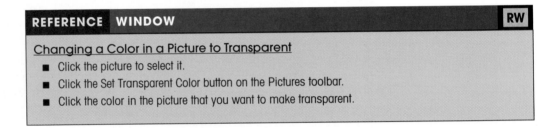

REFERENCE WINDOW   RW

Changing a Color in a Picture to Transparent
- Click the picture to select it.
- Click the Set Transparent Color button on the Pictures toolbar.
- Click the color in the picture that you want to make transparent.

Amanda asks you to change the blue background of the logo to transparent so that it will be consistent with the logo in the home page.

To change a color in a picture to transparent:

1. Click the **logo** to select it. Selection handles appear at the edge of the picture to indicate that it is selected and the Pictures toolbar appears.

2. Click the **Set Transparent Color** button ![button] on the Pictures toolbar.

3. Point to the **logo**. The pointer changes to a ![shape] shape. See Figure 3-26.

| Figure 3-26 | CREATING A TRANSPARENT PICTURE |

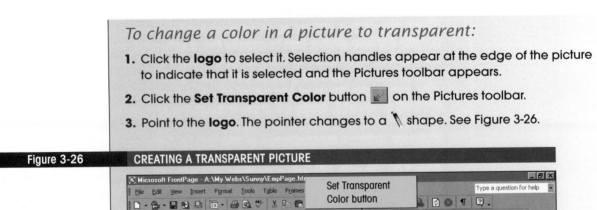

4. Make sure that the small arrow of the ✎ pointer points to the blue color that you want to make transparent, and then click the **blue** color. The blue background of the picture becomes transparent, allowing the background of the Web page to show through.

   TROUBLE? If you change the wrong color to transparent, click the Undo button 🔄 on the Standard toolbar, and then repeat Steps 2 through 4.

5. Click the **Save** button 💾 on the Standard toolbar. The Save Embedded Files dialog box opens, allowing you to overwrite the current version of this picture with the new version.

6. Make sure that the Employ.gif file will be saved in the Web site's images folder, and then click the **OK** button to overwrite the Employ.gif file with the transparent background.

The Employment Opportunities logo in the Web page looks more attractive with its new transparent background. Next, Amanda asks you to create a special hyperlink using the orange that appears in the logo.

Creating **Picture Hotspots**

Pictures can do more than add visual interest to your Web pages, they also can serve a functional purpose. For example, you can use a picture to link to a bookmark or to another Web page by creating one or more hotspots on it. A **hotspot**, or an **image map**, is an area of a picture that, when clicked, activates a hyperlink. A hotspot may have a rectangular, circular, or polygonal shape.

REFERENCE   WINDOW   **RW**

Creating a Picture Hotspot (Image Map)
- Click the picture in which to create a hotspot to select it.
- Click the button for the desired hotspot shape on the Pictures toolbar.
- Click and hold down the mouse button while you drag the pointer to specify the desired size of the hotspot, and then release the mouse button. The Insert Hyperlink dialog box opens.
- Specify the target of the hyperlink in the Insert Hyperlink dialog box.
- Click the OK button.

Amanda wants the orange in the Employment Opportunities logo to become a hotspot that serves as a hyperlink to the home page. You will create this hotspot as a circle.

To create a circular hotspot:

1. Click the **logo** to select it and to display the Pictures toolbar.

2. Click the **Circular Hotspot** button ⬭ on the Pictures toolbar, and then position the pointer in the middle of the orange in the logo. The pointer changes to a ✎ shape when it is pointing to the picture. See Figure 3-27.

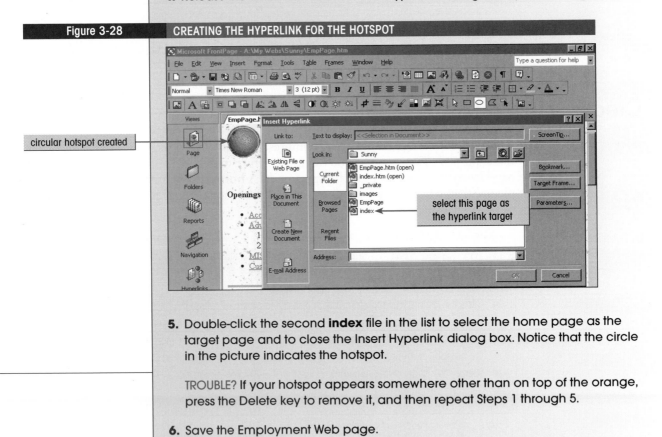

Figure 3-27   CREATING A PICTURE HOTSPOT

pointer for creating the hotspot positioned in the center of the orange

Circular Hotspot button

3. Hold down the mouse button and drag the pointer in any direction until you reach the edge of the orange. As you drag the pointer, you draw a circle to specify the size and location of the hotspot.

4. Release the mouse button. The Insert Hyperlink dialog box opens. See Figure 3-28.

Figure 3-28   CREATING THE HYPERLINK FOR THE HOTSPOT

circular hotspot created

select this page as the hyperlink target

5. Double-click the second **index** file in the list to select the home page as the target page and to close the Insert Hyperlink dialog box. Notice that the circle in the picture indicates the hotspot.

TROUBLE? If your hotspot appears somewhere other than on top of the orange, press the Delete key to remove it, and then repeat Steps 1 through 5.

6. Save the Employment Web page.

You have successfully created the hotspot and specified its hyperlink to the home page. Now users of the Sunny Web site can click either the orange in the logo or Home in the link bar to open the home page.

Highlighting Hotspots

When you create a hotspot, you can see its shape. Depending on the picture, however, it might be difficult to see its hotspots. By highlighting hotspots, you can see their location more clearly and confirm their placement.

Highlighting Hotspots on a Picture
- Click the picture that contains the hotspot(s) to select it.
- Click the Highlight Hotspots button on the Pictures toolbar.
- Click the Highlight Hotspots button again to turn off the hotspot highlights.

Next, you will check the location of the hotspot on the logo and verify its placement.

To highlight hotspots:

1. Make sure that the picture is still selected, and then click the **Highlight Hotspots** button [icon] on the Pictures toolbar. The hotspot in the logo appears as a dark circle in a white picture. See Figure 3-29.

| Figure 3-29 | HIGHLIGHTING A HOTSPOT IN A PICTURE |

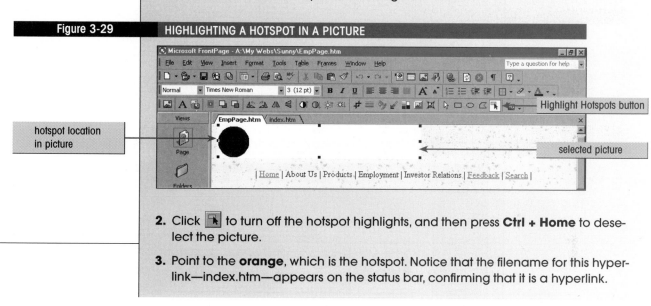

hotspot location in picture

Highlight Hotspots button

selected picture

2. Click [icon] to turn off the hotspot highlights, and then press **Ctrl + Home** to deselect the picture.

3. Point to the **orange**, which is the hotspot. Notice that the filename for this hyperlink—index.htm—appears on the status bar, confirming that it is a hyperlink.

Next, you will test the hotspot in the browser to verify that it works correctly.

To test a hotspot in the browser:

1. Click the **Preview in Browser** button [icon] on the Standard toolbar to open the Employment Web page in the browser. The Employment Opportunities logo appears with its transparent background.

2. Point to the **orange** in the logo. The pointer changes to a [icon] shape and the filename for the hyperlink appears on the status bar; both of these changes indicate that the orange is a hyperlink. Notice that the alternative text that you added to the logo is displayed as a ScreenTip and then disappears.

3. Click the **orange** to open the home page.

4. Click **Employment** in the link bar in the home page to return to the Employment page.

5. Close the browser window and, if necessary, return to FrontPage.

The hotspot in the Employment Opportunities logo provides users with another way to open the home page. Because you have made this change and many others to the Sunny Web site, Amanda wants you to check Hyperlinks view to ensure that no hyperlinks are missing or broken.

Viewing **Hyperlinks**

As you develop a Web site, you can get an overview of it by using Hyperlinks view to examine the hyperlinks that connect the site's pages. You should check Hyperlinks view periodically to verify that your links are set up correctly. Because it is easier to check your site's hyperlinks after you've added only a few hyperlinks to its pages, you might prefer to check smaller parts of the Web site as you go, instead of waiting until the entire Web site is completed. A completed Web site might contain hundreds of hyperlinks, so checking them as you create them ensures that they are set up as desired.

To view hyperlinks between Web pages:

1. Click the **Hyperlinks** button 🖼 on the Views bar. If necessary, click the **EmpPage.htm** page in the Folder List to display the Employment Web page as the center focus of Hyperlinks view.

2. If necessary, use the horizontal scroll bar to scroll the hyperlinks diagram in the Contents pane to the right until the diagram is centered in the window. See Figure 3-30.

Figure 3-30	HYPERLINKS VIEW FOR THE EMPLOYMENT WEB PAGE

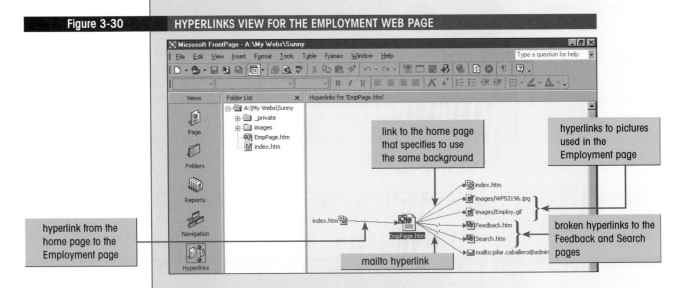

TROUBLE? If you do not see the links to the pictures, right-click any empty area in the Contents pane to open the shortcut menu, and then click Hyperlinks to Pictures.

Notice that the Employment Web page shows a hyperlink from the home page, a hyperlink to the home page, and a hyperlink to the mailto that you created. Amanda created the hyperlinks to the Feedback and Search Web pages, but their links are broken because these Web pages do not exist in the current Sunny Web site. Now you will check the hyperlinks in the home page.

3. Click **index.htm** in the Folder List to display the hyperlinks for that page. See Figure 3-31. Hyperlinks connect to and from the Employment Web page, as shown in Hyperlinks view. The diagram confirms that you have created the hyperlinks for navigating between these two pages. It also shows a link to the Minuet background sound that you added in Tutorial 2 as well as links to the pictures in this page (the background picture and the logo).

| Figure 3-31 | HYPERLINKS VIEW FOR THE HOME PAGE |

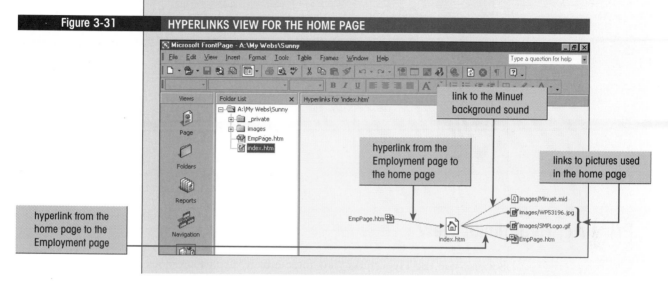

Three of the hyperlinks in Figure 3-31 end with a bullet and one ends with an arrow. An arrow indicates a hyperlink to another Web page in your Web site; a bullet indicates a hyperlink to a sound file or other type of multimedia file.

Notice also the plus (+) symbol in the upper-left corner of the EmpPage.htm file, located to the right of the index.htm icon. Recall from Tutorial 1 that an icon with a plus or minus sign means that you can expand or collapse the hyperlinks to and from that page.

There are actually two hyperlinks from the Employment Web page to the home page; one from the Home text in the link bar and one from the hotspot in the Employment Web page logo. When a single target of a hyperlink appears in more than one location in a Web page, it is called a **repeated hyperlink**. You can display and verify repeated hyperlinks in Hyperlinks view.

To display repeated hyperlinks:

1. Click **EmpPage.htm** in the Folder List to select this page as the center focus of Hyperlinks view. If necessary, use the horizontal scroll bar to center the hyperlinks diagram in the Contents pane.

2. Right-click any empty area in the Contents pane to open the shortcut menu, and then click **Repeated Hyperlinks** to display the repeated hyperlinks for this page. Three hyperlinks connect the Employment Web page to the home page. The hyperlink that ends with a bullet is an included style link that connects the background file used in the home page to the Employment Web page. The other two hyperlinks end with an arrow; one represents the hyperlink in the link bar and the other represents the hotspot.

3. Point to the **index.htm** icon to the right of the EmpPage.htm icon (the one that ends with a bullet). See Figure 3-32. An Included Style ScreenTip indicates the link to the background file in the home page.

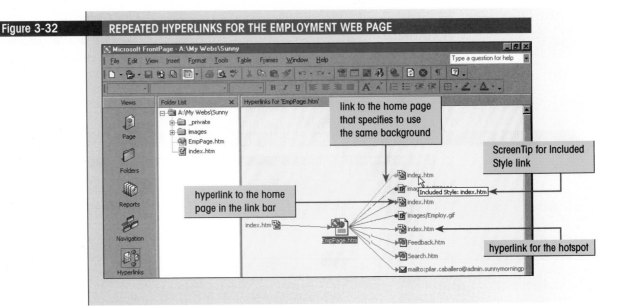

Figure 3-32 | REPEATED HYPERLINKS FOR THE EMPLOYMENT WEB PAGE

Printing **Hyperlinks View**

Because you use Hyperlinks view interactively, FrontPage does not provide a Print command that allows you to print this view. To print Hyperlinks view as a reference or a resource, however, you can copy it to the Windows Clipboard and then print it using WordPad or another word-processing program. Amanda asks you to bring the hyperlinks diagram with you to the next meeting of the Web site development team, so you need to print the view.

To print Hyperlinks view:

1. With the Employment Web page still displayed in Hyperlinks view, press the **Print Screen** key to copy the picture of the screen to the Windows Clipboard.

2. Click the **Start** button on the taskbar, point to **Programs**, point to **Accessories**, and then click **WordPad** to start WordPad and to open a new document. If necessary, maximize the WordPad program window.

3. Click the **Paste** button 📋 on the toolbar to insert your screenshot in the document.

   You'll need to change the page to landscape orientation to print it correctly.

4. Click **File** on the menu bar, click **Page Setup**, click the **Landscape** option button, and then click the **OK** button.

5. Click the **Print** button 🖨 on the WordPad Standard toolbar to print your screenshot of Hyperlinks view.

   Hyperlinks view changes frequently, so you don't need to save the document that you just created.

6. Click the **Close** button ✖ on the WordPad program window to close WordPad, and then click the **No** button to close WordPad without saving the document.

> **7.** Right-click any open area in the Contents pane in Hyperlinks view, and then click **Repeated Hyperlinks** on the shortcut menu to turn off this feature.
>
> **8.** Right-click any open area in the Contents pane in Hyperlinks view, and then click **Hyperlinks to Pictures** to turn off this feature.

With a printed copy of Hyperlinks view for the Employment Web page in hand, you can demonstrate to the Web site development team how the Web pages and files in the Sunny Web site are linked together. In the next session, you will use the Tasks list to organize the team's work on the Web site.

Session 3.2 QUICK CHECK

1. A(n) _____ is a named location in a Web page that identifies its position in the page.

2. If a bookmark is not associated with a text selection, then a(n) _____ appears in Page view to specify the bookmark's location.

3. How do you create a hyperlink to a bookmark in a Web page?

4. What does a pound sign (#) in a hyperlink indicate?

5. True or False: When using FrontPage to change a picture's background to transparent, the picture must be in the GIF file format.

6. A(n) _____ is an area of a picture that you can click to activate a hyperlink.

7. Which three shapes can you use to create a hotspot?

8. How do you include an e-mail address in a Web page?

9. True or False: FrontPage includes a Print command for printing Hyperlinks view.

SESSION 3.3

In this session, you will use the Tasks list to manage a Web site's development. You will add, modify, reassign, complete, and delete tasks. Finally, you will view the HTML code that implements the features of the Employment Web page.

Managing a Web Site's Development Using a Tasks List

In your meeting with the Web site development team, you presented your printout of Hyperlinks view for the Employment Web page. The team was pleased with the current structure and content of the Web site. Every team member is busy working on his or her contribution to the site, and you realize that building and testing a Web site is a group effort. At the meeting, Amanda suggests that you use a Tasks list to track and manage the tasks required to complete the Web site.

Recall from Tutorial 1 that a Tasks list is an organized, detailed listing of the activities or items necessary to complete a Web site. The Tasks list describes each task, indicates the person assigned to complete it, and specifies its priority. Once you have completed the initial design of your Web site, you can create a Tasks list that describes all of the pages you need to develop. You can add activities to a Tasks list, modify task names, assign developers, include descriptions, and remove a task from the list. After finishing a task, you can mark it as completed and then archive or delete it from the Tasks list. If the Web page that you need to create does not already exist, you can add the task of preparing the page and add a blank page to the Web site at the same time. When a task is linked to a page in this way, you can open the page in Page view directly from the Tasks list.

Adding a Task to the Tasks List

You can add a task to the Tasks list in any view or as you add new pages to the Web site. Amanda asks you to create the hyperlinks to the pages that are listed in the link bar of the home page. With the exception of the Employment Web page that you created in this tutorial and the home page, none of these pages has been created yet. For each hyperlink in the link bar, you will create a new page in the Sunny Web site and add the task of completing that page to the Tasks list at the same time.

REFERENCE WINDOW   **RW**

Creating a New Web Page and Adding It to the Tasks List
- In Page view, click the list arrow for the Create a new normal page button on the Standard toolbar, and then click Page.
- In the Page Templates dialog box, click the General tab (if necessary), and then click a page icon to select a page template on which to base the new Web page.
- Click the Just add Web task check box to select it, and then click the OK button.
- In the Save As dialog box, type the filename for the new page in the File name text box.
- Click the Change title button, type the title of the Web page in the Page title text box, and then click the OK button.
- Click the Save button.

The link bar in the home page contains several entries that you will eventually link to other Web pages. You will create the new pages using the Normal Page template and then use Page view to create the necessary hyperlinks.

To create a new Web page and add its task to the Tasks list:

1. If you took a break after Session 3.2, make sure that FrontPage is running, that your Data Disk is in the correct drive, and that the **Sunny** Web site is open.

2. Change to Folders view and then open the home page (**index.htm**) in Page view.

   The only hyperlink in the link bar is the one to the Employment Web page that you created in Session 3.2. You'll create the About Us page first. To create a new page using the default settings, you can click the Create a new normal page button on the Standard toolbar. To use the options for adding the page to the Tasks list, however, you must create the page using the Page Templates dialog box.

3. Click the **list arrow** for the Create a new normal page button 🗋 on the Standard toolbar, and then click **Page**. The Page Templates dialog box opens. You can use the options in this dialog box to create new Web pages based on a variety of templates. For now, Amanda asks you to use the Normal Page template for all of the new pages.

4. Make sure that the **General** tab is selected and that the **Normal Page** icon is selected, and then click the **Just add Web task** check box to select it.

5. Click the **OK** button. The Save As dialog box opens. You use this dialog box to indicate the location in which to save the new Web page, the page's filename and title, and the type of page to create. The About Us page will be a Web page in the Sunny Web site, the filename will be Company, and the title will be Company Profile.

6. Type **Company** to replace the selected filename new_page_1, and then click the **Change title** button. The Set Page Title dialog box opens. See Figure 3-33.

Figure 3-33	CREATING A NEW WEB PAGE

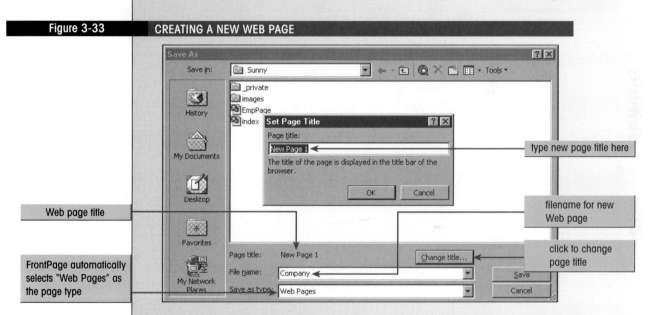

You'll add the page title "Company Profile" and then close the Set Page Title and Save As dialog boxes to finish creating the page.

7. Type **Company Profile**, and then click the **OK** button. The Set Page Title dialog box closes. Notice that the Save As dialog box now displays the new page title.

8. Make sure that the Save in list box shows the **Sunny** folder on your Data Disk, and then click the **Save** button. The Company Web page is created in the Sunny Web.

TROUBLE? If your Data Files are saved on a floppy disk, it will take a few seconds for FrontPage to create the Company Profile Web page. The page will open and then close in Page view. Wait for the page to close before continuing. If your Data Files are stored on a hard, Zip, or network drive, the Company Profile page will open and close quickly.

You added the Company Profile Web page to the Sunny Web site. You can use the Insert Hyperlink button to create the hyperlink from the home page to this new page. You'll use the "About Us" entry in the link bar to create the hyperlink.

To create the hyperlink from the home page to the Company Profile Web page:

1. Use the mouse to select the text **About Us** in the link bar in the home page.

2. Click the **Insert Hyperlink** button 🖴 on the Standard toolbar. The Insert Hyperlink dialog box opens.

3. If necessary, click the **Existing File or Web Page** button 🗐 on the Link to bar. The Look in list box should show the Sunny Web folder.

4. Click the **Company** page icon in the list box. See Figure 3-34.

| Figure 3-34 | CREATING THE HYPERLINK |

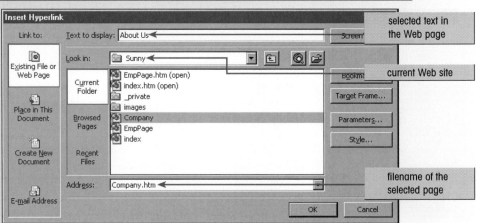

5. Click the **OK** button to close the Insert Hyperlink dialog box and to create the hyperlink. The "About Us" entry in the link bar is now a hyperlink that opens Company.htm.

When you created the Company.htm page, you also selected the option to create a new task in the Tasks list. You can change to Tasks view to see this task.

To view the task in Tasks view:

1. Click the **Tasks** button 🗐 on the Views bar. See Figure 3-35.

| Figure 3-35 | TASKS VIEW FOR THE SUNNY WEB SITE |

Tasks view shows the details for "Finish Company.htm," which is the task that FrontPage created when you created the Company.htm page. Notice that FrontPage assigned the task to you (or the name of the person currently logged on to the computer), gave it a high priority, and added a generic description. You will learn how to change these default entries later in this session.

Next, you will finish creating the hyperlinks to the Products and Investor Relations entries in the link bar in the home page. You'll create new pages using the Normal Page template and add these pages as tasks to the Tasks list.

To create the Products and Investor Relations pages and hyperlinks to them:

1. Click the **Page** button 🔲 on the Views bar to return to Page view for the home page.

2. Click the **list arrow** for the Create a new normal page button 🔲 on the Standard toolbar, and then click **Page**.

3. Make sure that the **General** tab is selected and that the **Normal Page** icon is selected, click the **Just add Web task** check box to select it, and then click the **OK** button.

4. Type **Products** in the File name text box, click the **Change title** button, type **Products** in the Page title text box, click the **OK** button, and then click the **Save** button.

   The Products Web page is created in the Sunny Web site. Next, create the hyperlink from the home page to the Products page.

5. Double-click **Products** in the link bar in the home page, click the **Insert Hyperlink** button 🔲 on the Standard toolbar, click the **Existing File or Web Page** button 🔲 on the Link to bar (if necessary), and then double-click **Products** in the Insert Hyperlink dialog box. You created a link in the home page to the Products page.

6. Repeat Steps 2 through 4 to create the Investor Relations page and a task for completing it. Use the **Normal Page** template, the filename **Investor**, and the page title **Investor Relations**.

7. Create the hyperlink from the Investor Relations entry in the link bar in the home page to the Investor page that you created in Step 6.

8. Save the home page.

You have now created three new pages—Company Profile, Products, and Investor Relations—in the Web site, added tasks for completing these pages to the Tasks list, and created the hyperlinks to these pages in the home page. The Web site will have two more Web pages—one each for Feedback and Search. Because Amanda doesn't want you to create these new pages using the Normal Page template, you will just add their tasks.

Adding a Task in Tasks View

■ Click the Tasks button on the Views bar.

■ Click the list arrow for the Create a new normal page button on the Standard toolbar, and then click Task.

■ Enter the required information for the task in the New Task dialog box.

■ Click the OK button to add the task to the list.

To add a task in Tasks view:

1. Click the **Tasks** button 🗐 on the Views bar to change to Tasks view. The three tasks for the three Web pages that you just created appear in the list.

2. Click the **list arrow** for the Create a new normal page button 🗋 on the Standard toolbar, and then click **Task**. The New Task dialog box opens, with the insertion point in the Task name text box.

3. Type **Create Feedback Web page** in the Task name text box, and then press the **Tab** key to move to the Assigned to list box. The default is to assign a new task to the person who is currently logged on to the computer. You don't know who will be responsible for this task, so you will change the assignment to "Team Member."

4. Type **Team Member** in the Assigned to list box, and then press the **Tab** key to move to the Description text box.

5. Type **Create a Web page that contains a form** in the Description text box. See Figure 3-36.

Figure 3-36	NEW TASK DIALOG BOX

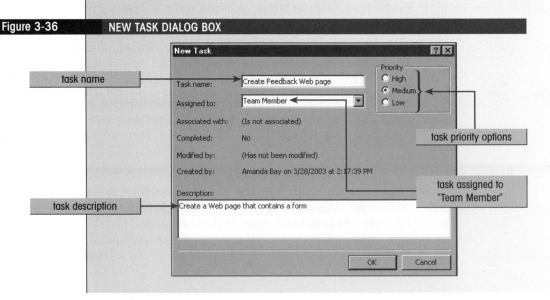

task name

task priority options

task assigned to "Team Member"

task description

When you create a new task in Tasks view, the default priority is medium. When you create a new Web page and add it to the Tasks list, however, FrontPage automatically assigns a high priority to the new task. Assigning the final priority to a task is up to the Web site developer; you might want to prioritize tasks or just accept the defaults. You will accept the default priority of medium, so you are ready to close the dialog box.

6. Click the **OK** button. The New Task dialog box closes, and the new task appears in Tasks view.

7. Repeat Steps 2 through 6 to add the second task to the Tasks list based on the following information:

Task name: **Create Search Web page**

Assigned to: **Team Member**

Description: **Create a Web page that searches the Sunny Web site**

You have finished entering the new tasks to the Tasks list. Next, Amanda wants to show you how to sort and edit tasks.

Sorting and Changing Tasks

A Tasks list might contain hundreds of tasks, so keeping it organized is important. You can sort a column of tasks by clicking the column heading. For example, clicking the Task column heading sorts the list in ascending alphabetical order by task; clicking the Task column heading again sorts the list in descending alphabetical order. Amanda wants you to sort and change tasks now, while the list is still small, so that you can practice this skill. As development of the Sunny Web site continues, you will most likely add many more tasks to the list.

To sort a Tasks list and change a task:

1. Click the **Task** column heading to sort the tasks alphabetically by task name.

2. Click the **Task** column heading again to sort the tasks in descending alphabetical order.

You can double-click any task to see its details.

3. Double-click the **Finish Company.htm** task to open the Task Details dialog box. In this dialog box, you can change the status of a task, its description, its priority, or the person assigned to complete it. The current description of this task in the Description text box shows that this task was added by a dialog box.

4. Type **Finish Company Profile Web page** in the Task name text box to provide a more descriptive name for the task.

5. In the Priority section, click the **Medium** option button to change the priority of this task. High priority is the default when you create a task in the Tasks list by adding a new page.

6. Click the **Assigned to** list arrow, and then click **Team Member** to reassign this task to the Web site development team.

7. Select the current description in the Description text box, and then replace it by typing **This page has been created and is ready to be imported into the Web site** as the new description.

You could click the Start Task button to have FrontPage open the page associated with this task in Page view (Company.htm), so you can begin working on the page. For now, you will simply close the Task Details dialog box.

8. Click the **OK** button to update the Tasks list. The updated task appears in Tasks view.

Now that you've successfully changed one of the tasks in the Tasks list, Amanda asks you to complete a task in the list. The process of completing a task in the Tasks list can entail anything from importing a new page to updating a hyperlink in an existing page. You will import the completed Company Profile Web page into the Sunny Web site as part of completing the Finish Company Profile Web page task that you just modified.

Importing a Web Page and Checking It for Broken Links

Amanda received the finished Company Profile Web page, Company.htm, from the team member who created it and then sent that page to you over the company intranet. You saved this page in the Tutorial.03 folder on your Data Disk. Now you need to import it into the Sunny Web site, replacing the blank Company Profile Web page that you created earlier in this session.

The Company Profile page's developer included some pictures in the page. When you import a page into a FrontPage Web site, however, you import only its HTML document. If the page's developer included pictures in the HTML document, they will be displayed as broken links until you add their files to the current Web site. As part of completing the task for the Company Profile Web page, you will import the page and insert its missing pictures.

To import the Company Profile Web page into the Sunny Web site:

1. Click the **Folders** button 🗀 on the Views bar.

2. Click **File** on the menu bar, and then click **Import** to open the Import dialog box.

3. Click the **Add File** button to open the Add File to Import List dialog box. If necessary, change to the drive or folder that contains your Data Disk, and then double-click the **Tutorial.03** folder to display its contents.

4. Double-click **Company** to return to the Import dialog box, and then click the **OK** button.

The Confirm Save dialog box opens, indicating that the page already exists in the Web site. Recall that you created this page when you added its task to the Tasks list. You will now replace it with the completed Company Profile page.

5. Click the **Yes** button. The page is replaced, and you return to Folders view.

Next, you will check the page that you just imported for broken hyperlinks. A **broken hyperlink**, or a **broken link**, references a Web page or multimedia file that does not exist in the current Web site.

To check the Web page for broken hyperlinks:

1. Click the **Hyperlinks** button ⬚ on the Views bar, and then click **Company.htm** in the Folder List to make that page the center focus of Hyperlinks view.

2. Right-click an empty area in the Contents pane to open the shortcut menu, and then click **Hyperlinks to Pictures**. Hyperlinks view now includes hyperlinks to pictures. See Figure 3-37.

Figure 3-37 **HYPERLINKS VIEW FOR THE COMPANY PROFILE WEB PAGE**

broken links to Web pages and pictures

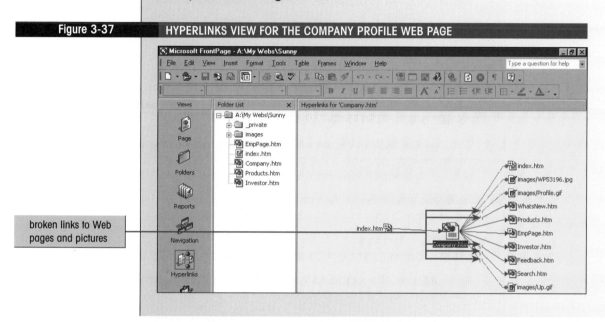

Two of the broken links shown in Figure 3-37 go to the Feedback.htm and Search.htm pages. You added these tasks to the Tasks list but have not created these pages yet, so these broken links are fine for now. There is also a broken link to the WhatsNew.htm page. You don't have any information about this page, so you will discuss it with the Web site development team in the next meeting.

Three pictures are used in the Company Profile page: WP53196.jpg, which is the background picture, and Profile.gif and Up.gif, which are pictures that the developer inserted in the page. These last two pictures are displaying as broken links, so you must insert them in your page. These files are stored in the Tutorial.03 folder on your Data Disk. To complete the Company Profile page, you will use Tasks view to open it.

Opening a Web Page from Tasks View

You can use the Tasks list to open a Web page that is associated with a task. Amanda asks you to complete the work necessary to finish the Finish Company Profile task. You will then mark this page as completed.

To access a Web page from the Tasks list:

1. Click the **Tasks** button 🗒 on the Views bar to switch to Tasks view, and then right-click the **Finish Company Profile Web page** task to select it and open the shortcut menu.

2. Click **Start Task**. The Company Profile page that you imported into the Sunny Web opens in Page view. A broken link icon ⊠ appears in a box at the top of the Web page. As Amanda explains, you must insert this picture in the page.

3. Right-click ⊠ to open the shortcut menu, click **Picture Properties** to open the Picture Properties dialog box, and then click the **General** tab. The Picture source text box contains the filename of the picture that the developer inserted (Profile.gif) and its expected location (the images folder of the current Web site). The Profile.gif file is missing from the Sunny Web site's images folder, but it is saved on your Data Disk.

4. Click the **Browse** button to the right of the Picture source text box to open the Picture dialog box, make sure that the drive or folder containing your Data Disk appears in the Look in text box, double-click the **Tutorial.03** folder, and then double-click **Profile**. The Picture Properties dialog box reappears, showing the correct path for the Profile.gif file.

5. Click the **OK** button. The picture now appears at the top of the Company Profile Web page, where the broken link previously was displayed. Because the picture is selected, the Pictures toolbar appears.

   Next, you will fix the broken link to the Up.gif picture that you discovered while viewing the Company Profile page in Hyperlinks view.

6. Press **Ctrl + End** to scroll to the bottom of the Web page. Notice the broken link to the picture that should be displayed to the left of the "Top of Page" hyperlink.

7. Repeat Steps 3 through 5 to insert the **Up.gif** picture at the location of the broken link. The Up.gif file is stored in the Tutorial.03 folder on your Data Disk.

   Now you need to save the Company Profile Web page and its embedded files in the Sunny Web site.

8. Click the **Save** button 🖫 on the Standard toolbar. A Microsoft FrontPage dialog box opens and asks whether you want to mark the task as completed. Click the **No** button for now. The Save Embedded Files dialog box opens, listing the files Profile.gif and Up.gif.

9. Make sure that the **images** folder is selected in the Save Embedded Files dialog box, and then click the **OK** button to save the Web page and to save the embedded GIF files in the images folder of the Sunny Web site.

After reviewing the page, you decide that it is finished, so you can mark its task as completed in the Tasks list.

Marking a Task as Completed

After finishing a task in your Tasks list, you can mark it as completed. It will remain in the Tasks list after you change its status.

REFERENCE WINDOW	RW

Marking a Task as Completed
- Click the Tasks button on the Views bar to display the Tasks list.
- Right-click the desired task to open the shortcut menu, and then click Mark Complete.

You are ready to mark the Finish Company Profile task as completed in your Tasks list. After marking this task as completed, you will set the Tasks list to show the task history.

To mark a task as completed and show the task history:

1. Click the **Tasks** button [icon] on the Views bar to display the Tasks list. The Finish Company Profile Web page task currently shows a status of "In Progress."

2. Right-click the **Finish Company Profile Web page** task to open the shortcut menu, and then click **Mark Complete**. After a few seconds, the status of this task changes from "In Progress" to "Completed," and its status symbol changes from a red dot to a green dot.

   When you mark a task as completed, it remains visible in the Tasks list. After you refresh the view, the task will no longer be visible unless you set the list to show the task history.

3. Click the **Refresh** button [icon] on the Standard toolbar. Notice that the Finish Company Profile Web page task no longer appears in the Tasks list. To display completed tasks, you must show the task history.

4. Right-click any blank area in the Tasks pane to open the shortcut menu, and then click **Show History**. The Tasks list is updated to reflect both unfinished and completed tasks. See Figure 3-38.

Figure 3-38   **UPDATED TASKS LIST**

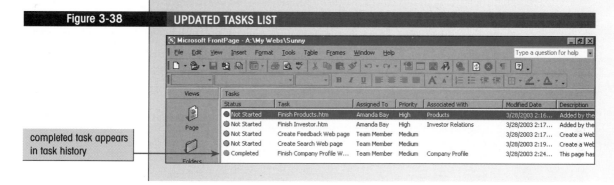

completed task appears in task history

Deleting a Task from the Tasks List

You can delete a task from the Tasks list. Deleting a task is a permanent action; you cannot reverse it.

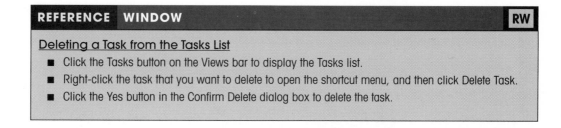

REFERENCE   WINDOW   **RW**

Deleting a Task from the Tasks List
■ Click the Tasks button on the Views bar to display the Tasks list.
■ Right-click the task that you want to delete to open the shortcut menu, and then click Delete Task.
■ Click the Yes button in the Confirm Delete dialog box to delete the task.

Because you have completed the Finish Company Profile Web page task, Amanda asks you to delete it from the Tasks list.

To delete a completed task from a Tasks list:

1. Right-click the **Finish Company Profile Web page** task to open the shortcut menu, and then click **Delete Task**. The Confirm Delete dialog box opens.

2. Click the **Yes** button to remove this task from the Tasks list.

3. Right-click any blank area in the Tasks pane, and then click **Show History** on the shortcut menu to turn off the task history. Because no completed tasks remain in the list, the list displays four tasks, all of which have a status of "Not Started."

You have now finished working with the Tasks list. Amanda asks you to view the HTML code for the work that you've done in the Employment Web page.

Viewing **HTML Code**

Earlier you changed the Employment Web page by creating a link to the background of the home page, adding bookmarks and internal hyperlinks, creating a hotspot, and including a mailto. Different HTML tags implement each of these features. For example, an HREF property of the A tag (the A indicates an anchor, which implements the hyperlinks) uses a pound sign (#), as in the example #MIS, to specify an internal hyperlink. In contrast, the NAME property uses a pound sign to specify a bookmark location in a Web page, as in the example #To Apply. The USEMAP tags were created by a FrontPage component to implement the hotspot in the logo. Amanda wants you to view the HTML code for the Employment Web page to gain a better understanding of the code that FrontPage created to build this page.

To view the HTML code of the Employment page and close FrontPage:

1. Click the **Folders** button 🗂 on the Views bar to change to Folders view, and then double-click **EmpPage.htm** in the Contents pane to open the Employment Web page in Page view.

2. Click the **HTML** button to switch to HTML Page view, and then scroll down the page until the BODY STYLESRC tag is at the top of the screen. See Figure 3-39. Notice the tags and code associated with various tasks, such as including a common background, implementing a hotspot, and creating a bulleted or numbered list.

Figure 3-39   HTML CODE FOR THE EMPLOYMENT WEB PAGE

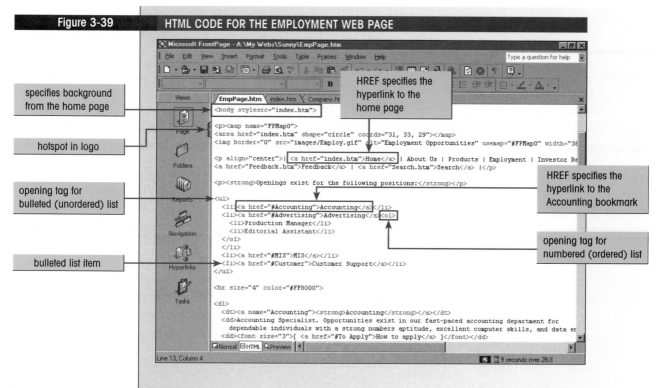

specifies background from the home page

hotspot in logo

opening tag for bulleted (unordered) list

bulleted list item

HREF specifies the hyperlink to the home page

HREF specifies the hyperlink to the Accounting bookmark

opening tag for numbered (ordered) list

3. Press the **Page Down** key to move down one page. See Figure 3-40. Notice the tags and code associated with creating a definition list and a defined term.

Figure 3-40   HTML CODE FOR THE EMPLOYMENT WEB PAGE (CONTINUED)

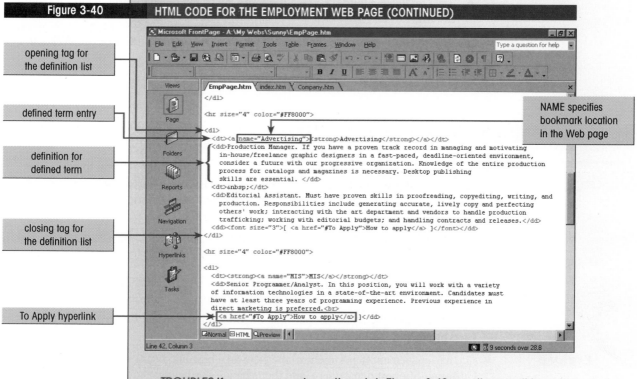

opening tag for the definition list

defined term entry

definition for defined term

closing tag for the definition list

To Apply hyperlink

NAME specifies bookmark location in the Web page

TROUBLE? If your screen doesn't match Figure 3-40, use the scroll bars to reposition the page.

4. Scroll down the page, examining the other tags that you created in this tutorial, such as the mailto.

5. Click the **Normal** button to return to Normal Page view.

6. Close the Sunny Web site, and then close FrontPage.

Amanda and Pilar are pleased with the Employment Web page. In the next tutorial, you will create Web pages that contain tables and frames.

Session 3.3 QUICK CHECK

1. A(n) _____ is a record of the details necessary for completing a Web site.

2. In the Page Templates dialog box, selecting the _____ check box lets you add a task to the Tasks list when you create a new page.

3. To add a new task to the Tasks list, click the list arrow on the _____ button on the Standard toolbar, and then click _____.

4. True or False: You can sort a Tasks list based on the values in any column in Tasks view.

5. To show a "Completed" status for a task, right-click the task in Tasks view, and then click _____ on the shortcut menu.

6. True or False: Deleting a task from the Tasks list permanently deletes it from the list.

7. True or False: You cannot reassign a task to another member of the Web site development team.

REVIEW ASSIGNMENTS

After reviewing the Employment Web page, Amanda and Pilar ask you to add a new department and job position. After completing the Employment Web page, you will import the What's New page into the Sunny Web site and update the hyperlinks in the link bar in the Company Profile Web page.

If necessary, insert your Data Disk in the appropriate disk drive, start FrontPage, and then do the following:

1. Open the **Sunny** Web site from your Data Disk, and then open the Employment Web page (**EmpPage.htm**) in Page view.

2. Create the bookmarks and hyperlinks for the items in the nested list in the table of contents at the top of the page.

Explore   3. Add a Management department to the page on a new line below the horizontal line for the Customer Support department, and then change this heading to bold. Format the heading as a defined term. On the next line, insert the contents of the file **CustMgr.doc** as its definition. Finish the new description by creating the "How to apply" hyperlink and inserting a horizontal line. (*Hint:* After entering the "How to apply" hyperlink, press the Enter key at the end of the line, and then use the Style list arrow to change the new line to the Normal style to end the definition list. You can copy a horizontal line from elsewhere in the page and paste it on the line with the Normal style.)

4. Add the department name for the position you created in Step 3 to the table of contents at the top of the page as a new bulleted item. Create the hyperlink from the new entry to the department heading in the body of the Web page. (*Hint:* Create a bookmark first.)

5. Create a bookmark named "Top" to the left of the logo at the top of the Employment Web page. Do not select any text or the logo for this bookmark.

6. Add the text "Top of Page" on a new line above the last updated date at the bottom of the Web page. Create a hyperlink from the Top of Page text to the Top bookmark you created in Step 5.

Explore ▶ 7. Insert the **Up.gif** picture from the Web site's images folder to the left of the Top of Page hyperlink that you created in Step 6, with one space separating the picture and the hyperlink. Create a hyperlink from the **Up.gif** picture to the Top bookmark. (*Hint:* To create a hyperlink using a picture, select the picture, and then click the Insert Hyperlink button on the Standard toolbar. If you have trouble selecting the picture, right-click it, and then click it again.)

8. Save the Employment Web page, and then use Preview Page view to test the bookmarks and hyperlinks in the page.

9. Open the Company Profile Web page (**Company.htm**) in Page view. The link bar in this page includes the What's New entry, which is already formatted as a hyperlink. However, this page does not exist in the Sunny Web site yet. Use Tasks view to add a new entry to the Tasks list for creating the What's New Web page, but do not create the new page. Include a description for this task to import the What's New page into the **Sunny** Web site and assign the task to Team Member.

10. Complete the task you added to the Tasks list in Step 9 by changing to Folders view and importing the What's New Web page (**WhatsNew.htm**) from the Tutorial.03 folder into the **Sunny** Web site. Add the page logo (**WhatLogo.gif**) where the broken hyperlink appears. Save the picture file in the Web site's images folder.

11. Use Preview Page view to test the hyperlinks connecting the What's New page and the Company Profile page, mark the task for the What's New page as completed, make sure that the task history is turned on, and then print the list. (*Hint:* Copy the screen and print it using WordPad.) Close WordPad without saving your changes, and then turn off the task history.

12. Display the What's New Web page as the center focus page in Hyperlinks view. Display the repeated hyperlinks and the hyperlinks to pictures, and then print Hyperlinks view using WordPad. Close WordPad without saving your changes. Turn off the display of the repeated hyperlinks and the hyperlinks to pictures.

Explore ▶ 13. Update the link bar in the Employment Web page so that each entry, with the exception of the Employment entry, contains a hyperlink that opens the correct page. Save the Employment Web page and then use HTML Page view to print its HTML code. On the printout, circle the HTML code for the Top bookmark; the Top of Page and Up button hyperlinks; and the new job heading, description, and How to apply hyperlink that you added.

14. Close the **Sunny** Web site and then close FrontPage.

CASE PROBLEMS

Case 1. Preparing an Information Page for Royal Hair Care Products The product launch for Quick Dry Solution at Royal Hair Care Products is well under way. Valerie Suarez met with Sharon Brock, the Quick Dry product manager, to discuss what type of support the company might offer through its Web site. Together, Valerie and Sharon decided to use the planned Company Information Web page to provide distributors and retailers with information about the product and its promotion. Valerie and Nathan Dubois, the information systems specialist, then met with Sharon and her staff to finalize their ideas on the Web page content. They agreed that the page should contain four sections: distribution, promotion, packaging, and legal. Sharon agreed to write a draft of the distribution information and provide Nathan with a copy of that file for use in the Company Information page. Nathan has started developing this page, and Valerie wants you to help him complete this task.

If necessary, start FrontPage, insert your Data Disk in the appropriate disk drive, and then do the following:

1. Read all of the questions for this case problem, and then prepare a planning analysis sheet for the revisions to the Web site.

2. Open the **Royal** Web site that you created in Tutorial 2 in Folders view. (If you did not create this Web site in Tutorial 2, ask your instructor for assistance.)

3. Import the partially completed Company Information (**RCompany.htm**) page from the Tutorial.03 folder on your Data Disk into the **Royal** Web site, and then open this page in Page view and examine its contents. If necessary, change the entries in the link bar in the home page that you created in Tutorial 2 to match the link bar in the Company Information page.

4. Insert the **RoyalHCP.gif** picture from the Tutorial.03 folder at the top of the page above the link bar.

5. Change the dark gray, outer background color of the **RoyalHCP.gif** picture to transparent.

6. Insert the text from the **Distrib.doc** file in the Tutorial.03 folder as a definition under the Distribution heading that appears between two horizontal lines.

7. Format the list containing the Distribution, Promotion, Packaging, and Legal section titles that make up the table of contents (located below the link bar) as a numbered list. Create a bookmark for each item where it is described in the body of the Web page. Then create a hyperlink from each of the table of contents items to its respective bookmark.

8. Include your e-mail address at the bottom of the Web page below the "For additional information contact us:" line. If you don't have an e-mail address, create one or use one provided by your instructor.

9. Create a bookmark named "Top" to the left of the **RoyalHCP.gif** picture at the top of the page. Do not select any text or the logo for the Top bookmark.

10. Place the text "Top of Page" on a new line below the mailto that you added in Step 8. Create a hyperlink from the "Top of Page" text to the "Top" bookmark.

11. Insert the **Up.gif** picture from the Tutorial.03 folder to the left of the Top of Page hyperlink with one space separating the picture and the hyperlink. Create a hyperlink from the **Up.gif** picture to the Top bookmark. (If you have trouble selecting the picture, right-click it and then click it again.)

12. Create a hyperlink in the link bar to the home page. Save the pictures in the Web site's images folder. Then create a hyperlink in the link bar in the home page to the Company Information page. Save the home page.

13. Use the link bar in the Company Information (**RCompany.htm**) page to create the following hyperlinks and new Web pages based on the Normal Page template. Add a task for creating each page in the Tasks list. Link the News entry in the link bar to the **RNews** page with the title "What's New," link the Feedback entry in the link bar to the **RFeedbak** page with the title "Feedback," and link the Employment entry in the link bar to the **REmploy** page with the title "Employment." Save the Company Information page.

14. Open the Tasks list, and then change the Finish task for the What's New page to "Import," add an appropriate description, assign the task to yourself (if necessary), and assign it medium priority. Change the Finish task for the Feedback page to "Create," add an appropriate description, assign the task to yourself (if necessary), and assign it medium priority.

15. Import the What's New page (**RNews.htm**) from the Tutorial.03 folder into the **Royal** Web site, replacing the current page. Insert the **Royal.gif** file from the Web site's images folder at the top of the page, press the spacebar, and then insert the **RNewsLog.gif** picture from the Tutorial.03 folder on the same line and to the right of the **Royal.gif** picture. Save the new picture file in the Web site's images folder.

Explore ▷ 16. Use drag and drop to create a hyperlink from the What's New (**RNews.htm**) page to the home page. Then use drag and drop to create a hyperlink from the home page to the What's New page. Edit the Home entry in the link bar so that it displays only the underlined text, "Home." Edit the What's New entry in the link bar in the home page so that it displays the text "News." (*Hint:* Use the Insert Hyperlink dialog box to change the text to display.) Save the What's New page and the home page.

17. Mark the task for the What's New page as completed in the Tasks list. Add a new task for creating the Search page to the Tasks list, but do not add this page to the Web site. Give the task an appropriate title, a medium priority, and a description, and assign the task to yourself.

18. Display the Company Information (**RCompany.htm**) page as the center focus page in Hyperlinks view. If necessary, center the hyperlinks diagram in the Contents pane. Display the repeated hyperlinks and the hyperlinks to pictures. Use WordPad to print Hyperlinks view, and then close WordPad without saving any changes. Turn off the display of the repeated hyperlinks and the hyperlinks to pictures.

Explore ▷ 19. Print the Company Information (**RCompany.htm**) page from Page view. Print the HTML code for this page. On the printout, circle the HTML code for the hyperlinks and bookmarks that you created.

20. Close the **Royal** Web site and then close FrontPage.

Case 2. Developing the Web Pages for Buffalo Trading Post The recycling business at Buffalo Trading Post remains strong. Donna Vargas and her sales staff receive approximately 50 phone calls each day from potential customers. To better serve these customers, Donna wants to add a page to the Buffalo Web site that provides information about the company's recycling process. Donna, Karla Perez, and the sales staff agree that the page should contain sections entitled "Frequently Asked Questions" and "How It Works" to describe the process of buying and selling clothing. They also want a "Choose To Re-Use" section that will describe Buffalo's overall commitment to recycling. Karla began the process of creating this page, and Donna wrote the text for the "How It Works" section. Karla asks you to help her complete the remaining Web development activities.

If necessary, start FrontPage, insert your Data Disk in the appropriate disk drive, and then do the following:

1. Read all of the questions for this case problem, and then prepare a planning analysis sheet for the revisions to the Web site.

2. Open the **Buffalo** Web site that you created in Tutorial 2 in Folders view. (If you did not create this Web site in Tutorial 2, ask your instructor for assistance.)

3. Import the partially completed How (**BHow.htm**) page in the Tutorial.03 folder into the Web site, and then open the How page in Page view and examine its contents. If necessary, change the entries in the link bar in the home page that you created in Tutorial 2 to match the link bar in the How page.

4. Insert the **BHowLogo.jpg** picture from the Tutorial.03 folder at the top of the How page above the link bar, and then center it.

5. Convert the JPG picture that you added in Step 4 to GIF format.

Explore   6. Use the **BWMark.gif** file from the Tutorial.03 folder as the background picture for the How page. Change the background picture to a watermark.

7. Insert the **HowWorks.doc** file in the Tutorial.03 folder as a definition below the How It Works heading that appears between two horizontal lines in the body of the How page.

Explore   8. Format the How It Works, Frequently Asked Questions, and Choose To Re-Use list that make up the table of contents (below the link bar) as a bulleted list with square bullet characters. (*Hint:* Select the items in the list, click Format on the menu bar, and then click Bullets and Numbering. On the Plain Bullets tab, select the square bullet character. If the square bullet character is not available, select any other bullet character that is not a small circle.)

9. Create a bookmark for each table of contents item where it is described in the body of the Web page. Create a hyperlink from each of the bulleted list items in the table of contents to its respective bookmark.

Explore   10. Include your e-mail address at the bottom of the Web page below the "For additional information please contact us:" line. If you don't have an e-mail address, create one or use one provided by your instructor. Change the style of your e-mail address to the Address style. Save the How page, and save its picture files in the Web site's images folder.

11. Create a bookmark named "Top" to the left of the logo at the top of the page.

12. Place the text "Top of Page" on a new line formatted with the Normal style below the mailto that you added in Step 10. Create a hyperlink from the Top of Page text to the Top bookmark.

Explore   13. Insert an appropriate clip-art picture that users can click to scroll to the top of the How page. Place it to the left of the Top of Page hyperlink that you added in Step 12. (*Hint:* To open the Insert Clip Art panel of the Task Pane, position the insertion point where you want to add the picture, click Insert on the menu bar, point to Picture, and then click Clip Art. Search using the text "up." When you find a picture, click its list arrow, and then click Insert. Click the Close button on the Task Pane to close it.) Insert one space between the picture and the text. If necessary, use the picture's sizing handles to reduce its size.

Explore   14. Create a hyperlink from the picture you added in Step 13 to the Top bookmark. Save the picture as **Up.gif** in the Web site's images folder. Test all of the internal hyperlinks using the browser.

15. Create a hyperlink in the link bar from the How page to the home page, and then create a hyperlink in the link bar from the home page to the How page. Save both pages.

Explore   16. Create a rectangular hotspot that encloses the "Buffalo Trading Post" text in the logo at the top of the How page. Link this hotspot to the home page.

17. Add a normal page to the **Buffalo** Web site with the filename **BWhat.htm** and the title "What." Add this page as a task in the Web site's Tasks list. Then select "What" in the link bar of the How page, and link it to the **BWhat.htm** page.

18. Import the Who page (**BWho.htm**) from the Tutorial.03 folder into the **Buffalo** Web site. Insert the **BWhoLogo.gif** picture from the Tutorial.03 folder at the top of the page, and then center it. Save the picture in the Web site's images folder.

19. Create the hyperlinks between the Home, Who, How, and What pages so that each page has an active hyperlink to the other three pages. (Do not create any links in the What page, which is blank.) Save each page after creating its hyperlinks. Use Preview Page view to test these hyperlinks.

20. Use Tasks view to add a new task to create the Where page in the Tasks list, but do not add this page to the Web site. Assign the task to yourself, add an appropriate description and task name, and give it a medium priority.

Explore　21. Change to Folders view. Change the title of the home page to "Buffalo Trading Post." (*Hint:* Click index.htm in the Contents pane, click the page's title to display the insertion point, type the new title, and then press the Enter key.) Preview the home page in a browser, and notice that the title bar in the browser displays the new name. Use the Source command on the View menu in Internet Explorer to access the page's source HTML code. In the HTML code, change the title back to "Home Page." (*Hint:* Look for the TITLE tags in the HTML code.) Close Notepad, save your changes, and then refresh the home page. Notice that the title bar in Internet Explorer now displays the title "Home Page." Close Internet Explorer, return to Folders view, click the Refresh button on the Standard toolbar, and verify that the title of the home page is correct in FrontPage.

22. Display the How page (**BHow.htm**) in Hyperlinks view. If necessary, center the hyperlinks diagram in the Contents pane. Display the hyperlinks to pictures in the page, and then use WordPad to print Hyperlinks view. Close WordPad without saving your changes. Turn off the display of hyperlinks to pictures within the page.

Explore　23. Use FrontPage to display the HTML code for the How page (**BHow.htm**), and then print it. On the printout, circle the HTML code for the pictures that you added to the page.

24. Close the **Buffalo** Web site and then close FrontPage.

Case 3. Completing the Employment Page for Garden Grill　Hiring and retaining the best possible staff is key to the continued growth of Garden Grill. Recently, Nolan Simmons and Shannon Taylor met with the corporate Human Resources director to discuss the content of the planned Employment Opportunities Web page. They want the page to emphasize that Garden Grill is a fun place to work and that employees are well rewarded. All agreed that the Employment Opportunities page should include information about both management and staff associate positions. The Human Resources director promised to create a Word document describing the manager's position and send that file to Shannon the next day. Shannon began developing the Employment Opportunities page based on the detailed requirements from the meeting. Nolan wants you to help Shannon complete the development and testing of this Web page.

If necessary, start FrontPage, insert your Data Disk in the appropriate disk drive, and then do the following:

1. Read all of the questions for this case problem, and then prepare a planning analysis sheet for the revisions to the Web site.

2. Open the **Garden** Web site that you created in Tutorial 2 in Folders view. (If you did not create this Web site in Tutorial 2, ask your instructor for assistance.)

3. Import the partially completed Employment Opportunities page (**GEmploy.htm**) from the Tutorial.03 folder on your Data Disk into the Web site. Open it in Page view and examine its contents.

4. Insert the **Garden.gif** picture from the **Garden** Web site's images folder on a new centered line above the broken picture link at the top of the Web page. Insert the **GNavBar.gif** picture from the Tutorial.03 folder in place of the broken link at the top of the page.

5. Specify the same background for this Web page that you used for the home page.

6. Insert the **Manager.doc** file from the Tutorial.03 folder on a new line that you create below the Managers heading that appears between two horizontal lines in the body of the Web page. Select the list of five items that appear under the description that you just added, and change them to a bulleted list. Use the Increase Indent button on the Formatting toolbar to indent the list by one additional tab stop.

Explore ▶ 7. Change the format of the bullets in the bulleted list that you created in Step 6 to a picture. (*Hint:* Select the bulleted list, click Format on the menu bar, and then click Bullets and Numbering. Click the Picture Bullets tab, click the Specify picture option button, click the Browse button, and then insert the **GBullet.gif** file from the Tutorial.03 folder.) Save the pictures in the Web site's images folder.

Explore ▶ 8. Select the bulleted list in the Staff Associates section, and apply the same bullets and indentation that you added in Step 7 to the items in the list. (*Hint:* Select the bulleted list, click Format on the menu bar, click Bullets and Numbering, and then apply the bullet picture that you saved in the Web site's images folder.)

9. Format as a numbered list the Managers and Staff Associates entries that make up the table of contents at the top of the page. Create a bookmark for each entry where it is described later in the Web page. Then create a hyperlink from each entry in the table of contents to its respective bookmark.

10. Include your e-mail address at the bottom of the Web page below the "For additional information contact us:" paragraph. If you don't have an e-mail address, create one or use one your instructor provides.

11. Create a bookmark named "Top" to the left of the Garden Grill logo at the top of the page.

12. Place the text "Top of Page" on a new line below the mailto that you added in Step 10. Create a hyperlink from the Top of Page text to the Top bookmark.

Explore ▶ 13. Insert the **Up.gif** picture from the Tutorial.03 folder to the left of the Top of Page hyperlink; one space should appear between the picture and the hyperlink. Create a hyperlink from the **Up.gif** picture to the Top bookmark. Save the picture in the Web site's images folder.

Explore ▶ 14. Create a hotspot in the link bar of the Employment Opportunities page that opens the home page.

Explore ▶ 15. Replace your text link bar in the home page with the **GNavBar.gif** picture that is saved in the **Garden** Web site's images folder. Center the new link bar picture, and then create a hotspot in the link bar in the home page that opens the Employment Opportunities page. Save the home page.

Explore ▶ 16. Use the link bar in the home page to create hyperlink hotspots to new Web pages that you add to both the Web and the Tasks list based on the Normal Page template. Link the About Us entry in the link bar to the **GAbout** page with the title "Company Profile," and link the Feedback entry in the link bar to the **GFeedbak** page with the title "Feedback." Save the home page.

17. Import the Company Profile page (**GAbout.htm**) from the Tutorial.03 folder into the **Garden** Web site, replacing the page that you created in Step 16. Open the page in Page view. Insert the **Garden.gif** picture located in the Web site's images folder at the top of the page. Create hotspots to open the home page, the Employment Opportunities page, and the Feedback page. Save the Company Profile page (**GAbout.htm**).

18. Mark the task for the Company Profile page as completed in the Tasks list. Add a new task for creating the Search page, but do not add this page to the Web site. Assign the task to yourself with medium priority, and provide an appropriate task name and description.

19. Display the Company Profile page (**GAbout.htm**) as the focus page in Hyperlinks view. If necessary, center the hyperlinks diagram in the Contents pane. Display the repeated hyperlinks and the hyperlinks to pictures. Use WordPad to print Hyperlinks view, and then close WordPad without saving changes. Turn off the display of the repeated hyperlinks and hyperlinks to pictures.

Explore

20. Create the hotspots in the link bar in the Employment Opportunities page to open the **GAbout.htm** and **GFeedbak.htm** pages. Then use FrontPage to print the HTML code for this page. On the printout, circle the code that specifies the hotspots that you created in the link bar, and the code that adds the background picture to the page.

21. Use Hyperlinks view to check your Web site for broken hyperlinks. Make sure that each page contains the appropriate hyperlinks, adding any that are needed and correcting any errors.

22. Close the **Garden** Web site and then close FrontPage.

Explore

Case 4. Creating a New Page for Replay Music Factory Business has been brisk at the Replay Music Factory. One frequently asked question (FAQ) concerns how the exchange process works for buying, selling, and trading compact discs (CDs). Charlene Fields and Alec Johnston met with the marketing manager to see how they might use the company's Web site to provide this information to customers. They are convinced that expanding the Web site in this way will translate into fewer phone calls from people asking for information about the exchange process. This call reduction, in turn, might allow the company to delay hiring additional sales associates to handle those calls.

Charlene and Alec decide to create a new Web page that describes the exchange process. In addition, they want you to create new, blank pages for the planned pages in the Web site. Charlene asks you to assist Alec with this enhancement of the company's Web site.

If necessary, start FrontPage, insert your Data Disk in the appropriate disk drive, and then do the following:

1. Read all of the steps for this case problem, and then prepare a planning analysis sheet for the revisions to the Web site.

2. Open the **Replay** Web site that you created in Tutorial 2. (If you did not create this Web site in Tutorial 2, ask your instructor for assistance.)

3. Open the home page in Page view. Use the link bar that you created in Tutorial 2 to add the planned pages to the Web site and to the Tasks list. Use the Normal Page template when creating the new pages and assign appropriate filenames and page titles. Create the hyperlinks in the link bar in the home page to connect to the new pages.

4. Design the new Web page that describes Replay's process for buying, selling, and trading used CDs. Include a table of contents with at least two entries, at least one bulleted list or numbered list, at least two defined terms and their associated definitions, internal hyperlinks from the table of contents to the detailed information for each table of contents entry in the document, a mailto, a link bar, at least one picture, and a hyperlink from the bottom of the page to a nontext-based bookmark at the top of the page. Use any sources available in developing your content, including browsing several commercial Web sites.

5. Open the Web page that you created in Step 3 and designed in Step 4 from Tasks view. This page will describe the exchange process at Replay Music Factory. Create this page using your design from Step 4. Apply the background from the home page to the new page.

6. Create a logo for the exchange-process page using any graphics program. (If you do not have a graphics program, skip to Step 7.) Save your logo as a GIF file in the Tutorial.03 folder on your Data Disk.

7. Insert the GIF file that you created in Step 6 at the top of the page. If you do not have access to a graphics program, use the **Replay.gif** file in the Tutorial.03 folder. Change the logo to use a transparent background.

8. Save the Web page, and save all of its pictures in the images folder of the **Replay** Web site.

9. Update the link bar in the page that you created in Step 5 to include hyperlinks to the other pages in the Web site that you added in Step 3.

10. Create a hotspot in the logo that you inserted in Step 7 to open the home page. Save the home page, and then save the new page. Use Preview Page view to test the new hyperlinks and bookmarks.

11. Mark the task for creating the page that describes the exchange process as completed in the Tasks list, but do not delete the task.

12. Display your new page as the focus page in Hyperlinks view. If necessary, center the hyperlinks diagram in the Contents pane. Display the repeated hyperlinks and the hyperlinks to pictures, and then print Hyperlinks view using WordPad. Close WordPad without saving your changes, and then turn off the display of the repeated hyperlinks and hyperlinks to pictures.

13. In FrontPage, print your new page and its HTML code. On the printout, circle and label the HTML code entries that create the hyperlinks, bookmarks, background picture, and hotspot.

14. Close the **Replay** Web site and then close FrontPage.

LAB ASSIGNMENTS

These Lab Assignments are designed to accompany the interactive Course Lab called Web Pages and HTML. To start the Web Pages and HTML Lab, click the Start button on the Windows taskbar, point to Programs, point to Course Labs, point to New Perspectives Applications, and then click Web Pages & HTML. If you do not see Course Labs on your Programs menu, see your instructor or technical support person.

Web Pages and HTML It's easy to create your own Web pages. As you learned in Tutorials 2 and 3, there are many software tools to help you become a Web author. In this Lab, you'll experiment with a Web authoring Wizard that automates the process of creating a Web page. You'll also try your hand at working directly with HTML code.

1. Click the Steps button to activate the Web Authoring Wizard and learn how to create a basic Web page. As you proceed through the Steps, answer all of the Quick Check questions. After you complete the Steps, you will see a Quick Check summary Report. Follow the instructions on the screen to print this report.

2. In Explore, click the File menu, and then click New to start working on a new Web page. Use the Wizard to create a home page for a veterinarian who offers dog day-care

and boarding services. After you create the page, save it on drive A or C, and print the HTML code. Your site must have the following characteristics:

   a. Title: Dr. Dave's Dog Domain

   b. Background color: Gold

   c. Picture: Dog.jpg

   d. Body text: Your dog will have the best care day and night at Dr. Dave's Dog Domain. Fine accommodations, good food, play time, and snacks are all provided. You can board your pet by the day or week. Grooming services also available.

   e. Text link: "Reasonable rates" links to www.cciw.com/np3/rates.htm.

   f. E-mail link: "For more information:" links to daveassist@drdave.com.

3. In Explore, use the File menu to open the HTML document called Politics.htm. After you use the HTML window (not the Wizard) to make the following changes, save the revised page on drive A or C, and then print the HTML code. Refer to the following table for a list of HTML tags you can use.

   a. Change the title to Politics 2000.

   b. Center the page heading.

   c. Change the background color to FFE7C6 and the text color to 000000.

   d. Add a line break before the sentence "What's next?".

   e. Add a bold tag to "Additional links on this topic:".

   f. Add one more link to the "Additional links" list. The link should go to the site http://www.elections.ca and the clickable link should read "Elections Canada".

   g. Change the last image to display the picture "next.gif".

4. In Explore, use the Web authoring Wizard and the HTML window to create a home page about yourself. You should include at least a screenful of text, a picture, an external link, and an e-mail link. Save the page on drive A, and then print the HTML code. Turn in your disk and printout.

HTML TAGS	MEANING AND LOCATION
`<HTML></HTML>`	States that the file is an HTML document. Opening tag begins the page; closing tag ends the page (required).
`<HEAD></HEAD>`	States that the enclosed text is the header of the page. Appears immediately after the opening HTML tag (required).
`<TITLE></TITLE>`	States that the enclosed text is the title of the page. Must appear within the opening and closing HEAD tags (required).
`<BODY></BODY>`	States that the enclosed material (all the text, pictures, and tags in the rest of the document) is the body of the document (required).
`<H1></H1>`	States that the enclosed text is a heading.
` `	Inserts a line break. Can be used to control line spacing and breaks in lines.
`<UL></UL>` `<OL></OL>`	Indicates an unordered list (list items are preceded by bullets) or an ordered list (list items are preceded by numbers or letters).
`<LI>`	Indicates a list item. Precedes all items in unordered or ordered lists.
`<CENTER></CENTER>`	Indicates that the enclosed text should be centered across the width of the page.
`<B></B>`	Indicates that the enclosed text should be bold.
`<I></I>`	Indicates that the enclosed text should be italic.
`<A HREF=" "></A>`	Indicates that the enclosed text is a hypertext link; the URL of the linked material must appear within the quotation marks after the equals sign.
`<IMG SRC=" ">`	Inserts picture into the document. The URL of the picture appears within the quotation marks following the SRC=" " attribute.
`<HR>`	Inserts a horizontal line.

QUICK | CHECK ANSWERS

Session 3.1

1. True
2. False
3. bulleted (unordered)
4. A list within another list
5. True
6. Increase Indent

Session 3.2

1. bookmark
2. icon
3. Create the bookmark in the page by selecting the text or location for it, clicking Insert on the menu bar, and then clicking Bookmark. Accept the default bookmark name or provide a new name, and then click the OK button. Select the text or location in the page that will contain the hyperlink to the bookmark, click the Insert Hyperlink button on the Standard toolbar, click the Place in This Document button on the Link to bar, select the bookmark, and then click the OK button.
4. A hyperlink to a location in the same Web page (an internal hyperlink)
5. True
6. hotspot (image map)
7. Circle, rectangle, polygon
8. Type it and then press the spacebar.
9. False

Session 3.3

1. Tasks list
2. Just add Web task
3. Create a new normal page, Task
4. True
5. Mark Complete
6. True
7. False

In this tutorial you will:

- Import a Web page from a Web server

- Create a table in a Web page

- Modify a table's appearance

- Split and merge table cells

- Enter data in a table

- Create a nested table

- Insert a picture in a table

- Create and edit a frames page

- Specify target frames in a frames page

- Print a frames page

- View the HTML code for a table and a frames page

CREATING

TABLES AND FRAMES IN A WEB PAGE

Completing the Investor Relations and Products Web Pages

CASE

Sunny Morning Products

During the design phase of the Sunny Morning Products Web site, Jacob Towle described his vision of the Investor Relations and Products pages to Amanda Bay, who is heading the Web site development team. Jacob wants the Investor Relations page to include the company's financial performance information and the Products page to include information about products available from the Sunshine Country Store. Based on this feedback, Amanda prepared sketches of these Web pages and asked Jacob to approve them before starting their development.

In this tutorial, you will create the Investor Relations and Products pages for Sunny Morning Products. You will import and use Amanda's partially completed Web pages. As you develop each page, you will review Amanda's design notes and documentation to familiarize yourself with the necessary planning activities. Your main activities in completing these Web pages include adding a table to the Investor Relations page and creating frames for the Products page. As a management intern in the marketing department, you are especially interested in the Products page, because it will be used to accept online orders from the Sunshine Country Store.

SESSION 4.1

In this session, you will create and format a table in a Web page. You will change the alignment of the table and its cells; insert, select, and delete rows and columns; split and merge cells; resize table cells; enter data and repetitive data in a table; create a nested table; insert a picture in a cell; add a caption to the table; and change the table's background color and format. Finally, you will test the table in a browser and examine its HTML code.

Reviewing the Tasks List

After the latest meeting with the Web site development team, Amanda asks you to review the Tasks list you created in Tutorial 3, which contains the tasks needed to complete the Sunny Web site. After you review the list, Amanda wants you to meet with her to discuss the Investor Relations Web page, which you will create first.

To open the Sunny Web site and review the Tasks list:

1. Make sure that your Data Disk is in the correct disk drive, start FrontPage, and then open the **Sunny** Web site from your Data Disk.

2. Click the **Tasks** button 📂 on the Views bar to open the Tasks list.

3. If necessary, click the **Task** column heading to sort the revised list in ascending alphabetical order. See Figure 4-1.

Figure 4-1	CURRENT TASKS FOR THE SUNNY WEB SITE

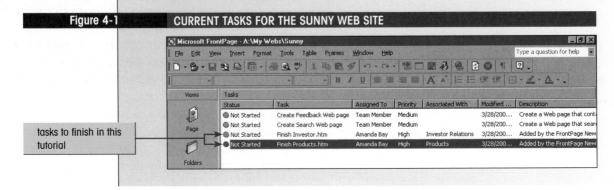

tasks to finish in this tutorial

The two Finish tasks show that you need to complete the Investor Relations and Products pages. You meet with Amanda, who asks you to finish her partially completed Investor Relations page first. Amanda stored this Web page on the World Wide Web site for Sunny Morning Products. You will retrieve her page from the site using a Web browser.

Importing a Web Page from a Web Server

In Tutorial 3, you learned how to import an HTML document stored on your Data Disk into a disk-based Web site. You can also import a Web page from a Web server into a FrontPage Web site. There are two methods for importing a Web page from a Web server. With the first method, you open the page in Internet Explorer, and then click the Edit button on the toolbar. This action starts FrontPage and opens the page in Page view, where you can edit and save the page. With the second method, you use the Import dialog box to specify the URL of the page that you are importing.

Amanda saved her partially completed Investor Relations Web page on the Web server for Sunny Morning Products. She asks you to replace the current, blank Investor Relations Web page that you created as part of the Tasks list in Tutorial 3 with the one stored on the company's Web server. When you replace a Web page, FrontPage overwrites the original Web page with the new one.

Regardless of the explicit copyrights placed on a Web page, you should never copy or revise a Web page without obtaining permission from the site's owner to do so. A **copyright** is a right granted by law to an author or other entity to control the reproduction, publication, or distribution of the author's or entity's original work. Amanda tells you that reproducing a Web page from a Web site from which you do not have permission is a violation of copyright law. In this case however, Sunny Morning Products owns the page that you will import, so you are not violating a copyright.

REFERENCE WINDOW   `RW`

Importing a Web Page from a Web Server

- Open the Web site into which you will save the page, connect to the Internet and open the Web page that you want to save in Internet Explorer, click the list arrow for the Edit button on the toolbar, click Edit with Microsoft FrontPage, and then save the page in the FrontPage Web site.
  or
- In Folders view, open the Web site into which you will import the page.
- Click File on the menu bar, and then click Import.
- Click the From Web button.
- Click the From a World Wide Web site option button, type the URL for the Web page in the Location text box, and then click the Next button.
- Make sure that the Limit to this page plus check box is selected, clear the Limit to and Limit to text and image files check boxes, and then change the value in the levels below text box to 0.
- Click the Next button, and then click the Finish button.
- If a dialog box opens and warns you about potential conflicts with themes, click the Yes button.

Note: You must be able to connect to the Internet with Internet Explorer to complete the following set of steps. You will navigate to the Course Technology Web site to simulate using the Web server for Sunny Morning Products.

To import a Web page from a Web server using Internet Explorer:

1. Start Internet Explorer and connect to your Internet service provider or log on to the network.

> **TROUBLE?** If you are not using Internet Explorer as your browser or if you cannot connect to the Internet, use the Import command on the File menu to import the Investor.htm file from the Tutorial.04 folder on your Data Disk into the Sunny Web site. Click the Yes button to overwrite the existing file, open the Investor.htm page in Page view, and then skip to Step 6.

2. Select the current URL in the Address bar, type **http://www.course.com/ downloads/newperspectives/fp2002/Investor.htm**, and then press the **Enter** key. The Investor Relations page opens in the browser. See Figure 4-2.

Figure 4-2	INVESTOR RELATIONS WEB PAGE

Edit button (your icon might look different)

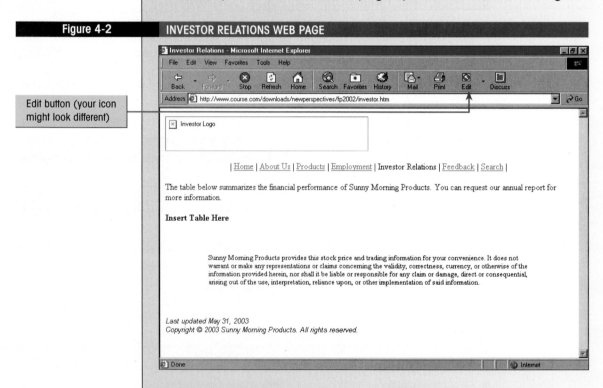

3. Click the list arrow for the **Edit** button [icon] on the toolbar, and then click **Edit with Microsoft FrontPage**. After a moment, FrontPage becomes the active program, and the investor.htm page opens in Page view. Depending on the speed of your Internet connection, it might take a few seconds to open the page from the server.

> **TROUBLE?** If your Edit button does not have an option to edit the page in FrontPage, return to FrontPage. In Folders view, use the Import command on the File menu to import the Investor.htm file from the Tutorial.04 folder on your Data Disk into the Sunny Web site. Click the Yes button to overwrite the existing file, open the Investor.htm page in Page view, and then skip to Step 6.

If you have the necessary permission, you could edit the Investor Relations page and then send the revised file back to the Web server to update it. Amanda asks you to save the Investor Relations page in the Sunny Web site, so you can edit it as part of your disk-based Web.

4. In FrontPage, click **File** on the menu bar, and then click **Save As**. The Save As dialog box opens. You need to specify the Sunny Web site on your Data Disk as the location in which to save the Web page.

5. Make sure that the **Sunny** folder on your Data Disk is open in the Look in list box and that the File name text box displays the filename "Investor," and then click the **Save** button. A dialog box opens and asks if you want to replace the Investor.htm page that you added with the Tasks list in Tutorial 3. Click the **Yes** button to continue.

   TROUBLE? If the Investor.htm page has a white background instead of the background picture from the home page, click Format on the menu bar, click Background, click the Browse button at the bottom of the dialog box, browse to (if necessary) and click index.htm in the Sunny Web site, click the OK button, and then click the OK button in the Page Properties dialog box. If the background picture still doesn't appear, ask your instructor or technical support person for help.

   Now the Investor Relations Web page is saved in the Sunny Web site. You'll need to add the logo to the page.

6. Right-click the **broken link** icon ⊠ at the top of the page to open the shortcut menu, click **Picture Properties**, click the **General** tab, and then click the **Browse** button to the right of the Picture source text box. Open the **Tutorial.04** folder on your Data Disk, and then double-click **Invest**. Click the **OK** button in the Picture Properties dialog box to close it.

   The logo now appears at the top of the Investor Relations page. Next, save the Web page and the embedded picture.

7. Click the **Save** button 🖫 on the Standard toolbar. The Save Embedded Files dialog box opens. Make sure that the location to save the file is the Sunny Web site's images folder, and then click the **OK** button.

8. Click the **Internet Explorer** program button on the taskbar to activate that program, and then click the **Close** button ⊠ on the title bar to close it. If necessary, close your dial-up connection as well.

The Investor Relations Web page will include a table that summarizes the company's financial performance over the past two years. Next, Amanda wants you to add this table to the Web page.

Understanding Tables

You are probably already familiar with the process of creating tables in Word documents. In FrontPage, just like in Word, a **table** consists of one or more rows of cells that organize and arrange data. A **cell** is the smallest component of a table. You can place text or a picture in a table cell. You can also create a **nested table**, which is a table within a table cell.

If your Web site development plan includes a Web page with a table, you should sketch out the desired appearance of the table before you create it using FrontPage. Sketching a table first helps you plan how many rows and columns you will need. Although you can add or delete columns after creating the table, it is easier to create the table correctly from the start.

The steps you take to create a table using FrontPage are similar to those you would use to create a table with Microsoft Word. For smaller tables, you use the **Insert Table button grid**, a toolbar button that displays a miniature table with four rows and five columns so you can specify the table's size. If your table is relatively small (fewer than four rows by five columns), you can click a cell in the grid to specify the desired table size. If your table will be larger than four rows by five columns, you can drag the last cell in the grid to enlarge it to the desired table size; when you release the mouse button, FrontPage creates the desired table.

When creating a table in FrontPage, you must specify table properties, such as the size of the border, the cell padding, the cell spacing, and the table width. A **border** is a line that surrounds each cell and the entire table. **Cell padding** is the distance between the contents of a cell and the inside edge of the cell, measured in pixels. **Cell spacing** is the distance between table cells, also measured in pixels. Increasing the cell spacing increases the distance between the borders that surround each cell.

You can specify the table width as a percentage of the width of the screen or as a fixed width in pixels. Remember that HTML documents will be displayed by a variety of computers that have monitors with different resolutions. For this reason, most developers set column widths for their tables as a percentage of the screen's width (such as 85%), rather than as a fixed measurement (such as 100 pixels wide). You should specify these types of settings to ensure that all users of your Web page will be able to view your tables correctly regardless of their particular monitors, computers, or Web browsers.

Figure 4-3 shows Amanda's sketch of the summary of financial performance table that you will create in the Investor Relations Web page. Amanda shows you the left, center, and right alignments used for the column headings and numbers in the table. Although her sketch is complete for now, she notes that you might need to revise the table's design and appearance as you work. After all, changes are a normal part of the evolution of any Web page.

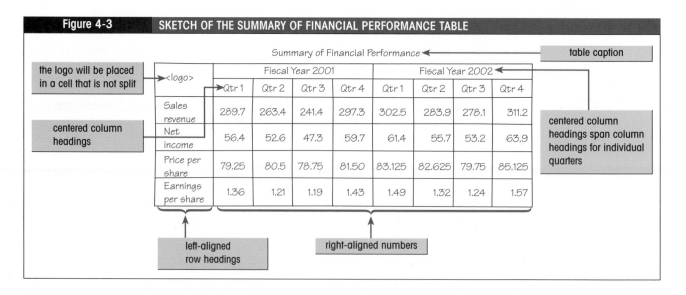

Figure 4-3   SKETCH OF THE SUMMARY OF FINANCIAL PERFORMANCE TABLE

Amanda also asks you to review the planning analysis sheet, shown in Figure 4-4, which she created when planning the development of the Investor Relations Web page.

Figure 4-4	AMANDA'S PLANNING ANALYSIS SHEET FOR THE INVESTOR RELATIONS WEB PAGE

Planning Analysis Sheet

Objective

Create an Investor Relations Web page that contains a table of financial performance information.

Requirements

Partially completed Investor Relations Web page

Financial performance information for the past two fiscal years, including sales revenue, net income, price per share, and earnings per share

Approval of table layout sketch

Logo for the first table cell

Results

Investor Relations Web page with the following information:

Company logo and link bar

Introductory paragraph

Financial performance information in a table format

Common background with the home page

Creating a Table in a Web Page

After sketching your table and securing the necessary approval from the Web site development team, you are ready to create the new table in the desired location in the Web page.

REFERENCE   WINDOW   **RW**

__Creating a Table in a Web Page__
- Click the location in the Web page where you want to insert the table.
- Click the Insert Table button on the Standard toolbar to open the Insert Table button grid.
- Click the grid cell that represents the desired table size, or drag the last cell in the Insert Table button grid to expand the grid to the desired table size, and release the mouse button.
  or
- Click Table on the menu bar, point to Insert, and then click Table. In the Insert Table dialog box, specify the number of rows and columns in the Rows and Columns text boxes, and then click the OK button.

When Amanda prepared the Investor Relations page, she typed a placeholder in the page indicating the intended location of the table. With the Investor Relations page now included in the Sunny Web site, you are ready to create the summary of financial performance table.

To insert the table:

1. With the Investor Relations Web page still displayed in Page view, select the **Insert Table Here** text. You will insert the table in this location.

2. Click the **Insert Table** button 🔲 on the Standard toolbar to open the Insert Table button grid. You might notice that it is the same Insert Table button grid that Word uses.

3. Point to the cell in the lower-right corner of the grid, and then click and hold down the mouse button while you drag the grid down and to the right to expand it to a size of five rows and nine columns. See Figure 4-5.

Figure 4-5	INSERT TABLE BUTTON GRID

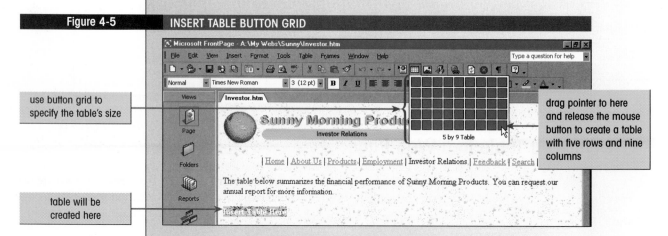

use button grid to specify the table's size

drag pointer to here and release the mouse button to create a table with five rows and nine columns

table will be created here

4. Release the mouse button. A table that contains five rows and nine columns replaces the selected "Insert Table Here" text. The insertion point is blinking in the first cell of the table.

   TROUBLE? If you clicked the cell in the lower-right corner of the grid and did not hold down the mouse button, a four-row by five-column table is inserted. Click the Undo button 🔲 on the Standard toolbar, and then repeat Steps 1 through 4.

5. Right-click anywhere in the new table to open the shortcut menu, and then click **Table Properties** to open the Table Properties dialog box. This dialog box lets you specify the table's properties and characteristics. See Figure 4-6.

Figure 4-6   **TABLE PROPERTIES DIALOG BOX**

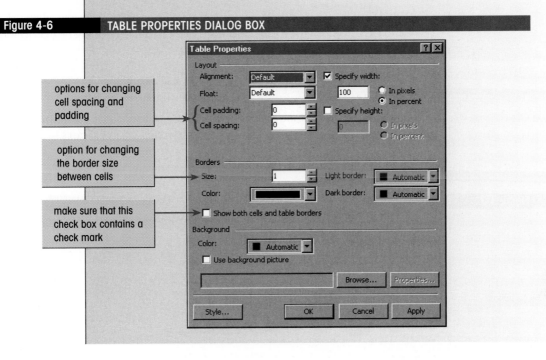

options for changing cell spacing and padding

option for changing the border size between cells

make sure that this check box contains a check mark

Amanda's sketch of the table (see Figure 4-3) indicates centered column headings and split and merged cells. The first cell in the table is not split. The row headings are left-aligned, and the numbers in the cells are right-aligned. The values in the table are fairly close together, which indicates lower padding and spacing values. You will format the table to Amanda's design specifications next. To help position the insertion point correctly, you will turn on the display of nonprinting characters. **Nonprinting characters** are symbols in a Web page, such as paragraph marks.

To format the table and turn on the nonprinting characters:

1. Make sure that the **Specify width** check box in the Layout section contains a check mark, select the current value in the Specify width text box and type **95**, and then make sure that the **In percent** option button is selected. This setting specifies that your table will be displayed at 95% of the browser's window size.

2. In the Layout section, click the **Cell padding up arrow** as necessary to change the cell padding to **4**, and then click the **Cell spacing up arrow** as necessary to change the cell spacing to **3**. These settings will increase the spacing between cells in the table, which will make the table's contents easier to read.

3. In the Borders section, click the **Size up arrow** as necessary to change the border size to **2**.

4. If necessary, click the **Show both cells and table borders** check box to select it so that the borders for the entire table and the individual cells will be displayed.

5. Click the **OK** button. The Table Properties dialog box closes, and the new properties are applied to the table.

6. If necessary, scroll down the page so you can see the entire table, which contains empty cells. Also notice that when a table is displayed, the Tables toolbar appears and provides options for working with tables.

   TROUBLE? If the Tables toolbar does not appear automatically, click View on the menu bar, point to Toolbars, and then click Tables. If necessary, drag the Tables toolbar to dock it below the Formatting toolbar.

   Amanda explains that it is easier to work with tables when you can see the nonprinting characters. She asks you to turn on this feature.

7. Click the **Show All** button ¶ on the Standard toolbar to turn on the display of nonprinting characters. See Figure 4-7. Notice that the cells have a left alignment, as indicated by the paragraph marks appearing in the left side of each cell.

| Figure 4-7 | INVESTOR RELATIONS PAGE WITH TABLE INSERTED |

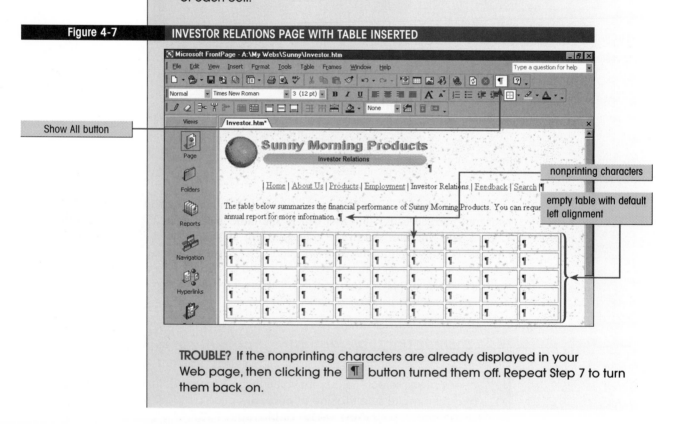

TROUBLE? If the nonprinting characters are already displayed in your Web page, then clicking the ¶ button turned them off. Repeat Step 7 to turn them back on.

You inserted the table in the correct location in the page, but Amanda now thinks that the table will look better if it is centered.

Aligning a Table

A table's alignment in a Web page differs from the alignment of the data in the table's cells. A table can have only one alignment, whereas each cell in the table can have a different alignment. The alignment of a table and the alignment of a table's cells are specified using different HTML tags. To specify a different alignment for the table, you need to change the table's properties.

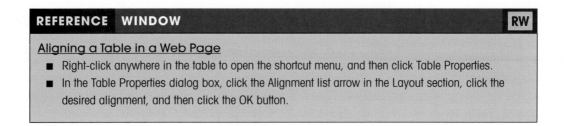

Aligning a Table in a Web Page
■ Right-click anywhere in the table to open the shortcut menu, and then click Table Properties.
■ In the Table Properties dialog box, click the Alignment list arrow in the Layout section, click the desired alignment, and then click the OK button.

The table that you inserted in the Investor Relations Web page is left-aligned, which is the default alignment. Amanda wants this table to be centered to give it a more balanced appearance when viewed in the browser. She asks you to center the table next.

To align a table in a Web page:

1. Right-click anywhere in the table to open the shortcut menu, and then click **Table Properties** to open that dialog box.

2. In the Layout section, click the **Alignment** list arrow, and then click **Center**. Selecting this option will center the table (but not the data in the table's cells) in the page.

3. Click the **OK** button. The Table Properties dialog box closes and the table's alignment changes to centered. See Figure 4-8.

Figure 4-8   CENTERED TABLE IN THE WEB PAGE

table's cells are still left-aligned

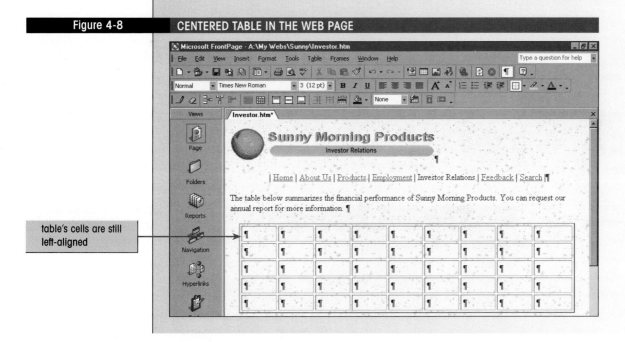

Inserting Rows and Columns in a Table

After creating a table, you can insert additional rows and columns as needed, either before or after entering data in the table's cells. After approving the table's initial design, Jacob decides to include additional data about the average annual return for earnings. Amanda asks you to accommodate this change by inserting one row and one column in the table. To accomplish this task, you can use the **Tables toolbar**, which provides tools specific to creating and formatting tables. Figure 4-9 describes the tools available on the Tables toolbar.

Figure 4-9	TABLES TOOLBAR BUTTONS AND THEIR DESCRIPTIONS

BUTTON NAME	BUTTON	FUNCTION
Draw Table		Lets you draw a new table or modify an existing table using the pointer, which changes to a ✐ shape, to draw lines to indicate rows and columns
Eraser		Lets you use the pointer, which changes to a ◇ shape, to merge cells
Insert Rows		Inserts a new row above the selected row
Insert Columns		Inserts a new column to the left of the selected column
Delete Cells		Deletes the selected cells
Merge Cells		Merges the selected cells into one larger cell
Split Cells		Splits the selected cell into one or more cells
Align Top		Vertically aligns the data in the selected cells at the top of the cells
Center Vertically		Vertically centers the data in the selected cells
Align Bottom		Vertically aligns the data in the selected cells at the bottom of the cells
Distribute Rows Evenly		Changes the height of the selected rows to equal measurements
Distribute Columns Evenly		Changes the width of the selected columns to equal measurements
AutoFit to Contents		Increases or decreases the sizes of selected columns in the table to best fit the data they contain
Fill Color		Lets you change the background color of the selected cells to a standard or custom color
Table AutoFormat Combo	None	Lets you apply a Table AutoFormat to an existing table by selecting the desired Table AutoFormat from a list
Table AutoFormat		Opens the Table AutoFormat dialog box, where you can select and apply a Table AutoFormat and special formats to an existing table
Fill Down		Copies data from the topmost cell in a range of selected cells and pastes it into the range of selected cells
Fill Right		Copies data from the leftmost cell in a range of selected cells and pastes it into the range of selected cells

REFERENCE WINDOW   RW

Inserting a Row in a Table

- Click any cell in the row above which you want to insert the new row, and then click the Insert Rows button on the Tables toolbar.
  or
- Click a cell adjacent to where you want to insert the new row, click Table on the menu bar, point to Insert, and then click Rows or Columns to open the Insert Rows or Columns dialog box.
- Click the Rows option button, and then enter the number of rows to insert in the Number of rows text box.
- Click the Above selection option button to insert the new row(s) above the currently selected row, or click the Below selection option button to insert the new row(s) below the currently selected row.
- Click the OK button.

REFERENCE   WINDOW   RW

<u>Inserting a Column in a Table</u>
- Click any cell in the column to the left of which to insert the new column, and then click the Insert Columns button on the Tables toolbar.
  or
- Click a cell adjacent to where you want to insert the new column, click Table on the menu bar, point to Insert, and then click Rows or Columns to open the Insert Rows or Columns dialog box.
- Click the Columns option button, and then enter number of columns to insert in the Number of columns text box.
- Click the Left of selection option button to insert the new column(s) to the left of the currently selected column, or click the Right of selection option button to insert the new column(s) to the right of the currently selected column.
- Click the OK button.

Because your table is empty, you could insert the new row and column anywhere in the table. You will insert a new fourth row and a new second-to-last column so that you will gain experience in adding rows and columns in different locations in the table.

To insert a row and a column in the table:

1. Click any cell in the third row. When you insert the new row, it will appear above the third row.

2. Click the **Insert Rows** button on the Tables toolbar. A new row is inserted. The insertion point is now blinking in a cell in the fourth row.

   Next, insert a column to the left of the last column in the table.

3. Click any cell in the last column of the table. When you insert the new column, it will appear to the left of the selected column.

4. Click the **Insert Columns** button on the Tables toolbar. A new column is added to the left of the selected column. The insertion point is now blinking in a cell in the last column of the table, which is narrower than the other columns. Your table now contains 6 rows and 10 columns.

With the addition of the new row and column to the table, Amanda is concerned about the readability of the table for users who have monitors with lower screen resolutions. She has another idea for handling Jacob's request, so she asks you to delete the row and column that you just added. You could click the Undo button on the Standard toolbar twice to cancel the insertion of the column and the row, but Amanda wants you to learn how to select and delete rows and columns as part of your training.

Selecting and Deleting Rows or Columns

Even when you sketch a table before inserting it in a Web page, sometimes you might need to add or delete rows and columns to create the right table for your data. The process of deleting rows or columns is straightforward. First, you select the row or column that you want to delete, or drag the pointer over a group of cells in several rows and columns. If you need to select additional rows or columns at the same time, hold down the Ctrl key while you select them. These selection methods are similar to how you would select table cells in Word. After selecting the cells, rows, or columns to delete, click the Delete Cells button on the Tables toolbar.

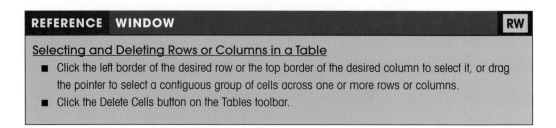

REFERENCE   WINDOW   **RW**

Selecting and Deleting Rows or Columns in a Table
- Click the left border of the desired row or the top border of the desired column to select it, or drag the pointer to select a contiguous group of cells across one or more rows or columns.
- Click the Delete Cells button on the Tables toolbar.

Amanda wants you to delete the third row and the last column from the table.

To select and delete a row and column from a table:

1. Move the pointer to the left border of the third row in the table so that it changes to a ➡ shape, and then click the left border to select the third row of the table. See Figure 4-10.

| Figure 4-10 | SELECTING AND DELETING A ROW IN A TABLE |

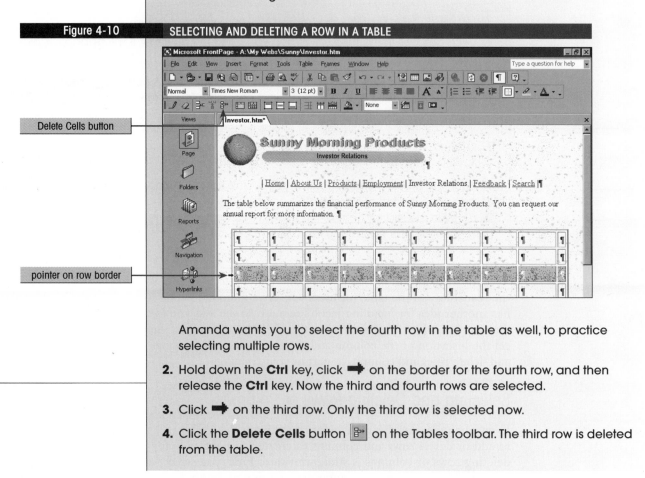

Amanda wants you to select the fourth row in the table as well, to practice selecting multiple rows.

2. Hold down the **Ctrl** key, click ➡ on the border for the fourth row, and then release the **Ctrl** key. Now the third and fourth rows are selected.

3. Click ➡ on the third row. Only the third row is selected now.

4. Click the **Delete Cells** button 📑 on the Tables toolbar. The third row is deleted from the table.

5. Move the pointer to the top border of the last column in the table so that it changes to a ↓ shape, and then click the top border to select the last column in the table.

6. Click the 🔲 button to delete the selected column. Now your table contains five rows and nine columns.

Next, Amanda asks you to create the column headings for the summary of financial performance table.

Splitting **and Merging Table Cells**

FrontPage provides many ways to arrange the information in a table. One popular method is to include column headings that identify the data displayed in each column. You can arrange the cells to span a row or column by splitting and merging cells. **Splitting cells** is the process of dividing a single cell into two or more rows or columns, whereas **merging cells** is the process of combining two or more cells in a row or column to form a single cell.

Splitting Table Cells

For the summary of financial performance table, Amanda wants you to split the cells in the eight columns that will contain the column headings for each quarter. You will not split the first cell in the first column because you will insert a picture in this cell later.

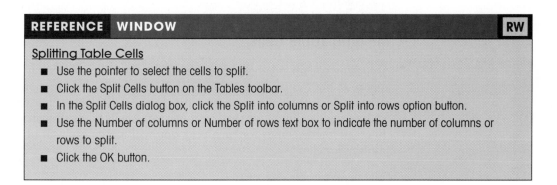

REFERENCE   WINDOW   **RW**

Splitting Table Cells
- Use the pointer to select the cells to split.
- Click the Split Cells button on the Tables toolbar.
- In the Split Cells dialog box, click the Split into columns or Split into rows option button.
- Use the Number of columns or Number of rows text box to indicate the number of columns or rows to split.
- Click the OK button.

Next, split the cells that will contain the column headings for the table.

To split cells:

1. Use the ➡ pointer to select the first row in the table, press and hold down the **Ctrl** key, click the cell in row 1, column 1, and then release the **Ctrl** key. Now cells 2 through 9 in the first row are selected.

2. Click the **Split Cells** button 🔲 on the Tables toolbar. The Split Cells dialog box opens. See Figure 4-11.

Figure 4-11 | SPLIT CELLS DIALOG BOX

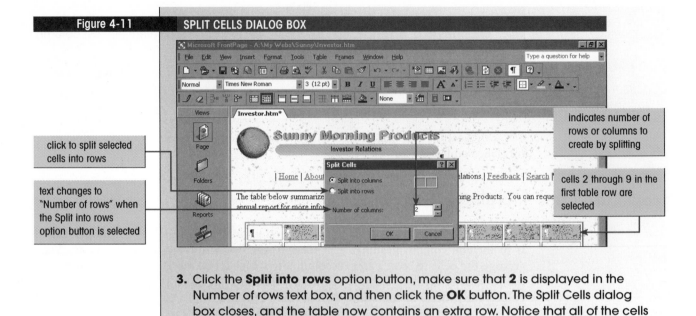

click to split selected cells into rows

text changes to "Number of rows" when the Split into rows option button is selected

indicates number of rows or columns to create by splitting

cells 2 through 9 in the first table row are selected

3. Click the **Split into rows** option button, make sure that **2** is displayed in the Number of rows text box, and then click the **OK** button. The Split Cells dialog box closes, and the table now contains an extra row. Notice that all of the cells in the first row, except for the cell in the first column, were split into two rows. The first cell in the table spans the first two rows of the table. This design matches Amanda's sketch.

Now that you have split the cells, you are ready to create the cells that will contain the year column headings in the table.

Merging Table Cells

According to Amanda's sketch of the table, the cells containing the year headings should appear at the top of those columns that contain the information for their respective four quarters. Unlike some spreadsheet programs, HTML does not provide tags to center text across several columns, so you must merge the cells that will span multiple rows or columns. To create the headings for each year, you will merge each set of four cells in the first row into single cells.

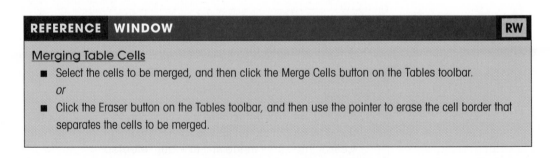

REFERENCE WINDOW   **RW**

Merging Table Cells

- Select the cells to be merged, and then click the Merge Cells button on the Tables toolbar.

  or

- Click the Eraser button on the Tables toolbar, and then use the pointer to erase the cell border that separates the cells to be merged.

Next, Amanda asks you to merge the cells for the year headings.

To merge cells:

1. Click the cell in row 1, column 2, press and hold down the **Shift** key, click the cell in row 1, column 5, and then release the mouse button and the **Shift** key to select cells 2 through 5 in row 1. See Figure 4-12.

| Figure 4-12 | TABLE WITH SELECTED CELLS |

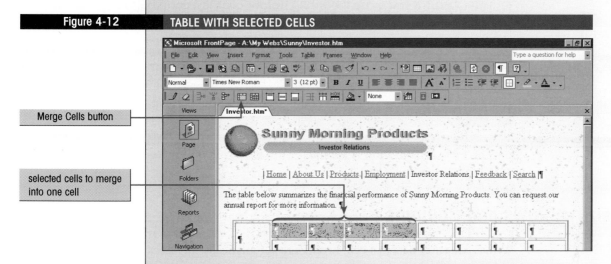

Merge Cells button

selected cells to merge into one cell

2. Click the **Merge Cells** button [ ] on the Tables toolbar. Click the cell in row 1, column 1, to deselect the merged cell, which is now one long cell in the row that spans the four columns below it. You will enter the column heading "Fiscal Year 2001" in this merged cell later. Now you can merge the cells for the "Fiscal Year 2002" column heading. Amanda wants you to use the Eraser to merge the second set of cells.

3. Click the **Eraser** button [ ] on the Tables toolbar to select this tool.

4. Slowly move the pointer over the border between the cells in row 1 and columns 6 and 7. As you move the pointer back and forth across the border, the pointer changes from a ◄──► shape to a ⌓ shape. See Figure 4-13.

| Figure 4-13 | USING THE ERASER TO MERGE CELLS |

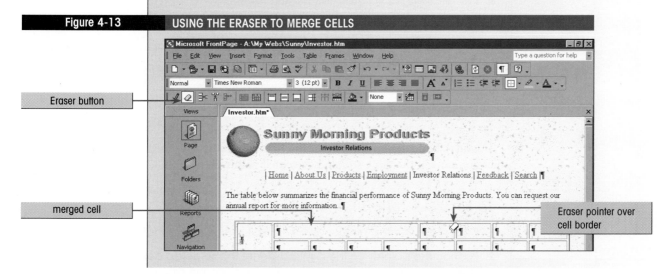

Eraser button

merged cell

Eraser pointer over cell border

5. With the ✏ pointer positioned in row 1, column 6, click and hold down the mouse button, and then drag the pointer across the border between the cells in row 1, columns 6 and 7. The border turns red while you are erasing it. Release the mouse button to merge these cells.

TROUBLE? If you erase the wrong border, click the Undo button 🔄 on the Standard toolbar to undo your change, and then repeat Step 5.

6. Repeat Step 5 to erase the borders between the cells in row 1, columns 7 and 8, and in row 1, columns 8 and 9. Now the first row contains two merged cells that will serve as your column headings.

7. Click 🖉 on the Tables toolbar to turn off the Eraser.

The table organization is complete: You have split and merged the appropriate cells to match Amanda's table design.

Resizing **Rows and Columns**

When you enter data in a cell, FrontPage automatically increases the size of the cell and the column in which it appears to accommodate the text that you entered. You can also manually resize a table's rows and columns to affect the overall appearance of your table.

Your next task is to widen the first column to make room for the headings that Amanda designed for these rows. The easiest way to resize a column is to use the pointer—you just drag the column's right border to the left to decrease the column's width, or drag the column's right border to the right to increase the column's width. You can also use the pointer to drag the bottom border of a row up to decrease its height or down to increase its height.

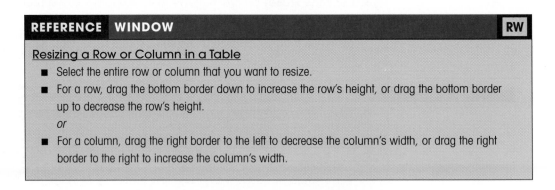

REFERENCE WINDOW   RW

Resizing a Row or Column in a Table
- Select the entire row or column that you want to resize.
- For a row, drag the bottom border down to increase the row's height, or drag the bottom border up to decrease the row's height.
  or
- For a column, drag the right border to the left to decrease the column's width, or drag the right border to the right to increase the column's width.

Amanda's table design shows that the first column is wider than the other columns. The other columns in the table should have equal widths.

To resize a column in a table:

1. Click ⬇ on the top border of the first column to select that column.

2. Position the pointer on the right border of the selected column so it changes to a ◄—► shape, and then click and hold down the mouse button as you drag the right border of the selected column to the right. When the dotted vertical line is positioned as shown in Figure 4-14, release the mouse button.

Figure 4-14   RESIZING A COLUMN'S WIDTH

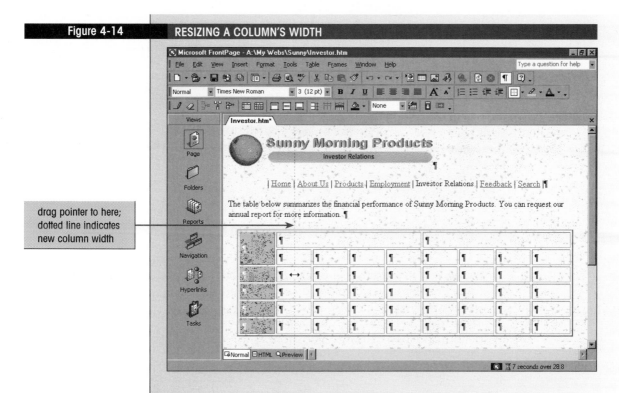

drag pointer to here; dotted line indicates new column width

TROUBLE? If you do not see the dotted vertical line, drag the pointer to approximately the same location shown in Figure 4-14 and then release the mouse button.

3. Click the cell in row 1, column 1 to deselect the first column.

Notice that the width of the second column decreased by more than half of its original size when you resized the first column. You could increase the size of each column in columns 2 through 9 individually, but a faster and more accurate way of resizing columns is to select them as a group and use the Distribute Columns Evenly button on the Tables toolbar.

To distribute the columns evenly:

1. Click the cell in row 2, column 2, press and hold down the **Shift** key, click the cell in the last row and last column (row 6, column 9), and then release the mouse button and the **Shift** key. The cells are selected. See Figure 4-15.

| Figure 4-15 | SELECTING A GROUP OF CELLS |

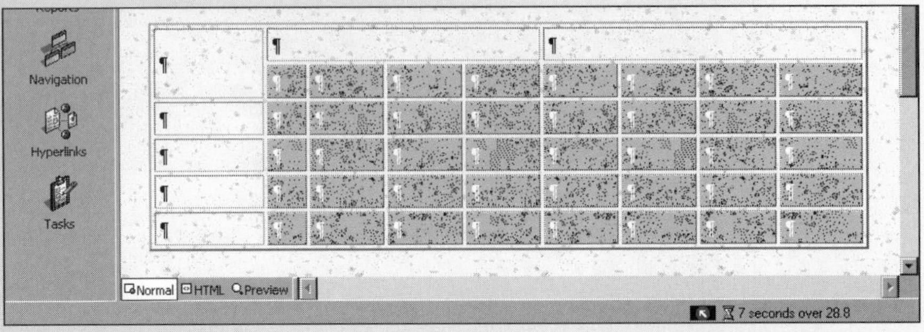

2. Click the **Distribute Columns Evenly** button ⊞ on the Tables toolbar. Now all of the selected cells have the same width.

TROUBLE? If the widths of the selected cells do not look the exactly same, click Table on the menu bar, point to Table Properties, and then click Cell. Click the Specify width check box to select it (you might need to click it twice), type 10 in the text box below the Specify width check box, click the In percent option button, and then click the OK button.

3. Click the cell in row 1, column 1 to deselect the cells.

You can select rows and use the Distribute Rows Evenly button on the Tables toolbar to change the heights of a group of selected rows to the same measurement as well. Now you can enter the data into the table.

Entering Data in a Table

Entering data in a table in a Web page is similar to entering table data in a Word document or in an Excel worksheet. You position the insertion point in the appropriate cell and then type the data. You move the insertion point into a cell by clicking the cell or by pressing the appropriate arrow keys or the Tab key to move to the desired cell.

When your table contains repetitive data, you can type the data once and then use the Fill Down or Fill Right buttons on the Tables toolbar to copy and paste data into adjacent cells. You'll begin by adding the text for the column headings.

To enter data in a table:

1. Click the cell in row 1, column 2, and then type **Fiscal Year 2001**.

TROUBLE? If you aren't sure where to enter the column heading in the table, refer to the table's sketch in Figure 4-3.

2. Select the current cell and the cell to its right. See Figure 4-16.

Figure 4-16 | USING THE FILL RIGHT BUTTON

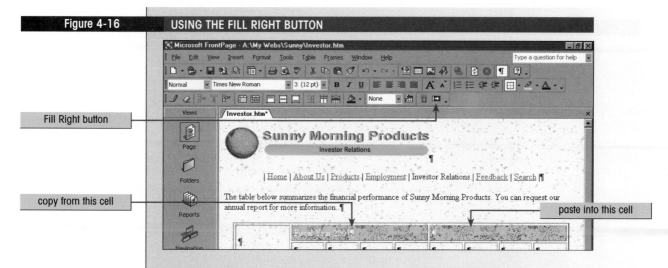

Fill Right button

copy from this cell

paste into this cell

3. Click the **Fill Right** button ⊡ on the Tables toolbar. The content of the first cell is copied into the second cell. Now you can edit the text in the second cell to change it to "Fiscal Year 2002."

4. Click to the right of 2001 in the second cell, press the **Backspace** key, and then type **2**. The column headings are complete.

5. Press the **Tab** key to move to the cell in row 2, column 2, and then type **Qtr 1**.

6. Select cells 2 through 9 in the second row, and then click the ⊡ button. The text "Qtr 1" is copied into the selected cells.

7. Use Figure 4-17 to edit the data that you just copied into the second row and to enter the data in the rest of the table. Press the **Tab** key after typing the data in a cell to move to the next cell. Do not press the Tab key after typing the data in the last cell in the table or you will create a new row. Because you manually set the width of the first column, FrontPage does not automatically increase the size of that column to fit the data; instead, the automatic line wrap feature expands the height of the cells containing the row headings (Sales revenue, Net income, Price per share, and Earnings per share) as necessary so that all of the text fits in one cell. Your completed table should look like Figure 4-17.

Figure 4-17   COMPLETED TABLE WITH DATA ENTERED

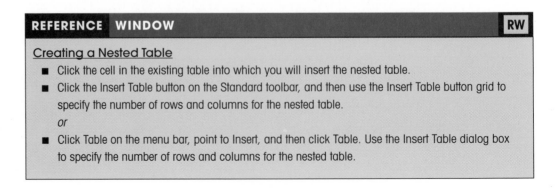

TROUBLE? If the row headings in the first column don't wrap to a second line automatically, don't worry. Depending on your monitor's size and resolution, the entries in your table might look different. Continue with Step 8.

8. Click the **Save** button on the Standard toolbar to save the page.

Jacob would still like to include the average earnings per share amount for each year's data in the table. Amanda asks you to create a nested table to store the new data instead of entering it in a new row and column.

Creating a Nested Table

When you need to add more data in a cell, but not to an entire table, you can use a nested table to hold the new data. A **nested** table is a table that exists within the cell of another table.

REFERENCE WINDOW   RW

Creating a Nested Table
- Click the cell in the existing table into which you will insert the nested table.
- Click the Insert Table button on the Standard toolbar, and then use the Insert Table button grid to specify the number of rows and columns for the nested table.

  or
- Click Table on the menu bar, point to Insert, and then click Table. Use the Insert Table dialog box to specify the number of rows and columns for the nested table.

Amanda asks you to create two nested tables—one for each year in the current table.

To create the nested tables:

1. Scroll the page so that you can see all of the table, click the cell in column 5 of the last row (row 6, column 5) to select it, and then press the **End** key to position the insertion point at the end of the data in this cell.

2. Click the **Insert Table** button 🔲 on the Standard toolbar, and then click the first cell in the second row in the Insert Table button grid (a 2 by 1 table). A table with two rows and one column appears in the selected cell below the current cell value.

3. With the insertion point positioned in the first cell of the nested table, type **Average return**.

4. Press the **Tab** key, and then type **1.2975**.

5. Click the last cell in the last row of the main table, press the **End** key, and then repeat Step 2 to create a nested table with two rows and one column. Type **Average return** in the first cell of the nested table, press the **Tab** key, and then type **1.405** in the second cell of the nested table. See Figure 4-18.

| Figure 4-18 | TABLE WITH TWO NESTED TABLES |

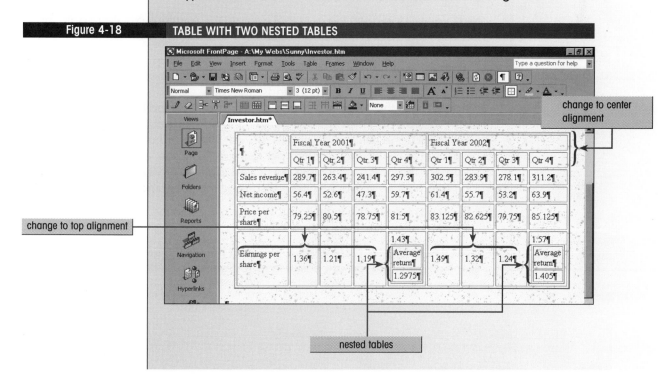

change to center alignment

change to top alignment

nested tables

The data that you entered in the table's cells is left-aligned, which is the default alignment for cells. According to Amanda's sketch of the table, some of this data should be right-aligned. You also need to center the table's headings. The nested tables that you added to the main table caused the fourth-quarter earnings per share amounts to display higher in their cells than the values for the other quarters. You will correct all of these problems next.

Aligning Cell Contents

In addition to the horizontal alignment of left, center, and right, you can select a vertical alignment of top, middle, or bottom for cells. These two alignments—horizontal and vertical—are specified using different HTML tags. Middle is the default vertical alignment, and left is the default horizontal alignment.

You align cell contents by selecting the cells and specifying the desired alignment. You specify a selected cell's horizontal alignment using the alignment buttons on the Formatting toolbar. You specify a selected cell's vertical alignment using the alignment buttons on the Tables toolbar.

To align table data:

1. Use the pointer to select rows 1 and 2 at the top of the table. These rows contain the year and quarter number column headings and the empty cell in row 1, column 1.

2. Click the **Center** button 🔳 on the Formatting toolbar to center the data horizontally in these cells. The default vertical alignment for cells is middle (centered), so these cells are correctly aligned.

   Next, you will top-align the cells that contain the earnings per share data for the first, second, and third quarters of fiscal year 2001.

3. Click the cell in column 1 of the last row (containing the "Earnings per share" text), press and hold down the **Shift** key, click the cell in column 4 of the last row (containing the data 1.19), release the mouse button and the **Shift** key, and then click the **Align Top** button 🔳 on the Tables toolbar. The row heading for the last row and the cells that contain the earnings per share data for the first, second, and third quarters of fiscal year 2001 now have a top vertical alignment to match the earnings per share data for the fourth quarter of fiscal year 2001. The cells that contain the nested tables already appear to have the top alignment, so you don't need to change their alignments.

4. Select cells 6 through 8 in the last row (which contain the data 1.49, 1.32, and 1.24), and then click the 🔳 button to apply the top alignment to these cells.

5. Click the cell in row 1, column 1 to deselect the cells. Now the values in the Earnings per share row are easier to read. See Figure 4-19.

| Figure 4-19 | TABLE WITH TOP-ALIGNED CELLS IN LAST ROW |

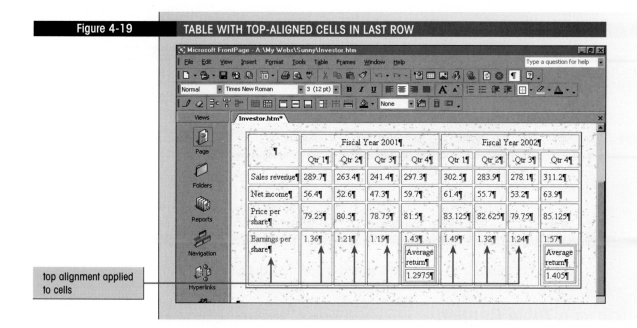

top alignment applied to cells

Next, Amanda wants you to change the horizontal alignment of the numeric data in the table to right. Right-aligning financial data is the standard when including currency amounts in a financial document.

To right-align numeric data in a table:

1. Select the cells in rows 3 through 6 and columns 2 through 9.

2. Click the **Align Right** button ▤ on the Formatting toolbar to right-align the data in these cells.

3. Click the cell in row 1, column 1 to deselect the cells.

4. Save the page.

Inserting a Picture in a Table

You can insert a picture in any table cell. If the picture is larger than the cell that holds it, FrontPage adjusts the size of the cell automatically to accommodate the picture's size. You follow the same process for inserting a picture in a cell as when inserting a picture elsewhere in a Web page. The only difference is that you select a cell as the location for the picture, instead of selecting a line in the Web page. Amanda already created a logo file that she wants you to include as a picture in the first cell of the table.

To insert a picture in a table cell:

1. With the insertion point in the cell in row 1, column 1, click the **Insert Picture From File** button 🖾 on the Standard toolbar to open the Picture dialog box.

2. Open the **Tutorial.04** folder on your Data Disk, and then double-click **FinPerf**. The Picture dialog box closes, and the logo appears in the first cell of the table. Because the picture is wider than the cell that contains it, the cell's size adjusted automatically to accommodate the picture. See Figure 4-20.

| Figure 4-20 | PICTURE INSERTED IN THE FIRST TABLE CELL |

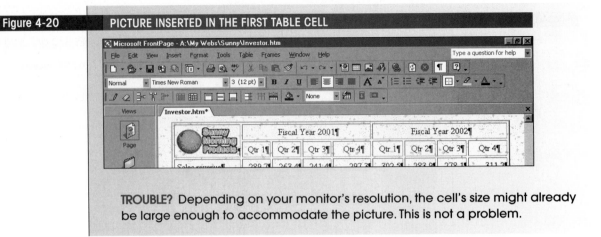

TROUBLE? Depending on your monitor's resolution, the cell's size might already be large enough to accommodate the picture. This is not a problem.

Amanda also wants you to add a caption to the table to identify its contents.

Adding a Table Caption

A **table caption** is a title that appears either above or below a table. It can contain one or more lines of text. Although the table caption appears to be a part of the table, it actually resides outside of the table's border and is created by a separate HTML tag. When you insert a caption, its default location is above the table. You can relocate the caption by clicking the Caption Properties command on the table's shortcut menu.

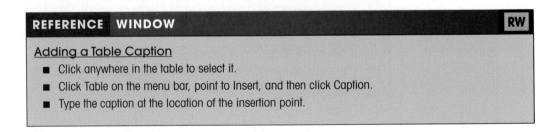

REFERENCE WINDOW   **RW**

Adding a Table Caption
- Click anywhere in the table to select it.
- Click Table on the menu bar, point to Insert, and then click Caption.
- Type the caption at the location of the insertion point.

Amanda asks you to add a caption at the top of the table.

To add a table caption:

1. Click **Table** on the menu bar, point to **Insert**, and then click **Caption**. A new line appears above the table, and the insertion point moves to the new line. This new line is the table's caption. Although the caption *looks* like any other line in Page view, it is formatted as an HTML caption and not as a new line.

2. Type **Summary of Financial Performance**.

3. Select the **Summary of Financial Performance** caption, and then click the **Bold** button **B** on the Formatting toolbar to change the caption to bold text.

4. Click anywhere in the **Summary of Financial Performance** caption to deselect it.

After adding a caption to a table, you can change its properties. For example, you might want to display the caption on two lines, or place one or more blank lines between the caption and the table. You can press Shift + Enter to create a new line in a caption. Another way to change an existing caption's properties is to use the settings in the Caption Properties dialog box.

Amanda wants you to move the caption to below the table to see if this positioning looks better.

To change caption properties and save the Web page:

1. Right-click the **Summary of Financial Performance** caption to open the shortcut menu, and then click **Caption Properties** to open that dialog box. See Figure 4-21.

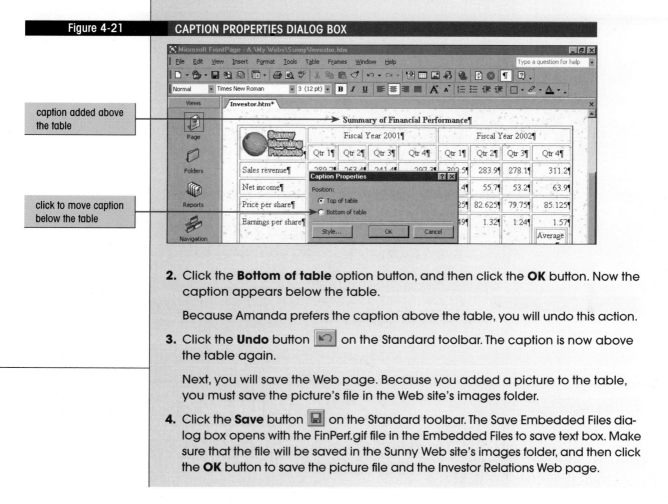

Figure 4-21   **CAPTION PROPERTIES DIALOG BOX**

caption added above the table

click to move caption below the table

2. Click the **Bottom of table** option button, and then click the **OK** button. Now the caption appears below the table.

   Because Amanda prefers the caption above the table, you will undo this action.

3. Click the **Undo** button on the Standard toolbar. The caption is now above the table again.

   Next, you will save the Web page. Because you added a picture to the table, you must save the picture's file in the Web site's images folder.

4. Click the **Save** button on the Standard toolbar. The Save Embedded Files dialog box opens with the FinPerf.gif file in the Embedded Files to save text box. Make sure that the file will be saved in the Sunny Web site's images folder, and then click the **OK** button to save the picture file and the Investor Relations Web page.

You are almost finished with the table. However, Amanda has some additional table properties that she wants you to set to enhance the table's appearance.

Setting Table Properties

After you create a table, you might decide to enhance its appearance with a background color and complementary cell and table border colors. You can also use a Table AutoFormat, which applies different formats to your table.

Applying a Table AutoFormat

When you apply a **Table AutoFormat**, FrontPage enhances the table with a predefined combination of colors, colored borders, and other special effects. A Table AutoFormat might be simple, colorful, classic, or three-dimensional. After applying an AutoFormat, you can use the Table Properties dialog box to change the AutoFormat to customize your table's appearance.

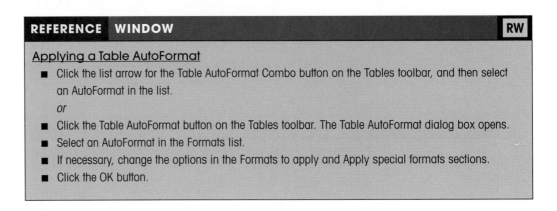

REFERENCE WINDOW — RW

Applying a Table AutoFormat
- Click the list arrow for the Table AutoFormat Combo button on the Tables toolbar, and then select an AutoFormat in the list.
  or
- Click the Table AutoFormat button on the Tables toolbar. The Table AutoFormat dialog box opens.
- Select an AutoFormat in the Formats list.
- If necessary, change the options in the Formats to apply and Apply special formats sections.
- Click the OK button.

Although Amanda is pleased with the appearance of the table in the Investor Relations page, she thinks that an AutoFormat might further enhance it.

To apply a Table AutoFormat to the table:

1. Click the **list arrow** for the Table AutoFormat Combo button | None ▼ | on the Tables toolbar, and then click **Simple 2**. See Figure 4-22. The table's format changes to use a white background color in the cells. The cell and table borders are hidden.

Figure 4-22   SIMPLE 2 TABLE AUTOFORMAT APPLIED TO TABLE

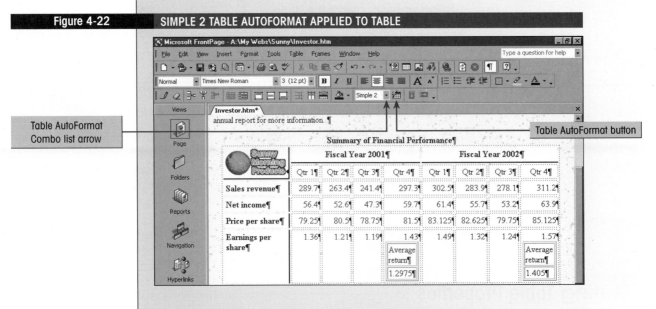

Table AutoFormat Combo list arrow

Table AutoFormat button

You could continue clicking the Table AutoFormat Combo list arrow and selecting different formats. However, an easier way to find a suitable Table AutoFormat is to use the Table AutoFormat dialog box.

2. Click the **Table AutoFormat** button 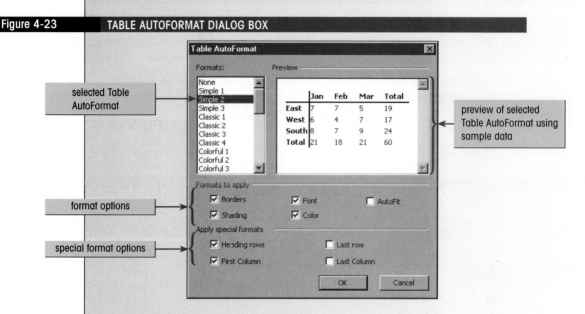 on the Tables toolbar. The Table AutoFormat dialog box opens. See Figure 4-23.

Figure 4-23   TABLE AUTOFORMAT DIALOG BOX

selected Table AutoFormat

preview of selected Table AutoFormat using sample data

format options

special format options

The Simple 2 format is selected, and a preview of its appearance is shown in the Preview box. Notice that you can also use this dialog box to control which formats are applied to your table. For example, deselecting a check box in the Formats to apply section omits those elements from the AutoFormat. In addition, you might want to apply or deselect special formats in your tables. A heading row is the first row in a table; it usually contains column headings. The table's first column usually contains row headings. You can also apply special formats to the last row and last column in a table when these table elements require special formatting.

Amanda wants to see whether any of the AutoFormats are more appealing than the Simple 2 format that you applied.

3. Click **Classic 3** in the Formats list. The Preview box shows the appearance for the Classic 3 format. This format's dark background might make the page difficult to read. In addition, the AutoFormat's color scheme doesn't match well with the current colors used in the Investor Relations page.

4. Scroll down the Formats list and click **3D Effects 1**. This format uses alternating dark and light background colors to distinguish rows in the table.

5. Scroll up the Formats list and click **Colorful 2**. This AutoFormat complements the colors in the Investor Relations page, so Amanda asks you to apply it.

6. Click the **OK** button. The table now uses the table's AutoFormat styles. See Figure 4-24.

| Figure 4-24 | COLORFUL 2 TABLE AUTOFORMAT APPLIED TO TABLE |

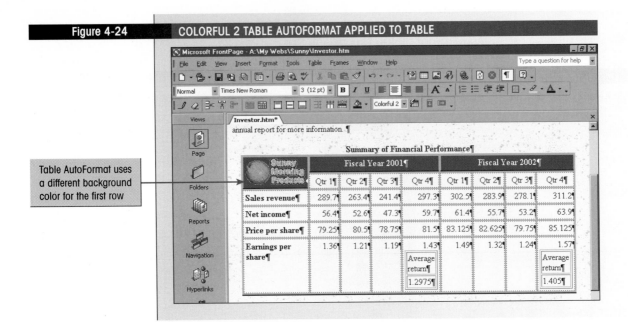

Table AutoFormat uses a different background color for the first row

Amanda thinks that the nested tables might stand out better with a different background color. The background color for a table or a specific cell is separate from the background specified for the Web page that contains the table. When you change a background color, you can either select from a list of common colors or open the More Colors dialog box and choose from a wide color spectrum.

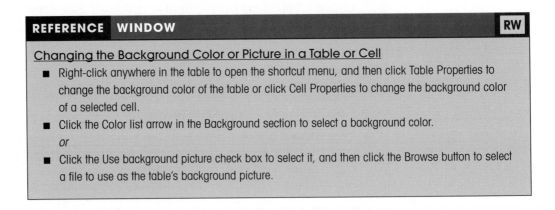

REFERENCE WINDOW   **RW**

Changing the Background Color or Picture in a Table or Cell
- Right-click anywhere in the table to open the shortcut menu, and then click Table Properties to change the background color of the table or click Cell Properties to change the background color of a selected cell.
- Click the Color list arrow in the Background section to select a background color.
 or
- Click the Use background picture check box to select it, and then click the Browse button to select a file to use as the table's background picture.

Amanda wants you to change the current background color of the nested tables to white.

To change the background color of the nested tables:

1. Right-click the first nested table to open the shortcut menu, and then click **Table Properties** to open that dialog box.

2. In the Background section, click the **Color** list arrow to display a list of available colors, and then click the **white** color.

3. Click the **OK** button. The white background is applied to the table.

TROUBLE? If the table's borders change to white, but the background color remains the same, then you changed the border color of the nested table instead of the background color. Click the Undo button 🔄 on the Standard toolbar, and then repeat Steps 1 through 3.

4. Repeat Steps 1 through 3 to change the background color of the second nested table to white.

Now Amanda wants you to change the color of the borders in the nested tables to maroon to match the color scheme used in the Colorful 2 Table AutoFormat.

REFERENCE WINDOW   **RW**

Changing a Table's Border Color
- Right-click the table to open the shortcut menu, and then click Table Properties.
- In the Borders section, click the Color list arrow, and then select a color for the table's borders.
- To change the cell's border colors, click the Light border list arrow and select a color for the bottom and right borders of each cell, and then click the Dark border list arrow and select a color for the top and left borders of each cell. Choose complementary colors to create a three-dimensional appearance or choose the same colors to create a solid cell border.
- Click the OK button.

To change the border colors of the table and cells:

1. Right-click the first nested table to open the shortcut menu, and then click **Table Properties**.

2. In the Borders section, click the **Color** list arrow, and then click the **maroon** color.

3. Click the **Light border** list arrow, and then click the **maroon** color.

4. Click the **Dark border** list arrow, and then click the **maroon** color.

5. Click the **OK** button to close the Table Properties dialog box. The first nested table appears with the new border colors.

6. Repeat Steps 1 through 5 to change the second nested table's border colors to maroon. The completed table is shown in Figure 4-25.

Figure 4-25   BACKGROUND AND COLORED BORDER ADDED TO NESTED TABLES

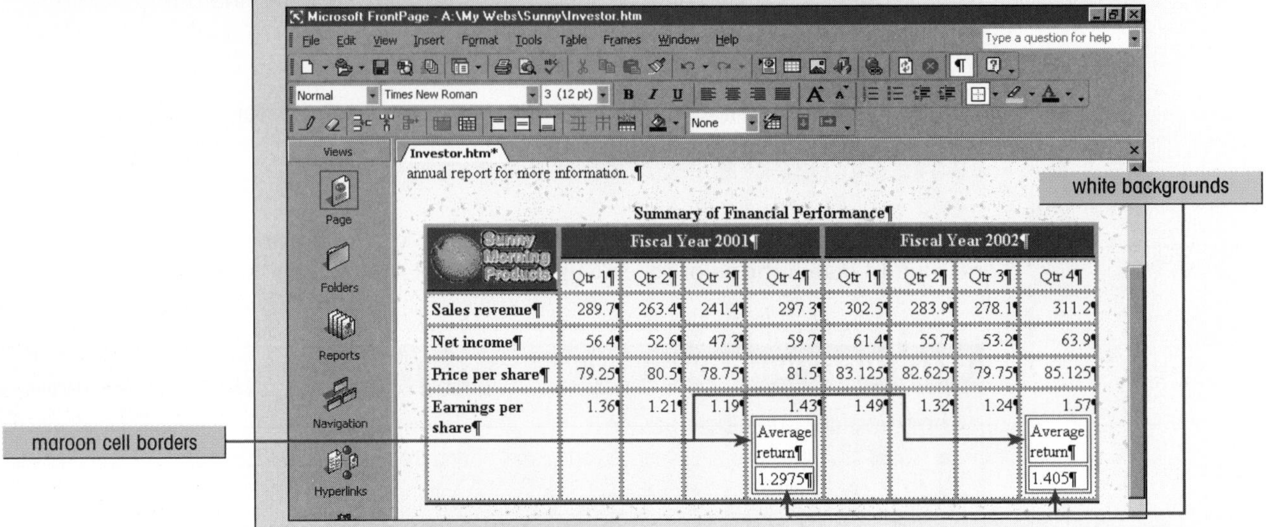

white backgrounds

maroon cell borders

7. Click the **Show All** button ¶ on the Standard toolbar to turn off the display of nonprinting characters.

8. Save the page.

Now that you've completed these table property changes, you are finished creating the table. Your task is not complete, however, until you test the appearance of the table in the browser. In this case, testing is especially important because you formatted the table to occupy a percentage of the window's width.

To test a table in the browser:

1. Click the **Preview in Browser** button on the Standard toolbar. If necessary, scroll down the page to review the table's appearance. Notice the appearance of the caption, background, picture, and nested tables.

2. Close the browser and return to FrontPage.

If you are more comfortable creating a table using a spreadsheet program (such as Excel) or a word processor (such as Word), you can create a table in another format and then insert the file in the Web page. FrontPage will recognize the table and convert it to HTML code. The HTML code that FrontPage produces for a table originally created in another program is the same, and you can use the tools in FrontPage to edit the inserted table as if you had originally created it using FrontPage.

Viewing **HTML Tags for a Table**

When you create a table in a Web page, whether using FrontPage or another program, you create a complex HTML document. For example, the <TABLE> and </TABLE> tags specify the beginning and end of the table. The <TR> and </TR> tags indicate the beginning and end of one row in the table, whereas individual <TD> and </TD> tags indicate the beginning and end of each cell. FrontPage generates a separate line for each cell in a table. The <DIV> tag and CENTER attribute cause the table to be centered in the page.

So that you can gain a better understanding of the HTML code that FrontPage used to create the Investor Relations page, Amanda asks you to view the page's HTML code.

To view the HTML code for a table and close FrontPage:

1. Click the **HTML** button to switch to HTML Page view, and then scroll the page until the <DIV ALIGN="CENTER"> tag appears at the top of the window. See Figure 4-26.

| Figure 4-26 | HTML CODE FOR THE SUMMARY OF FINANCIAL PERFORMANCE TABLE |

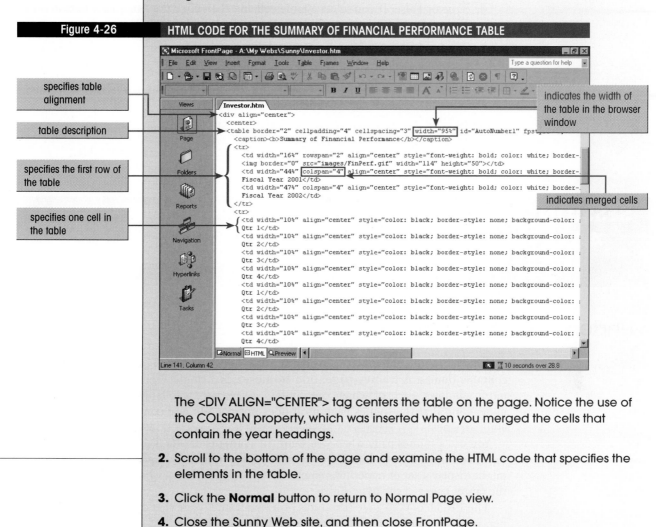

The <DIV ALIGN="CENTER"> tag centers the table on the page. Notice the use of the COLSPAN property, which was inserted when you merged the cells that contain the year headings.

2. Scroll to the bottom of the page and examine the HTML code that specifies the elements in the table.

3. Click the **Normal** button to return to Normal Page view.

4. Close the Sunny Web site, and then close FrontPage.

The Web site development team is happy with your progress. Your next assignment is to create a frames page in which to display the link bar, table of contents, and individual product Web pages.

Session 4.1 QUICK CHECK

1. What is the smallest component of a table?

2. Why should you create a table in a Web page using a percentage of the window size, instead of using fixed measurements such as inches or pixels?

3. _____ is the distance between the contents of a cell and its inside edge.

4. True or False: If you select a table cell and then click the Align Left button on the Formatting toolbar, you will left-align the selected cell's contents.

5. True or False: Clicking the Center button on the Formatting toolbar will center a table in a Web page.

6. When you insert a row in a table using the Tables toolbar, the new row appears _____ the currently selected row.

7. Describe two ways to merge two adjacent cells into a single cell.

8. The default location for a table's caption is _____ the table.

SESSION 4.2

In this session, you will create a new frames page using a template, import Web pages into the Sunny Web site to use in the frames page, and then specify the pages to open in the frames page. You will specify target frames for pages displayed in the frames page and use predefined frame names. Finally, you will test the frames page in a browser and examine its HTML code.

Understanding Frames

In Tutorial 1, you examined the Products Web page, which is an example of a Web page that contains frames. A **frames page**, or a **frameset**, is a single Web page divided into two or more windows, each of which can contain a separate, scrollable page. It is important to understand that the frames page itself does not contain any content—it contains only the empty frames.

You use a frames page when you want the contents of one frame in the browser window to remain unchanged while the contents of other frames change. For example, one frame might display a set of hyperlinks (such as a table of contents), while a second frame displays the target pages of the hyperlinks.

The Products Web page (Products.htm) is a frames page that contains three frames: banner, contents, and main. The Products Web page itself is just a set of empty frames; its HTML code specifies each frame's name and size. Amanda created a Web page that contains a link bar to open in the banner frame and a Web page that contains a table of contents with hyperlinks to open in the contents frame. The target pages of the hyperlinks in the contents frame will open in the main frame.

When you open a frames page in a browser, the browser first displays the frames page and then opens the pages that are specified to load into the individual frames. If the frames page contains three frames, your browser is really displaying *four* separate Web pages—the frames page and one page in each of the three frames. Figure 4-27 shows the Products frames page and describes how it works.

Figure 4-27	PRODUCTS FRAMES PAGE ACTIONS

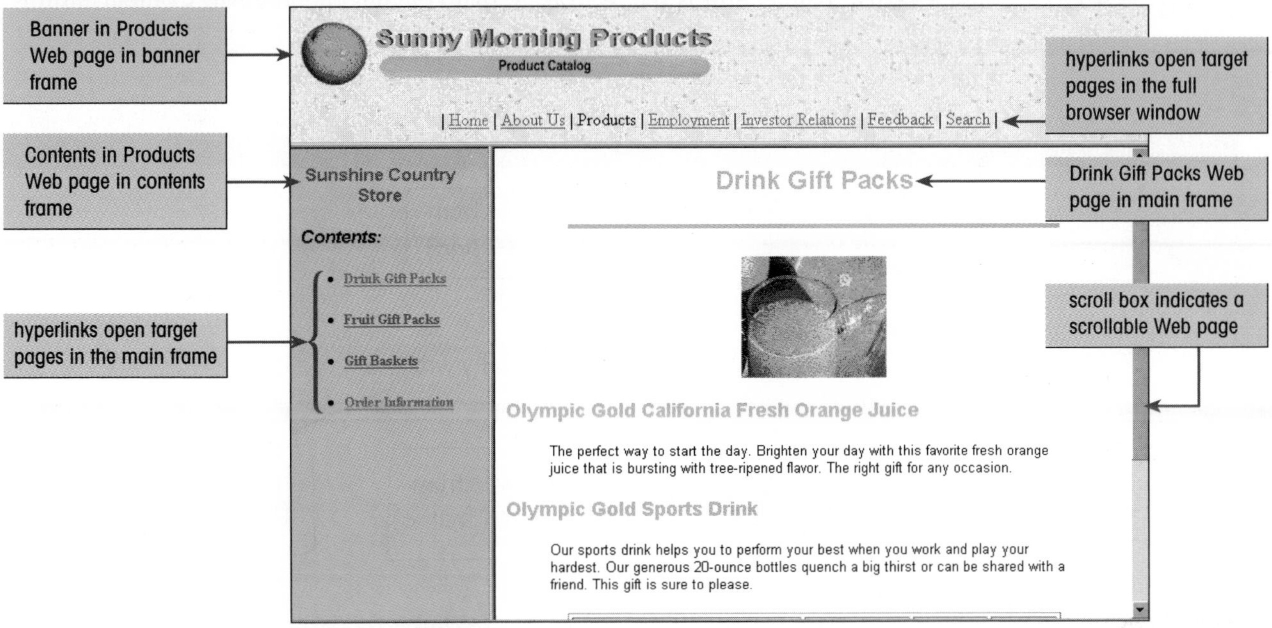

Banner in Products Web page in banner frame

Contents in Products Web page in contents frame

hyperlinks open target pages in the main frame

hyperlinks open target pages in the full browser window

Drink Gift Packs Web page in main frame

scroll box indicates a scrollable Web page

Frames provide Web site developers with a means to display two or more Web pages at once. An advantage of displaying multiple Web pages simultaneously is that a link bar or table of contents is always visible, making it easier to navigate the site. Using a frames page has some disadvantages as well. Some browsers cannot display Web pages that contain frames, which means that some visitors to your Web site might not see the frames page with the different Web pages. Therefore, you should use frames only when you are certain that your Web site's users will be able to display them. Another concern when using a frames page is that the page displayed in the main frame appears in a smaller window than when it is displayed in the full browser window. If the page in the main frame contains a lot of text, the user will need to scroll the page frequently to read its contents, which can be very distracting.

Creating a Frames Page

FrontPage includes many frames page templates that you can use to create a frameset. A **frames page template** is a Web page that contains the specifications for the individual locations and sizes of the frames in a frames page. When you create a frames page using a template, FrontPage assigns a default name to each frame. You can resize any of the frames in the frames page and change other frame properties after creating them.

Figure 4-28 shows Amanda's sketch of the Products Web page. Products.htm is the frames page, Banner.htm is the Web page that contains the link bar, Contents.htm is the Web page that contains the table of contents, and Drink.htm is one of the pages that will open in the main frame.

Figure 4-28	SKETCH OF THE PRODUCTS FRAMES PAGE

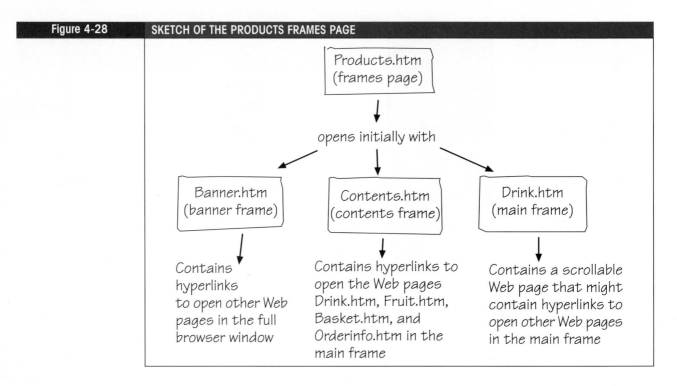

Figure 4-29 shows Amanda's planning analysis sheet for the development of the Products Web page.

Figure 4-29   AMANDA'S PLANNING ANALYSIS SHEET FOR THE PRODUCTS WEB PAGE

Planning Analysis Sheet

Objective

Create a frames page for displaying product information and accepting online orders. The page should include a link bar with hyperlinks to other Web pages in the Sunny Web site, a table of contents with hyperlinks that open Web pages in the main frame, and the individual product pages.

Requirements

Page for banner frame

Page for contents frame

Pages for main frame—one for each hyperlink in the contents frame

Picture files

Results

Products Web page with three frames: the banner frame will contain links to other Sunny Web pages, the contents frame will contain links that open pages in the main frame, and the main frame will display pages with product information

Clicking a hyperlink in the contents frame will open the target page in the main frame

Clicking a hyperlink in the banner frame will open the target page in the full browser window, replacing the frames page

Amanda wants you to create the Products Web page. She already created the pages that will open in the main frame.

REFERENCE   WINDOW   **RW**

Creating a Frames Page

- In the New from template section of the Task Pane, click Page Templates.
- In the Page Templates dialog box, click the Frames Pages tab.
- Click a template to see its preview and description.
- Double-click a template icon to close the Page Templates dialog box and to create the new frames page.

You will create the Products Web page using a frames page template.

To create a frames page:

1. Make sure that your Data Disk is in the appropriate disk drive, start FrontPage, and then open the **Sunny** Web site from your Data Disk.

2. If necessary, click the **Page** button 📄 on the Views bar to change to Page view.

3. In the New from template section of the Task Pane, click **Page Templates**. The Page Templates dialog box opens.

   TROUBLE? If the Task Pane is not open, click View on the menu bar, and then click Task Pane.

4. Click the **Frames Pages** tab to display the list of available frames page templates.

   You can preview a template to see its description and appearance before using it.

5. If necessary, click the **Banner and Contents** icon. A preview and description of the selected template appear on the right side of the Page Templates dialog box. See Figure 4-30.

Figure 4-30	PAGE TEMPLATES DIALOG BOX

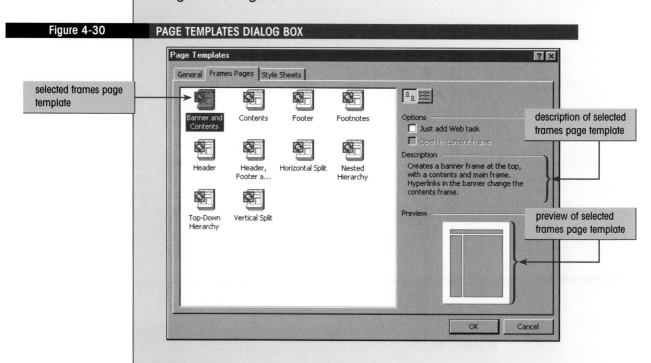

selected frames page template

description of selected frames page template

preview of selected frames page template

6. Select other templates and examine their previews and descriptions.

   The plan you reviewed with Amanda most closely matches the Banner and Contents template. This template has a banner frame, a contents frame, and a main frame.

7. Double-click the **Banner and Contents** icon to close the Page Templates dialog box and to create a new page. The new frames page opens in Page view using the title new_page_1.htm. (Your page might use a different number in the filename.) See Figure 4-31.

Figure 4-31	NEW FRAMES PAGE IN NORMAL PAGE VIEW

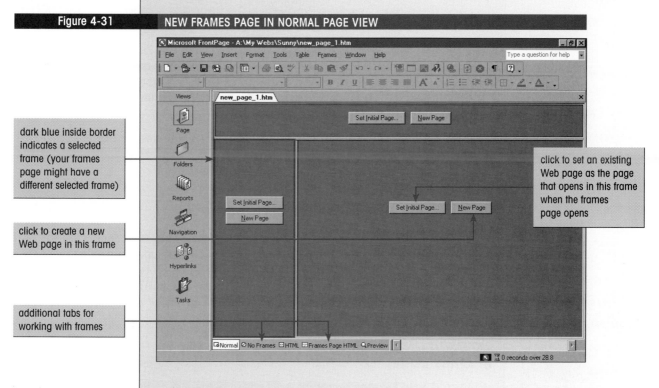

dark blue inside border indicates a selected frame (your frames page might have a different selected frame)

click to set an existing Web page as the page that opens in this frame when the frames page opens

click to create a new Web page in this frame

additional tabs for working with frames

Amanda asks you to save the new page.

8. Click the **Save** button 🖫 on the Standard toolbar. The Save As dialog box opens. See Figure 4-32.

Figure 4-32	SAVE AS DIALOG BOX

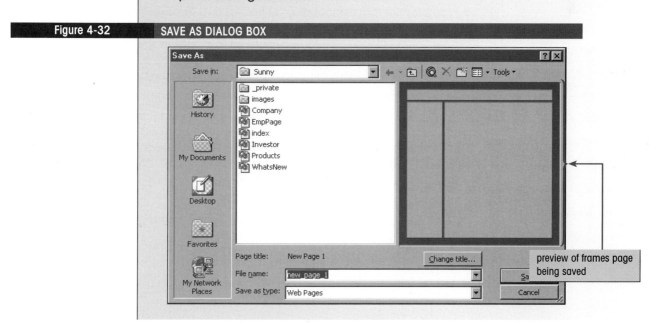

preview of frames page being saved

Notice that the Save As dialog box shows a preview of the frames page that you will save. The frames page contains three frames, as indicated by the thin borders. The frames page itself appears with a dark border.

9. Type **Products** as the filename, click the **Change title** button to open the Set Page Title dialog box, type **Products** in the Page title text box, click the **OK** button, make sure that the Save in list box displays the Sunny folder, and then click the **Save** button in the Save As dialog box.

   A message box opens, informing you that the Products.htm file already exists. Amanda reminds you that you added a page to the Web site in Tutorial 3 when you added the associated task to the Tasks list. The existing Products.htm file is blank, so you can replace the page.

10. Click the **Yes** button to replace the existing page. The frames page is saved in the Web site using the filename Products.htm.

Examining the HTML Code for a Frames Page

The Products Web page that you just created is only a single Web page with no content, except for three empty frames named banner, contents, and main. Notice that two new buttons—No Frames and Frames Page HTML—appear at the bottom of the Contents pane. These options appear when a frames page is open in Page view. Amanda wants you to examine the HTML code that created the frames page to learn more about frames pages.

To examine the No Frames page and the HTML code for a frames page:

1. Click the **No Frames** button at the bottom of the Contents pane. A new page opens in Page view and completely replaces the frames page. This page contains the text, "This page uses frames, but your browser doesn't support them." FrontPage created this page automatically with your frames page. If a Web browser that cannot display frames tries to open the frames page, this page will open in its place. Amanda explains that you could change the content of this page to include hyperlinks to pages that would otherwise be available in the frames page. Because you expect the Sunny Web site users to have current releases of browsers that support frames, you will not modify this No Frames page.

2. Click the **Frames Page HTML** button. The HTML code for the Products.htm page—the frameset—appears in this view. See Figure 4-33. Notice that the FRAME NAME tags identify the three frames—banner, contents, and main. Also notice that the title of the page, as specified by the TITLE tags, is Products.

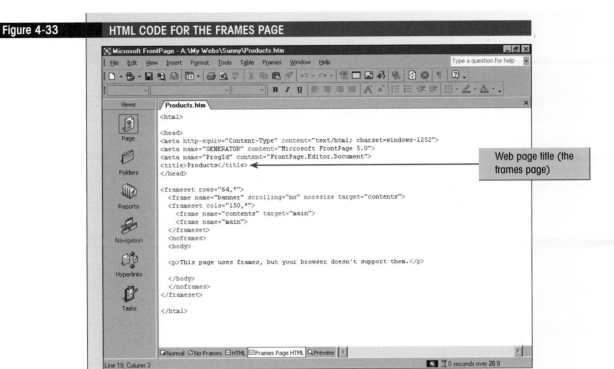

Figure 4-33   HTML CODE FOR THE FRAMES PAGE

3. Click the **Normal** button to return to Normal Page view.

Your next task is to set the page that opens in each frame when the Products Web page is opened in the browser. Amanda already created these pages for you. You can import them into the Sunny Web site and use them in the Products Web page.

Importing Web Pages for Use in a Frames Page

Before you can use Amanda's existing pages in the Products frames page, you must import them into the Sunny Web site. Then you will set these pages to open in the frames page.

To import pages for a frames page:

1. Click **File** on the menu bar, and then click **Import** to open the Import dialog box.

2. Click the **Add File** button to open the Add File to Import List dialog box. If necessary, open the **Tutorial.04** folder on your Data Disk, and then click **Banner** in the file list.

Rather than import the rest of the files from the list one at a time, you can select the remainder of the files to import all of the files you'll need at the same time.

3. Press and hold down the **Ctrl** key, click the files **Basket**, **Contents**, **Drink**, **Fruit**, **Ordrform**, and **Ordrinfo**, and then release the **Ctrl** key. All seven files are selected.

4. Click the **Open** button. The seven files you selected in Steps 2 and 3 are displayed and selected in the Import dialog box.

5. Click the **OK** button to import the files into the Sunny Web site.

TROUBLE? If you are storing your Web site on a floppy disk, it might take a few minutes to import these pages.

The pages that will open in the Products frames page are now saved in the Sunny Web site.

Setting Initial Pages for Frames

When you created the frames page, it displayed three frames, each containing a Set Initial Page button and a New Page button. Clicking the Set Initial Page button lets you specify an existing Web page (from the current Web site or from another location) as the page that opens in the selected frame. Clicking the New Page button lets you create a new blank page in the Web site and open it in the frame so you can enter its content. Creating a new page for use in any of the frames in the frames page is the same as creating a new Web page in Page view—the only difference is that you are creating and editing the new page in a frame. Because you previously imported the Web pages that will be used with the frames page, they already exist in the Sunny Web site.

Amanda wants you to specify, or set, the initial page to open for each frame in the Products Web page.

To set the initial pages for a frames page:

1. Click the **Set Initial Page** button in the banner frame. The banner frame is selected and the Insert Hyperlink dialog box opens. When you set the page, you are really creating a hyperlink to it.

2. Double-click **Banner**. The Insert Hyperlink dialog box closes and the Banner.htm page (Banner in Products) appears in the banner frame. Notice that the page contains a broken link, and you cannot see the page's content. You will fix these problems later.

TROUBLE? If you accidentally set the wrong page to open in a frame, right-click in the frame to select it and to open the shortcut menu, click Frame Properties, click the Browse button to the right of the Initial page text box to browse for and select the correct file, click the OK button, and then click the OK button again.

3. Repeat Steps 1 and 2 to set the **Contents** page (Contents in Products) to open in the contents frame on the left side of the frames page.

4. Repeat Steps 1 and 2 to select the **Drink** page (Drink Gift Packs) to open in the main frame on the right side of the frames page. Notice that a broken link to a picture appears in the Drink Gift Packs Web page. See Figure 4-34.

Figure 4-34 **INITIAL PAGES DISPLAYED IN THE FRAMES PAGE**

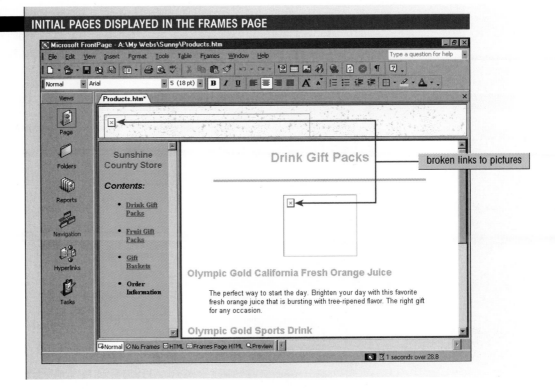

Editing the Frames in a Frames Page

The Web pages that you imported into the Sunny Web site and then set to open in the frames contain some problems that you must fix. First, the pages in the banner and main frames contain broken links to pictures, so you need to add these picture files to the Web site. The page in the banner frame is not visible, so you need to increase its height to see the page correctly. Finally, depending on your screen resolution, the page in the contents frame may contain a vertical scroll bar and possibly a horizontal scroll bar. Although the scroll bars allow users to scroll the contents of the page, the frame would be easier to view if they did not need to scroll the page, so you will resize the contents frame as well.

First, you will edit the frames to display the Web pages correctly.

To edit the frames:

1. Click the banner frame to select it. A dark blue border appears inside the banner frame to indicate that it is selected.

2. Move the pointer to the bottom frame border of the banner frame so that the pointer changes to a ↕ shape.

3. Click and hold down the mouse button on the bottom border of the banner frame, drag the frame border down about one inch, and then release the mouse button. After you release the mouse button, the link bar should be visible. (See Figure 4-35.)

   Now the contents frame contains a vertical scroll box in the vertical scroll bar. You can widen the contents frame so users won't need to scroll the page and to make the hyperlinks in that page appear on one line.

4. Click the contents frame to select it, and then click and drag its right border to the right about one-half inch so that each hyperlink is displayed on a single line. Now the vertical scroll box disappears and it is easier to view the hyperlinks in the contents frame. See Figure 4-35.

| Figure 4-35 | FRAMES PAGE AFTER RESIZING THE BANNER AND CONTENTS FRAMES |

banner frame now displays the full page

contents frame is wider

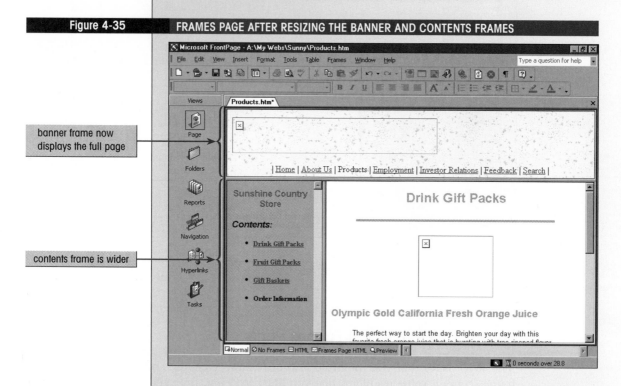

When you changed the sizes of the frames, you changed the HTML document that contains information about the frames. When you display a frames page in Page view, clicking the Save button saves the changes that you made to the pages in the frameset and to the frameset itself.

5. Click the **Save** button 🖫 on the Standard toolbar to save the frames page with these initial page settings.

Next, you need to embed the two missing picture files—one in the Banner in Products Web page and one in the Drink Gift Packs Web page. In Tutorial 3, you learned that when you import an existing Web page into a Web site, its embedded picture files are not imported along with the pages.

To embed pictures in the imported Web pages:

1. Right-click the **broken picture** icon ⊠ in the banner frame page to select it and open the shortcut menu, and then click **Picture Properties**. The Picture Properties dialog box opens.

2. Click the **General** tab, click the **Browse** button in the Picture source section to open the Picture dialog box, and then browse to and open the **Tutorial.04** folder on your Data Disk.

3. Double-click **Catalog** in the list to close the Picture dialog box, and then click the **OK** button to close the Picture Properties dialog box. The picture appears in the banner frame.

4. Click the **Save** button 🖫 on the Standard toolbar to open the Save Embedded Files dialog box, make sure that the Catalog.gif file will be saved in the Sunny Web site's images folder, and then click the **OK** button in the Save Embedded Files dialog box to save the picture.

   Next, insert the missing picture in the Drink Gift Packs page.

5. Repeat Steps 1 through 4 to add the **Juice** picture from the Tutorial.04 folder to the Drink Gift Packs Web page, and then save the file in the images folder.

Now that you have updated and saved the pages that open in the frames page, Amanda asks you to specify the other pages that should open in the main frame.

Specifying the Target Frame

A **target frame** is the designated frame in a frames page in which a Web page opens. For example, the target frame for the Drink Gift Packs Web page is the main frame of the Products Web page. When Amanda created the Contents.htm page, she specified the hyperlinks, including their target frames, except for the hyperlink to the Ordering Information page. Amanda asks you to modify the Contents page to include the hyperlink that opens the Ordering Information page in the main frame of the Products Web page.

To specify the target frame for a Web page:

1. In the contents frame, select **Order Information** as the text for the hyperlink, and then click the **Insert Hyperlink** button 🖳 on the Standard toolbar to open the Insert Hyperlink dialog box.

2. Scroll down the list of files until you see Ordrinfo, and then click **Ordrinfo** to select the Ordering Information page.

3. Click the **Target Frame** button. The Target Frame dialog box opens. See Figure 4-36.

   Look at the Common targets list box and verify that "Page Default (main)" is specified as the frame where the Ordering Information page will open. When you specify a hyperlink in the contents frame, the default setting is for the linked document to open in the main frame.

Figure 4-36	TARGET FRAME DIALOG BOX

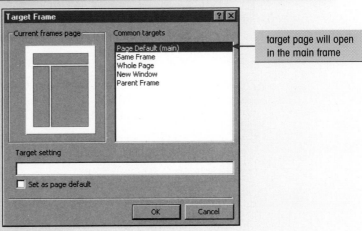

target page will open
in the main frame

4. Click the **OK** button to close the Target Frame dialog box, and then click the **OK** button to close the Insert Hyperlink dialog box.

5. Click **Order Information** in the contents frame to deselect it. The "Order Information" text now appears as a hyperlink.

6. Click the **Save** button 💾 on the Standard toolbar to save the Contents in Products page.

Examining a Frame's Properties

After creating a frames page, you can verify that the pages will open in the correct frames by checking the values in the Frame Properties dialog box. Amanda asks you to verify that the Drink Gift Packs page was specified as the default target page that opens in the main frame of the Products Web page.

To examine a frame's properties:

1. Right-click the main frame to select it and open the shortcut menu, and then click **Frame Properties**. The Frame Properties dialog box opens. See Figure 4-37.

| Figure 4-37 | FRAME PROPERTIES DIALOG BOX |

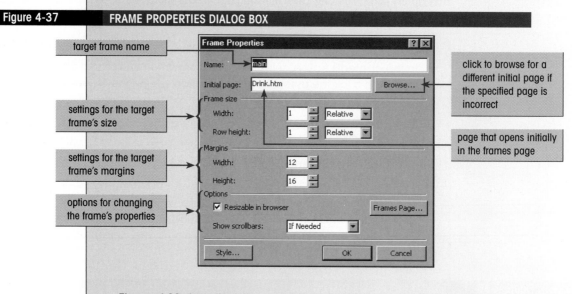

Figure 4-38 describes the changes that you can make to a selected frame using this dialog box.

Figure 4-38	OPTIONS IN THE FRAME PROPERTIES DIALOG BOX AND THEIR DESCRIPTIONS
OPTION	**DESCRIPTION**
Name	The name of the selected frame in the frames page.
Initial page	The filename of the page that opens in the named frame when the frames page is opened in the browser. Click the Browse button to change or set the page that opens initially.
Width (Frame size section)	The frame's width. Use the list box to specify the frame's width relative to other frames, to set the width as a percentage of the browser window's size, or to set the width as a fixed number of pixels. The default width is 1 with relative sizing.
Row height (Frame size section)	The frame's height. Use the list box to specify the frame's height relative to other frames, to set the height as a percentage of the browser window's size, or to set the height as a fixed number of pixels. The default height is 1 with relative sizing.
Width (Margins section)	The frame's margin width (in pixels), which indicates the amount of left and right space to indent the content in the frame from the inside frame border.
Height (Margins section)	The frame's margin height (in pixels), which indicates the amount of top and bottom space to indent the content in the frame from the inside frame border.
Resizable in browser check box	Select this check box to let users resize the current frame using a Web browser. Clear this check box to prevent users from resizing the frame.
Frames Page button	Opens the Page Properties dialog box with the Frames tab selected so that you can change the spacing between frames or turn the display of frame borders on or off.
Show scrollbars list box	Lets you specify whether to display scroll bars as needed for longer pages or to always or never display scroll bars.
Style button	Lets you change the style of the frames in the page; this topic is beyond the scope of this tutorial.

2. Verify that the Name text box displays the value "main" and that the Initial page text box has the value "Drink.htm." These values were set automatically when you set the Drink Gift Packs page to open in the main frame of the frames page. If you needed to revise any of these values, you could. For the Products frames page, they are correct.

3. Click the **OK** button to close the Frame Properties dialog box.

Now that you have specified all of the pages, you can test the frames page in a browser.

To test a frames page using a browser:

1. Click the **Preview in Browser** button [icon] on the Standard toolbar, and then click the **Yes** button to save your changes. The Products Web page opens in the browser and displays the Web pages that you specified in each frame.

2. Click the **Order Information** hyperlink in the contents frame. The Order Information page opens in the main frame.

3. Click the **Home** hyperlink in the link bar in the banner frame. The home page, which should open in the full browser window, opens in the contents frame. This indicates that a problem exists with the target frame for this hyperlink. See Figure 4-39.

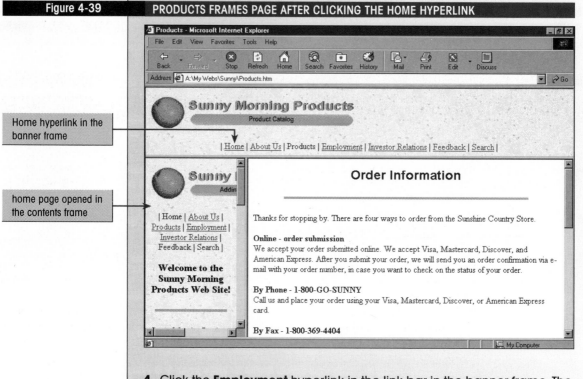

Figure 4-39   PRODUCTS FRAMES PAGE AFTER CLICKING THE HOME HYPERLINK

Home hyperlink in the banner frame

home page opened in the contents frame

4. Click the **Employment** hyperlink in the link bar in the banner frame. The Employment Web page replaces the entire Products Web page and opens in the full browser window. This action is the one that you want to occur when any page is opened from the link bar in the banner frame.

5. Click the **Products** hyperlink in the link bar. The Products Web page opens and replaces the Employment page in the browser window.

6. Close the browser.

When you clicked the link to the home page in the link bar in the banner frame, the page did not completely replace the Products frames page. Instead, the home page opened in the contents frame. You need to change the target frame for the home page by modifying its hyperlink in the link bar in the Banner in Products page so that the frames page will close before the home page opens. In other words, the target of the hyperlink should open in the full browser window without any frames.

Using Predefined Frame Names

When you use a FrontPage frames page template to create a frames page, the navigation between frames is already set up for you. For example, the Banner and Contents frames page template specifies that pages opened using hyperlinks in the contents frame will open in the main frame. For the Products frames page, you imported the pages that open into each frame into the Web site and included their existing hyperlinks into each frame, instead of creating them as new pages from within the frames page. Sometimes you might need to change the target frame for a hyperlink. For example, your testing in the previous section revealed that the Home hyperlink in the Banner in Products page did not open the home page correctly.

Four predefined frame names tell a Web browser where to open hyperlinked pages in a frames page. A **predefined frame name** is an HTML value that specifies which Web page to open and in which frame to open it. Figure 4-40 describes the four predefined frame names that you can use to specify target frames.

Figure 4-40	PREDEFINED FRAME NAMES	
HTML CODE	**PREDEFINED FRAME NAME**	**DESCRIPTION**
_self	Same Frame	The target of the hyperlink opens in the same frame as the page containing the hyperlink.
_top	Whole Page	The target of the hyperlink replaces the frames page and opens in the full browser window.
_blank	New Window	The target of the hyperlink opens in a new window. A new window means that a second instance of the browser starts and opens the page. Use this option to open a page that is related to the frames page's contents, but is not part of the frames page. For example, a page that contains information about eye discomfort might include a hyperlink that opens a page related to diseases of the eye in a new browser window.
_parent	Parent Frame	The target of the hyperlink opens a page that replaces the entire frameset that defines the frame containing the hyperlink.

The default target frame for a hyperlink is Page Default (*frame name*), where *frame name* is the name of the frame in which the page will open. For example, if you create a hyperlink in a page that appears in the contents frame, the default target frame for the hyperlinked page would be Page Default (main). If you do not specify a predefined frame name when creating a hyperlink, the target of the hyperlink will open in the main frame.

When Amanda created the link bar in the Banner in Products page, she specified the _top target frame for every hyperlink except for the Home hyperlink. In your testing, you confirmed this problem: The home page opened in the contents frame, whereas the Employment page opened correctly in the full browser window. Amanda wants you to learn how to change the target frame of a hyperlink, so she asks you to specify the _top target frame for the hyperlink to the home page.

To change the target frame for a hyperlink and test it in the browser:

1. Right-click the **Home** hyperlink in the link bar in the banner frame to open the shortcut menu, and then click **Hyperlink Properties** to open the Edit Hyperlink dialog box. The index.htm filename appears in the Address text box.

2. Click the **Target Frame** button to open the Target Frame dialog box. The current target frame, Page Default (contents), is selected in the Common targets list box, and the Target setting text box is empty. You need to change the target frame so that the home page opens in the full browser window, replacing the entire frames page. To do so, you must specify the Whole Page (_top) target setting.

3. Click **Whole Page** in the Common targets list box. FrontPage adds the HTML equivalent, _top, to the Target setting text box. See Figure 4-41.

Figure 4-41 | SETTING A NEW FRAME TARGET

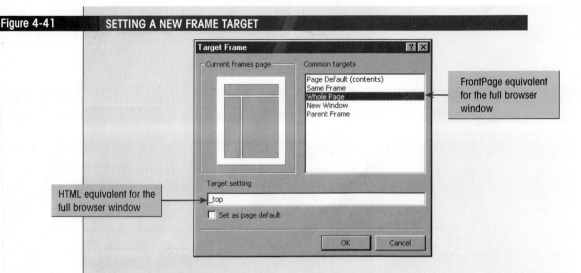

4. Click the **OK** button to close the Target Frame dialog box and return to the Edit Hyperlink dialog box. Notice that the Target frame section now displays the correct target frame, _top.

5. Click the **OK** button to close the Edit Hyperlink dialog box, and then click the **Save** button 🖫 on the Standard toolbar to save your changes.

6. Click the **Preview in Browser** button 🔍 on the Standard toolbar to open the revised Products frames page in the browser.

   Now test the page again to make sure that it works correctly.

7. Click the **Home** hyperlink in the link bar in the banner frame. The home page replaces the entire Products frames page in the browser. Your test is successful.

8. Close the browser.

You will need to change a target frame only when the desired target frame was not set correctly when you created your frames pages. Creating hyperlinks that open pages in frames can be a complicated chore, so it is important to test your frames pages thoroughly to ensure that all of the hyperlinked pages open correctly. You can also use Hyperlinks view to examine all of the hyperlinks to and from a frames page, and use Reports view to search for broken links.

Adding a New Frame to an Existing Frames Page

After creating a frames page, you can add a new frame to it by dividing an existing frame into two separate frames. To divide one existing frame into two frames, you hold down the Ctrl key while dragging the border of the existing frame that you want to divide to create a new frame. After adding the new frame, you can specify a Web page to open in the new frame by using the same procedure you followed for creating other pages in the frames page.

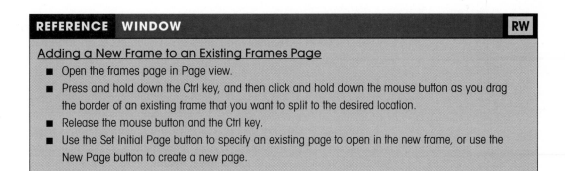

Amanda wants to add a sales slogan in a new frame in the Products frames page. She asks you to split the current main frame into two frames.

To add a new frame to an existing frames page:

1. Click the main frame to select it.

2. Press and hold down the **Ctrl** key, point to the bottom border of the main frame so the pointer changes to a ↕ shape, click and hold down the mouse button as you drag the border up about one inch, and then release the mouse button and the **Ctrl** key. A new frame is created, containing the Set Initial Page and New Page buttons. See Figure 4-42.

Figure 4-42   CREATING A NEW FRAME IN A FRAMES PAGE

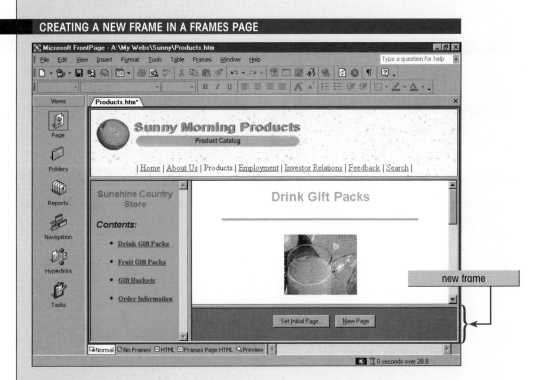

You could add the sales slogan to the new frame, but as Amanda looks at the entire frames page, she realizes that the main frame is now too small to display its content effectively. She asks you to restore the main frame to its original size.

3. Click the new frame to select it, click **Frames** on the menu bar, and then click **Delete Frame**. The new frame is deleted and the main frame returns to its original size.

4. Save the page.

FrontPage lets you divide existing frames within a frames page easily and quickly to provide the best presentation for your Web pages. Nevertheless, you must exercise care to avoid making a frame too small to be useful.

Now the Products frames page and its accompanying Web pages are complete. You will test all of the pages in the frameset in the Review Assignments.

Printing a Frames Page

Printing a frames page is not as straightforward as printing a Web page that does not contain frames. In FrontPage, you can print the individual Web pages that appear in each frame in a frames page, but you cannot print the frames page itself. For example, if you select the outer border for the frames page in Page view, the Print button on the Standard toolbar and the Print command on the File menu become disabled. If you select an individual frame in the frames page, you can use either of these methods to print the page that appears in that frame.

When you view a frames page in the browser, you have more options for printing the frames page. If you click File on the menu bar and then click Print, you can use the Print dialog box to select what to print. Figure 4-43 shows the Print dialog box in Internet Explorer.

Figure 4-43	PRINT DIALOG BOX IN INTERNET EXPLORER

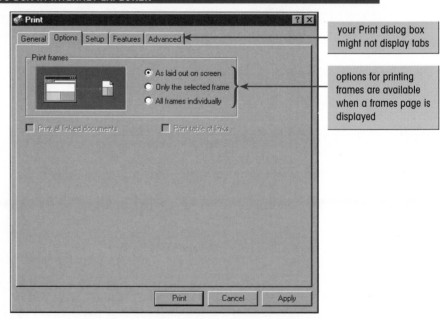

your Print dialog box might not display tabs

options for printing frames are available when a frames page is displayed

When a frames page is open in the browser, the Print frames section displays three options:

- The "As laid out on screen" option prints the frames page as it appears on the screen. In other words, this option prints the full content of the pages that you see in the browser window.

■ The "Only the selected frame" option prints the active frame. This is the default option; when you click the Print button on the toolbar, the selected frame prints automatically.

■ The "All frames individually" option prints the full content of each page in the frames page on a separate sheet of paper.

Amanda wants you to print the frames page, not just the individual pages contained within the frames page.

To print the frames page:

1. Click the **Preview in Browser** button 🔍 on the Standard toolbar to open the Products Web page in the browser.

2. Click **File** on the menu bar, and then click **Print**. The Print dialog box opens. If necessary, click the **Options** tab to display those settings.

   TROUBLE? If you are using Netscape Navigator, you must click each frame to select it, and then click the Print button on the toolbar to print each frame's contents individually. Navigator does not have an option to print the frames page. Skip to Step 4 to after printing each of the three frames.

3. Click the **As laid out on screen** option button in the Print frames section, and then click the **Print** button (or the **OK** button). Internet Explorer prints the contents of the frames page as it appears on the screen.

4. Close the browser.

Viewing HTML Tags for a Frames Page

When you viewed the HTML code for the frames page earlier in this session, you saw only the HTML code that created the frames page. Now Amanda wants you to examine the HTML code for the frames page again, so you can see the HTML code that FrontPage created to display the Web pages in the frames page. The FRAMESET tags indicate the beginning and end of the frameset and specify each frame in the frames page. Within the FRAME tag, the SRC property indicates the filename for the target page, and the NAME property identifies the name of the frame in which to display the target page. The ROWS and COLUMNS properties of the FRAMESET tag indicate the layout of the frames as a percentage of the size of the page when it is displayed in the browser.

To view the HTML code for a frames page:

1. Click the **Frames Page HTML** button to display the HTML code for the Products frames page. See Figure 4-44. For each frame in your frames page, the HTML code specifies the frame's name (FRAME NAME), the page to open initially (SRC), and the size of the frame (FRAMESET COLS).

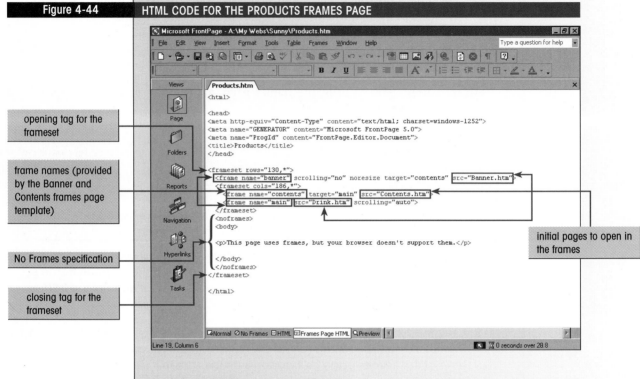

Figure 4-44   HTML CODE FOR THE PRODUCTS FRAMES PAGE

2. Click the **HTML** button. The HTML code for each page displayed in the frames page appears in each frame.

3. Click the **Normal** button to return to Normal Page view.

4. Close the Sunny Web site, and then close FrontPage.

With the Investor Relations and Products pages complete, you review your progress with Amanda and the rest of the Web site development team. The summary of financial performance table adds key information to the Investor Relations page in an organized and attractive format. The Products frames page lets customers easily examine the categories of products available from the Sunshine Country Store. In the next tutorial, you will learn how to enhance the appearance of the Web site by applying a Web theme.

Session 4.2 QUICK CHECK

1. True or False: A frames page does not contain any content; it contains only the specifications that define the empty frames.

2. A frames page that displays two frames will display _____ Web pages when it is opened in the browser.

3. True or False: You can use a frames page without hesitation because all browsers can display frames.

4. Click the _____ button in Page view to examine the HTML code for a frames page.

5. Click the _____ button in an empty frame to specify an existing Web page to open when the browser loads the frames page.

6. Which predefined frame name causes the browser to remove all loaded frames pages before displaying the target of a selected hyperlink?

7. The HTML tag that specifies the beginning of a frames page is _____.

REVIEW ASSIGNMENTS

During your meeting with the Web site development team, you received feedback on how to improve the Investor Relations and Products Web pages. The team suggests adding two additional tables of information to the Investor Relations page. They also suggest creating a new Web page for the company's new clothing line, which includes T-shirts, tote bags, and other items. You will create the Clothing Web page and set it to open in the main frame of the Products Web page.

If necessary, insert your Data Disk in the appropriate disk drive, start FrontPage, and then do the following:

1. Open the **Sunny** Web site from your Data Disk in Folders view.

2. Open the Investor Relations page (**Investor.htm**) in Page view, and then display the non-printing characters (if necessary). Change the cells in row 2, columns 2 through 9, to bold.

Explore

3. Insert a new row at the bottom of the summary of financial performance table. (*Hint:* Use the Table menu to insert the new row below the existing last row in the table.) Then use the Eraser to merge all of the cells in the new row into a single cell and change the cell's vertical alignment to centered.

4. Add the following text to the cell you created in Step 3: "Note: All amounts in millions, except per share amounts, which are in dollars." Center the text in the cell, decrease the font size to 10 points, and then change the text color to red.

Explore

5. Add the table of stock trading information shown in Figure 4-45 below the summary of financial performance table. Separate the two tables on the page with one blank line. Use the same properties for the new table (alignment, size, cell padding, Table AutoFormat, and so on) as for the summary of financial performance table. Change the data in the third column to bold, add the caption "Stock Trading Information" at the top of the table, and then change it to bold.

Figure 4-45

Sunny Morning Products (SNY) New York Stock Exchange (NYSE)			
Last Traded at	**85.125**	Date/Time	**May 31 15:54:00**
$ Change	**2.125**	% Change	**2.59**
Volume (000)	84.7	# of Trades	104
Open	82.5	Previous Close	81.875
Day Low	82.25	Day High	83.25
52-Week Low	73.25	52-Week High	87.25

Explore   6. Apply a custom background color of your choice to the two nested tables in the summary of financial performance table that you created in the tutorial. (*Hint:* Right-click the first nested table to open the shortcut menu, click Table Properties, click the Color list arrow in the Background section, and then click More Colors to open the More Colors dialog box. Click the Custom button to open the Color dialog box. Click any color in the Basic colors section, and then click in the color spectrum and look at the Color | Solid preview boxes to see the color. When you find a color that you like and one that will not interfere with the readability of the text in the cell, click the Add to Custom Colors button, and then click the OK button. Close the remaining dialog boxes. To apply the same color to the second nested table, select the color in the Document's colors section on the Background Color palette.) Save the Investor Relations Web page.

Explore   7. Use a word processor or spreadsheet program to create a third table for the Investor Relations page. Your table should include the following information about shareholders: Fiscal Year 2001: 251,215 shareholders, 74,512,255 shares transacted, 16% increase; and Fiscal Year 2002: 352,584 shareholders, 84,752,922 shares transacted, 29% increase. Determine the best way to present this information using a table. If you use a word processor to create the table, make sure that you use its Table commands. Save the file as **Shareholder** in the Tutorial.04 folder on your Data Disk with the default file extension, and then close your word processor or spreadsheet program.

Explore   8. Insert two blank lines after the stock trading information table, and then click the second blank line. (If necessary, use the Decrease Indent button on the Formatting toolbar to delete the tab stops on this line.) Insert the file that you created in Step 7 in the Investor Relations Web page. Add an appropriate caption at the top of the table, and then change it to bold. Use the same properties for the new table (alignment, size, cell padding, Table AutoFormat, and so on) as for the other tables in this page.

9. Save the Investor Relations Web page, and then turn off the display of nonprinting characters. Preview the page in the browser, and then use the browser to print the page and its HTML code. Close the browser.

Explore   10. Return to FrontPage, and then design and create a new Web page named and titled **Clothing** to introduce the company's new line of T-shirts, sweatshirts, and tote bags. Write and format the page based on the writing style, format, and content of other pages in the Web site. Save the page.

11. Open the Products Web page (**Products.htm**) in Page view, and then create a new entry in the bulleted list in the contents frame page with a hyperlink to open the Clothing Web page in the main frame. (*Hint:* Click the line below the Order Information bullet, and then click the Bullets button. Otherwise, the spacing between items will not be equal.) If necessary, change the font and style of the new hyperlink to match the other hyperlinks in the contents frame. Save your changes.

12. Open the Products Web page in the browser and test all of its hyperlinks. If necessary, return to FrontPage and correct the problems that you discover, including fixing broken links to picture files. Specify the **OrgBack.jpg** file as the background picture for the Ordering Information page (**Ordrinfo.htm**). Save the picture files for each page in the Web site's images folder. (*Hint:* The picture files are saved in the Tutorial.04 folder on your Data Disk.)

Explore   13. Revise the Banner in Products page in the Products frames page by creating a table that contains each of the navigation entries. (*Hint:* Rather than using the vertical bar to separate navigation choices, display them in a table with a single row. Use the Help system to learn more about the Convert Text to Table command on the Table menu. Use the vertical bar symbol as the "Other" separator value.) Change the border colors of the cells and the table to navy. If any extra cells are created when you convert the text to a table, select and then delete them. If necessary, adjust the banner frame's size so that the link bar is completely visible. Save your changes, and then test the revised frames page in the browser. Open the Clothing page in the main frame, and then print the Products page as it appears in the browser. Close the browser.

14. Open the Tasks list and mark the Finish Investor.htm and Finish Products.htm tasks as completed.

Explore

15. Open the Products Web page in HTML Page view, and then print the HTML code for the individual Web pages displayed in the frames page. (*Hint:* Select a frame, and then click the Print button on the Standard toolbar. Print the HTML code for each frame separately.)

16. Close the **Sunny** Web site, and then close FrontPage.

CASE PROBLEMS

Case 1. Building an Investors Page for Royal Hair Care Products   Sales of Quick Dry Solution have boosted the profitability of Royal Hair Care Products' operations. Valerie Suarez met with the company's senior managers to present an update on the company's Web site. The management team asked Valerie to expand the Web site to include information required by the company's investors, such as information about the company's financial and stock performance. After the meeting, Valerie revised her Web site plan to include a new Web page and collected the necessary information for its content from the appropriate individuals. She asked Nathan Dubois to sketch and create a Web page of the stock market performance information. Valerie wants you to help Nathan complete the financial information page.

If necessary, start FrontPage, insert your Data Disk in the appropriate disk drive, and then do the following:

1. Read all of the questions for this case problem, and then prepare a planning analysis sheet for the changes to the Web site.

2. Open the **Royal** Web site from your Data Disk in Page view. (If you did not create this Web site in Tutorial 2 and change it in Tutorial 3, ask your instructor for assistance.)

Explore

3. Create a frames page using the Banner and Contents template. Save the frames page with the filename **RInvest** and the title "Financial Information."

4. Create the new Financial Performance Web page in the main frame, and then save it using the filename **RFinInfo** and the title "Financial Performance." Display the non-printing characters, and then create the table shown in Figure 4-46 in the page in the main frame. Use the Fill commands as necessary to enter the data. Add the caption "Financial Performance Information" above the table, and then change it to bold.

Figure 4-46

	Fiscal Year 2002			
	Qtr 1	Qtr 2	Qtr 3	Qtr 4
Sales revenue	421.3	474.2	508.1	480.3
Net income	14.0	14.1	14.5	14.2
Price per share	34.250	33.625	36.125	32.250
Earnings per share	2.20	2.19	2.30	2.01
Note: All amounts in thousands, except per share amounts, which are in dollars.				

5. Apply an appropriate AutoFormat to the table. Change the alignment of numeric data to right, and center the column headings. Change the style of the row and column headings to bold.

6. Import the **RStock.htm** file from your Data Disk into the Web site. This page contains the stock performance information and will open in the main frame of the frames page.

Explore ▶ 7. Create a new page in the banner frame named and titled **Banner**. Insert a centered, user-defined link bar that contains the same entries as the link bar in the home page. (*Hint:* Use the Windows Clipboard to copy the link bar from the home page and paste it into the Banner page. You will create the hyperlink to the home page in Step 8.) Change the link bar to use a table with a single row. (*Hint:* Use the Help system to learn more about the Convert Text to Table command on the Table menu.) Delete any extra cells that are created after the conversion. When a user clicks a hyperlink in the link bar in the banner frame, the target page should replace the frames page and open in the full browser window. (*Hint:* Use the Edit Hyperlink dialog box to verify and change the target frame of any existing hyperlinks in the link bar.) The link bar should have active hyperlinks to the following pages: **RCompany.htm**, **RNews.htm**, **REmploy.htm**, and **RFeedbak.htm**.

Explore ▶ 8. Create a hyperlink in the banner frame that opens the home page in the full browser window. Center the data in the new cell. Save your changes.

9. Create a new page in the contents frame named and titled **Contents**. The entries in the table of contents should appear on separate lines in the contents frame. Create hyperlinks to the pages that will open in the main frame (**RFinInfo.htm** and **RStock.htm**).

10. Verify that the **RFinInfo.htm** page is the default page that opens in the main frame when the frames page is opened in the browser. Save your changes.

Explore ▶ 11. Use the browser to test the frames page and make sure that each of the hyperlinks results in the appropriate action. If necessary, return to FrontPage to create new hyperlinks in the link bars in other pages in the Web site that open the new **RInvest.htm** frames page. Save your changes to each page. Then use the browser to print all three pages individually in the frames page with the Financial Performance Web page displayed in the main frame. Close the browser.

12. Use FrontPage to print the HTML code for the frames page (**RInvest.htm**) and the Banner page (**Banner.htm**).

13. Display the **RInvest.htm** page as the center focus in Hyperlinks view, expand the hyperlinks for the **Contents.htm** page, and then print Hyperlinks view using WordPad.

14. Close the **Royal** Web site, and then close FrontPage.

Case 2. Creating a "What" Page for Buffalo Trading Post   Retail-clothing customers usually want to know which items are the current best-sellers. At Buffalo Trading Post, Donna Vargas and Karla Perez decided that a list of the current top 10 hot items would be a great addition to the Web site. As you discuss this concept with a sales associate, you conclude that there are three main areas of interest: women's clothing, children's clothing, and accessories. Karla asks you to help create the "What" page.

If necessary, start FrontPage, insert your Data Disk in the appropriate disk drive, and then do the following:

1. Read all of the questions for this case problem, and then prepare a planning analysis sheet for the changes to the Web site.

2. Open the **Buffalo** Web site from your Data Disk in Page view. (If you did not create this Web site in Tutorial 2 and change it in Tutorial 3, ask your instructor for assistance.)

3. Donna wants you to use a frames page to implement the top 10 list of hot items by creating a separate Web page for each of the following categories: women's clothing, children's clothing, and accessories. Use the Banner and Contents frames page template to create a new frames page with the filename **BWhat** and the title "What." Replace the existing **BWhat.htm** file that you created with the Tasks list in Tutorial 3.

Explore ▷ 4. Create a new Web page in the banner frame with the filename and title **Banner**. Design and create a table that will contain the entries for the link bar. Your table design should include a cell with a picture for each of the following navigation choices: Home, Who, How, Where, and Contact.

Explore ▷ 5. Change the background, light border, and dark border colors of the table that you created in Step 4 to white so that the table's borders are not visible. Insert the **BWhatLog.gif** picture as a centered logo in this page, and then insert the following pictures in the appropriate cells in the table that you created in Step 4: **BNavHome.gif**, **BNavWho.gif**, **BNavHow.gif**, **BNavWhre.gif**, and **BNavCon.gif**. (*Hint:* The picture files are saved in the Tutorial.04 folder on your Data Disk. Turn on the nonprinting characters to see the table cells.) Center the pictures in the cells. Add appropriate alternative text to each picture. Change the height of the banner frame so that the logo and table contents are visible. Save the picture files in the Web site's images folder.

6. Create the hyperlinks for the Home, Who, and How pictures to open the appropriate pages in the full browser window.

7. Create a new page in the contents frame with the filename and title **Contents**. Create a list that you will format as hyperlinks to each page that will open in the main frame, and then format the list as a bulleted list.

Explore ▷ 8. Design one table for the hot items list for each category. Each table should include the name of the item, a brief description, and a current price range. Then create separate Web pages to open in the main frame of the frames page for each table, using appropriate filenames and titles for each page. Set the page for the women's category to open as the default page in the main frame. Format the list in the Contents page as hyperlinks that open the appropriate pages in the main frame. Save each page.

Explore ▷ 9. Test the frames page in a browser and verify that clicking each hyperlink results in the appropriate action. If you encounter any problems during testing, return to FrontPage and correct them. Then use the browser to print the frames page as it appears in the browser with the Accessories page displayed in the main frame. Close the browser.

Explore ▷ 10. Use FrontPage to print the HTML code for the frames page. Circle the FRAME tags that specify the name of each default page that opens in a frame and the name of the frame in which the page opens.

Explore ▷ 11. Display the What page (**BWhat.htm**) as the center focus in Hyperlinks view, expand the hyperlinks from the **Contents.htm** page, and then print Hyperlinks view using WordPad.

Explore ▷ 12. Run a Site Summary report to discover any broken hyperlinks, and then correct the problems.

13. Close the **Buffalo** Web site, and then close FrontPage.

Case 3. Developing the Menu Pages for Garden Grill   Nolan Simmons and Shannon Taylor, members of the Web site development team at Garden Grill, just returned from a meeting with Don Cook, who runs the marketing department. During the meeting, Don described his vision of the restaurant menu Web pages that will allow Garden Grill to remain competitive in the casual, full-service restaurant industry. Ideally, customers should be able to view the menu from their homes or offices before coming to the restaurant. The Web site will contain four separate menu pages—one each for appetizers, sandwiches, entrees, and desserts. Don wants to use a table to arrange the entries in each menu. He asks you to help Shannon develop these Web pages.

If necessary, start FrontPage, insert your Data Disk in the appropriate disk drive, and then do the following:

1. Read all of the questions for this case problem, and then prepare a planning analysis sheet for this enhancement to the Web site.

2. Open the **Garden** Web site from your Data Disk in Page view. (If you did not create this Web site in Tutorial 2 and change it in Tutorial 3, ask your instructor for assistance.)

3. Use the Contents frames page template to create the menu as a frames page. Save the page with the filename **GMenu** and the title "Menu."

4. Sketch the design and contents of each table that will contain the menu items in each menu category. Each table should include at least three menu choices and cells for each item's name, description, and price.

5. Create a new page to open in the contents frame with the filename and title **Contents**. The Contents Web page should include hyperlinks to each menu page, with the main frame being the target for the four menu category pages. Create an appropriate target for the home page so that it replaces the entire frames page and opens in the full browser window.

6. Create the four Web pages according to your design. Create appropriate filenames and titles for each page.

7. Insert the **Garden.gif** picture from the **Garden** Web site's images folder at the top of each page that you created in Step 6. Save each page as you complete it.

8. Edit the frames page so that the Appetizers Web page opens first when the Menu frames page is opened in the browser.

Explore ▶ 9. Apply complementary background and border colors to the table in each of the menu category pages. Then change the background color of the Contents page to use the same background as the home page. Save each page as you finish it.

10. Create a hyperlink from the home page to the Menu Web page. Make sure that each Web page in the Web site contains active hyperlinks to the site's other pages. Test each of the hyperlinks in the frames page using the browser. If you encounter any problems during testing, return to FrontPage and correct them.

Explore ▶ 11. Create a new frame in the Menu page by splitting the contents frame. Drag the bottom border of the contents frame up approximately two inches to create the new frame. Next, create a new Web page in the new frame with the filename **Contact** and the title "Contact Us." Apply the same background to the Contact Us Web page that you applied to the home page, and then enter the following text: "Didn't find your favorites? Send your menu suggestions to" and then press the spacebar and create a mailto with your e-mail address. (Don't worry if your e-mail address is longer than the frame's width.) Save the page.

12. Test the frames page in a browser. If necessary, use the pointer to increase the height and width of the contents and contact frames so they do not contain any scroll bars. Use the browser to print the frames page as it is laid out with the Desserts Web page displayed in the main frame. Close the browser.

Explore   13. Use FrontPage to print the HTML code for the frames page. Circle the FRAME tags that specify the name of each default page that opens in a frame and the name of the frame in which the page opens.

14. Display the Menu Web page (**GMenu.htm**) as the center focus in Hyperlinks view, expand the hyperlinks for the **Contents.htm** Web page, and then print Hyperlinks view using WordPad.

Explore   15. Run a Site Summary report to discover any broken hyperlinks, and correct any problems.

16. Close the **Garden** Web site, and then close FrontPage.

Explore   *Case 4. Preparing a Specials Page for Replay Music Factory*   Charlene Fields is pleased with your progress in assisting Alec Johnston with the development of the company's Web site. During a recent management meeting, Charlene presented the content of the current Replay Web site and received feedback from members of Replay's senior management team. Cassady Spruiell, senior marketing manager, suggested including a Specials Web page in the Web site that would contain a list of the CDs for which Replay wants to provide additional exposure. Cassady wants to use the Specials page to promote several different music categories. She approved a design using a frames page in which the contents page would display the selection of music types and the main page would display the available specials for that music type. Furthermore, Cassady wants you to arrange the specials for each music type as a table so that the information in each page is easy to read. Charlene asks you to assist Alec with this Web revision.

If necessary, start FrontPage, insert your Data Disk in the appropriate disk drive, and then do the following:

1. Read all the questions for this case problem, and then prepare a planning analysis sheet for this enhancement to the Web site.

2. Open the **Replay** Web site from your Data Disk in Page view. (If you did not create this Web site in Tutorial 2 and change it in Tutorial 3, ask your instructor for assistance.)

3. Sketch the appearance of the Specials frames page. Your frames page should include at least one frame for the table of contents with each of the types of music and one frame to display the individual page with the details of each type of music. At least one of the tables should contain a nested table.

4. Create a new frames page using a template that closely matches your design. (*Hint:* If you do not find a frames page template that matches your design, adjust your design to match an existing template.) Save the frames page with the filename **MSpecials.htm** and the title "Specials."

5. Sketch the design of each of the tables that you will use on each music category page. Include a minimum of three different music types of your choice. Each special music offering should include information that indicates the artist, title, identification number, and current price.

6. Create all the Web pages for your design using real or fictitious data. The user should be able to return to the home page using a hyperlink displayed in a contents page. Format the links in the contents page that open pages in the main frame as a table. Apply an appropriate AutoFormat to this table.

7. Specify the hyperlinks for displaying each of the pages for the type of music in a main frame. Adjust the sizes of the frames in the frames page as necessary to accommodate the text that they contain.

8. Using either the Contents Web page or a page displayed in another frame, specify the hyperlinks for all the other pages that are opened from this frames page. For any page that is not part of the frames page, that page should replace the entire frames page and open in the full browser window.

9. Display one of the music type pages as the initial page in the main frame when the frames page is opened in the browser.

10. Use the browser to test the frames page to make sure each of the hyperlinks results in the appropriate action. If you discover any problems during testing, return to FrontPage and correct them. (*Hint:* Make sure that each page in the Web site that contains content includes a link to the new Specials page.) Close the browser.

11. Use FrontPage to print each of the pages that opens in your frames page.

12. Run a Site Summary report to discover any broken links, and then correct the problems.

13. Close the **Replay** Web site, and then close FrontPage.

QUICK | CHECK ANSWERS

Session 4.1

1. One cell
2. Creating a table using percentages ensures that all users will see the table correctly, regardless of their computer's monitor size and resolution.
3. Cell padding
4. True
5. False
6. above
7. Select the cells, and then click the Merge Cells button; or click the Eraser button, and then use the pointer to erase the border between the cells to merge.
8. above

Session 4.2

1. True
2. three
3. False
4. Frames Page HTML
5. Set Initial Page
6. _top (Whole Page)
7. FRAMESET

In this tutorial you will:

- Create a thumbnail picture

- Change a picture's characteristics

- Create a hover button

- Add dynamic HTML effects and a page transition to a Web page

- Create a subweb

- Create and change the navigation structure of a Web site

- Change a Web site to use shared borders and link bar components

- Apply a theme to a Web site

- Customize a theme and apply it to a Web site

- Create a Photo Gallery in a Web page

- Create a WordArt object in a Web page

USING
PICTURES, SHARED BORDERS, AND THEMES

Creating a Map Web Page and the Recipes Subweb

CASE

Sunny Morning Products

The basic content for the Web site is complete, and now the Web site development team decides to focus on the site's appearance. Amanda Bay wants you to change the appearance of pictures that you include in the Sunny Web site, not only to add visual interest, but also to use them as hyperlinks that open other pages. In addition, she asks you to use hover buttons, a page transition, and animation in the pages. These special effects are created using dynamic HTML code that FrontPage adds to your page automatically.

Tyler Vanauken manages the marketing department at Sunny Morning Products. In the past, he has successfully used print advertising and telephone sales to promote the Sunshine Country Store. The store generates a large profit from in-store sales and through direct-mail campaigns. The store also receives many calls from customers seeking driving directions, so Tyler suggests including a picture of a map on the Sunny Morning Products home page. He has already created the map and saved it on your Data Disk so that you can insert it in the Sunny Web site.

Tyler also reports that many customers have requested recipes for some of the products sold at the store, such as cakes, pies, and baked breads. At the weekly meeting of the Web site development team, he suggests including a few recipes for popular products in the Web site. Tyler wants to include several recipes in the Web site initially and then add new recipes each month to increase the overall number of recipes slowly. He has already created several pages with recipes, which are stored on the company's Web server. Tyler wants the pages for the recipes to have a different appearance from other pages in the Sunny Web site. Amanda suggests creating a subweb in the existing Sunny Web site to give the marketing department separate control over the site's appearance, access, and function.

In this tutorial, you will include the map in the Sunny Web site and then create and format the new Recipes subweb. When you are finished, patrons can use the Web site to obtain directions to the Sunshine Country Store and to print recipes for the store's products.

<table>
<tr><td>**SESSION 5.1**</td><td>In this session, you will create a thumbnail picture in a Web page, change its appearance, and add text to it. You will create a hover button with a hyperlink to the home page. Finally, you will add a page transition and animate text in a Web page.</td></tr>
</table>

Creating a Thumbnail Picture

So far in this book, you have included pictures in your Web pages and formatted some of them with transparent backgrounds and hotspots. You can use FrontPage to change a picture's appearance in other ways, as well. For example, you can create a smaller version of a picture, a picture with washed-out colors, or a picture with an enhanced border. In addition, you can change the way that a picture behaves in a Web page by applying special effects to it, such as changing the picture's color when the user points to it. Amanda wants you to enhance the appearance of the home page by adding a picture with some of these effects applied to it.

A **thumbnail picture** is a small picture that contains a hyperlink to a larger version of the same picture, or to any other specified location. Using a thumbnail picture is appropriate when some users might not need the larger version. Users who want to view the larger picture can click the thumbnail picture, which contains a hyperlink to open a new Web page containing the larger picture. Thumbnail pictures are commonly used in Web pages that contain catalog items, such as a clothing or shoe store.

The hyperlink in a thumbnail picture might connect to a picture file or to Web page that contains the picture and some text. When the thumbnail opens a picture file, the browser opens the picture file; the user must then click the browser's Back button to return to the previous Web page. If the hyperlink opens a Web page that contains the larger picture, the page can include hyperlinks to other Web pages, just like any other Web page. When you create a thumbnail of a larger picture, FrontPage automatically creates the thumbnail picture, inserts it in place of the larger picture, and then creates a hyperlink from the thumbnail picture to the larger picture.

In response to Tyler's request for a map in the home page, Amanda asks you to create a thumbnail of the map that he provided with a hyperlink to the full-sized map. Using a thumbnail in the home page—instead of the full-sized picture—ensures that the page will download quickly. To help plan your work, Amanda asks you to review the planning analysis sheet shown in Figure 5-1 that she prepared after her meeting with Tyler.

Figure 5-1	AMANDA'S PLANNING ANALYSIS SHEET FOR THE SUNSHINE COUNTRY STORE WEB PAGE

Planning Analysis Sheet

Objective

Create a new Web page that identifies the location of the Sunshine Country Store and uses special effects to enhance the page's appearance.

Requirements

Map picture showing the location of the Sunshine Country Store

Sunshine Country Store Map Web page to import into the Web site

Results

A Web page that includes the following elements:

>   A map picture with directions for locating the Sunshine Country Store
>
>   A hover button with a hyperlink to return to the home page
>
>   A page transition that occurs when the page is opened
>
>   Animated text

The Sunshine Country Store Map Web page will open when the user clicks a thumbnail picture of the map in the home page.

REFERENCE   WINDOW   **RW**

<u>Creating a Thumbnail Picture</u>
- If necessary, insert the full-sized picture in the Web page in the desired location.
- Select the picture.
- Click the Auto Thumbnail button on the Pictures toolbar.

Amanda asks you to create the thumbnail picture in the home page. First, you will open the home page in the Sunny Web site.

To open the home page and to create the thumbnail:

1. Make sure that your Data Disk is in the appropriate disk drive, start FrontPage, open the Sunny Web site from your Data Disk, and then open the home page in Page view.

   TROUBLE? If you are storing your Data Files on drive A, you might not have enough disk space to complete this tutorial. To create more space on your Data Disk, open your Data Disk in Windows Explorer, and then delete the Tutorial.02, Tutorial.03, and Tutorial.04 folders and their contents from your Data Disk. If your Data Files are stored on a hard drive or a network, then no action is necessary.

2. Press **Ctrl + End** to scroll to the bottom of the home page, click anywhere in the last line in the paragraph above the marquee, press the **End** key to position the insertion point at the end of the line, press the **Enter** key to insert a new line in which to place the picture, and then click the **Center** button 📄 on the Formatting toolbar to center the line.

   Now you are ready to import the map picture that shows the Sunshine Country Store's location.

3. Click the **Insert Picture From File** button 🖼 on the Standard toolbar, browse to and open the **Tutorial.05** folder on your Data Disk, and then double-click **Map**. The map that Tyler created is inserted in the home page.

4. If necessary, scroll down the home page so that you can see the entire map, and then click the **map picture** to select it and to display the Pictures toolbar.

   TROUBLE? If the Pictures toolbar doesn't appear automatically, click View on the menu bar, point to Toolbars, and then click Pictures.

5. Click the **Auto Thumbnail** button 🖼 on the Pictures toolbar to create the thumbnail picture. See Figure 5-2.

| Figure 5-2 | HOME PAGE WITH THUMBNAIL MAP PICTURE |

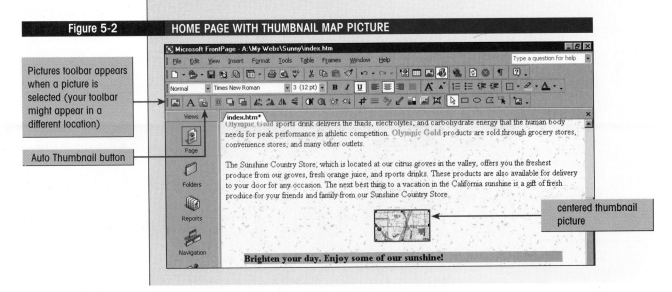

Pictures toolbar appears when a picture is selected (your toolbar might appear in a different location)

Auto Thumbnail button

centered thumbnail picture

The thumbnail picture replaces the full-sized picture in the home page. FrontPage created a hyperlink from the thumbnail to the Map.gif file in the Tutorial.05 folder on your

Data Disk, which is the location of the original, full-sized picture from which the thumbnail was created. When you save the home page, you will need to save this smaller picture in the Sunny Web site. Before you save the picture, however, Amanda wants you to change its characteristics.

Changing Picture Characteristics

You can use FrontPage to change many picture characteristics. For example, you can convert a picture to black and white, rotate it, change its contrast or brightness level, add a beveled edge to the picture's frame, or wash out a picture. When you **wash out** a picture, you reduce its brightness and contrast to create a faded appearance. You can also change the way that the picture appears in the page. For example, you can position it in front of or behind text and other page elements.

Amanda wants you to make several changes to the thumbnail picture. Although you could make the same types of changes to the Map.gif file or to any other GIF picture, for now you will concentrate on the appearance of the thumbnail picture.

To change picture characteristics:

1. With the thumbnail picture still selected, click the **Color** button on the Pictures toolbar. A list opens, providing four options: Automatic, Grayscale, Black & White, and Wash Out. Only the Grayscale and Wash Out effects are enabled for a color picture. If you select the Grayscale option, FrontPage will convert the picture to use shades of gray instead of colors. When it is enabled, the Black & White option lets you change a picture to use only black and white, with no shading. This option is available for pictures without any shading.

2. Click **Grayscale**. The picture changes to a black-and-white image.

3. Click the button and then click **Grayscale** to restore the colors to the thumbnail picture.

4. Click the **Rotate Left** button on the Pictures toolbar. The picture flips on its left side. Click the **Rotate Right** button to return the picture to its original orientation.

5. Click the button and then click **Wash Out**. Notice that the colors become faded in the picture, but the picture still contains colors.

6. Click the **Restore** button on the Pictures toolbar to remove the wash-out effect and restore the picture to its original state. Clicking the Restore button removes all previously applied, unsaved picture effects.

   Amanda feels that the wash-out effect provides the best appearance for the thumbnail picture, so she wants you to use it. You will also apply a new effect to the picture's edges.

7. Click the **Undo** button on the Standard toolbar to return to the thumbnail picture with the wash-out effect.

8. Click the **Bevel** button on the Pictures toolbar. Notice that the edges of the picture change to include a raised effect. The picture now has a wash-out effect and a beveled edge. Amanda asks you to save the page.

9. Click the **Save** button on the Standard toolbar to open the Save Embedded Files dialog box. You need to save the original picture file, Map.gif, and the thumbnail picture, which FrontPage automatically named

> Map_small.gif in the images folder of the Sunny Web site. FrontPage names a thumbnail by appending "_small" to the filename of the full-sized picture.
>
> **10.** Make sure that the files will be saved in the Sunny Web site's images folder, and then click the **OK** button. The picture files are saved in the Sunny Web site.

Amanda asks you to enhance the thumbnail picture by adding text over it so that users can easily identify its function.

Adding Text Over a Picture

When you insert a GIF picture that you plan to use as a hyperlink in a Web page, a good design practice is to add descriptive text on top of the picture to identify its function. You place text over a picture by selecting the picture and then using the Text button on the Pictures toolbar to add the text.

REFERENCE WINDOW	RW

Adding Text Over a Picture
- In Page view, click the picture to select it.
- Click the Text button on the Pictures toolbar to open a text box on top of the selected picture.
- Type the desired text. If necessary, press the Enter key to start a new line.
- Click anywhere in the Web page to close the text box.

Amanda wants you to place text on the thumbnail picture to indicate that it opens a map to the Sunshine Country Store.

To add text to a picture:

1. If necessary, click the **thumbnail picture** to select it and to display the Pictures toolbar.

2. Click the **Text** button [A] on the Pictures toolbar to open a text box on top of the picture.

3. Type **Store**, press the **Enter** key to start a new line, and then type **Map**. This text will appear on top of the picture.

Next, you will change the color of the text that you added to the picture to the same orange color that you used for the "Olympic Gold" text in the home page.

4. Select the **Store Map** text, click the **list arrow** for the Font Color button [A] on the Formatting toolbar to open the color palette, and then click the **orange** color in the Document's Colors section. The text that you added on top of the thumbnail picture changes to orange.

5. Click outside the picture to deselect it and the text. See Figure 5-3.

Figure 5-3   THUMBNAIL WITH DESCRIPTIVE TEXT

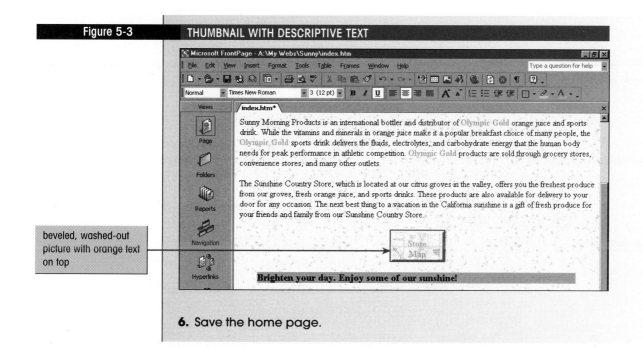

beveled, washed-out picture with orange text on top

6. Save the home page.

You have now created a thumbnail picture, changed several of its characteristics, and added text over it. Amanda wants you to test the thumbnail picture to make sure the hyperlink works correctly by opening the full-sized map picture.

To test the thumbnail picture:

1. Click the **Preview in Browser** button 🔍 on the Standard toolbar to open the home page in the browser, and then scroll to the bottom of the page (if necessary) so you can see the thumbnail picture.

2. Point to the **thumbnail picture**. The pointer changes to a 🖑 shape. The pathname listed in the status bar indicates that this picture contains a hyperlink to the Map.gif file.

3. Click the **thumbnail picture**. The Map.gif file opens as a separate Web page in the browser window. The URL in the Address bar indicates that this page is a GIF file and not an HTML document. A GIF file cannot contain hyperlinks, so you will need to use the browser's Back button to return to the home page.

4. Click the **Back** button ⬅ on the Standard Buttons toolbar to return to the home page, and then close the browser.

To return to the previous Web page, you had to click the Back button on the toolbar. Some Web users might not know to do this, so Amanda asks you to provide navigation options for returning to the home page. To do so, you need to include the full-sized map picture in a Web page. Tyler created a Web page that contains the map picture, so you need only to import that page into the Sunny Web site and then create the appropriate hyperlinks.

To import the Web page for the full-sized picture:

1. Return to FrontPage (if necessary), and then click the **Folders** button 📁 on the Views bar.

2. Click **File** on the menu bar, and then click **Import** to open the Import dialog box.

3. Click the **Add File** button to open the Add File to Import List dialog box, open the **Tutorial.05** folder on your Data Disk, and then double-click **MapPage**. The MapPage.htm file is listed in the Import dialog box.

4. Click the **OK** button to import the Web page into the Sunny Web site.

With the Web page imported into the Sunny Web site, you are ready to add the link back to the home page. First, you'll change the link from the thumbnail picture in the home page to the imported Sunshine Country Store Map page (MapPage.htm). Then you'll create the link from the Map page to the home page.

To edit the hyperlink for the thumbnail picture:

1. Double-click **index.htm** in the Contents pane to open the home page in Page view.

2. Right-click the **thumbnail picture** (not the "Store Map" text) to select it and open the shortcut menu, and then click **Hyperlink Properties**. The Edit Hyperlink dialog box opens. The Address text box displays the current hyperlink to the Map.gif file in the Web site's images folder.

   TROUBLE? If the Insert Hyperlink dialog box opens and the Address text box is empty, then you right-clicked the picture's text box. Click the Cancel button, and then repeat Step 2.

3. Scroll down the list box and double-click **MapPage** to change the thumbnail picture's hyperlink to this Web page and to close the Edit Hyperlink dialog box.

4. Save the home page.

After making this revision to the hyperlink to the Map page, you need to test the page to verify that the hyperlink from the thumbnail picture opens the correct Web page.

To test the hyperlink from the thumbnail picture:

1. Click the **Preview in Browser** button 🔍 on the Standard toolbar.

2. Scroll down the home page until you see the thumbnail picture (if necessary), and then click the **Store Map picture** to open the Sunshine Country Store Map page. The URL in the Address bar specifies the MapPage.htm Web page, and not the Map.gif file. Tyler did not include a link on this page to return to the home page.

3. Close the browser and return to FrontPage (if necessary).

4. Right-click the **thumbnail picture** (not the "Store Map" text) to open the short-cut menu, and then click **Follow Hyperlink**. The MapPage.htm file opens in Page view.

You have successfully created the link from the home page to the Sunshine Country Store Map page. Now you need to complete the link in the other direction—from the Sunshine Country Store Map page back to the home page. A fun way to do this is to use a hover button.

Creating a Hover Button

A **hover button** is a special button that contains a hyperlink. A hover button is just like any other button that appears in a Web page, except that you can add animation and special effects to it. You can set an effect from a list of available effects, or you can use the custom option to create a picture that changes on mouse over. **Mouse over**, or **mouse fly over**, is the act of moving the pointer over a hover button or picture. When you point to a hover button, the appearance of the button changes to match the mouse-over effect specified for that button.

Amanda wants you to create a hover button in the Sunshine Country Store Map page that changes on mouse over and contains a hyperlink that opens the home page.

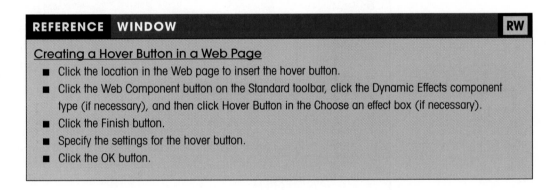

REFERENCE WINDOW   **RW**

Creating a Hover Button in a Web Page
- Click the location in the Web page to insert the hover button.
- Click the Web Component button on the Standard toolbar, click the Dynamic Effects component type (if necessary), and then click Hover Button in the Choose an effect box (if necessary).
- Click the Finish button.
- Specify the settings for the hover button.
- Click the OK button.

Amanda explains that there are many options for creating hover buttons. She asks you to create a hover button that displays the text "Return to Home Page," contains a hyperlink that opens the home page, and has coordinated colors for the hover button's effects.

To create a hover button:

1. If necessary, scroll to the bottom of the Sunshine Country Store Map page. Tyler created a table at the bottom of the Web page into which you will insert the hover buttons. You'll need to turn on the nonprinting characters to see the table.

    TROUBLE? If the nonprinting characters are already displayed, skip Step 2.

2. Click the **Show All** button ¶ on the Standard toolbar to display the nonprinting characters.

    The table below the map contains two empty cells. You could not see this table when you viewed it in the browser because the table's cells do not have colored borders.

3. Click in the left cell of the table to select it. You will insert the hover button in this cell.

4. Click the **Web Component** button  on the Standard toolbar, make sure that **Dynamic Effects** is selected in the Component type list box and that **Hover Button** is selected in the Choose an effect list box, and then click the **Finish** button. The Hover Button Properties dialog box opens. See Figure 5-4.

| Figure 5-4 | HOVER BUTTON PROPERTIES DIALOG BOX |

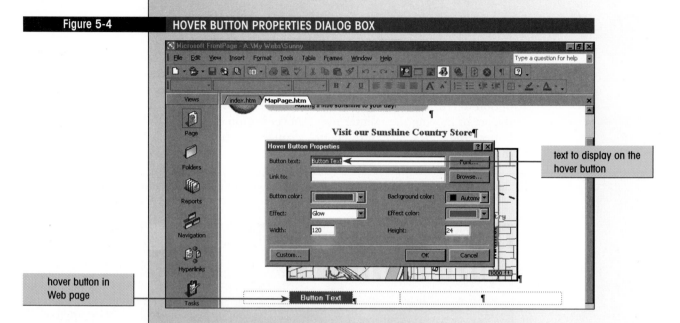

The text that appears in the Button text text box will be displayed on the hover button. You will enter text to indicate that clicking this button opens the home page. Amanda wants you to change the default font, size, style, and color of this text, as well.

5. Type **Return to Home Page** as the Button text, and then click the **Font** button in the dialog box to open the Font dialog box.

6. Click the **Font** list arrow and then click **Arial**, click the **Size up** arrow four times to change the size to **18**, and then click the **Color** list arrow and click the **yellow** color in the Standard colors section. See Figure 5-5.

| Figure 5-5 | COMPLETED FONT DIALOG BOX |

7. Click the **OK** button to close the Font dialog box and return to the Hover Button Properties dialog box.

Next, choose the target page for the hyperlink. In this case, you will select the file for the home page.

8. Click the **Browse** button to open the Select Hover Button Hyperlink dialog box. Make sure that the folder for the Sunny Web site appears in the Look in list box, and then scroll down and double-click **index** to select the home page and to return to the Hover Button Properties dialog box. The Link to text box now displays the filename for the home page.

Next, specify the colors and effect for the hover button.

9. Click the **Button color** list arrow, and then click the **green** color in the Standard colors section.

10. Click the **Effect** list arrow, and then click **Reverse glow**.

11. Click the **Effect color** list arrow, click **More Colors** to open the More Colors dialog box, click the **orange** color (second to last row, third color from the left), and then click the **OK** button to close the More Colors dialog box. See Figure 5-6.

| Figure 5-6 | COMPLETED HOVER BUTTON PROPERTIES DIALOG BOX |

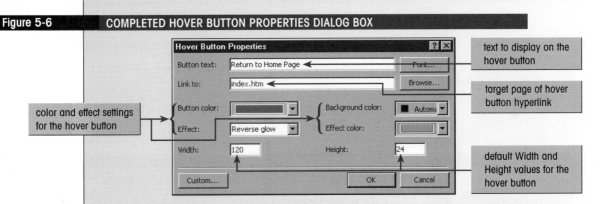

FrontPage specified a default width and height for your hover button and displayed these measurements (in pixels) in the Width and Height text boxes. Usually, it is easier to accept the default measurements and then to resize the button using the pointer, if necessary, in Page view.

12. Click the **OK** button to create the hover button. The button appears in the table, but some of its text is not visible. See Figure 5-7.

| Figure 5-7 | HOVER BUTTON IN THE WEB PAGE |

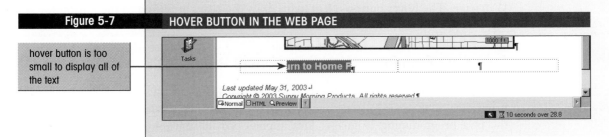

The default size of the hover button is too small for the text that you set to be displayed on the button. You can resize the button by selecting it and dragging one of its sizing handles until it is the desired size. Amanda asks you to increase the size of the hover button and then to test it in the browser.

To resize a hover button and test it in the browser:

1. Click the **hover button** to select it. Sizing handles appear around the button.

2. Drag the center-right sizing handle to the right to increase the size of the hover button so all of the text appears. See Figure 5-8. (Because Tyler set the table's borders so they will not be displayed in the browser, the hover button does not need to fill the table cell in which it appears.)

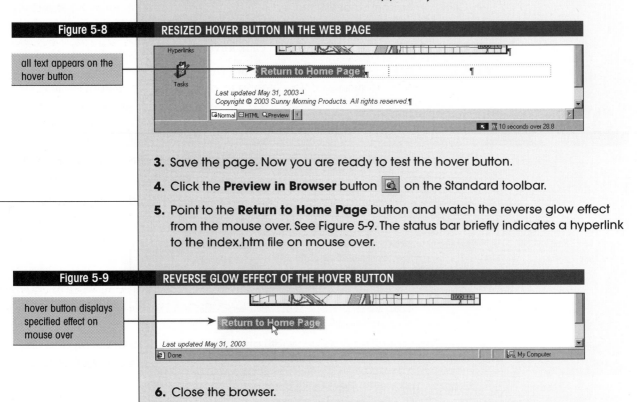

Figure 5-8	RESIZED HOVER BUTTON IN THE WEB PAGE

all text appears on the hover button

Figure 5-9	REVERSE GLOW EFFECT OF THE HOVER BUTTON

hover button displays specified effect on mouse over

3. Save the page. Now you are ready to test the hover button.

4. Click the **Preview in Browser** button 🔍 on the Standard toolbar.

5. Point to the **Return to Home Page** button and watch the reverse glow effect from the mouse over. See Figure 5-9. The status bar briefly indicates a hyperlink to the index.htm file on mouse over.

6. Close the browser.

The hover button provides an attractive, animated way of creating a hyperlink to another Web page. The hover button effect helps draw the user's attention to the button for selecting the hyperlink.

Changing FrontPage Web Component Properties

A hover button is created using a Java applet that is one of several components built into FrontPage. The user's browser executes a Java applet, which is a short program written in the Java programming language. Java applets provide dynamic features in a Web page, including the hover button's animation effects. After creating a hover button or other Web component, you can modify its action or appearance by changing its properties.

Amanda asks you to change the properties of the hover button by revising the button's background color.

To change and test a FrontPage Web component property:

1. In Page view, right-click the **Return to Home Page** hover button to open the shortcut menu, and then click **Hover Button Properties** to open the Hover Button Properties dialog box.

2. Click the **Button color** list arrow, and then click the **maroon** color in the Standard colors section.

3. Click the **Effect** list arrow, and then click **Glow**.

4. Click the **OK** button to close the dialog box, and then save the page. The hover button is now maroon.

5. Preview the page again in a browser, and then point to the **hover button**. The orange glow now appears with the maroon background.

   Amanda feels that this color combination is more appealing. Next, she asks you to test the action of the hover button in the browser.

6. Click the **Return to Home Page** button. The home page opens in the browser. Now test the link to the Sunshine Country Store Map page.

7. Click the **Store Map picture**. The Sunshine Country Store Map page opens in the browser.

8. Close the browser.

The hover button provides the desired effect of increased attention when the pointer moves over the button. As with other Web page features, you should apply these effects carefully to avoid overwhelming or distracting users.

Using **Dynamic HTML**

Dynamic HTML (DHTML) gives you the ability to control the display of elements in a Web page. When a DHTML command is applied to text or a picture, Internet Explorer (and other Web browsers that support this feature) will animate the text or picture (or apply other effects that you specify) by executing the relevant HTML code. Because DHTML does not require additional information from the Web server that stores the Web page, it is very efficient and presents the user with a lively, interesting page without consuming network resources. Page transitions and animations are two methods of making a Web page more interesting. You will apply each of these features to enhance the Sunshine Country Store Map page.

Creating a Page Transition

A **page transition** is an animated effect that you can apply to one or more Web pages in a Web site. When a user opens a page with a transition, the specified transition animates while the page is being loaded. You can specify a closing transition for a page, as well. Amanda tells you to use transitions sparingly, because having too many can overwhelm users and make opening and closing pages occur much more slowly than when no transitions are used.

REFERENCE WINDOW   **RW**

<u>Applying a Page Transition</u>
- With the desired page open in Page view, click Format on the menu bar, and then click Page Transition to open the Page Transitions dialog box.
- Click the Event list arrow, and then select the desired event.
- Enter a value (in seconds) for the duration in the Duration (seconds) text box.
- Click the desired Transition effect.
- Click the OK button.

Amanda asks you to apply the Wipe right transition effect to the Sunshine Country Store Map page.

To add a page transition:

1. Click **Format** on the menu bar, and then click **Page Transition** to open the Page Transitions dialog box. See Figure 5-10.

Figure 5-10   **PAGE TRANSITIONS DIALOG BOX**

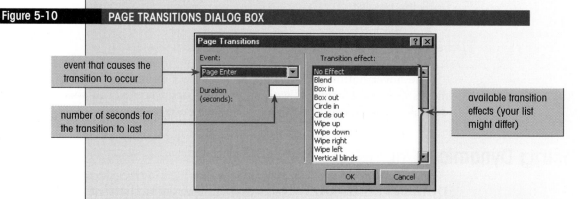

The default Event is **Page Enter**, which means that the transition will occur when the page is opened or refreshed in the browser. Three other options are available: **Page Exit**, which applies the transition when the user leaves the page; **Site Enter**, which applies the transition when the user opens any page in the Web site; and **Site Exit**, which applies the transition when the user leaves the Web site.

2. Click the **Event** list arrow, and then click **Page Exit**. The transition will occur when you leave the page.

3. Click in the **Duration (seconds)** text box, and then type **5** as the number of seconds that the transition should last.

4. In the Transition effect list box, click **Wipe right** to select that effect.

TROUBLE? If you do not have the Wipe right transition, select another transition effect.

5. Click the **OK** button to complete the page transition specifications.

In addition to page transitions, you also can control the manner in which individual objects, such as text or pictures, are displayed in a Web page.

Creating Animated Text in a Web Page

You can apply animation to selected page elements. **Animation** is an effect that causes an element to "fly" into view from a corner or side of the page or in some other eye-catching way, such as using a spiraling motion. You can apply animation to either text or pictures.

REFERENCE   WINDOW   **RW**

Creating Animated Text or Pictures in a Web Page
■ Select the text or picture that you want to animate.
■ Click Format on the menu bar, and then click Dynamic HTML Effects to display the DHTML Effects toolbar.
■ Click the On list arrow, and then select an event on which you want the effect to occur.
■ Click the Apply list arrow, and then select an effect to apply.
■ If it is active, click the Effect list arrow and select a direction in which to apply the effect.

Amanda wants you to apply animation to the text that appears above the map for additional emphasis.

To add text animation:

1. Select the text **Visit our Sunshine Country Store**. Amanda wants this text to bounce into view from the right side of the screen when the page is opened or refreshed in the browser.

2. Click **Format** on the menu bar, and then click **Dynamic HTML Effects**. The DHTML Effects toolbar appears in the Contents pane, as either a docked or floating toolbar. If necessary, drag this toolbar to the top of the Contents pane so that it does not block the text that you selected in Step 1. Then make sure that the Highlight Dynamic HTML Effects button 📄 on the DHTML Effects toolbar has a white background to indicate that this feature is turned on, so that DHTML elements will be highlighted in Page view, making them easier to locate.

   Next, specify the effects for the selected text.

3. Click the **On** list arrow on the DHTML Effects toolbar, and then click **Page load**. This setting will apply the effect when the page is opened or refreshed in the browser.

   You can specify three other effects for pictures: **Click**, which causes the animation to occur when the user clicks the element; **Double click**, which causes the animation to occur when the user double-clicks the element; and **Mouse over**, which causes the animation to occur on mouse over.

4. Click the **Apply** list arrow on the DHTML Effects toolbar, and then click **Elastic**. This setting will cause the selected text to bounce into place. When you select certain effects, you must also indicate the direction from which to apply the effect. You will know that you need to select a direction if the Effect list arrow becomes active.

5. Click the **Effect** list arrow on the DHTML Effects toolbar, which displays the text "< Choose Settings >" when it is active, and then click **From right**. See Figure 5-11. This setting indicates that the specified effect will occur from the right side of the window. Notice that the DHTML element in your Web page is highlighted with a light blue background; this background will not be visible in the browser.

Figure 5-11	ANIMATED TEXT IN A WEB PAGE

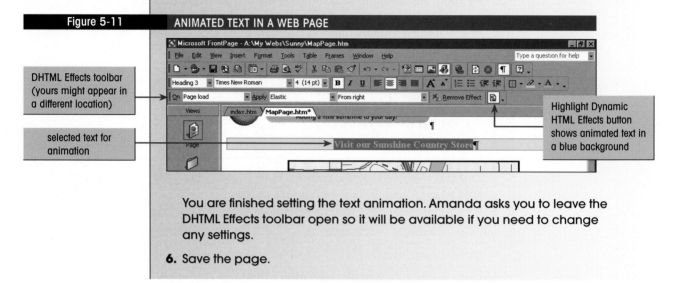

DHTML Effects toolbar (yours might appear in a different location)

selected text for animation

Highlight Dynamic HTML Effects button shows animated text in a blue background

You are finished setting the text animation. Amanda asks you to leave the DHTML Effects toolbar open so it will be available if you need to change any settings.

6. Save the page.

Amanda asks you to open the Sunshine Country Store Map page from the home page so you can see the full effect in the browser. If a browser is not capable of handling these effects, then it ignores them and opens the page anyway. To verify that your effects work correctly, Amanda asks you to test the page transition and text animation that you created for the Sunshine Country Store Map page.

To test the text animation and page transition:

1. Click the **index.htm** page tab at the top of the Contents pane to display the home page in Page view.

2. Click the **Preview in Browser** button 🔍 on the Standard toolbar to open the home page in the browser.

3. Click the **Store Map picture**, and watch the Elastic animation. Keep in mind that you must have Internet Explorer 5.0 or higher to see special effects.

TROUBLE? If you do not see the text animation in the page, click the Refresh button 🔄 on the Standard Buttons toolbar. When you store a Web site's file on a floppy disk, the files load more slowly than when the Web site's files are stored on a hard drive or on a Web server, and sometimes you cannot see the effects.

4. Click the **Return to Home Page** hover button. The Wipe Right page transition occurs and then the home page opens.

5. Close the browser and return to FrontPage.

You have successfully included several animation effects in the Web page. Amanda asks you to view the HTML code that FrontPage used to create these effects.

Viewing **HTML Code for Web Components**

When you created the hover button for the Sunshine Country Store Map page, FrontPage created a Java applet and inserted it into the HTML document. The page transition and text animation were implemented with Java scripts. An **applet** uses a series of parameters that specify an object's behavior. A **script** is code that is included in the Web page and executed by the Web browser. Amanda asks you to examine the HTML code for the hover button that is implemented using an applet.

To view the HTML code for a Java applet:

1. Click **View** on the menu bar, point to **Toolbars**, and then click **DHTML Effects**. The DHTML Effects toolbar closes.

2. Click the **MapPage.htm** page tab at the top of the Contents pane, and then click the **HTML** button to switch to that view.

3. Scroll the page until the SCRIPT tag appears at the top of the window. See Figure 5-12. Notice the parameters for the text value and the effect value.

Figure 5-12	HTML CODE FOR THE SUNSHINE COUNTRY STORE MAP PAGE

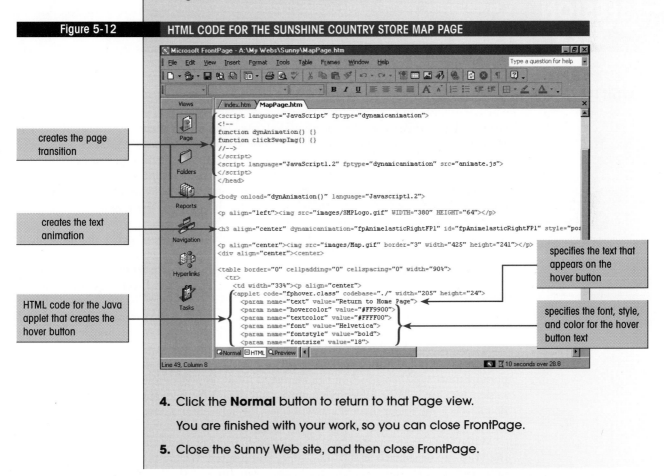

4. Click the **Normal** button to return to that Page view.

   You are finished with your work, so you can close FrontPage.

5. Close the Sunny Web site, and then close FrontPage.

Amanda and Tyler are pleased with the changes that you have made to the home page. These changes will make the home page easier and more interesting for patrons to use. In the next session, you will create the new Recipes subweb, which will include shared borders, link bar components, and a Web theme.

Session 5.1 QUICK CHECK

1. When you create a thumbnail picture in a Web page, FrontPage automatically creates a(n) _____ to the full-sized picture that was used to create the thumbnail.

2. List three effects that you can apply to a picture using the Pictures toolbar.

3. Describe the process for adding text over a picture in a Web page.

4. Moving the pointer over a hover button is called _____.

5. True or False: A Java applet creates a hover button in a Web page.

6. True or False: You can add a page transition to only one page in a Web site.

7. True or False: Animation is an effect that causes an element to "fly" into view from a corner or side of the page.

8. What are two effects that you can create in a Web page using DHTML?

SESSION 5.2

In this session, you will create a subweb and import pages into it at the same time. You will also create shared borders and link bars in the subweb.

Using a Wizard to Create a Subweb

A **subweb** is a Web site within another Web site. You can create one or more subwebs in the Web site's main folder, which is called the **root Web**. In most cases, Web site developers use subwebs to control the appearance of and access to the pages within it. For example, a company might have a Web site that includes a root Web named Widgets. The Widgets root Web, in turn, might contain subwebs for the different company departments, such as accounting, human resources, and receiving. In this case, each subweb will contain its own home page and other pages that support the site. The Web site's administrator, or webmaster, might assign different access to each subweb. For instance, the webmaster might specify that only members of the accounting department will be permitted to create new pages in the accounting subweb.

To create a subweb, right-click the Web site's root folder in the Folder List in Folders view to open the shortcut menu, point to New, and then click Folder. FrontPage will create a new folder and change to editing mode, allowing you to type the folder's name. Press the Enter key to finish creating the folder. At this point, you have created a Windows folder in your Web site. To convert the folder into a subweb, right-click the folder in the Folder List, and then click Convert to Web on the shortcut menu. After you click the Yes button, FrontPage will convert the Windows folder to a Web folder by adding the files and folders necessary to support a FrontPage Web site. You can identify a folder as a Web folder, rather than a Windows folder, because a Web folder contains a blue dot in its folder icon. To open the subweb, double-click the folder. FrontPage will open the subweb in a new program window. You can add new pages to the subweb just as you would in a root Web.

When you need to create a new FrontPage Web site or a subweb and also import pages into the Web site or subweb at the same time, you can use the Import Web Wizard, which is an option in the Web Site Templates dialog box. The **Import Web Wizard** creates a Web site (or subweb) in the location that you specify and then adds pages to it from the location or Web server that you specify.

Tyler has already created the Web pages that you will use to create the Recipes subweb. He saved these pages in the Tutorial.05 folder on your Data Disk. Amanda wants you to import these pages from your Data Disk to create the Recipes subweb in the Sunny Web site. Figure 5-13 shows her planning analysis sheet for the Recipes subweb.

Figure 5-13	AMANDA'S PLANNING ANALYSIS SHEET FOR THE RECIPES SUBWEB

Planning Analysis Sheet

Objective

Create a subweb in the Sunny Web site that includes recipes for items sold by the Sunshine Country Store. The subweb will include top, left, and bottom shared borders. The top and left shared borders will include link bars created by FrontPage; the bottom shared border will include the date on which the recipe was added to the subweb. The subweb will use a theme to add visual interest to its pages.

Requirements

Files for the subweb's home page and pages that contain the recipes

Picture files for the home page

Results

A home page that includes an introduction, hyperlinks to the recipes pages, and
  a Photo Gallery of recipe categories (cakes, pies, breads, and icings)

Link bars with links to same-level and child pages and the home page

Each recipe should appear in its own Web page and include links to related recipes

A Web site that uses a colorful, casual Web theme and other enhancements to
  make the site visually appealing

REFERENCE **WINDOW**   **RW**

Using the Import Web Wizard to Create a Subweb

- Open the root Web in Folders view.
- If necessary, click View on the menu bar and then click Task Pane to display the Task Pane.
- Click Empty Web in the Task Pane.
- In the Web Site Templates dialog box, click in the Specify the location of the new web text box, and then type the full path to the root Web site, a backslash, and the subweb name.
- Double-click the Import Web Wizard icon to create the subweb and to start the Wizard.
- Select the location from which to import the existing Web pages, and then click the Next button.
- Select any files to exclude from the specified location, and then click the Exclude button.
- Click the Next button, and then click the Finish button.

Next, you will create the Recipes subweb using Tyler's existing files.

To create a subweb using the Import Web Wizard:

1. Make sure that your Data Disk is in the appropriate disk drive, start FrontPage, and then open the **Sunny** Web site from your Data Disk in Folders view.

   Before creating a subweb, you must select the root Web folder in which you want the subweb to be created.

2. Click the **Sunny** folder in the Folder List. This is the root Web. If necessary, display the Task Pane by clicking **View** on the menu bar, and then clicking **Task Pane**.

3. In the New section of the Task Pane, click **Empty Web**. The Web Site Templates dialog box opens. Recall from Tutorial 2 that you can use the templates and Wizards in this dialog box to create a new FrontPage Web. You can also use these options to create a subweb.

4. Click in the **Specify the location of the new web** text box, and then type **A:\My Webs\Sunny\Recipes**. This path will create a subweb named Recipes in the Sunny Web site on your Data Disk.

   TROUBLE? If you are using a different drive or folder for your Data Disk, use the appropriate path for it.

5. Double-click the **Import Web Wizard** icon to create the Recipes subweb. After a few moments, the subweb is created in the Sunny Web site, and the Wizard starts and opens the Import Web Wizard – Choose Source dialog box, in which you specify the location from which to import your existing files. You can import the files from a disk location or from a World Wide Web site. You will import the files from your Data Disk.

6. Click the **From a source directory of files on a local computer or network** option button, select the text in the Location text box, and then type **A:\Tutorial.05** (or the path to the Tutorial.05 folder on your Data Disk).

7. Click the **Next** button. The Import Web Wizard – Edit File List dialog box opens. In this dialog box you can choose either to import all files from the location that you just specified or to exclude files that you don't need. The Tutorial.05 folder on your Data Disk includes files that you used in Session 5.1 and the files that you will use in Session 5.3 and in the end-of-tutorial exercises. You don't need to include these files in the Recipes subweb, so you will select and exclude them.

8. Press and hold down the **Ctrl** key, click the files **Beach.gif**, **Map.gif**, **MapPage.htm**, **Italy.gif**, **Mexico.gif**, **US.gif**, and **Bullet.gif** to select them, and then release the **Ctrl** key. Click the **Exclude** button to display the list of the nine files that you will import.

   TROUBLE? If necessary, exclude any other files so that only the files Pie.htm, Icing.htm, Cake.htm, Bread.htm, P_Cake.jpg, P_Bread.jpg, P_Pie.jpg, P_Icing.jpg, and Recipes.htm are imported.

9. Click the **Next** button, and then click the **Finish** button in the Import Web Wizard – Finish dialog box to import the specified pages into the Recipes subweb. After a few moments, the pages are imported into the Recipes subweb. The original Sunny Web site is open in one FrontPage program window, and the new Recipes subweb is open in a second FrontPage program window.

10. Click the **Microsoft FrontPage** program button on the taskbar that is not active (the one for the Sunny Web site). Notice that the Recipes subweb now appears in the Folder List.

11. Close the Sunny Web site, and then close FrontPage program window that contained it.

Note: Because a subweb and a root Web are both FrontPage Web sites, you can do almost everything in a subweb that you can do in a root Web. The discussion throughout the rest of this tutorial applies equally well to root Webs and subwebs.

Tyler did not create a home page for the subweb. When a Web browser opens a Web site or a subweb, it searches for a page named index.htm or default.htm to open as the Web's home page.

REFERENCE WINDOW | **RW**

Renaming a Page's Filename and Title in Folders View
- In Folders view, click the page to select it, and then click the page's filename again to change to editing mode and to display the insertion point.
- Type the new filename and extension, and then press the Tab key to select the page's title and change to editing mode.
- Type the new title and then press the Enter key.

Amanda asks you to rename the Recipes.htm page to index.htm so that a Web browser will open this page as the subweb's home page automatically. She also wants you to change this page's title to "Country Recipes." You can change a page's filename and title in Folders or Navigation view. Amanda asks you to complete these tasks in Folders view:

To rename a page's filename and title in Folders view:

1. Change to Folders view for the Recipes subweb (if necessary), click **Recipes.htm** in the Contents pane to select it, and then click **Recipes.htm** again to change to editing mode. The filename is selected, a text box appears around the filename, and the insertion point appears in the text box. You can just type the new name to change the page's filename.

2. Type **index.htm** and then press the **Tab** key. The Rename dialog box opens while FrontPage changes the page's filename to index.htm. Then FrontPage selects the page's title and adds the text box with an insertion point in it.

You will change the page's title to "Country Recipes."

3. Press the **Home** key to place the insertion point before the "R" in Recipes.

4. Type **Country**, press the **spacebar**, and then press the **Enter** key. The page's title is renamed to Country Recipes. See Figure 5-14.

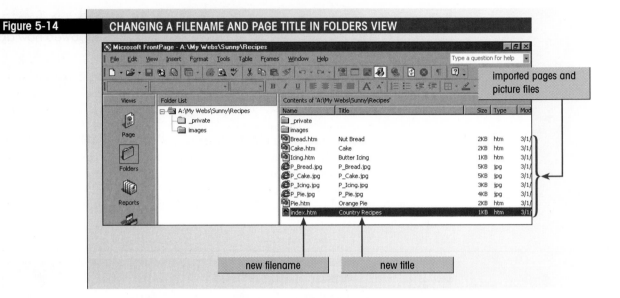

Figure 5-14   CHANGING A FILENAME AND PAGE TITLE IN FOLDERS VIEW

Understanding Shared Borders and Link Bars

When your Web site contains many pages, you can use shared borders and a link bar component to ensure a consistent appearance for all pages. A **shared border** presents information common to all Web pages in a consistent manner across selected Web pages or the entire Web site.

In Tutorials 2 and 3, you entered and formatted a user-defined link bar for the pages in the Sunny Web site. Creating a user-defined link bar is easy and useful, but you must ensure that all subsequent changes made to the navigation structure, including adding and deleting pages, are updated in every Web page that includes a user-defined link bar. In contrast, when you use a **link bar component** to create a link bar, FrontPage maintains and updates the link bar entries automatically, thus saving you some time and ensuring that the links to other pages are always consistent and accurate.

Before you can create shared borders or a link bar component in a Web site, you must use Navigation view to add pages from your Web site in a **navigation structure**, which identifies the pages in your Web site and shows how they are related to each other. The navigation structure resembles an organization chart. Usually, the home page appears at the top level of the Web site, with some pages below it, additional levels of pages below those pages, and so on. In this context, the home page is the parent page, the pages under the home page are child pages of the home page, and so on. You can add any Web page from the Web site to its navigation structure. Some pages that appear in a frames page, such as a banner or contents page, are usually omitted from the navigation structure, because these pages are relevant only to the frameset.

After creating the navigation structure and turning on the shared borders, you add the content of the shared border(s) to your Web site in any page that uses the border. A shared border appears with a thin border line in Page view to indicate its location in a Web page; this border is not displayed in the browser.

Shared borders typically appear in every Web page in a Web site that uses them. FrontPage lets you set a top, bottom, left, or right border, or any two or more such borders, for the entire Web site. A shared border often includes button or text hyperlinks to other pages in the Web site, as well as other text or pictures that should appear in every page in the site.

When you edit the content of a shared border in a single Web page, your changes apply to *all* pages in the Web site that use the same shared border. For example, adding a company name and logo to a top shared border in one Web page will cause all other pages in the Web site that use the top shared border to display the same name and logo in the same location in the shared border.

You could add a shared border with a link bar component to the Sunny Web site, but Amanda doesn't feel that this change is necessary because all of the hyperlinks in the link bar are already in place and active. However, Amanda believes that the Recipes subweb that you created for the marketing department is an excellent candidate for shared borders. You will set the home page as the parent for the Recipes subweb, with child pages that include recipes for cakes, pies, and breads. Those child pages will have child pages to icings, crusts, and butters, respectively. This structure will ensure that when a recipe for a cake is displayed in the browser, the page containing a recipe for an icing for that cake will be included as a hyperlink in the recipe page.

Now you are ready to create the navigation structure for the Recipes subweb. The Country Recipes page will be the top-level page in the Recipes subweb. You will add the Nut Bread, Cake, and Orange Pie pages as child pages of the Country Recipes Web page. Then you will add the Butter Icing page as a child of the Cake page.

Creating a Navigation Structure

After you import or create Web pages in a Web site, they are available for use in the Web site's navigation structure. You add a file to the navigation structure by dragging its filename from the Folder List to the Navigation pane and positioning the page icon so that the connector specifies the desired level and order for the page in the structure. Amanda wants you to create the navigation structure for the Recipes subweb next.

To add existing Web files to the navigation structure:

1. Click the **Navigation** button 🗂 on the Views bar to change to Navigation view.

   TROUBLE? If the Navigation toolbar blocks the navigation structure, drag it to the top of the Navigation pane to move it out of the way.

   TROUBLE? If necessary, click the Toggle Pane button 🖼 on the Standard toolbar to display the Folder List.

   The subweb's current navigation structure includes only the top-level page in the Web site, Country Recipes (index.htm). To create the navigation structure, you will drag a filename from the Folder List to the Navigation pane, and then release the mouse button when the page is in the correct position.

2. Click **Pie.htm** in the Folder List, and then drag it to the Navigation pane. Position the Pie.htm page so that it is below the Country Recipes page. See Figure 5-15.

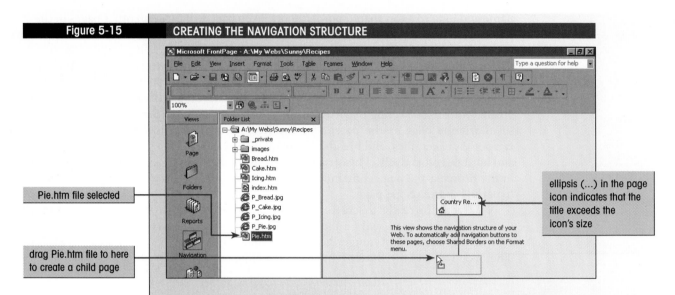

Figure 5-15   CREATING THE NAVIGATION STRUCTURE

3. When the page is correctly positioned (see Figure 5-15), release the mouse button. The page's title, Orange Pie, appears in the page icon. If you need to know the filename of a page in the navigation structure, you can click it and the page's filename will appear on the status bar.

4. Repeat Steps 2 and 3 to add the **Bread.htm** and **Cake.htm** pages to the Navigation pane as child pages of the Country Recipes page and to the right of the Orange Pie page, and then click anywhere in a blank area of the Navigation pane to deselect the pages. See Figure 5-16.

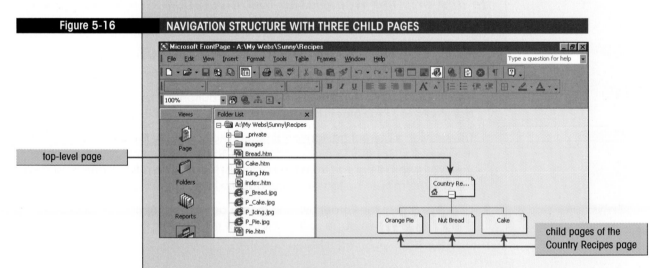

Figure 5-16   NAVIGATION STRUCTURE WITH THREE CHILD PAGES

TROUBLE? If you add a page in the wrong position, click the page that you need to fix and drag it into the correct position so your Navigation pane looks like Figure 5-16.

5. Drag the **Icing.htm** page from the Folder List into the Navigation pane, position it as a child page of the Cake page, and then release the mouse button. See Figure 5-17.

Figure 5-17   COMPLETED NAVIGATION STRUCTURE

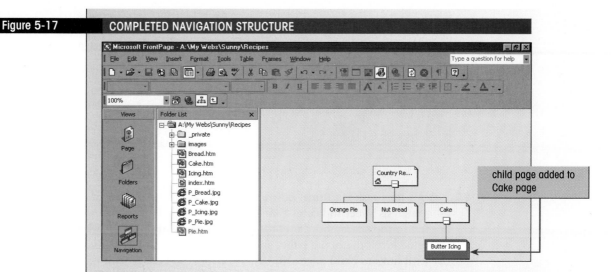

Because the kitchen might add several recipes for different cakes, Amanda recommends that you change the title of the Cake page to "Orange Cake." Because Navigation view is currently displayed, you will change the title in Navigation view.

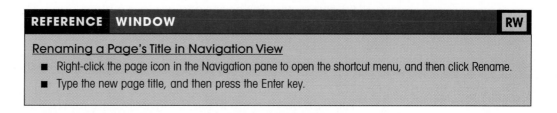

REFERENCE   WINDOW   **RW**

<u>Renaming a Page's Title in Navigation View</u>
■ Right-click the page icon in the Navigation pane to open the shortcut menu, and then click Rename.
■ Type the new page title, and then press the Enter key.

To rename a page's title in Navigation view:

1. Right-click the **Cake** page icon in the Navigation pane to select it and open the shortcut menu, click **Rename**, and then type **Orange Cake**. You are changing the title of the Web page, but not the filename, which is still Cake.htm.

2. Press the **Enter** key to rename the page. This title change will also be displayed in Folders view and when the page is viewed with a browser.

Now that you have created the navigation structure, you can turn on the shared borders and start creating the link bar components.

Creating **Shared Borders in a Web Site**

When you created the navigation structure, you were really telling FrontPage about the relationships between the Web pages in your Web site. For example, without the navigation structure, FrontPage would not know that the Butter Icing page is a child of the Orange Cake page. The navigation structure identifies these relationships so that FrontPage will create the correct link bar in the shared border for each page that uses one.

REFERENCE WINDOW   **RW**

Turning on Shared Borders for a Web Site

- If necessary, create the navigation structure for the Web site in Navigation view.
- Click Format on the menu bar, and then click Shared Borders.
- Select the option button for applying the shared border to all or selected pages, select the shared border(s) to add, select the option to include navigation buttons if desired, and then click the OK button.

Your next task is to turn on the shared borders for the Recipes subweb. Amanda's planning analysis sheet indicates that the pages in the Recipes subweb will have three shared borders: a top shared border containing the page's title and a link bar with links to pages at the same level, the home page, and the parent page; a left shared border containing a link bar with links to child pages; and a bottom shared border with the date on which the recipe was added to the Web site. All pages in the Recipes subweb will share the same borders, so you can turn on the shared borders with any page selected in the Navigation pane.

To turn on the shared borders:

1. Click **Format** on the menu bar, and then click **Shared Borders**. The Shared Borders dialog box opens and displays a blank page. You have not added any shared borders to the Recipes subweb yet, so no options are selected.

2. If necessary, click the **All pages** option button to indicate that the shared borders you will select should be applied to all pages that appear in the Navigation pane.

   You must add a page to the Navigation pane before you can display a shared border in that page. If you select the All pages option button but do not add a particular Web page to the navigation structure, then that page will display a message in Page view reminding you to add the page to the navigation structure for it to be able to use the shared border.

3. Click the **Top** check box to select it, and then click the **Include navigation buttons** check box, which becomes active after you click the Top check box. This change adds a top shared border with a link bar to every page in the navigation structure.

4. Click the **Left** check box to select it, and then click the **Include navigation buttons** check box to add the left shared border with a link bar to every page in the navigation structure.

5. Click the **Bottom** check box to add a bottom shared border to every page in the navigation structure. See Figure 5-18.

Figure 5-18   SHARED BORDERS DIALOG BOX

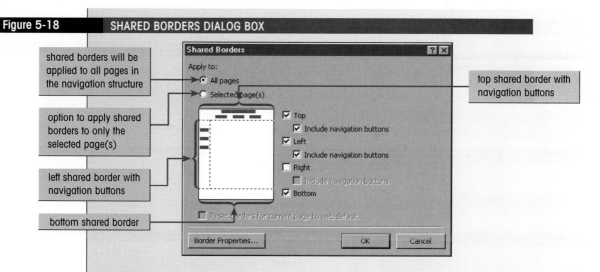

shared borders will be applied to all pages in the navigation structure

option to apply shared borders to only the selected page(s)

left shared border with navigation buttons

bottom shared border

top shared border with navigation buttons

6. Click the **Border Properties** button. The Border Properties dialog box opens. See Figure 5-19.

Figure 5-19   BORDER PROPERTIES DIALOG BOX

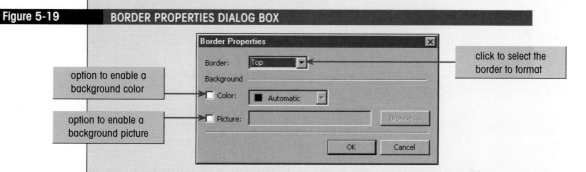

option to enable a background color

option to enable a background picture

click to select the border to format

You can use the options in the Border Properties dialog box to control the appearance of the shared borders in your Web pages. For example, you might choose a different background color and a picture to include in the shared border. Amanda doesn't want to include these options, so you will close the Border Properties dialog box and then finish creating the shared borders.

7. Click the **Cancel** button to close the Border Properties dialog box, and then click the **OK** button to close the Shared Borders dialog box and to create the top, bottom, and left shared borders. The status bar will display some messages indicating that the Web site's shared borders are being created. This process will take a few seconds if you are storing your Data Files on a floppy disk.

Although FrontPage has created the shared borders, you can't see them in your Web site in Navigation view. When you open any page that appears in the navigation structure in Page view, however, you will see the borders. Next, you will open the Orange Cake page in Page view.

To open the Orange Cake page in Page view:

1. Double-click the **Orange Cake** page icon in the Navigation pane to open that page in Page view. See Figure 5-20.

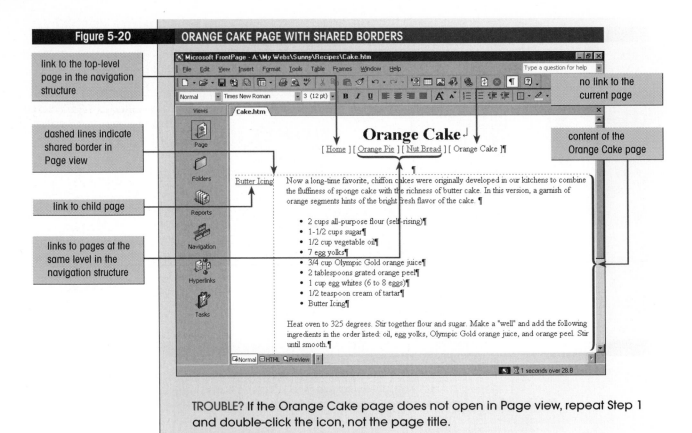

Figure 5-20   ORANGE CAKE PAGE WITH SHARED BORDERS

link to the top-level page in the navigation structure

no link to the current page

dashed lines indicate shared border in Page view

content of the Orange Cake page

link to child page

links to pages at the same level in the navigation structure

TROUBLE? If the Orange Cake page does not open in Page view, repeat Step 1 and double-click the icon, not the page title.

The top shared border includes the page's title (Orange Cake) and the navigation options for the top-level page (Home) and the pages at the same level as the Orange Cake page (Orange Pie, Nut Bread, and Orange Cake). The page's title appears in a page banner. A **page banner**, or **Web banner**, is a text or picture object that appears at the top of each page that uses a top shared border. Its text is taken from the page's title in Navigation view. The hyperlinks below the page banner and in the left shared border appear in a link bar. The option for including the home page was automatically selected for the top shared border. When this option is selected, FrontPage inserts the link named "Home" in the link bar and creates a link to the site's top-level page.

The Orange Cake page is the only child page in the Web site with its own child page, and the link to that page (Butter Icing) appears automatically in the left shared border. For pages without links in any border, a message indicates that you can click the border to add content to it. The Country Recipes page does not contain any links in the top shared border, as you will see next.

To examine the shared borders for the Country Recipes page:

1. Click the **Navigation** button on the Views bar to change to Navigation view.

2. Double-click the **Country Recipes** page icon to open this page in Page view. See Figure 5-21.

Figure 5-21 COUNTRY RECIPES PAGE WITH SHARED BORDERS

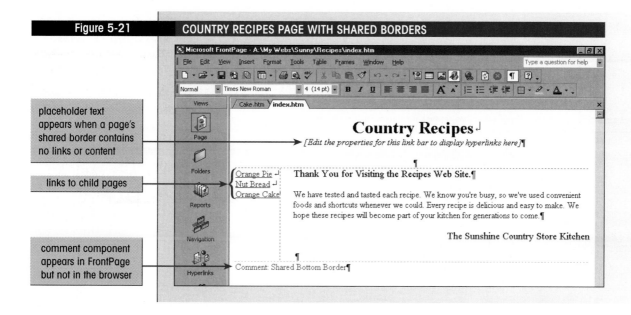

placeholder text appears when a page's shared border contains no links or content

links to child pages

comment component appears in FrontPage but not in the browser

The top shared border displays the page's title and a message. The top shared border does not contain a link bar because the Country Recipes page is the top-level page in the Web site and no "higher" or same-level "equal" pages exist. The left shared border contains links to the child pages of the Country Recipes Web page. The bottom shared border contains a comment that you will replace with your own content.

Next, Amanda wants you to view the shared borders in the browser.

To test the shared borders and link bars in the browser:

1. Click the **Preview in Browser** button 🔍 on the Standard toolbar. The Country Recipes page opens in the browser. The top shared border displays the page's title, and the left shared border displays the links to this page's child pages. See Figure 5-22.

Figure 5-22 COUNTRY RECIPES PAGE IN THE BROWSER

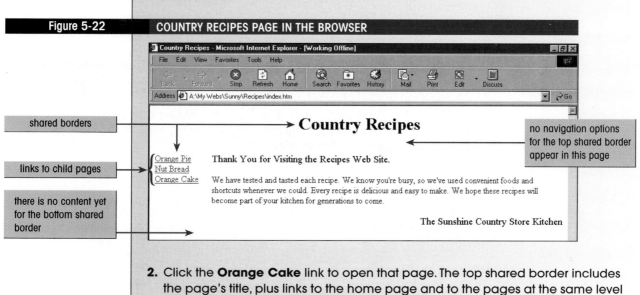

shared borders

links to child pages

there is no content yet for the bottom shared border

no navigation options for the top shared border appear in this page

2. Click the **Orange Cake** link to open that page. The top shared border includes the page's title, plus links to the home page and to the pages at the same level as the Orange Cake page. The left shared border includes a link to a child page, Butter Icing.

3. Click the **Butter Icing** link to open that page. The left shared border does not appear because this page has no child pages. The top shared border includes links to "Home" and "Up." Clicking the Home link will open the Country Recipes page. Clicking the Up link will open the parent page, which is the Orange Cake page. See Figure 5-23.

Figure 5-23	BUTTER ICING PAGE IN THE BROWSER

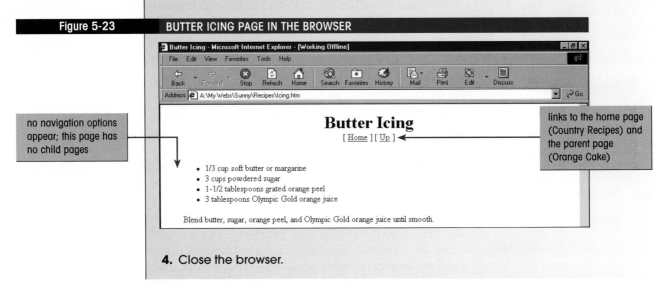

no navigation options appear; this page has no child pages

links to the home page (Country Recipes) and the parent page (Orange Cake)

4. Close the browser.

After examining the pages in the browser, you decide to add a horizontal line in the top shared border to separate the link bar from the recipes. You can make this change by editing the top shared border.

Editing a Shared Border

After creating a shared border, you can modify it by opening in Page view any page that uses the shared border and then making the desired changes. Remember that all of the Web pages included in the Web site's navigation structure use the *same* shared borders, so any changes that you make to any single shared border are automatically applied to all pages that use it. You can change the content of the shared border by using the same techniques that you would use to revise any other Web page in Page view.

Amanda wants you to add a horizontal line below the link bar component in the top shared border to separate the border from the actual page content. She also wants you to add a component to the bottom shared border that displays the date on which the page was added to the Recipes subweb. You will make these changes in Page view for the Country Recipes page. You could also make these changes using any page in the Web site because all of the pages use the same shared borders.

To edit the top and bottom shared borders:

1. Move the pointer over the text that begins "Edit the properties" in the link bar in the top shared border of the home page until your pointer changes to a 🗒️ shape, and then click the **link bar placeholder text** to select it.

2. Press the **Down arrow** key ↓ on the keyboard to position the insertion point on the next line, and then press the **Delete** key to remove this line.

3. Click **Insert** on the menu bar, and then click **Horizontal Line**. A horizontal line appears in the shared border below the link bar placeholder text.

4. Click the **comment placeholder text** in the bottom shared border to select it, press the **Enter** key, type **Added on** and then press the **spacebar**.

   FrontPage includes a component that adds the date on which the page was last edited. You will use this component to add the date.

5. Click **Insert** on the menu bar, click **Date and Time**, click the **OK** button, and then type a **period**. Today's date is added to the bottom shared border, using the format MM/DD/YYYY. You can use the Date and Time dialog box to format the date to appear in other formats, as well.

6. Click the **Align Right** button ▤ on the Formatting toolbar to right-align the content in the bottom shared border.

7. Save the home page.

8. Click the **Cake.htm** page tab to open the Orange Cake page in Page view. Notice that the horizontal line appears in the top shared border for this page. Scroll down the page, if necessary, to see the bottom shared border.

Changes to any of the other shared borders are made in the same manner. Next, Amanda asks you to review the link bars to see whether you can improve them.

Revising a Link Bar

After you create a link bar component, you might need to revise it occasionally to change the hyperlinks or to change the format of the links (text or buttons). Amanda asks you to check the current link bar properties next.

To open the Link Bar Properties dialog box:

1. Right-click the **link bar** in the top shared border to open the shortcut menu, and then click **Link Bar Properties** to open the Link Bar Properties dialog box. See Figure 5-24. Notice that most of the choices are option buttons, so only one selection is permitted.

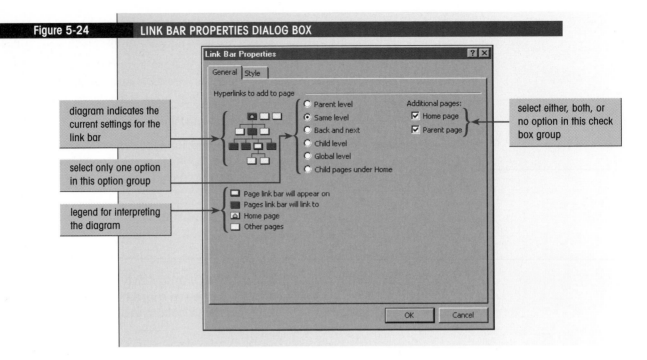

Figure 5-24   LINK BAR PROPERTIES DIALOG BOX

Figure 5-25 describes the settings on the General tab in the Link Bar Properties dialog box and provides examples of how these settings would apply to the Orange Cake page. When you change an option in this dialog box, the sample diagram changes to reflect the new links. Make sure that you study these settings and understand how they work before continuing.

Figure 5-25   LINK BAR PROPERTY DESCRIPTIONS AND EXAMPLES

OPTION	DESCRIPTION	EXAMPLE FOR THE ORANGE CAKE PAGE IN THE RECIPES SUBWEB
General tab: Select one option button and one or both check boxes.		
Parent level option button	All pages will include a link to the parent-level page.	Home link only (the parent page)
Same level option button	All pages will include links to pages at the same level as the currently displayed page.	Nut Bread, Orange Cake, and Orange Pie
Back and next option button	All pages will include links to the left and right of the currently displayed page, based on how the pages were added to the navigation structure.	Back and Next links, which open the Nut Bread and Orange Pie pages, respectively
Child level option button	All pages will include a link to the currently displayed page's child pages, if applicable.	Link to the Butter Icing page
Global level option button	All pages will include a link to the top-level page in the Web site.	Home link only (the top-level page in Navigation view)
Child pages under Home option button	All pages will include links to the child pages of the home page.	Links to Nut Bread, Orange Cake, and Orange Pie

Figure 5-25	LINK BAR PROPERTY DESCRIPTIONS AND EXAMPLES, continued	
OPTION	**DESCRIPTION**	**EXAMPLE FOR THE ORANGE CAKE PAGE IN THE RECIPES SUBWEB**
Home page check box	All pages will include a link to the home page, regardless of what other options are selected.	Home link, plus any other links included by the option button selected in the Hyperlinks to add to page section
Parent page check box	All pages will include a link to the page's parent-level page, regardless of what other options are selected.	Home link (which is the Orange Cake's parent page), plus any other links included by the option button selected in the Hyperlinks to add to page section

To change the link bar:

1. Click the **Back and next** option button to select it. The Home page and Parent page check boxes are still selected. Notice that the diagram in the dialog box shows these changes to the hyperlinks included in the link bar.

2. Click the **Same level** option button to select it and to return to the original configuration.

3. Click the **Style** tab. See Figure 5-26.

Figure 5-26	STYLE TAB OF THE LINK BAR PROPERTIES DIALOG BOX

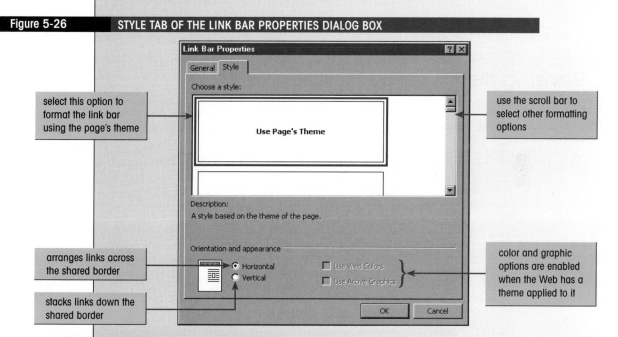

select this option to format the link bar using the page's theme

use the scroll bar to select other formatting options

arranges links across the shared border

stacks links down the shared border

color and graphic options are enabled when the Web has a theme applied to it

The options on the Style tab control the appearance of the buttons that you selected for inclusion on the General tab. By scrolling the Choose a style list box, you can select a theme or text style as the basis for formatting your links. In the Orientation and appearance section, clicking the Horizontal option button arranges the hyperlinks in the link bar across the shared border; clicking the Vertical option button vertically stacks the hyperlinks in the link bar in the shared border. When you select a theme to format the hyperlinks, the Use Vivid Colors and Use Active Graphics check boxes become active so you can choose those options, as well.

For now, Amanda asks you to keep the buttons arranged horizontally across the top shared border and to select the default style, which is to use the page's theme. You'll apply a theme to the Recipes subweb in Session 5.3.

4. Make sure that the **Use Page's Theme** option and the **Horizontal** option button are selected, and then click the **OK** button. You can also examine the selections in the left shared border.

5. Right-click the **link bar** in the left shared border (the Butter Icing hyperlink) to select it, and then click **Link Bar Properties** on the shortcut menu. The Link Bar Properties dialog box for the left shared border opens. The top shared border will include a link to the home page, so you don't need to repeat that link in the left shared border.

6. Make sure that the **Child level** option button is selected and that the **Home page** and **Parent page** check boxes do not contain check marks, and then click the **Style** tab.

7. Scroll up the Choose a style list and click the **Use Page's Theme** button, make sure that the **Vertical** option button is selected, and then click the **OK** button. The Link Bar Properties dialog box for the left shared border closes.

8. Save the page.

These changes to the shared borders will appear in every page in the Web site that uses them.

Revising the Navigation Structure

After creating the navigation structure, turning on shared borders, and changing the link bar's properties, you might need to revise the navigation structure. For example, you can delete or add pages to the navigation structure or change the existing page titles. You can also drag the page icons in the Navigation pane to rearrange their order in the link bars.

Deleting a Page from the Navigation Structure

When you use Navigation view to delete a page from the Web site, you can delete the page from the navigation structure only or from the entire Web site. If you delete the page from the navigation structure only, then the page is deleted from the structure and from any link bars, but it remains in the Web site. Deleting the page from the Web site permanently removes the page from the navigation structure, from the link bars, and from the Web site.

REFERENCE WINDOW   **RW**

Deleting a Page from the Navigation Structure
- In Navigation view, right-click the page icon in the Navigation pane that you want to delete to select the page and open the shortcut menu.
- Click Delete to open the Delete Page dialog box.
- Click the Remove this page from the navigation structure option button to delete the page from the navigation structure, or click the Delete this page from the Web option button to delete the page from the Web site.
- Click the OK button.

Tyler still has to prepare the butter recipe that complements the nut bread recipe, so he doesn't want the nut bread recipe link to appear in the shared borders right now. To meet Tyler's needs, Amanda asks you to delete the Nut Bread page from the navigation structure, but not from the Web site.

To delete a page from the navigation structure:

1. Click the **Navigation** button 🖼 on the Views bar to return to Navigation view.

2. Right-click the **Nut Bread** page icon to open the shortcut menu, and then click **Delete** to open the Delete Page dialog box.

3. Click the **Remove page from the navigation structure** option button to select it (if necessary), and then click the **OK** button. The Nut Bread Web page is deleted from the navigation structure. The Bread.htm page remains in the Folder List, indicating that this Web page still exists in the subweb.

To replace the Nut Bread recipe, Tyler wants you to create a new Web page for a cranberry bread recipe that the kitchen is preparing. You will create this new page in Navigation view and add it to the navigation structure, which will automatically update the link bars. Tyler will send you the actual recipe later.

Adding a New Web Page in Navigation View

When you use Navigation view to create a new Web page, you add it to the navigation structure and to the Web site at the same time. Next, you will add a blank page to the Web site as a child page of the Country Recipes Web page. You have already set the Web site to include shared borders and a link bar component, so FrontPage will automatically update the hyperlinks to this new page and include the top, bottom, and left shared borders in it.

REFERENCE WINDOW   **RW**

Adding a New Page in Navigation View
- Click the page icon that is the parent for the new page.
- Click the Create a new normal page button on the Standard toolbar to add the page as a child of the selected parent page and to assign the new page a default title and filename.
- Right-click the new page icon to open the shortcut menu, click Rename, enter the page's title, and then press the Enter key.

FrontPage automatically assigns a filename that is the same as the title you enter, although it changes any spaces in your Web page's title to underscore characters. After adding the new page to the navigation structure, you will rename it.

To add a new page to the Web site and change its title:

1. Click the **Country Recipes** page icon in the Navigation pane to select it. When you add a new page, you must first select the parent page.

TROUBLE? If the navigation structure collapses when you click the Country Recipes page icon, then you clicked the minus box on the page icon. Click the plus box on the Country Recipes page icon to expand the navigation structure.

2. Click the **Create a new normal page** button ⬜ on the Standard toolbar. A new page with the default title of "New Page 1" and the temporary filename of new_page_1.htm is added to the Web site.

   TROUBLE? If your default page title includes another number, don't worry. Just make sure that a new page was created.

   Next, rename the new page.

3. Right-click the **New Page 1** page icon to open the shortcut menu, and then click **Rename**.

4. Type **Cranberry Bread** as the page's title, and then press the **Enter** key. The new page does not appear in the Folder List until you open it in Page view or change to Folders view.

5. Double-click the **Cranberry Bread** page icon. The page opens in Page view, which creates the file in the Recipes subweb. Notice the shared borders at the top, bottom, and left side of the Web page. See Figure 5-27. These are the same shared borders that you set for all pages in the Web site. Also notice that FrontPage corrected the top shared border to reflect the deletion of the Nut Bread page and the addition of the Cranberry Bread page.

Figure 5-27	CRANBERRY BREAD PAGE IN PAGE VIEW

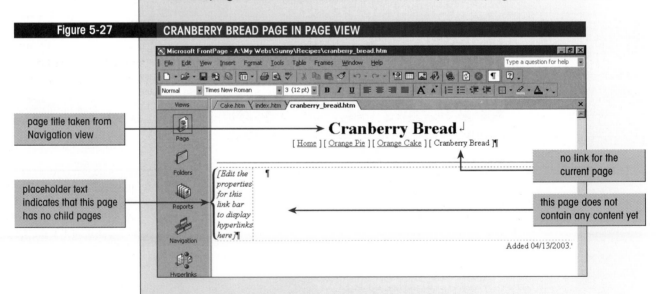

page title taken from Navigation view

placeholder text indicates that this page has no child pages

no link for the current page

this page does not contain any content yet

6. Click the **Folders** button 🗀 on the Views bar to change to Folders view. Notice that the Cranberry Bread page was added to the Web site with the filename cranberry_bread.htm.

Turning Off Shared Borders for a Single Page

If the content of a shared border is not appropriate for any particular Web page, you can turn off its display in that Web page. For example, the Country Recipes Web page does not include any links in the top shared border, because it is the top-level page in the Web site and the top shared border includes only links to the top-level and same-level pages. Because the top border of the Country Recipes page does not contain any links, Amanda asks you to turn it off. She asks you to turn off the left and bottom shared borders on this page as well.

REFERENCE WINDOW   **RW**

Turning Off Shared Borders for a Single Web Page
- Open the page in Page view.
- Click Format on the menu bar, and then click Shared Borders to open that dialog box.
- Click the Current page option button.
- Click the Top, Left, Right, and Bottom check boxes, as necessary, to turn off the appropriate shared borders.
- Click the OK button.

To turn off shared borders for a single Web page:

1. Double-click **index.htm** to open the Country Recipes page in Page view.

2. Click **Format** on the menu bar, and then click **Shared Borders** to open the Shared Borders dialog box.

3. Click the **Current page** option button to select it, and then click the **Top**, **Left**, and **Bottom** check boxes to clear them. The sample diagram changes to show that this page does not contain any shared borders.

4. Click the **OK** button to close the Shared Borders dialog box and to turn off the top, left, and bottom shared borders for this page.

Without the presence of any shared borders, the Country Recipes page no longer has a page title or link bar. The other pages in the Recipes subweb use link bars in the top and left shared borders and include their titles in the top shared border. You could enter and format a user-defined link bar for this page, but an easier option is to create a new link bar component that will appear only in this page.

Adding a Link Bar Component to a Web Page

You can add a link bar component to any Web page, not just to a shared border. Amanda wants you to include a link bar component in the Country Recipes page that provides links to the recipes (child pages) in the Web site. Using a separate link bar component for the Country Recipes page will free up more space for recipes that will be added to the Recipes subweb in the future. In addition, you can use a different arrangement of hyperlinks than what is available in the shared borders. You could create a user-defined link bar to accomplish the same objective, but it would require more work to maintain than using a link bar component, which is automatically created and maintained by FrontPage.

To add a link bar component to a Web page:

1. Create a blank line at the top of the home page, place the insertion point there, and then click the **Center** button 🔲 on the Formatting toolbar to center this line. You will insert the link bar component here.

2. Click **Insert** on the menu bar, and then click **Navigation**. The Insert Web Component dialog box opens, with the Link Bars component type selected. You can choose from three styles of link bars: a bar with custom links to pages in the current Web site or to pages in other Web sites, a bar with Back and Next links to pages in the current site, or a bar based on the arrangement of pages in Navigation view. You'll choose the third option so that the hyperlinks will match the other link bars in the subweb.

3. In the Choose a bar type list box, click **Bar based on navigation structure**, and then click the **Next** button. The second dialog box opens, in which you choose a style for the link bar.

4. Make sure that the **Use Page's Theme** button is selected, and then click the **Next** button. The third dialog box opens, in which you select an option for the arrangement of the hyperlinks. You'll use the horizontal option, which is the default.

5. Click the **Finish** button. The Link Bar Properties dialog box opens. The default setting is for the link bar to contain links to child-level pages.

6. Click the **OK** button. The link bar is inserted at the top of the page.

7. Save the home page.

You added a link bar component to the Country Recipes page that is separate from the link bar component that appears in the top shared borders of the other Web pages in the Recipes subweb. When the marketing department adds new pages to the Recipes subweb, FrontPage will update this link bar automatically to include hyperlinks to the new pages after you add those pages to the Web site's navigation structure.

When you turned off the top shared border for this page, you deleted the page's title from the page. You want the page to include a title, but not a shared border. Amanda explains that you can add a page banner to identify a page's content.

Creating a Page Banner

A page banner is a text or picture object that usually appears at the top of each page in a Web site. You can add a page banner to any page, but first you must include the page in the Web site's navigation structure.

REFERENCE WINDOW   **RW**

Creating a Page Banner

- Click the location where you want the banner to appear in the Web page.
- Click Insert on the menu bar, and then click Page Banner.
- Select the Picture or Text option button to indicate the type of banner to create.
- Edit the text in the Page banner text text box as necessary.
- Click the OK button.

You already created a navigation structure, so you will create a FrontPage page banner next.

To add a page banner to a Web page:

1. Create a new, centered line at the top of the home page and then position the insertion point on the new line. You will add the page banner here.

2. Click **Insert** on the menu bar, and then click **Page Banner**. The Page Banner Properties dialog box opens. See Figure 5-28.

| Figure 5-28 | PAGE BANNER PROPERTIES DIALOG BOX |

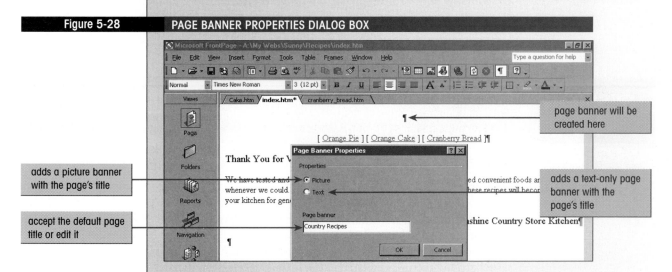

adds a picture banner with the page's title

accept the default page title or edit it

page banner will be created here

adds a text-only page banner with the page's title

Tyler wants the title of this page to be "Sunny Morning Products," so that visitors will know that it is part of the Sunny Web site. You will change the page title in the Page Banner Properties dialog box.

3. Make sure that the **Picture** option button is selected, select the text in the Page banner text box, type **Sunny Morning Products**, and then click the **OK** button to insert the page banner in the page. FrontPage automatically updates the page title in Navigation and Folders view, too.

4. Save the home page. The page banner, Sunny Morning Products, appears at the top of the Web page. You ask Amanda why the page banner is displayed as regular text, even though you selected the picture option. Amanda explains that you could use the Formatting toolbar to change the appearance of the page banner, but an easier way is to apply a Web theme that automatically formats the entire page—including the page banner—using predefined pictures and fonts.

5. Close the Recipes subweb, and then close FrontPage. Click the **Yes** button if you are asked to save any open pages.

In the next session, you will apply a Web theme to the Recipes subweb and finish formatting the home page.

Session 5.2 QUICK CHECK

1. How many shared borders can you add to a Web site?

2. What information does a top shared border usually contain?

3. What is the advantage of using a link bar component instead of a user-defined link bar?

4. In which views can you change a page's filename and title?

5. How does FrontPage use the navigation structure to create a link bar component?

6. A hyperlink named _____ in a link bar component will open the parent page for the current page.

SESSION 5.3

In this session, you will apply a theme to the Recipes subweb and then customize the existing theme. Finally, you will create a Photo Gallery in a Web page and format text in the home page using WordArt.

Applying a Theme to a Web Site

The work that you have done so far—creating shared borders and a link bar component, and adding a page banner—have all made the Recipes subweb easy to navigate. However, remember that Tyler wants the subweb to have a fun, interesting appearance. You could add a background picture and change the format of text that appears in each page in the subweb to add this visual interest. Amanda explains that an easier way of applying the same formatting to all pages in a subweb is to use a Web theme.

A **theme** is a collection of design elements, such as bullets, backgrounds, table borders, fonts, and pictures, that you can apply to an entire subweb or Web site, or to a single Web page. A Web site with a theme applied to it has a consistent, professional appearance. Everything in the page—from its bullets to its background picture—is professionally designed to fit together. When you insert new bullets, horizontal lines, page banners, link bars, and other graphical elements in a page that uses a theme, these elements automatically match the theme. Also, if you add a new page to a Web site that has a theme applied to it, the new page will use the same theme automatically. FrontPage includes many themes with styles ranging from conservative to flashy. (Not all of these themes are installed by default, however.) When you apply a theme, you can change it to use vivid colors, active graphics, or a background picture. You can even modify a theme to customize it for your needs.

REFERENCE WINDOW   **RW**

Applying a Theme to a Web Site

- In Page view, Folders view, or Navigation view, click Format on the menu bar, and then click Theme.
- In the Themes dialog box, click the All pages option button.
- Click the theme names and examine the Sample of Theme box to find one that you like.
- Click the Vivid colors, Active graphics, and Background picture check boxes to select or deselect these options.
- Click the OK button.
- Click the Yes button to apply the theme to the current Web site.

FrontPage offers many themes. You will look for a casual theme that adds color and visual interest.

To apply a theme to a subweb:

1. Make sure that your Data Disk is in the appropriate disk drive, start FrontPage, open the **Recipes** subweb from your Data Disk, and then open the home page in Page view.

2. Click **Format** on the menu bar, and then click **Theme**. The Themes dialog box opens. The selected theme is "(No Theme)", which indicates that the subweb does not use themes.

3. If necessary, click the **All pages** option button to indicate a site-wide change.

4. Click some of the themes in the list. Notice that the theme's name might indicate its contents. For example, the Checkers theme displays a checkerboard in its page elements.

   TROUBLE? Depending on your installation of FrontPage and other Microsoft Office programs, you might see a different list of themes than those identified in the text. If you don't have a specified theme, select another theme.

   TROUBLE? If you see a message in the Sample of Theme box indicating that the theme needs to be installed, either insert your Microsoft Office XP CD into the appropriate drive and click the Install button, or select another theme in the list box until you find one that is already installed.

5. Scroll down the list of available themes until you see Poetic, and then click **Poetic** to preview it in the Sample of Theme box.

   You can change a theme to use vivid colors, active graphics, a background picture, and a cascading style sheet (CSS), which defines the styles used in your document (such as those used in headings).

6. If necessary, select the **Active graphics** and **Background picture** check boxes, and clear the **Vivid colors** and **Apply using CSS** check boxes. See Figure 5-29.

Figure 5-29	THEMES DIALOG BOX

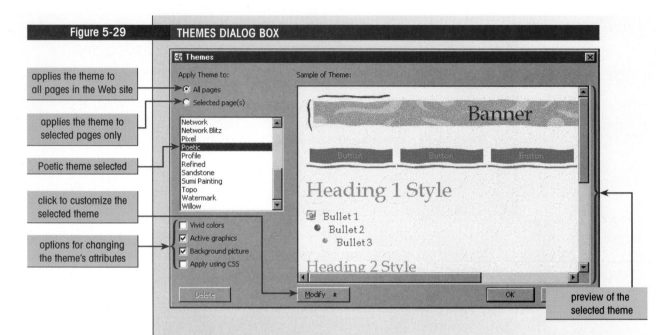

applies the theme to all pages in the Web site

applies the theme to selected pages only

Poetic theme selected

click to customize the selected theme

options for changing the theme's attributes

preview of the selected theme

7. Click the **Background picture** check box to preview the theme without the background picture. Notice that the page's background is now white. You may have previewed some sample themes in Step 4 that used dark background colors. In these cases, you could use the theme without the background picture if the text in your page would not be readable after applying the theme.

8. Click the **Vivid colors** check box to select it. The white background changes to yellow. The yellow color is part of this theme's vivid color settings.

9. Click the **OK** button. A Microsoft FrontPage dialog box opens and indicates that this action will permanently replace some of the existing formatting information.

10. Click the **Yes** button to apply the theme to the Recipes subweb. Several messages are displayed on the status bar while this action is being performed— uploading, applying theme, and loading web. After the theme has been applied, the home page is displayed in Page view. See Figure 5-30. The style of the headings, page banner, background, and link bar component has changed to match the new theme.

Figure 5-30	COUNTRY RECIPES PAGE WITH THEME APPLIED

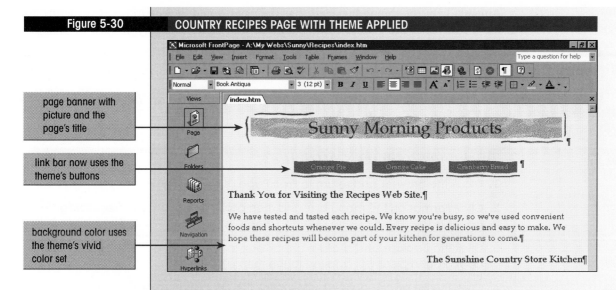

page banner with picture and the page's title

link bar now uses the theme's buttons

background color uses the theme's vivid color set

TROUBLE? It will take several minutes to apply the theme if your Web site is saved on a floppy disk. If you are storing your Web site on a hard drive, themes are applied and saved much faster.

Next, you will open the home page in the browser and test the link bar component.

To view the page in the browser and test the link bar:

1. Preview the home page in a browser.

2. Point to the **Orange Cake** button in the link bar. The button's appearance changes to reverse the colors. This animation occurs because you chose the active graphics option when you applied the theme.

3. Click the **Orange Cake** button in the link bar to open that page. See Figure 5-31. The link bar in the top and left shared borders, page banner, and horizontal line all use elements that match the theme. You selected these settings when you created the link bar in the top and left shared borders and the page banner.

Figure 5-31	ORANGE CAKE PAGE WITH THEME APPLIED

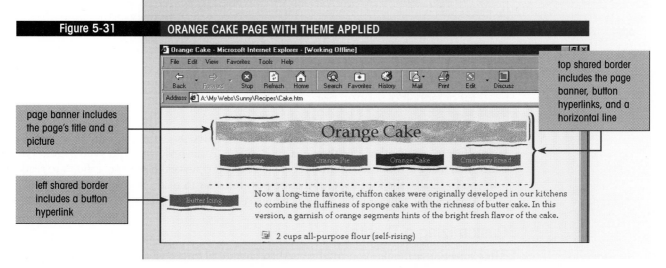

top shared border includes the page banner, button hyperlinks, and a horizontal line

page banner includes the page's title and a picture

left shared border includes a button hyperlink

Amanda likes the theme but feels that the page would look better with a picture background, instead of the yellow color. To make this modification, you need to change the theme's attributes.

Changing a Theme's Attributes

You can change a theme's attributes using the Themes dialog box. You will apply the Poetic theme's background picture next.

To change a theme's attributes:

1. Close the browser and return to FrontPage (if necessary).

2. Click **Format** on the menu bar, and then click **Theme**. The Themes dialog box opens again. This time, the selected theme is "(Default) Poetic."

3. Click the **Background picture** check box to select that option. The theme's background picture is applied to the theme's preview.

4. Click the **All pages** option button, click the **OK** button to apply the background picture to the theme, and then click the **Yes** button. The home page is displayed using the theme's background picture. See Figure 5-32.

| Figure 5-32 | COUNTRY RECIPES PAGE WITH THEME'S BACKGROUND PICTURE |

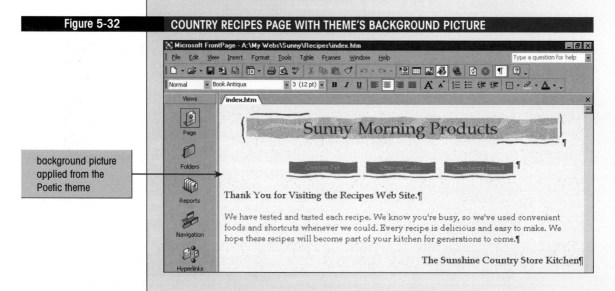

background picture applied from the Poetic theme

TROUBLE? If you see broken links in the page banner and link bar, close the Web site and FrontPage. Then restart FrontPage, open the Sunny Web site, and open the home page in Page view. If you still see broken links, ask your instructor or technical support person for help.

The revised theme has been applied to the entire Recipes subweb. You ask Tyler to visit your office to see whether this theme is appropriate. After reviewing the Web pages, Tyler is concerned that the font used in the Web page's body text makes the recipe difficult to read. He asks you to change the font to see if the recipes are easier to read. After discussing this change with Amanda, she tells you that Tyler's change requires you to customize the existing theme.

Customizing a Theme

After selecting a theme, you might need to change it to better suit your needs. You could select and change the font in the body of every Web page to meet Tyler's request, but an easier way is to customize the existing theme so that all existing and future Web pages will include the revised font.

To customize the Poetic theme:

1. Click **Format** on the menu bar, and then click **Theme**. The Themes dialog box opens.

2. Click the **Modify** button in the dialog box. The dialog box changes to add the "What would you like to modify?" section, which includes buttons to change the theme's colors, graphics, and text. Also notice the Save and Save As buttons, which let you save a customized Web theme with a new name for future use. You need to change the font used by the theme, so you will click the Text button to open a dialog box that lets you change the text options.

3. Click the **Text** button. The Modify Theme dialog box opens and displays the preview of the current theme, an Item list box, and a list of fonts available on your system. You need to change the style of the Body text, so the Item list box is already set for you. You could click the list arrow and change the style of headings used in the theme as well.

4. Make sure that the Item list box displays the **Body** option, click **Arial** in the Font list box, and then preview the change in the Sample of Theme box. See Figure 5-33.

Figure 5-33	MODIFY THEME DIALOG BOX

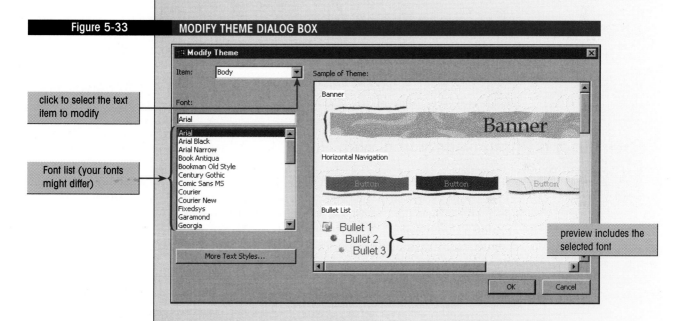

click to select the text item to modify

Font list (your fonts might differ)

preview includes the selected font

TROUBLE? If you do not have the Arial font on your system, select a similar font.

5. Click the **OK** button to close the Modify Theme dialog box. The Themes dialog box is redisplayed.

6. Click the **All pages** option button (if necessary), click the **OK** button to close the Themes dialog box. A dialog box opens and asks whether you want to save the changes to the Poetic theme.

7. Click the **Yes** button, click the **OK** button to accept "Copy of Poetic" as the new theme name, and then click the **Yes** button (if necessary). The Themes dialog box closes, and the Arial font is applied to the body text in the pages in the Recipes subweb. See Figure 5-34.

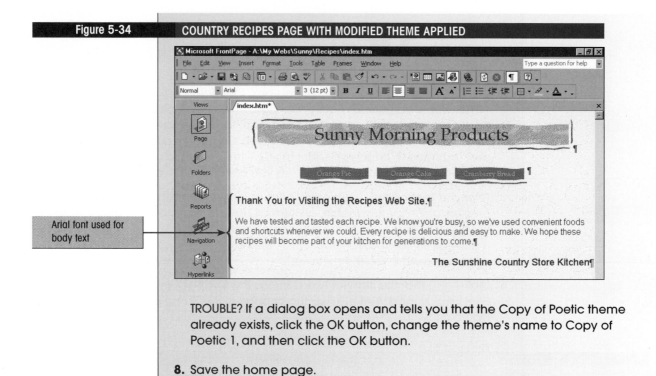

Figure 5-34 **COUNTRY RECIPES PAGE WITH MODIFIED THEME APPLIED**

Arial font used for body text

TROUBLE? If a dialog box opens and tells you that the Copy of Poetic theme already exists, click the OK button, change the theme's name to Copy of Poetic 1, and then click the OK button.

8. Save the home page.

The new theme is attractive and the text in the Web page is easier to read. The final change that Tyler asks you to make is to add pictures to the home page.

Creating a Photo Gallery in a Web Page

A **Photo Gallery** is a FrontPage Web component that lets you add pictures with captions and descriptions to your Web pages. The advantage of using a Photo Gallery is that you can create and format the captions, descriptions, and thumbnail pictures automatically. After creating a Photo Gallery, you can change its properties, just like any other FrontPage Web component, by revising the captions and descriptions or by adding and deleting pictures.

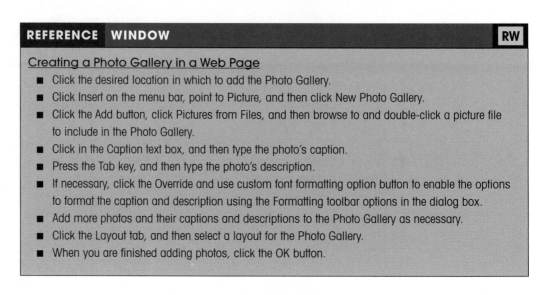

REFERENCE WINDOW   **RW**

Creating a Photo Gallery in a Web Page
- Click the desired location in which to add the Photo Gallery.
- Click Insert on the menu bar, point to Picture, and then click New Photo Gallery.
- Click the Add button, click Pictures from Files, and then browse to and double-click a picture file to include in the Photo Gallery.
- Click in the Caption text box, and then type the photo's caption.
- Press the Tab key, and then type the photo's description.
- If necessary, click the Override and use custom font formatting option button to enable the options to format the caption and description using the Formatting toolbar options in the dialog box.
- Add more photos and their captions and descriptions to the Photo Gallery as necessary.
- Click the Layout tab, and then select a layout for the Photo Gallery.
- When you are finished adding photos, click the OK button.

You will add the Photo Gallery at the bottom of the page.

To create a Photo Gallery on the home page:

1. Click the blank line at the bottom of the home page.

2. Click **Insert** on the menu bar, point to **Picture**, and then click **New Photo Gallery**. The Photo Gallery Properties dialog box opens. Tyler saved the pictures that you will add to the Photo Gallery on your Data Disk.

3. Click the **Add** button, and then click **Pictures from Files**. The File Open dialog box opens. If necessary, open the **Tutorial.05** folder on your Data Disk, and then double-click **P_Cake**. The picture's filename and a preview appear in the dialog box. See Figure 5-35.

Figure 5-35	PHOTO GALLERY PROPERTIES DIALOG BOX

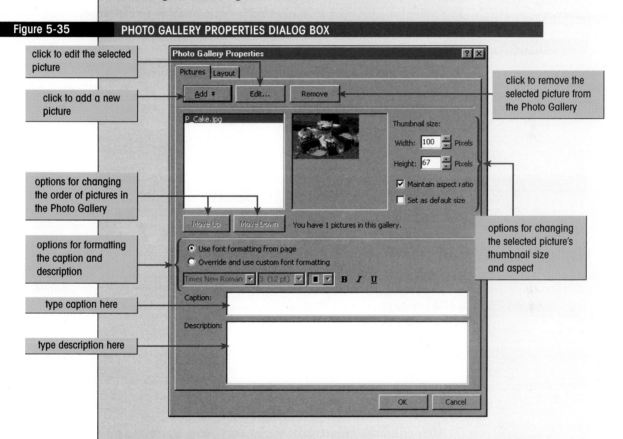

click to edit the selected picture

click to add a new picture

click to remove the selected picture from the Photo Gallery

options for changing the order of pictures in the Photo Gallery

options for formatting the caption and description

options for changing the selected picture's thumbnail size and aspect

type caption here

type description here

The next step is to add the caption and description for this photo. Notice the two option buttons in the middle of the dialog box. If you want the caption and description to use the same formatting as other text in the page, click the Use font formatting from page option button. If you want to format the caption and description using the formatting options in the dialog box, click the Override and use custom font formatting option button.

Because the home page uses a theme, you will not use custom formatting, which will ensure that the Photo Gallery has the same font style as other text in the page.

4. Click in the **Caption** text box, and then type **Cakes**.

5. Press the **Tab** key to move to the Description text box, and then type **Try one of our delicious cake recipes today.**

6. Repeat Steps 3 through 5 to add the **P_Pie** picture to the Photo Gallery with the caption **Pies** and the description **Our pies are sure to become some of your favorites.**

7. Add the **P_Bread** picture to the Photo Gallery using the caption **Breads** and the description **You'll love our specialty breads. They make excellent gifts.**

8. Add the **P_Icing** picture to the Photo Gallery using the caption **Icings** and the description **Our icings are terrific with our cakes, but we're sure that you'll love them with your favorite cake recipes, too.**

9. Click the **OK** button. FrontPage creates the Photo Gallery in the home page. See Figure 5-36.

Figure 5-36	PHOTO GALLERY ADDED TO THE HOME PAGE

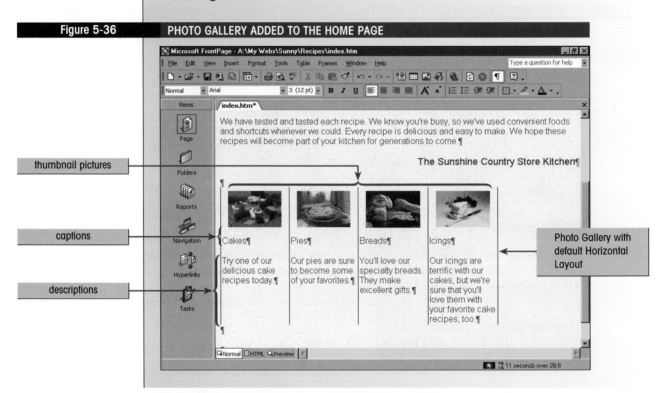

After creating a Photo Gallery, you can change its characteristics or the way that the text in the captions and descriptions is formatted. After viewing the Photo Gallery, Tyler asks you to change its alignment to centered and to see whether another arrangement of the pictures would work better than the default option.

To change the Photo Gallery's alignment and style:

1. Click the **Photo Gallery** to select it, and then click the **Center** button 🔳 on the Formatting toolbar. The Photo Gallery is centered on the page.

2. Right-click the **Photo Gallery** to open the shortcut menu, click **Photo Gallery Properties,** and then click the **Layout** tab. The Layout tab contains options for arranging the pictures in the Photo Gallery. The default, Horizontal Layout, displays each picture, its caption, and its description in a row format. You can change the number of pictures to display in each row by changing the value in the Number of pictures per row box. The default value is to display five pictures in each row.

3. Click the **Montage Layout** option. This layout arranges pictures as a collage. When you point to a picture in the collage, its caption appears. This layout does not let you use descriptions.

4. Click the **Slide Show** layout. This layout arranges the pictures in a scrollable format, with the selected image being displayed in its full size with a description below it.

5. Click the **Vertical Layout** option. This layout displays pictures in columns with their captions and descriptions.

   Tyler likes the Slide Show layout, so you will select that one.

6. Click **Slide Show** in the list box, and then click the **OK** button. The Photo Gallery changes to the Slide Show layout.

   To view the Photo Gallery, you can switch to Preview Page view.

7. Click the **Preview** button, and then scroll down the page so you can see the entire Photo Gallery.

8. Click the **Pies** picture. The Slide Show changes to display the Pies picture and its caption and description. See Figure 5-37.

| Figure 5-37 | PREVIEW PAGE VIEW OF PHOTO GALLERY WITH SLIDE SHOW LAYOUT |

arrows for scrolling through the pictures (when more pictures are included in the Photo Gallery)

click a thumbnail picture to display the full-sized picture and its caption and description

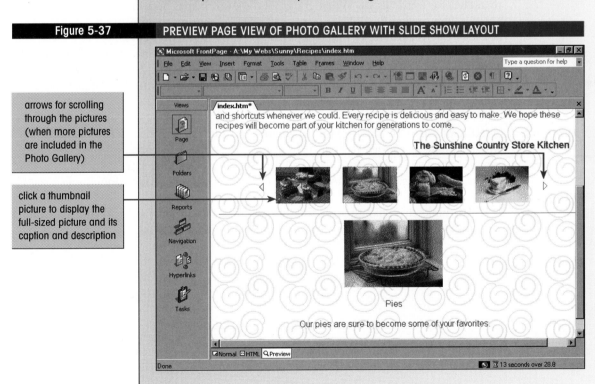

9. Click the **Normal** button.

10. Save the home page, and save the embedded files in the Recipes subweb's images folder.

The last change that Tyler wants you to make is to format the home page so the first and last lines of text on the page stand out more. Although you could format these lines as headings, Tyler wants you to try formatting them as WordArt.

Using Drawings, AutoShapes, and WordArt in a Web Page

Sometimes the content of your Web pages requires you to draw objects, such as arrows and callouts, or shapes, such as hearts or smiling faces. In other cases, you might want to format text in a special way by controlling its color, font, and appearance. In these cases, you can insert a drawing, AutoShape, or WordArt in the page.

A **drawing** is a canvas object that contains objects such as text boxes and arrows. For example, you might use a drawing object to create a simple diagram. To insert a drawing, click Insert on the menu bar, point to Picture, and then click New Drawing. A canvas object opens in the Web page, along with the Drawing Canvas toolbar. You use the buttons on the Drawing toolbar to draw lines, change colors, and add text boxes. Clicking the Fit, Expand, or Scale Drawing buttons on the Drawing toolbar lets you control the size of the canvas object.

An **AutoShape** is a predesigned shape, such as an arrow, bracket, square, circle, banner, star, or callout. You can insert an AutoShape in a Web page by clicking the AutoShapes button on the Drawing toolbar or by clicking Insert on the menu bar, pointing to Picture, and then clicking AutoShapes. When you click the AutoShapes button on the Drawing toolbar, a menu with several AutoShape categories opens. Pointing to an AutoShape category, such as Lines, opens a palette of line styles that you can insert. After clicking a line style, you use the pointer to draw a line in a Web page. FrontPage then automatically generates the HTML code required to position and draw the object on the page. If you use the Insert menu to place an AutoShape on a Web page, the AutoShapes toolbar opens and provides buttons for accessing the same AutoShape styles.

WordArt is a text object to which you can apply a font, font size, and special effects. To create a WordArt object in a Web page, you can either select existing text or insert new text while creating the WordArt object. In either case, when you create a WordArt object, you can select the style, font, font size, and font style for your text. After creating the WordArt object, you can use the WordArt toolbar to change its attributes or double-click the object to edit the text.

Tyler thinks that changing the first line of text on the home page to WordArt would create additional visual interest for this page.

REFERENCE WINDOW   RW

Creating a WordArt Object in a Web Page

- If necessary, select the existing text that you will format as a WordArt object.
- Click Insert on the menu bar, point to Picture, and then click WordArt. The Word Art Gallery dialog box opens.
- Click the WordArt style to use for your text, and then click the OK button. The Edit WordArt Text dialog box opens.
- Select the font, font size, and font style for your text. If necessary, type or edit the text for the WordArt object in the Text text box.
- Click the OK button.
- Use the WordArt toolbar to change the color, shape, letter height, direction, alignment, or character spacing of the WordArt object, if desired.

To create WordArt objects using existing text:

1. Scroll up the home page, and then select the text **Thank You for Visiting the Recipes Web Site.** (make sure that you select the period).

2. Click **Insert** on the menu bar, point to **Picture**, and then click **WordArt**. The WordArt Gallery dialog box opens and shows the WordArt styles that you can apply to text. See Figure 5-38.

Figure 5-38   WORDART GALLERY DIALOG BOX

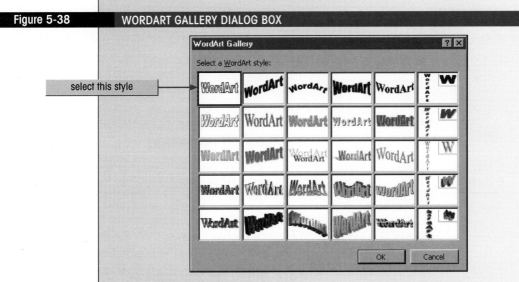

select this style

3. Click the first style in the first row, and then click the **OK** button. The Edit WordArt Text dialog box opens. See Figure 5-39. You use this dialog box to specify the font, font size, and font style for your WordArt object. Notice that the text you selected in Step 1 appears in the Text text box. If necessary, you can edit the text now. If you did not select existing text before opening the WordArt Gallery dialog box, the default "Your Text Here" text would appear in the Text text box. You could then select and replace that text before continuing.

Figure 5-39   EDIT WORDART TEXT DIALOG BOX

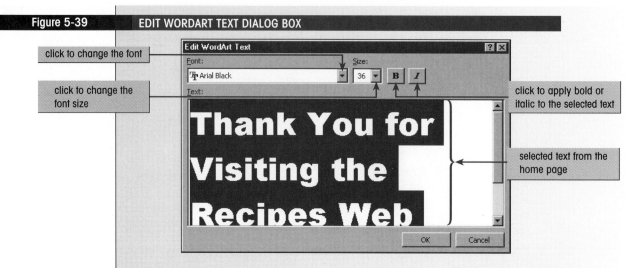

Tyler suggests that you use the default font for this WordArt style, Arial Black, but change its size to 14.

4. Click the **Size** list arrow, and then scroll up and click **14**. The text changes to use the new specifications.

5. Click the **OK** button. The WordArt object appears in the Web page, and the WordArt toolbar opens. See Figure 5-40.

Figure 5-40   WORDART OBJECT ADDED TO THE HOME PAGE

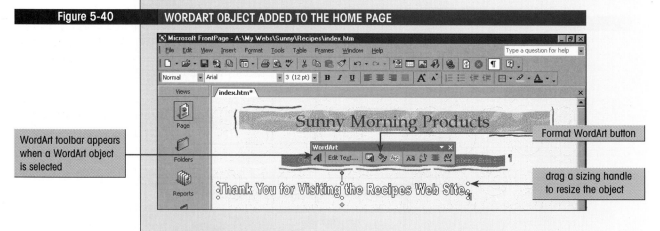

TROUBLE? If the WordArt toolbar blocks the WordArt object in the Web page, drag it to another location or dock it below the Formatting toolbar.

TROUBLE? If normal text appears to the right of the WordArt object, position the insertion point at the beginning of the normal text and then press the Enter key. Click the WordArt object to select it again.

When a WordArt object is selected, the WordArt toolbar appears. The buttons on the WordArt toolbar let you change the WordArt text, style, color, shape, letter height, direction, alignment, and character spacing of the letters in the WordArt object. Tyler likes the WordArt object but suggests that you change it to use the same purple color that appears in the theme.

To change a WordArt object:

1. With the WordArt object selected, click the **Format WordArt** button 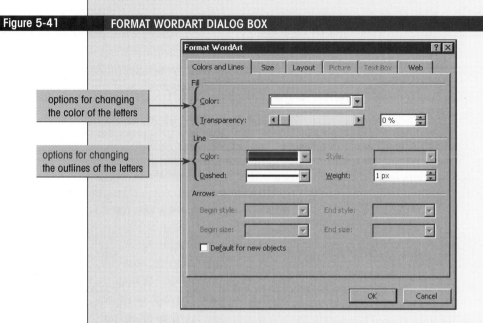 on the WordArt toolbar. The Format WordArt dialog box opens. See Figure 5-41.

Figure 5-41   FORMAT WORDART DIALOG BOX

options for changing the color of the letters

options for changing the outlines of the letters

You can use the Colors and Lines tab in this dialog box to control the color, style, and weight of the lines and the fill color of the letters in the WordArt object. The Size tab lets you control the size, rotation, and scale of a WordArt object; the Layout tab lets you control the positioning style of the WordArt object. Usually, you can accept the default options on the Size and Layout tabs.

2. In the Fill section, click the **Color** list arrow, and then click the **violet** color (use the ScreenTips to identify the correct color). This change will fill the letters with a violet (purple) color.

3. In the Line section, click the **Color** list arrow, and then click the **lavender** color. This change will draw the lines that surround each letter using a lavender (light purple) color.

4. Click the **OK** button, and then click an empty area in the Web page to deselect the WordArt object. The WordArt object changes to purple with light purple letter outlines. See Figure 5-42.

Figure 5-42   COMPLETED WORDART OBJECT

WordArt object with purple letters and outlines

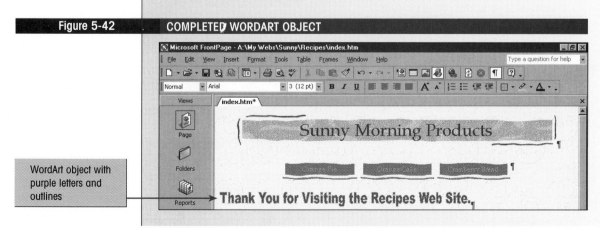

5. Save the home page, and then preview it in the browser. Use the hyperlinks to view all of the pages that you created in this tutorial.

6. Close the browser and return to FrontPage (if necessary).

Amanda wants you to view the HTML code that FrontPage used to implement your changes.

Viewing HTML Code for FrontPage Web Components and Themes

FrontPage stores the files needed to support the Photo Gallery in the Web's photogallery folder. FrontPage hides most of the HTML code for hover buttons and animations, shared borders, link bars, and themes in hidden folders and files that it automatically creates. The _borders and _themes folders are the primary folders in which the theme's shared border and theme files are stored. FrontPage does not display hidden folders in Folders view unless you configure it to do so. If you like, you can see these folders and the files they contain using Windows Explorer.

Shared borders and themes are implemented in FrontPage using META tags (which were described in Tutorial 2). These META tags are created automatically by FrontPage and inserted in each page in the Web site. FrontPage then uses these META tags to display the desired arrangement of borders and themes, using the files that are stored in the theme's and border's hidden folders. For the Recipes subweb, FrontPage created the top, left, and bottom shared borders as Web pages in the _borders folder.

The banners and link bars were created using FrontPage Web components, which are identified in each page's HTML document with a comment tag (<!-- ... -->). If a Web browser that does not support a FrontPage Web component opens a Web page that contains such a component, the browser will ignore those components that it cannot process and display. When you use HTML Page view to view the HTML code for a Web page that contains components, FrontPage displays the component's HTML code in a different color to distinguish it.

To view the HTML code for themes and FrontPage components:

1. Click the **HTML** button, and then press **Ctrl + Home** to scroll to the top of the page. See Figure 5-43. Examine the code in the page and identify the changes that you made in this session.

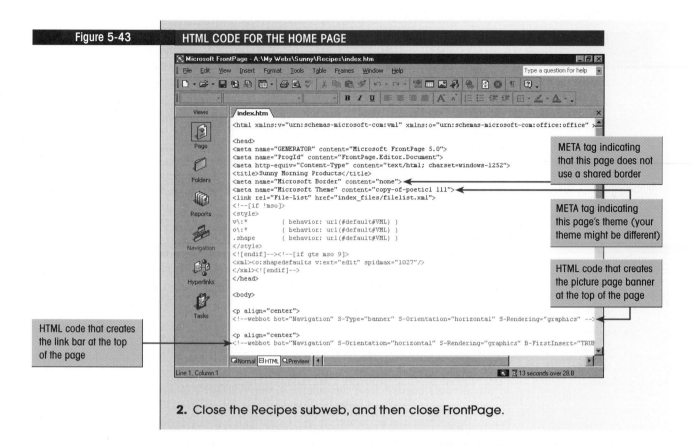

Figure 5-43   HTML CODE FOR THE HOME PAGE

2. Close the Recipes subweb, and then close FrontPage.

Tyler is pleased with the new Recipes subweb and feels that the FrontPage shared borders and link bars will make it easy to maintain and update the site as new recipes are added to it. In Tutorial 6, you will publish the Sunny Web site to a Web server and create pages that use FrontPage components for processing them.

Session 5.3 QUICK CHECK

1. To change a theme, click the _____ button in the Themes dialog box.

2. True or False: You must apply the same theme to every page in a Web site.

3. Which button would you click in the Themes dialog box to modify the theme's color scheme?

4. True or False: When you create a caption in the Photo Gallery, you have the option of applying custom formatting to the text.

5. How do pictures in a Photo Gallery appear on the page when you apply the Montage Layout to the Photo Gallery?

6. Arrows, callouts, and special graphics such as a heart shape are examples of _____.

7. The files that create the shared borders in a Web site are stored in the Web's _____ folder.

REVIEW ASSIGNMENTS

After examining the Recipes subweb and gathering input from other members of the marketing department, Tyler asks you to make some changes to improve the site's functionality. He asks you to create two new recipe pages as placeholders in the Web site until he obtains the final recipes from the kitchen. Amanda also asks you to modify the Sunny Web site to link it to the Recipes subweb. In addition, you will enhance the Clothing Web page that you created in Tutorial 4 to add a picture.

If necessary, insert your Data Disk in the appropriate disk drive, start FrontPage, and then do the following:

1. Open the **Sunny** Web site from your Data Disk in Folders view.

2. Open the **Clothing.htm** Web page that you created in Tutorial 4 in Page view. On a new line above the footer, add a centered hover button with the text "Return to Home Page" that contains a hyperlink to open the home page. Select a font and colors of your choice and an appropriate mouse over effect for the hover button. If necessary, change the hover button's size so that the text is displayed correctly.

3. On a new centered line below the hover button that you added in Step 2, insert the **Beach.gif** picture from the Tutorial.05 folder on your Data Disk in the Clothing Web page. If necessary, resize the picture to make it smaller, and then apply a beveled edge to the picture's border. Save the picture in the Web site's images folder. Next, preview the page in a browser and print it. Test your hover button to verify that it links to the home page. Close the browser.

Explore   4. Open the Sunshine Country Store Map page (**MapPage.htm**) in Page view. Create a second hover button with your choice of colors and mouse over effect in the Sunshine Country Store Map page in the right cell of the table that appears below the map picture. Use the text "Go to Recipes Site" for the hover button and format it using 18-point, bold, Arial font. Then create a hyperlink to the home page in the **Recipes** subweb on your Data Disk. If necessary, change the size of the hover button to accommodate its text. Save your changes, and then test the new hover button in the browser. Use the browser's Back button to return to the Sunshine Country Store Map page, and then print it.

Explore   5. Use the hover button in the Sunshine Country Store Map to open the Sunny Morning Products home page, use a hyperlink to open the Investor Relations page, and then click the Edit button on the Standard Buttons toolbar to edit the Investor Relations page in FrontPage. Apply a page exit transition of your choice to the Investor Relations page that has a duration of four seconds, save the page, and then test the transition in the browser. (*Hint:* You must leave the page to test the transition.)

Explore   6. Animate the link bar in the Investor Relations page so that the words in the link bar fly across the screen from the upper-left corner of the page. Save the page, and then test the animation in the browser. (*Hint:* You might need to refresh the page to see the text animation.) Close the browser.

7. Close the DHTML Effects toolbar, close the **Sunny** Web site, and then open the **Recipes** subweb from your Data Disk.

8. Use Navigation view to create two new pages in the **Recipes** subweb (you will create the pages, but will not enter the recipes). The first page will contain a recipe for Hard Candy. Add this page at the same level as the Orange Cake page. Then create another new page for a recipe for Christmas Candy. Add this page as a child page to the Hard

Candy page. Open the Christmas Candy Web page in Page view, and then apply a theme of your choice to only this page. Choose the options to use vivid colors, active graphics, and a background picture. After applying the theme, save the Christmas Candy page.

Explore ▷ 9. On a new, right-aligned line in the bottom shared border of all pages in the **Recipes** subweb, except for the Country Recipes Web page, type the text "To order items from Sunny Morning Products," press the spacebar, and then add a hover button at the end of the sentence that includes the text "click here". The hover button should include a link to the appropriate page in the **Sunny** Web site. Select colors and a mouse over effect of your choice. Save and test your changes in the browser, and then close the browser.

Explore ▷ 10. Print Navigation view for the **Recipes** subweb. (*Hint:* Use a toolbar button.) Use FrontPage to print the Christmas Candy page and its HTML code.

11. Close the **Recipes** subweb, and then close FrontPage.

CASE PROBLEMS

Case 1. Changing the Appearance of the Royal Hair Care Products Web Site   Valerie Suarez is pleased with the financial performance and current stock market activities tables that you added to the Web site in Tutorial 4. Now that the Web site includes many different pages of information, Valerie asks you to improve its appearance to ensure that it is visually interesting and easy to use. First, you will change the user-defined link bar to include hover buttons. Then you will change the appearance of the pages that open in the main frame of the frames page. After you have finished making these changes, Valerie will meet with the rest of the Web site development team to test the site and gather feedback.

If necessary, start FrontPage, insert your Data Disk in the appropriate disk drive, and then do the following:

1. Read all of the questions for this case problem, and then prepare a planning analysis sheet for the changes to the Web site.

2. Open the **Royal** Web site from your Data Disk in Folders view. (If you did not create this Web site in Tutorial 2 and change it in Tutorials 3 and 4, ask your instructor for assistance.)

3. Open the Financial Information Web page (**RInvest.htm**) that you created in Tutorial 4 in Page view.

Explore ▷ 4. In the upper-left cell of the table in the Financial Performance page, which opens in the main frame, create a thumbnail of the **Royal.gif** picture that is saved in the Web site's images folder. Change the picture to use a beveled edge. Then create a hyperlink from the thumbnail picture to the Royal Hair Care Products home page so that the home page opens and replaces the frames page in the browser. Add appropriate alternative text to the picture. Save the picture with the default filename in the site's images folder. Test the page in the browser, and then close the browser.

Explore ▷ 5. Change the user-defined link bar in the banner frame to include a hover button for each item in the link bar with links to the corresponding pages. Use the default hover button settings for each button, and create hyperlinks that open the pages in the full browser window, replacing the frames page. (*Hint:* Create a hover button for the link to the current page, but do not assign a hyperlink to it. Change the table's properties to the center alignment and to use 95% of the browser window's width. There is no Search page in the Web site. When you create the hyperlink for the Search hover button, enter the filename **RSearch.htm** as the hyperlink, even though this page does not yet exist. You will create this page in Tutorial 6.) If one of the hover buttons is not horizontally aligned with the others, turn on the nonprinting characters and delete any extra lines in the table's cell. After creating all of the hover buttons, resize them until they are only as wide as the text they contain. Save your changes, test the link bar in the browser, and then close the browser. Use FrontPage to print the HTML code for the page that is displayed in the banner frame.

6. Animate the words in the contents frame with an animation of your choice. Experiment with the different effects, and then select the one that you like the best. Save the page.

7. Add a page transition of your choice to the home page. This transition should occur when the user opens the page and should last for five seconds. Preview the Financial Information page in the browser to test the animation that you applied in Step 6, and then click the Home hyperlink in the banner frame to test the transition that you applied to the home page.

8. Apply an appropriate theme to the entire Web site. Before applying the theme, make sure that it includes vivid colors, active graphics, and a background picture, and that it coordinates well with the colors that you have used in the site's pages.

9. Test the Web site using a browser. If necessary, apply a different theme to ensure that all text in the Web site is clear and readable. Close the browser.

10. Use FrontPage to print the HTML code for the Financial Performance page (**RFinInfo.htm**) and for the Banner page (**Banner.htm**).

11. Close the **Royal** Web site, and then close FrontPage.

Case 2. Adding Shared Borders and a Theme to the Buffalo Trading Post Web Site Donna Vargas and Karla Perez realize that as business at the Buffalo Trading Post (BTP) continues to grow, they will be adding more Web pages to the company's Web site. They are pleased with the appearance of the site so far. Donna wants to make sure that it is easy to update the site when new pages are added. She asks you to change the existing link bars to ones generated by FrontPage, which will be updated automatically when new pages are added to the site. Also, Karla wants you to add a theme to the pages to present a consistent appearance.

If necessary, start FrontPage, insert your Data Disk in the appropriate disk drive, and then do the following:

1. Read all of the questions for this case problem, and then prepare a planning analysis sheet for the changes to the Web site.

2. Open the **Buffalo** Web site from your Data Disk in Navigation view. (If you did not create this Web site in Tutorial 2 and change it in Tutorials 3 and 4, ask your instructor for assistance.)

Explore ▶ 3. Create a navigation structure for the Web site using the existing pages. The home page should be the top-level page; the What, How, and Who pages should be child pages of the home page; and the Accessories, Women's Clothing, and Children's Clothing pages should be child pages of the What page. After creating the navigation structure, print Navigation view. (*Hint:* To print Navigation view, use a toolbar button.)

4. Open the home page in Page view, and then add a bottom shared border to all pages in the Web site.

5. Select both lines of the footer that appear at the bottom of the home page. Cut the footer from the page, select the comment placeholder text that appears in the bottom

shared border, and then paste the footer into the bottom shared border. (Choose the option to keep the source formatting.) If necessary, insert one blank line at the top of the bottom shared border. On a new third line in the bottom shared border, add the text "Last updated" and then insert the date and time when the page was last edited using a date/time format of your choice. Save your changes.

Explore

6. Change the background color of the bottom shared border to use the light orange color with the value Hex={FF,CC,99}. (*Hint:* Use the Border Properties dialog box and the More Colors dialog box to make this change.)

Explore

7. Use FrontPage Help to learn how to add a comment to the home page in Page view (insert a normal text comment, not an HTML comment), and then close the Help window. Insert the following comment at the top of the page, on a new line above the link bar, as a reminder to add the new company logo to the Web page: "Update the BTP logo when the new one is available next week." Save the home page, view the changes you made in a browser, and then close the browser.

Explore

8. Apply a customized version of the Axis theme to the entire Web site. (If you do not have this theme, select another theme.) The theme should use vivid colors, active graphics, and a background picture. Before applying the theme, click the Graphics button and use the Modify Theme dialog box to change the bullet list picture for List Bullet 1 so that it uses the **Bullet.gif** file that is saved in the Tutorial.05 folder on your Data Disk. Save the new theme using the default name.

9. Open the Who page in Page view, and scroll to the bottom of the page. Change the numbered list that appears under the line "Why are we here?" to a bulleted list. Make sure that the bullets use the picture identified in Step 8. Save the Who page.

Explore

10. Open the home page in Page view. Change the heading that you created for the home page into a page banner. (*Hint:* Select and cut the heading from the page. Create a new, centered line at the top of the page and below the comment to contain the page banner. Open the Page Banner Properties dialog box, choose the Picture option, select the text in the Page banner text box, and then press Ctrl + V to paste the heading.) If necessary, edit your banner text to make it fit on a single line. Save the home page, and then view it in the browser. Test the links throughout the Web site to ensure that they work correctly. Close the browser.

Explore

11. Use FrontPage to print the home page, and then print the HTML code for the home page. On the printout, circle the HTML code that implements the comment, page banner, and bottom shared border.

12. Close the **Buffalo** Web site, and then close FrontPage.

Case 3. Enhancing the Appearance of the Menu Pages for Garden Grill Nolan Simmons and Shannon Taylor want to make sure that the new menu pages that you added to the Web site in Tutorial 4 are easy and fun to read. According to Nolan, the menu pages should be similar in appearance to the restaurant's menus that are provided to patrons. He asks you to use FrontPage to add logos and themes to the menu pages so that they have the same professional appearance as the menus provided at the restaurant.

If necessary, start FrontPage, insert your Data Disk in the appropriate disk drive, and then do the following:

1. Read all of the questions for this case problem, and then prepare a planning analysis sheet for the changes to the Web site.

2. Open the **Garden** Web site from your Data Disk in Folders view. (If you did not create this Web site in Tutorial 2 and change it in Tutorials 3 and 4, ask your instructor for assistance.)

Explore

3. Change the **Garden.gif** picture, found at the top of the Appetizers page that you created in Tutorial 4, to have a beveled edge. Save the page and overwrite the existing **Garden.gif** file in the Web site's images folder. Open the home page in Page view. Why does the logo in this page now have a beveled edge?

4. Change to Folders view and create a new normal page using the filename **Specials.htm** and the title "Specials." Open the page in Page view, and then enter content to describe one weekly restaurant special of your choice. Insert the **Garden.gif** picture from the Web site's images folder in the Specials page.

Explore

5. Insert a Photo Gallery in the Specials page. Use the pictures **US.gif, Italy.gif**, and **Mexico.gif**; the captions "America," "Italy," and "Mexico;" and write descriptions about a food item from each country for each picture. (For example, the special for the America picture might be chicken fried steak.) Select a layout of your choice (but not the Montage layout) for the Photo Gallery and use the font formatting from the page. Center the Photo Gallery on the page.

Explore

6. Change the style of the photo captions in the Photo Gallery to 14-point, bold, blue Tahoma font. Change the style of the description text to 12-point Tahoma font. Save the pictures in the Web site's images folder.

7. On a new line below the Photo Gallery in the Specials page, create a centered hover button with the text "Return to Home Page" that contains a hyperlink to the home page. Use 18-point, bold, MS Sans Serif font on the hover button, and add colors and a mouse over effect of your choice. If necessary, resize the hover button so that all text is visible, and then save the Specials page.

8. In the home page, create a centered hover button on a new centered line below the marquee that includes the text "Go to Specials Page" and that contains a hyperlink to the **Specials.htm** page. Use 18-point, bold, MS Sans Serif font on the hover button, and add colors and a mouse over effect of your choice. Save the home page.

9. Select and apply a page exit transition of your choice to the Specials page.

Explore

10. Change the **Garden.gif** picture that you inserted in the Specials page to use a fly in from bottom animation effect when the user opens the page. (*Hint:* Select the picture, and then use the DHTML Effects toolbar to create the effect.) Save the Specials page, and then test it and its link to the home page in the browser. Close the browser.

Explore

11. Use FrontPage to print the Specials page and then print its HTML code. On the printout, circle the HTML code that creates the picture animation, the page transition, the hover button, and the code that creates the Photo Gallery in the Web page.

12. Close the **Garden** Web site, and then close FrontPage.

Explore

Case 4. Enhancing the Replay Music Factory Web Site Charlene Fields and Alec Johnston are pleased with the Specials page that you added to the Web site. Based on feedback from the marketing department, Charlene asks you to add a picture to the Specials page and then to create hover buttons with hyperlinks to navigate the Web site. She also wants you to create a navigation structure to make it easier for her to add pages based on current market trends in the industry.

If necessary, start FrontPage, insert your Data Disk in the appropriate disk drive, and then do the following:

1. Read all of the questions for this case problem, and then prepare a planning analysis sheet for the changes to the **Replay** Web site.

2. Open the **Replay** Web site from your Data Disk in Folders view. (If you did not create this Web site in Tutorial 2 and change it in Tutorials 3 and 4, ask your instructor for assistance.)

3. Open the **MSpecials.htm** page in Page view, and then apply a theme of your choice to each page that opens in the main frame, but not to the entire Web site. Set the theme's options to ensure that the text in the music type pages is readable.

4. Create a hover button in the home page that contains a hyperlink to the Specials page. Create a second hover button in the contents frame of the **MSpecials.htm** page that returns the user to the home page. (If necessary, delete any other link in the contents frame that opens the home page.) Save your changes, test the hover buttons in the browser, and then close the browser.

5. Create a navigation structure that contains the home page and its child pages, and then print the navigation structure. (*Hint:* Do not add pages that open in a frames page to the navigation structure.)

6. Change the headings in the three music type pages to WordArt objects with your choice of style and colors. Save each page.

7. Replace the existing link bar in the home page with a link bar component with pages from the navigation structure and that is based on a theme of your choice. (*Hint:* Scroll the Choose a bar style list to make a selection.) Arrange the hyperlinks horizontally and choose the option to include links to child-level pages. Save the page.

8. Replace the existing link bar in the page that describes Replay's process for buying, selling, and trading used CDs which you created in Tutorial 3 with a link bar component with the same specifications as the link bar in the home page, except include links to same-level pages and to the home page. Save the page.

9. Use a browser to test the Web site, making sure that your hyperlinks work correctly. (Some of the pages might be blank; this is correct.)

10. Use FrontPage to print the HTML code for one of the music type pages that opens in the Specials frames page. On the printout, circle the HMTL code that identifies the theme you applied to the page and the code that creates the WordArt object.

11. Use FrontPage to print the home page and its HTML code. On the printout, circle the HTML code that creates the link bar and the hover button.

12. Close the **Replay** Web site, and then close FrontPage.

QUICK | CHECK ANSWERS

Session 5.1

1. hyperlink
2. Any three of: add text over a picture; create a thumbnail; rotate; increase or decrease contrast or brightness; crop; set transparent color; change to black and white; wash out; bevel the edges; create a hotspot; or restore
3. Select the picture, click the Text button on the Pictures toolbar, type the text, and then click anywhere outside the picture.
4. mouse over or mouse fly over
5. True
6. False

7. True

8. A page transition; animated text and pictures

Session 5.2

1. Any number from zero to four

2. A top shared border usually contains a page banner and hyperlinks to same-level pages, along with a link to the home page and to the parent page.

3. When you use a user-defined link bar, you must create and maintain it. When you use a link bar component, FrontPage automatically creates and maintains the link bar, which is usually a more accurate and efficient method.

4. Navigation view and Folders view

5. FrontPage uses the information you provide in the navigation structure to establish the relationships among Web pages.

6. Up

Session 5.3

1. Modify

2. False

3. Colors

4. True

5. The photos appear as a collage. Selecting a photo in the collage displays a caption. You cannot include descriptions with this layout.

6. AutoShapes

7. _borders

OBJECTIVES

In this tutorial you will:

- Create a new Web page using a template

- Change the properties of the search component

- Add a form component to a Web page

- Add form fields to a form and set their properties

- Validate form fields

- Use a form handler

- Open an Office document from a Web site

- Use a Web server

- Publish a Web site

- Process Web pages on a server

- Create a hit counter and a banner ad in a Web page

- Drag and drop files in a Web site

- Use the Find and Replace commands

- Recalculate and verify hyperlinks in a Web site

- Set permissions for a Web site

PUBLISHING
A WEB SITE

Preparing the Search and Feedback Web Pages

CASE

Sunny Morning Products

In her design of the user-defined link bar for the Sunny Web site, Amanda Bay included a hyperlink to the Search Web page that you will create in this tutorial. The Web site development team requested this page, which will allow users to easily search the entire Web site for information about specific products or employment positions. In addition, users will be able to search the Internet for information using the same page.

Because the Web site is a new way of marketing Sunny Morning Products, Jacob Towle wants to gather as much data as possible from the people who use the Web site. In response to Jacob's request, Amanda's Web site plan includes a Feedback Web page that will let users enter information into a form and submit it to Sunny Morning Products. This form will ask for the user's name and e-mail address, and provide options for commenting on the Web site, products, and services of Sunny Morning Products. The marketing department will then use this information to make decisions about expanding and updating the site.

The Search and Feedback Web pages that you will create in this tutorial will require a Web server for processing. You will create these pages and then publish the Sunny Web site to your computer's Web server. After publishing the Web site, you will enhance it by adding other server-based functions that analyze, update, and monitor the completed Web site. When you complete this tutorial, you will have finished the Web site that Sunny Morning Products will publish on its Web server so that Internet users can visit it. In addition, you will be fully trained in creating, maintaining, and updating a Web site for the management department at Sunny Morning Products.

SESSION 6.1

In this session, you will use a template to create a new Web page that contains a search component for searching the Sunny Web site and the Internet. You will also add a form component to a Web page and add form fields to it.

Reviewing the Tasks List

In this week's meeting with the members of the Web site development team, you received a preliminary outline describing the features that the team wants to include in the Search and Feedback Web pages. Before beginning these tasks, Amanda asks you to open the Sunny Web site and assign the tasks for completing these pages to yourself.

To open the Sunny Web site and update the Tasks list:

1. Start FrontPage, insert your Data Disk in the appropriate disk drive, and then open the **Sunny** Web site from your Data Disk.

   TROUBLE? If you are storing your Data Files on drive A, you will not have enough space on your Data Disk to complete this tutorial. To create space on your Data Disk, open it in Windows Explorer, and then delete all folders from the disk except Tutorial.06 and My Webs. If your Data Files are stored on a hard drive or a network, then no action is necessary.

2. Click the **Tasks** button 🗹 on the Views bar to open the Tasks list. The Tasks list includes two tasks—one each for creating the Feedback and Search Web pages.

3. Double-click the **Create Feedback Web page** task. The Task Details dialog box opens. You assigned this task to "Team Member" when you created it in Tutorial 3.

4. Click in the **Assigned to** text box to select the current entry, type your first and last names separated by a space, and then click the **OK** button. The Task Details dialog box closes, and the Tasks list is revised to show that this task is assigned to you.

5. Repeat Steps 3 and 4 to assign the **Create Search Web page** task to yourself.

Figure 6-1 shows Amanda's planning analysis sheet for creating the Search Web page, which you will create first.

Figure 6-1	AMANDA'S PLANNING ANALYSIS SHEET FOR THE SEARCH WEB PAGE

Planning Analysis Sheet

Objective

Create a Search Web page that accepts text entered by the user, and then is processed by the server to return a list of hyperlinks to pages in the Web site or on the Internet that contain that text.

Requirements

Template for creating a Search Web page
Picture file for the logo

Results

A Search Web page that contains search components that the server uses to process requests for information in the Sunny Web site and on the Internet. The page should include the Sunny Morning Products logo and a title.

Creating the Search Web Page Using a Template

In Tutorial 3, you used the Normal Page template to create new Web pages that did not contain any specific formatting or text. Recall that a Web page template provides formatting and content related to a specific type of page. When creating a new Web page, you can base it on a template that contains the approximate content you need. For example, if you are creating a Web page into which users will enter personal information, you might create your page using the Guest Book template, which includes Web components and sample text that are commonly found in a printed guest book. After creating a new Web page that is based on a template, you can edit it just like any other Web page. Figure 6-2 describes several FrontPage templates that you can use to create new Web pages.

Figure 6-2	SELECTED TEMPLATE WEB PAGES AND WIZARDS AND THEIR DESCRIPTIONS

NAME	DESCRIPTION
Confirmation Form	A page that confirms the receipt of information from a user of a form, discussion, or registration page
Feedback Form	A page that collects data entered by a user, such as comments and personal information
Form Page Wizard	A Wizard that creates a Web page containing a form with appropriate data fields to collect information
Frequently Asked Questions	A page with popular questions about a topic and their answers
Photo Gallery	A page that contains a Photo Gallery with pictures, captions, and descriptions that you supply
Search Page	A page that accepts keywords entered by a user and then returns a list of hyperlinks to pages with matching entries
Table of Contents	A page that contains a list of hyperlinks to every page in the current Web site

Amanda asks you to preview the Search Page template to determine whether its content is appropriate for the Search Web page that you will create for the Sunny Web site. To use a template for creating a new Web page, you must be in Page view.

To create a Web page using a template:

1. Click the **Page** button 🔲 on the Views bar to change to Page view. If the Task Pane is not open, click **View** on the menu bar, and then click **Task Pane**.

2. In the "New from template" section of the Task Pane, click **Page Templates**, and then if necessary, click the **General** tab. The Page Templates dialog box opens and displays a scrollable list of icons that represent different types of pages and Wizards that you can use to create a new Web page.

3. Scroll down the template list until you see the Search Page icon, and then click the **Search Page** icon to select it. See Figure 6-3. The description and preview indicate that this page will provide the capability for searching the entire Web site, so it is the correct template to use.

Figure 6-3	PAGE TEMPLATES DIALOG BOX

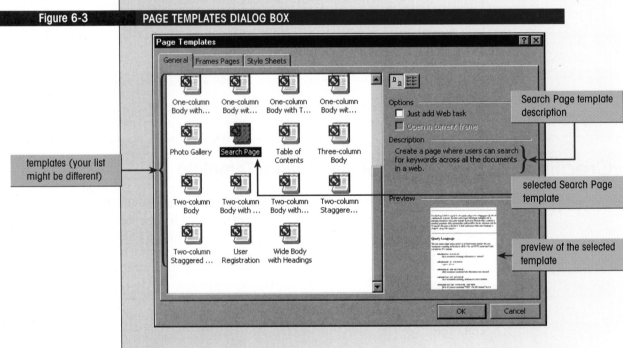

4. Click the **OK** button to create a new Web page based on the Search Page template. See Figure 6-4.

Figure 6-4   NEW WEB PAGE CREATED USING THE SEARCH PAGE TEMPLATE

default page name
(your page name might
be different)

comment text

dashed line indicates a
FrontPage component

Search for text box

explanatory text for
using the template

Start Search and Reset
buttons

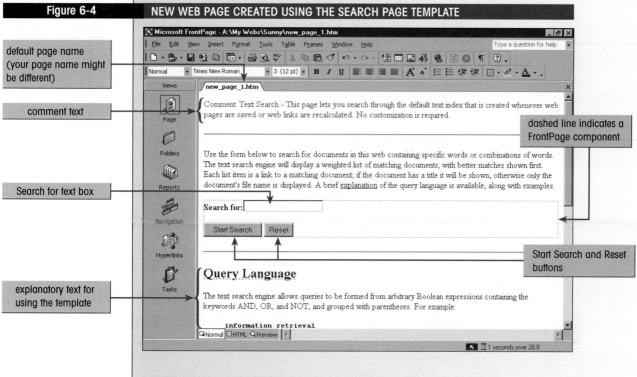

5. Scroll down the new Web page and examine its contents. The page contains a comment at the top of the page, text that describes how to use the page, a Web component that contains a Search for text box and the Start Search and Reset buttons, and an "explanation" hyperlink that links to a Query Language section with details about using the page. The bottom of the page contains a "Back to Top" hyperlink to a bookmark at the top of the page and a footer with sample copyright information.

6. Press **Ctrl + Home** to scroll to the top of the page.

The overall design and content of the new page is very similar to the page that the Web site development team requested. You can make some minor changes to convert this generic Search page into the specific Search Web page you need. You will remove the comment from the top of the page, link the background to the home page, insert the Sunny Morning Products logo at the top of the page, and then change the title of the page and the page's filename to "Search."

To revise a Web page created using a template:

1. Point to the purple "Comment: Text Search - This page..." text at the top of the page. The pointer changes to the Web component pointer 🖳 to identify the location of the Web component. The comment includes text you can see in Page view, but not in a Web browser.

2. Right-click the purple comment text to select it and open the shortcut menu, and then click **Cut**. The comment is deleted, and a blank line appears above the horizontal line at the top of the page.

Next, enter the page's title and format it as a heading.

3. Type **Search** on the blank line at the top of the page, click the **Style** list arrow on the Formatting toolbar, and then click **Heading 2**.

Next, change the page to use the same background as the home page.

4. Click **Format** on the menu bar, click **Background**, click the **Get background information from another page** check box to select it, and then click the **Browse** button to open the Current Web dialog box.

5. Double-click **index.htm** in the list of files to select the home page and return to the Page Properties dialog box, and then click the **OK** button. The Page Properties dialog box closes and the Web page displays the background picture.

Next, you will insert the Sunny Morning Products logo at the top of the page.

6. Press **Ctrl + Home** to move the insertion point to the top of the page, press the **Enter** key to insert a new line, and then press the **Up** arrow key ↑. The insertion point moves to the blank line that you created, where you will insert the logo.

7. Click the **Insert Picture From File** button 🖾 on the Standard toolbar to open the Picture dialog box, open the **Tutorial.06** folder on your Data Disk, and then double-click **Search**. The logo is inserted at the top of the page.

Finally, save the page using the new filename and title and save the logo file in the Web site's images folder.

8. Click the **Save** button 🖫 on the Standard toolbar to open the Save As dialog box, make sure that the **Sunny** folder appears in the Save in text box and that the Page title and filename are both **Search**, and then click the **Save** button. The Save As dialog box closes. Because you added a picture to the page, the Save Embedded Files dialog box opens.

9. Make sure that the **Search.gif** file will be saved in the Sunny Web site's images folder, and then click the **OK** button.

Changing the Search Component's Properties

When you created the Search page from the template, FrontPage automatically included a search component that searches the Web site using keywords entered by the user. You can also add a search component to an existing page by clicking the Web Component button on the Standard toolbar, clicking the Web Search Component type, and then following the instructions in the dialog boxes. Regardless of how you create the search component, you can change its properties as necessary. Because Amanda wants you to increase the size of the text box into which users will type keywords, you will change the search component's properties.

To change the properties of the search component:

1. If necessary, scroll down the Search page so you can see the Search for text box and the Start Search and Reset buttons, and then place the pointer anywhere in the dashed-line box that contains these objects. The pointer changes to a 🖾 shape.

2. Right-click anywhere in the search component to open the shortcut menu, and then click **Search Form Properties** to open the Search Form Properties dialog box. See Figure 6-5.

Figure 6-5	SEARCH FORM PROPERTIES DIALOG BOX

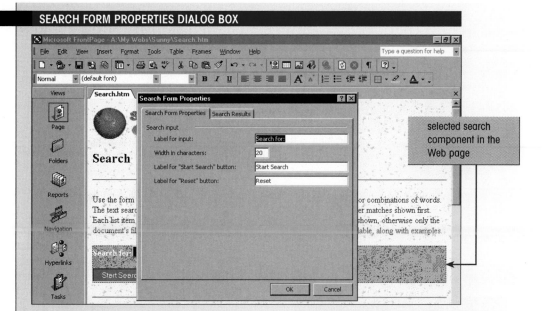

selected search component in the Web page

The Search Form Properties tab includes options for changing the defaults for the label and width of the text box as well as the labels for the two buttons that are created by the page's template. You can accept these defaults or change them, when necessary, to match your requirements. You will change the width of the Search for text box so that users can enter more characters.

3. Select the current value in the Width in characters text box, and then type **24** to increase the size of the Search for text box. The other default settings are acceptable, so you can close the dialog box.

4. Click the **OK** button to close the dialog box and return to the Search Web page, and then click anywhere in the paragraph above the search component to deselect it. Notice that the size of the Search for text box was increased to 24 characters.

Next, you will change the default footer text at the bottom of the page to match the content of the other page footers in the Sunny Web site. Instead of typing this information, you will copy and paste it from the home page.

5. Click the **Folders** button on the Views bar to change to Folders view, double-click **index.htm** to open the home page in Page view, press **Ctrl + End** to scroll to the bottom of the home page, select both lines of the footer, and then click the **Copy** button on the Standard toolbar.

6. Click the **Search.htm** page tab on the Contents pane, press **Ctrl + End** to scroll to the bottom of the Search page, and then select the three lines in the existing footer.

7. Click the **Paste** button on the Standard toolbar to paste the footer from the home page into the Search page. You will accept the default option to keep the source formatting, so you don't need to click the Paste Options button that appears.

8. Save the Search page.

Amanda also wants to include a search component that visitors can use to search the Internet. FrontPage provides a variety of components that you can use to create a link to a map at Expedia.com; to display stock market information; and to display business, living, travel, news, sports, and technology headlines, as well as weather forecasts from MSNBC. All of these components are available in the Insert Web Component dialog box.

To insert the search the Web component:

1. Scroll up the Web page until the "Query Language" heading appears at the top of the Contents pane, click to the left of the letter **Q** in Query Language, press the **Enter** key, and then press the **Up** arrow key ↑ to move to the new line.

2. Click the **Web Component** button 📇 on the Standard toolbar. The Insert Web Component dialog box opens.

3. Scroll down the list of Component types, and then click **MSN Components**. The two MSN components—Search the Web with MSN and Stock quote—appear in the Choose a MSN component list box. See Figure 6-6.

Figure 6-6	INSERT WEB COMPONENT DIALOG BOX

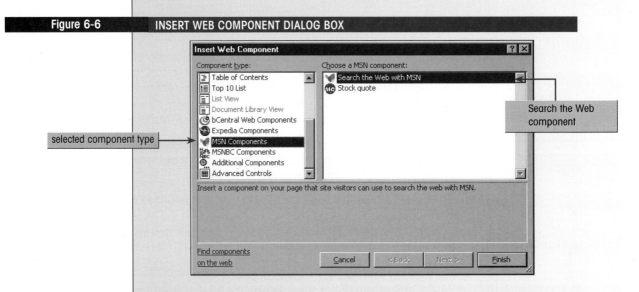

4. Make sure that the **Search the Web with MSN** component is selected, and then click the **Finish** button. The Search the Web component appears in the Web page. See Figure 6-7.

Figure 6-7	SEARCH THE WEB COMPONENT ADDED TO SEARCH PAGE

> TROUBLE? If a Dial-up Connection dialog box opens, click the Close button ☒ to close it. You do not need an Internet connection to complete these steps.
>
> The Search Web page now contains a component that will let users enter keywords to search the Internet. In Session 6.3, you will publish the Sunny Web site on a server and use this page to search the site and the Internet.
>
> **5.** Save the Search page.

Now that the Search Web page is complete, you are ready to work on the Feedback Web page.

Creating a Web Page That Contains a Form

Next, you will prepare the Feedback Web page, which will contain a form. A **form** is a collection of form fields in a Web page that gathers information. A **form field** is a data-entry field in a form, such as a text box or an option button. A user enters data into the form by typing directly into a text box, by selecting an option button or a check box, or by selecting a value from a drop-down menu. After completing the form, the user submits it to the server, where a form handler processes it. A **form handler** is a program that collects and processes the form's data in a predetermined manner. For example, you might select a form handler to save the form's data in an HTML file or to send the form's data to an e-mail address. FrontPage includes many form handlers to process common requests, but you can also design your own form handlers if you like.

During your meeting with the Web site development team, the team members indicated a desire to collect information about the site's users and their impressions of the Web site, the company, and the company's products. The team wants users to be able to enter their names and e-mail addresses and have an option to ask for a response after submitting the form. In addition, users should be able to enter brief, open-ended comments. Finally, the team wants to ask users how many times they have visited the Sunshine Country Store. This information will help the marketing department determine who is visiting the site as well as obtain positive and negative feedback in several categories. Figure 6-8 shows a sketch of the Feedback Web page that the team wants you to create.

Figure 6-8   **DESIGN SKETCH OF THE FEEDBACK WEB PAGE**

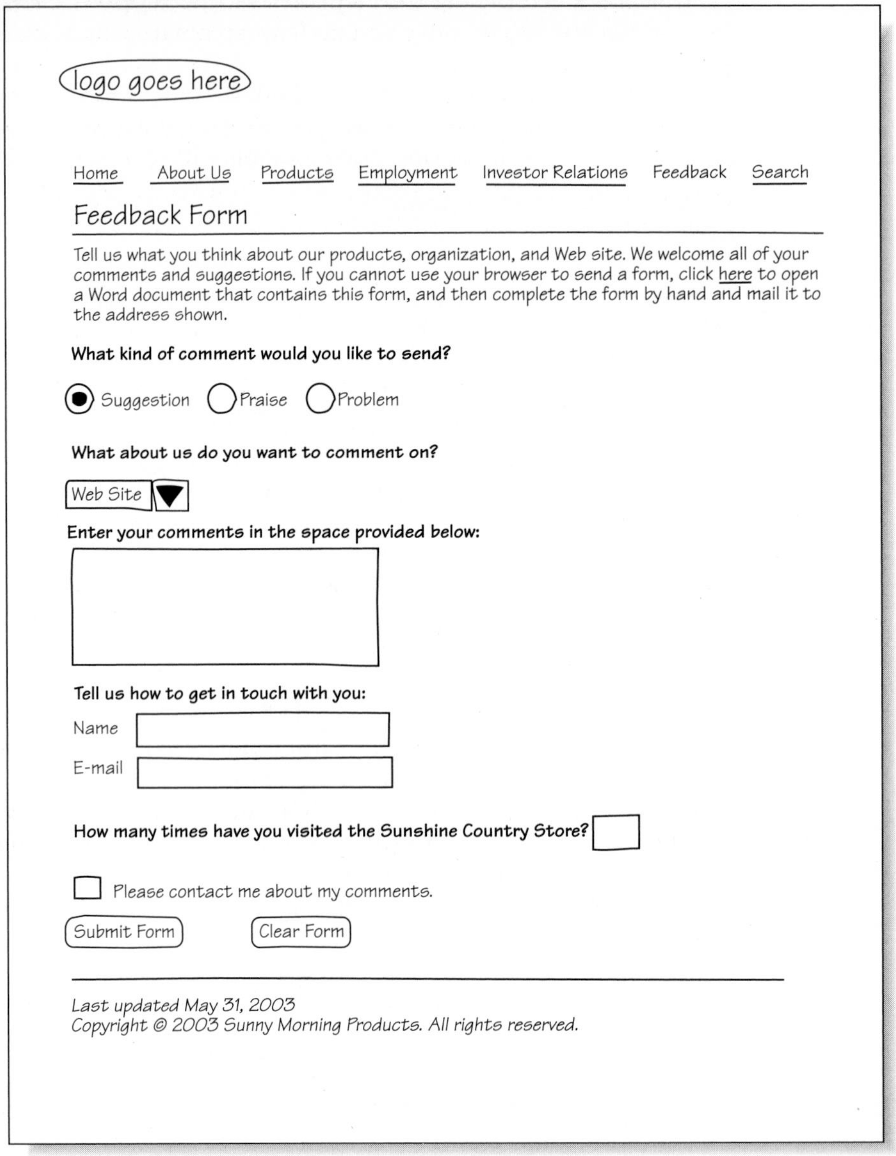

(logo goes here)

Home   About Us   Products   Employment   Investor Relations   Feedback   Search

Feedback Form

Tell us what you think about our products, organization, and Web site. We welcome all of your comments and suggestions. If you cannot use your browser to send a form, click here to open a Word document that contains this form, and then complete the form by hand and mail it to the address shown.

What kind of comment would you like to send?

(●) Suggestion   ( ) Praise   ( ) Problem

What about us do you want to comment on?

[Web Site ▼]

Enter your comments in the space provided below:

[   ]

Tell us how to get in touch with you:

Name [   ]

E-mail [   ]

How many times have you visited the Sunshine Country Store? [   ]

[ ] Please contact me about my comments.

(Submit Form)   (Clear Form)

Last updated May 31, 2003
Copyright © 2003 Sunny Morning Products. All rights reserved.

There are two ways to create a form. First, you can use the **Form Page Wizard**, which asks questions about the type of form that you want to create and lets you select the form's options to create a new Web page containing the form with the fields you specified using the Wizard. To use this option, double-click the Form Page Wizard icon in the Page Templates dialog box. You can use this method when you want to create a standard type of form, such as a form that contains billing and shipping addresses or information about products, such as quantity ordered.

Second, you can create a form by creating a new Web page using the Normal Page template and then inserting a form component in the page. The form component appears as a box with a dashed outline in Page view. You use the Form command on the Insert menu to insert the form's fields in the form. After adding a form field, you can accept its default settings or change its properties.

Regardless of how you create the form, you edit it in the same way as any other Web page. For example, if you click to the left of a form field and start typing the text to serve as its label, the form field moves to the right to make room for the text. Pressing the Enter key to the left of a form field inserts a new paragraph, which causes the form field to appear at the beginning of the next line. You can cut or copy form fields to the Windows Clipboard and paste them into a form. Although a single Web page can contain more than one form, the most popular approach is to create a single form in a Web page. You will create one form in the Feedback Web page.

In addition to reviewing the sketch provided by the Web site development team, it is important to define other steps that you will use to create the new form. The sketch should identify which form fields you want to use and their approximate locations in the form component. Amanda's planning analysis sheet, shown in Figure 6-9, specifies how to validate the form fields, collect data from the form, and confirm the form's submission to the server for the user. You will learn more about the information shown in the planning analysis sheet as you complete this tutorial.

| Figure 6-9 | AMANDA'S PLANNING ANALYSIS SHEET FOR THE FEEDBACK WEB PAGE |

Planning Analysis Sheet

Objective

Create a Feedback Web page that contains a form with form fields for collecting user feedback and contact information.

Requirements

Sketch of the page's planned appearance from the Web site development team, including the form fields to use to collect the desired data

Feedback logo to include in the page

Option button group with only one selection permitted

Drop-down box that shows three categories with only one selection permitted

Text area box that is 50 characters wide and five lines high

Text boxes that are 35 characters wide for the user's name and e-mail address

A text box that stores only integers from zero to 100

A check box to request a response

Submit Form and Clear Form push buttons to submit and reset the form, respectively

Results

A Feedback Web page that includes the Sunny Morning Products logo, a title, and form fields that collect the desired data from users. The user's data is stored in a results file on the server, which the marketing department will use to collect positive feedback and to respond to problems. The results file will also be sent to the general e-mail address for the marketing department.

Before adding form fields to a form, you need to create a Web page that contains a form component. Rather than asking you to create a new blank page and type the necessary text, Amanda created the Feedback Web page and entered some of the form's text for you. First, you will import Amanda's existing page into the Sunny Web site. Then you will create the necessary form fields and change their properties, as needed, to match Amanda's plan.

To import the Feedback Web page into the Sunny Web site:

1. Click the **Folders** button on the Views bar to change to Folders view.

2. Click **File** on the menu bar, and then click **Import**. The Import dialog box opens.

3. Click the **Add File** button to open the Add File to Import List dialog box, open the **Tutorial.06** folder on your Data Disk, and then double-click **Feedback**. The path to the Feedback.htm file on your Data Disk appears in the Import dialog box.

4. Click the **OK** button to import the Feedback page into the Sunny Web site.

5. Double-click **Feedback.htm** in the Contents pane to open the Feedback page in Page view. The page that Amanda created contains a broken link to a picture at the top of the page. You need to insert the picture in the page and then save it in the Web site's images folder. The file for the logo is saved in the Tutorial.06 folder on your Data Disk.

6. Right-click the **broken link** icon at the top of the page, click **Picture Properties** on the shortcut menu, click the **General** tab, click the **Browse** button to the right of the Picture source text box, open the **Tutorial.06** folder on your Data Disk, and then double-click **FormLogo**. You return to the Picture Properties dialog box.

7. Click the **OK** button to close the Picture Properties dialog box. The logo is inserted at the top of the page and the Pictures toolbar is displayed because the picture is selected.

8. Click the **Save** button on the Standard toolbar. Save the FormLogo.gif file in the Sunny Web site's images folder.

Now you are ready to modify the Feedback Web page to add a form component. You will then insert the form fields in the form component and modify their properties to meet Amanda's specifications.

Adding a Form Component to a Web Page

Before adding a form field to the Web page, you must add the form component that will contain all of the form's fields. If you used the Form Page Wizard to create your Web page, FrontPage added the form component to the page automatically. Amanda's Feedback Web page does not yet contain a form component. When you add a form component to a page, FrontPage creates the component and inserts the Submit and Reset buttons in it automatically.

REFERENCE WINDOW **RW**

<u>Creating a Form Component and Adding a Form Field to It</u>
- Position the insertion point where you want to insert the form.
- Click Insert on the menu bar, point to Form, and then click Form.
- Place the insertion point inside the form component where the first form field should appear.
- Click Insert on the menu bar, point to Form, and then click the desired form field to add it to the form.
- Right-click the form field object, and then click Form Field Properties on the shortcut menu to open the form field's Properties dialog box.
- Enter the appropriate values for the form field's properties.
- Click the OK button.

After you add the form component to the page, you must cut Amanda's existing content from the page and paste it into the form component. The form handler on the server will process only form fields that are contained in a form component.

To insert a form component in the Feedback Web page:

1. Click to the left of the word **Tell** in the paragraph that appears under the horizontal line to position the insertion point there. This line of text is the first one that will appear in the form.

2. Click **Insert** on the menu bar, point to **Form**, and then click **Form**. FrontPage inserts a form component on a new line below the horizontal line. The form component contains the Submit and Reset buttons.

   You will cut the text that Amanda created for the form and paste it into the form component. The insertion point appears to the left of the Submit button in the form component, which is where you will paste the existing text.

3. Select all of the lines of text beginning with "Tell us…" and ending with "Please contact me about my comments."

4. Click the **Cut** button 🗷 on the Standard toolbar to cut the selected text from the page.

5. Click to the left of the Submit button, but inside the form component, to place the insertion point there. You will paste the text that you just cut here.

   TROUBLE? If you see selection handles around the Submit button, then you selected the button instead of the space between the form component and the Submit button. Repeat Step 5.

6. Click the **Paste** button 📋 on the Standard toolbar to paste the text into the form component. You will keep the source formatting, so you do not need to click the Paste Options button that appears. The form component now contains the text that Amanda created. See Figure 6-10.

Figure 6-10	FORM COMPONENT INSERTED INTO THE FEEDBACK WEB PAGE

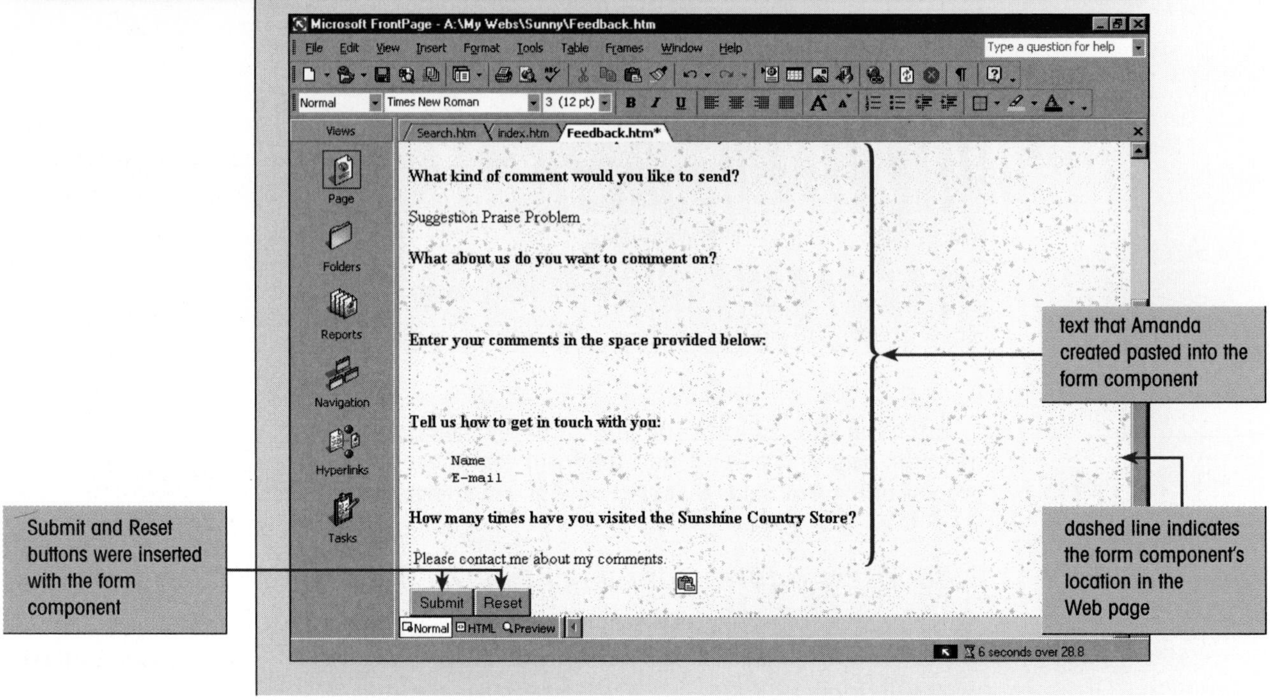

text that Amanda created pasted into the form component

dashed line indicates the form component's location in the Web page

Submit and Reset buttons were inserted with the form component

Now you are ready to add fields to the form.

Adding Option Buttons to a Form

Option buttons, (also known as **radio buttons**) are usually arranged in groups in a form. An **option group name** identifies a related set of option buttons. Within a group of option buttons, only one button can be selected at a time—selecting any option button automatically deselects any other selected option button. You create labels for option buttons by typing the appropriate text next to the button. For example, a form might have a section with the group name "Age" that contains corresponding option buttons with the labels "Under 25," "25-40," "41-65," and "Over 65." Option buttons are appropriate when only a few choices are available, such as when specifying age groups. A form can contain more than one option button group.

The first option button you add to a form will be selected automatically when you open the form in the browser, unless you change the default settings. Therefore, the first button should be the most common response, so users won't need to select it if it is their choice. You can also design an option button group so that no single option button is selected, thereby forcing the form's user to make a selection instead of accepting the default selected option button in a group.

When you create option button groups in a form, consider the following design suggestions:

■ Use option buttons when you want to limit the user to selecting one of a few related and mutually exclusive choices.

■ The minimum number of option buttons in a group is two, and the recommended maximum is seven.

■ Clearly label each option button in a group so that users can easily determine the appropriate button to select.

■ Use a heading or text to identify the group name for the option buttons.

Amanda already included the labels for each option button and asks you to insert the option button form fields to the left of the labels. If necessary, refer to Figure 6-8 while creating the form to determine where to place the form fields.

To add an option button to a form:

1. If necessary, scroll the Feedback Web page so you can see the "Suggestion Praise Problem" text. These words will be the labels for three option buttons.

2. Click to the left of the word **Suggestion** to position the insertion point where you will insert the first option button.

3. Click **Insert** on the menu bar, point to **Form**, and then click **Option Button** to insert the first option button in the form to the left of the "Suggestion" label. Notice that the option button is selected, as indicated by the black dot that appears within the white circle. See Figure 6-11.

Figure 6-11	OPTION BUTTON FORM FIELD INSERTED IN THE FORM

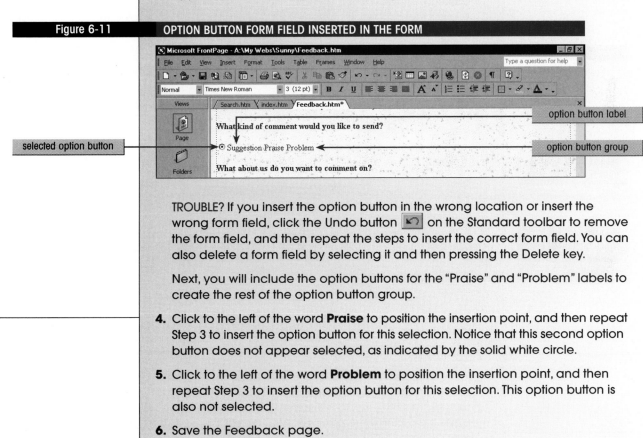

TROUBLE? If you insert the option button in the wrong location or insert the wrong form field, click the Undo button on the Standard toolbar to remove the form field, and then repeat the steps to insert the correct form field. You can also delete a form field by selecting it and then pressing the Delete key.

Next, you will include the option buttons for the "Praise" and "Problem" labels to create the rest of the option button group.

4. Click to the left of the word **Praise** to position the insertion point, and then repeat Step 3 to insert the option button for this selection. Notice that this second option button does not appear selected, as indicated by the solid white circle.

5. Click to the left of the word **Problem** to position the insertion point, and then repeat Step 3 to insert the option button for this selection. This option button is also not selected.

6. Save the Feedback page.

The Suggestion, Praise, and Problem option buttons now belong to a group that appears below the "What kind of comment would you like to send?" heading. Within any option button group, the user can select only one option button.

After placing a form field in the form, you can change its properties to more closely match your needs. For example, FrontPage assigned the group name R1 to the option button group, the value V1 to the Suggestion option button, the value V2 to the Praise option button, and the value V3 to the Problem option button. You could accept these default values for the group and button names, but Amanda suggests that you modify the current option button properties by changing the group name to MessageType and the button names to match their labels. Using more meaningful names will make the responses easier to examine and locate in the file that stores the form's results. Amanda tells you that names for groups and form fields may not contain spaces.

To change option button properties:

1. Right-click the **option button** to the left of the Suggestion label to select it and open the shortcut menu, and then click **Form Field Properties** to open the Option Button Properties dialog box. You will change the group name and the value name for the option button.

2. Type **MessageType** in the Group name text box, press the **Tab** key to select the value in the Value text box, and then type **Suggestion**. Now the option button group is named MessageType, and the option button form field is named Suggestion. See Figure 6-12. In the Initial state section, the Selected option button is selected, indicating that the Suggestion option button is the default selection. You will learn more about the other options in this dialog box later in this tutorial.

Figure 6-12	COMPLETED OPTION BUTTON PROPERTIES DIALOG BOX

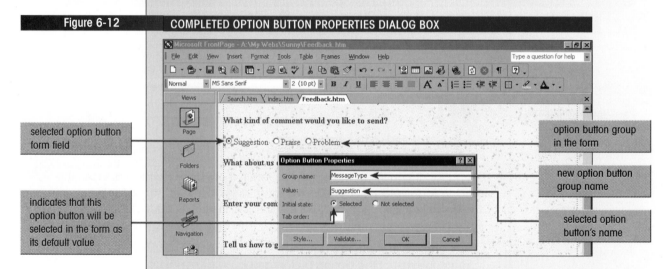

3. Click the **OK** button to accept the changes to the option button's properties and close the dialog box.

   TROUBLE? If a message box opens and tells you that the name is not valid, click the OK button to continue and make sure that "MessageType" in the Group name text box does not contain a space. Click the OK button and then repeat Steps 1-3.

   Next, you will change the properties for the other two option buttons and assign them to the same group as the Suggestion option button.

4. Right-click the **option button** to the left of the Praise label, and then click **Form Field Properties** to open the Option Button Properties dialog box for this option button. The default for the Praise option button is "Not selected;" only one option button can be selected in a group at a time.

5. Type **MessageType** in the Group name text box, press the **Tab** key, type **Praise**, and then click the **OK** button.

> **6.** Right-click the **option button** to the left of the Problem label, click **Form Field Properties** to open the Option Button Properties dialog box for this option button, type **MessageType** in the Group name text box, press the **Tab** key, type **Problem**, and then click the **OK** button.
>
> **7.** Save the Feedback page.

You have specified that the MessageType option button group will include each of the three option button form fields you placed in the form. Next, you will add another type of form field—a drop-down box.

Adding a Drop-Down Box to a Form

Option buttons are useful when you want a user to select a response from only a few choices. When you want to present several choices in a single form field, a **drop-down box** (also called a **drop-down menu**) is an appropriate choice because it saves space by organizing choices in a list. The user displays the list and then selects the correct choice. Although a user could select one or more choices from a drop-down box, usually only one selection is permitted.

When you create drop-down boxes in a form, consider the following design suggestions:

- Use a drop-down box when you want the user to select a choice from a list.
- Drop-down boxes should contain a minimum of three choices.
- Arrange items in the list so that the most commonly selected entries appear first, or arrange items in ascending order alphabetically, numerically, or chronologically.
- The default selection in a drop-down box should be either the most used choice or the first choice in the list.

Amanda wants you to insert a drop-down box in the form to provide a list of categories from which the user can select when sending comments to Sunny Morning Products. The marketing department supplied the following categories for the list: Web Site, Company, and Products.

> ### To add a drop-down box to a form:
>
> **1.** Click the line immediately below the "What about us do you want to comment on?" heading to position the insertion point in the correct location for the drop-down box.
>
> **2.** Click **Insert** on the menu bar, point to **Form**, and then click **Drop-Down Box**.

FrontPage creates a drop-down box that displays only two characters. Amanda wants you to change the default settings to increase the width of the drop-down box, to insert the list items, and to change the default form field names.

> ### To add choices to a drop-down box and change its properties:
>
> **1.** Right-click the **drop-down box** to select it and open the shortcut menu, and then click **Form Field Properties**. The Drop-Down Box Properties dialog box opens. FrontPage automatically assigned the name D1 to the drop-down box. The dialog box shows that there are no choices in the list and that multiple selections are not permitted. You will rename the drop-down box, and then you will create the choices that will appear in the list.

2. In the Name text box, select **D1**, and then type **Subject**. The drop-down box form field now has the name Subject.

3. Click the **Add** button to open the Add Choice dialog box. You use this dialog box to create entries in the list. First, you will supply the item's name, or choice, which is how the item will appear in the list. Then you will supply the item's value, which is the name of the list item in the results file. Finally, you will indicate whether the item is selected or not selected in the drop-down box.

4. Type **Web Site** in the Choice text box, and then click the **Specify Value** check box to select it. FrontPage automatically adds the value "Web Site" to the Specify Value text box.

5. Click to the left of the letter **S** in the Specify Value text box, press the **Backspace** key to delete the space, and then click the **Selected** option button in the Initial state section to select it. See Figure 6-13.

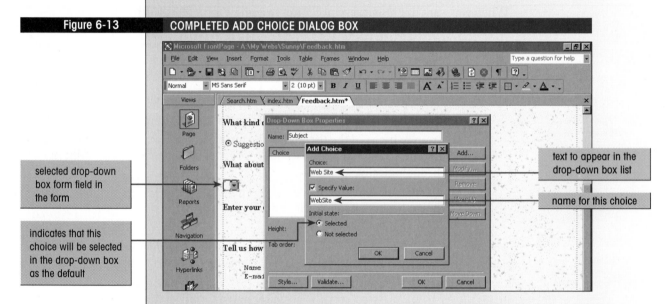

Figure 6-13	COMPLETED ADD CHOICE DIALOG BOX

selected drop-down box form field in the form

indicates that this choice will be selected in the drop-down box as the default

text to appear in the drop-down box list

name for this choice

6. Click the **OK** button to finish adding this choice to the drop-down box and to close the Add Choice dialog box. The other two choices, Company and Products, will have the same choice name and value, so you will not need to check the Specify Value check box. FrontPage will use the choice name as the value.

7. Click the **Add** button in the Drop-Down Box Properties dialog box, type **Company** in the Choice text box, make sure that the **Not selected** option button is selected, and then click the **OK** button to close the Add Choice dialog box.

8. Click the **Add** button in the Drop-Down Box Properties dialog box, type **Products** in the Choice text box, make sure that the **Not selected** option button is selected, and then click the **OK** button to close the Add Choice dialog box. See Figure 6-14.

Figure 6-14   COMPLETED DROP-DOWN BOX PROPERTIES DIALOG BOX

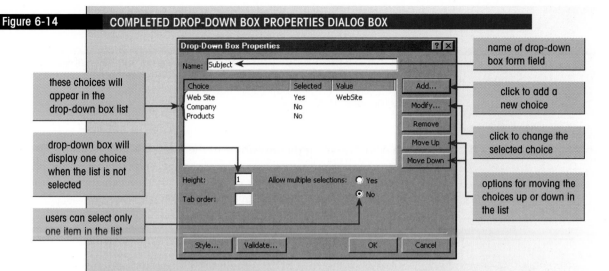

9. Click the **OK** button to close the Drop-Down Box Properties dialog box. The drop-down box appears in the form, with Web Site displayed as the default choice.

10. Save the Feedback page.

If you click the list arrow on the drop-down box in Page view, you will select the form field instead of displaying the list. To see the list, you must open the page in a browser or Preview Page view and then click the list arrow. You will test all of the form fields in the browser after completing the form. Next, Amanda asks you to add a text box form field to the form.

Adding a Text Box to a Form

When you need a user to supply limited information in a form field that is unique or uncommon, such as a phone number or an e-mail address, you can use a text box to collect the data. A **text box** accepts a single line of typed information. You can also use a text box form field to permit users to enter a password, in which case the password appears as a series of asterisks to conceal it while it is being typed.

When you create text boxes in a form, consider the following design suggestions:

- Use a text box when you want the user to enter a limited amount of unique or uncommon information.
- A text box limits the number of characters that a user can enter.
- A text box can serve as a password field.

In addition to being unique, a user's name and e-mail address usually are short so they are suitable candidates for text box form fields.

To add a text box to a form:

1. Press **Ctrl + End** to scroll down the Feedback Web page so you can see the "Tell us how to get in touch with you:" heading and the Name and E-mail labels for the text boxes that you will create.

2. Click anywhere in the **Name** label, and then press the **End** key to place the insertion point a few spaces to the right, where Amanda inserted a tab stop.

3. Click **Insert** on the menu bar, point to **Form**, and then click **Textbox**. FrontPage places a text box form field in the form.

4. Click in the **E-mail** label, press the **End** key, and then repeat Step 3 to add a text box a few spaces to the right of the E-mail label.

5. Save the Feedback page.

Now that you've added the text boxes to the form, you need to set their widths. Amanda wants you to change their current properties so that each text box can display a maximum of 35 characters, rather than the default of 20 characters. You can also open the Properties dialog box for a form field by double-clicking it, as you will see next.

To change the properties of a text box:

1. Double-click the **text box** for the Name label to open the Text Box Properties dialog box. FrontPage assigned the name T1 to the text box. If you want a default value to appear in the text box when the form is opened in the browser, you can set it by entering a value in the Initial value text box. You can also change the width of the text box (using a measurement indicating the maximum number of characters that will be displayed in the text box), change the text box to accept a password, or change the order in which the user selects text boxes in the form when pressing the Tab key. Amanda wants you to rename the text box and then increase its width.

2. Type **UserName** in the Name text box, press the **Tab** key twice to select the value in the Width in characters text box, and then type **35** to set the text box to display a maximum of 35 characters. See Figure 6-15.

Figure 6-15	COMPLETED TEXT BOX PROPERTIES DIALOG BOX

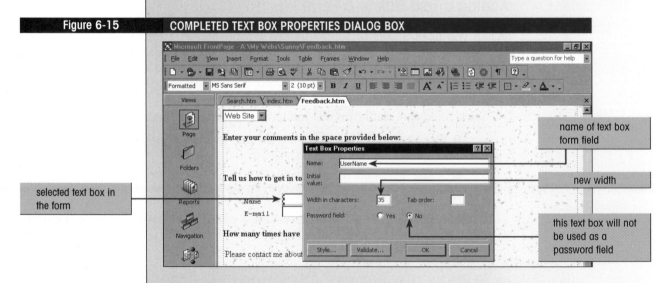

3. Click the **OK** button. The Name text box increases to a width of 35 characters.

4. Repeat Steps 1–3 to set the E-mail text box properties to have the name **UserEmail** and a width of **35** characters.

5. Save the Feedback page.

The text boxes will let a user enter a name and e-mail address and display a maximum of 35 characters each. Some text information, such as user comments or problem descriptions, requires more space. When you need to accept unique passages of longer text, you can use a text area form field.

Adding a Text Area to a Form

A **text area** (also called a **scrolling text box**) has the same basic characteristics as a text box, except that it accepts multiple lines of text information and it cannot serve as a password field. A text area is an effective form field when asking a user to provide open-ended feedback about a particular product or service.

When you create a text area in a form, consider the following design suggestions:

■ Use a text area when you want a user to supply information that might include more than one line.

■ A text area accepts and displays multiple lines of text entered by the user. The size of the text area should be large enough to display several lines of text at a time.

Amanda's design of the Feedback Web page includes a text area form field that allows users to enter multiple lines of text. You will add this form field next.

To add a text area to a form:

1. Scroll up the Feedback Web page so you can see the heading "Enter your comments in the space provided below:" (if necessary), and then click the blank line below that heading. You will insert the text area here.

2. Click **Insert** on the menu bar, point to **Form**, and then click **Text Area**. FrontPage inserts a text area in the form.

To match the Web site development team's form design, you will change the default properties for the text area from 20 characters wide and two lines to 50 characters wide and five lines.

To change the properties of a text area:

1. Double-click the **text area** to open the TextArea Box Properties dialog box. FrontPage automatically assigned the name S1 to the text area. Notice that you can specify an initial value for the text area; if you leave this text box empty, then the text area will be empty when the Web page that contains it is opened in the browser. You can also set the properties for a text area so as to change its width and the number of lines of text displayed in the box. If the user enters more text than can be displayed in the text area, the form field will scroll the lines automatically.

You will change the default name to be more descriptive of the text area, and then you will change the form field's size.

2. Type **Comments** in the Name text box, press the **Tab** key twice to move to the Width in characters text box, type **50**, press the **Tab** key twice to move to the Number of lines text box, and then type **5**. See Figure 6-16.

Figure 6-16	COMPLETED TEXT AREA BOX PROPERTIES DIALOG BOX

selected text area in the form

no initial value specified

name of text area form field

new width

new height

3. Click the **OK** button. The text area is displayed with the new properties—it is five lines high and 50 characters wide.

4. Save the Feedback page.

5. Close the Sunny Web site, and then close FrontPage.

You will test the Feedback and Search Web pages after you publish the Web site in Session 6.3. In the next session, you will create the rules used by FrontPage to verify that the form's fields accept the correct data from users.

Session 6.1 QUICK CHECK

1. True or False: When you use a template to create a new Web page, FrontPage automatically enters content and components that are relevant to the page.

2. What two methods can you use to determine the location of a Web component in a Web page?

3. True or False: You cannot change the properties of a component in a Web page that was created by a template.

4. What is a form field?

5. Before adding a form field to a Web page, you must first create a(n) _____ in the Web page that will contain the form field.

6. What is a form handler?

7. Why is it a good idea to change the default group name and value for an option button group?

8. You are designing a Web page for a Canadian company that includes a list of the Canadian provinces. Which form field would you use to collect the data, which properties would you assign to the form field, and which option would be the default selection? Defend your selections.

SESSION 6.2

In this session, you will validate a form field to verify data entered by a user. You will add a check box form field and push buttons to a form and then change their default properties. In addition, you will specify and configure a form handler to process the form and test the form on a client. You will open an Office document from a Web site and create a hyperlink to it. Finally, you will view the HTML code for a Web page that contains a form.

Validating a Form Field

The text boxes and text area that you added to the Feedback Web page in Session 6.1 accept unique text information entered by a user. In some situations, you might want to validate the information that a user enters into these form fields. For example, if you ask a user to enter a product number in a text box and all product numbers contain four digits, you might set the properties of the text box so that it must contain four digits. By ensuring that the user enters four digits, you can reduce data-entry errors.

Validation is the process of checking the information entered by a user into one or more form fields to verify that the information is acceptable. If the data entered by a user fails the validation test, then the user must change it before the browser will send the form to the server for processing. You specify data validation criteria using the form field's Properties dialog box.

The sketch of the Feedback Web page (see Figure 6-8) includes a text box that lets users enter the number of times that they have visited the Sunshine Country Store. Amanda wants to ensure that users can enter only a positive, whole number (or an **integer**) into this form field. In other words, a user shouldn't be able to enter a negative number, a number containing a decimal, or letters into this form field. Amanda wants you to set this form field so that it must accept an integer that is in the range zero to 100. To ensure that users will not inadvertently skip this form field, you will also validate this form field so that it must contain an acceptable value. In other words, users cannot submit the form if this form field is empty or contains an invalid response.

To create the text box and change its properties:

1. Start FrontPage, insert your Data Disk in the appropriate drive, and then open the **Sunny** Web site from your Data Disk in Folders view.

2. Double-click **Feedback.htm** in the Contents pane to open the Feedback Web page in Page view.

3. Press **Ctrl + End**, click in the "How many times have you visited the Sunshine Country Store?" heading, and then press the **End** key. Now the insertion point is positioned in the correct location for the text box.

4. Click **Insert** on the menu bar, point to **Form**, and then click **Textbox**. A text box is added to the form. You will change the form field's name to "Visits" and change its width to three characters.

5. Double-click the **text box** that you created in Step 4 to open the Text Box Properties dialog box, type **Visits** in the Name text box, press the **Tab** key twice to move to the Width in characters text box, type **3**, and then click the **OK** button. The dialog box closes and the text box is displayed with the new width.

Next, you will set the validation criteria for the Visits text box.

To validate a text box in a form:

1. Double-click the **Visits text box** to open the Text Box Properties dialog box, and then click the **Validate** button. The Text Box Validation dialog box opens. Currently, there are no validation criteria placed on the data entered into the Visits text box, as indicated by the "No Constraints" setting in the Data type list box.

2. Click the **Data type** list arrow. You can select Text, Integer, or Number as the data type to validate. You want to make sure that this form field accepts whole numbers, so you will select Integer as the data type.

3. Click **Integer** to specify that data type. The settings in the Numeric format section become active.

4. In the Numeric format section, click the **None** option button in the Grouping category, because the data should not contain a comma or a period. You use this option to display a number with a period or a comma, such as 4.5 or 10,000.

5. In the Data length section, click the **Required** check box to select it, press the **Tab** key to move to the Min length text box, type **1**, press the **Tab** key to move to the Max length text box, and then type **3**. You have specified 1 as the minimum number of digits and 3 as the maximum number of digits that a user can enter into this form field. Selecting the Required check box means that the user must enter a value—even zero—into this form field before the server will accept the form for processing.

6. In the Data value section, click the **Field must be** check box to select it, click the **Field must be** list arrow, click **Greater than or equal to** (if necessary), press the **Tab** key to move to the Value text box, and then type **0** (the number zero—not the capital letter "O"). These settings specify that the integer must be greater than or equal to zero.

7. In the Data value section, click the **And must be** check box to select it, click the **And must be** list arrow, click **Less than or equal to** (if necessary), press the **Tab** key to move to the Value text box, and then type **100**. These settings specify that the integer must be less than or equal to 100. See Figure 6-17.

Figure 6-17	COMPLETED TEXT BOX VALIDATION DIALOG BOX

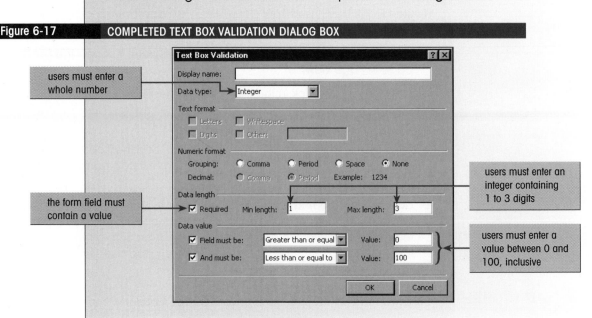

users must enter a whole number

users must enter an integer containing 1 to 3 digits

the form field must contain a value

users must enter a value between 0 and 100, inclusive

8. Click the **OK** button to close the Text Box Validation dialog box, and then click the **OK** button to close the Text Box Properties dialog box.

9. Save the Feedback page.

Now users must enter an integer between zero and 100 in the Visits text box before the server will process the form. Next, Amanda asks you to add a form field that will alert the Web site development team when a user requests a response to his or her submission.

Adding a Check Box to a Form

You can use a **check box** by itself to collect a yes/no response to a question, or you can use check boxes in a group to let users answer yes or no to more than one option. Unlike with option button groups, selecting one check box in a check box group does not automatically deselect another check box in the same check box group. You can set the properties for each check box so that it is selected or not selected when the form opens in the browser.

When you create check boxes in a form, consider the following design suggestions:

- Use check boxes when you want a user to select from a group of one or more independent and nonexclusive choices.
- Set the default selection to the most frequently occurring selection.
- Clearly label each check box in a group.
- When necessary, use a heading or text to identify the subject of the check box group.

You will add a check box to the form that lets a user request a response from Sunny Morning Products.

To add a check box to a form and change its properties:

1. Click anywhere in the text "Please contact me about my comments," and then press the **Home** key to place the insertion point at the beginning of the line. You will add the check box to the left of the text that describes it.

2. Click **Insert** on the menu bar, point to **Form**, and then click **Checkbox**. FrontPage inserts a check box at the beginning of the line.

3. Double-click the **check box** to open the Check Box Properties dialog box. You will change the default name and value of this form field. The default value that is stored in the results file when the user selects the check box is "ON." You will change this value to "Yes;" a "Yes" value in the results file means the user requested a response.

4. Type **ContactMe** in the Name text box, press the **Tab** key to move to the Value text box, and then type **Yes**. In the Initial state section, the Not checked option button is selected, indicating that this check box will not contain a check mark when the Feedback Web page is opened in the Web browser. See Figure 6-18.

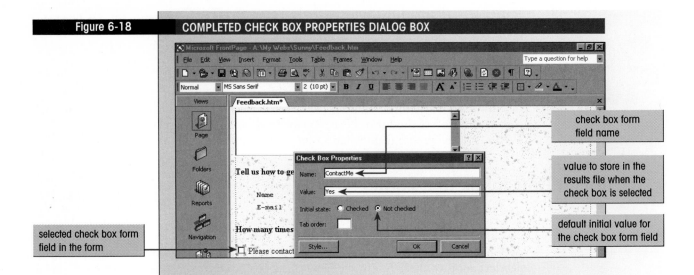

Figure 6-18   COMPLETED CHECK BOX PROPERTIES DIALOG BOX

check box form field name

value to store in the results file when the check box is selected

default initial value for the check box form field

selected check box form field in the form

5. Click the **OK** button to close the Check Box Properties dialog box. The check box form field looks the same—changing the Name property did not affect this form field's appearance. Your changes affected only how the server will process this form field.

You have finished adding all of the form fields that collect data from the user. To finish this form, you need to supply the user with a way of sending the Web page to the server for processing.

Adding **Push Buttons**

Push buttons (also called **command buttons**) are used to submit a form to the server, to clear the form's fields, or to perform specific functions programmed by the developer. You can create three types of push buttons in a form; each type implements a different processing action. You use a **Submit push button** to let a user submit a form to the server for processing. Clicking a **Reset push button** clears any previously entered data from the form. Clicking a **Normal push button** initiates a user-defined script (an advanced Web page feature that is beyond the scope of this tutorial). When you create a form, FrontPage automatically creates and programs the Submit and Reset push buttons for you. By default, the Submit push button is associated with the FrontPage form handler that processes the submitted form results on the Web server. Because these two buttons are automatically included in the form, you can either accept their default values or edit them to better suit your needs. If you add a new push button to a form, FrontPage automatically creates a Normal push button with the value "Button." You must change the properties of the new button to change its name and function.

Amanda asks you to edit the Submit and Reset push buttons in the form. To match the sketch shown in Figure 6-8, you will change the label for the Submit push button to "Submit Form" and the label for the Reset push button to "Clear Form."

To change the properties of the Submit push button:

1. Double-click the **Submit push button** to open the Push Button Properties dialog box.

2. Type **Submit** in the Name text box, press the **Tab** key to move to the Value/label text box, press the **End** key, press the **spacebar**, and then type **Form**. In the Button type section, the Submit option button is selected, indicating that this button submits the form's data to the Web server. See Figure 6-19.

Figure 6-19	COMPLETED PUSH BUTTON PROPERTIES DIALOG BOX

- push button form field name
- label for the push button in the form
- this push button submits the form to the server

3. Click the **OK** button to close the Push Button Properties dialog box. The Submit button now displays the label "Submit Form." FrontPage automatically resized the push button to accommodate the new label.

Next, you will change the default settings for the Reset push button to change its name to "Clear" and its label to "Clear Form."

To change the properties of the Reset push button:

1. Double-click the **Reset push button** to open the Push Button Properties dialog box.

2. Type **Clear** in the Name text box, press the **Tab** key to move to the Value/label text box, and then type **Clear Form**. The Reset option button is selected in the Button type section, indicating that this button resets the values in the form's fields to their default settings.

3. Click the **OK** button to close the Push Button Properties dialog box. The Reset push button now displays the label "Clear Form."

4. Save the Feedback page.

You have finished placing all of the form fields that collect data in the form and provided a means for the user to submit the form to the server for processing. When a form is submitted to the server, you must tell the server how to process it by specifying a form handler.

Using a Form Handler

A form handler is a program on a Web server that communicates with a browser to process form data received from the browser. FrontPage installs several form handlers that use the FrontPage Server Extensions and reside on the Web server to perform their functions. You select a form handler based on how you want to process the data collected in your form. For the Feedback Web page, you will use the FrontPage Save Results form handler, which collects and saves form data in a variety of file formats.

The **Save Results form handler** collects data from a browser and stores it in the specified format on the server. You have the option of sending the results to a file, to an e-mail address, or to a database. The data entered by the user in the form, or the **form results**, is stored on the server in a format that you specify. The two most popular methods of storing form results are as a text file, with one line for each form that was submitted to the server, or as an HTML file, with a line for each form field name and its value (known as a **field name-data value pair**). In the text file method, the first entry, or row, contains the names of the form fields from which the data was obtained. In the HTML file method, each form field name is included as a field name-data value pair, with the name being repeated with the data from each form submission. When using either of these formats to store form results, most developers will set the results file to add the form results at the end of the file for each form submitted to the server.

In addition to storing the results in a file on the server, you can send the results to an e-mail address. To send the form results to an e-mail address, the FrontPage Server Extensions must be configured so that the server can send e-mail messages. Normally, the Web site's administrator, or **webmaster**, configures the FrontPage Server Extensions for this type of processing. Check with your instructor or technical support person to determine whether your FrontPage installation and server are enabled to send a form's results to an e-mail address.

When you configure the Save Results form handler, you must specify a format for your results file. You can use a text file to collect the data in each form field, along with optional information, such as the date on which the form was submitted and the Internet Protocol (IP) address of the user. If you collect data in a text file, the file is stored in the _private folder of your FrontPage Web site, where it is hidden from Internet users. Data collected in an HTML file is also stored in the _private folder.

Amanda asks you to use the Save Results form handler to specify the processing method for the data collected by the Feedback Web page.

To configure the Save Results form handler:

1. Right-click anywhere in the **form component** to open the shortcut menu, and then click **Form Properties**. The Form Properties dialog box opens. See Figure 6-20.

Figure 6-20	FORM PROPERTIES DIALOG BOX

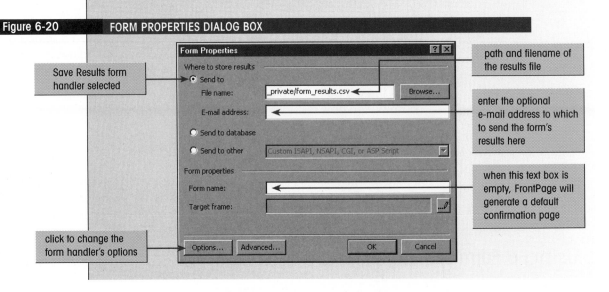

Save Results form handler selected

path and filename of the results file

enter the optional e-mail address to which to send the form's results here

when this text box is empty, FrontPage will generate a default confirmation page

click to change the form handler's options

The settings in this dialog box let you choose the filename in which to store your results file and the optional e-mail address to which to send the results from each form submission. You can also send your form results to a database or to a location defined by a script. You use the Form properties section to supply the filename that will serve as your confirmation page. (You will learn more about confirmation pages in Session 6.3.) To change the options for any of these settings, click the Options button.

Amanda's planning analysis sheet shows that the form results will be stored in a text file and sent to an e-mail address at Sunny Morning Products. You will configure these settings next.

2. In the Where to store results section, verify that the **Send to** option button is selected, select the default value in the File name text box, and then type **_private/Feedback.txt**. You will store your results in a file named Feedback.txt in the _private folder of the Sunny Web site.

3. Press the **Tab** key twice to move to the E-mail address text box, and then type **results@sunnymorning.com**. The form results will also be sent to this e-mail address.

4. Click the **Options** button to open the Saving Results dialog box. See Figure 6-21. Make sure that **Text database using comma as a separator** appears in the File format list box and that the **Include field names** and **Latest results at end** check boxes in the Optional second file section contain check marks. When you select the option to use a comma as the data separator, a comma will separate the data entered into each form field. This format, which is known as **comma-delimited text**, is a popular choice for storing data because many different programs can read and use it.

Figure 6-21 FILE RESULTS SETTINGS

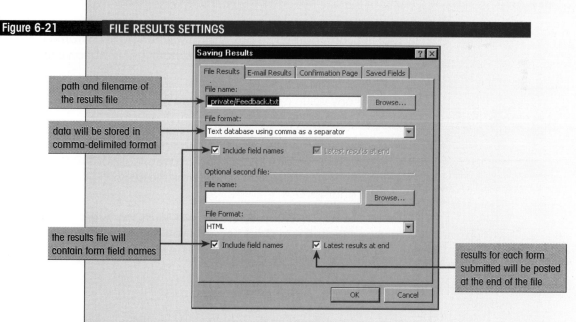

path and filename of the results file

data will be stored in comma-delimited format

the results file will contain form field names

results for each form submitted will be posted at the end of the file

TROUBLE? If "Text database using comma as a separator" does not appear in the File format list box, click the File format list arrow and then click this option to select it.

5. Click the **Saved Fields** tab to display those settings. See Figure 6-22. In the Additional information to save section, click the **Remote computer name** check box to select it. This setting will save the user's IP address in the results file with the field name "Remote Name." The Form fields to save list box displays a list of all form fields in the Feedback Web page. The form fields are easy to distinguish because you gave them meaningful names, instead of accepting the defaults names of V1, S1, and so on.

Figure 6-22	SAVED FIELDS SETTINGS

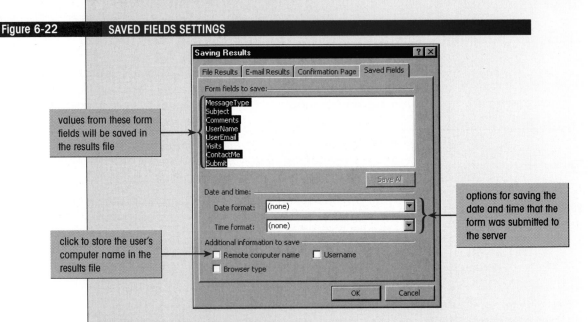

values from these form fields will be saved in the results file

options for saving the date and time that the form was submitted to the server

click to store the user's computer name in the results file

6. Click the **OK** button to return to the Form Properties dialog box, and then verify that the Form name text box is empty. When no form name is specified, FrontPage automatically generates a default confirmation page, which is the action you want.

TROUBLE? If any value appears in the Form name text box, select it and then press the Delete key to remove it.

7. Click the **OK** button. A Microsoft FrontPage message box opens, indicating that you are creating the form in a disk-based Web that does not have the required FrontPage Server Extensions to send e-mail messages. For now, you will delete the e-mail address.

8. Click the **Yes** button to display the E-mail Results tab, press the **Delete** key to delete the selected e-mail address that you entered in Step 3, and then click the **OK** button. The dialog boxes close and you return to the form.

9. Save the Feedback page.

Now that you have identified the form handler, including specifying the file in which the results will be stored on the server, you need to test the form.

Testing a Form on the Client

Unlike the case with other Web pages, you should test a page that contains a form on the client *and* on the server. When testing the form on a client, you test each form field by entering data into it. For example, you can enter text in text boxes or use drop-down boxes to ensure that they display the choices you specified. Also, you can clear all data from the form and then reenter it. Any form fields that use data validation, such as the Visits text box, require a server for verification. Therefore, you cannot test form fields that are validated until you can submit the form to a server for processing.

At this point in the development of the form, Amanda asks you to test it on the client. Your test of the form will include reviewing the layout of form fields in the form and testing their operation. You will finish testing the form in Session 6.3 after publishing the Web site on a server.

To test a form on the client:

1. Click the **Preview in Browser** button 🔍 on the Standard toolbar, and then, if necessary, click the **OK** button in the message box that reminds you that some form elements won't work in a disk-based Web. The Feedback Web page opens in the browser.

2. Scroll down the page until you see the form fields, and then click the **Praise** option button under the "What kind of comment would you like to send?" heading to select it.

3. Click the **What about us do you want to comment on?** list arrow, and then click **Products**.

4. Click in the **Enter your comments in the space provided below** text area, and then type **This is a test.**

5. Press the **Tab** key to move to the Name text box, type your first and last names separated by a space, press the **Tab** key to move to the E-mail text box, and then type your e-mail address.

6. Press the **Tab** key to move to the Visits text box, and then type **200**.

7. Click the **Please contact me about my comments** check box to select it. Now you can simulate submitting the form to the server.

8. Click the **Submit Form** button. The FrontPage Run-Time Component Page opens to advise you that a server is required for the page to function correctly. You will test the page using a server later in this tutorial.

9. Click the **Back** button ⇦ on the toolbar to return to the Feedback Web page, and then click the **Clear Form** button. The data you previously entered is cleared from the form; this action does not require a server. Your test of the form on the client is successful.

10. Close the browser.

Although the browser performs data validation, a server is required to generate the error messages that appear when the Visits text box contains an invalid entry.

Opening an Office Document from a Web Site

The Web site development team wants to make sure that people who cannot submit forms to the server—for whatever reason—will still be able to submit feedback to Sunny Morning Products. You could ask users to use a browser to print the Feedback Web page and complete the form, but then the default option buttons would be selected and users could not indicate their comment type because they cannot use a drop-down box on a paper form. In response to the development team's request, Amanda saved the form as a Microsoft Word 2002 document and then modified it to make it easier to complete. She asks you to create a link to the document and to open it. First, you will import the file into the Sunny Web site.

To import the Word document into the Sunny Web site:

1. Click the **Folders** button [icon] on the Views bar to change to Folders view.

2. Click **File** on the menu bar, click **Import**, click the **Add File** button, open the **Tutorial.06** folder on your Data Disk, double-click **Form**, and then click the **OK** button in the Import dialog box to import the file.

3. Double-click **Form.doc** in the Contents pane. Microsoft Word starts and opens the document. Amanda wants to give users some additional space in which to enter comments, so she asks you to increase the size of the text area.

   TROUBLE? If Microsoft Word does not open, your installation of FrontPage is not configured to open Office documents in the program that created them. If necessary, close the program that opened. In FrontPage, click Tools on the menu bar, click Options, and then click the Configure Editors tab. Select the Open web pages in the Office application that created them check box, and then click the OK button. Repeat Step 3. If Word still doesn't open, ask your instructor or technical support person for help.

4. Scroll down the document, click the **text area** to select it, and then drag the middle-right sizing handle to the right to enlarge the text area to approximately the same size as shown in Figure 6-23.

Figure 6-23	WORD DOCUMENT OPENED FROM THE SUNNY WEB SITE

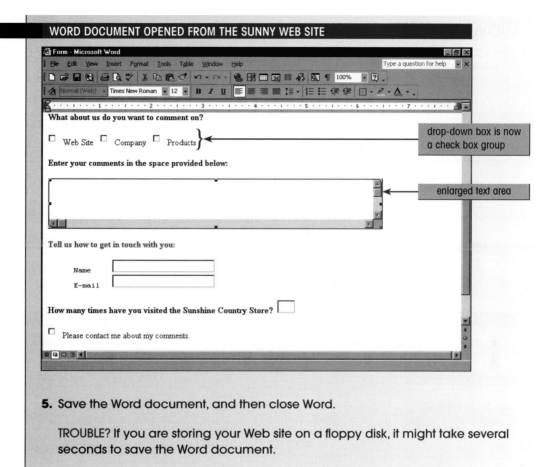

5. Save the Word document, and then close Word.

TROUBLE? If you are storing your Web site on a floppy disk, it might take several seconds to save the Word document.

Next, you will create the hyperlink to the Word document.

To create a hyperlink to a Word document:

1. In FrontPage, double-click **Feedback.htm** in the Contents pane to open the Feedback Web page in Page view.

2. Scroll to the top of the page, and then double-click the word **here** in the third sentence of the paragraph that appears below the horizontal line.

3. Click the **Insert Hyperlink** button on the Standard toolbar to open the Insert Hyperlink dialog box, scroll down the list of files in the Sunny Web site, and then double-click **Form**. The Insert Hyperlink dialog box closes and the "here" text now contains a link to the Word document.

4. Click the **here** hyperlink to deselect it, and then save the Feedback page.

5. Press and hold down the **Ctrl** key, and then click the **here** link. Microsoft Word starts and opens the document.

6. Close Word.

In Session 6.3, you will publish the Sunny Web site to a server and then test the Feedback and Search Web pages again. Next, Amanda asks you to examine the HTML code for the Feedback Web page.

Viewing HTML Code for a Form

Creating a form using HTML code is a complicated chore. All of the form fields are nested within the FORM tags, which specify the beginning and end of the form in the Web page. The POST value for the METHOD property specifies that the data in the form will be processed by or posted to the server. The WEBBOT tag specifies the properties for the Save Results form handler. The option button, text box, and check box form fields are implemented using the INPUT tag. The drop-down box form field is implemented using the SELECT tag, and the text area form field is implemented using the TEXTAREA tag. Each tag includes properties that specify the appearance of the form field in the form and its settings.

To view the HTML code for the Feedback Web page:

1. Click the **HTML** button to display the HTML code for the Feedback Web page.

2. Scroll the page until the opening FORM tag appears at the top of the Contents pane. See Figure 6-24.

Figure 6-24	HTML CODE FOR THE FEEDBACK WEB PAGE

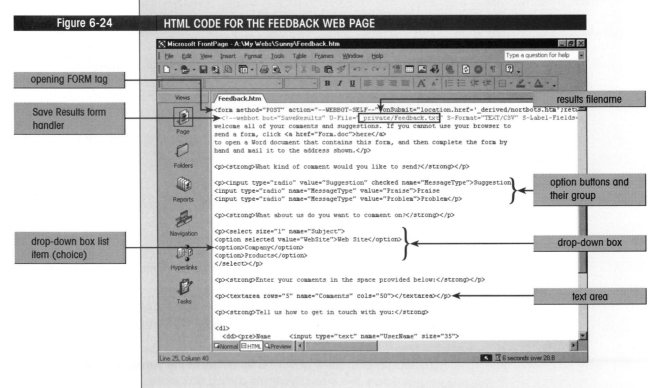

3. Press **Ctrl + End** to scroll to the end of the page. See Figure 6-25. Scroll the page to the right to view the HTML code that creates and validates the Visits text box.

Figure 6-25   **HTML CODE FOR THE FEEDBACK WEB PAGE (CONTINUED)**

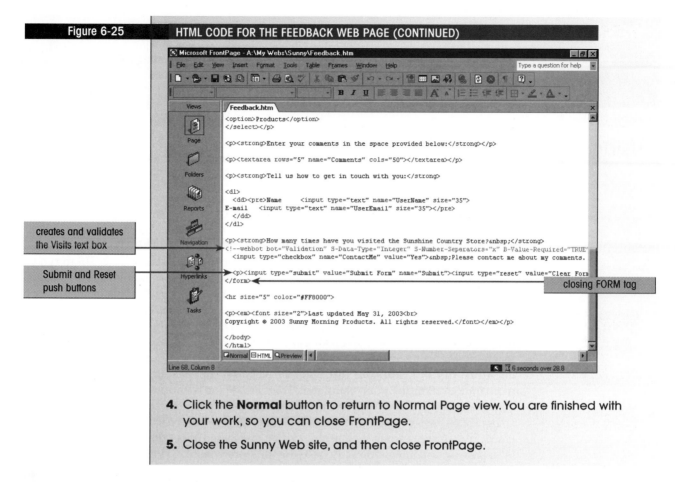

creates and validates
the Visits text box

Submit and Reset
push buttons

closing FORM tag

4. Click the **Normal** button to return to Normal Page view. You are finished with your work, so you can close FrontPage.

5. Close the Sunny Web site, and then close FrontPage.

In Session 6.3, you will publish the Sunny Web site to a server and test the Web site. You will also enhance the Web site by adding Web components that require a server for processing.

Session 6.2 QUICK CHECK

1. True or False: When validating a text box form field, you can set the field to accept only numbers, integers, or letters as valid values.

2. To ensure that users will enter data into a form field, click the _____ check box in the form field's Validation dialog box.

3. Name and describe three validation criteria that you can set for a form field that will contain integers.

4. Name and describe the three types of push buttons that you can create in a form.

5. The name and value of a form field in a results file is known as a(n) _____.

6. A Web site's administrator is called a(n) _____.

7. The choices in a drop-down box list are specified in HTML using the _____ tag.

SESSION 6.3

In this session, you will publish a disk-based Web to a server, process forms using a server, and examine form results stored on a server. You will create a hit counter, include a banner ad, move files using drag and drop, use the Find and Replace commands, and recalculate and verify hyperlinks. Finally, you will learn how permissions are used to restrict access in a Web site.

Using a Desktop Web Service

To function as a Web server, a computer requires a Web server program, which is special software that works with the computer's operating system to receive and execute requests for Web pages. The steps in this tutorial use **Microsoft Internet Information Services (IIS)** version 5.0, which is installed with Windows 2000 Professional. You can usually tell that IIS is running on your computer when the IIS icon 🐾 is displayed on the Windows taskbar. Sometimes IIS is running, but its icon on the taskbar is hidden. You can set IIS to run when Windows starts (the default setting) or you can start it from the Windows Control Panel.

To access a site stored on IIS, you do not need to use the "www" prefix or the server type suffix in the URL; instead, you use the computer name or the default name of **localhost**. Most Web developers use a desktop Web service to develop and test a Web site before publishing it on a Web server and making the site available to Internet users. Because the specifications for using a desktop Web service vary from one computer to another, it is important to work with your instructor or technical support person to determine the correct configuration for your computer. Your instructor will note any differences that you might encounter as you complete the steps in this session.

Figure 6-26 shows the differences between using a disk-based Web and using a server-based Web to access your Web pages. With a disk-based Web, the Web browser opens each Web page by obtaining it directly from the file stored on disk. With a server-based Web, the Web browser uses the TCP/IP network protocol to send the request for a Web page to the server. The server then obtains a copy of the file stored on disk and sends it back to the browser by way of the TCP/IP network connection, and the browser subsequently opens the file. Thus, with a local Web server, the TCP/IP network software uses the same network processing to obtain the requested files as if it were connecting to a Web server.

Figure 6-26	FILE TRANSFER COMPARISON OF A DISK-BASED AND SERVER-BASED WEB

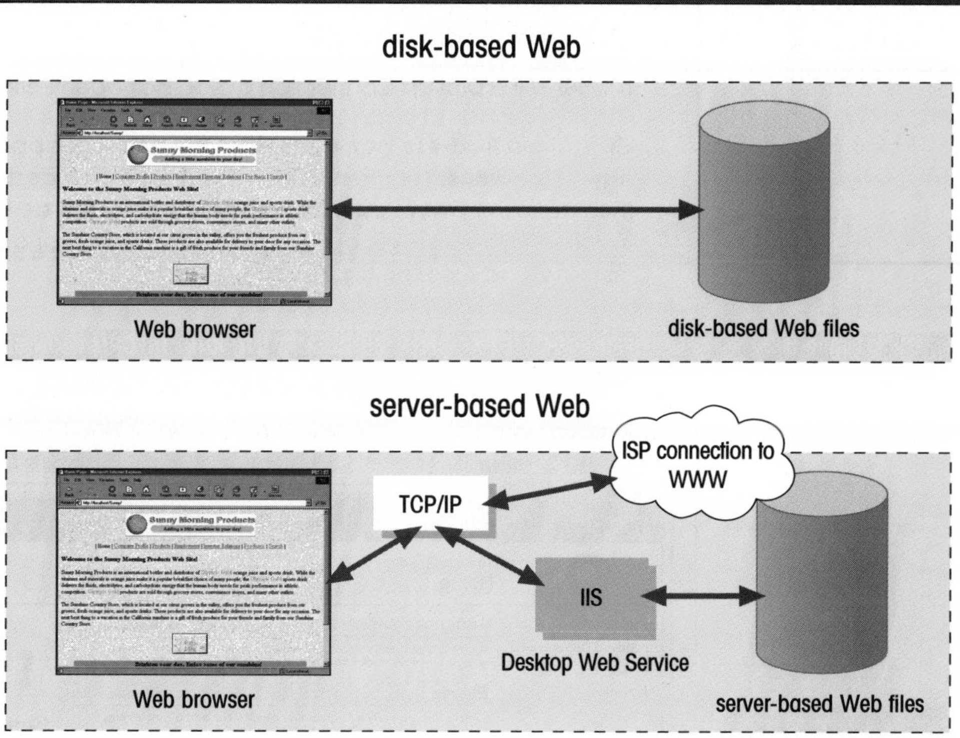

The technical support person at Sunny Morning Products has installed and configured IIS and the FrontPage 2002 Server Extensions on Amanda's computer. The technical support person assigned the name "localhost" to Amanda's computer (your computer's name might be different). You will test IIS to make sure that it is installed and operating correctly and that you can access it using your Web browser. Your instructor or technical support person will inform you of any differences that you might encounter in the lab. These steps assume a default installation of IIS and a default URL of localhost to access it.

To test IIS:

1. Make sure that IIS is running by confirming that the IIS icon 🐾 appears on the taskbar.

    TROUBLE? If the IIS icon has a red "X" or a yellow triangle on it, then it is stopped or paused. Right-click the IIS icon on the taskbar, and then click Start Service or Continue Service.

    TROUBLE? If you do not see the IIS icon on the taskbar, click the Start button on the taskbar, point to Settings, and then click Control Panel. Double-click the Administrative Tools icon, and then double-click the Personal Web Manager icon. (If you do not see a Personal Web Manager icon, ask your instructor or technical support person for help; IIS might not be installed.) In the Personal Web Manager dialog box, click the Start button to start IIS, and then click the Close button ✖ to close the dialog box. If you see a Stop button in the Personal Web Manager dialog box, then IIS is already running. Close the dialog box and Control Panel.

2. Start Internet Explorer, but do not connect to the Internet. You do not need an Internet connection to complete these steps.

TROUBLE? If a Dial-up Connection dialog box opens, click the Close button X.

3. Click in the **Address bar**, make sure any URL that appears is selected, type **http://localhost** (or the name or IP address provided by your instructor), and then press the **Enter** key. The IIS home page or the default home page that was installed for your server opens, confirming that IIS or another Web server is installed and functioning. See Figure 6-27.

Figure 6-27	DEFAULT HOME PAGE FOR MICROSOFT INTERNET INFORMATION SERVICES 5.0

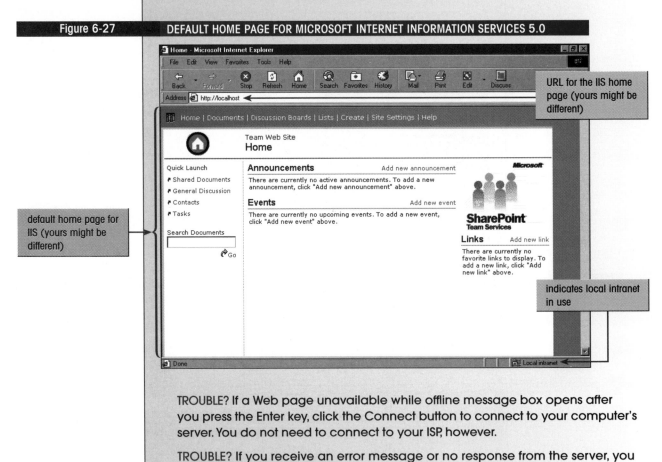

URL for the IIS home page (yours might be different)

default home page for IIS (yours might be different)

indicates local intranet in use

TROUBLE? If a Web page unavailable while offline message box opens after you press the Enter key, click the Connect button to connect to your computer's server. You do not need to connect to your ISP, however.

TROUBLE? If you receive an error message or no response from the server, you might need to start, install, or configure the server. Ask your instructor or technical support person for help.

You need to move the folders and files from your disk-based Web to the server so that you can continue testing the Sunny Web site.

Publishing a Web Site

You **publish** a Web site by copying the Web site's folders and files to your computer's server or to a Web server that is connected to the Internet. When you publish a Web site to IIS, the default server-based folder containing all server-based Webs is C:\Inetpub\wwwroot; any Web sites that are published to IIS are stored as subfolders, or subwebs, in this path.

Note: You will need to know how your computer is organized before publishing your Web site to ensure that the server-based Web folder contains the FrontPage 2002 Server Extensions. Your instructor will inform you of any differences that you might encounter in the lab.

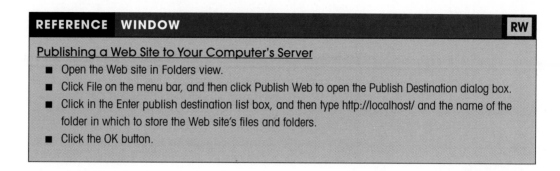

REFERENCE   WINDOW   RW

Publishing a Web Site to Your Computer's Server
- Open the Web site in Folders view.
- Click File on the menu bar, and then click Publish Web to open the Publish Destination dialog box.
- Click in the Enter publish destination list box, and then type http://localhost/ and the name of the folder in which to store the Web site's files and folders.
- Click the OK button.

You can publish a disk-based Web site to a server using the same or a different Web site name. Before publishing a Web site, check with the server's administrator to find out if you need to use any special naming conventions, such as using only lowercase letters or omitting spaces in Web folder names and filenames. Even though a disk-based Web site and a server-based Web site can have the same name, you access a disk-based Web using a path to a folder on a floppy or hard drive. For a server-based Web, you use the HTTP protocol, the server name (in this case, localhost), and the name of the Web site, as in http://localhost/Sunny.

When you publish a Web site to IIS, the site is added as a subfolder in the C:\Inetpub\wwwroot folder on your hard drive. If you are publishing changes to an existing server-based Web site, you can click the Publish Web button on the Standard toolbar and FrontPage will automatically publish the changes to the correct Web site on the server without reopening the Publish Destination dialog box.

Amanda wants you to publish the Sunny Web site to IIS to create a server-based Web.

Note: You must be able to publish files to your computer's hard drive or network drive to complete the steps in Session 6.3. If you cannot access one of these drives, read Session 6.3 without completing the steps at the computer so that you will know how to publish a Web site.

To publish a disk-based Web to IIS:

1. Start FrontPage, and then open the **Sunny** Web site from your Data Disk in Folders view.

2. Click **File** on the menu bar, and then click **Publish Web**. The Publish Destination dialog box opens. See Figure 6-28.

Figure 6-28   PUBLISH DESTINATION DIALOG BOX

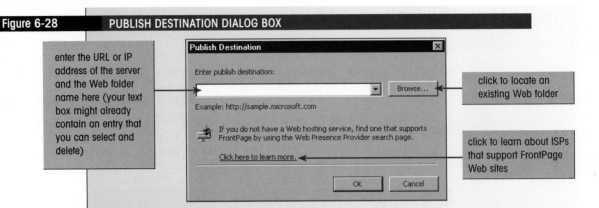

enter the URL or IP address of the server and the Web folder name here (your text box might already contain an entry that you can select and delete)

click to locate an existing Web folder

click to learn about ISPs that support FrontPage Web sites

You will change the publish destination by typing the path to IIS or your server.

3. Select any text in the Enter publish destination text box (if necessary), type **http://localhost/Sunny**, and then click the **OK** button.

TROUBLE? If your instructor provides you with a different path or computer name, or an IP address for publishing your Web site, use that path and computer name instead of the one provided in Step 3. If you are connected to a network server and your computer's name contains a period, then use the IP address, rather than the computer's name provided in Step 3.

TROUBLE? If the Enter Network Connection dialog box opens, enter your network user name, password, and domain in the appropriate text boxes. If you do not have a user name and password, ask your instructor or technical support person for help.

A Microsoft FrontPage message box opens, indicating that a Web site does not exist at the location you specified. You need to create the Web folder, so you'll click the OK button.

4. Click the **OK** button. The Publish Web dialog box opens. See Figure 6-29.

Figure 6-29   PUBLISH WEB DIALOG BOX

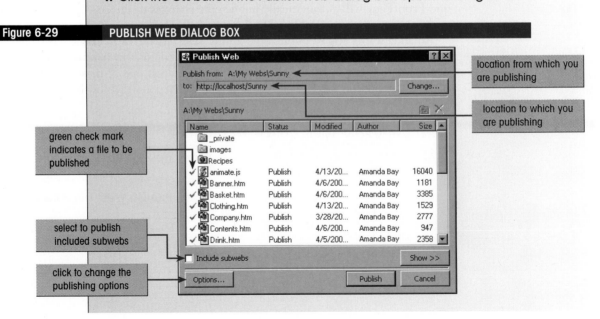

location from which you are publishing

location to which you are publishing

green check mark indicates a file to be published

select to publish included subwebs

click to change the publishing options

TROUBLE? If a Sunny Web site already exists on the server, rename the Web using "Sunny" plus your name and then continue with the steps.

The Publish Web dialog box identifies the location from which you are publishing and the location to which you are publishing. In this case, you are publishing your disk-based Web (A:\My Webs\Sunny) to IIS (http://localhost/Sunny). To change this publish destination, you can click the Change button to return to the Publish Destination dialog box and then make the necessary changes.

The dialog box also lists all of the folders and files in your Web site. Each file has a status of "Publish" and a green check mark to the left of the filename. If you had set any page so that it would not be published, the status would be "Don't publish" and a red "X" would appear instead of the green check mark. (You can set a page so that it is not published by right-clicking the filename and then clicking Don't Publish on the shortcut menu.)

Finally, if your Web site contains a subweb, you must select the Include sub-webs check box to publish the subweb with the root Web.

If you need to change the options for publishing a Web site, you can click the Options button.

5. Click the **Options** button. The Options dialog box opens. See Figure 6-30.

Figure 6-30   OPTIONS DIALOG BOX

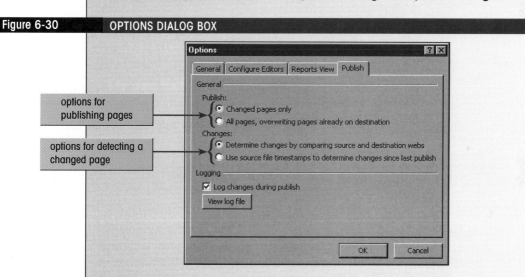

You can change the default settings to publish either all pages or only those pages that contain changes. The advantage of publishing only changed pages is that it will speed up the publishing process. You can specify which method to use to determine a changed page: by comparing the source and destination Web sites, or by comparing the date and time that pages in the source Web site were last saved. You'll accept the default settings.

6. Click the **OK** button to close the Options dialog box, click the **Include subwebs** check box to select it, and then click the **Publish** button in the Publish Web dialog box. FrontPage begins publishing the disk-based Web to IIS. Several messages appear on the status bar and in the dialog box while FrontPage publishes your disk-based Web to IIS. The "Web site published successfully!" message shown in Figure 6-31 appears when the publishing process is finished.

Figure 6-31   DIALOG BOX THAT OPENS AFTER SUCCESSFULLY PUBLISHING A WEB SITE

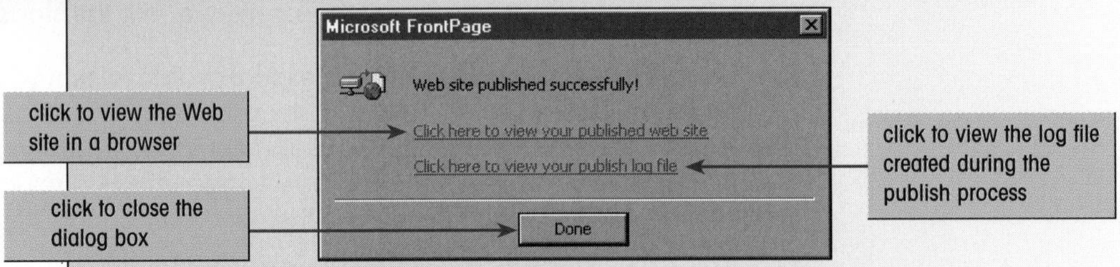

click to view the Web site in a browser

click to view the log file created during the publish process

click to close the dialog box

> **TROUBLE?** If a dialog box opens and tells you that FrontPage cannot locate the FrontPage Server Extensions, then you either typed the wrong computer name in Step 3 or the Server Extensions are not configured correctly. Ask your instructor or technical support person for help.

While publishing your Web site to IIS, FrontPage automatically changed the filename of your disk-based home page from index.htm to Default.htm. FrontPage also updated any links to the file named index.htm to Default.htm. This naming convention also works in reverse. If you publish a Web site from IIS to a disk-based Web, then the file Default.htm is renamed index.htm. Some developers publish a server-based Web to a folder on a hard drive to create a backup copy of the Web site because all of the FrontPage Server Extensions and the Web site's contents are also copied to the disk.

Now that you have published the Sunny Web site to IIS, you can open it using the hyperlink created by FrontPage.

7. Click the **Click here to view your published web site** hyperlink in the Microsoft FrontPage dialog box. The home page for the server-based Web site opens in the browser.

> **TROUBLE?** If the logo in the home page does not appear, click the Refresh button [icon] on the toolbar to reload the page.

Notice that the URL of the home page is now http://localhost/Sunny/. The HTTP protocol in the URL indicates that your Web browser is communicating with a server to process requests, instead of opening files directly from your computer's hard drive. The server is opening the files from the path C:\Inetpub\wwwroot\Sunny folder on your hard drive. You can perform the same activities using this server-based Web as you did with the disk-based Web. In addition, when you open a server-based Web in FrontPage, you can edit pages, update hyperlinks, and perform other tasks, just as you did in the disk-based Web. The main difference between the two Web sites is that the server-based Web will process several key elements of the Web site, including the form that you created earlier in this tutorial.

Publishing Changes to Pages in a Web Site

Your disk-based Web site is still open in FrontPage. Amanda reminds you that you did not create the hyperlinks in the home page to open the Feedback and Search Web pages that you completed earlier in this tutorial. So that you can practice publishing changes to pages, you will update the home page using the disk-based Sunny Web and then publish these changes to the server-based Sunny Web. When you modify a server-based Web, you usually don't need to take the extra step of publishing your changes because they are made directly in the server-based Web. Some changes, however, must be published to work correctly, even if you make them in a server-based Web.

REFERENCE WINDOW **RW**

Publishing Changes to a Server-Based Web Site

- In Page view, open the Web page that you need to edit, make the changes, and then save the page.
- Edit and save other Web pages, as necessary.
- Click the Publish Web button on the Standard toolbar.

To update the link bar in the home page and publish the changes:

1. Close the browser, and then in FrontPage click the **Done** button in the dialog box to close it. The disk-based Sunny Web site is still open in FrontPage, as indicated by the path A:\My Webs\Sunny in the title bar.

2. Double-click **index.htm** in the Contents pane to open the home page in Page view.

3. Double-click **Feedback** in the link bar, click the **Insert Hyperlink** button 🖼 on the Standard toolbar to open the Insert Hyperlink dialog box, and then scroll down the list of files and double-click **Feedback**.

4. Repeat Step 3 to create the **Search** hyperlink in the link bar that opens the **Search** page.

5. Save the home page. You need to publish it to the server to update your changes in the server-based Web.

6. Click the **Publish Web** button 🖼 on the Standard toolbar. Because you have already published this Web site, you do not have to specify a location to which to publish it. A Microsoft FrontPage dialog box opens and processes the updates to the server-based Sunny Web site. After a few moments, the "Web site published successfully!" message appears again.

7. Click the **Click here to view your published web site** hyperlink to open the home page of your server-based Web site in the browser, and then click the **Refresh** button 🖼 on the toolbar (if necessary) to load the new version of the home page. The Feedback and Search hyperlinks in the link bar are now active.

Processing Web Pages on a Server

After a server processes a Web page that contains a form, it usually sends a confirmation page to the browser that sent the page. A **confirmation page** is a Web page that contains a copy of the data entered by the user and often is used for verification purposes. FrontPage can return a default confirmation page or you can create, save, and specify a custom confirmation page. When you specify a custom confirmation page, FrontPage automatically inserts the data entered by the user in the correct locations in the confirmation page and then sends it to the browser. You will not create a custom confirmation page in this tutorial, but you can search for the topic "Create a confirmation page and assign it to a form" in the FrontPage Help system to learn more about creating one.

Next, you will test the Search and Feedback Web pages to make sure that the server processes these pages correctly.

To test the Search Web page in a browser:

1. Click the **Search** hyperlink in the link bar in the home page. The Search page opens in the browser. The page's URL references the page in the server-based Web.

   TROUBLE? If a Dial-up Connection dialog box opens, click the Close button 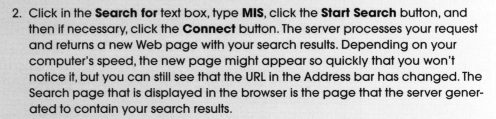.

2. Click in the **Search for** text box, type **MIS**, click the **Start Search** button, and then if necessary, click the **Connect** button. The server processes your request and returns a new Web page with your search results. Depending on your computer's speed, the new page might appear so quickly that you won't notice it, but you can still see that the URL in the Address bar has changed. The Search page that is displayed in the browser is the page that the server generated to contain your search results.

   TROUBLE? If a page opens with the message "Service is not running" and you published the Sunny Web site on IIS, you will need to start the Indexing Service. Click the Start button on the taskbar, point to Settings, and then click Control Panel. Double-click the Administrative Tools icon, double-click the Component Services icon, and then click Services (Local) in the pane on the left. Scroll down the list of services on the right and double-click Indexing Service. Click the Start button, click the OK button, and then close the remaining windows. It might take

   TROUBLE? If you published the Sunny Web site to IIS, it might take several minutes for the server to index the pages you just published. If you see the message, "No documents found. Please try again." you may need to wait a few minutes for the index to show the search results. a few minutes for IIS to index your site and provide the search results.

   TROUBLE? If an Internet Explorer dialog box opens and says that you are sending information to the local intranet, click the Yes button to continue.

3. Scroll down the Search page so you can see the search results. See Figure 6-32. The server generated this revised version of the Search page. The Search Results table contains one entry that is formatted as a hyperlink. The Employment Web page contains the search text that you specified. Pages identified in the search results are hyperlinks that you can click to open those pages.

Figure 6-32 **SEARCH WEB PAGE WITH SEARCH RESULTS**

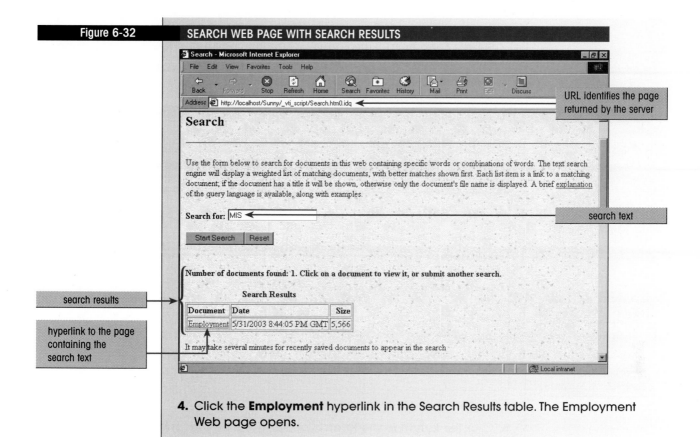

URL identifies the page returned by the server

search text

search results

hyperlink to the page containing the search text

4. Click the **Employment** hyperlink in the Search Results table. The Employment Web page opens.

Now you can test the Feedback Web page, which contains the form that must be processed by a server.

To test the Feedback Web page using Internet Explorer:

1. Click the **Feedback** hyperlink in the link bar in the Employment page to open the Feedback page.

2. Click the **Praise** option button, select **Company** in the drop-down box list, type **This is a test.** in the text area, type your name and e-mail address into the text boxes, type **155** in the Visits text box, and then click the **Please contact me about my comments** check box to select it.

3. Click the **Submit Form** button. The form validation error message box opens, indicating that this data does not meet the validation criteria. See Figure 6-33.

Figure 6-33 **ERROR MESSAGE FOR THE VISITS TEXT BOX**

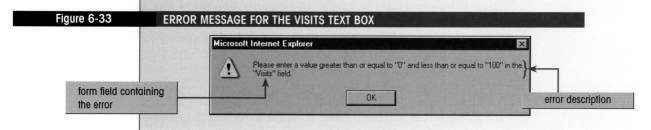

form field containing the error

error description

4. Click the **OK** button, select **155** in the Visits text box, type **15**, and then click the **Submit Form** button. The Form Confirmation page opens with a copy of the data you entered into the form. The server generated this page automatically. See Figure 6-34.

Figure 6-34	FORM CONFIRMATION PAGE

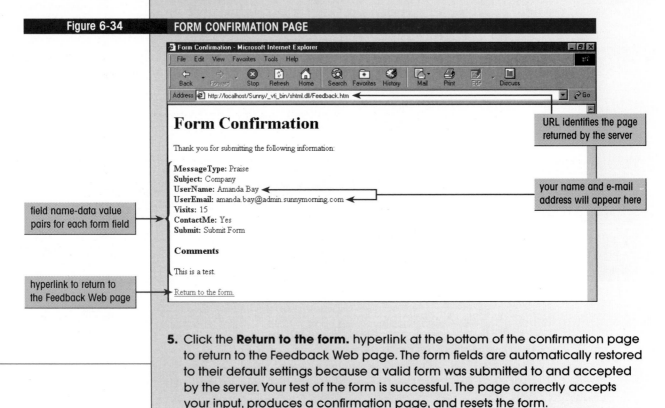

5. Click the **Return to the form.** hyperlink at the bottom of the confirmation page to return to the Feedback Web page. The form fields are automatically restored to their default settings because a valid form was submitted to and accepted by the server. Your test of the form is successful. The page correctly accepts your input, produces a confirmation page, and resets the form.

When the confirmation page was sent to your browser, the form's results were also written to the Feedback.txt file that you specified when you created the form. The Feedback.txt file is stored in the Web site's _private folder, which is a hidden file that you can examine from FrontPage. It is a good practice to examine the data collected by a form to help improve customer service or identify problems. For example, you might create a separate report of "problem" information to discuss with the customer service manager.

Examining a Form Results File

When you set the Save Results form handler to store the form's results, you specified a comma-delimited text file format. In a **comma-delimited text file**, the name of each form field appears in the first line of the file. The form results from each form submission are then added as a new line at the end of the file. Unless you submitted your form more than once, the results file contains only two lines—one containing the form field names and another containing the form results from your form submission. You can examine the contents of the results file on the server at any time.

Amanda asks you to view this file to increase your understanding of how the data submitted to the server is stored. First, however, you must close the disk-based Sunny Web and open the server-based Sunny Web.

To open a server-based Web:

1. Close the browser, and then click the **Done** button to close the dialog box. The title bar indicates that the current Web site is stored on your Data Disk. You will close this Web site and then open the published Web site.

2. Click **File** on the menu bar, and then click **Close Web**. The disk-based Web closes.

3. Click the **list arrow** for the Open button ⤷ on the Standard toolbar, and then click **Open Web** in the list. The Open Web dialog box opens. You need to access the folder on your computer that contains server-based Webs.

4. Click the **My Network Places** button in the Look in column, and then click the **Sunny on localhost** folder to select it. See Figure 6-35.

Figure 6-35	MY NETWORK PLACES

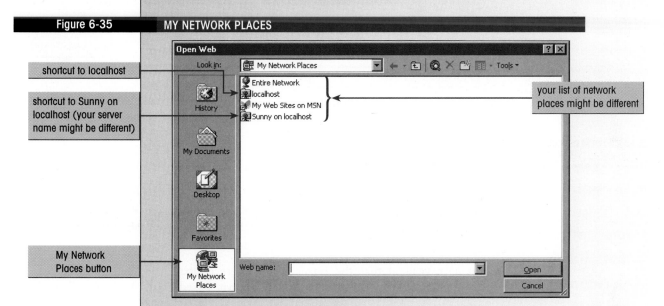

shortcut to localhost

shortcut to Sunny on localhost (your server name might be different)

your list of network places might be different

My Network Places button

TROUBLE? If you see localhost or your server's name in the list box, double-click it to open it. The Sunny Web site should appear as a folder that you can select.

5. Click the **Open** button, and then change to Folders view (if necessary). The Web site contains the file Default.htm instead of index.htm, which is the home page in a server-based Web. The FrontPage title bar indicates that the current Web is stored at http://localhost/Sunny.

TROUBLE? If the Sunny Web site does not open, double-click the Sunny folder in the Folder List to open it in a new FrontPage window. Close the other FrontPage window that is open.

Now that the server-based Web is open, you can examine the results file.

To examine a results file:

1. Click the **_private** folder in the Folder List, and then double-click **Feedback.txt** in the Contents pane. The file opens in Notepad or the default text editor for your installation of FrontPage. The file contains the results from one form. Each value in quotation marks represents the value for one form field in the form. See Figure 6-36.

Figure 6-36	FORM RESULTS TEXT FILE

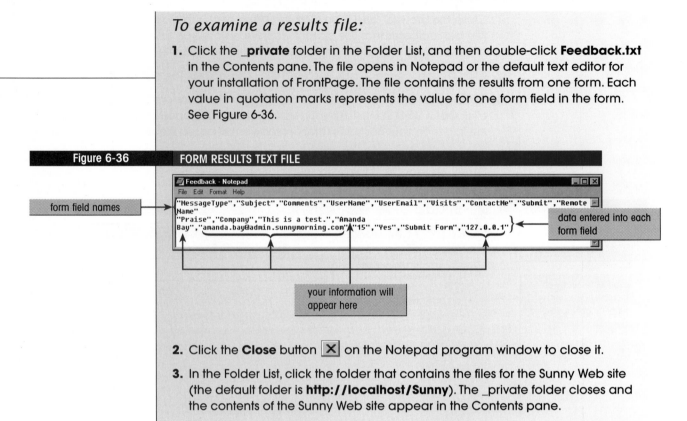

form field names

data entered into each form field

your information will appear here

2. Click the **Close** button ☒ on the Notepad program window to close it.

3. In the Folder List, click the folder that contains the files for the Sunny Web site (the default folder is **http://localhost/Sunny**). The _private folder closes and the contents of the Sunny Web site appear in the Contents pane.

You have verified that the forms results were collected correctly and stored in the Feedback.txt file in the _private folder of the server-based Sunny Web site. Amanda wants you to add the remaining features to the Web site before preparing the site for publication on the Web server for Sunny Morning Products.

Using a Hit Counter

The Web site development team is interested in counting the number of visitors to the site. A **hit counter** is a Web component that counts the number of times a page in a Web site has been opened or refreshed using a Web browser. Usually a hit counter appears in the Web site's home page, although you can create hit counters in other pages, as well. A hit counter requires a server for processing, so you can test it only in a server-based Web. Because a hit counter is a built-in Web component, you simply insert it in the appropriate location in a Web page, and FrontPage then creates its complex HTML code automatically. You can accept the default settings for the hit counter or change the counter style and other properties if desired. The counter style is implemented using a default or custom-designed GIF picture that contains the digits zero through nine.

REFERENCE WINDOW   **RW**

Creating a Hit Counter in a Web Page
- ■ Click the location in the Web page where you want to insert the hit counter.
- ■ Click the Web Component button on the Standard toolbar.
- ■ In the Component type list box, click Hit Counter.
- ■ In the Choose a counter style list box, click the desired hit counter style, and then click the Finish button.
- ■ Set the options to reset the counter or to display a fixed number of digits as needed.
- ■ Click the OK button.

Amanda asks you to insert a hit counter in the home page. The hit counter will begin at 1000 and display six digits.

To create a hit counter in a Web page:

1. Double-click **Default.htm** in the Contents pane to open the home page in Page view. You will insert the hit counter above the footer.

2. Press **Ctrl + End**, click to the left of **Last** in the first line of the footer, press the **Enter** key to create a new line above the footer, press the **Up** arrow key ↑, click the **Center** button ▤ on the Formatting toolbar, and then click the **Bold** button **B** on the Formatting toolbar.

3. Type **You are visitor number** as the text that precedes the hit counter, and then press the **spacebar**.

4. Click the **Web Component** button 🖳 on the Standard toolbar, and then in the Component type list box click **Hit Counter**. The Choose a counter style list box displays five styles of hit counters.

5. Click the third hit counter style in the Choose a counter style list box, and then click the **Finish** button. The Hit Counter Properties dialog box opens. See Figure 6-37.

Figure 6-37   **HIT COUNTER PROPERTIES DIALOG BOX**

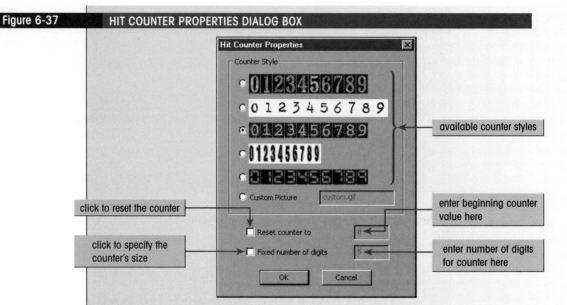

available counter styles

click to reset the counter

enter beginning counter value here

click to specify the counter's size

enter number of digits for counter here

6. Click the **Reset counter to** check box to select it, press the **Tab** key to move to its text box, and then type **1000**. The hit counter will start at 1000, instead of at zero. Starting the hit counter at a number other than zero or one is a common practice on the Internet.

7. Click the **Fixed number of digits** check box to select it, press the **Tab** key to move to its text box, and then type **6**. The counter will display six digits.

8. Click the **OK** button to close the Hit Counter Properties dialog box and to insert the hit counter. The placeholder "[Hit Counter]" indicates the hit counter's location in the Web page.

   Next, complete the rest of the sentence that contains the hit counter.

9. Press the **spacebar**, and then type **to our Web site.** as the text that follows the hit counter.

10. Save the home page.

Now you can test the hit counter.

To test the hit counter:

1. Click the **Preview in Browser** button 🔍 on the Standard toolbar to open the home page in a browser.

2. Press **Ctrl + End** to scroll to the bottom of the home page to see the hit counter. You are visitor number 1001.

3. Click the **Refresh** button 🔁 on the toolbar to refresh the page. Now you are visitor number 1002. Each time the page is opened or refreshed, the hit counter is incremented by one. See Figure 6-38.

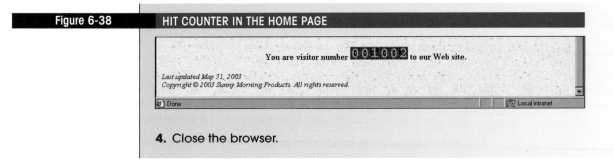

Figure 6-38 | **HIT COUNTER IN THE HOME PAGE**

You are visitor number 001002 to our Web site.

Last updated May 31, 2003
Copyright © 2003 Sunny Morning Products. All rights reserved.

Done   Local intranet

4. Close the browser.

The hit counter will count the number of visitors to the Sunny Web site. By measuring this traffic, the Web site development team will have information on which to base future decisions when enhancing the Sunny Web site.

Your next task is to include a banner ad in the home page.

Using the Banner Ad Manager

Banner ads are dynamic billboards that display a series of images, such as pictures of products or the text of a company slogan. As each new image appears, the Web browser applies a visual transition effect so that the transition from one image to the next is not noticeable. If desired, you can associate a hyperlink with a banner ad.

The **Banner Ad Manager** is a Java applet that controls the continuous display of images in the Web page. For the Banner Ad Manager to work correctly, you need to test it using a server-based Web.

Before creating a banner ad, you need to create the GIF files that you will use in it. You can use an image-editing program to create these images, or you can obtain them from some other source. (Creating an image is beyond the scope of this tutorial.)

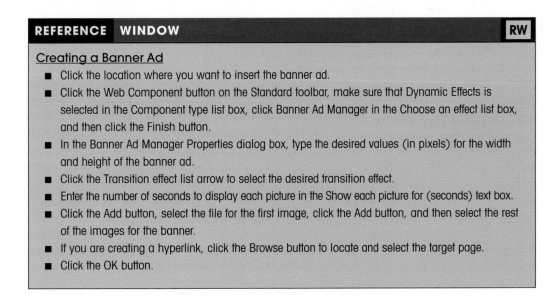

REFERENCE WINDOW   **RW**

Creating a Banner Ad
- Click the location where you want to insert the banner ad.
- Click the Web Component button on the Standard toolbar, make sure that Dynamic Effects is selected in the Component type list box, click Banner Ad Manager in the Choose an effect list box, and then click the Finish button.
- In the Banner Ad Manager Properties dialog box, type the desired values (in pixels) for the width and height of the banner ad.
- Click the Transition effect list arrow to select the desired transition effect.
- Enter the number of seconds to display each picture in the Show each picture for (seconds) text box.
- Click the Add button, select the file for the first image, click the Add button, and then select the rest of the images for the banner.
- If you are creating a hyperlink, click the Browse button to locate and select the target page.
- Click the OK button.

Amanda asks you to replace the current Sunny Morning Products logo in the home page with a banner ad.

To include a banner ad in the home page:

1. On the home page, click the **Sunny Morning Products** logo to select it, and then press the **Delete** key. The logo is deleted; you will insert the banner ad in its place.

2. Click the **Web Component** button 🖼 on the Standard toolbar, make sure that **Dynamic Effects** is selected in the Component type list box, click **Banner Ad Manager** in the Choose an effect list box, and then click the **Finish** button. The Banner Ad Manager Properties dialog box opens. See Figure 6-39.

Figure 6-39	BANNER AD MANAGER PROPERTIES DIALOG BOX

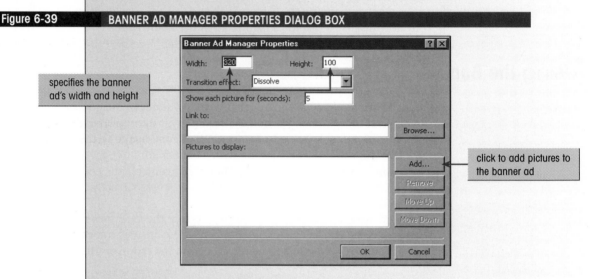

specifies the banner ad's width and height

click to add pictures to the banner ad

Amanda gave you the dimensions for the pictures that will be displayed by the Banner Ad Manager. The default value is selected in the Width text box, so you can just type the new value.

3. Type **380** in the Width text box, press the **Tab** key to move to the Height text box, and then type **65**. You will accept the default transition values, which are a Dissolve transition and a five-second display of each picture. The banner ad will not serve as a hyperlink, so you will leave the Link to text box empty.

Next, specify the picture files for the banner ad.

4. Click the **Add** button to open the Add Picture for Banner Ad dialog box, open the **Tutorial.06** folder on your Data Disk, and then double-click **Banner1**. The Add Picture for Banner Ad dialog box closes, and the Banner1.gif file appears in the Pictures to display list box.

5. Repeat Step 4 to select **Banner2** as the second file. Now both filenames appear in the Pictures to display list box.

6. Click the **OK** button. Only the first picture that you specified appears in Page view. The pictures that Amanda created for use in the banner ad have a white background. She explains that after inserting a picture in a banner ad, you cannot change the picture's characteristics. If the pictures should have a certain appearance, such as a transparent background, you need to make the desired changes before inserting the file in the Banner Ad Manager.

7. Click the **Save** button 🖫 on the Standard toolbar. The Save Embedded Files dialog box opens and displays the two files used in the Banner Ad Manager. The two banner ad pictures—Banner1.gif and Banner2.gif—do not have a folder location specified, which means that they will be saved in the root folder of the Sunny Web site. Amanda wants you to save the files for the banner ad there for now, instead of in the site's images folder.

TROUBLE? If images/ or any folder name appears in the Folder column for the Banner1.gif and Banner2.gif files, click the Change Folder button, click the Sunny folder that appears in the Look in list box, and then click the OK button to return to the Save Embedded Files dialog box. Continue with Step 8.

8. Click the **OK** button to save the page.

With the banner ad included in the home page, you are ready to test it to make sure that it operates correctly.

To test the Banner Ad Manager:

1. Click the **Preview in Browser** button 🔍 on the Standard toolbar to open the home page in a browser. Watch the logo as the picture changes every five seconds.

2. Close the browser.

This banner ad should increase the visual appeal of the home page, as Jacob had anticipated.

Moving a File Using Drag and Drop

In Tutorial 5, you learned how to use drag and drop to arrange the pages in your Web site in a navigation structure. You can also use drag and drop to move one or more files in your Web site from one folder to another. When you use drag and drop, FrontPage automatically updates any pages that contain hyperlinks to the files that you move. Amanda wants you to use drag and drop to move the files used in the banner ad into the Web site's images folder, so they will be in the same folder as other multimedia files in the Web site. After moving the files, you will confirm that FrontPage updated the location of the files.

To use drag and drop to move files:

1. Click the **Folders** button 🗀 on the Views bar to change to Folders view. Make sure that the Folder List is displayed.

2. Click the **Refresh** button 🔃 on the Standard toolbar to refresh the file listing in the Contents pane.

3. Click **Banner1.gif** in the Contents pane to select that file, and then press and hold down the **Shift** key and click **Banner2.gif** to select both files.

4. Point to the file icon for the **Banner1.gif** file, press and hold down the left mouse button, and then move the pointer to the images folder in the Folder List. The pointer changes to a ⬚ shape when you point to the images folder.

5. Release the mouse button. The Rename dialog box opens, and then the files are moved to the images folder. FrontPage automatically updates the references in the Banner Ad Manager, as you will see next.

6. Double-click **Default.htm** in the Contents pane to open the home page in Page view, and then double-click the **banner ad** in the page. The Banner Ad Manager Properties dialog box opens. The Pictures to display list box shows that the pictures for the banner ad are now stored in the images folder.

7. Click the **Cancel** button to close the Banner Ad Manager Properties dialog box.

Although drag and drop is similar to moving files in Windows Explorer, it is important to note that moving files using Windows Explorer will not automatically update the hyperlinks to those files. You should use only FrontPage to move files to ensure that your hyperlinks are updated using the files' new location.

Global Find and Replace

When you need to find a specific occurrence of text in a Web page or make a site-wide change, you can use the Find and Replace commands on the Edit menu to search each page in the Web site. When you use the Replace command, you can tell FrontPage to find and replace text with new text that you specify. The Find and Replace commands search only for text in a Web page; you cannot use them to search for specific settings in dialog boxes, such as a page's title. The options in the Find and Replace dialog box let you search only the current page or the entire Web site; you can also specify options for finding text, such as matching the case of letters in the word ("Letter" instead of "letter") and locating only whole words ("pen" but not words that contain "pen," such as "pencil").

After reviewing the published Web site, the Web site development team suggests changing the "About Us" text in the user-defined link bar in each Web page to "Company Profile." The team feels that renaming the hyperlink for the Company.htm page will make it easier to identify the page. You can make this change using the Replace command, instead of changing the hyperlink manually in every page in the Web site.

To use the Replace command to replace text in the Web site:

1. Click **Edit** on the menu bar, and then click **Replace**. The Find and Replace dialog box opens.

2. In the Find what text box, type **About Us**.

3. Press the **Tab** key to move to the Replace with text box, and then type **Company Profile**.

4. In the Search options section, make sure that the **All pages** option button is selected, and then click the **Match case** check box to select this option. See Figure 6-40.

Figure 6-40	FIND AND REPLACE DIALOG BOX

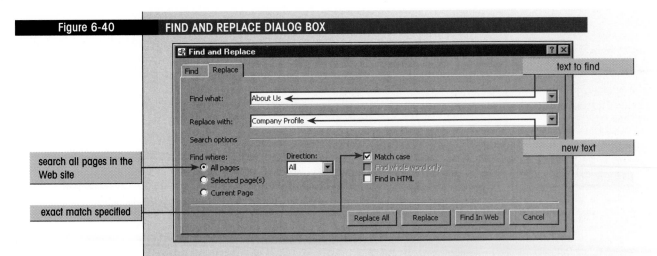

search all pages in the Web site

exact match specified

text to find

new text

5. Click the **Find In Web** button. After a few moments, FrontPage lists the pages in the Sunny Web site that contain at least one occurrence of the "About Us" text. The bottom of the dialog box indicates that FrontPage found 6 occurrences of the About Us text in 6 Web pages and searched a total of 17 Web pages. See Figure 6-41.

Figure 6-41	FIND AND REPLACE DIALOG BOX WITH DETAILS

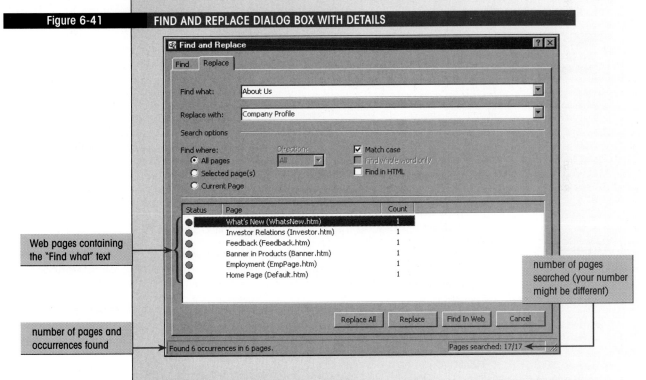

Web pages containing the "Find what" text

number of pages searched (your number might be different)

number of pages and occurrences found

To replace all occurrences of text without first examining them, click the Replace All button. You cannot undo this action, however. To replace occurrences one at a time, after examining them first, click the Replace button. In this case, FrontPage will open each page and select the "Find what" text in the page; you can click the Replace button to change it or edit the text as usual. After completing the replace operation in the first page, a dialog box opens and gives you the option of continuing to the next page in the list or returning to the list of pages.

You'll use the Replace All button to replace every occurrence of "About Us" with "Company Profile."

6. Click the **Replace All** button. A message box opens and warns that you will not be able to undo this operation.

7. Click the **Yes** button to continue. Now the Find and Replace dialog box shows that each page was edited and that six occurrences of the "Find what" text in six pages were updated. See Figure 6-42.

Figure 6-42	COMPLETED FIND AND REPLACE DIALOG BOX

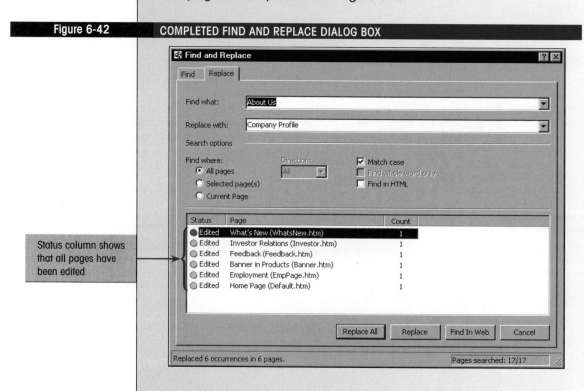

Status column shows that all pages have been edited

8. Click the **Cancel** button to close the Find and Replace dialog box. The link bar now contains a hyperlink named "Company Profile," indicating that FrontPage correctly replaced the "About Us" text in this page.

9. Point to the **Company Profile** hyperlink in the link bar. The status bar displays the file named Company.htm, indicating that the hyperlink still references the correct file.

Because the home page was open when you executed the Replace All command, you must save it. The other pages in the Web that were updated by the Replace All command were closed, and the changes were saved automatically.

10. Save the home page.

Changing a Filename in Folders View

After creating your Web pages, you might want to change the page filenames to have more meaningful descriptions. Because filenames are used as hyperlinks throughout the Web site, it would be a tedious and error-prone activity for you to search for each hyperlink and change each filename manually. When you use Folders view to change a page's filename, FrontPage automatically updates the links to that page using the new filename.

REFERENCE WINDOW **RW**

Renaming a File in Folders View
- Right-click the filename that you want to change, and then click Rename.
- Type the new filename, and then press the Enter key.
- Click the Yes button to rename the hyperlinks in the Web site.

You have already changed the hyperlink text for the "About Us" hyperlink to "Company Profile." This hyperlink references the Company.htm file with a page title of "Company Profile." Amanda would like you to rename the Company.htm file to Profile.htm so that the filename will match the page title, similar to the manner in which other files are named in the Sunny Web site.

To rename a file in Folders view:

1. Click the **Folders** button 🗗 on the Views bar to change to Folders view.

2. Right-click **Company.htm** in the Contents pane to open the shortcut menu, and then click **Rename**. The filename changes to editing mode. To change the filename, simply type a new one.

3. Type **Profile.htm** as the new filename, and then press the **Enter** key. The Rename dialog box opens and asks whether you want to update the hyperlinks in the six pages containing links to the Company Profile Web page.

4. Click the **Yes** button. FrontPage renames the page and updates the hyperlinks to it.

   Amanda asks you to verify this update by checking the hyperlink in the home page.

5. Double-click **Default.htm** to open the home page in Page view, and then point to the **Company Profile** hyperlink in the link bar. The filename Profile.htm appears on the status bar, confirming the update of the hyperlink.

6. Close the home page.

You have confirmed that the hyperlink to the Company Profile Web page was updated. Amanda thinks that now is a good time to see if there are any problems with any of the other hyperlinks in the Web site.

Recalculating **and Verifying Hyperlinks**

When you are working on a Web site, it is a good idea to recalculate the hyperlinks contained in it periodically. **Recalculating hyperlinks** is the process of updating the display of all views of the Web site in which you are working, including updating the text index created by a FrontPage search component (when one is used), deleting files for unused themes, and repairing any broken hyperlinks. You can recalculate the hyperlinks in a disk-based or server-based Web. When it recalculates the hyperlinks in a server-based Web, FrontPage updates the index that it maintains for the search component as well.

Verifying hyperlinks is the process of checking all of the hyperlinks in a Web site to identify any internal or external broken hyperlinks. An **external hyperlink** is a hyperlink to a location that is not in the current Web site, such as a hyperlink to a URL on a different Web server. Any broken hyperlinks will be listed in Reports view so you can repair them.

You can recalculate and verify hyperlinks to detect and repair broken hyperlinks. One of the primary differences between these two commands relates to how broken hyperlinks are displayed. Both commands list broken hyperlinks, but verifying hyperlinks provides a report of all broken hyperlinks (both internal and external). Both commands also provide information that is useful in locating and correcting hyperlink problems.

Recalculating Hyperlinks

First, Amanda asks you to recalculate the hyperlinks in the server-based Sunny Web site.

To recalculate hyperlinks:

1. Click the **Hyperlinks** button 🖼 on the Views bar, and then click **Default.htm** in the Folder List to make this page the center focus.

2. Click **Tools** on the menu bar, and then click **Recalculate Hyperlinks**. The Recalculate Hyperlinks dialog box opens and describes the actions that will occur after clicking the Yes button. See Figure 6-43.

Figure 6-43	RECALCULATE HYPERLINKS DIALOG BOX

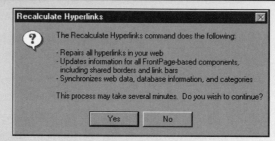

3. Read the information in the dialog box, and then click the **Yes** button. The "Updating hyperlinks and text indices..." message appears on the status bar. After a few seconds, Hyperlinks view is refreshed with the home page as the center focus in the Contents pane, and all hyperlinks are updated. FrontPage also deleted any unnecessary files in the Sunny Web site.

The hyperlinks have been recalculated, and their display has been updated to reflect any changes. No broken links are visible for the home page.

Verifying Hyperlinks

When you recalculated the hyperlinks for the Sunny Web site, only the selected page—the home page—was visible in Hyperlinks view. To see the hyperlinks for the remaining pages in the Sunny Web site, you would need to select and examine each page in Hyperlinks view. A better way of identifying broken links in a Web site is to use Reports view. When you verify hyperlinks, FrontPage checks each Web page for missing or broken hyperlinks and then displays a report of its findings.

Amanda wants you to verify the hyperlinks in the Sunny Web site to identify any problems, so you can fix them.

To verify hyperlinks:

1. Click the **Reports** button 🗊 on the Views bar to change to Reports view. If necessary, click **View** on the menu bar, point to **Toolbars**, and then click **Reporting** to display the Reporting toolbar.

   TROUBLE? If the Reporting toolbar blocks the report, drag the toolbar to another location on your screen.

2. Click the **Verifies hyperlinks in the current web** button 🖳 on the Reporting toolbar. The Verify Hyperlinks dialog box opens.

3. Click the **Verify all hyperlinks** option button, and then click the **Start** button. See Figure 6-44. The Broken Hyperlinks report lists several broken links in the current Web site. If your computer is connected to the Internet, FrontPage will also verify some of the hyperlinks to the search the Web component that you added to the Search Web page.

Figure 6-44	BROKEN HYPERLINKS REPORT IN REPORTS VIEW

five broken hyperlinks in the Sunny Web site and in the Recipes subweb and one verified hyperlink

these broken hyperlinks to the search the Web component require an Internet connection to be verified

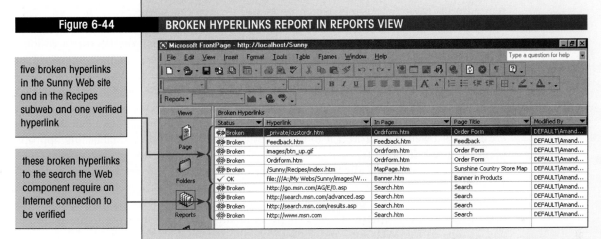

   TROUBLE? If a Dial-up Connection dialog box opens, click the Close button ☒.

   TROUBLE? If your list differs from that in Figure 6-44, then you probably introduced some errors while working on the Review Assignments for Tutorials 2 through 5. To edit a page and correct an error, double-click the page in the list. The page will open in Page view so that you can correct the error. Save the page and then return to Reports view. Repeat this process to correct any other errors in your Sunny Web site that don't appear in Figure 6-44.

4. Close the Sunny Web site, and then close FrontPage.

Recalculating and verifying hyperlinks has helped you to isolate several broken hyperlinks, and possibly other problems in your Web site. Amanda will use your report in her next meeting with the Web site development team so they can finalize the site. After fixing any problems that you find, it is a good idea to recalculate and verify the hyperlinks again, so you can check the changes that you made.

Setting Permissions for a Web Site

Permissions allow a Web site developer to control who can browse, author, or administer a Web site after it has been published. When the Web server is properly configured for using permissions, you can use FrontPage to administer the permissions for a Web site or a subweb. Three types of permissions exist: browsing, authoring, and administering. **Browsing permissions** authorize a user to browse (open) all of the pages in a Web site, including hidden files, but the user cannot make changes to the pages. **Authoring permissions** allow a user to browse and change a site's pages by opening them in Page view. Finally, **administering permissions** allow a user to browse and change a site's pages and to set other users' permissions. For example, if you do not want a user to be able to change the content of a Web site, you would set that user's permission to browsing. Permissions are hierarchical; for example, a user with administering permissions also has authoring and browsing rights, whereas authoring permissions give a user browsing rights but not administering rights.

When you run IIS on a Windows NT or Windows 2000 computer, users and groups are set up and maintained in Windows and cannot be created in FrontPage. In this case, the system administrator determines which users and groups can set security for Web sites that reside on that server. You will be able to set permissions for a Web site only if you have the necessary permissions to do so for the client or network on which the IIS server resides.

If the server allows permissions and the settings have not been changed, the permissions established for the root Web are inherited by all other Web sites. The Sunny Web site that you published to the server is a subweb in the FrontPage root Web, which is C:\Inetput\wwwroot. Thus any permissions that were set for the root Web also apply to the Sunny Web site that you published. You can change the permissions for a subweb at any time; in fact, one advantage of creating a subweb is to protect it independently of the root Web by establishing appropriate permissions for different users.

You create and update the permissions for an individual Web site by opening the site in FrontPage, clicking Tools on the menu bar, pointing to Server, and then clicking Permissions. If you have permission to administer the server's security settings, a page will open in the browser where you can create or change the Web site's permissions, add users and groups to the Web site, and set and change permissions for individual users and for groups. For example, at Sunny Morning Products, Amanda and other members of the Web site development team have administering permissions, whereas employees who are not involved in the development of the Web site have only browsing permissions.

Going Live

Going live is the process of publishing your Web site on a Web server to make it accessible to other users. In this tutorial, you published a disk-based Web to a server and tested it to ensure that its features work as expected. Before publishing a Web site on a Web server, most commercial Web site developers also test the Web site using different Web browsers, screen resolutions, and connection speeds to confirm that the Web site works consistently for the many ways in which people will access it. After thoroughly testing the site, the developer or administrator publishes it on the designated Web server.

You published the Sunny Web site to the server on your computer. After thorough testing and analysis, you will be ready to publish the Web site to the Web server for Sunny Morning Products. You would use the Publish Web command in FrontPage to publish your Sunny Web site from your computer's server to the Web server for Sunny Morning Products. To publish the site to a World Wide Web server, you need the URL for the Web server and you must have the correct user name, password, and permission to publish and maintain a Web site.

Generally, an individual designated as its administrator manages a Web server. The administrator is responsible for the overall management of the server, including the management of user access to it. The administrator determines how and where a Web site will be located on the server based on the procedures that have been established for the Web server by the company or ISP that owns and operates the server. The procedures for publishing a Web site on Web server vary; check with your site's administrator for more information about publishing Webs on your server.

Acceptable Use Policies

Most companies and ISPs maintain an **acceptable use policy** (**AUP**). An AUP typically consists of a published or online document that an ISP or company creates to indicate the acceptable activities permitted on the Web server. For example, an AUP for an educational institution might prohibit users from using the network to engage in commercial activities, or an AUP for an ISP might prohibit users from creating Web sites on the network that include objectionable material. It is the responsibility of the Web site's administrator to verify that the Web site will meet these standards.

FrontPage 2002 Server Extensions

In this tutorial, you learned that the FrontPage 2002 Server Extensions must be installed and properly configured before certain features of the Sunny Web site, such as the hit counter and the form processing will work correctly. Some ISPs do not accept Web sites with FrontPage Server Extensions because the extensions can sometimes compromise the security of the Web server on which they reside. Before creating your Web site, it is important to identify any restrictions imposed by the operator of the Web server on which your Web site will ultimately reside. You might learn that the ISP will not accept Webs with FrontPage Server Extensions. In this case, you can either search for another ISP to host your Web site or set your installation of FrontPage to disable features disallowed by the ISP. If you must disable features that use the extensions, create the Web site as usual but, before creating any of its pages, click Tools on the menu bar, click Page Options, and then click the Compatibility tab. You can use this tab to disable features that use the FrontPage Server Extensions and other Web elements, as necessary.

Fortunately, most ISPs have a technical support staff available to answer questions about publishing a Web site. Your best course of action is to find and communicate with an ISP before creating your Web site to gather information about the ISP's AUP and policy for accepting Web sites that contain FrontPage Server Extensions. In most cases, the ISP can provide alternative means for creating pages in the event that the server cannot accept server extensions.

Now that you have finished your Web site development-training course, you are ready to return to the marketing department to help create, manage, and update its Web site.

Session 6.3 QUICK | CHECK

1. True or False: To connect to your computer's Web server, you must also connect to your ISP.

2. What is the default directory in which FrontPage publishes Web sites?

3. After publishing a disk-based Web site, FrontPage automatically renames the file for the home page to _____.

4. What is a confirmation page?

5. A text file that contains form results, where the first line contains form field names and subsequent lines contain data submitted by each form, is called a(n) _____ file.

6. True or False: You can include only one hit counter in a Web site.

7. How do you update the text index used by a FrontPage search component?

8. What is the primary difference between recalculating and verifying the hyperlinks in a Web site?

9. What are three types of permissions that you can set for a FrontPage Web site?

REVIEW ASSIGNMENTS

Before preparing the Sunny Web site for publication on the Sunny Morning Products Web server, Amanda asks you to test the pages again and to make any necessary adjustments.

If necessary, start FrontPage, insert your Data Disk in the appropriate disk drive, and then do the following:

1. Use My Network Places to open the **Sunny** Web site that you published to the server in Folders view.

2. Mark the tasks for completing the Feedback and Search Web pages as completed.

3. Open the Search Web page (**Search.htm**) in Page view. Add a link bar to the Search Web page below the logo. (*Hint:* Copy the link bar from the home page, paste it into the Search Web page, and then update the link bar to include a link to the home page and to remove the link to the Search page.) Save the Search Web page.

4. Open the Feedback Web page (**Feedback.htm**) in Page view. Change the Subject drop-down box form field to include two new choices: Employee and Other. These new choices should not be selected, and their choice and value names should be the same. If necessary, use the Move Down button to move these choices so they appear fourth and fifth in the list. Then change the drop-down box form field so that two items are displayed in the browser when the list is not selected. Save the Feedback Web page, and then use Preview Page view to check the page's appearance.

Explore   5. Start Microsoft Excel, and then open the **Feedback.txt** file from the _private folder of the Web site. (*Hint:* Use My Network Places to access the **Sunny** Web site folder. You will need to select the All Files option in the Files of type list box to find the file.) When the Text Import Wizard starts, click the Delimited option button (if necessary), click the Next button, click the Comma check box and clear the Tab check box in the Delimiters section, and then click the Finish button. The form results data is displayed in the worksheet using the form field names as the column headings. Resize each column to its best fit and then print the worksheet in landscape orientation. Close Excel without saving your changes.

Explore
6. Modify the banner ad that you created in the home page by adding the **Banner3.gif** file as its third image. (This file is saved in the Tutorial.06 folder on your Data Disk.) Then change the time that images are displayed to three seconds. After inserting the new image, save this GIF file in the Web site's images folder. Test the banner ad in the browser, and then close the browser.

Explore
7. Use FrontPage to print the HTML code for the home page. On the printout, circle the code that adds the **Banner3.gif** file to the Banner Ad Manager and changes the duration time for each image.

Explore
8. Recalculate and verify the hyperlinks in the Web site and correct any problems that you can. (*Hint:* If you can connect to the Internet before verifying hyperlinks, FrontPage will verify all of the links. You probably won't be able to correct all of the broken links.) When you are finished, save any pages in which you made changes, recalculate and verify the site's hyperlinks again, and then use WordPad to print the Broken Hyperlinks report. Close WordPad without saving your changes.

9. Close the **Sunny** Web site, and then close FrontPage.

CASE PROBLEMS

Case 1. Constructing Search and Feedback Pages for Royal Hair Care Products Customer response to Quick Dry Solution has exceeded company expectations. Many customers have written letters to Royal Hair Care Products to praise the product. Valerie Suarez met with Nathan Dubois to share this information and to discuss the Feedback Web page that they will include in the Web site. They decided to design this page to gather specific information from customers on how well the product works, how often customers use it, and so forth. They also decided to create a Search Web page that lets users search the entire Royal Web site. Valerie asks you to help Nathan complete the necessary design and development activities for the Feedback and Search Web pages.

If necessary, start FrontPage, insert your Data Disk in the appropriate disk drive, and then do the following:

1. Read all of the questions for this case problem, and then prepare a planning analysis sheet for the enhancements to the Web site.

2. Open the **Royal** Web site from your Data Disk. (If you did not create this Web site in Tutorial 2 and change it in Tutorials 3, 4, and 5, ask your instructor for assistance.)

3. Create the Search Web page using the Search Page template. Delete the comment at the top of the page, and then insert the **Royal.gif** file from the Web site's images folder. Copy the link bar from the home page, and then paste it on a new line below the logo. Change the link bar to include the links to the home page and to other pages in the Web site. Save the page using the filename **RSearch.htm** and the title "Search."

Explore

4. Open the Feedback Web page (**RFeedbak.htm**) that you created with the Tasks list in Tutorial 3 in Page view. Insert the **Royal.gif** file at the top of the page, copy and paste a link bar in the page, and then revise the link bar so that it includes active links to the other pages in the Web site. Write and enter an appropriate introduction below the link bar. Insert a form component in the page, and then create and design the Feedback page using the following information:

   ■ Three types of comments and feedback exist: Testimonial, Suggestion, and Problem.

   ■ The customer should be able to indicate the average weekly number of applications of Quick Dry Solution. Apply criteria to this field so that it will not accept values higher than 15 or inappropriate values.

   ■ The customer should be able to indicate where the product is purchased most often by selecting one of the following choices: Drug Store, Discount Store, Department Store, Salon, Supermarket, or Other. If the response is "Other," ask the customer to enter the location into a separate text box.

   ■ The customer should be able to enter comments and feedback in a text area box that is 50 characters wide and displays five lines.

   ■ The customer should be able to provide his or her name, e-mail address, and home phone number in text boxes that display 35 characters.

   ■ The customer should be able to give or deny permission to use his or her comments in company advertisements. (*Hint:* Create the appropriate group but do not include a default selection.)

   ■ The customer should be able to send the form to the server or clear the form's fields.

5. Save the form's results as comma-delimited text in the **RFeedbak.txt** file in the _private folder of the Web site. Save the Feedback Web page.

6. Examine each page in the Web site and update the link bars to ensure that all links are active and created properly. Save your changes and close any open pages in Page view.

7. Use the Publish Web command on the File menu to publish the **Royal** Web to the server using the same folder name, and then use the hyperlink created by FrontPage to open the published Web site in the browser. Test the Search and Feedback Web pages that you created. Print the results page and the confirmation page that you receive from the server. Make any corrections required in your disk-based **Royal** Web site, and then republish the Web site to the server. Close the browser.

Explore

8. Close your disk-based Web and then use My Network Places to open the server-based **Royal** Web site. Recalculate the hyperlinks in the Web site, and then verify all hyperlinks. Correct any errors that you find. If you cannot correct an error, create a new task for that page.

9. Mark the tasks for creating the Search and Feedback Web pages as completed.

10. Add a hit counter to the home page with your choice of specifications, location, and style.

11. Find and replace all occurrences of the hyperlink name that you used for the **RInvest.htm** page with "Performance."

12. Thoroughly test the Web site in the browser. If necessary, return to the server-based Web site and make any necessary corrections. If you find any pages that have no content, make sure that a task for completing them appears in the Tasks list. Close the browser.

13. Use FrontPage to print the home page and its HTML code.

14. Close the **Royal** Web site, and then close FrontPage.

Case 2. Preparing a Contact Page for Buffalo Trading Post Many Buffalo Trading Post (BTP) customers have told a sales associate that they would like to use the BTP Web site to request more information and to add their names to a mailing list. During a recent Web site development meeting, the company's sales associates encouraged Donna Vargas to develop a Contact Web page for customers. They agreed that the page's design should include a way for customers to add their names and addresses to the company's mailing list. Customers should also be able to send comments to BTP about items they would like to buy or sell using the categories of women's clothing, children's clothing, and accessories. The sales associates also were interested in finding out how many times a customer had visited a BTP retail store. Donna organized the ideas from the meeting and then met with Karla Perez to review the Contact page requirements. Donna asks you to help Karla make these enhancements to the BTP Web site.

If necessary, start FrontPage, insert your Data Disk in the appropriate disk drive, and then do the following:

1. Read all of the questions in this case problem, and then prepare a planning analysis sheet for the Web site enhancements.

2. Open the **Buffalo** Web site from your Data Disk. (If you did not create this Web site in Tutorial 2 and change it in Tutorials 3, 4, and 5, ask your instructor for assistance.)

3. Create the Contact page using the information supplied in the Case Problem description. Use form fields as necessary to create the form, and define any necessary validation criteria to ensure that data is input correctly. Insert the **B_Contac.gif** picture from the Tutorial.06 folder on your Data Disk at the top of the page, copy and paste a link bar in the page, and then revise the link bar so that it includes active links to the other pages in the Web site. Write and enter an appropriate introduction below the link bar. Save the results collected by this form as comma-delimited text in the **Contact.txt** file in the _private folder of the Web site. Save the page using the filename and title **Contact**. Save the **B_Contac.gif** file in the Web site's images folder.

Explore 4. Use FrontPage to print the Contact page and its HTML code. On the printout, circle the code that implements the FrontPage Save Results form handler.

5. Examine each page in the Web site, and update the link bar as needed to ensure that all links are active and properly created. Save your changes.

6. Use the Publish Web command on the File menu to publish the **Buffalo** Web to the server using the same folder name, and then use the hyperlink created by FrontPage to open the published Web site in a browser. Test the Contact Web page that you created, and then print the confirmation page that you receive from the server. Make any corrections required in your disk-based **Buffalo** Web site, and then republish the Web site to the server. Close the browser.

Explore 7. Close your disk-based Web and then use My Network Places to open the server-based **Buffalo** Web site. Recalculate the hyperlinks in the Web site, and then verify all hyperlinks. Correct any errors that you find. If you cannot correct an error, create a new task for that page.

Explore 8. Create a new Web page using the Confirmation Form page template to confirm data submitted by the Contact Web page. Modify the form using the appropriate form field names in the form. Make any other appearance-related revisions to the form. Save the Web page using the filename **Confirm** and the page title "Confirmation" in the _private folder of the Web site. Return to the Contact Web page, and then open the Form Properties dialog box. Click the Options button, and then click the Confirmation Page tab. Type _private/Confirm.htm in the URL of confirmation page (optional) text box to use the new Confirmation page with the form. Save the Contact page, and use the browser to submit a form to the server. Print the Confirmation page created by the server and then close the browser.

Explore   9. Design and create a new Web page using the filename and title **Where**. This page will provide information on the nearest BTP store location. Insert the **B_Where.gif** picture from the Tutorial.06 folder on your Data Disk as the page's logo and save it in the Web site's images folder. The page should also include a link bar with links to the other pages in the Web site. Update the link bars in the other pages in the Web site to activate the hyperlink to the Where page. Use the browser to print the Where page, and then close the browser.

10. Close the **Buffalo** Web site, and then close FrontPage.

Case 3. Developing Search and Feedback Pages for Garden Grill Nolan Simmons is pleased with Shannon Taylor's progress on the Garden Grill Web site. The Web site development team's next priorities are creating the Feedback and Search Web pages. After a meeting with Beau Walker, who directs the company's marketing department, Nolan directs Shannon to create a new Web page to gather customer information and customer feedback about their eating habits and impressions about the restaurant's menu, prices, service, and Web site. Nolan also asks Shannon to use a template to create a Search Web page.

If necessary, start FrontPage, insert your Data Disk in the appropriate disk drive, and then do the following:

1. Read all of the questions for this case problem, and then prepare a planning analysis sheet for these revisions to the Web site.

2. Open the **Garden** Web site from your Data Disk. (If you did not create this Web site in Tutorial 2 and change it in Tutorials 3, 4, and 5, ask your instructor for assistance.)

3. Create a Search Web page using a template. After creating the page, delete the comment, and then insert the **Garden.gif** picture from the Web site's images folder as the logo for this page. Copy the link bar from the home page, and then paste it in approximately the same location as the one in the home page. Update the hyperlinks in the link bar in the Search Web page to include active links to other pages in the Web site and an inactive link to the Search Web page. Set the page to use the same background as the home page. Save the page using the filename and title **Search**.

Explore   4. Design and create the Feedback Web page for Garden Grill using the information provided in the Case Problem description. Use different form fields and validation as necessary to gather and validate the data. Insert the **Garden.gif** picture as the logo for this page, copy the link bar from the home page, and then paste it in the same location in this page. Update the link bar so that it contains links to pages in the Web site. Save the form results as comma-delimited text in the **Feedback.txt** file in the _private folder of the Web site. Save the page using the title "Feedback" and the filename **GFeedbak.htm** (replace the existing file with the same name).

5. Use FrontPage to print the HTML code for the Feedback page. On the printout, circle the FORM, SELECT, and INPUT tags as well as the code that implements the FrontPage Save Results form handler.

6. Examine each page in the Web site and update the link bars to ensure that all links are active and created properly. Save your changes.

7. Use the Publish Web command on the File menu to publish the **Garden** Web site to the server using the same folder name, and then use the hyperlink created by FrontPage to open the published Web site in a browser. Test the Feedback and Search Web pages that you created, and print the confirmation and the search results pages that you receive from the server. Make any corrections required in your disk-based **Garden** Web site, and then republish the Web site to the server. Close the browser.

Explore   8. Close your disk-based Web and then use My Network Places to open the server-based **Garden** Web site. Recalculate the hyperlinks in the Web site, and then verify all hyperlinks. Correct any errors that you find. If you cannot correct an error, create a new task for that page.

Explore

9. Modify the Feedback Web page in the server-based Web so that the Save Results form handler also stores the results in an HTML file named **Feedback.htm** in the _private folder of the Web site. (*Hint:* Specify the second results file using the Options button.) Use a browser to test the Feedback Web page using realistic data that you create. Enter data for three different users. Close the browser, and then use FrontPage to print the **Feedback.htm** page that contains the form results.

Explore

10. Design and create the Franchise Information page that provides information about applying for and managing a Garden Grill franchise. This page should include a link bar with links to the other pages in the Web site. Insert the **Garden.gif** picture from the Web site's images folder as the logo for the page. Save the page using the filename **FranInfo.htm** and the title "Franchise Information." Update the links in the rest of the Web site to activate the Franchise link. Save your changes to each page, and then use FrontPage to print the HTML code for the Franchise Information page.

Explore

11. Start Microsoft Excel, and then open the **Feedback.txt** file from the _private folder. (*Hint:* Use My Network Places to access the **Garden** Web site folder. Select the Text Files option in the Files of type list box to find the file.) When the Text Import Wizard starts, click the Delimited option button (if necessary), click the Next button, click the Comma check box and clear the Tab check box in the Delimiters section, and then click the Finish button. The form results data is displayed in the worksheet using the form field names as the column headings. Print the worksheet in landscape orientation, and then close Excel without saving your changes.

12. Close the **Garden** Web site, and then close FrontPage.

Explore

Case 4. Producing Search and Feedback Pages for Replay Music Factory Many of Replay Music Factory's satisfied customers have traded their old CDs for different ones. Based on the success of the Specials Web page, Charlene Fields asked to meet with Alec Johnston to review the current Web site. Charlene described her plans to include a Search Web page and a form that collects data to help the company make sound marketing decisions. Charlene was particularly interested in gathering information about CDs that Replay does not currently stock. This information should include different categories of music and performers as well as specific titles of interest. Charlene asks you to help Alec make these enhancements to the Web site.

If necessary, start FrontPage, insert your Data Disk in the appropriate disk drive, and then do the following:

1. Read all of the questions for this case problem, and then prepare a planning analysis sheet for the modifications to the Web site.

2. Open the **Replay** Web site from your Data Disk. (If you did not create this Web site in Tutorial 2 and change it in Tutorials 3, 4, and 5, ask your instructor for assistance.)

3. Create a new Web page in Page view, with an appropriate heading to identify the page contents, a logo, and a FrontPage link bar with links to same-level pages in the site. (*Hint:* Use the same link bar settings that you used for other pages in the site.) Insert a search component and a search the Web component. For the search component, change the Search for text box so that it holds 30 characters and uses the label "Search the Replay Web site for:", and then change the push button labels to "Search Now" and "Clear Fields." Change the label for the push button in the Search the Web component to "Search the Web now." Save the page using the filename and title **Search**.

4. Design and create the Feedback Web page based on information you determine the user will provide. Use appropriate form fields and validation criteria to collect the desired data. Include a page heading and logo in this page, and create a FrontPage link bar. Save the form results as comma-delimited text in the **Feedback.txt** file and also as **Feedback.htm** in the _private folder of the Web site. Save the page using the filename **Feedback.htm** and the title "Feedback."

5. Use FrontPage to print the HTML code for the Feedback page. On the printout, circle the FORM, SELECT, and INPUT tags as well as the code that implements the FrontPage Save Results form handler.

6. Examine each page in the Web site, making sure that pages that contain content have been created properly. Save your changes.

7. Use the Publish Web command on the File menu to publish the **Replay** Web site to the server with the same name, and then use the hyperlink created by FrontPage to open the published Web site in a browser. Test the Feedback and Search Web pages that you created, and print the confirmation and search results pages that you receive from the server. Make any corrections required in your disk-based **Replay** Web site, and then republish the Web site to the server. Close the browser.

8. Close your disk-based Web and then use My Network Places to open the server-based **Replay** Web site. Recalculate the hyperlinks in the Web site, and then verify all hyperlinks. Correct any errors that you find. If you cannot correct an error, create a new task for that page.

9. Create a new Web page using the Confirmation Form template to confirm data submitted by the Feedback Web page. Modify the form using the appropriate form field names in the form. Make any other appearance-related revisions to the form. Save the Web page using the filename **Confirm.htm** and the page title "Confirmation" in the _private folder of the Web site. Open the Feedback Web page, and then open the Form Properties dialog box. Click the Options button, and then click the Confirmation Page tab. Type _private/Confirm.htm in the URL of confirmation page (optional) text box to use the new Confirmation page with the form. Save the page.

10. Use the Frequently Asked Questions template to create a new page. Include several questions that Replay customers might ask. Make the pages similar to the other pages in the Web site. Save the page using the filename and title **FAQ**.

11. Design and create a banner ad containing at least three pictures in an appropriate page in the Web site. If possible, create the GIF files that you will use in the banner ad. (If you cannot create the files, use the Clip Art Gallery to locate appropriate GIF files that are approximately the same size, or use the files **Replay1.gif**, **Replay2.gif**, and **Replay3.gif** in the Tutorial.06 folder on your Data Disk.) Save the images in the Web site's images folder.

12. Thoroughly test the site in a browser. Use the browser to print the FAQ page and its HTML code, the confirmation page returned by the Feedback Web page, and the HTML code for the page in which you created the banner ad. Close the browser.

13. Close the **Replay** Web site, and then close FrontPage.

QUICK CHECK ANSWERS

Session 6.1

1. True
2. The pointer changes to the Component pointer when you point to the component, and a dashed outline surrounds the component.
3. False
4. A data-entry field in a form, such as a text box or option button, that is used to collect data from a user.

5. form component

6. A program on a Web server that collects and processes a form's data in a predetermined manner.

7. It will make the group name and the button values easy to locate and identify in the results file.

8. Use a drop-down box with the name "Province" and assign each value in the list a name that is equivalent to the province's name. Using a drop-down box gives the user several mutually exclusive choices. The option that should be selected in the drop-down box would be the most populated province, or the province that is closest to the company's location.

Session 6.2

1. True

2. Required

3. Grouping, which edits the value to insert a comma or period; data length, which specifies the minimum and maximum number of integers that the form field can contain; and data value, which lets you specify that the entered value must be greater than, equal to, less than, or in a certain range based on a predetermined value.

4. Submit, which lets a user send the form to the server for processing; Reset, which clears the form's fields of any previously entered data; and Normal, which initiates a user-defined script.

5. field name-data value pair

6. webmaster

7. OPTION

Session 6.3

1. False

2. C:\Inetpub\wwwroot

3. Default.htm

4. A Web page that contains a copy of the data entered into a form, which the server sends to the browser to confirm a form's submission.

5. comma-delimited text

6. False

7. Recalculate the Web site's hyperlinks by clicking Tools on the menu bar and then clicking Recalculate Hyperlinks from Hyperlinks view.

8. Verifying hyperlinks checks for broken external and internal links and presents findings as a report in Reports view, making it easy to identify all broken links quickly and easily.

9. Browsing permissions allow a user to browse (open) pages in a Web site. Authoring permissions allow a user to browse and change a site's pages by opening them in Page view. Administering permissions allow a user to browse and change a site's pages and set other users' permissions.

New Perspectives on

MICROSOFT®

FRONTPAGE® 2002

Read This Before You Begin

To the Student

Data Disks

To complete the Tutorials, Review Assignments, Case Problems, and Additional Case Problems in this book, you will need three Data Disks. Your instructor will either provide you with these Data Disks or ask you to make your own.

If you are making your own Data Disks, you will need **three** blank, formatted high-density disks. You will need to copy a set of folders from a file server or standalone computer or the Web onto your disks. Your instructor will tell you which computer, drive letter, and folders contain the files you need. You could also download the files by going to **www.course.com**, clicking Data Disk Files, and following the instructions on the screen.

The information below shows you which folders go on each of your disks:

Data Disk 1

Write this on the disk label: Data Disk 1: Tutorials 7-9
Put these folders on the disk:
Tutorial.07
Tutorial.08
Tutorial.09

Data Disk 2

Write this on the disk label: Data Disk 2: Additional Case Problems 1 and 2
Put these folders on the disk:
AddCase1
AddCase2

Data Disk 3

Write this on the disk label: Data Disk 3: Additional Case Problem 3
Put this folder on the disk:
AddCase3

Hard Drive Disk Structure

For these tutorials, you must be able to create FrontPage Web sites on a Web server. The steps in this book are written for Internet Information Services (IIS) 5.0, although you can create your Web sites on any Web server with the FrontPage 2002 Server Extensions. You or your instructor must install the starting Data Files for Case Problems 1 through 4 before you can begin working on them. You can obtain these files by going to **www.course.com** and following the instructions on the screen.

When you begin each tutorial, be sure you are using the correct Data Disk. Refer to the "File Finder" chart at the back of this text for more detailed information on which files are used in which tutorials. See the inside front or inside back cover of this book for more information on Data Disk files, or ask your instructor or technical support person for assistance.

Course Labs

The FrontPage tutorials feature two interactive Course Labs to help you understand database and spreadsheet concepts. There are Lab Assignments at the end of Tutorials 8 and 9 that relate to these Labs.

To start a Lab, click the **Start** button on the Windows taskbar, point to **Programs**, point to **Course Labs**, point to **New Perspectives Course Labs**, and then click the name of the Lab you want to use.

Using Your Own Computer

If you are going to work through this book using your own computer, you need:

- ■ **Computer System** Microsoft Windows NT, 2000 Professional, or higher must be installed on your computer. This book assumes a typical installation of Microsoft FrontPage 2002, Microsoft Excel 2002, and Microsoft Access 2002. You also must have Internet Information Services version 5.0 or higher and the Microsoft FrontPage 2002 Server Extensions. The recommended browser for viewing Web pages is Internet Explorer 5.0 or higher.

- ■ **Data Disk(s)** You will not be able to complete the tutorials or exercises in this book using your own computer until you have your Data Disks.

- ■ **Course Labs** See your instructor or technical support person to obtain the Course Lab software for use on your own computer.

Visit Our World Wide Web Site

Additional materials designed especially for you are available on the World Wide Web.
Go to www.course.com/NewPerspectives.

To the Instructor

The Data Disk files and Course Labs are available on the Instructor's Resource Kit for this title. Follow the instructions in the Help file on the CD-ROM to install the programs to your network or standalone computer. For information on creating Data Disks or the Course Labs, see the "To the Student" section above.

You are granted a license to copy the Data Files and Course Labs to any computer or computer network used by students who have purchased this book.

OBJECTIVES

In this tutorial you will:

- Use the Import Web Wizard to import a Web site from a URL

- Change a Web site's settings

- Assign Web pages to categories, and create a site map

- Use source control

- Create a shared template

- Use absolute positioning to place text and pictures in a Web page

- Use a Wizard to create a discussion group

- Post, reply to, and search for messages in a discussion group

- Display and examine the hidden folders in a Web site

- Change the properties of a discussion group

CREATING A NEW WEB SITE ON A WEB SERVER

Creating the Recipes Web Site and a Discussion Group

CASE

Sunny Morning Products

Microsoft FrontPage, or simply **FrontPage**, is a program that lets you develop, maintain, and publish a Web site. Using this program, you can create, view, and edit your Web pages; insert and edit text and pictures; import and export files; and add, test, and repair hyperlinks to and within your pages.

Amanda Bay is a marketing manager at Sunny Morning Products, a California-based international bottler and distributor of Olympic Gold brand fresh orange juice and thirst-quencher sport drinks. Olympic Gold products are sold in grocery stores, convenience stores, and many other outlets. Sunny Morning Products also sells fresh produce, such as oranges and grapefruit, at the Sunshine Country Store located at its California groves and through the company's Web site. At the request of the company's president, Jacob Towle, Amanda created a Web site development training course to teach people in the different departments at Sunny Morning Products how to use the Internet and the company's Web site to increase sales and improve communication with customers.

In addition to selling fresh produce and Olympic Gold products, the Sunshine Country Store specializes in baked goods, such as cakes, breads, and pies. To help promote the store and its products, Tyler Vanauken, another marketing manager, created a Web site to share recipes for the store's products. Initial customer reaction to the recipes Web site has been favorable. Jacob gave Tyler his permission to expand the site to include additional recipes and a discussion forum, and he authorized the marketing department to manage the site as needed.

In this tutorial, you will import the recipes Web site from a World Wide Web server to your server and then help the marketing department set up and enhance the site.

SESSION 7.1

In this session, you will use the Import Web Wizard to import a Web site from a URL and then change the new Web site's settings to make it compatible with different browsers and servers. You will enable source control for the new Web site, thereby restricting access to the site's pages to one Web author at a time. Finally, you will create a template for the Web site to ensure that all new recipes pages will have a consistent appearance.

Using the Import Web Wizard to Import a Web Site

When you use the Import Web Wizard, you can simultaneously create a new Web site and import pages into it, either from a file location or from a World Wide Web server. Tyler published the existing recipes Web site on the Sunny Morning Products Web server, but he needs you to include additional features in the Web site. You will import his pages and create a new FrontPage Web site on your computer's server.

Note: The steps in this tutorial assume that you are running Windows 2000 Professional and Microsoft Internet Information Services (IIS) version 5.0. To complete this tutorial, you must have an Internet connection, and you must be able to publish Web pages to your computer's hard drive or network drive using IIS. If you are using a different Web server, ask your instructor or technical support person for help.

To create the new Web site and import pages from a URL:

1. Start FrontPage and then change to Folders view. If necessary, close any open Web page or Web site and display the Task Pane.

2. In the New section of the Task Pane, click **Empty Web**. The Web Site Templates dialog box opens and displays a list of templates and Wizards that you can use to create a new FrontPage Web site.

3. Click the **Import Web Wizard** icon to select it. A description of this Wizard appears in the Description section.

4. Click in the **Specify the location of the new web** text box to select its current entry, and then type **http://localhost/recipes**, where *localhost* is the name of your computer or your computer's IP address. If you are using a different computer name, enter that name instead. You will create a new Web site named "recipes" on the specified server.

   It is a good practice to create the Web site name using all lowercase letters, with no spaces or other punctuation marks, so that it will be a legal folder name on any operating system on which it might reside. Although IIS and many other servers would accept "Recipes" as a legal filename, you will use all lowercase letters to ensure that the Web site name is acceptable on all servers. You will also apply this standard to all files created in the site.

5. Click the **OK** button. The Create New Web dialog box opens and FrontPage creates the new Web site on the server. After a moment, the Import Web Wizard – Choose Source dialog box opens. You will import the files from a World Wide Web site. For this tutorial, you will use the Course Technology Web site to simulate using the Sunny Morning Products Web site.

6. If necessary, click the **From a World Wide Web site** option button to select it, click in the **Location** text box to select the current entry, and then type **http://www.course.com/downloads/newperspectives/fp2002**.

TROUBLE? If you cannot make an Internet connection, click the From a source directory of files on a local computer or network option button to import the appropriate files from your Data Disk. Browse to the Tutorial.07 folder on your Data Disk, click the Open button, and then click the Next button. In the Import Web Wizard - Edit File List dialog box, press and hold the Ctrl key as you select all of the files *except* for b_icing.htm, chifcake.htm, chifpie.htm, Default.htm, nut_brd.htm, and site_map.htm. Click the Exclude button, and then continue with Step 9.

7. Click the **Next** button. The Import Web Wizard–Choose Download Amount dialog box opens. See Figure 7-1. You can use this dialog box to limit the number and size of the pages to download. You can also limit the download process so that you retrieve only text and image files.

| Figure 7-1 | IMPORT WEB WIZARD – CHOOSE DOWNLOAD AMOUNT DIALOG BOX |

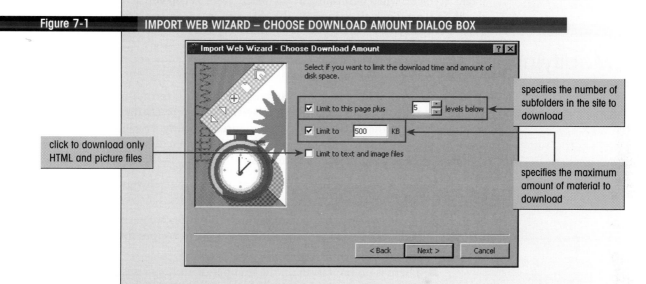

specifies the number of subfolders in the site to download

click to download only HTML and picture files

specifies the maximum amount of material to download

8. Click the **Limit to this page plus** and **Limit to** check boxes to clear them, as you will not need to enforce any restrictions on what to download.

9. Click the **Next** button to display the final dialog box of the Import Web Wizard, and then click the **Finish** button. The Import Web Progress dialog box opens while FrontPage imports the files from the URL into the new recipes Web site on the server. Depending on the speed of your Internet connection, this process might take from a few seconds to several minutes. After the import process is finished, the files are displayed in Folders view. See Figure 7-2.

| Figure 7-2 | FOLDERS VIEW OF THE RECIPES WEB SITE |

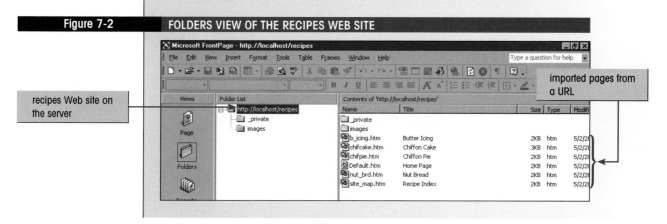

recipes Web site on the server

imported pages from a URL

TROUBLE? If a Dial-up Connection dialog box opens, enter your user name and password, and then click the Connect button. You must have an Internet connection to import the pages. (If you cannot make an Internet connection, see the Trouble? for Step 6.)

TROUBLE? If a dialog box opens and warns you that the Web site must use the current themes and elements, click the Yes button to continue.

You created the new recipes Web site directly on the server when you specified the path to your server as the site's location. Because you created a server-based Web site, you won't need to publish the Web site's pages to the server by using the Publish Web command on the File menu as you do when publishing a disk-based Web. When you access a FrontPage Web using the HTTP protocol, all changes to the Web site are made on the server automatically.

Modifying the New Web Site

After creating a new Web site, you can begin formatting and adding pages to it immediately. Before you start working on the pages, Tyler asks you to change some of the default Web settings to ensure that the Web site is configured properly. During his testing of the recipes Web site on the Sunny Morning Products Web server, Tyler encountered the following problems that he would like you to address:

■ The site's pages have different appearances when viewed using older browser versions.

■ Users currently have no method for isolating recipes in the different categories. For example, if a user wants a list of recipes for cakes, he or she must use the page titles to infer the pages' contents.

■ There is no limitation on the number of authors revising any single Web page at one time, which leads to server errors when one author attempts to save a page that is in use by another author.

■ There is no forum for users of the Web site to discuss cooking techniques, submit recipes, or recommend changes or enhancements to existing recipes.

With these problems in mind, Tyler created the planning analysis sheet shown in Figure 7-3. You will solve these problems for Tyler as you complete this tutorial.

| Figure 7-3 | TYLER'S PLANNING ANALYSIS SHEET FOR THE RECIPES WEB SITE |

Planning Analysis Sheet

Objective

Create a new FrontPage Web site on a server using files available on the Sunny Morning Products server. Set the Web site to function for specific browsers and servers and to enable the FrontPage Server Extensions and certain Internet technologies. Create a site map and a discussion group. The Web site should use source control. The pages in the Web site will feature recipes, with pictures, using products from the Sunshine Country Store.

Requirements

Files for current Web pages on the Sunny Morning Products server

Categories to use in the site map

Picture files to use in the recipes pages

Results

A new Web site that has the following characteristics:

       Pages for recipes, with pictures

       An index for locating the site's recipes

       Source control

       FrontPage link bars in all pages

       A theme

       A discussion group that is accessible to all site visitors

Specifying a Browser Version

As part of the recipes Web site's initial development and testing, Tyler tested the site's pages using computers with different browser versions and operating systems. He also collected data from the site's current users and determined that all of them use Windows 2000 and either Internet Explorer or Netscape Navigator as their browsers. The Sunny Morning Products Web site currently is stored using Microsoft Internet Information Services; it is the only Web server that will store the site's pages. In addition, the Sunny Morning Products Web site is enabled with the FrontPage Server Extensions and can run programs and scripts.

With these criteria in mind, Tyler asks you to set the recipes Web site to match these settings. When you change the default settings for a single Web site, FrontPage will use the new settings for all future Web sites. Therefore, it is a good idea to check these settings for all new Web sites that you create to ensure their accuracy.

To change the settings of a FrontPage Web site:

1. In Folders view, click **Tools** on the menu bar, and then click **Page Options**. The Page Options dialog box opens.

2. Click the **Compatibility** tab to display those settings. Read the message at the top of the Compatibility tab, which indicates that changing these settings might disable some menu and dialog box options so as to ensure that Web sites you create will contain only those features supported by the options that you select. In the future, if you attempt to create a feature in a Web site and that feature's menu command is disabled, you can check the Web site's settings to see whether that feature has been disabled.

3. Click the **Browsers** list arrow, and then click **Both Internet Explorer and Navigator**. FrontPage will allow you to use only those features supported by both of these popular browsers.

4. Click the **Browser versions** list arrow, and then click **5.0 browsers and later**. FrontPage will allow you to use only those features supported by versions 5.0 and later of the specified browsers.

5. Click the **Servers** list arrow, and then click **Microsoft Internet Information Server 3.0 and later**.

6. If necessary, click the **Enabled with Microsoft FrontPage Server Extensions** check box to select it, and then make sure that every check box, except for the ActiveX controls and VBScript check boxes in the Available Technologies section, contains a check mark. See Figure 7-4. When you selected the browsers and their versions, FrontPage automatically deselected the ActiveX controls and VBScript check boxes; the browsers, browser versions, and servers that you selected do not support these technologies. If you clicked one of these check boxes, you would override the default settings for the selected browsers, browser versions, and servers. In such a case, one or all of the settings for the browser, browser version, and server would change to "Custom," indicating that you have customized the default configuration.

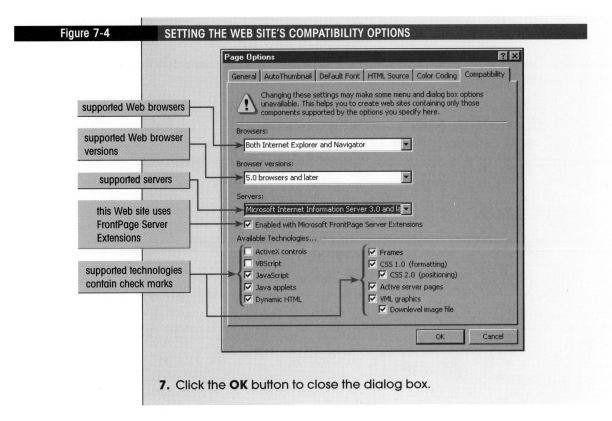

Figure 7-4   **SETTING THE WEB SITE'S COMPATIBILITY OPTIONS**

supported Web browsers

supported Web browser versions

supported servers

this Web site uses FrontPage Server Extensions

supported technologies contain check marks

7. Click the **OK** button to close the dialog box.

Next, Tyler asks you to create a site map so that users can locate specific recipes more easily.

Creating a Site Map

If you have surfed the Web, you may have noticed that some Web sites include a hyperlink to a site map. A **site map** is a list of hyperlinks that shows how the pages in the site are related to one another or organizes them in some other meaningful way. In a small Web site, the site map might contain a list of hyperlinks to pages. In a large Web site, the site map might contain hyperlinks to subcategories and to other Web pages.

Assigning Web Pages to Categories

Before you can create a site map Web page, you must decide how to organize the pages in the Web site. Tyler wants to group recipes using categories such as cakes, icings, and pies. You create **categories** to identify the topic of each Web page. You can then use the FrontPage table of contents component to tell FrontPage how to organize the Web pages within the site map. FrontPage supplies a variety of predefined categories, but you can also create your own categories. You delete the default categories or categories that you do not use, as necessary.

When you assign a page to a category, you can also assign the page to a particular member of the Web site development team and specify a review status for it. A **review status** is a way to select the type of review or approval that the page needs before being considered final. For example, if the page contains legal material that requires verification by an attorney, you might select the "Legal Review" category.

<u>Creating Categories and Assigning Pages to Them</u>

- In Folders view, right-click any Web page filename in the Contents pane to open the shortcut menu, and then click Properties.
- Click the Workgroup tab, and then click the Categories button.
- In the Master Category List dialog box, type the name of a new category in the New category text box, and then press the Enter key or click the Add button. Repeat this process as many times as necessary to add the remaining categories for the entire Web site.
- Click the OK button.
- Click the check box for the appropriate category for the page that you selected. (The selected page's name appears in the title bar of the Properties dialog box.)
- If necessary, click the Assigned to list arrow and select the team member to whom the page is assigned, or click the Names button to enter a new name.
- If necessary, click the Review status list arrow and select a review status for the page, or click the Statuses button to enter a new status.
- Click the OK button in the Properties dialog box to close it.
- To assign other Web pages to categories, right-click the page's filename in Folders view to open the shortcut menu, click Properties, click the Workgroup tab, and then click the check box for the appropriate category in the Available categories list box.
- Click the OK button.

First, you will create all of the categories for the recipes Web site. Tyler suggests that you use the categories Cakes, Pies, Breads, Icings, Butters, and New Recipes. After creating these categories, you will assign pages containing recipes to the appropriate categories. After creating the categories, you will use the table of contents component to create the site map.

To create the categories:

1. Right-click **nut_brd.htm** in the Contents pane to open the shortcut menu, and then click **Properties**. The nut_brd.htm Properties dialog box opens.

2. Click the **Workgroup** tab. See Figure 7-5. FrontPage contains several default categories that appear in the Available categories list box. You could select one of these default categories, but Tyler wants you to create new categories for this Web site. When you add or delete categories, your changes apply only to the current Web site and do not affect the default categories supplied by FrontPage in other Web sites.

Figure 7-5   WORKGROUP TAB

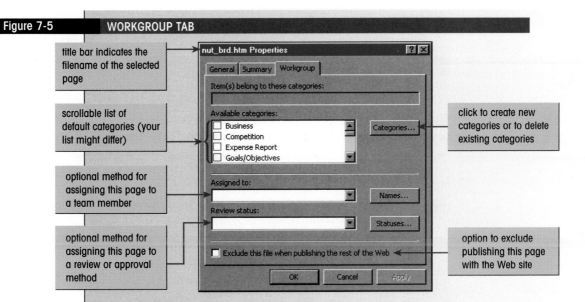

title bar indicates the filename of the selected page

scrollable list of default categories (your list might differ)

optional method for assigning this page to a team member

optional method for assigning this page to a review or approval method

click to create new categories or to delete existing categories

option to exclude publishing this page with the Web site

TROUBLE? If your Properties dialog box does not contain a Workgroup tab, then the FrontPage 2002 Server Extensions are not installed and properly configured on the server. Ask your instructor or technical support person for help.

3. Click the **Categories** button. The Master Category List dialog box opens.

4. Type **Breads** in the New category text box, and then press the **Enter** key. The Breads category is added to the list. See Figure 7-6.

Figure 7-6   MASTER CATEGORY LIST DIALOG BOX

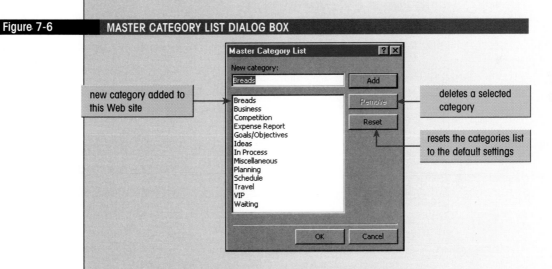

new category added to this Web site

deletes a selected category

resets the categories list to the default settings

To add the next category, simply type its name and then press the Enter key.

5. Type **Pies** and then press the **Enter** key. The Pies category is added to the list.

6. Repeat Step 5 to add the following categories to the list: **Cakes**, **Icings**, **Butters**, and **New Recipes**. After pressing the Enter key for the New Recipes category, click the **OK** button. You return to the Properties dialog box for the nut_brd.htm file.

Before closing the dialog box, you need to assign the nut_brd.htm page to a category. You will not assign this page to any member of the Web site development team, nor will you select a review status.

> **7.** Click the **Breads** check box in the Available categories list box to select it, and then click the **OK** button. The Properties dialog box closes, and the nut_brd.htm page is now assigned to the Breads category.

You have now created all of the categories. The next step is to assign the other pages in the Web site to the appropriate categories. You won't assign a category to either the site_map.htm or Default.htm page. It is not necessary to assign every page in the Web site to a category.

To assign pages to categories:

1. Right-click **chifcake.htm** in the Contents pane to open the shortcut menu, click **Properties**, and then click the **Workgroup** tab.

2. Click the **Cakes** check box in the Available categories list, and then click the **OK** button.

3. Repeat Steps 1 and 2 to assign the **chifpie.htm** page to the **Pies** category and the **b_icing.htm** page to the **Icings** category.

You can assign a page to more than one category by clicking the appropriate check boxes in the Available categories list box. If you need to delete a category assignment for a page, clear the check box for that category. You can use Reports view to view the categories assigned to pages in the Web site to verify that you categorized them correctly.

To run a Categories report:

1. Click the **Reports** button 🗔 on the Views bar. If necessary, display the Reporting toolbar by clicking **View** on the menu bar, pointing to **Toolbars**, and then clicking **Reporting**.

TROUBLE? If the Reporting toolbar blocks the report, drag it out of the way or dock it below the Formatting toolbar.

2. Click the **Reports** list arrow on the Reporting toolbar, point to **Workflow**, and then click **Categories**. The Categories report appears in Reports view. You can sort the list using any of the column headings, just as you would sort the Tasks list.

3. Click the **Category** column heading to sort the Categories list by category name. Notice that the home page (Default.htm) and the Recipe Index page (site_map.htm) are not assigned to categories.

Using the Table of Contents Component

Now that you have created categories and assigned pages to them, you are ready to insert the FrontPage table of contents component in the page. When you add new Web pages to the Web site, you can assign them to categories, creating new categories as necessary. FrontPage will automatically update the site map Web page and display the new Web pages in the appropriate categories.

REFERENCE   WINDOW   RW

Creating a Site Map

- Create or open the page that will contain the site map in Page view. If necessary, enter text and format the page.
- Click the Web Component button on the Standard toolbar, click Table of Contents in the Component type list box, and then click Based on Page Category in the Choose a table of contents list box.
- Click the Finish button.
- Click the check box for the appropriate category in the Choose categories to list files by list box.
- If necessary, click the check boxes to include the date on which the file was last modified and/or comments to the file.
- Click the OK button.
- Repeat the steps to add more table of contents components to the page as necessary.

You will add the component for each category to Tyler's existing Web page. The site_map.htm page will include a page banner and a FrontPage link bar, so you will need to add the page to the Web site's navigation structure.

To create the site map:

1. Click the **Folders** button 🗔 on the Views bar to change to Folders view.

2. Double-click **site_map.htm** in the Contents pane to open this page in Page view. The message in the top shared border reminds you to add this page to the navigation structure so that it can use the page banner and link bar.

3. Click the **Navigation** button 🗗 on the Views bar, and then drag the **site_map.htm** file from the Folder List to the navigation structure to make it a child page of the home page.

4. Double-click the **Recipe Index** icon in the navigation structure to open that page in Page view. See Figure 7-7. Now a centered page banner and a link bar appear at the top of the page. Tyler has already created bookmarks to each category and inserted a blank line below each category heading. You will insert the table of contents component for each category on the blank line below its heading.

Figure 7-7   RECIPE INDEX WEB PAGE IN PAGE VIEW

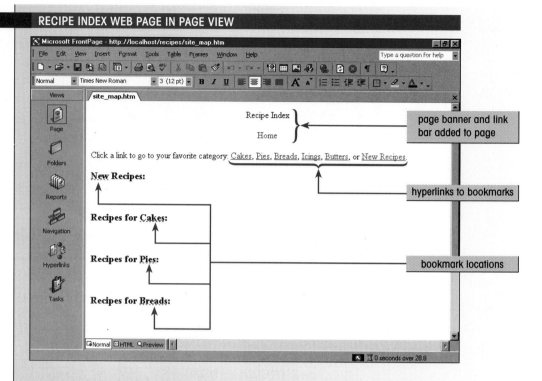

5. Click the blank line below the New Recipes heading, click the **Web Component** button on the Standard toolbar, click **Table of Contents** in the Component type list box, click **Based on Page Category** in the Choose a table of contents list box, and then click the **Finish** button. The Categories Properties dialog box opens.

   TROUBLE? If the Based on Page Category component is not available, then your server does not have the FrontPage 2002 Server Extensions installed. Ask your instructor or technical support person for help.

6. Scroll down the list of available categories, click the **New Recipes** check box to select it, and then click the **OK** button. The Recipe Index page now displays three "Page in Category" placeholders for the New Recipes category. The table of contents component always displays three placeholders, but they do not represent the number of Web pages that are currently in the category. To see the Web pages in this category, you must open the page in a browser.

   TROUBLE? If you do not see the three "Page in Category" placeholders, then you did not click the New Recipes check box. Repeat Steps 5 and 6.

7. Repeat Steps 5 and 6 to insert the appropriate table of contents component below each heading in the page.

8. Click the **Save** button on the Standard toolbar, and then click the **Preview in Browser** button on the Standard toolbar. See Figure 7-8. The table of contents component added the correct hyperlinks for each category to the page. There are no recipes in the Butters and New Recipes categories, so no hyperlinks appear below these headings. (You might need to scroll down the page to see the Butters heading.)

Figure 7-8	RECIPE INDEX WEB PAGE IN THE BROWSER

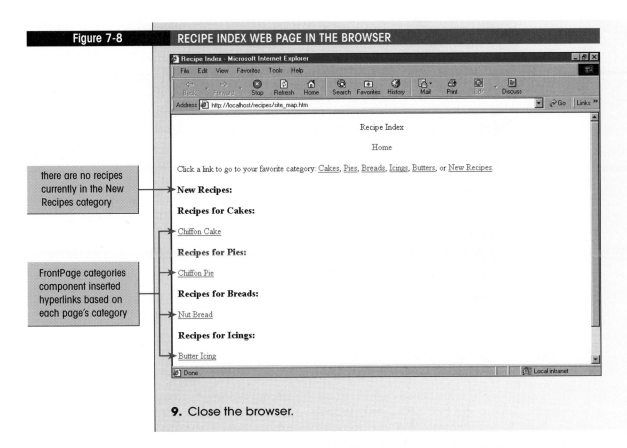

there are no recipes currently in the New Recipes category

FrontPage categories component inserted hyperlinks based on each page's category

9. Close the browser.

As the marketing department adds new pages to the Web site and assigns them to categories, the table of contents component will update the site map to keep it current. As the Web site continues to grow, site visitors will appreciate the site map because it will allow them to readily find the desired recipes.

Using Source Control to Manage Multiple Authors

Tyler is concerned about the way that pages are updated in the recipes Web site. Because more than one person will contribute to the work required to complete the pages, he wants to ensure that only one author can work on a particular page at a time. For example, he doesn't want the author who is coordinating the product pictures to work on a page at the same time as the author who enters the actual recipe, because one author's changes to the Web page could be lost.

Fortunately, FrontPage has a built-in source control feature in Web sites that are enabled with FrontPage 2002 Server Extensions. **Source control** lets you ensure that only one copy of a Web page can be edited at a time. Multiple authors can view a page simultaneously, but only *one* author can be editing the page and saving changes at any time.

Normally, a Web site that is developed by multiple authors is stored on an intranet, making it accessible to everyone with access to the site. When an author checks out a page to edit it, other authors can open the page, but they cannot edit it. When a page is checked out to the current author, a check mark appears to the left of the page's filename in Folders view. Other authors will see a padlock icon, which indicates that the page is in use. A green dot indicates a page that is available for editing.

REFERENCE WINDOW   RW

Enabling and Using Source Control for a Web Site

- Close all open pages in the Web site that you are going to enable with source control.
- In Folders view, click Tools on the menu bar, and then click Web Settings.
- If necessary, click the General tab.
- Click the Use document check-in and check-out check box to select it.
- Click the OK button, and then click the Yes button.
- To check out a page, double-click it in Folders view, and then click the Yes button. Edit and save the page as usual.
- To check in a page, close it in Page view, change to Folders view, right-click the filename to open the shortcut menu, and then click Check In.
- To cancel all changes (including saved changes) made in a Web page that you checked out, click Undo Check-Out on the shortcut menu when you check in the page, and then click the Yes button.

Tyler asks you to enable source control for the recipes Web site to ensure that only one author can edit a page at a time.

To enable source control for the recipes Web site:

1. Click the **Close** button ☒ on the Contents pane to close the Recipe Index page (site_map.htm). Because any open pages will not be enabled, you must close all Web pages in the Web site before enabling source control.

2. Click the **Folders** button 📁 on the Views bar to change to Folders view.

3. Click **Tools** on the menu bar, click **Web Settings**, and then make sure that the **General** tab is selected.

4. Click the **Use document check-in and check-out** check box to select it, and then click the **OK** button. A dialog box opens and tells you that you have changed the source control for this Web site and that FrontPage must recalculate the Web site to proceed.

5. Click the **Yes** button. The dialog box closes. Now a green dot appears to the left of the filenames for the pages in the Web site. See Figure 7-9. Any new pages added to the Web site will also use source control.

| Figure 7-9 | WEB SITE ENABLED WITH SOURCE CONTROL |

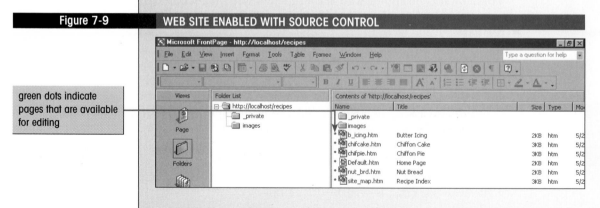

green dots indicate pages that are available for editing

TROUBLE? If you don't see the green dots, click the Refresh button 🔄 on the Standard toolbar.

The green dots to the left of the filenames indicate that the pages are not in use by you or any other author. To check out a page so that you can edit it, double-click it.

To check out a Web page:

1. Double-click **site_map.htm** in the Contents pane. A dialog box tells you that this page uses source control. See Figure 7-10.

Figure 7-10   **MICROSOFT FRONTPAGE DIALOG BOX**

Microsoft FrontPage

? site_map.htm
The file is under source control and has read only attributes.

Do you want to check it out?

[Yes]   [No]   [Cancel]

message indicates the page's filename and status

2. Click the **Yes** button to check out the page. The page opens in Page view. You could now edit it just like any other page.

3. Click the **Folders** button 🗀 on the Views bar. A red check mark appears to the left of the site_map.htm page, indicating that this page is in use. If another author logged on to the server on which this Web site is stored, that person would see a padlock icon to the left of the page's filename, indicating that the file is locked.

Next, you will close the page and check it in.

To check in a Web page:

1. Click the **Page** button 🗀 on the Views bar to return to the Recipe Index page in Page view.

2. Click the **Close** button ✕ on the Contents pane to close the page.

3. Click the **Folders** button 🗀 on the Views bar to change to Folders view. You closed the page, but it is still checked out to you. If you close the Web site without checking in the page, the page would remain locked and no other author could edit it.

4. Right-click **site_map.htm** in the Contents pane to open the shortcut menu.

You have two options for checking in a page. The first option, Check In, lets you check in the page and accept all of the changes that you made in that page. The second option, Undo Check Out, lets you check in the page and discard all of the changes that you made—even those changes that you saved. Both of these options will release the lock on the page so that other authors can check out the page for editing.

5. Click **Check In**. FrontPage checks in the page, releases the lock, and changes the red check mark to a green dot. Now other authors can edit the page.

To disable source control for a Web site, return to the Web Settings dialog box, and then clear the Use document check-in and check-out check box on the General tab. Usually, a site's administrator is the only person who can enable and disable source control for a Web site. When you are using IIS on a client, however, you can usually enable source control without obtaining permission.

Creating a Shared Template

Tyler wants to make sure that all of the pages in the recipes Web site have a common presentation and appearance. One way to accomplish this goal is to apply a theme to the entire Web site. The theme changes only the appearance of a Web site's pages; it does not ensure that every page has a heading, footer, and other elements in common, as Tyler desires for the recipes Web site.

You have learned that FrontPage includes a variety of templates that you can use to create new Web pages. You can also create your own template and save it in the Web site so that other authors can use it to create new pages. When you create a template and make it available to other authors, the template is called a **shared template**. Shared templates are saved in the Web site in which you create them, as well as on the drive on which the FrontPage program is stored, so you can also use them in other Web sites.

The template that Tyler wants you to create will contain a page banner, a FrontPage link bar, an introductory paragraph, a bulleted list of the recipe's ingredients, a photo of the finished product, a description for making the recipe, and a footer with the date on which the page was last edited and the company's copyright information. Tyler has already started work on the page and saved it in the Tutorial.07 folder on your Data Disk. You will import this page into the recipes Web site, open it in Page view, make some changes to it, and then save it as a shared template.

To import the page and add components to it:

1. Click **File** on the menu bar, click **Import**, click the **Add File** button, click the **Look in** list arrow, change to the drive or folder that contains your Data Disk, open the **Tutorial.07** folder, double-click **style**, and then click the **OK** button to import the style.htm page into the Web site. This page automatically is enabled with source control, as indicated by the green dot to the left of its filename.

2. Double-click **style.htm** in the Contents pane, and then click the **Yes** button to check out the page and open it in Page view. See Figure 7-11. Tyler wants the template to include a page banner and a link bar. The page already contains placeholder text that tells authors how to enter information into the page.

| Figure 7-11 | STYLE.HTM PAGE THAT WILL BECOME A SHARED TEMPLATE |

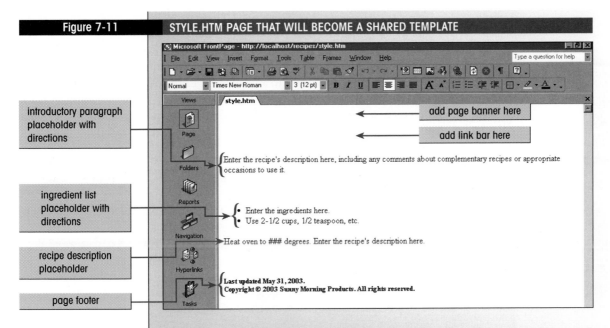

introductory paragraph placeholder with directions

ingredient list placeholder with directions

recipe description placeholder

page footer

add page banner here

add link bar here

Enter the recipe's description here, including any comments about complementary recipes or appropriate occasions to use it.

- Enter the ingredients here.
- Use 2-1/2 cups, 1/2 teaspoon, etc.

Heat oven to ### degrees. Enter the recipe's description here.

Last updated May 31, 2003.
Copyright © 2003 Sunny Morning Products. All rights reserved.

3. With the insertion point positioned on the centered line at the top of the page, click **Insert** on the menu bar, and then click **Page Banner**. The default settings in the Page Banner Properties dialog box are correct, so click the **OK** button. Because this page has not been added to the Web site's navigation structure, a placeholder appears in place of the page banner. When authors use this template to create new pages, the placeholder will remind them to add the page to the navigation structure so that this element will work correctly.

4. Press the **Down arrow** key ↓ to move to the next blank, centered line, click **Insert** on the menu bar, and then click **Navigation**. The Insert Web Component dialog box opens. Link Bars is already selected in the Component type list.

5. In the Choose a bar type list box, click **Bar based on navigation structure**, and then click the **Next** button.

6. Scroll down the list of bar styles to the bottom, and then scroll up and click the **Dots** style in the list (use the ScreenTips to identify the Dots style; it is the fifth style from the end of the list). This style displays links across the page, with the links being separated by dots.

7. Click the **Finish** button. The Link Bar Properties dialog box opens.

8. Click the **Same level** option button, click the **Home page** check box to select it, click the **Parent page** check box to select it, and then click the **OK** button. The Link Bar Properties dialog box closes and the link bar placeholder appears in the page.

Before you save the page as a template, Tyler asks you to format the page by creating an area in which to insert a photo of the finished product. For example, a recipe for a cake should include a picture of the finished cake. The marketing department will coordinate with the kitchen staff to obtain these product shots.

Using Absolute Positioning for Text and Pictures

So far in these tutorials, you have used the insertion point to position text and pictures on an existing line in a Web page. Using **absolute positioning**, or simply **positioning**, lets you place text or a picture in an exact location in a page without regard to blank or existing lines. You can use positioning to place text or a picture anywhere in a page, including in front of or behind other elements. When you use absolute positioning, you can format text that surrounds the positioned text or object to flow on top of, behind, or around the object.

REFERENCE WINDOW   **RW**

Inserting Text or a Picture in a Web Page Using Absolute Positioning

- Enter the text or insert the picture that you want to position in the page.
- Select the text or picture that you inserted.
- Click View on the menu bar, point to Toolbars, and then click Positioning to display the Positioning toolbar.
- Click the Position Absolutely button on the Positioning toolbar. (The Position Absolutely button also appears on the Pictures toolbar.)
- Drag the position box to an exact location in the page; drag a sizing handle to resize the position box.

Tyler's planning analysis sheet shows that each recipe's picture should appear to the right of the bulleted list containing the recipe's ingredients. You will use positioning to place a text box with instructions in this location. When an author creates a new page using the template, he or she can replace the text with the appropriate picture and then use the mouse to adjust the picture's size or placement as necessary.

To position text using absolute positioning:

1. Click **View** on the menu bar, point to **Toolbars**, and then click **Positioning**. The Positioning toolbar opens. If necessary, drag the Positioning toolbar so that it does not block the Web page or dock it below the Formatting toolbar.

2. Click the blank line that appears between the "Enter the recipe's description here..." paragraph and the first bulleted item in the bulleted list.

   When using absolute positioning, you can insert the text or picture anywhere in the page; the original location is not important. Nevertheless, it is a good practice to insert the text or picture on a blank line, which makes it easier to select the text or picture later.

3. Type **Replace this text with the product shot and resize it, if necessary.** This text is a placeholder to remind authors to insert the photo in the correct location in the page. See Figure 7-12.

Figure 7-12   USING ABSOLUTE POSITIONING

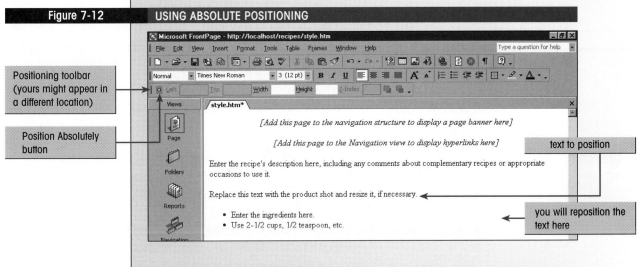

Positioning toolbar (yours might appear in a different location)

Position Absolutely button

text to position

you will reposition the text here

4. Select the text that you typed in Step 3, and then click the **Position Absolutely** button [icon] on the Positioning toolbar. See Figure 7-13. FrontPage places a position box with sizing handles around the selected text. You will correct the awkward appearance of the text after you resize the position box.

Figure 7-13   POSITION BOX AROUND THE SELECTED TEXT

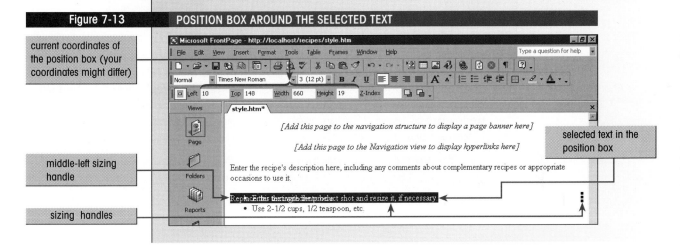

current coordinates of the position box (your coordinates might differ)

middle-left sizing handle

sizing handles

selected text in the position box

5. Point to the middle-left sizing handle so that the pointer changes to a ◆━━◆ shape, click and drag the pointer to the right until the position box is the same size as the one shown in Figure 7-14, and then release the mouse button. If necessary, use the pointer to resize the position box so that it has approximately the same coordinates shown on the Positioning toolbar in Figure 7-14, or use the ◆┼◆ pointer to drag the position box to a new location. You could also type the same coordinates in the text boxes on your Positioning toolbar as the ones shown in Figure 7-14.

Figure 7-14	RESIZED POSITION BOX

new coordinates of the position box (yours might differ)

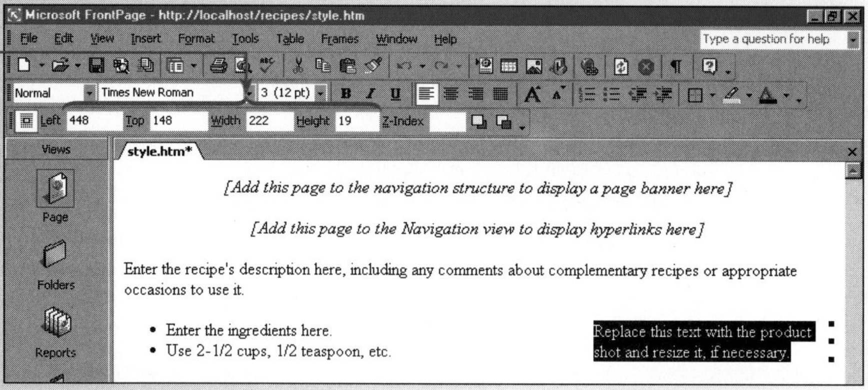

6. Click the **Preview** button. The text is now absolutely positioned in the page. When the page's author uses the position box, he or she will need to verify that the position box appears in the correct location when the Web page is viewed using different browsers and monitors. It is easy to resize and move the position box as necessary by using a sizing handle or the pointer, or by typing new coordinates in the text boxes on the Positioning toolbar when the object is selected.

7. Click the **Normal** button to return to Normal Page view, click **View** on the menu bar, point to **Toolbars**, and then click **Positioning** to close the Positioning toolbar.

8. Save the style.htm page.

Now that you have finished formatting the page, you can save it as a shared template.

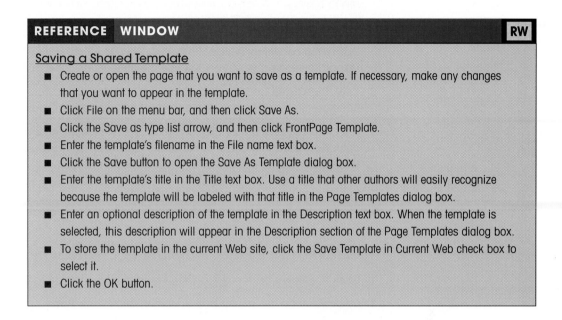

Saving a Shared Template
- Create or open the page that you want to save as a template. If necessary, make any changes that you want to appear in the template.
- Click File on the menu bar, and then click Save As.
- Click the Save as type list arrow, and then click FrontPage Template.
- Enter the template's filename in the File name text box.
- Click the Save button to open the Save As Template dialog box.
- Enter the template's title in the Title text box. Use a title that other authors will easily recognize because the template will be labeled with that title in the Page Templates dialog box.
- Enter an optional description of the template in the Description text box. When the template is selected, this description will appear in the Description section of the Page Templates dialog box.
- To store the template in the current Web site, click the Save Template in Current Web check box to select it.
- Click the OK button.

You will save the shared template in the recipes Web site.

To save the shared template:

1. Click **File** on the menu bar, and then click **Save As**. The Save As dialog box opens.

2. Click the **Save as type** list arrow, and then click **FrontPage Template**.

3. Click the **Save** button. The Save As Template dialog box opens.

4. Type **Style Page** in the Title text box. This title will identify the template's name in the Page Templates dialog box. This title differs from the value in the Name text box, which is the filename of the template.

5. Press the **Tab** key three times to move to the Description list box, and then type **Use this template to create a new recipe page.**

6. Click the **Save Template in Current Web** check box to select it. See Figure 7-15.

Figure 7-15   COMPLETED SAVE AS TEMPLATE DIALOG BOX

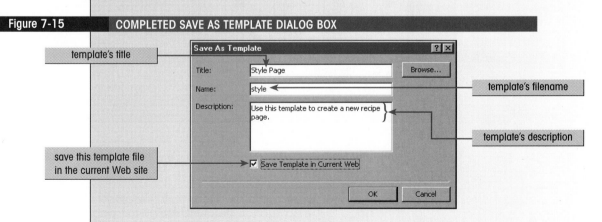

7. Click the **OK** button. FrontPage creates the template in two places: in the Web site in a hidden folder named sharedtemplates and in the default folder on the hard drive where FrontPage user information is saved (the default folder is Documents and Settings*user name*\\Application Data\\Microsoft\\FrontPage\\Pages\\stylet\\). The next time you open the Page Templates dialog box, you will see the Style Page icon in the list.

8. Click the **Close** button ⊠ on the Contents pane to close the style.htm page. Because source control is enabled for this page, you must check it in.

9. Click the **Folders** button ⧉ on the Views bar to change to Folders view, right-click **style.htm** in the Contents pane to open the shortcut menu, and then click **Check In**.

You can verify that you created the template correctly by creating a new Web page.

To use the Style Page template to create a new Web page:

1. Click the **Page** button ⧉ on the Views bar to change to Page view.

2. Click **View** on the menu bar, and then click **Task Pane**. The Task Pane opens.

3. In the New from template section of the Task Pane, click **Page Templates**.

4. Scroll down the list of icons until you see the Style Page icon, and then click the **Style Page** icon. See Figure 7-16.

Figure 7-16	PAGE TEMPLATES DIALOG BOX

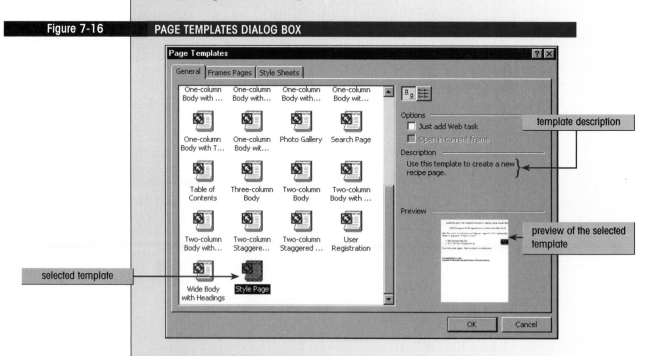

5. Click the **OK** button. A new page named new_page_1.htm is created using the Style Page template.

An author would replace the existing text in this page to create a new recipe, add the page to the navigation structure, assign the page to an appropriate category, and then save the page in the recipes Web site. You don't need to save this page, so you will close it without saving changes.

6. Click the **Close** button ☒ on the Contents pane to close the page without saving it.

7. Close the recipes Web site, and then close FrontPage.

In the next session, you will create a discussion group for the recipes Web site.

Session 7.1 QUICK CHECK

1. True or False: When developing a Web site using FrontPage, you must use the FrontPage Server Extensions.

2. True or False: You can set a FrontPage Web site to enable and disable certain Internet technologies, such as Java applets or ActiveX controls.

3. A Web page that shows how the pages in a Web site are related to one another and that provides hyperlinks to these pages is called a(n) _____.

4. Why must you create categories for Web pages and assign the site's pages to categories before creating a site map?

5. Suppose that you are creating a personal Web site on your computer's server. Would you enable source control for that Web site? Why or why not?

6. When a Web page that is enabled with source control is checked out to another author, you will see a(n) _____ icon to the left of the page's filename in Folders view on your computer.

7. How do you check in a Web page that is enabled with source control and permanently save the changes that you made in the page?

8. You can use _____ to precisely place text or pictures in a Web page.

SESSION 7.2

In this session, you will use a Wizard to create a discussion group. You will post messages to the site, reply to messages, and search for a message. You will display and examine a Web site's hidden folders and change the properties of a discussion group. Finally, you will view the HTML code for the discussion group's contents page.

Creating and Using a Discussion Group

In his planning analysis sheet for the recipes Web site (see Figure 7-3), Tyler wanted to create a way for users of (that is, visitors to) the Web site to exchange ideas and information. A **discussion group** is a specialized Web site that can stand alone or act as part of an existing Web site. It accepts messages from users, catalogs and indexes the information in these messages, and lets users reply to messages. The discussion group can be accessible to everyone or it can be protected so that only registered users can read and post messages.

When you use the Discussion Web Wizard to create a discussion group, the Wizard asks you a series of questions. Based on your answers, it creates the discussion group and its pages, as well as a hidden folder in which to store the discussion group's files. Figure 7-17 describes the pages that the Wizard can create. In the following sections, you will develop a discussion group for the recipes Web site and learn about each page and the hidden folder in more detail.

Figure 7-17	PAGES CREATED BY THE DISCUSSION WEB WIZARD	
PAGE NAME	**PAGE DESCRIPTION**	**REQUIRED?**
Confirmation	A page confirming the server's receipt of a new message.	No. You do not need to confirm the receipt of a message.
Frameset	A frames page containing the Table of Contents and Welcome pages.	No. You can specify that frames be used all the time, only when the visitor's browser supports them, or not at all.
Search Form	A page containing a search form that site visitors can use to search for keywords in posted messages.	No. However, including a search form in a discussion group does make it easier for visitors to locate messages related to a specific topic.
Submission Form	The page that visitors use to submit comments to the discussion group.	Yes. A discussion Web site must have a Submission Form.
TOC (Table of Contents)	The page that functions as the site's index. FrontPage creates hyperlinks to every message in the discussion group. Clicking a hyperlink opens the message.	No. However, it is suggested that you do include this page in your discussion group; without it, users have no way to view the site's contents.
Welcome	The discussion Web site's home page, containing default instructions for using the site and hyperlinks to the Submission Form and the Search Form Web pages.	No. You can specify that the site uses an existing home page, or you can ask FrontPage to create the Welcome page for you. Any single Web site can contain only one home page.

Planning a Discussion Group

Before you create a discussion group, it is a good idea to think about how visitors will use the site and consider any special requirements that you will need to implement. For example, when using the Discussion Web Wizard to create a new discussion group, you must decide whether to create a new Web site or to add the discussion group to the current Web site. Keep in mind that an active discussion group can receive hundreds of messages a day. These messages require processing resources and take up space on the server on which the discussion group is published. Before creating a discussion group on a Web server, you must make sure that the server has the necessary resources to maintain and store it.

During the planning phase, you must also consider how you will manage the messages submitted to the discussion group. There is no way to automatically detect and deal with messages containing inappropriate language or content. The site's administrator could try to find and delete all unsuitable messages. Deleting messages is not a good idea, however, because it would interfere with the hyperlinks that connect the site's messages. Instead, the site's administrator could replace the contents of an inappropriate message with "Contents Deleted" or similar text. However, this solution places a heavy burden on the site's administrator, who must read every message to determine its usefulness and appropriateness to the site.

A better way to manage messages is to decrease the risk of inappropriate content by creating a secure Web site that allows only authorized visitors to participate in the discussion group. Typically, the site's administrator sets up accounts with logons and passwords for qualified visitors. If a particular discussion participant repeatedly submits inappropriate messages, the site's administrator can invalidate his or her privileges.

Using a Wizard to Create a Discussion Group

Although you could create a discussion group by developing the individual Web pages required to support the discussion group, it is much easier to let the Discussion Web Wizard do the work for you. The files that run and administer the discussion group are hidden files that contain FrontPage components. The FrontPage 2002 Server Extensions run the discussion group, so they must be installed and properly configured on the Web server on which the discussion group is created and published.

REFERENCE WINDOW   **RW**

Using the Discussion Web Wizard to Create a Discussion Group

- In Folders view, open the Web site to which you will add the discussion group. If you want to create a new Web site for the discussion group, close any open Web pages or Web sites.
- In the New section of the Task Pane, click Empty Web. The Web Site Templates dialog box opens.
- If you are creating a new Web site, click in the Specify the location of the new web list box, and then type http://, the server name on which to create the new Web site, and the name of the Web site. If you are adding the discussion group to an existing Web site, click the Add to current Web check box.
- If you are creating the discussion group on a Web server that requires Secure Socket Layer (SSL) communication, click the Secure connection required (SSL) check box.
- Double-click the Discussion Web Wizard icon. Use the Discussion Web Wizard's dialog boxes to specify the pages to create, a title for the discussion group, a name for the hidden folder that will store the discussion group pages, the input fields to create in the Submission Form, the site's security status (open versus closed), the sort order for the index (oldest to newest or newest to oldest), whether to replace the existing home page or create a new one, the information that the Search Form should supply with hyperlinks to matching pages, an optional theme, and the frames page options.
- Click the Finish button to create the discussion group.

Tyler asks you to add a discussion group to the recipes Web site using the title "Recipe Discussion" and the hidden folder name "_disc." The Recipe Discussion will be an unprotected site; any visitor can read and submit messages. Tyler wants you to create all of the Wizard's available default pages. The Submission Form will contain the Subject, Category, and Comments fields; the table of contents will be sorted with the newest message listed first; you will not create a new home page; the Search Form will supply hyperlinks to matching pages with each message's subject, size, and date; and you will create a frames page. Because you are adding the discussion group to an existing Web site, the Wizard will not prompt you to select a theme. You can apply a theme later, if necessary.

After creating the initial discussion group, you can format its pages just as you would any other Web page. However, it is very important that you retain the file structure created by the Wizard. For example, you should not move pages or hidden files or rename any form fields created in the Submission Form or the Search Form. Such changes will cause the discussion group to stop functioning correctly. Conversely, formatting the pages by adding pictures, themes, and other visual interest is appropriate—and suggested—because the Wizard creates the basic content with only minimal formatting.

Before creating the discussion group, you need to open the recipes Web site from the server. Because you are the only user for the server, you will disable source control to make your work go faster.

To open the recipes Web site from the server and disable source control:

1. Start FrontPage and change to Folders view.

2. Click the **list arrow** for the Open button 📂 on the Standard toolbar, and then click **Open Web**. The Open Web dialog box opens.

3. If necessary, click the **My Network Places** button in the Open Web dialog box. See Figure 7-18.

Figure 7-18	OPENING A WEB SITE FROM A SERVER

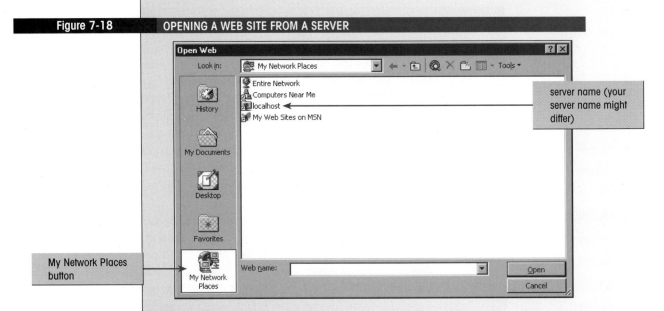

4. Double-click the name of your Web server. The default name is **localhost**.

TROUBLE? If you see a "recipes on localhost" folder instead of the localhost folder, click the recipes on localhost folder to select it, click the Open button, and then skip Step 5.

5. Click the **recipes** folder, and then click the **Open** button. The recipes Web site opens in Folders view. Notice that your files use source control, as indicated by the green dots to the left of each filename.

TROUBLE? If your Web site does not open in Folders view, click the Folders button 📁 on the Views bar.

6. Click **Tools** on the menu bar, and then click **Web Settings**. If necessary, click the **General** tab to display those settings.

7. Click the **Use document check-in and check-out** check box to clear it, and then click the **OK** button.

8. Click the **Yes** button to recalculate the Web site. The files in the Web site no longer have green dots to the left of their filenames, indicating that you have disabled source control for this Web site.

Now that the recipes Web site is open, you can create the discussion group.

To create the discussion group:

1. Click **View** on the menu bar, and then click **Task Pane**.

2. In the New section of the Task Pane, click **Empty Web**. The Web Site Templates dialog box opens.

3. Click the **Add to current Web** check box to select it. FrontPage dims the Specify the location of the new web list box.

   TROUBLE? If your Web server requires SSL communication, click the Secure connection required (SSL) check box to select it. Usually you do not need to select this option when creating Web sites on a desktop Web service such as IIS. If you are unsure about the need for SSL communication, ask your instructor or technical support person for help.

4. Double-click the **Discussion Web Wizard** icon. FrontPage starts the Discussion Web Wizard and opens the first dialog box. Read the information provided.

5. Click the **Next** button. The second dialog box opens. See Figure 7-19. You use this dialog box to select the pages and features that you want to create in the discussion group. You have already learned about the Submission Form, Table of Contents, Search Form, and Confirmation pages (see Figure 7-17).

Figure 7-19	SELECTING THE DISCUSSION GROUP PAGES AND FEATURES

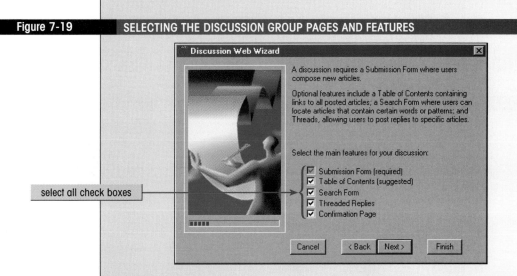

select all check boxes

Selecting the Threaded Replies option enables the site to index messages based on their topics, along with the replies to those messages. When the Threaded Replies option is selected, the original message appears flush with the left margin, and replies to that message appearing indented on a new line below the original message. If you do not select the Threaded Replies option, then all messages in the discussion group will be listed in chronological order using the sort order you specified in the Wizard.

6. If necessary, click any empty check box to select it, and then click the **Next** button. This dialog box asks you to enter a title and name for the discussion group. Type **Recipe Discussion** in the Enter a descriptive title for this discussion text box, press the **Tab** key to move to the Enter the name for the discussion folder text box, and then type **_disc** (if necessary). See Figure 7-20.

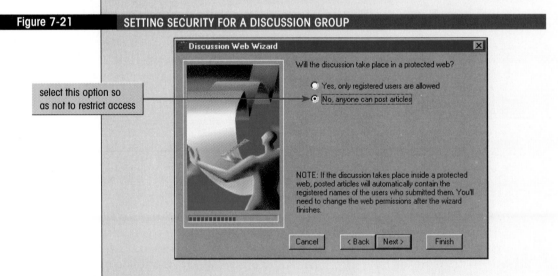

Figure 7-20 — ENTERING THE TITLE AND NAME OF THE DISCUSSION GROUP

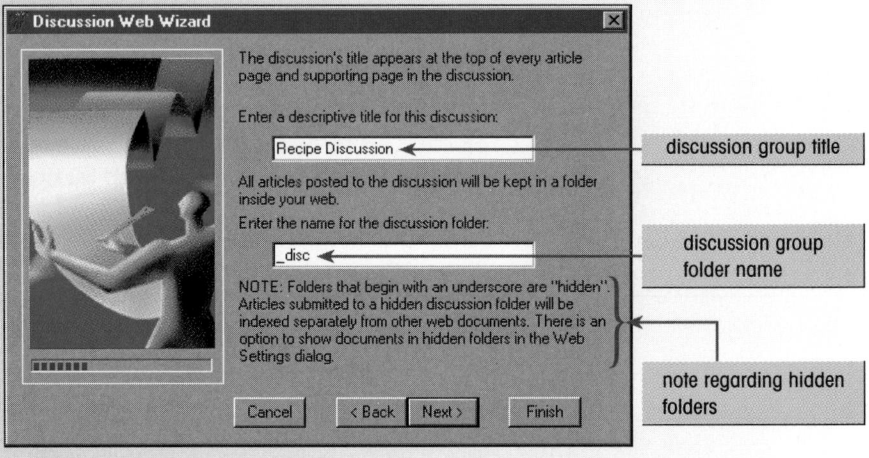

discussion group title

discussion group folder name

note regarding hidden folders

The note in the dialog box reminds you that the discussion folder's name must begin with an underscore character so that FrontPage can index the messages submitted to the discussion group. Folders that have an underscore as the first character are hidden.

7. Click the **Next** button. If necessary, click the **Subject, Category, Comments** option button to select it so that the Wizard will create these form fields in the Submission Form, and then click the **Next** button. The next dialog box asks whether your discussion group is protected. See Figure 7-21.

Figure 7-21 — SETTING SECURITY FOR A DISCUSSION GROUP

select this option so as not to restrict access

8. If necessary, click the **No, anyone can post articles** option button to select it, and then click the **Next** button. The next dialog box asks how you want to sort the messages listed in the table of contents.

9. If necessary, click the **Newest to oldest** option button to select it, and then click the **Next** button. The next dialog box asks if you want to create a new home page. See Figure 7-22. The recipes Web site already has a page named Default.htm, so you do not need to create a home page.

Figure 7-22 | SELECTING THE HOME PAGE FOR THE DISCUSSION GROUP

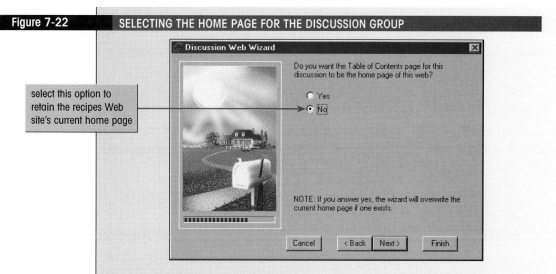

select this option to retain the recipes Web site's current home page

10. If necessary, click the **No** option button, and then click the **Next** button. The next dialog box asks you to select the information that will appear with the search results created by the Search Form.

11. If necessary, click the **Subject, Size, Date** option button to select it, and then click the **Next** button. The next dialog box asks you to specify a frame option. See Figure 7-23.

Figure 7-23 | SELECTING A FRAME OPTION

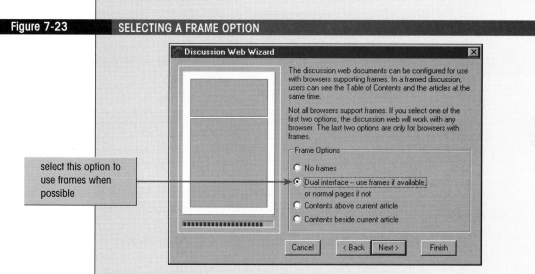

select this option to use frames when possible

A preview of the selected frame option appears on the left side of the dialog box. The most appropriate option is the dual interface, which creates a frames page when the browser can display frames, and normal pages when the browser cannot display frames.

12. If necessary, click the **Dual interface -- use frames if available, or normal pages if not** option button to select it, and then click the **Next** button. The final dialog box of the Discussion Web Wizard tells you how to display the Web site's hidden files and reviews the contents of the main pages you selected. See Figure 7-24. If you need to change any options, you can click the Back button to return to a previous dialog box.

Figure 7-24	FINAL DIALOG BOX OF THE DISCUSSION WEB WIZARD

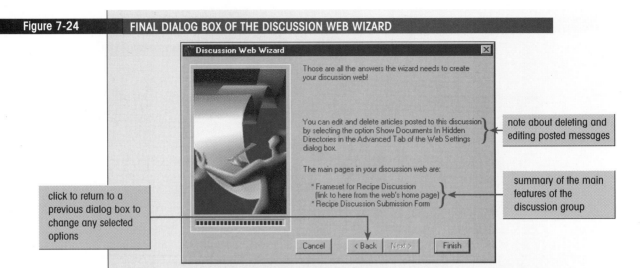

click to return to a previous dialog box to change any selected options

note about deleting and editing posted messages

summary of the main features of the discussion group

13. Read the information in the final dialog box, and then click the **Finish** button.

FrontPage creates the pages in the discussion group as well as the hidden folder and files that will maintain and run it. The default Web pages created by the Discussion Web Wizard have the prefix "Recipe Discussion" and the default page title. The filenames of pages that belong to the discussion group all begin with "disc," which is the same as the folder name (without the leading underscore character) that you specified when you created the discussion group.

It is very easy to participate in the discussion group; most pages contain instructions for users. To learn how to use the discussion group, you will post and reply to a message to simulate the experience of a visitor to the page.

Posting a Message

When you **post** a message, or article, to a discussion group, you actually submit a form to a server for processing. The FrontPage Server Extensions process the form and store its contents in the discussion group's hidden folder in the Web site. The Discussion Web Wizard creates all of the default forms required to run the discussion group, so the discussion group is ready to use immediately. You could start your work by formatting the pages created by the Wizard, but for now, you decide to begin by using the discussion group so that you will understand how it works. Your practice work will also give you an opportunity to examine the pages created by the Wizard and to consider ways to improve them.

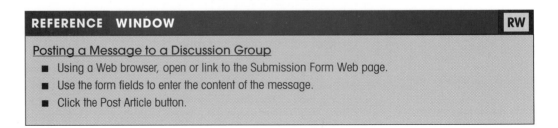

REFERENCE WINDOW   RW

Posting a Message to a Discussion Group
- Using a Web browser, open or link to the Submission Form Web page.
- Use the form fields to enter the content of the message.
- Click the Post Article button.

You will post a message to the discussion group by opening the site's Welcome page and navigating to the Submission Form page. You must use the browser to post a message to the discussion group.

To post a message to the discussion group:

1. Click the **Recipe Discussion Welcome** page (disc_welc.htm) in the Contents pane to select it, and then click the **Preview in Browser** button 🔍 on the Standard toolbar. The Welcome page opens in the browser. See Figure 7-25. Notice that the page created by the Wizard contains only basic content, without any special formatting.

Figure 7-25 | **WELCOME PAGE IN THE BROWSER**

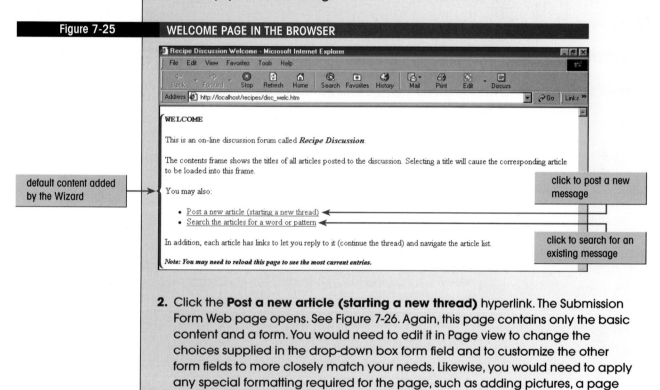

default content added by the Wizard

click to post a new message

click to search for an existing message

2. Click the **Post a new article (starting a new thread)** hyperlink. The Submission Form Web page opens. See Figure 7-26. Again, this page contains only the basic content and a form. You would need to edit it in Page view to change the choices supplied in the drop-down box form field and to customize the other form fields to more closely match your needs. Likewise, you would need to apply any special formatting required for the page, such as adding pictures, a page background, and hyperlinks to other pages in the recipes Web site.

Figure 7-26   POSTING A NEW MESSAGE

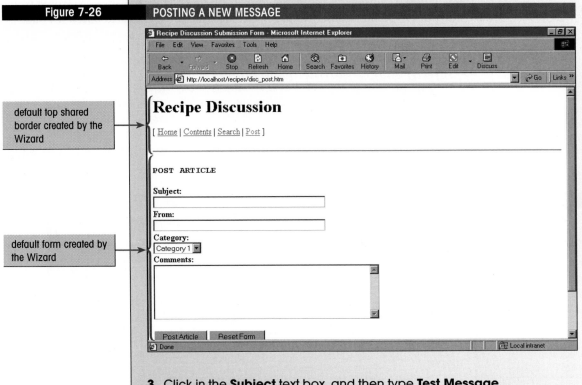

default top shared border created by the Wizard

default form created by the Wizard

3. Click in the **Subject** text box, and then type **Test Message**.

4. Press the **Tab** key to move to the From text box, and then type **Tyler Vanauken**.

5. Click the **Category** list arrow, and then click **Category 3**. You can see that you will need to change this form field to create appropriate choices for the recipes Web site in the drop-down list. For example, you might change the choices to "Recipe Enhancement," "Recipe Correction," "Recipe Comments," and "Other."

6. Click in the **Comments** text box, and then type **This is a test.**

7. Scroll down the page as necessary, and then click the **Post Article** button. A confirmation page opens, indicating that the server received your message. See Figure 7-27. The page includes a message that reminds you to refresh the main page (Contents) to see your message in the list.

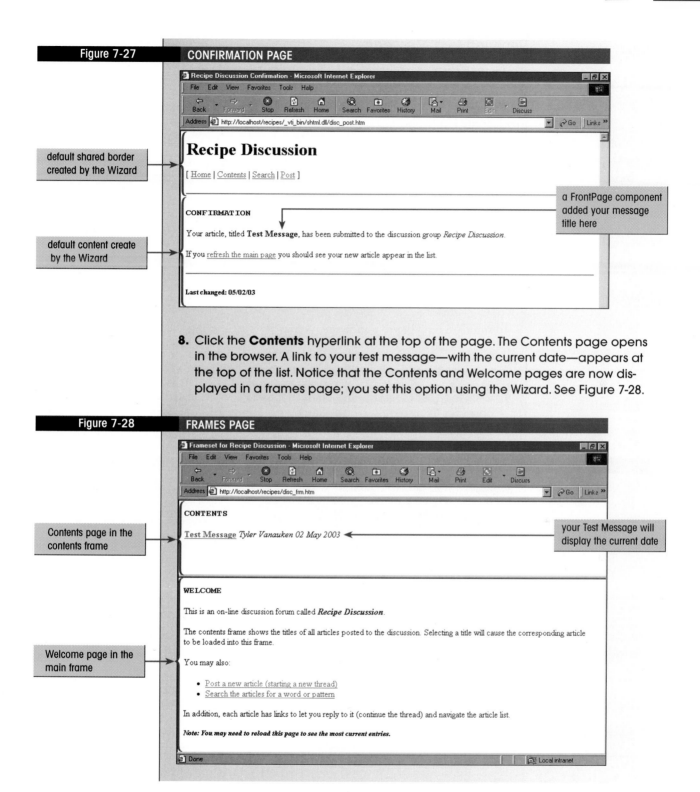

Figure 7-27   CONFIRMATION PAGE

default shared border created by the Wizard

default content create by the Wizard

a FrontPage component added your message title here

8. Click the **Contents** hyperlink at the top of the page. The Contents page opens in the browser. A link to your test message—with the current date—appears at the top of the list. Notice that the Contents and Welcome pages are now displayed in a frames page; you set this option using the Wizard. See Figure 7-28.

Figure 7-28   FRAMES PAGE

Contents page in the contents frame

your Test Message will display the current date

Welcome page in the main frame

Now your discussion group contains one message. You can reply to that message to see how threads work. A **thread** is a series of messages on a related topic and their replies.

Replying to a Message

The Test Message that you created in the previous set of steps is now stored in the recipes Web site. Notice that the Test Message is formatted as a hyperlink in the contents frame. To reply to a message, you click its hyperlink to the original message. You then use a hyperlink to select the Reply option.

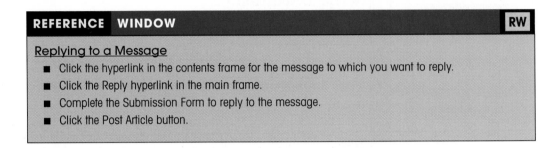

REFERENCE WINDOW   **RW**

Replying to a Message
- Click the hyperlink in the contents frame for the message to which you want to reply.
- Click the Reply hyperlink in the main frame.
- Complete the Submission Form to reply to the message.
- Click the Post Article button.

To simulate replying to a message, you will reply by using the name "Amanda Bay."

To reply to a message:

1. Click the **Test Message** hyperlink in the contents frame. The main frame changes to display a page with the contents and details of the Test Message you submitted. See Figure 7-29.

Figure 7-29   REPLYING TO A MESSAGE

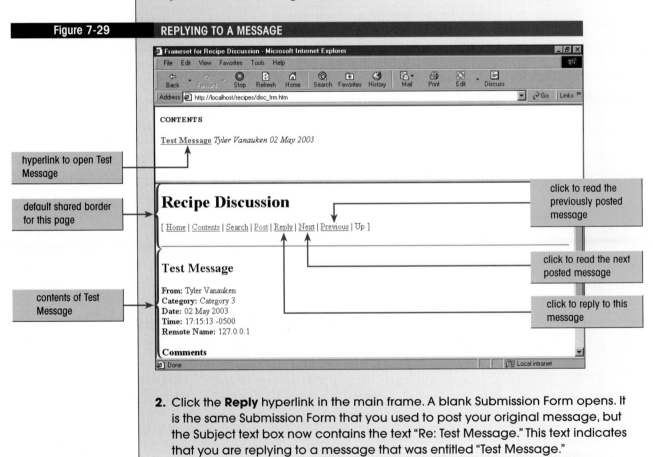

hyperlink to open Test Message

default shared border for this page

contents of Test Message

click to read the previously posted message

click to read the next posted message

click to reply to this message

2. Click the **Reply** hyperlink in the main frame. A blank Submission Form opens. It is the same Submission Form that you used to post your original message, but the Subject text box now contains the text "Re: Test Message." This text indicates that you are replying to a message that was entitled "Test Message."

3. Click in the **From** text box, and then type **Amanda Bay**.

4. Click the **Category** list arrow, and then click **Category 3**.

5. Click in the **Comments** text box, and then type **I am replying to your test message.**

6. Scroll down the page as necessary, and then click the **Post Article** button. The Confirmation page opens.

7. Click the **Contents** hyperlink to return to the frames page. See Figure 7-30. Your reply is now indented below the original message. This indentation indicates a threaded reply, or a message with the same topic. As additional replies are submitted to the discussion group, they will also be indented in the Contents pane. New messages (threads) will appear flush with the left margin.

| Figure 7-30 | THREADED REPLY IN THE CONTENTS PAGE |

reply appears as an indented message under the original message

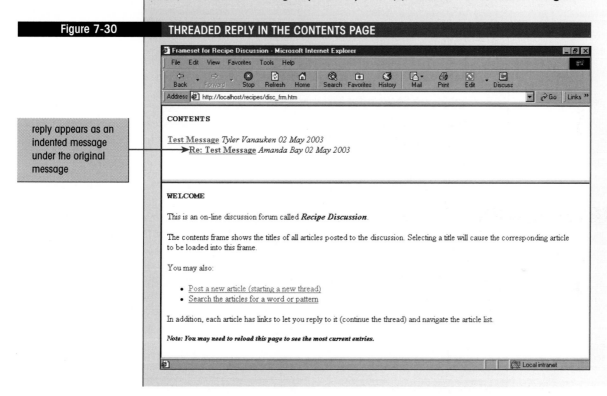

Now the discussion group contains two messages. To help you understand the Search Form, you will search for your messages.

Searching a Discussion Group

The page in the main frame contains a hyperlink that lets you search the messages in the discussion group for a word or pattern (phrase). The Search Form page contains the same FrontPage search component that you use to search a Web site.

REFERENCE WINDOW **RW**

Searching a Discussion Group
- Click the Search the articles for a word or pattern hyperlink, in the Welcome page to open the Search Form page.
- Click in the Search for text box, and then type the word or phrase that you want to find.
- Click the Start Search button.
- Click a hyperlink in the results page to open the page(s) that contain your search text.

You will search for the word "test." The search component should find this word in both of your messages.

To search a discussion group:

1. Click the **Search the articles for a word or pattern** hyperlink in the main frame. The Search Form Web page opens in the main frame.

2. Click in the **Search for** text box, and then type **test**.

3. Click the **Start Search** button. Scroll down the page as necessary to see the search results area, which shows that both of your messages contain this text.

   TROUBLE? Depending on the server in use, it might take several minutes to create an index, and you might receive the message, "No documents found. Please try again." If this message appears, wait a few minutes, and then click the Start Search button again. If you don't want to wait for the index, click the Test Message hyperlink in the contents frame instead of the one in the search results (as specified in Step 4) and continue with Step 5.

4. Click the **Test Message** hyperlink in the search results to open that message. The hyperlinks at the top of the page include one named "Next." Clicking this hyperlink will open the next message, which in this case is the reply from Amanda Bay. The "next" message is not always a reply; it is just the next message in the list.

5. Click the **Next** hyperlink. The Re: Test Message message opens.

6. Click the **Microsoft FrontPage** program button on the taskbar to return to FrontPage. Do not close the browser.

Tyler wants to confirm that you can view and, if necessary, edit the messages in the discussion group.

Displaying **and Examining a Web Site's Hidden Folders**

To see the hidden folders and files for the discussion group, you need to change the Web site to display them.

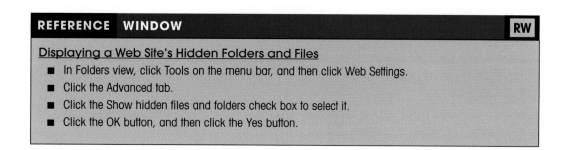

REFERENCE WINDOW   **RW**

<u>Displaying a Web Site's Hidden Folders and Files</u>
- In Folders view, click Tools on the menu bar, and then click Web Settings.
- Click the Advanced tab.
- Click the Show hidden files and folders check box to select it.
- Click the OK button, and then click the Yes button.

Tyler asks you to display the hidden folders in the recipes Web site. You will see the hidden folder created by the Discussion Web Wizard, along with the _sharedtemplates folder that was created in Session 7.1.

To display the Web site's hidden folders:

1. Click **Tools** on the menu bar, and then click **Web Settings**. The Web Settings dialog box opens.

2. Click the **Advanced** tab to display those settings.

3. Click the **Show hidden files and folders** check box to select it, and then click the **OK** button. The Web Settings dialog box closes and a Microsoft FrontPage dialog box opens. See Figure 7-31.

Figure 7-31   **DIALOG BOX ASKING TO REFRESH THE WEB SITE**

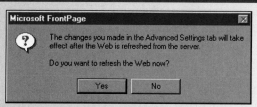

4. Click the **Yes** button. Folders view is refreshed, and all of the site's files and folders are displayed in Folders view. See Figure 7-32.

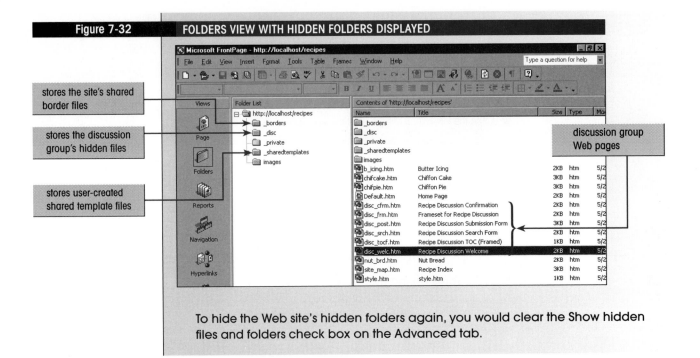

Figure 7-32   FOLDERS VIEW WITH HIDDEN FOLDERS DISPLAYED

stores the site's shared border files

stores the discussion group's hidden files

stores user-created shared template files

discussion group Web pages

To hide the Web site's hidden folders again, you would clear the Show hidden files and folders check box on the Advanced tab.

When you post a message to a discussion group, FrontPage names the HTML document from that message using a sequential filename. For example, the Test Message has the filename 00000001.htm. The reply to the Test Message has the filename 00000002.htm. As additional messages are submitted to the discussion group, they will have sequential filenames. To open the HTML documents that contain the posted messages, you double-click them.

Tyler asks you to open the Test Message and edit its content, simulating how you might handle a message that contains inappropriate content.

To open a posted message and the table of contents in FrontPage:

1. Click the **_disc** folder in the Folder List to open it. The files in this folder appear in the Contents pane. Unless you submitted additional messages, you should see your Test Message, your reply to the Test Message, and a file named tocproto.htm. See Figure 7-33.

Figure 7-33	CONTENTS OF THE_DISC HIDDEN FOLDER

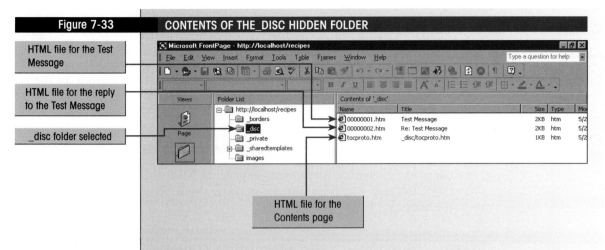

HTML file for the Test Message

HTML file for the reply to the Test Message

_disc folder selected

HTML file for the Contents page

2. Double-click **00000001.htm** in the Contents pane. The Test Message opens in Page view.

3. Scroll down the page as necessary, select the word **test** in the Comments section, and then type **[comment deleted]**.

4. Click the **Save** button 🔲 on the Standard toolbar.

   Next, view the page in the browser.

5. Click the browser's program button on the taskbar, click the **Test Message** hyperlink in the contents frame, and then click the **Refresh** button 🔲 on the toolbar. Scroll down the page (if necessary) to see the Test Message text, noticing the update you made to that message.

   You can also edit the discussion group's table of contents by opening the tocproto.htm file in Page view.

6. Click the **Microsoft FrontPage** program button on the taskbar, and then click the **Folders** button 🔲 on the Views bar to return to Folders view.

7. Double-click **tocproto.htm** in the Contents pane. The Contents page opens in Page view. You can edit this page as well. Be careful not to delete any hyperlinks, as such a change will affect the way that messages in the discussion group are linked together. Normally, you would not need to edit a page in the discussion group, but you can do so when necessary.

8. Delete the word **Message** in the Test Message hyperlink so it becomes just "Test."

9. Click 🔲, switch to the browser, and then click 🔲 on the toolbar. The hyperlink for the Test Message is now "Test."

10. Click the **Test** hyperlink in the contents frame. The Test Message appears in the main frame. Your changes are displayed in the contents frame, but the hyperlink to the Test Message still works.

11. Close the browser, and then close the 00000001.htm and tocproto.htm pages in Page view.

You have posted and replied to a message, searched the discussion group, and edited a message. The discussion group works correctly and should serve your needs. As with most Web pages created using a Wizard, however, you can always improve their appearance and utility by adding your own content and formatting. Tyler asks you to change some of the default pages to make them easier to use, and then to apply a Web theme to the entire recipes Web site.

Changing the Properties of a Discussion Group

The first thing that you will do is add the site's pages to Navigation view. Next, you will create FrontPage link bars and page banners in some pages. Finally, you will apply a Web theme to the entire Web site.

To add new pages to the navigation structure:

1. Click the **Navigation** button on the Views bar. The navigation structure currently contains the home page (Default.htm) and the Recipe Index page (site_map.htm) that you added in Session 7.1.

2. Drag the pages from the Folder List and drop them into the navigation structure so that it looks like Figure 7-34.

| Figure 7-34 | NAVIGATION STRUCTURE FOR THE RECIPES WEB SITE |

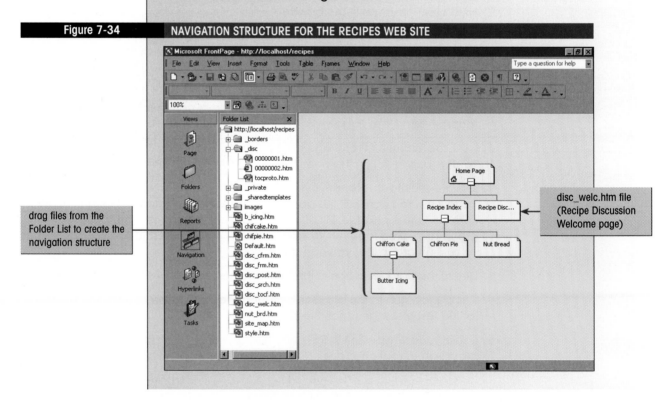

drag files from the Folder List to create the navigation structure

disc_welc.htm file (Recipe Discussion Welcome page)

Changing the Discussion Group's Shared Borders

You may have noticed that the pages in the discussion group use a text page banner and a FrontPage link bar with text hyperlinks to the discussion group's pages and to the home page. When you initially develop a discussion group, FrontPage creates a shared border that only the discussion group Web pages use. Hyperlinks to the pages in the discussion group are added to the shared border automatically. If you need to rename or add a hyperlink to the discussion group's shared border, you can edit it just like any other shared border.

Tyler thinks that the top shared border for the discussion group pages would be more effective if it contained hyperlinks to the Welcome page and to the home page of the recipes Web site. These changes will make it easier for the site's visitors to navigate the Web site.

To edit a discussion group's shared border:

1. Click the **Folders** button 🗀 on the Views bar to change to Folders view.

2. Click the **_borders** folder in the Folder List. This folder contains the files that create the shared borders for the discussion Web site. The disc_aftr.htm file is the footer for pages that display messages, the disc_ahdr.htm file is the header for pages that display messages (with the page banner and hyperlinks), the disc_foot.htm file is the footer for pages that do not display messages, and the disc_head.htm file is the header for pages that do not display messages.

3. Double-click **disc_head.htm** in the Contents pane to open it in Page view. See Figure 7-35. To make Tyler's suggested changes, you will need to change the hyperlinks.

| Figure 7-35 | SHARED BORDER FOR THE DISCUSSION GROUP PAGES |

4. Point to the **Home** hyperlink. Notice that the status bar displays Default.htm, which is the target of the hyperlink. This hyperlink opens the home page for the recipes Web site. To make the target of this hyperlink clearer, Tyler suggests that you change it to "Recipes Home Page."

5. Select the **Home** hyperlink, and then type **Recipes Home Page**. Point to the new hyperlink and make sure that Default.htm is still the target.

Next, you will add the hyperlink to the Welcome page.

6. Click to the right of the first vertical bar separator (the one that appears after the Recipes Home Page hyperlink), press the **spacebar**, type **Welcome Page**, press the **spacebar**, and then type **|** (the vertical bar separator). See Figure 7-36.

7. Select **Welcome Page**, click the **Insert Hyperlink** button 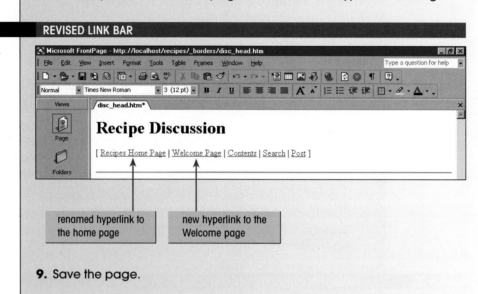 on the Standard toolbar, scroll down the list of files, and then double-click **disc_welc**. The Insert Hyperlink dialog box closes, and FrontPage creates the hyperlink to the Welcome page.

8. Click anywhere in the Web page to deselect the hyperlink. See Figure 7-36.

Figure 7-36	REVISED LINK BAR

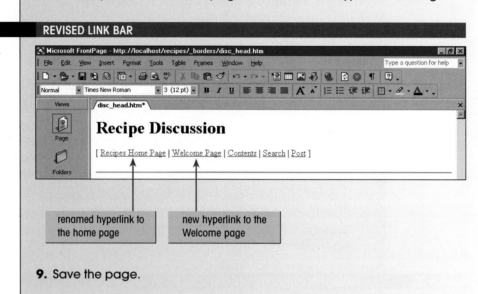

renamed hyperlink to
the home page

new hyperlink to the
Welcome page

9. Save the page.

You made this change to the top shared border for the pages that do not contain messages. You can test this change in the browser.

To test the shared border in the browser:

1. Click the **Preview in Browser** button on the Standard toolbar, click the **Welcome Page** hyperlink, and then click the **Post a new article (starting a new thread)** hyperlink in the main frame. The page displays the changes that you made to the link bar in the main frame.

2. Close the browser.

Adding a Page Banner and Link Bar to the Welcome Page

Tyler suggests that you change the discussion pages to include page banners instead of the default page headings and that you add a FrontPage link bar to the Welcome page. These changes will make it easier for users to navigate the site. After making these changes, you will apply a theme to the Web site to create some visual interest.

To include a page banner and link bar in the Welcome page:

1. Press and hold down the **Ctrl** key, click the **Welcome Page** hyperlink that you created in the disc_head.htm page, and then release the **Ctrl** key. The Welcome page opens in Page view.

2. Select the **WELCOME** heading at the top of the Welcome page, click **Insert** on the menu bar, and then click **Page Banner**.

3. Click the **OK** button to insert the page banner with the default settings.

4. Click the **Center** button 🗐 on the Formatting toolbar to center the page banner.

5. Press the **Enter** key to create a new centered line.

6. Click **Insert** on the menu bar, and then click **Navigation**. The Insert Web Component dialog box opens, with the Link Bars component type selected.

7. Click the **Bar based on navigation structure** bar type in the Choose a bar type list box, and then click the **Next** button.

8. Scroll down the list of bar styles, click the **Dots** style (the fifth style from the end of the list), and then click the **Finish** button. The Link Bar Properties dialog box opens.

9. Click the **Same level** option button, click the **Home page** check box to select it, click the **Parent page** check box to select, and then click the **OK** button. A link bar appears below the page banner.

10. Save the Recipe Discussion Welcome page.

Applying a Theme to the Recipes Web Site

Your Web site's navigation structure is complete, so you are ready to select a theme.

To apply a Web theme:

1. Click **Format** on the menu bar, and then click **Theme**. The Themes dialog box opens.

2. If necessary, click the **All pages** option button to select it.

3. Scroll down the list of themes (if necessary), and then click **Blends**.

   TROUBLE? If the Blends theme is not installed on your computer, select another theme.

4. If necessary, click the **Vivid colors**, **Active graphics**, and **Background picture** check boxes to select them, and then click the **OK** button.

5. Click the **Yes** button to apply the theme. After a few moments, the Recipe Discussion Welcome page is displayed with the theme's elements. See Figure 7-37.

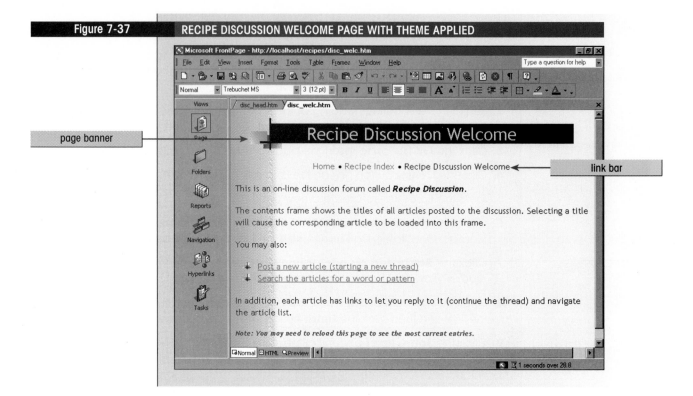

| Figure 7-37 | RECIPE DISCUSSION WELCOME PAGE WITH THEME APPLIED |

Tyler likes the theme but doesn't like the background picture used by the theme. He asks you to modify the background picture.

To modify the background picture:

1. Click **Format** on the menu bar, and then click **Theme**. The Themes dialog box opens.

2. If necessary, click the **All pages** option button to select it.

3. Click the **Modify** button, and then click the **Graphics** button. The Modify Theme dialog box opens with the Item list box set to Background Picture.

   You will change the background picture to use a GIF file that Tyler saved in the Tutorial.07 folder.

4. Click the **Browse** button. The Open File dialog box opens.

5. Click the **Look in** list arrow, open the **Tutorial.07** folder on your Data Disk, and then double-click **netbkgnd**.

   The Modify Theme dialog box reappears and displays the revised theme. The Background Picture text box lists the file that you selected, netbkgnd.gif.

6. Click the **OK** button to close the Modify Theme dialog box, and then click the **OK** button in the Themes dialog box. A message box opens, asking you to save your changes.

7. Click the **Yes** button to save the theme with the suggested name, and then click the **Yes** button to apply the theme to all pages in the Web site.

TROUBLE? If the suggested theme name already exists, change it by appending a digit or taking some other action to create a unique name.

8. Click the **Preview in Browser** button on the Standard toolbar. The Recipe Discussion Welcome page opens in the browser, showing the new background picture. See Figure 7-38.

| Figure 7-38 | NEW BACKGROUND PICTURE ADDED TO THEME |

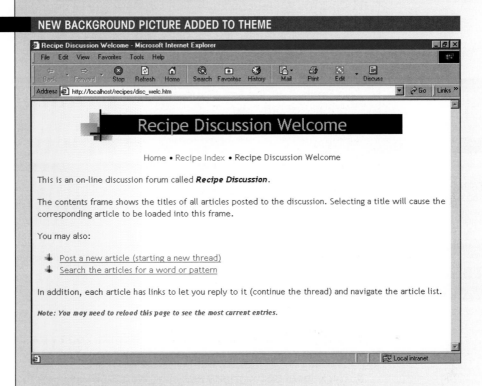

9. Use the hyperlinks that you created in the top shared border to navigate the Web site. When you are finished, close your browser.

Now the Web site is visually interesting and easier to use. You will finish revising the discussion pages in the Review Assignments.

Tyler wants you to examine the HTML code for the Contents page created by the Wizard to see how messages are added to the discussion group's table of contents.

Viewing **HTML Code for a Contents Page**

The Discussion Web Wizard created several Web pages, a hidden folder, and several hidden files, all of which maintain and run the discussion group. Many of these pages contain HTML elements with which you are already familiar. For example, the discussion group contains a frames page, a page with a form component, and a page with a search component.

The Contents page is a new type of HTML document that you have not used previously. The discussion form handler inserts the results of a form in the Contents page and creates a hyperlink to the form (message). In addition, the discussion form handler names the form (message) sequentially as the server receives forms and then stores them in the _disc folder of the Web site.

Tyler wants you to examine the HTML code for the Contents page.

To view the HTML code for the Contents page:

1. Click the **Folders** button [icon] on the Views bar to change to Folders view, click the **_disc** folder in the Folder List, and then double-click **tocproto.htm** in the Contents pane. The Contents page opens in Page view.

2. Click the **HTML** button to display the HTML code for the Contents page. You might need to scroll the page to the right to view the HTML code shown in Figure 7-39. The FrontPage components that create the content of this page appear as gray text.

Figure 7-39	HTML CODE FOR THE CONTENTS PAGE

FrontPage component that adds the first message

first message (Test)

second message (Re: Test Message)

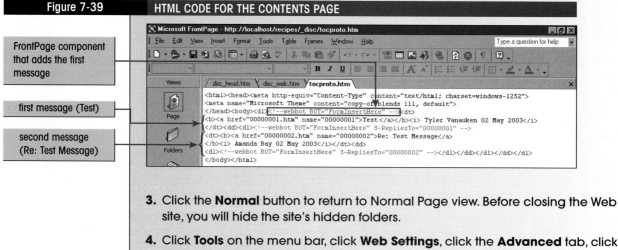

3. Click the **Normal** button to return to Normal Page view. Before closing the Web site, you will hide the site's hidden folders.

4. Click **Tools** on the menu bar, click **Web Settings**, click the **Advanced** tab, click the **Show hidden files and folders** check box to clear it, click the **OK** button, and then click the **Yes** button.

You are finished with your work, so you can close the recipes Web site and FrontPage.

5. Close the recipes Web site, and then close FrontPage.

In the next tutorial, you will create a Web page that stores information about the recipes Web site's visitors in an Access database.

Session 7.2 QUICK | CHECK

1. Suppose you are creating a discussion group for benefits administrators affiliated with a statewide agency. Would you use a protected Web for the discussion group? Why or why not?

2. True or False: You must install and configure the FrontPage 2002 Server Extensions to publish a discussion group on a server.

3. The easiest way to create a discussion group in FrontPage is to use the _____.

4. Which page created by the Discussion Web Wizard is not optional?

5. In FrontPage, how can you identify hidden folders in a Web site?

6. How do you display a FrontPage Web site's hidden folders?

7. True or False: You can post a message to a discussion group from FrontPage.

8. Which filename does FrontPage use to store the first message posted to a new discussion group?

9. What is the filename of the top shared border for a discussion group Web page that does not display a message?

REVIEW ASSIGNMENTS

Tyler asks you to enhance the recipes Web site by making several changes. First, you will use absolute positioning to add product shots to some of the recipes pages. Next, you will import several new pages that Tyler just received into the Web site. After importing the pages, you will assign them to the appropriate categories. Tyler also asks you to change the Wizard's default term of "article" to "message." You will change the Submission Form to include appropriate content for accepting information from users regarding cooking and the site's recipes. Finally, you will customize the Wizard's default confirmation page to personalize it for visitors.

If necessary, start FrontPage, insert your Data Disk in the appropriate disk drive, and then do the following:

1. Open the **recipes** Web site from your computer's server in Folders view.

Explore ▶ 2. Open the Chiffon Cake page (**chifcake.htm**) in Page view. Use absolute positioning to place the picture saved as **c_cake.jpg** in the Tutorial.07 folder on your Data Disk to the right of the bulleted list. (*Hint:* Insert the picture anywhere in the page, select the picture, click the Position Absolutely button on the Pictures toolbar, and then drag the picture to the correct location. You will need to resize the picture to make it fit correctly.) Save the picture in the Web site's images folder, and then preview the page in the browser. If necessary, return to the Chiffon Cake page and make any adjustments required. When you are finished, print the page, and then close both the browser and the Chiffon Cake page.

3. Change to Folders view, and then import the following pages from the Tutorial.07 folder into the Web site: **pecan_br**, **org_cake**, and **orgicing**. Select these three pages in Folders view, and then apply the Web site's default theme to only the selected pages.

4. Change to Navigation view, add the Orange Pecan Bread (**pecan_br.htm**) and Orange Cake (**org_cake.htm**) pages as child pages of the Recipe Index page, and then add the Orange Icing page (**orgicing.htm**) as a child page of the Orange Cake page.

5. Open each new page that you imported into the Web site in Step 3 in Page view, and drag the position box as necessary to place it to the right of the bulleted list. Save each page as you finish it.

6. For the Orange Cake page, change the Orange Icing ingredient to a hyperlink to the Orange Icing page (**orgicing.htm**). Replace the text in the position box with the picture saved as **org_pic.jpg** in the Tutorial.07 folder. Absolutely position the picture to the right of the bulleted list in the Orange Cake page. (*Hint:* Select the text in the position box, and then insert the picture. With the picture selected, click the Position Absolutely button on the Pictures toolbar. Resize and move the picture as necessary to position it correctly.) Save the **org_pic.jpg** file in the Web site's images folder. (You will not insert pictures in the Orange Icing and Orange Pecan Bread Web pages.)

7. Assign the three pages that you imported in Step 3 to the New Recipes category. Open the Recipe Index page (**site_map.htm**) in Page view, and then preview the page in the browser. Make sure that the table of contents component correctly added the three new recipes below the New Recipes heading. Close the browser.

Explore ▶ 8. Use the Replace command to search all pages in the Web site to find all occurrences of the word "article" and replace them with the word "message." (*Hint:* Search all pages in the Web site, and click the Replace All button to make the changes automatically.)

9. Open the Submission Form Web page (**disc_post.htm**) in Page view. Change the "POST message" heading to "POST MESSAGE" and the Heading 1 style.

Explore ▶ 10. Make the following changes to the form component in the Submission Form Web page:

   a. Delete the comment component that appears to the right of the Category drop-down box form field.

   b. Change the label for the Subject text box to "Message Subject:". (Do not change the name of the text box form field.) Change the width of the Subject text box form field to 65 characters.

   c. Change the label for the From text box to "From (please type your first and last names):". (Do not change the name of the text box form field.) Change the width of the From text box form field to 65 characters.

   d. Enter the following label to the left of the drop-down box form field: "Select a category for your comments:" Press the spacebar twice to insert two spaces, and then change the new label to bold. Delete the existing "Category:" label and the line on which it appears. Change the properties of the drop-down box form field to include the following choices: Recipe Enhancement, Recipe Correction, Recipe Comment, General Cooking, and Other. The value for each choice should be the same as its choice name, but with any spaces omitted. The Recipe Enhancement choice should be the default selection. The drop-down box form field should have a height of 1 and should not allow multiple selections.

   e. Change the width of the Comments text area to 65 characters.

   f. Change the default value/label of the form's Submit button to "Post Message."

   g. Save your changes to the Submission Form Web page, and then preview the page using the browser. (If necessary, use the Refresh button to reload the current version of the page, which includes the theme.) Use your browser to print the form's HTML code, and then close the browser. On the printout, circle the HTML code that implemented the changes you made in Step 10.

Explore ▶ 11. Return to FrontPage and examine the form properties for the Submission Form Web page. What is the name of the form handler that processes this form? Click the Cancel button to close the dialog box without making any changes.

Explore

12. Open the Confirmation Web page (**disc_cfrm.htm**) in Page view. Change the "CONFIRMATION" heading to the Heading 1 style. Press the End key to reposition the insertion point, and then press the Enter key to insert a new line. On the new line, type "Dear", press the spacebar, and then insert a confirmation field that uses the name entered in the From field in the Submission Form. (*Hint:* Click the Web Component button on the Standard toolbar, scroll down and click the Advanced Controls Component type, and then click the Confirmation Field control. Click the Finish button, and then type the name of the form field to be inserted. The confirmation field's name is From.) Type a comma after the confirmation field component. Save the Confirmation Web page.

13. Open the Search Form Web page (**disc_srch.htm**) in Page view. Change the "SEARCH FOR message" heading to "SEARCH FOR MESSAGE" and the Heading 1 style. Change the width of the Search for text box to 50 characters. Save the Search Form page.

14. Open the home page in Page view, and then change the link bar component so that it contains links to child pages. Save the home page, and then preview it in a browser, verifying that all pages work correctly. Use the browser to print the Submission Form Web page. (*Hint:* You will need to post a new message to print this page; type your name in the From text box.)

15. Close the browser, the **recipes** Web site, and FrontPage.

CASE PROBLEMS

Case 1. Creating a Discussion Group for Royal Hair Care Products   Royal Hair Care Products, established in 1984, is a leader in hair care products for women, men, and children. Its current product line includes shampoos, conditioners, hair sprays, and styling gels. The company's newest product is Quick Dry Solution; when applied to wet hair, this solution dries it quickly without the need for a hair dryer. Quick Dry Solution is available in either a gel form or a liquid spray. The easy-to-use product leaves hair feeling natural and manageable.

Valerie Suarez, president of Royal Hair Care Products, and Nathan Dubois, an information systems specialist, are responsible for creating and maintaining the Web site for Royal Hair Care Products. This Web site currently includes the following main pages: a home page; an About Us page with distribution, promotion, packaging, and legal information; a Financial Information page with information about the company's financial performance and stock; a What's New page with information about Quick Dry Solution; a Feedback page that contains a form for commenting about Royal Hair Care Products; and a Search page that lets users search the Web site using a keyword or phrase.

Valerie wants to expand the Web site to include a discussion group where consumers can comment about Royal Hair Care Products and industry trends. As a progressive company, Royal Hair Care Products is always looking for new product ideas that will save people time and money and keep them looking their best.

If necessary, start FrontPage, insert your Data Disk in the appropriate disk drive, and then do the following:

1. Read all the questions for this case problem, and then prepare a planning analysis sheet for the enhancements to the Web site.

2. Open the **royal** Web site from the server. (*Note:* The files for the **royal** Web site must be installed on the Web server before you can complete this case problem. Contact your instructor or technical support person for assistance.) Change the Web site's settings to enable it with the FrontPage Server Extensions, for Internet Explorer and Navigator versions 5.0 and later, and for Microsoft Internet Information Server 3.0 and later.

3. Use the Discussion Web Wizard to add a discussion group to the Web site. The discussion group should have the following features:

   a. It should include all of the main features (Submission Form, Table of Contents, Search Form, Threaded Replies, and a Confirmation Page).
   b. The title of the discussion group is Royal Discussion. The discussion folder name is _disc.
   c. Choose the Subject, Product, and Comments input fields for the Submission Form.
   d. The discussion group is not protected.
   e. Sort the messages in order from newest to oldest.
   f. Do not replace the existing home page in the **royal** Web site.
   g. The Search Form should report only the Subject for matching documents.
   h. Use a dual interface frames page.

4. Open the Submission Form Web page (**disc_post.htm**) in Page view. Change the form component as follows:

   a. Delete the comment component that appears to the right of the drop-down box form field, and delete the "Product:" label and the line on which it appears from the form component.
   b. Enter the following label to the left of the drop-down box form field: "Select a category for your comments:" Press the spacebar twice to insert two spaces, and then change the new label to bold. Change the properties of the drop-down box form field to include the following choices: Suggestion, Feedback, Quick Dry Solution, Shampoo, Conditioner, Hair Spray, and Styling Gel. The default selected entry should be Suggestion. The value for each choice should be the same as its choice name, but with any spaces omitted. The drop-down box form field should have a height of 1 and should not allow multiple selections.
   c. Change the width of the Comments text area to 75 characters.
   d. Save the page.

5. Add the Royal Discussion Welcome page (**disc_welc.htm**) to the navigation structure as a child page of the home page. Position the Royal Discussion Welcome page to the right of the Search page.

6. Open the Royal Discussion Welcome page in Page view, and then replace the existing "WELCOME" heading with a centered page banner that uses the default settings. On a new, centered line below the page banner, insert a FrontPage link bar with text links separated by dots to same-level pages and to the home page. (The link bar might span two lines in Page view.)

7. Place the insertion point at the end of the first line of text in the Royal Discussion Welcome page ("This is an on-line discussion forum called Royal Discussion."). Press the spacebar, and then insert the following text: "We encourage you to use this discussion group to comment on Royal Hair Care Products, to offer your suggestions, and to ask questions about product usage. Other users can reply to your comments and share their experiences. Please use the Search option to find topics of interest." Save the page.

Explore

8. Modify the header for all pages in the discussion group to change the existing heading to "Royal Hair Care Products" and to add a hyperlink to the Royal Discussion Welcome page. Change the existing Home hyperlink to "Royal Home Page." (*Hint:* To access the header files for the discussion Web pages, display the Web site's hidden folders. You will need to make this change in both header files for the discussion group pages.) Save your changes.

9. Open the home page (**Default.htm**) in a browser. Use the link bar to open the Royal Discussion Welcome page, and then print it.

10. Use a hyperlink in the Royal Discussion Welcome page to post a new message using data that you make up. Before posting the message, print the Submission Form Web page. After submitting the form, click the link in the Confirmation page to refresh the main page.

11. Post another new message to the discussion group (do not reply to the message that you posted in Step 10). Refresh the main page, and then print only the Contents page. Close the browser.

12. Use FrontPage to print the Submission Form page and its HTML code. On the print-out of the HTML code, circle the code for the changes that you made to this page.

13. Close the **royal** Web site, and then close FrontPage.

Case 2. Creating an Online Forum for Buffalo Trading Post   Buffalo Trading Post (BTP) is a regional retail clothing business that specializes in buying, selling, and trading used clothing. The company buys all of its merchandise from people who bring items to one of BTP's trading post stores. BTP accepts only clothing in good condition for resale, and it attracts a loyal following of fashion enthusiasts and bargain hunters.

Donna Vargas, BTP's president, and Karla Perez, a systems analyst, are the primary developers of the Web site. This Web site currently includes the following main pages: a home page; a "What" page that lists the top 10 selling items in different categories; a "How" page that describes how BTP buys and sells merchandise; a "Who" page that describes the history of BTP; a "Where" page that provides a toll-free number for locating a BTP store; and a "Contact" page that includes a form component for submitting comments and feedback to BTP.

Donna and Karla met with a group of sales representatives from different stores and learned that many clothing genres have a distinct customer following. In response, Donna proposed creating an online forum in the BTP Web site that would permit customers to interact with one another. In addition to providing a service to customers, BTP would benefit from the free nature of the comments and could use this information to spot emerging fashion trends.

If necessary, start FrontPage, insert your Data Disk in the appropriate disk drive, and then do the following:

1. Read all the questions for this case problem, and then prepare a planning analysis sheet for the enhancements to the Web site.

2. Open the **buffalo** Web site from the server. (*Note:* The files for the **buffalo** Web site must be installed on the Web server before you can complete this case problem. Contact your instructor or technical support person for assistance.) Change the Web site's settings to enable it with the FrontPage Server Extensions, for Internet Explorer and Navigator versions 5.0 and later, and for Microsoft Internet Information Server 3.0 and later.

3. Use the Discussion Web Wizard to add a discussion group to the Web site. The discussion group should have the following features:
   a. It should include all of the main features (Submission Form, Table of Contents, Search Form, Threaded Replies, and a Confirmation Page).
   b. The title of the discussion group is Fashion Trends. The discussion folder name is _disc.
   c. Choose the Subject, Category, and Comments input fields for the Submission Form.
   d. The discussion group is not protected.

    e. Sort the messages in order from newest to oldest.

    f. Do not replace the existing home page in the **buffalo** Web site.

    g. The Search Form should report only the Subject for matching documents.

    h. Use a dual interface frames page.

Explore

4. Open the Submission Form Web page (**disc_post.htm**) in Page view. Change the form component as follows:

    a. Delete the comment component that appears to the right of the drop-down box form field, and delete the existing "Category:" label and the line on which it appears.

    b. Enter the following label to the left of the drop-down box form field: "Select a category for your comments:" Press the spacebar twice to insert two spaces, and then change the new label to bold. Change the properties of the drop-down box form field to include the following choices: The Sixties, The Seventies, The Eighties, The Nineties, and Requests. The value for each choice should be the same as its choice name, but with any spaces omitted. The default selected entry should be Requests, and this choice should appear first in the list. The drop-down box form field should have a height of 1 and should not allow multiple selections.

    c. Change the width of the Comments text area to 70 characters and the number of lines to 5.

    d. Change the properties of the discussion form handler so that it will collect the date and time that the message was posted and the user name of the person who posted the form. (*Hint:* Right-click the form component to open the shortcut menu, click Form Properties, and then click the Options button.)

    e. Save the page.

5. Add the Fashion Trends Welcome page (**disc_welc.htm**) for the discussion group to the navigation structure as a child page of the home page. Position the Fashion Trends Welcome page to the right of the Contact page.

6. Open the Fashion Trends Welcome page in Page view, and then change the existing "WELCOME" heading to a centered page banner with the default settings. On a new, centered line below the page banner, insert a FrontPage link bar based on the navigation structure; the links should use the page's theme and target same-level pages and the home page. Return to Navigation view, and then change the page title for the Fashion Trends Welcome page to "Fashion Forum."

7. Rewrite the default content in the Fashion Forum page that the Wizard created to make it more closely match Donna's vision of how visitors might use this page. Do not change the default hyperlinks. Save the page.

8. Change the background picture used in the Web site's theme to **toptxtr.jpg**; this file is saved in the Tutorial.07 folder on your Data Disk. Save the revised theme using the suggested name.

9. Open the Fashion Forum Web page (**disc_welc.htm**) in the browser, and then print the page.

10. Post a new message to the discussion group using data that you make up. Before posting the message, print the page. Click the link in the Confirmation page to refresh the main page.

Explore

11. Reply to the message that you posted in Step 10. Return to FrontPage, open the Contents page (**tocproto.htm**) in Page view, and then print its HTML code. On the printout, circle the HTML code that inserted the message you posted in Step 10.

12. Close the **buffalo** Web site, FrontPage, and the browser.

Case 3. Creating a Site Map for Garden Grill   Garden Grill is a national chain of casual, full-service restaurants. Its moderately priced menu features delicious dishes taken from various locations around the world. Shannon Taylor and Nolan Simmons manage the company's Web site. This Web site currently includes the following main pages: a home page; a Franchise Information page with information about opening a new restaurant; a Company Profile page with information about the restaurant; a Career Opportunities page with information about current employment opportunities; a Feedback page that allows customers to comment on the restaurant; and a Search page that customers can use to search the site.

Nolan wants to add several new pages to the Web site featuring new entrees at the restaurant. After adding these pages, he wants to create a site map to make it easier for the Web site's visitors to locate new pages. Finally, Nolan wants to include pictures of the new entrees along with their descriptions.

If necessary, start FrontPage, insert your Data Disk in the appropriate disk drive, and then do the following:

1. Read all the questions for this case problem, and then prepare a planning analysis sheet for the enhancements to the Web site.

2. Open the **garden** Web site from the server in Folders view. (*Note:* The files for the **garden** Web site must be installed on the Web server before you can complete this case problem. Contact your instructor or technical support person for assistance.) Change the Web site's settings to enable it with the FrontPage Server Extensions, for Internet Explorer and Navigator versions 5.0 and later, and for Microsoft Internet Information Server 3.0 and later.

3. Import the files **angel.htm**, **pasta.htm**, **pudding.htm**, and **pecan.htm** from the Tutorial.07 folder on your Data Disk into the Web site. Select these files in Folders view, and then apply the Web site's default theme to the pages.

Explore

4. Create the following categories in the Web site: Appetizers, Desserts, Entrees, Specials, Sandwiches, and New Menu Items. Delete all other default categories from the Web site.

5. Examine each page in the Web site. Assign those pages containing a menu item or dealing with general menu categories to an appropriate category. (*Hint:* You can assign a page to a category from Page view by clicking File on the menu bar and then clicking Properties.) Categorize the pages that you imported in Step 3 as both new menu items and the appropriate category for the featured food item.

6. Run a report to check the pages in the Web site to confirm that you assigned the pages containing menu items and menu information to the appropriate categories.

7. In Page view, add a new Normal page to the Web site with the filename **site_map.htm** and the title "Menu Options." After saving the page, add it to the Web site's navigation structure as a child page of the home page. Position the page to the right of the Franchise Information page in the navigation structure.

Explore

8. Add each page that you imported in Step 3 (**pecan.htm**, **angel.htm**, **pudding.htm**, and **pasta.htm**) and each existing food page (**appetize.htm**, **dessert.htm**, **entrees.htm**, **sandwich.htm**, and **special.htm**) to the Web site's navigation structure as a child page of the Menu Options page. In four of these pages (**pecan.htm**, **angel.htm**, **pudding.htm**, and **pasta.htm**), use absolute positioning to center a photo below the existing text. Use the photos **p_pie**, **p_angel**, **p_puddng**, and **p_pasta** in the Pecan Pie, Angel Food Cake, Banana Pudding, and Pasta Salad Web pages, respectively. These picture files are saved in the Tutorial.07 folder on your Data Disk. After positioning each picture, save the picture in the Web site's images folder.

9. Create the content of the Menu Options page using the categories you created in Step 4. Use any design that you like, but make sure that the new menu items appear at the top of the page. Use the appropriate FrontPage component to list the pages based on their categories. When you are finished, save the page, preview it in the browser, and then print it. Use a hyperlink in the Menu Options page to open the Pasta Salad Web page in the browser. Use the browser to print the page and its HTML code. On the printout of the code, circle the HTML code that identifies this page's category as well as the code that absolutely positions the picture in this page.

10. Close the browser, the **garden** Web site, and FrontPage.

Explore

Case 4. Creating a Discussion Group for Replay Music Factory Replay Music Factory (RMF) is a regional music store that specializes in buying, selling, and trading used compact discs (CDs). RMF buys used CDs from three sources: the Internet, customers, and brokers. This strategy allows RMF to offer a wide variety of music to its highly discriminating listeners. The company's quality control division keeps the firm's defect rate below 1%, so all of its products are 100% guaranteed.

Charlene Fields, the company's president, and Alec Johnston, a systems analyst, are in charge of the content and development of RMF's Web site. This Web site currently includes the following main pages: a home page; a Specials page for special buys on CDs in three categories (country & western, classic rock, and contemporary music); a frequently asked questions page; a page explaining how RMF conducts business; a feedback page with a form for submitting comments to RMF; and a search page that lets users search the site using key terms.

Charlene wants to expand the current Web site by creating a discussion group that will enable RMF to monitor current trends in the music industry.

If necessary, start FrontPage, insert your Data Disk in the appropriate disk drive, and then do the following:

1. Read all the questions for this case problem, and then prepare a planning analysis sheet for the enhancements to the Web site.

2. Open the **replay** Web site from the server. (*Note:* The files for the **replay** Web site must be installed on the Web server before you can complete this case problem. Contact your instructor or technical support person for assistance.) Change the Web site's settings to enable it with the FrontPage Server Extensions, for Internet Explorer and Navigator versions 5.0 and later, and for Microsoft Internet Information Server 3.0 and later.

3. Use the Discussion Web Wizard to add a discussion group to the Web site. The discussion group should have the following features:
   a. It should include all of the main features except for Threaded Replies.
   b. The title of the discussion group is Music Trends. The discussion folder name is _disc.
   c. Choose the Subject, Category, and Comments input fields for the Submission Form.
   d. The discussion group is not protected.
   e. Sort the messages in order from newest to oldest.
   f. Do not replace the existing home page in the **replay** Web site.
   g. The Search Form should report only the Subject for matching documents.
   h. Use a dual interface frames page.

4. Open the Submission Form Web page (**disc_post.htm**) in Page view. Change the form component as follows:

   a. Delete the comment component that appears to the right of the drop-down box form field, and delete the existing "Category:" label and the line on which it appears.

   b. Enter the following label to the left of the drop-down box form field: "Select a category:" Press the spacebar twice to insert two spaces, and then change the new label to bold. Change the properties of the drop-down box form field to include the following choices: Purchase, Trade, Sell, and Other. The default selected entry should be Sell, and this choice should appear first in the list. The value for each choice should be the same as its choice name. The drop-down box form field should have a height of 1 and should not allow multiple selections.

   c. Change the width of the Comments text area to 75 characters and the number of lines to 4.

   d. Change the properties of the discussion form handler so that it collects the date and time that the message was posted and the user name of the person who posted the form. (*Hint:* Right-click the form component to open the shortcut menu, click Form Properties, and then click the Options button.)

   e. Save the page.

5. Add the Music Trends Welcome Web page (**disc_welc.htm**) to the navigation structure as a child page of the home page. Position the Welcome page to the right of the Search page. Open the Music Trends Welcome Web page in Page view, and add a centered page banner and a centered link bar at the top of the page. The link bar should include links to same-level pages and to the home page, with the hyperlinks formatted using the page's theme.

6. In Navigation view, rename the Music Trends Welcome Web page (**disc_welc.htm**) as "Music Trends."

7. Rewrite the default content in the Music Trends Web page created by the Wizard make the text more closely match how visitors might use this page. Do not change the default hyperlinks. Save the page.

8. For each page created by the Discussion Web Wizard, change the page's title (which appears in all uppercase letters) to centered and the Heading 1 style. Save each page.

9. Open the Music Trends Web page in a browser, and then print the page.

10. Post a new message to the discussion group using data that you make up. Before posting the message, print the page. Click the link in the Confirmation page to refresh the main page.

11. Can you reply to the message that you posted in Step 10? If not, why not?

12. Close the browser, the **replay** Web site, and FrontPage.

QUICK CHECK ANSWERS

Session 7.1

1. False
2. True
3. site map
4. FrontPage uses the categories to insert hyperlinks to appropriate pages in the correct location in the Web page that contains the FrontPage table of contents component (the site map).
5. If you are the only author of the site, then you do not need to enable source control for the site, because no other author will be checking out and editing pages.
6. padlock
7. Close and save the page, right-click the filename in the Contents pane of Folders view, and then click Check In on the shortcut menu.
8. absolute positioning

Session 7.2

1. Answers will vary. You would probably want to secure the site to keep the discussion focused on topics that apply only to benefits administrators.
2. True
3. Discussion Web Wizard
4. Submission Form
5. The names of hidden folders begin with an underscore character.
6. Click Tools on the menu bar, click Web Settings, click the Advanced tab, click the Show hidden files and folders check box to select it, click the OK button, and then click the Yes button.
7. False
8. 00000001.htm
9. disc_head.htm

OBJECTIVES

In this tutorial you will:

- Start Access and open and examine a database

- Create a database connection to a Web site

- Verify a database connection and set a Web site to run scripts

- Insert a Database Results region in a Web page

- Use a Web page to query a database

- Create a form that sends data to an Access database

- Create and use a data access page

INTEGRATING
A DATABASE WITH A FRONTPAGE WEB SITE

Using Web Pages to View and Store Data in an Access Database

CASE

Sunny Morning Products

Tyler Vanauken is pleased with your progress in developing the recipes Web site. The process of adding new recipes to the site should be easy because FrontPage will automatically update the link bars in every page. New pages will use the same theme and have a consistent appearance thanks to the shared template that you created.

Tyler's next expansion of the Web site is to connect an existing database to the recipes Web site and then to compile an electronic guest book, which is similar to a guest book that you might find at a wedding reception or an open house. Tyler wants to collect information from visitors to the recipes Web site, who are customers of Sunny Morning Products. He will then use this information to create an electronic mailing list of people who want to receive promotional materials and notices of new recipes. Tyler realizes that direct marketing using e-mail addresses is much less expensive than using printed materials. In addition, he believes that the e-mail mailing list will be directed to a much more specific target audience, because the recipients have already used the Web site and expressed an interest in receiving additional materials.

To collect the information that Tyler needs, you will use a Web page to collect the Web site visitors' information. Instead of storing this information in a text file in the _private folder of the Web site, you will store the data in an Access database in the Web site. Data stored in a database is easily sorted, retrieved, and printed. Members of the marketing department, who will be the users of this database, will utilize this data for many purposes, including the e-mail mailing list. To make it easier for a user to view the data in the database, you will create a Web page that displays this information and lets the user update, add, delete, and sort records.

SESSION 8.1

In this session, you will learn about databases. You will start Access and open and examine a database. You will import a database into a Web site and use it in a Web page. Finally, you will use a Web page to query a database.

Understanding **Databases**

Databases

A **database**, or a **relational database**, is a collection of related **tables** that store data about an object. Each table is made up of fields and records. A **field** is a single characteristic of an object. The set of fields in a table related to one particular object makes up a **record**. For example, Sunny Morning Products currently maintains a database of items for sale at the Sunshine Country Store. This database contains two tables that store the product description, characteristics, cost, and selling price of each item. The Product table contains the fields ProductID, Name, Description, and Size. The Price table contains the fields ProductID, Cost, and RetailPrice.

The tables in a single database can be linked together—or *related*—using a common field. A **common field** appears in two or more tables in the database. For example, the Product and Price tables are linked together using a common field that identifies each item's product number (ProductID). Figure 8-1 shows the Product and Price tables and indicates how they are related.

Figure 8-1	RELATED TABLES IN A DATABASE

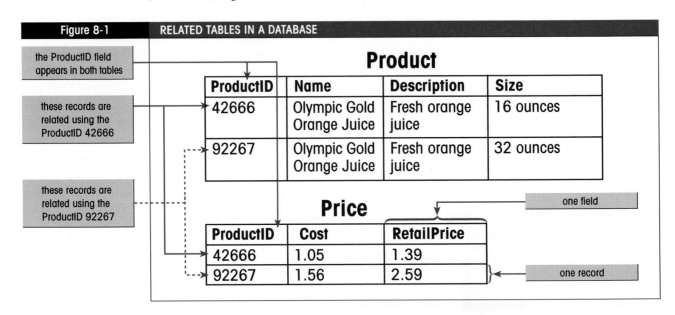

Microsoft Access 2002, or simply **Access**, is a relational database management program that enables you to create and maintain databases. Tyler used Access to create the recipes database using data collected by the Feedback Web page in the current Sunny Web site. This Web page collects each customer's first and last names, e-mail address, and comments about Sunny Morning Products. Tyler's staff was assigned the task of inputting information collected in the feedback.txt file in the _private folder of the Sunny Web site into the Access database. The information could not be easily imported directly from the feedback.txt file because it was not stored in the correct format. For example, Tyler's database stores the customer's name in two fields, FirstName and LastName, whereas the feedback.txt file stores the customer's name in one field, with the names separated by a space. The recipes database contains three tables: Customers, Category, and Subject.

Starting **Access and Opening an Existing Database**

Tyler wants you to open the recipes database and become familiar with its content and organization.

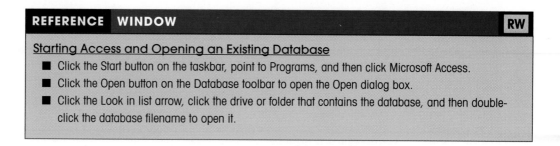

REFERENCE WINDOW   RW

Starting Access and Opening an Existing Database
- Click the Start button on the taskbar, point to Programs, and then click Microsoft Access.
- Click the Open button on the Database toolbar to open the Open dialog box.
- Click the Look in list arrow, click the drive or folder that contains the database, and then double-click the database filename to open it.

The recipes database is saved in the Tutorial.08 folder on your Data Disk.

To start Access and open the recipes database:

1. Click the **Start** button on the taskbar, point to **Programs,** and then click **Microsoft Access.** The Access 2002 start-up screen opens for a moment, and then the Microsoft Access program window opens.

2. Click the **Open** button 🗁 on the Database toolbar. The Open dialog box opens.

3. Click the **Look in** list arrow, change to the folder or drive that contains your Data Disk, double-click the **Tutorial.08** folder, and then double-click **recipes.** The recipes database opens in the Access program window.

4. Click the **Maximize** button ☐ on the Database window.

5. If necessary, click the **Tables** object in the Database window to display the tables list. See Figure 8-2.

Figure 8-2	DATABASE WINDOW FOR THE RECIPES DATABASE

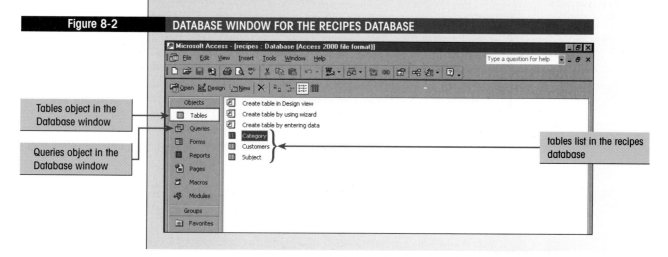

Tables object in the Database window

Queries object in the Database window

tables list in the recipes database

The recipes database contains three tables—Category, Customers, and Subject. The Category and Subject tables contain values that Access uses to look up the values in the Category and Subject fields in the Customers table. Tyler's design for the Customers table appears in Figure 8-3.

Figure 8-3	CUSTOMERS TABLE DESIGN IN THE RECIPES DATABASE		
FIELD NAME	**DATA TYPE**	**FIELD SIZE**	**DESCRIPTION**
CustomerID	AutoNumber	Long Integer	An Access AutoNumber field adds the CustomerID. CustomerIDs are assigned sequentially as new records are added to the table.
FirstName	Text	30	The customer's first name.
LastName	Text	30	The customer's last name.
EmailAddress	Text	50	The customer's e-mail address.
PhoneNum	Text	30	The customer's telephone number, which is entered in the format ##########. An input mask formats and stores the value in the format (###) ###-#### in the database.
Category	Text	50	A lookup field that selects any of the following values from the Category table: Web Site, Company, or Products.
Subject	Text	50	A lookup field that selects any of the following values from the Subject table: Suggestion, Praise, or Problem.

The recipes database also contains one query named Customer Feedback. A **query** is a database object that displays data to answer a question. For example, you might ask the question, "Which records in the Customers table have the value 'Praise' in the Subject field?" When you run this query, Access selects the records that answer your question. The Customer Feedback query, as you will see, lists all of the Customers table records; however, it lists those records in a specific order and displays only some of the fields for each record.

Next, you will examine the Customers table and the Customer Feedback query objects.

To open the table and query:

1. Double-click **Customers** in the tables list. The Customers table opens in Table Datasheet view, also called the Table window. See Figure 8-4. The Customers table contains 20 records, each of which has a unique CustomerID field value. The field that uniquely identifies each table record is called a **primary key**. Thus, the primary key of the Customers table is the CustomerID field, which is an AutoNumber field whose value was assigned by Access.

Figure 8-4   **CUSTOMERS TABLE IN TABLE DATASHEET VIEW**

field names (column headings)

current record indicator

Close Window button for the Table window

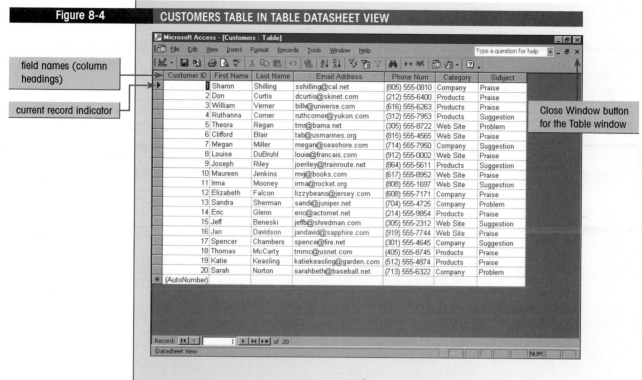

2. Click the **Close Window** button ⊠ on the menu bar to close the Table window. The Database window for the recipes database is displayed again.

3. Click the **Queries** object in the Database window to display the queries list, and then double-click **Customer Feedback** in the queries list to open the query in Query Datasheet view, also called the Query window. This query displays all records in the Customers table in ascending order by last name. The CustomerID values do not appear in the query results because the CustomerID field is not included in the query design. See Figure 8-5.

Figure 8-5   **CUSTOMER FEEDBACK QUERY IN THE QUERY WINDOW**

Close Window button for the Query window

Close button for the Microsoft Access program window

query results are sorted in alphabetical order by last name

the CustomerID field does not appear in the query results

the LastName column appears first in the query results

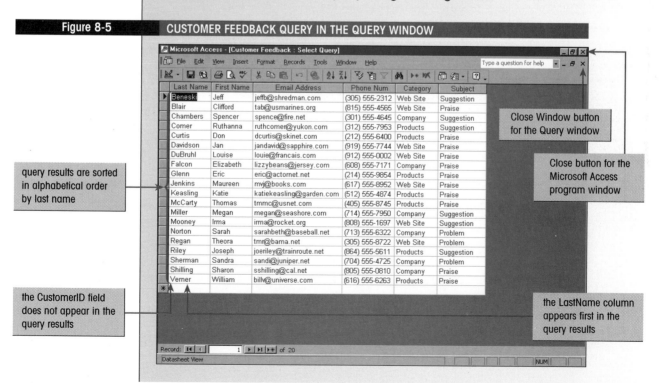

4. Click ☒ on the menu bar to close the Query window.

5. Click the **Close** button ☒ on the Access title bar to close both the recipes database and Access.

Tyler's planning analysis sheet for the incorporation of two databases into the recipes Web site appears in Figure 8-6. The recipes database is the first one that you will import into the recipes Web site.

Figure 8-6	TYLER'S PLANNING ANALYSIS SHEET FOR INCORPORATING A DATABASE

Planning Analysis Sheet

Objective

Create two database connections and new Web pages with the following capabilities: display records from the Customer Feedback query in the recipes database, filter the records in the Customer Feedback query in the recipes database using information supplied by the user, accept data entered in a form from a Web page and store it in the guest database, and display records from the Results table in the guest database.

Requirements

Access file for the recipes database

Access file for the guest database

Web page that contains a form component

Results

• A Web page that connects to a database and allows the marketing department to see who is using the Sunny Web site.

• A separate Web page stored in the recipes Web site into which customers can enter their names, e-mail addresses, phone numbers, and areas of interest. The marketing department will use this information to target advertising to the appropriate individuals and to plan future enhancements to the Web site.

• A new database that contains data about people who use the recipes Web site. The form will collect the person's name, address, city, state/province, postal code, country, phone number, and e-mail address and store this information in a database.

• A data access page that displays records from the guest database and that permits authorized employees to view, add, delete, sort, filter, and update records using a Web page.

Creating **a Database Connection**

You can import an existing database into a Web site by copying the database file in Windows Explorer and then pasting it into the open Web site. This method is an extremely easy way to integrate an existing database into a Web site because FrontPage creates the database connection for you. By creating a connection between a Web site and an Access database, you can display and query database data using a Web page. A **database connection** specifies the name, location, and type of database that you want to access. You can make four kinds of database connections between a FrontPage Web site and an Access database:

- A **file-based connection** is made when you import an Access database into a FrontPage Web site. FrontPage creates the database connection automatically when you import a database into it.

- A **System DSN** (or **System Data Source Name**) **connection** is made when you connect a database that is stored on a Web server to a FrontPage Web site.

- A **network connection** is made to a database server, which is a server that is dedicated to managing a database. Microsoft SQL Server is one example of a database server. (Database servers are beyond the scope of this tutorial.)

- A **custom connection** is one in which you use a file that contains the commands to define the necessary connection information between the database and the FrontPage Web site. (Creating a custom connection is beyond the scope of this tutorial.)

When you paste a database into a Web site, the Add Database Connection dialog box opens and requests a connection name for the database. After you provide a connection name and click the Yes button to continue, a Microsoft FrontPage dialog box opens and asks where to store your database files. When you import a database, FrontPage automatically creates a folder named **fpdb** (for FrontPage database) and configures it so that it is inaccessible to visitors of your published Web site.

REFERENCE   WINDOW   **RW**

Importing an Access Database into a Web Site
- Click the Start button on the taskbar, point to Programs, point to Accessories, and then click Windows Explorer.
- Browse to the database that you want to import into the Web site, right-click it to open the shortcut menu, and then click Copy. Close Windows Explorer.
- Start FrontPage and open the Web site in Folders view.
- Right-click the Folder List to open the shortcut menu, and then click Paste.
- Enter the database connection name, click the Yes button, and then click the Yes button again.

Tyler asks you to import the recipes database into the recipes Web site. First, you will copy the recipes database. You will then start FrontPage, open the recipes Web site, and paste the database into it.

To import an existing database into a Web site:

1. Click the **Start** button on the taskbar, point to **Programs**, point to **Accessories**, and then click **Windows Explorer**. Windows Explorer opens and displays the files and folders on your computer.

2. If necessary, open **My Computer** in the Folders list, and then click the **3½ Floppy (A:)** drive in the Folders list to display the contents of your Data Disk.

   TROUBLE? If your Data Files are stored in another location, click that location to display the contents of your Data Disk. This tutorial assumes that you are storing your Data Files on drive A.

3. Open the **Tutorial.08** folder to display its contents.

4. Right-click **recipes** (or **recipes.mdb** if Windows is configured to show filename extensions) to open its shortcut menu, and then click **Copy**. A copy of the recipes database is stored on the Windows Clipboard. You will close Windows Explorer before starting FrontPage.

5. Click the **Close** button ☒ on the Windows Explorer title bar to close it.

6. Start FrontPage, open the **recipes** Web site from the server, and then change to Folders view (if necessary).

7. Right-click any empty area in the Folder List to open the shortcut menu, and then click **Paste**. The Importing Files dialog box opens, and then the Add Database Connection dialog box opens on top of it. See Figure 8-7. You use the Add Database Connection dialog box to provide a name for the database connection. The URL for the database is its Windows filename. You can use the same connection name and URL for a database, although you need not do so.

Figure 8-7	ADD DATABASE CONNECTION DIALOG BOX

default database connection name

filename of the imported database

8. Type **Recipes** in the Name text box, and then click the **Yes** button. The Importing Files dialog box reappears, and the status bar indicates that FrontPage is creating the fpdb folder in which to store the database files. After a few seconds, a dialog box opens and asks whether you want to store your database files in the fpdb folder.

   TROUBLE? If a Microsoft FrontPage dialog box opens and tells you that the database name must be unique, then a database connection named Recipes already exists in your Web site. Click the OK button, change the database connection name to Recipes1 (or to another name that is not in use), and then click the Yes button to continue.

9. Click the **Yes** button. After a few seconds, the Importing Files dialog box closes. Folders view now shows the fpdb folder that FrontPage created. Notice that a new page named global.asa appears in the Contents pane (you might need to scroll down to see the filename). This file stores the VBScript that connects the Web site to the recipes database. A **VBScript** is a program written in the Visual Basic programming language that contains programming instructions for a Web page. The VBScript is embedded in the HTML document in which it resides so that Web browsers can read and execute its commands.

TROUBLE? If you do not see the Web's hidden folders in the Folder List, click Tools on the menu bar, click Web Settings, click the Advanced tab, click the Show hidden files and folders check box to select it, click the OK button, and then click the Yes button.

10. Click the **fpdb** folder in the Folder List to display its contents. The Access file for the recipes database is stored in this folder.

11. Click the folder for the **recipes** Web site (the default folder is http://localhost/recipes) in the Folder List to redisplay its contents.

Verifying a Database Connection

After importing the database, you can verify the database connection by using the Web Settings dialog box. When you **verify** a database connection, FrontPage tests the connection to ensure that it is properly configured.

REFERENCE   WINDOW   **RW**

Verifying a Database Connection
- Click Tools on the menu bar, click Web Settings, and then click the Database tab.
- Click the connection name in the list box, and then click the Verify button.
- Click the OK button.

To verify the database connection:

1. Click **Tools** on the menu bar, click **Web Settings**, and then click the **Database** tab. A question mark appears in the Status column for the recipes database, indicating that the database connection has not yet been verified.

2. Click the **Recipes** connection, and then click the **Verify** button. The question mark in the Status column changes to a green check mark, indicating a valid connection. See Figure 8-8.

Figure 8-8	WEB SETTINGS DIALOG BOX

check mark indicates a verified database connection

database connection name

click to remove the selected database connection

click to create a new database connection

click to modify the selected database connection

click to verify the selected database connection

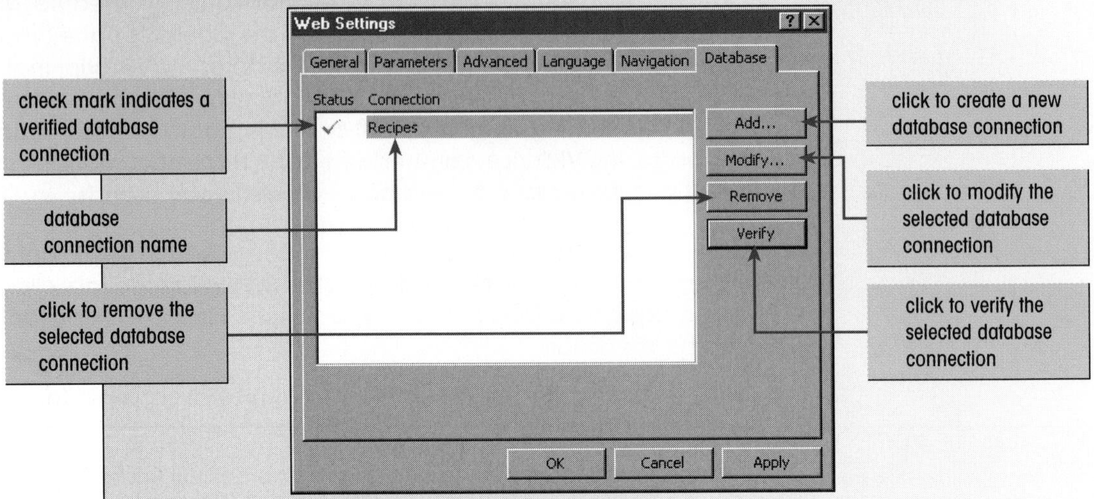

3. Click the **OK** button to close the Web Settings dialog box.

The recipes database now exists on the server as part of the recipes Web site; it also exists as a separate file in the Tutorial.08 folder on your Data Disk. These two files have the same name, but they are not linked in any way. As a result, if you open the recipes database from the Tutorial.08 folder on your Data Disk and make changes to it, the recipes database that is stored in your Web site will not reflect these changes. After you import a database into a Web site, it is important that you make changes only to the database that is stored in the fpdb folder in the Web site. To start Access and open the database stored in the Web site, just double-click the database filename in the fpdb folder.

Now that you have imported the recipes database into your Web site and verified its connection, you can create a new Web page and use the Database Results Wizard to display the Customer Feedback query in the recipes database in a Web page.

Setting the Web Site to Run Scripts

Before you can work with the Database Results Wizard, the Web site must be enabled to run Active Server Pages (ASP). An **Active Server Page** is a Web page with an .asp filename extension that includes client-side and server-side scripts that process the page. Because these scripts must be set to run on the server, you must also configure your Web site's folder to run scripts. A folder on a Web server that permits the execution of scripts is called an **executable folder**.

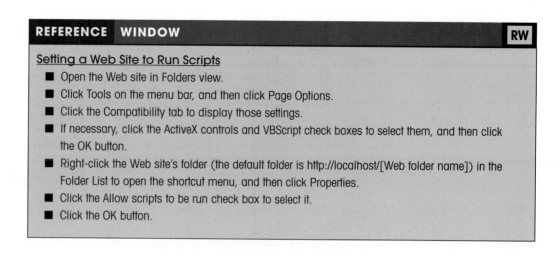

REFERENCE WINDOW   RW

Setting a Web Site to Run Scripts

- Open the Web site in Folders view.
- Click Tools on the menu bar, and then click Page Options.
- Click the Compatibility tab to display those settings.
- If necessary, click the ActiveX controls and VBScript check boxes to select them, and then click the OK button.
- Right-click the Web site's folder (the default folder is http://localhost/[Web folder name]) in the Folder List to open the shortcut menu, and then click Properties.
- Click the Allow scripts to be run check box to select it.
- Click the OK button.

You will change the recipes Web site's settings before using the Database Results Wizard to create the page. Normally, only the Web site's administrator can change a Web site's settings. If you are working on a server other than a Microsoft IIS, your instructor will provide you with alternative instructions.

To change the Web site's settings to run scripts:

1. Click **Tools** on the menu bar, and then click **Page Options**. The Page Options dialog box opens.

2. Click the **Compatibility** tab to display those settings.

3. If necessary, click the **Enabled with Microsoft FrontPage Server Extensions** check box to select it.

4. Make sure that every check box in the Available Technologies section contains a check mark. The Browser versions list box now shows the "Custom" setting. See Figure 8-9.

| Figure 8-9 | ENABLING SCRIPTS FOR THE RECIPES WEB SITE |

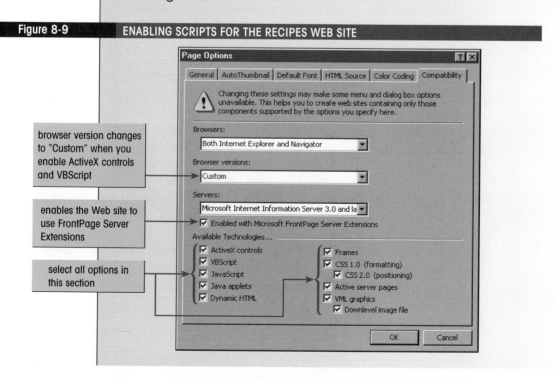

browser version changes to "Custom" when you enable ActiveX controls and VBScript

enables the Web site to use FrontPage Server Extensions

select all options in this section

5. Click the **OK** button to close the Page Options dialog box. You also need to configure the Web site's folder to allow scripts to be run.

6. Right-click the Web site's folder in the Folder List (the default folder is http://localhost/recipes) to open the shortcut menu, and then click **Properties**. The Properties dialog box for the recipes Web site opens.

7. If necessary, click the **Allow scripts to be run** and the **Allow files to be browsed** check boxes to select them, and then click the **OK** button. The Properties dialog box closes.

Now the Web site is configured to run scripts. Next, you will insert the Database Results region in a new Web page.

Inserting a Database Results Region in a Web Page

Tyler's planning analysis sheet indicates that you will create a new Web page and insert database data into it. When you insert data from a database into a Web page, FrontPage calls it a Database Results region. A **Database Results region** is a component in a Web page that contains HTML code and client-side and server-side scripts that retrieve and display database data in the Web page. After you insert the Database Results region, the Database Results Wizard starts. The **Database Results Wizard** asks you a series of questions about the database, the database object to be inserted, and special filters (if any) to be applied to that database object. A **filter** is a set of restrictions that you place on the records in a table or query to display a subset of a table's or query's records. For example, a filter might display records that contain the value TX in a State field to select only records for people who live in Texas. A filter differs from a query in that a filter only *temporarily* displays a subset of data.

REFERENCE WINDOW   **RW**

Using the Database Results Wizard to Insert a Database Results Region in a Web Page

- Open the existing page in which to insert the Database Results region in Page view, or create a new page in Page view.
- Position the insertion point where you want to insert the Database Results region.
- Click Insert on the menu bar, point to Database, and then click Results. The Database Results Wizard starts.
- Click the Use an existing database connection option button, and then, if necessary, click the list arrow and select the database name. Click the Next button.
- Click the Record source option button, click the list arrow, click the object in the database that contains the data you want to display, and then click the Next button.
- If necessary, click the Edit List button to select and/or reorder the desired fields to display in the Web page, and then click the OK button. To apply a filter to the records, click the More Options button, use the More Options dialog box to create the filter, and then click the OK button. Click the Next button.
- Select a formatting option for displaying the data, and then click the Next button.
- Select an option for displaying returned records in the Web page, and then click the Finish button.

After inserting a Database Results region in a Web page, you can change its properties to customize its default appearance to meet your needs.

To insert a Database Results region in a new Web page:

1. Click the **Page** button 🔲 on the Views bar to change to Page view, and then, if necessary, click the **Create a new normal page** button 🔲 on the Standard toolbar to create a new page. The new page uses the background picture from the Web site's theme and has the filename new_page_1.htm.

2. Click **Insert** on the menu bar, point to **Database**, and then click **Results**. The Database Results Wizard starts. By default, FrontPage assumes that you will use the Recipes database for your Database Results region, because the Recipes database connection is the only one in the Web site. See Figure 8-10.

Figure 8-10	USING AN EXISTING DATABASE CONNECTION

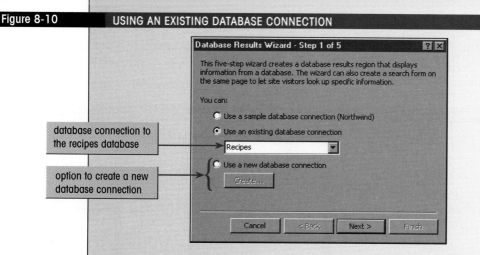

database connection to the recipes database

option to create a new database connection

3. Click the **Next** button. The second dialog box lets you specify the database object that contains the data to be used in the Web page. The recipes database contains four objects—the Customers, Subject, and Category tables, and the Customer Feedback query. The Category table is selected in the Record source list box because it is first alphabetically in the list of objects. If you don't find a suitable object in the list, you can open the database from the fpdb folder of the Web site and use Access to create the correct object, or you can click the Custom query option button and click the Edit button to create a query using SQL. You will use the existing Customer Feedback query object as the record source.

4. Click the **Record source** list arrow, and then click **Customer Feedback (VIEW)**. The "VIEW" notation indicates that you will see the query datasheet in the Web page.

5. Click the **Next** button to continue. The third dialog box lets you specify the fields to include in the Web page, their order, and an optional filter. See Figure 8-11. Tyler wants the person's phone number to be displayed in the third column of the Database Results region, so you need to change the field order.

Figure 8-11   SELECTING AND ORDERING THE FIELDS TO USE IN THE DATABASE RESULTS REGION

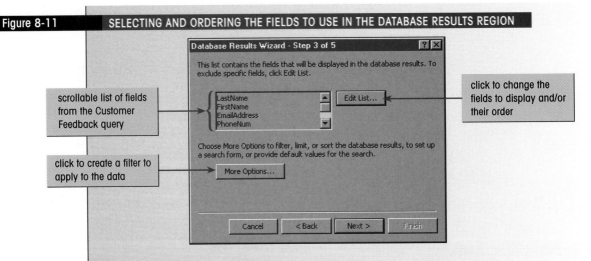

scrollable list of fields from the Customer Feedback query

click to change the fields to display and/or their order

click to create a filter to apply to the data

6. Click the **Edit List** button. The Displayed Fields dialog box opens. All fields from the Customer Feedback query appear in the Displayed fields list box. See Figure 8-12.

Figure 8-12   DISPLAYED FIELDS DIALOG BOX

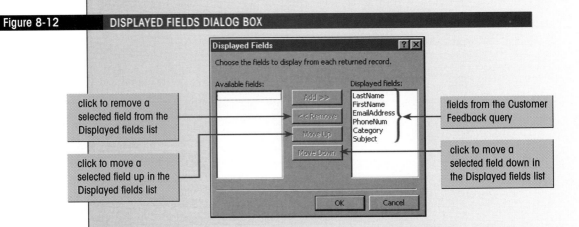

click to remove a selected field from the Displayed fields list

fields from the Customer Feedback query

click to move a selected field up in the Displayed fields list

click to move a selected field down in the Displayed fields list

7. Click the **PhoneNum** field in the Displayed fields list box, and then click the **Move Up** button. Now the PhoneNum field appears as the third entry in the list.

8. Click the **OK** button to close the Displayed Fields dialog box. You will not create a filter for the database region, so click the **Next** button to go to the next dialog box. See Figure 8-13. In this dialog box, you select the formatting options to use in the Web page. The default settings are to display one record from the database object in each row, to format the table in the results page using a border and a header row with the object's field names, and to expand the table to the width of the page. You will accept these settings.

Figure 8-13 | **SELECTING THE FORMATTING OPTIONS FOR THE DATABASE RESULTS REGION**

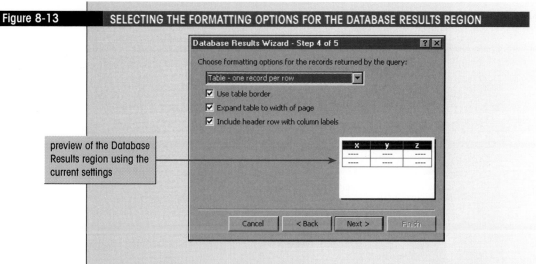

preview of the Database Results region using the current settings

9. Make sure that your default settings match those shown in Figure 8-13, and then click the **Next** button. The last dialog box lets you set the number of records to display in the results page. The default is to group five records on each results page.

10. If necessary, click the **Split records into groups** option button to select it, click in the **Split records into groups** text box, and then type **5**.

11. Click the **Finish** button. The Web page now contains a Database Results region. See Figure 8-14.

Figure 8-14 | **DATABASE RESULTS REGION IN THE WEB PAGE**

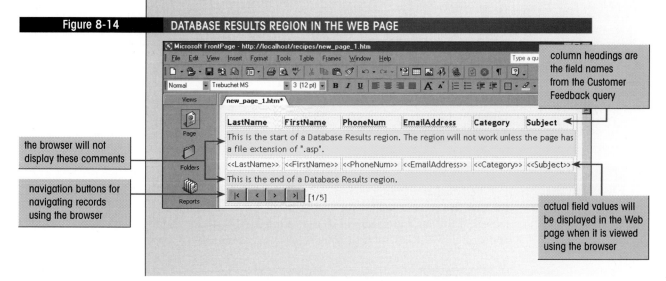

column headings are the field names from the Customer Feedback query

the browser will not display these comments

navigation buttons for navigating records using the browser

actual field values will be displayed in the Web page when it is viewed using the browser

Saving and Previewing the Database Results Region

FrontPage used the fonts and styles from the Web site's theme to format the Database Results region. Before previewing the page in the browser, you must save the page.

To save the Web page and preview it in the browser:

1. Click the **Save** button 🖫 on the Standard toolbar. The Save As dialog box opens.

2. Make sure that the **recipes** folder appears in the Save in list box, type **cust_qry** in the File name text box, make sure that the Save as type list box is set to **Active Server Pages**, and then click the **Save** button. The Web page now has an .asp filename extension, indicating that it is an Active Server Page. (The comment in the Database Results region reminds you that this page must have an .asp filename extension to work correctly.)

3. Click the **Preview in Browser** button 🔍 on the Standard toolbar to open the first results page in the browser. See Figure 8-15.

Figure 8-15	FIRST RESULTS PAGE IN THE BROWSER

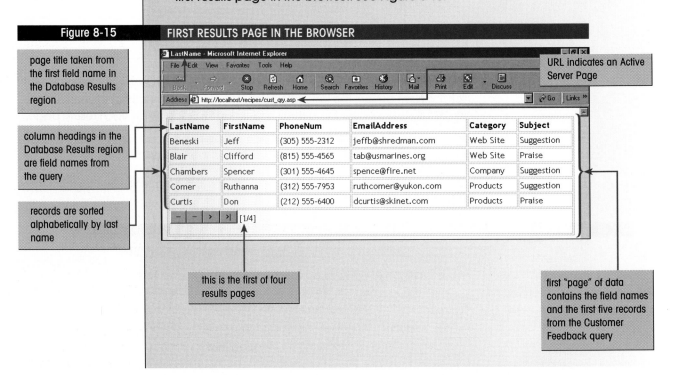

page title taken from the first field name in the Database Results region

column headings in the Database Results region are field names from the query

records are sorted alphabetically by last name

URL indicates an Active Server Page

this is the first of four results pages

first "page" of data contains the field names and the first five records from the Customer Feedback query

The Database Results region correctly grouped the records from the query and displayed the first five records in alphabetical order by last name. Notice that the PhoneNum column appears third, as you specified in the Wizard. Also notice the four navigation buttons that appear below the last record. You can click these buttons to scroll through the records.

To scroll the records:

1. Click the **Go to Next Page** button 🔳. The browser displays the second results page. The text "[2/4]" now appears to the right of the navigation buttons, indicating that you are viewing the records on the second of a total of four results pages. The first two navigation buttons, which you can use to navigate to an earlier results page, are now active. As you use the navigation buttons to scroll the records, the buttons change to reflect the current options.

TROUBLE? If an Internet Explorer dialog box opens and asks whether you want to send information to the local intranet, click the Yes button.

2. Click the **Go to Last Page** button ⧉ on the navigation bar. The browser displays the fourth (and final) results page.

3. Click the **Go to First Page** button ⧉. The browser redisplays the first results page.

Although the correct data is displayed, you can improve the appearance of this page. First, consider the page's title of "LastName," which is the first field name displayed in the Database Results region. You can change the page's title in Folders view to "Customer Feedback" to better reflect its content. Second, note that the column headings for the Database Results region are the field names from the Customer Feedback query. You can change these column headings to more meaningful names, and then format them with a more attractive style.

Changing the Page Title and Formatting the Database Results Region

Tyler asks you to return to FrontPage to correct the problems that you previously identified.

To change the page title and format the Database Results region:

1. Close the browser.

2. In FrontPage, click the **Folders** button ⧉ on the Views bar to change to Folders view.

3. Right-click **cust_qry.asp** in the Contents pane to select the page and to open the shortcut menu, click **Rename**, and then press the **Tab** key to select the page's title and change to editing mode.

4. Type **Customer Feedback** and then press the **Enter** key.

5. Click the **Page** button ⧉ on the Views bar to change to Page view.

Red, wavy lines appear under the LastName, FirstName, PhoneNum, and EmailAddress column headings, indicating that these words are not in the FrontPage dictionary. You can right-click a column heading to open a shortcut menu for the Spelling dialog box and then click a suggested replacement. Alternatively, you can edit a column heading just like any other text in the page.

6. Right-click the **LastName** column heading to open the shortcut menu, and then click **Last Name**. The column heading changes to "Last Name" and the red, wavy line disappears.

7. Right-click the **FirstName** column heading and click **First Name**, right-click the **EmailAddress** column heading and click **Email Address**, and then edit the PhoneNum field to change it to **Phone #**.

8. Select the first row in the Database Results region (the one that contains the column headings), click the **Style** list arrow on the Formatting toolbar, and then click **Heading 3**. The column headings change to the Heading 3 style.

9. With the column headings still selected, click the **Center** button ⧉ on the Formatting toolbar to center the headings.

10. Save the page and then preview it in a browser. See Figure 8-16. The Web page looks better with the new title, column headings, and formatting.

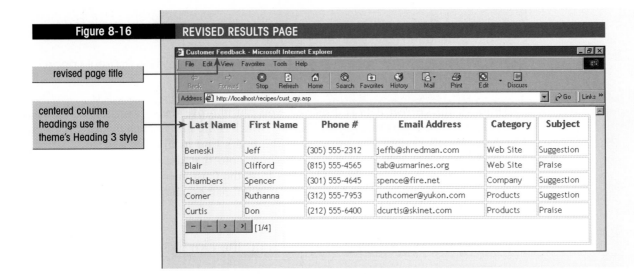

Figure 8-16   **REVISED RESULTS PAGE**

revised page title

centered column headings use the theme's Heading 3 style

Last Name	First Name	Phone #	Email Address	Category	Subject
Beneski	Jeff	(305) 555-2312	jeffb@shredman.com	Web Site	Suggestion
Blair	Clifford	(815) 555-4565	tab@usmarines.org	Web Site	Praise
Chambers	Spencer	(301) 555-4645	spence@fire.net	Company	Suggestion
Comer	Ruthanna	(312) 555-7953	ruthcomer@yukon.com	Products	Suggestion
Curtis	Don	(212) 555-6400	dcurtis@skinet.com	Products	Praise

[1/4]

Using a Web Page to Query a Database

In addition to displaying all of the records from a database object, such as a query, you might want to let users search for specific records within an object. You can do so by creating a page that contains a Database Results region and a search form.

Tyler asks you to create another Web page to display only those records from the Customer Feedback query that match a category entered by the user. Instead of re-creating the Database Results region, you will copy the existing Customer Feedback Web page, rename its filename and title, and then create a search form in the new page.

To create a copy of a Web page and change its filename and title:

1. Close the browser, and then click the **Close** button ⊠ on the Contents pane to close the Customer Feedback page.

2. Click the **Folders** button 🗀 on the Views bar to change to Folders view.

3. Right-click **cust_qry.asp** in the Contents pane to open its shortcut menu, and then click **Copy**.

4. Right-click any open area of the Contents pane to open the shortcut menu, and then click **Paste**. FrontPage creates a new Web page named cust_qry_copy(1).asp and titled Customer Feedback. (You might need to scroll down the Contents pane to see the new filename.) You will rename this page, and then open it in Page view.

5. Right-click **cust_qry_copy(1).asp** in the Contents pane to select it and to open the shortcut menu, click **Rename** to change to editing mode, type **custsrch.asp**, press the **Tab** key to select the page title and change to editing mode, press the **End** key, press the **spacebar**, type **Search**, and then press the **Enter** key. The new Web page is now named custsrch.asp, and its title is "Customer Feedback Search."

6. Double-click **custsrch.asp** to open the Customer Feedback Search page in Page view. This page contains a copy of the Database Results region that you created in the Customer Feedback page.

Now that you have copied and renamed the page, you can run the Database Results Wizard again to create the search form.

Creating a Search Form to Query a Database

The search form that you will create to let users query the database is similar to the search form used to search a Web site for keywords. You must rerun the Database Results Wizard to create the search form. FrontPage will program the search form to query the database using the object from the database that you specify.

REFERENCE WINDOW   **RW**

Creating a Search Form in a Web Page That Queries a Database

- Open the existing page that contains a Database Results region. Right-click the Database Results region to open the shortcut menu, and then click Database Results Properties. The Database Results Wizard starts.

or

- Create a new Web page, click Insert on the menu bar, point to Database, and then click Results. The Database Results Wizard starts.
- Confirm or set the options in the first two dialog boxes.
- In the third dialog box (Step 3 of 5), click the More Options button. The More Options dialog box opens.
- Click the Criteria button to open the Criteria dialog box.
- Click the Add button. The Add Criteria dialog box opens.
- Select the field name and comparison operator to use in the query.
- Click the Use this search form field check box to select it.
- Click the OK button. Click the Add button to specify additional criteria (if necessary), or click the OK button to close the Criteria dialog box.
- Click the OK button to close the More Options dialog box.
- Confirm or set the options in the remaining dialog boxes, and then click the Finish button.

To create a search form in a page that queries a database:

1. Double-click the Database Results region. The Database Results Wizard starts.

2. Click the **Next** button twice to advance to the dialog box that contains the text "Step 3 of 5" in the title bar.

3. Click the **More Options** button. The More Options dialog box opens.

4. Click the **Criteria** button. The Criteria dialog box opens.

5. Click the **Add** button. The Add Criteria dialog box opens. See Figure 8-17. You need to specify the Category field as the search field. Stated in FrontPage language, you must specify that *Category equals Category*, which means that only those records whose Category field value matches the category entered by the user in the search text box will be displayed in the results page.

| Figure 8-17 | CREATING A FILTER FOR A DATABASE RESULTS REGION |

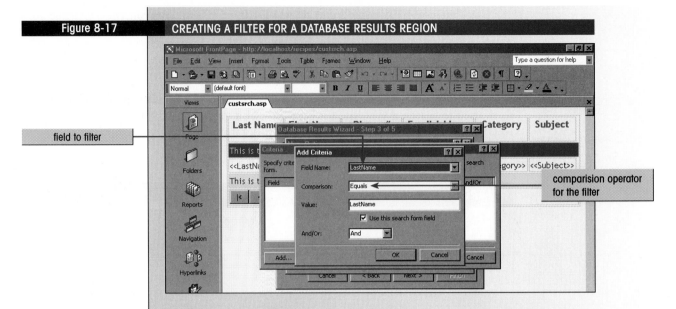

field to filter

comparision operator
for the filter

6. Click the **Field Name** list arrow, and then click **Category**. The Comparison list box should display the operator "Equals" and the Value text box should display the field name "Category."

7. If necessary, click the **Use this search form field** check box to select it, and then click the **OK** button. The Add Criteria dialog box closes, and the Criteria dialog box displays the filter criteria. See Figure 8-18. You could specify additional criteria by clicking the Add button again. However, Tyler needs to search using only the Category field, so you can finish the Database Results Wizard now.

| Figure 8-18 | CRITERIA DIALOG BOX |

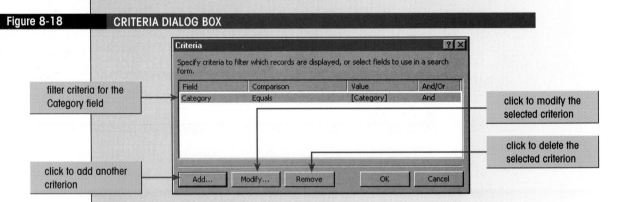

filter criteria for the
Category field

click to modify the
selected criterion

click to delete the
selected criterion

click to add another
criterion

8. Click the **OK** button to close the Criteria dialog box, click the **OK** button to close the More Options dialog box, click the **Next** button twice, and then click the **Finish** button. The Database Results Wizard closes, and the Customer Feedback Search page now displays the search form. See Figure 8-19.

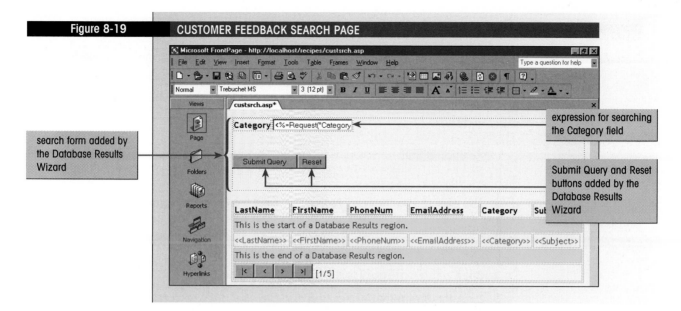

Figure 8-19   CUSTOMER FEEDBACK SEARCH PAGE

search form added by the Database Results Wizard

expression for searching the Category field

Submit Query and Reset buttons added by the Database Results Wizard

The Database Results Wizard reset the column headings in the Database Results region to their field-name equivalents from the query. Next, you will change the column headings to make them match the ones in the Customer Feedback Web page.

To change and format the column heading names:

1. Right-click the **LastName** column heading to open the shortcut menu and click **Last Name**, right-click the **FirstName** column heading and click **First Name**, right-click the **EmailAddress** column heading and click **Email Address**, and then edit the PhoneNum field to change it to **Phone #**.

2. Select the first row in the Database Results region (the one that contains the column headings), click the **Style** list arrow on the Formatting toolbar, and then click **Heading 3**. The column headings change to the Heading 3 style.

3. With the column headings still selected, click the **Center** button ▤ on the Formatting toolbar to center the headings.

You can test the search form by saving the page and opening it in the browser.

To test the database search form:

1. Save the page and then preview it in the browser. See Figure 8-20.

Figure 8-20 | CUSTOMER FEEDBACK SEARCH PAGE IN THE BROWSER

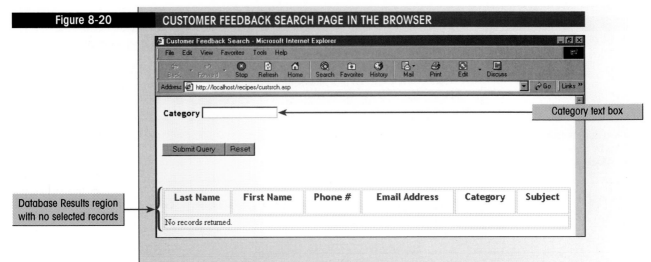

2. Click in the **Category** text box, and then type **Web Site**.

3. Click the **Submit Query** button. The browser displays the first of the two results pages containing records that match your request. Each record contains the value "Web Site" in the Category column. See Figure 8-21.

Figure 8-21 | QUERY RESULTS USING THE "WEB SITE" FILTER

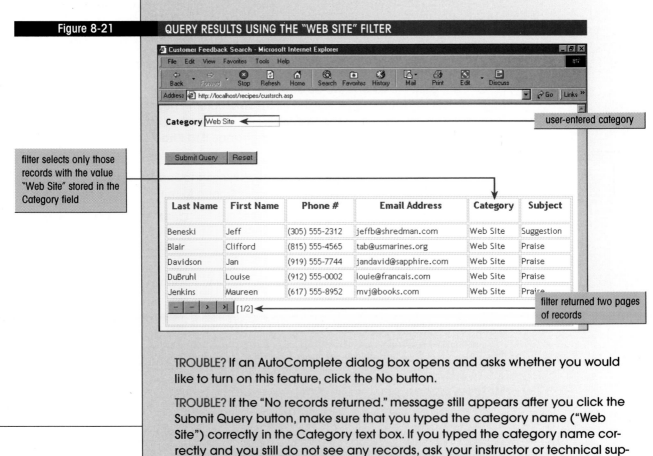

TROUBLE? If an AutoComplete dialog box opens and asks whether you would like to turn on this feature, click the No button.

TROUBLE? If the "No records returned." message still appears after you click the Submit Query button, make sure that you typed the category name ("Web Site") correctly in the Category text box. If you typed the category name correctly and you still do not see any records, ask your instructor or technical support person for help.

4. Select the text in the Category text box, type **Products**, and then click the **Submit Query** button. The browser displays the first results page of records containing the value "Products" in the Category field.

The query works correctly, but you realize that users will need some instructions for using this page. Otherwise, users will not know what the Category values are. You can add the instruction text to the page in Page view.

To add text to the Customer Feedback Search page:

1. Close the browser.

2. Press **Ctrl + Home** to move the insertion point to the top of the page, and then press the **Enter** key to insert a new line. The insertion point appears on the new blank line.

3. Type the following text on the new line: **Type one of the following categories in the Category text box, and then click the Submit Query button: Web Site, Products, or Company.**

4. Save the page and then preview it in the browser. See Figure 8-22. Now users of the page will know how to submit queries.

| Figure 8-22 | REVISED CUSTOMER FEEDBACK SEARCH PAGE |

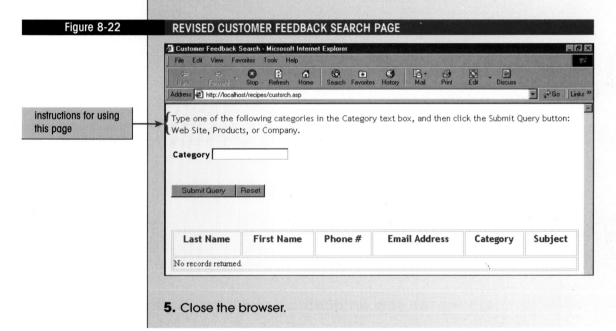

instructions for using this page

5. Close the browser.

The real power and utility of the connection to a database derive from the ability to query the database stored on the server after changes have been made to it. Next, you will update the database and use the same Web page to view the changes.

Updating a Database and Viewing the Changes in a Web Page

As more people visit the Sunny Web site, more names will be added to the Customers table in the recipes database. Tyler wants to ensure that the Customer Feedback and Customer Feedback Search Web pages always reflect the most current data in the database, not the data as it existed when you originally created the database connection and its Web pages. As long as the changes are made in the database that is stored in the Web site, any Web page that uses the database connection will always reflect the most up-to-date data. If you add, change, or delete records in the database, the Web pages that use the database connection will also reflect these changes. Next, you will add a record to the Customers table in Access to simulate the addition of a record by the database connection.

To add a record to the Customers table:

1. Click the **Folders** button [icon] on the Views bar to change to Folders view, and then click the **fpdb** folder in the Folder List to open it.

2. Double-click **recipes.mdb** in the Contents pane. Microsoft Access starts and opens the recipes database. You will open the Customers table and add a new record to it.

3. If necessary, click the **Tables** object on the Objects bar, and then double-click **Customers** in the tables list to open the Customers table in Table Datasheet view.

4. Click the **New Record** button [icon] on the Table Datasheet toolbar. The current record indicator moves to row 21, the (AutoNumber) text in the CustomerID field is selected, and Access is ready to accept a new record.

5. Press the **Tab** key. The insertion point moves to the First Name column. Type **Betty**, press the **Tab** key to move to the Last Name column, type **Brask**, and then press the **Tab** key to move to the Email Address column.

6. Continue entering data and pressing the **Tab** key to enter the entire record with the following data: Email Address: **bettybrask@golden.net**; Phone Num: **8085558751**; Category: **Web Site**; Subject: **Praise**. As you enter text in the Category and Subject fields, the Lookup Wizard will complete your entries. The input mask in the PhoneNum field automatically formats the phone number in the format (###) ###-####.

7. Press the **Tab** key after entering the Subject field value to save the record in the table. The navigation bar at the bottom of the Table window now displays "Record 22 of 22" and "(AutoNumber)" is selected in row 22.

8. Click the **Close** button [X] on the Access program window title bar to close the table, the recipes database, and Access.

Next, you will open the Customer Feedback Search page in the browser to confirm that the new record you added to the Customers table appears in the Web page.

To view the new database record in the Web page:

1. Click the Web site's folder in the Folder List (the default folder is http://localhost/recipes) to display all of its pages in the Contents pane, and then click **custsrch.asp** in the Contents pane to select it.

2. Click the **Preview in Browser** button [icon] on the Standard toolbar to open the Customer Feedback Search page in the browser.

3. Click in the **Category** text box, type **Web Site**, and then click the **Submit Query** button. The new record for Betty Brask appears in the search results, so you know that the database was updated. See Figure 8-23.

Figure 8-23	NEW RECORD IN THE CUSTOMER FEEDBACK SEARCH PAGE

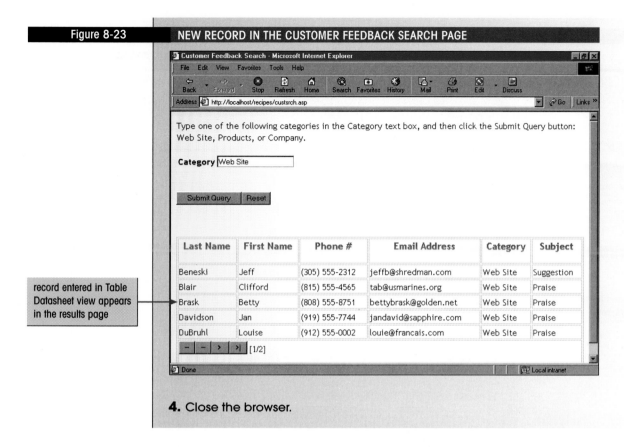

record entered in Table Datasheet view appears in the results page

4. Close the browser.

Tyler wants you to examine the HTML code that created the search form and the Database Results region. To do so, you will view the HTML code for the Customer Feedback Search page.

Viewing HTML Code for a Page with a Database Connection

The Customer Feedback Search Web page contains complex HTML code that creates the querying capability for the Web page, the connection to the Access database, and the capability to display matching field values.

To view the HTML code:

1. Double-click **custsrch.asp** in the Contents pane to open the Customer Feedback Search Web page in Page view, click the **HTML** button to display the HTML code for the page, and then scroll down the page until the FORM tag appears at the top of the Contents pane. See Figure 8-24.

Figure 8-24   HTML CODE FOR THE CUSTOMER FEEDBACK SEARCH PAGE

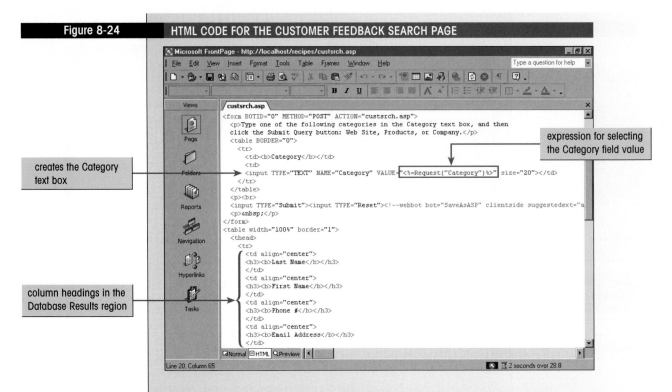

creates the Category text box

expression for selecting the Category field value

column headings in the Database Results region

2. Press the **Page Down** key to scroll the window down one page, and then scroll the page so that the TBODY tag appears at the top of the Contents pane. See Figure 8-25.

Figure 8-25   HTML CODE FOR THE CUSTOMER FEEDBACK SEARCH PAGE, CONTINUED

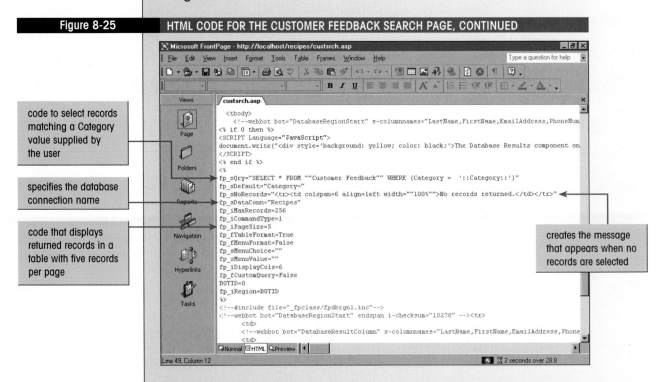

code to select records matching a Category value supplied by the user

specifies the database connection name

code that displays returned records in a table with five records per page

creates the message that appears when no records are selected

3. Continue pressing the **Page Down** key to scroll the window down one page at a time. Examine the HTML code that creates the database connection and the Database Results region.

> **4.** After you have examined all of the HTML code, close the recipes Web site and FrontPage.

In the next session, you will create a form into which site visitors can enter information that will be stored in the recipes database. You will also create a data access page.

Session 8.1 QUICK CHECK

1. What is a database connection?

2. Describe how to import a database into a FrontPage Web site.

3. What must you do before inserting a Database Results region in a Web page?

4. What is a Database Results region?

5. When you temporarily select a subset of records from a database table or query, you are using a(n) _____.

6. True or False: You cannot limit the number of records displayed in a Web page by a Database Results region.

7. True or False: You cannot change the properties of a Database Results region.

8. True or False: If you update a database that has a connection to a FrontPage Web site and is stored in the Web site, any Web pages that use the database connection will display the revised data from the database.

SESSION 8.2

In this session, you will use a form in a Web page to send data to an Access database, and then you will view the changes in the Access database. You will also create a data access page to view, add, delete, browse, filter, and sort database records using a browser.

Creating a Form for Data Input

Tyler wants you to create a form in the recipes Web site that will serve as an electronic guest book. This form will collect each visitor's first and last names, e-mail address, street address, city, state or province, postal code, country, and telephone number. Tyler also wants the form to include a form field that asks for permission to send promotional materials to the visitor's e-mail address.

The visitor will submit the form to the server, where it will be processed. The form results will be stored in an Access database, which will make the data accessible for many different needs. For example, the marketing department will use the mailing addresses to send printed promotional materials, the e-mail addresses to send electronic messages to promote new products at the Sunshine Country Store or new recipes in the Web site, and the phone numbers to contact visitors for open-ended marketing research studies. By storing visitor data in an Access database, the marketing department gains the flexibility to produce reports about the data, to query the database for specific records, and to manage the data in many ways. These advantages are not easily realized when you collect a form's results in an HTML or text file.

When creating a new database connection, you have the option of importing an existing database into the Web site; in that case, FrontPage will create the database connection. Alternatively, you can use the Database tab in the Web Settings dialog box to add a new database connection to a database that exists on the same file system or server as the Web site. For the guest book, you will import an existing database into the Web site. After importing the database, you will import into the recipes Web site a Web page created by Tyler that contains a form for collecting data.

Importing an Existing Database into a Web Site

Tyler's existing database is stored in the Tutorial.08 folder on your Data Disk. The guest database contains one table named Results, which has the structure shown in Figure 8-26.

Figure 8-26	RESULTS TABLE DESIGN IN THE GUEST DATABASE		
FIELD NAME	**DATA TYPE**	**FIELD SIZE**	**DESCRIPTION**
ID	AutoNumber	Long Integer	An Access AutoNumber field that adds the ID. IDs are assigned sequentially as new records are added to the table.
FirstName	Text	35	The visitor's first name.
LastName	Text	35	The visitor's last name.
Address	Text	70	The visitor's street address.
City	Text	35	The visitor's city.
State/Prov	Text	10	The visitor's state or province.
PostalCode	Text	10	The visitor's postal code.
Country	Text	10	The visitor's country.
Phone	Text	15	The visitor's phone number, including the area code.
EmailAddress	Text	45	The visitor's e-mail address.
Promotion	Text	3	A Yes or No response to indicate whether the guest wants to receive promotional materials via e-mail.

To import the guest database into the recipes Web site:

1. Start Windows Explorer, open the drive or folder that contains your Data Disk, and then open the **Tutorial.08** folder to display its contents.

2. Right-click the **guest** file to open the shortcut menu, and then click **Copy**.

3. Close Windows Explorer.

4. Start FrontPage, open the **recipes** Web site from the server, and then change to Folders view (if necessary). Because the fpdb folder already exists in the Web site, you can paste the file directly into that folder.

5. Click the **fpdb** folder in the Folder List to open it in the Contents pane, right-click any open area of the Contents pane to open the shortcut menu, and then click **Paste**. The Importing Files dialog box opens, and then the Add Database Connection dialog box opens on top of it. You will create a database connection named Guest.

> **TROUBLE?** If you do not see the fpdb folder in the Folder List, display the Web site's hidden folders.

6. Type **Guest** in the Name text box, and then click the **Yes** button. The Importing Files dialog box becomes visible again for a few moments, and then it closes. The database is now stored in the fpdb folder of the recipes Web site. You can verify the database connection by using the Web Settings dialog box.

7. Click **Tools** on the menu bar, click **Web Settings** to open the Web Settings dialog box, and then click the **Database** tab. The Recipes database connection appears with a verified status, and the Guest database connection is shown with an unverified status.

8. Click the **Guest** connection, and then click the **Verify** button. The question mark in the Status column changes to a green check mark, indicating a valid connection. The recipes Web site now has two valid database connections.

9. Click the **OK** button to close the Web Settings dialog box.

Now that the guest database is stored in the Web site and the database connection has been verified, you can use the database connection to send data from a Web page to the database. Tyler has already created a Web page named guest_bk.asp that contains a form for collecting data. You will import this page into the Web site from the Tutorial.08 folder on your Data Disk. You will then configure the form to send data to the guest database.

To import the guest_bk Web page into the recipes Web site:

1. Click the Web site's root folder (the default is http://localhost/recipes) to select it, click **File** on the menu bar, and then click **Import**. The Import dialog box opens.

2. Click the **Add File** button. The Add File to Import List dialog box opens. You need to import the file from the Tutorial.08 folder on your Data Disk.

3. Click the **Look in** list arrow, change to the drive or folder that contains your Data Disk, open the **Tutorial.08** folder, and then double-click **guest_bk**. The Import dialog box appears again with guest_bk.asp selected.

4. Click the **OK** button to import the Guest Book Web page into the Web site. If necessary, scroll down the Contents pane to see the imported file.

Now you can open the Guest Book Web page and change it so that the server will send data collected from this Web page to the guest database. You must add this new page to Navigation view so that the page banner and link bar components will appear correctly.

To open the Guest Book Web page and add it to Navigation view:

1. Double-click **guest_bk.asp** in the Contents pane to open the Guest Book Web page in Page view. The placeholders at the top of the page remind you to add the page to Navigation view.

2. Click the **Navigation** button on the Views bar to change to Navigation view, and then drag **guest_bk.asp** from the Folder List to the navigation structure, as shown in Figure 8-27.

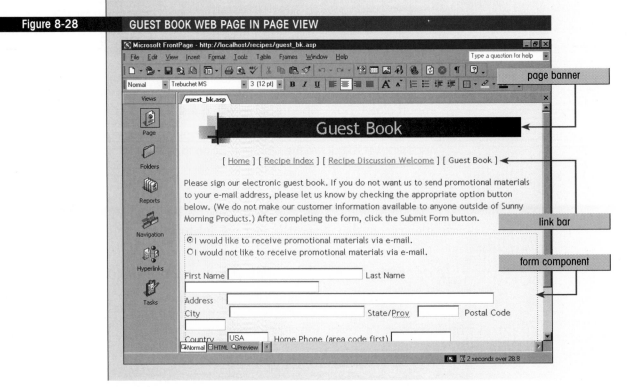

Figure 8-27   ADDING THE GUEST BOOK WEB PAGE TO NAVIGATION VIEW

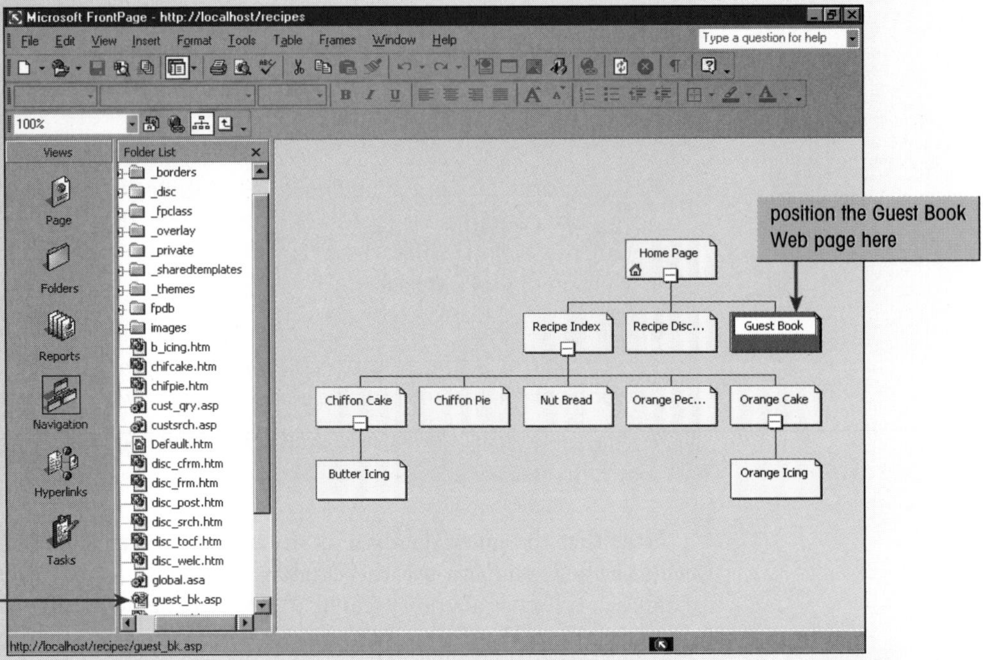

position the Guest Book Web page here

guest_bk.asp (Guest Book) page in the Folder List

3. Double-click the **Guest Book** page icon in the navigation structure to open the page in Page view. Now the page banner and link bar are correct. See Figure 8-28.

Figure 8-28   GUEST BOOK WEB PAGE IN PAGE VIEW

page banner

link bar

form component

Configuring a Form to Send Results to a Database

Now you can configure the existing form to send its results to the guest database in the Web site.

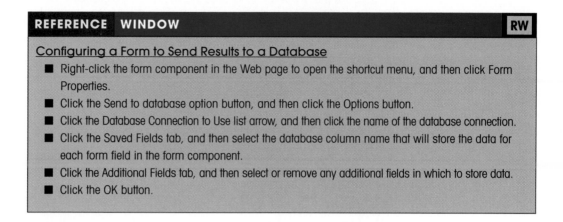

REFERENCE WINDOW   **RW**

Configuring a Form to Send Results to a Database
- Right-click the form component in the Web page to open the shortcut menu, and then click Form Properties.
- Click the Send to database option button, and then click the Options button.
- Click the Database Connection to Use list arrow, and then click the name of the database connection.
- Click the Saved Fields tab, and then select the database column name that will store the data for each form field in the form component.
- Click the Additional Fields tab, and then select or remove any additional fields in which to store data.
- Click the OK button.

To configure the form to save results to the database:

1. Right-click the form component in the Web page to open the shortcut menu, and then click **Form Properties**. The Form Properties dialog box opens.

2. Click the **Send to database** option button to select this form handler, and then click the **Options** button. The Options for Saving Results to Database dialog box opens. You need to change the database connection to Guest.

3. Click the **Database Connection to Use** list arrow, and then click **Guest**. FrontPage uses the Guest database connection to connect to the guest database stored on the server, and it selects the Results table in the guest database. See Figure 8-29.

Figure 8-29   OPTIONS FOR SAVING RESULTS TO DATABASE DIALOG BOX

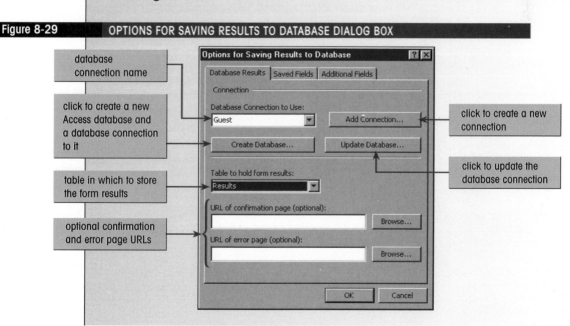

4. Click the **Saved Fields** tab to display those settings. See Figure 8-30. By default, FrontPage selected each field from the Results table in the guest database. Now you need to tell FrontPage the name of the database column in which to store the values. The values in the Form Field list are the form field names that Tyler used when he created the form. For example, the form field name of the text box labeled "E-mail Address" is "EmailAddress."

Figure 8-30	SAVED FIELDS FOR THE RESULTS TABLE

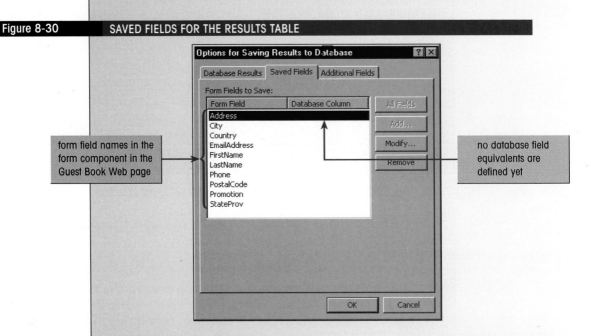

form field names in the form component in the Guest Book Web page

no database field equivalents are defined yet

5. Double-click **Address** in the Form Field list. FrontPage connects to the database, reviews the Results table structure, and then opens the Modify Field dialog box. FrontPage selected the Address field in the Results table as the one in which to store form results from the Address field. This selection is correct—the Address form field in the Web page will send data to the Address field in the Results table in the guest database. If you need to change the field in which to save data, you could click the Save to database column list arrow and select a different field.

6. Make sure that **Address** is selected in the Save to database column list box, and then click the **OK** button to close the Modify Field dialog box. The Database Column value for the Address Form Field now displays the Address field. With the exception of the State/Prov field, Tyler's form fields and database columns have the same names; FrontPage should correctly select each database field in which to store the data. The State/Prov database column appears as "StateProv" in FrontPage, because the slash is not a valid character for a FrontPage form field.

7. Repeat Steps 5 and 6 to supply the Database Column value for each field in the database.

8. Click the **Additional Fields** tab to display those settings. See Figure 8-31.

Figure 8-31	ADDITIONAL FIELDS TAB

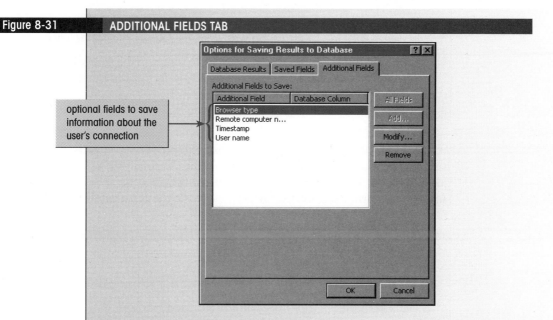

optional fields to save information about the user's connection

Tyler doesn't want to save information about the visitor's browser, his or her user name, or time data, so you will remove these fields from the form results. If you select these options, the database connection will automatically add these fields to the table structure in the database.

9. Click **Browser type** in the Additional Fields to Save list box (if necessary), and then click the **Remove** button. The Browser type field is deleted, and the Remote computer name field is selected.

10. Click the **Remove** button three times to remove the rest of the fields from the Additional Fields to Save list box, and then click the **OK** button to close the Options for Saving Results to Database dialog box.

11. Click the **OK** button in the Form Properties dialog box to close it.

12. Save the page.

Now you can open the Guest Book Web page in the browser and submit a form to the server. You will examine the guest database afterward to confirm that the server stored the form results as a record in the Results table.

To open the Web page in the browser and submit a form:

1. Click the **Preview in Browser** button 🔍 on the Standard toolbar.

2. Click the **I would not like to receive promotional materials via e-mail** option button to select it.

3. Click in the **First Name** text box, and then type **Tyler**.

4. Press the **Tab** key to move to the Last Name text box, and then type **Vanauken**.

5. Continue pressing the **Tab** key to enter the following data in the text boxes: Address: **8336 Seashore Drive**; City: **Los Angeles**; State/Prov: **CA**; Postal Code: **90028**; Country: **USA**; Home Phone: **213-555-0725**; and E-mail Address: **tvanauken@admin.sunnymorning.com**.

6. Click the **Submit Form** button. The default Form Confirmation page opens and confirms that the information was correctly submitted to the server.

7. Click the **Return to the form** hyperlink to return to the Guest Book page. The form fields are cleared, and the page is ready to accept another form submission.

8. Close the browser.

When you submitted the Guest Book page to the server, the server used the Guest database connection that you defined in the recipes Web site to send the form results to the guest database. You can open both Access and the guest database from FrontPage to make sure that the form results were correctly stored in the Results table.

To open the Access database and view the form results in a query:

1. Click the **Folders** button 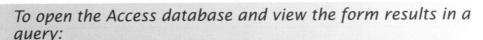 on the Views bar to change to Folders view.

2. Click the **Refresh** button 🗊 on the Standard toolbar to refresh the Web site's contents.

3. Click the **fpdb** folder in the Folder List to display its contents in the Contents pane, click 🗊, and then double-click **guest.mdb** in the Contents pane. Access starts and opens the guest database.

4. If necessary, click the **Tables** object in the Objects bar, double-click **Results** in the tables list, and then click the **Maximize** button ☐ on the Table window to maximize it. The Table window displays the record that you entered using the Guest Book Web page. See Figure 8-32.

Figure 8-32	RESULTS TABLE IN THE GUEST DATABASE

record added using the
Guest Book Web page →

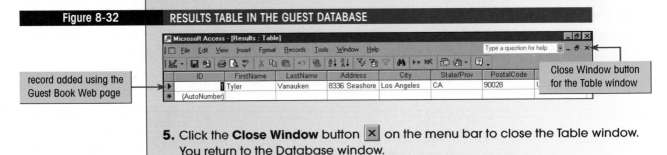

Close Window button
for the Table window

5. Click the **Close Window** button ☒ on the menu bar to close the Table window. You return to the Database window.

The form you used to store data in the database accepts only user input. If you want to use a Web page to display data from the table on which the form is based, you must use Access to create a data access page.

Creating a Data Access Page

A **data access page** is a Web page that uses a form to display data from the Access table or query on which it is based. You use a data access page in the same way that you would use a form in an Access database. A data access page includes controls that let you add, delete, sort, filter, and change the records displayed. You need Internet Explorer 5.0 or higher (or Netscape Navigator 4.7x or higher) to display data access pages.

Sometimes a data access page is available only on an intranet, or it is hidden in a published Web site so that only authorized users can view its data. For example, in the recipes Web site, site visitors should not be able to access the records stored in the Results table in the guest database. You will therefore exclude this page when publishing the recipes Web site to make it unavailable to site visitors.

You must use Access to create a data access page. You will save the data access page in the recipes Web site.

REFERENCE WINDOW   **RW**

<u>Creating a Data Access Page</u>
- Double-click the database in the fpdb folder in the Web site to start Access and open the database.
- Click the Pages object in the Objects bar of the Database window.
- Double-click Create data access page by using wizard in the pages list.
- Select the table or query on which to base the data access page, select the fields to include in the data access page, and then click the Next button.
- Select an optional grouping level, and then click the Next button.
- Use the drop-down list(s) to select an optional sort order, and then click the Next button.
- Either edit the suggested title or accept the default title, and then click the Finish button.
- Click the Save button on the Page Design toolbar, open the Web site in which to store the page, click the Save button, enter the page's filename, and then click the Save button.

Tyler wants you to create a data access page in Access that is based on the Results table. Then, instead of checking the records in the database by starting Access and opening the database and table, he can check the records by using the data access page stored in the recipes Web site. Because the data access page will display customer information, you will set this page so that it is not published with the rest of the site on the server for Sunny Morning Products. The guest database is already open in Access, so you are ready to create the data access page.

To create a data access page:

1. Click the **Pages** object in the Objects bar of the Database window, and then double-click **Create data access page by using wizard** in the pages list. The Page Wizard starts and opens the first dialog box. In this dialog box, you can select the table or query in the current database that contains the fields you want to include in your data access page. Because only one object—the Results table—appears in the guest database, the Tables/Queries list box is already set. The Available Fields list box shows all of the fields in the Results table. See Figure 8-33.

Figure 8-33   USING THE PAGE WIZARD TO CREATE A DATA ACCESS PAGE

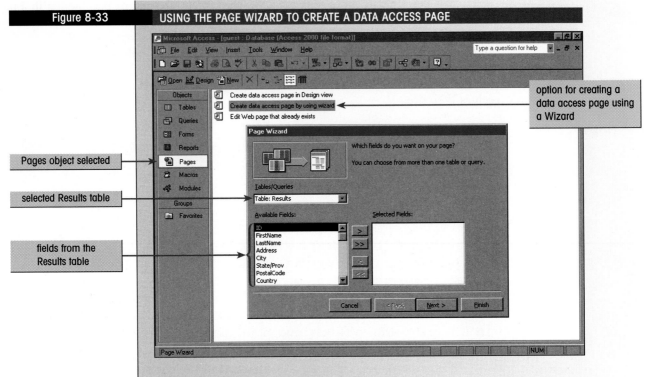

You'll select all fields in the Results table.

2. Click the ⟩⟩ button to move all available fields to the Selected Fields list box. Use the scroll bar to make sure that the following fields appear in the Selected Fields list box: ID, FirstName, LastName, Address, City, State/Prov, PostalCode, Country, Phone, EmailAddress, and Promotion.

TROUBLE? If any other field besides those listed in Step 2 appears in the Selected Fields list box, click the extra field, and then click the ⟨ button to remove it. Repeat this process to remove all extra fields.

3. Click the **Next** button. The next dialog box asks you to specify an optional grouping level for the data. You will not group the data.

4. Click the **Next** button. The next dialog box asks you to specify an optional sort order for the data. Tyler wants to sort the records alphabetically by last name.

5. Click the **list arrow** for the first text box, and then click **LastName**. See Figure 8-34. An ascending sort order is already specified, so you can continue to the next dialog box.

Figure 8-34	SPECIFYING THE SORT ORDER FOR THE DATA ACCESS PAGE

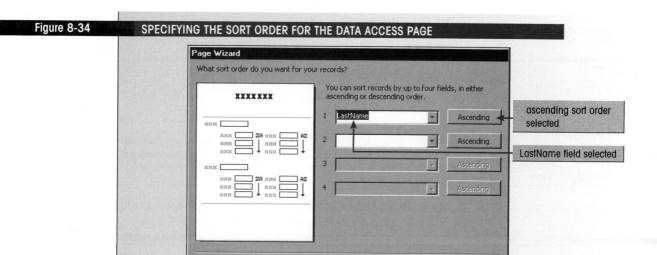

6. Click the **Next** button. The final dialog box asks you for a page title. You will accept the default title of "Results," so click the **Finish** button. After a few seconds, Access creates the data access page and opens it in Page Design view. If necessary, click the **Maximize** button 🔲 on the Page Design window to maximize it. See Figure 8-35.

Figure 8-35	DATA ACCESS PAGE IN PAGE DESIGN VIEW

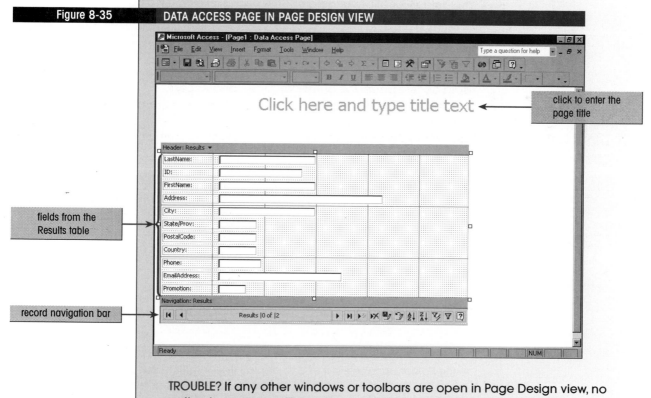

TROUBLE? If any other windows or toolbars are open in Page Design view, no action is necessary. They will not affect your work in Access.

7. Click the text at the top of the page (**Click here and type title text**), type **Guest Book Results**, and then click anywhere outside of the title to deselect it.

Saving a Data Access Page

You will not make any other design changes to the data access page, so you can save and close it. When you save a data access page, it is saved in two places: as an object in the database and as an HTML file on the server or a hard drive. You will save the data access page in the recipes Web site on the server.

> ### To save the data access page in the FrontPage Web site:
>
> **1.** Click the **Save** button 🔲 on the Page Design toolbar to open the Save As Data Access Page dialog box.
>
> **2.** Click the **My Network Places** button, type the full path to the **recipes** Web site on your server in the File name text box (the default is http://localhost/recipes), and then click the **Save** button.
>
> TROUBLE? If your Web site is stored in another location, type the path to the recipes Web site on your server.
>
> **3.** Select the text in the File name text box (if necessary), type **rslt_dap**, make sure that the Save as type list box is set to **Microsoft Data Access Pages**, and then click the **Save** button. Access saves the data access page as an object in the database and as an HTML file in the recipes Web site.
>
> TROUBLE? If a dialog box opens and asks whether you want to set this folder as the default location for data access pages, click the No button.
>
> TROUBLE? If a dialog box opens and informs you that the page contains a connection string to an absolute path, click the OK button.
>
> **4.** Click the **Close** button ☒ on the Access program window title bar to close the data access page, the guest database, and Access.

The data access page is stored in the recipes Web site. You can now open the data access page and use FrontPage to format it.

Modifying a Data Access Page in FrontPage

You stored the data access page in the recipes Web site. You will use FrontPage to open this page so you can edit it. Tyler wants you to apply the Web site's theme to the data access page so that its appearance will match that of the other pages in the Web site. Then you will save the page and open it in the browser.

> ### To open the data access page in Page view, apply the default Web theme, and preview it in the browser:
>
> **1.** Click the root folder of the recipes Web site (the default is http://localhost/recipes) in the Folder List to select it and to display its contents in the Contents pane, and then click the **Refresh** button 🔁 on the Standard toolbar to refresh the Web site.
>
> **2.** Scroll down the list of files as necessary, and then double-click **rslt_dap.htm** to open it in Page view. Tyler wants you to apply the Web site's theme to this new page.

TROUBLE? If you do not see the rslt_dap.htm file in the Contents pane, then you may have saved it in the wrong folder of the Web site. Locate the file in one of the other folders of the recipes Web site, use drag and drop to move it to the Web site's root folder (http://localhost/recipes), and then repeat Step 2.

TROUBLE? If the data access page opens in Access instead of in Page view, close Access. Click the No button when asked to replace the file on the server. Right-click rslt_dap.htm in the Contents pane to open the shortcut menu, and then click Open With. In the Open With Editor dialog box, click FrontPage (frontpg.exe), and then click the OK button. The Guest Book Results page will open in Page view. Continue with Step 3.

3. Click **Format** on the menu bar, and then click **Theme**. The Themes dialog box opens.

4. Click the **Selected page(s)** option button to select it (if necessary), and then click **(Default) Copy of Blends**.

TROUBLE? If the customized theme that you applied to the Web site in Tutorial 7 has a different name, select that name in the list.

5. Click the **OK** button. The page now uses elements from the Web site's theme.

6. Save the page and then preview it in a browser. See Figure 8-36. The record that you entered in the Guest Book Web page appears in the Guest Book Results page. As more records are added to the Results table, Tyler will be able to use this data access page to view, delete, sort, and filter records as necessary.

| Figure 8-36 | DATA ACCESS PAGE IN THE BROWSER |

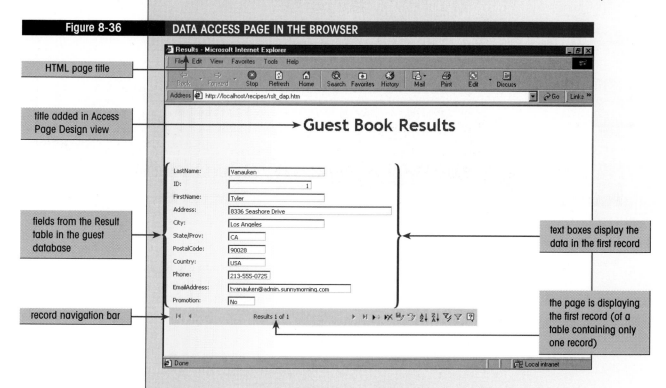

TROUBLE? If Internet Explorer opens a page and indicates that you need to change the browser's security settings, ask your instructor or technical support person for help. If you are working on your own computer, follow the directions in the page to change the browser's security settings. Do *not* change the security settings for a public or lab computer.

TROUBLE? If Internet Explorer opens a Microsoft Data Access Components dialog box that asks whether if you want to allow the page to access data on another domain, click the Yes button.

The data access page contains the title that you created in Access Page Design view, the fields from the Results table in the guest database, the values for the first record in the Results table, and a record navigation bar.

When a data access page is based on a table, you can use the **record navigation bar** to display, add, change, delete, save, sort, and filter records in the table on which that page is based. If the data access page is based on a query, depending on the type of query you might not be able to use it to add, change, delete, or save records. Figure 8-37 describes the buttons that appear on the record navigation bar.

Figure 8-37	DATA ACCESS PAGE RECORD NAVIGATION BAR BUTTONS AND THEIR DESCRIPTIONS	
BUTTON	**BUTTON NAME**	**DESCRIPTION**
	First	Displays the first record
	Previous	Displays the previous record
	Next	Displays the next record
	Last	Displays the last record
	New	Clears the fields in the data access page so that a new record can be entered
	Delete	Deletes the current record
	Save	Saves the current record
	Undo	Reverses the previous action
	Sort Ascending	Sorts the records in ascending order based on the current active field
	Sort Descending	Sorts the records in descending order based on the current active field
	Filter by Selection	Lets you set a filter to display a subset of the records using the value in the current active field
	Filter Toggle Button	Applies a filter or removes the currently applied filter
	Help	Opens the Microsoft Access Data Pages Help window

Adding a Record Using a Data Access Page

You can use the data access page to enter a new record in the Results table, just as you would use the Guest Book Web page and its form component to add a new record. A site visitor won't use the data access page to enter a record, but Tyler wants you to do so to practice using the data access page.

REFERENCE   WINDOW   **RW**

Adding a Record to a Database Table Using a Data Access Page
- ■ Click the New button on the record navigation bar in the Web page.
- ■ Enter the data into the text boxes. Press the Tab key to move the insertion point to the next text box.
- ■ After entering data in all of the text boxes, click the Save button on the record navigation bar to save the record.

To add a record to a table using a data access page:

1. Click the **New** button [►] on the record navigation bar in the Web page. The browser clears the form fields and positions the insertion point in the LastName text box.

2. Type **Bay** in the LastName text box, and then press the **Tab** key. The insertion point moves to the FirstName text box, skipping over the ID text box because Access automatically generates the ID field value.

3. Type **Amanda**, and then press the **Tab** key to move to the Address text box.

4. Enter the following data into the remaining text boxes, using the Tab key to move to the next field (do not press the Tab key after entering the data in the Promotion text box): Address: **5942 Los Verdes Drive**; City: **Los Angeles**; State/Prov: **CA**; PostalCode: **90026**; Country: **USA**; Phone: **213-555-0810**; Email Address: **abay@admin.sunnymorning.com**; and Promotion: **Yes**.

5. After entering the data in the Promotion text box, click the **Save** button [💾] on the record navigation bar, and then click the **Refresh** button [🔁] on the toolbar. See Figure 8-38. Amanda's record is record 1 of 2 because the sort order that you specified—alphabetically by LastName—sorts the record with the LastName "Bay" before the record with the LastName "Vanauken."

Figure 8-38   **ADDING A NEW RECORD**

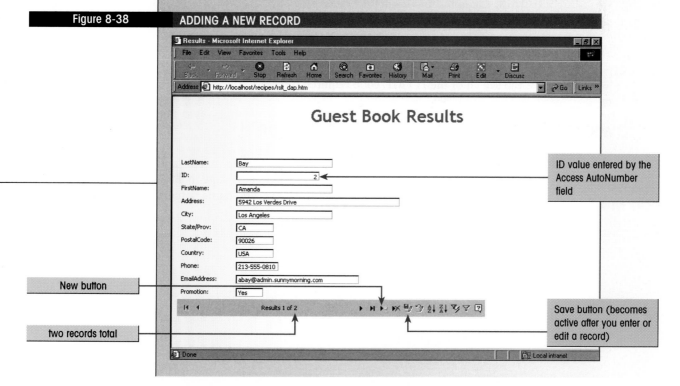

- ID value entered by the Access AutoNumber field
- New button
- two records total
- Save button (becomes active after you enter or edit a record)

Viewing Records Using a Data Access Page

The Results table in the guest database currently contains two records, but it will eventually include hundreds of records. Tyler wants you to use the buttons on the record navigation bar to practice sorting and browsing records.

To view the records in the table using the data access page:

1. Click the **Last** button ▶| on the record navigation bar. The browser displays the last record (for Tyler Vanauken), which has an ID of 1.

2. Click the **Previous** button ◀ on the record navigation bar. The browser displays the first record (for Amanda Bay), which has an ID of 2.

3. Click in the **FirstName** text box, and then click the **Sort Descending** button ⬇ on the record navigation bar. The browser sorts the records in descending order by the FirstName field and then moves the insertion point to the LastName field. The record for Tyler Vanauken is displayed because the FirstName "Tyler" comes first in descending alphabetical order. You can sort records based on any field by clicking the field and then clicking a sort button.

4. Click in the **State/Prov** text box, and then click the **Filter by Selection** button ⬇ on the record navigation bar. The filter will select only those records that contain the current value ("CA") in the State field. Two records are selected, as indicated by the "Results 1 of 2" text on the record navigation bar.

5. Click the **Filter Toggle Button** button 🔽 on the record navigation bar to remove the filter.

6. Click in the **PostalCode** text box, and then click 🔽. Only one record is selected, because only one record in the Results table contains this postal code.

7. Click 🔽 on the record navigation bar to remove the filter.

8. Close the browser.

Now the database on the server contains the record that you added using the browser. Tyler wants you to view the HTML code for the Guest Book Results page so that you can see all of the HTML code required to create it.

Viewing **HTML Code for a Data Access Page**

When you created the Results data access page using Access and then saved it, Access created the HTML code for the page. The data access page includes code to define each field in the page, including its formatting properties and name, label, and position in the page.

To view the HTML code for the data access page:

1. Click the **HTML** button.

TROUBLE? If a Confirm Save dialog box opens, click the Yes button to replace the fpdb/guest.mdb file on the server.

2. Press **Ctrl + Home** to scroll to the top of the page, and then scroll down the page so that the META tag for the theme appears at the top of the Contents pane (this tag appears about three-fourths of the way down the page). See Figure 8-39. Each object in the data access page requires several lines of code to define its properties.

| Figure 8-39 | HTML CODE FOR THE DATA ACCESS PAGE |

theme for this page

title added in Access Page Design view

code that displays records and formats data in the access page

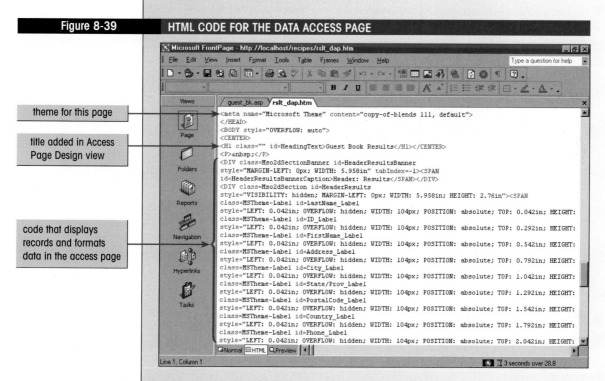

3. Press the **Page Down** key, and then scroll the page until the TBODY tag appears at the top of the Contents pane. Figure 8-40 shows the HTML code that creates the buttons in the record navigation bar.

Figure 8-40	HTML CODE FOR THE DATA ACCESS PAGE, CONTINUED

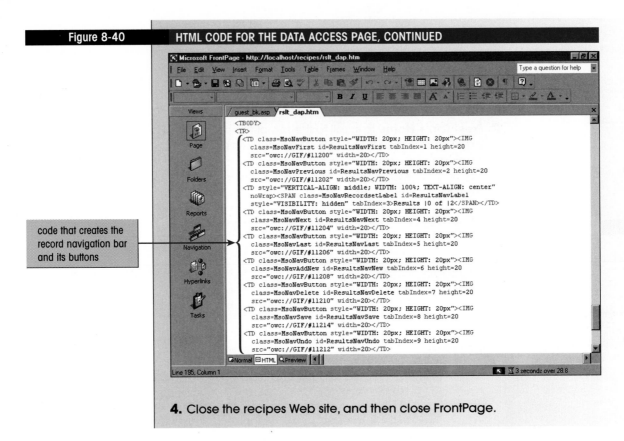

code that creates the record navigation bar and its buttons

4. Close the recipes Web site, and then close FrontPage.

In the next tutorial, you will learn how to create Office components and styles in a Web page.

Session 8.2 QUICK CHECK

1. FrontPage saves database files used with database connections in the _____ folder of the Web site.

2. True or False: You use the Form Properties dialog box to configure the form fields to save in a database table using a database connection.

3. True or False: You can use a database connection to store information about the Web page user's browser type and computer name.

4. What is a data access page?

5. True or False: You can use FrontPage to create a data access page.

6. What settings are available when you use the Page Wizard to create a new data access page?

7. To add a new record to a table using a data access page, you click the _____ button on the record navigation bar.

REVIEW ASSIGNMENTS

The Web pages that you created in this tutorial have the functionality that Tyler needs, but the default pages created by the Wizards do not have the same appearance as other pages in the recipes Web site. Tyler asks you to format the Web pages and to finalize their appearance. In addition, you will change the settings for pages that contain visitor data so that they are not included when the Web site is ultimately published to the Sunny Morning Products Web server.

If necessary, start FrontPage, insert your Data Disk in the appropriate disk drive, and then do the following:

1. Open the **recipes** Web site from the server in Folders view.

2. Open the Customer Feedback page (**cust_qry.asp**) in Page view. Create a centered heading at the top of the page with the text "Customer List." (*Hint:* With the insertion point at the beginning of the first cell in the table, press the Enter key.) Apply the Heading 1 style to the heading.

Explore ▷ 3. Start the Database Results Wizard and use it to make the following changes to the existing Database Results region in the Customer Feedback page:
   a. Change the message that appears when no records are returned in the query to "There are no records matching your request." (*Hint:* Click the More Options button in the Database Results Wizard – Step 3 of 5 dialog box.)
   b. Change the formatting options to display a list with one field per item. Add labels for all field values, place a horizontal separator between records, and use the Paragraphs list option.
   c. Choose the option to display all records together, and then click the Finish button.

4. Change the headings for the form fields in the Customer Feedback page as necessary to Last Name, First Name, Phone Number, Email Address, Category, and Subject. (Keep the colon that follows each heading name.)

5. Add a normal, left-aligned paragraph below the heading that you added in Step 2 with the following text: "This customer list displays current data collected from the Feedback Web page in the Sunny Web site. Refresh the page to update the data. Records are sorted alphabetically by last name."

6. Save the page, and then preview it using the browser. Use the browser to print the first page of the Customer Feedback page, and then close the browser.

7. Change the settings for the Customer Feedback page to exclude it when publishing the Web site. Save and close the page.

8. Open the Customer Feedback Search page (**custsrch.asp**) in Page view. Create a centered heading at the top of the page with the text "Customer List Search." (*Note:* The heading will appear in the search form component in Page view, but it will appear correctly as a heading when viewed in the browser.) Apply the Heading 1 style to the heading. Exclude this page when publishing the Web site, and then save and close the page.

Explore ▷ 9. In Folders view, change the page title of the data access page (**rslt_dap.htm**) to "Guest Book Results." Open the page in Page view. Change the labels that appear to the left of the LastName, FirstName, PostalCode, and EmailAddress text boxes to Last Name, First Name, Postal Code, and Email Address, respectively. (*Hint:* Click a label to edit it.) Save the Guest Book Results Web page.

10. Open the Guest Book Results page in a browser, and then add a new record using your name and address information. Use the browser to print the new record, and then close the browser. (*Note:* If you receive an error message and the browser cannot load the records into the data access page, ask your instructor for assistance.)

11. Close the **recipes** Web site, and then close FrontPage.

CASE PROBLEMS

Case 1. Integrating a Database with the Web Site for Royal Hair Care Products As part of a new promotional campaign, Valerie Suarez wants to provide customers with a means of obtaining a sample from a new product line of styling gels made from all-natural ingredients, including herbs and fruits. Royal Hair Care Products will use the styling gels to roll out a new product line of shampoos and conditioners. Valerie wants to include a new Web page in the Web site that collects each interested visitor's first and last names, address, city, state/province, postal code, country, and telephone number.

Valerie asks you to create the following new pages: a "Request Product" page that includes a form that sends its results to an Access database; an Active Server Page named "Customer Information" that displays data in the royal database; and a data access page named "Customer Data Access Page" that displays data in a table in the royal database containing the data stored by the Request Product Web page.

If necessary, start FrontPage, insert your Data Disk in the appropriate disk drive, and then do the following:

1. Read all the questions for this case problem, and then prepare a planning analysis sheet for the enhancements to the Web site.

2. Open the **royal** Web site from the server. (If you did not create this Web site in Tutorial 7, ask your instructor for assistance.)

3. Import the **royal** database from the Tutorial.08 folder on your Data Disk into the **royal** Web site. Use "Royal" as the database connection name, and store all database files in the fpdb folder of the Web site.

4. Create a new page in Page view with the title "Request Product" and the filename **sendinfo.asp**.

5. Add the Request Product page (**sendinfo.asp**) to Navigation view as a child page of the home page. Position the Request Product page between the What's New and Feedback pages in the navigation structure.

Explore   6. Add a brief introductory paragraph below the link bar in the Request Product page. Use the information in the case problem description to determine the appropriate content.

Explore   7. Insert a form component below the paragraph that you added in Step 6. The form component should contain the following text box form fields: First Name, with the name FirstName and a width of 50 characters; Last Name, with the name LastName and a width of 50 characters; Address, with the same name and a width of 70 characters; City, with the same name and a width of 50 characters; State/Province, with the name StateProv and a width of 10 characters; Postal Code, with the name PostalCode and a width of 10 characters; Country, with the same name, a width of 10 characters, and an initial value of USA; and Phone, with the same name and a width of 15 characters. Choose the layout for the form fields in the form component.

Explore   8. Verify the Royal database connection, and then set the form to send its results to the **Customer** table in the **royal** database stored in the fpdb folder of the **royal** Web site. The database column names and form field names are the same. Do not collect any additional fields.

9. Save the Request Product page, and then preview it in the browser. Complete the Request Product page using your own name and address information, print the page, and then submit the form to the server. Close the browser.

10. Open the **royal** database stored in the Web site from FrontPage, open the **Customer** table in the Table window, and then confirm that the form handler correctly stored your data. Close Access.

11. Close the Request Product page, and then create a new page in Page view with the title "Customer Information" and the filename **custinfo.asp**. Change the setting for the Customer Information page to exclude it when publishing the Web site. Turn off the display of the top shared border for only this page, and then save the page.

12. Add a centered heading with the Heading 1 style at the top of the page with the text "Customer Information." Create a Database Results region that displays the records from the **Customer Feedback** query in the **royal** database. Include all fields from the query, accept the default formatting options, and display all records together. After inserting the Database Results region in the Web page, change the column headings to more meaningful names, and then apply the Heading 4 style and center them. Save the page, preview it in the browser, use the browser to print the page, and then close the browser.

13. Open the **royal** database stored on the server from FrontPage, and then click the Pages object in the Database window. Use a Wizard to create a data access page based on the **Customer** table. Include all fields in the page, do not use a grouping level, sort the records in ascending alphabetical order by LastName, and change the default title to "Customer Data Access Page."

14. Enter the page title "Customer Data Access Page" at the top of the new data access page, and then save it as **cust_dap** in the root folder of the **royal** Web site. Close Access.

15. Refresh the Web site, and then open the Customer Data Access Page (**cust_dap.htm**) in Page view. (*Hint:* You might need to right-click the filename, click Open With, and then select the FrontPage option to open the page in Page view.) Apply the Web site's theme to the page, and then exclude the page when publishing the Web site. Save the page, and then preview it in the browser. Use the data access page to add a new record to the table using real or fictitious data. Print the page using the browser, and then close the browser.

16. Close the **royal** Web site, and then close FrontPage.

Case 2. Integrating a Database with the Web Site for Buffalo Trading Post Donna Vargas, president of Buffalo Trading Post (BTP), knows that customer service is an important ingredient in BTP's success. She realizes that many of her loyal customers might use a computer for business, but they do not want to receive personal correspondence via their e-mail addresses. In response to customer requests, Donna wants to create a database of information that the promotion department can use to send advertisements about sales and promotions to customers. She asks you to create a Web page that will accept input from the user, a Web page that displays customer information, and a data access page that displays all records in the database and provides functionality to update them.

If necessary, start FrontPage, insert your Data Disk in the appropriate disk drive, and then do the following:

1. Read all the questions for this case problem, and then prepare a planning analysis sheet for the enhancements to the Web site.

2. Open the **buffalo** Web site from the server. (If you did not create this Web site in Tutorial 7, ask your instructor for assistance.)

3. Import the **buffalo** database from the Tutorial.08 folder on your Data Disk into the **buffalo** Web site. Use "Buffalo" as the database connection name, and store all database files in the fpdb folder of the Web site.

4. Create a new page in Page view with the title "Add to Mailing List" and the filename **mailinfo.asp**.

5. Add the Add to Mailing List page (**mailinfo.asp**) to Navigation view as a child page of the home page. Position the Add to Mailing List page to the left of the What page in the navigation structure.

Explore

6. Enter a brief introductory paragraph on the first line (but not in the bottom shared border of the Web page) of the Add to Mailing List Web page. Use the information in the case problem description to determine the appropriate content. At the top of the page, insert a centered picture page banner and a centered link bar based on the navigation structure with hyperlinks formatted using the page's theme to same-level pages and to the home and parent pages.

Explore

7. Insert a form component below the paragraph that you added in Step 6. The form component should contain the following text box form fields: First Name, with the name FirstName and a width of 50 characters; Last Name, with the name LastName and a width of 50 characters; Address, with the same name and a width of 70 characters; City, with the same name and a width of 50 characters; State/Province, with the name StateProv and a width of 10 characters; Postal Code, with the name PostalCode and a width of 10 characters; Country, with the same name, a width of 12 characters, and an initial value of USA; Phone, with the same name and a width of 15 characters; and Email Address, with the name EmailAddress and a width of 50 characters. Choose the layout for the form fields in the form component.

Explore

8. Verify the Buffalo database connection, and then set the form to send its results to the **Customers** table in the **buffalo** database stored in the fpdb folder of the **buffalo** Web site. The database column names and the form field names are the same. Do not collect any additional fields.

9. Save the Add to Mailing List page, and then preview it in the browser. Complete this page using your own name and address information, print the page, and then submit the form to the server. Close the browser.

10. Open the **buffalo** database stored in the Web site from FrontPage, open the **Customers** table in the Table window, and then confirm that the form handler correctly stored your data. Close Access.

11. Close the Add to Mailing List page, and then create a new page in Page view with the title "Mailing List Information" and the filename **maillist.asp**. Change the settings for the Mailing List Information page to exclude it when publishing the Web site, and then save the page.

12. Add a centered heading with the Heading 1 style at the top of the page using the text "Mailing List Information." Create a Database Results region that displays the records from the **Mailing List** query in the **buffalo** database. Include all fields from the query, accept the default formatting options, and display all records together. After inserting the Database Results region in the Web page, change the column headings to more meaningful names, and then apply the Heading 4 style and center them. Select the database fields (the row between the start and end of the Database Results region), and then change the fields to 10-point text. Save the page, preview it in the browser, use the browser to print the page, and then close the browser. Close the Mailing List Information page in Page view.

13. Open the **buffalo** database stored in the Web site from FrontPage, and then click the Pages object in the Database window. Use a Wizard to create a data access page based on the **Customers** table. Include all fields in the page, do not use a grouping level, sort the records in ascending order by ID, and change the default title to "Mailing List Data Access Page."

14. Enter the page title "Mailing List Data Access Page" at the top of the new data access page, and then save it as **mail_dap** in the root folder of the **buffalo** Web site. Close Access.

15. Refresh the Web site, and then open the Mailing List Data Access Page (**mail_dap.htm**) in Page view. (*Hint:* You might need to right-click the filename, click Open With, and then select the FrontPage option to open the page in Page view.) Apply the Web site's theme to the page, and then exclude the page when publishing the Web site. Save the page, and then preview it in the browser. Use the data access page to add a new record to the table using real or fictitious data. Use the browser to print this new record, and then close the browser.

16. Close the **buffalo** Web site, and then close FrontPage.

Case 3. Integrating a Database with the Web Site for Garden Grill Nolan Simmons wants to include a new Web page in Garden Grill's Web site that lets customers enter comments into a form whose results are stored in an Access database. Nolan hopes to use this database to gather information about regional trends, which might lead to the introduction of new menu items. The form should contain a text area that lets users enter information about whatever is on their minds—including the restaurant, service, and menu. When the menu is updated, Nolan can use the information stored in the database to provide mailing lists to the marketing department, which can then mail coupons and new menus to current and past customers.

If necessary, start FrontPage, insert your Data Disk in the appropriate disk drive, and then do the following:

1. Read all the questions for this case problem, and then prepare a planning analysis sheet for the enhancements to the Web site.

2. Open the **garden** Web site from the server. (If you did not create this Web site in Tutorial 7, ask your instructor for assistance.)

3. Import the **garden** database from the Tutorial.08 folder on your Data Disk into the **garden** Web site. Use "Garden" as the database name, and store all database files in the fpdb folder of the Web site.

4. Create a new page in Page view with the title "Customer Comments" and the filename **comments.asp**.

5. Add the Customer Comments page (**comments.asp**) to Navigation view as a child page of the home page. Position the Customer Comments page between the Career Opportunities and Feedback Web pages.

Explore   6. Add a brief introductory paragraph under the link bar in the Web page. Use the information in the case problem description to determine the appropriate content.

Explore   7. Insert a form component below the paragraph that you added in Step 6. The form component should contain the following text box form fields: First Name, with the name First and a width of 50 characters; Last Name, with the name Last and a width of 50 characters; Address, with the same name and a width of 70 characters; City, with the same name and a width of 50 characters; State/Province, with the name StateProv and a width of 10 characters; Postal Code, with the name PostalCode and a width of 10 characters; Country, with the same name, a width of 10 characters, and an initial value of USA; Phone, with the same name and a width of 15 characters; and Email Address, with the name Email and a width of 50 characters. Create a text area named Comments, with the same name, a width of 70 characters, and a height of 5 lines. Choose the layout for the form fields in the form component.

Explore   8. Verify the Garden database connection, and then set the form to send its results to the **Comments** table in the **garden** database stored in the fpdb folder of the **garden** Web site. The database column names and form field names are the same. Do not collect any additional fields.

9. Save the Customer Comments page, and then preview it in the browser. Complete the Customer Comments page using your own name and address information, print the page, and then submit the form to the server. Close the browser.

10. Open the **garden** database stored in the Web site from FrontPage, open the **Comments** table in the Table window, and then confirm that the form handler correctly stored your data. Close Access.

11. Close the Customer Comments page, and then create a new page in Page view with the title "Customer Comments" and the filename **custinfo.asp**. Change the settings for the Customer Comments page to exclude it when publishing the Web site. Turn off the top shared border for this page, and then save it.

Explore   12. At the top of the page, add a centered heading that uses the Heading 2 style and the text "Customer Comments." Create a Database Results region that displays the records from the **Customer Feedback** query in the **garden** database. Include all fields except ID from the query. Accept the default formatting options, and display all records together. After inserting the Database Results region in the Web page, change the column headings to more meaningful names, and then apply the Heading 5 style and center them. Select the database fields (the row between the start and end of the Database Results region), and then change the fields to 10-point text. Save the page, preview it in the browser, use the browser to print the page, and then close the browser.

Explore   13. Open the **garden** database stored in the Web site from FrontPage, and then click the Pages object in the Database window. Use a Wizard to create a data access page based on the **Comments** table. Include all fields in the page except for the ID field, group the records using the State/Prov field, sort the records in ascending order by City, and change the default title to "Customer Comments Data Access Page."

14. Enter the page title "Customer Comments Data Access Page" at the top of the new data access page, and then save it as **cust_dap** in the root folder of the **garden** Web site. Close Access.

Explore   15. Refresh the Web site, and then open the Customer Comments Data Access Page (**cust_dap.htm**) in Page view. (*Hint:* You might need to right-click the filename, click Open With, and then select the FrontPage option to open the page in Page view.) Apply the Web site's theme to the page, and then exclude the page when publishing the Web site. Save the page, and then preview it in the browser. How did the grouping option that you set using the Database Results Wizard affect the appearance of the data in the page? What happens when you click the plus box to the left of the State/Prov label? How might Garden Grill use grouping levels to improve a Web page that contains menu items? Print the page, and then close the browser.

16. Close the **garden** Web site, and then close FrontPage.

Explore   **Case 4. Integrating a Database with the Web Site for Replay Music Factory** Charlene Fields wants to let customers browse the inventory of Replay Music Factory (RMF) by using a Web page. Customers should be able to select a category of music and then view a list of the store's inventory of CDs in that category. Alec Johnston will be in charge of entering the records for in-stock items into a database. While he is working on this extensive project, Charlene asks you to create the Web pages in the Web site that will let customers browse the site. Eventually, she will add additional pages to the Web site that accept online orders.

If necessary, start FrontPage, insert your Data Disk in the appropriate disk drive, and then do the following:

1. Read all the questions for this case problem, and then prepare a planning analysis sheet for the enhancements to the Web site.

2. Open the **replay** Web site from the server. (If you did not create this Web site in Tutorial 7, ask your instructor for assistance.)

3. Import the **replay** database from the Tutorial.08 folder on your Data Disk into the **replay** Web site. Use "Replay" as the database connection name, and store all database files in the fpdb folder of the Web site.

4. Verify the Replay database connection.

5. Open the **replay** database stored in the Web site from FrontPage, and then click the Pages object in the Database window. Use a Wizard to create a data access page based on the **Inventory** table. Include all fields in the page, do not specify a grouping level or a sort order, and change the default title to "Replay Music Factory Inventory."

6. Enter the page title "Replay Music Factory Inventory" at the top of the new data access page, and then save it as **inv_dap** in the root folder of the **replay** Web site. Close Access.

7. Refresh the Web site, and then open the Replay Music Inventory page (**inv_dap.htm**) in Page view. (*Hint:* You might need to right-click the filename, click Open With, and then select the FrontPage option to open the page in Page view.) Apply the Web site's theme to the page. Save the page, and then preview it in the browser. Use the data access page to enter one record for a real or fictitious CD. Save the record. (*Hint:* Valid categories are Pop, Rock and Roll, Country & Western, Classical, Spanish, Children's, and Comedy. Valid ratings are Adult, General, Youth, and Not Rated. The ID field is an AutoNumber field. The StockID field can contain letters and digits to make a product code.) Use the browser to print the new record.

8. Navigate to the first record in the data access page, sort the records in ascending order based on the Artist field, and then navigate to the record that you added in Step 7. Use a button on the record navigation bar to delete the record that you entered in Step 7.

9. Use a filter to sort the data access page so that it displays only those records in the Country & Western category.

10. Remove the filter that you applied in Step 9. Sort the records in ascending alphabetical order by CD title. Print the first record.

11. Sort the records in descending order by artist. Print the first record, and then close the browser.

12. Close the **replay** Web site, and then close FrontPage.

LAB ASSIGNMENTS

Databases

These Lab Assignments are designed to accompany the interactive Course Lab called Databases. To start the Databases Lab, click the Start button on the Windows taskbar, point to Programs, point to Course Labs, point to New Perspectives Applications, and then click Databases. If you do not see Course Labs on your Programs menu, see your instructor or technical support person.

Databases The Databases Lab demonstrates the essential concepts of file and database management systems. You will use the Lab to search, sort, and report the data contained in a file of classic books.

1. Click the Steps button to review basic database terminology and to learn how to manipulate the classic books database. As you proceed through the Steps, answer the Quick Check questions that appear. After you complete the Steps, you will see a Quick Check Summary Report. Follow the instructions on the screen to print this report.

2. Click the Explore button. Make sure you can apply basic database terminology to describe the classic books database by answering the following questions:

   a. How many records does the file contain?
   b. How many fields does each record contain?
   c. What are the contents of the Catalog # field for the book written by Margaret Mitchell?
   d. What are the contents of the Title field for the record with Thoreau in the Author field?
   e. Which field has been used to sort the records?

3. In Explore, manipulate the database as necessary to answer the following questions:
   a. When the books are sorted by title, what is the first record in the file?
   b. Use the Search button to search for all books in the West location. How many do you find?
   c. Use the Search button to search for all books in the Main location that are checked in. What do you find?

4. In Explore, use the Report button to print a report that groups the books by Status and sorts them by title. On your report, circle the four field names. Draw a box around the summary statistics showing which books are currently checked in and which books are currently checked out.

QUICK | CHECK ANSWERS

Session 8.1

1. A database connection specifies the name, location, and type of database that you want to access from a FrontPage Web.

2. Copy the database file in Windows Explorer, open the Web site in FrontPage, right-click the Folder List, click Paste on the shortcut menu, enter the name of the database connection, and then click the Yes button. Click the Yes button again to store the database's files in the fpdb folder of the FrontPage Web site.

3. You must enable the Web site to run Active Server Pages and to run scripts.

4. A component in a Web page that contains HTML code and client-side and server-side scripts that retrieve and display data from the database in the Web page.

5. filter

6. False

7. False

8. True

Session 8.2

1. fpdb

2. False

3. True

4. A Web page that uses a form to display data from the Access object on which it is based; the page includes controls that let you add, delete, sort, filter, browse, and change the data displayed, depending on the type of object on which the page is based.

5. False

6. Select the table or query on which to base the data access page, select the fields to display in the data access page, select an optional grouping level, select optional sort orders, and enter a title.

7. New

OBJECTIVES

In this tutorial you will:

- Insert a spreadsheet component in a Web page

- Insert a chart component in a Web page

- Resize Office components in a Web page

- Get Help for an Office component

- Insert a PivotTable list component in a Web page

- Create user-defined styles for fonts, paragraphs, and hyperlinks

- Link a Web page to a cascading style sheet

LAB

Spreadsheets

USING OFFICE COMPONENTS AND STYLES

Creating Interactive Components and Style Sheets for the Recipes Web Site

CASE

Sunny Morning Products

The recipes Web site will include hundreds of new pages within the next few months. Tyler Vanauken wants to make sure that the Web site development team has the resources it needs to make appropriate decisions on expanding and improving the site. Tyler is confident that the Web site will meet the company's original goals of featuring recipes for popular products and collecting information about the site's visitors.

Tyler wants you to insert two components in a Web page that he created so that the Web site development team can easily determine which Web pages are the most popular. He wants to include a spreadsheet in a Web page that contains data about the number of times each Web page in the Web site has been opened. This spreadsheet will show the results by category, and the team can use this information to determine whether some recipes are more popular than others. Tyler also wants this information to appear in a chart format to visually illustrate Web site usage.

In addition, Tyler wants to analyze sales data from late April and May, when some orange groves were heavily damaged by an infestation of black scale insects. He wants to compare this year's sales data with sales data from previous years to state the damage in financial terms; he will then provide this information to the company's board of directors.

In a recent meeting, the Web site development team expressed interest in using a different format for new Web pages to distinguish them from existing pages. Currently, all Web pages use the same Web theme. The team feels that this approach makes it difficult to identify Web pages that promote special sales and events. Tyler wants you to create a style sheet that authors can use to format new Web pages. This style sheet will include different styles for headings, text, and hyperlinks to distinguish Web pages with these elements from ones formatted with the Web theme.

When you are finished with this tutorial, the Web site development team will be ready to create new pages using your style sheet, and to use data collected by Sunny Morning Products to plan future enhancements to the Web site.

SESSION 9.1

In this session, you will insert a spreadsheet, chart, and PivotTable list component in a Web page. You will change the characteristics of these components by resizing them and changing their properties. You will also learn how to get Help while using a component.

Using Prebuilt Office Components

Most of the Office XP programs—including Word, Excel, Access, and PowerPoint—include commands that let you save their documents as Web pages, which you can then include in a Web site. In many cases, however, you must use the same Office XP program to update the Web page that you used to create the page; you cannot use FrontPage to make changes. To create a Web page that contains a chart, for example, you could use Excel to create the chart and then save the workbook that contains the chart as a Web page in a FrontPage Web site. In this case, you must use Excel to make any changes to that chart.

You could instead use FrontPage to create the chart in the Web page by inserting an Office component into the Web page. An **Office component** is a self-contained object in a Web page that includes the commands and tools required to use it. Note, however, that an Office component is *not* an embedded object from another Office program. You can create three types of Office components in a Web page: a spreadsheet, a chart, or a PivotTable list. A **spreadsheet**, or **worksheet**, is a tool that lets you analyze and summarize data. A **chart** displays data from a spreadsheet or other data source as a picture—for example, as a pie chart or a bar chart. A **PivotTable list** is an interactive spreadsheet that lets you quickly summarize, organize, and display large amounts of data.

When you insert an Office component in a Web page, FrontPage creates the object and provides the tools and commands needed to manipulate it. An Office component does not include the same powerful functionality as the Office XP programs, but it does contain tools to perform calculations, format the data's appearance, and change its characteristics.

You insert an object in a Web page by clicking the Web Component button on the Standard toolbar and then clicking the Spreadsheets and charts component type in the list box. If the Spreadsheets and charts component type is dimmed in the Component type list, then you might need to install the Office XP components on the server.

Tyler wants to include a spreadsheet and a chart in a Web page that detail the Web site's activity by category. He will display the data from the crop damage in a separate Web page. Figure 9-1 shows Tyler's planning analysis sheet for the enhancements that you will make to the recipes Web site.

| Figure 9-1 | TYLER'S PLANNING ANALYSIS SHEET FOR ENHANCING THE RECIPES WEB SITE |

Planning Analysis Sheet

Objective

Enhance the recipes Web site by adding spreadsheet and chart components to the Activity Report Web page to show the Web site's activity by category. Create a new Web page containing a PivotTable list component for analyzing the impact of crop damage in late April and May. Create a Web page that contains styles to use in future recipe pages.

Requirements

Activity Report Web page

Excel workbook that contains the Web site's statistics by category

Excel workbook that contains sales data for late April and May

Results

A Web page that includes a spreadsheet and chart showing the Web site's statistics by category, a Web page containing a PivotTable list component to analyze sales data, and a style sheet that authors can use to create special styles in future Web pages containing new recipes.

Inserting a Spreadsheet Component in a Web Page

Spreadsheets

When you need to display spreadsheet data in a Web page, you can use one of two methods to include the data. The first method is to create the workbook in Excel and then save it as a Web page by clicking File on the menu bar, clicking Save as Web Page, and then saving the file in the desired Web site as a Web page. For this method, you must have Excel installed on your computer.

Alternatively, regardless of whether Excel is installed on your computer, you can insert spreadsheet data in a Web page by inserting an Office spreadsheet component. The spreadsheet component allows you to enter, format, and update spreadsheet data using FrontPage. When you insert a spreadsheet component, you are really inserting an object that includes spreadsheet commands and tools similar to those found in Excel. In fact, the object itself looks like a miniature Excel program window, and the commands and tools provided by the spreadsheet component are similar to those found in Excel.

REFERENCE WINDOW   **RW**

Inserting and Using a Spreadsheet Component in a Web Page
- Create a new Web page to contain the spreadsheet component, or open an existing Web page and position the insertion point in the location in which to insert the component.
- Click the Web Component button on the Standard toolbar, click Spreadsheets and charts in the Component type list box, make sure that Office Spreadsheet is selected in the Choose a control list box, and then click the Finish button.
- Click the desired cell and then enter the data that you want to analyze using the spreadsheet component. Use the Tab key or the arrow keys to move to other cells as necessary to enter the data.
- Click the Commands and Options button on the spreadsheet component toolbar to open the Commands and Options dialog box. Use the commands and tools to calculate and format the data.
- Click anywhere outside the spreadsheet component to deselect it.

Tyler has been collecting information about the Web site's statistics in an Excel workbook that he saved in the Tutorial.09 folder on your Data Disk. He obtained this data from the network administrator at Sunny Morning Products, who used Reports view to generate various usage reports about the Web site. Tyler now wants to create a Web page in the recipes Web site that the Web site development team can use to determine which recipe categories are the most popular, as indicated by the number of times that users have opened pages from each category. For example, the usage statistics might indicate that recipes for cakes are opened frequently, but recipes for butters are rarely used. After examining this data, the team can make decisions about future expansions to the site.

Not all members of the Web site development team have Excel installed on their computers, but all of the team's computers do have the Office XP components installed and their browsers can display these components. (You must have Internet Explorer 4.01 or higher to view and change Office components in a Web page, and you must have Internet Explorer 5 or higher to view and interact with pivot tables.) For this reason, Tyler wants you to insert a spreadsheet component in the Web page to display the site's usage information. He has already created the Web page that will include the spreadsheet component and the Excel workbook that contains the data. You will import both of these files into the Web site from your Data Disk. After inserting the spreadsheet component in the Web page, you will use the Commands and Options dialog box to import the data from Tyler's Excel workbook into the spreadsheet component.

To import the Web page and data file, and then insert the spreadsheet component:

1. Start FrontPage, open the **recipes** Web site from the server, and then, if necessary, change to Folders view.

2. Click **File** on the menu bar, click **Import**, and then click the **Add File** button. The Add File to Import List dialog box opens.

3. Click the **Look in** list arrow, open the drive or folder that contains your Data Disk, and then double-click the **Tutorial.09** folder.

4. Click **activity**, press and hold the **Ctrl** key, click **openings**, release the **Ctrl** key, and then click the **Open** button.

5. Click the **OK** button to import the Activity Report and Openings files into the recipes Web site.

6. Scroll down the Contents pane (if necessary), and then double-click **activity.htm** to open the Activity Report Web page in Page view. Tyler included two placeholders in the page to indicate where you should insert the spreadsheet and chart components.

7. Select the text **Insert spreadsheet component here**, click the **Web Component** button 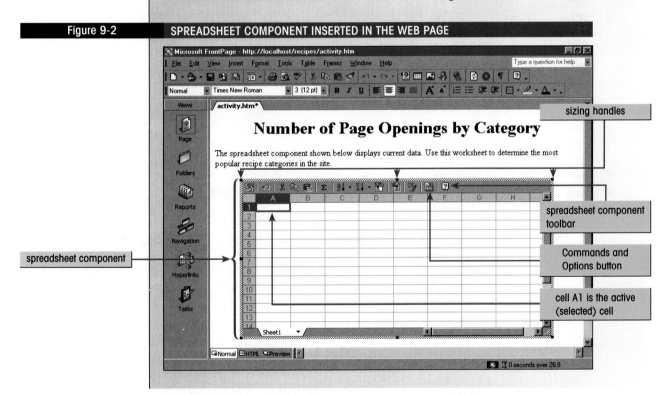 on the Standard toolbar, click **Spreadsheets and charts** in the Component type list box, make sure that **Office Spreadsheet** is selected in the Choose a control list box, and then click the **Finish** button. A spreadsheet component, containing its own toolbar, is inserted in the Web page.

   TROUBLE? If the Spreadsheets and charts option in the Component type list box is dimmed, click the Cancel button. Click Tools on the menu bar, click Page Options, and then click the Compatibility tab. If necessary, click the ActiveX controls and the VBScript check boxes to select them, click the OK button, and then repeat Step 7. If the Spreadsheets and charts option remains dimmed, ask your instructor or technical support person for help.

8. Click the cell in row 1, column A. Sizing handles and a slashed border appear around the component to indicate that it is selected. The dark border around cell A1 indicates that it is the active cell. See Figure 9-2.

Figure 9-2 | **SPREADSHEET COMPONENT INSERTED IN THE WEB PAGE**

After inserting the spreadsheet component, you can either click in a cell and enter data just as you would in Excel, or you can use the Commands and Options dialog box to import data into the spreadsheet component. Because Tyler has gathered the required data in a file that you have already imported into the Web site, you will use the Import Data command to enter his data into the spreadsheet component.

Importing Data into a Spreadsheet Component

You already imported the file that contains the data you will import into the spreadsheet component. After you insert a spreadsheet component in a Web page, you can use the commands in the Commands and Options dialog box to manipulate the data. This dialog box contains commands similar to those found in Excel.

To open the Commands and Options dialog box and import the data:

1. Click the **Commands and Options** button 📧 on the spreadsheet component toolbar to open the Commands and Options dialog box, and then click the **Import** tab. See Figure 9-3.

Figure 9-3	COMMANDS AND OPTIONS DIALOG BOX

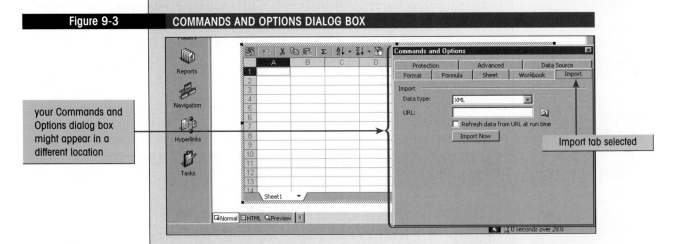

your Commands and Options dialog box might appear in a different location

Import tab selected

TROUBLE? Depending on your installation of FrontPage, the Commands and Options dialog box might appear in a different location on your screen. You can move the dialog box anywhere on the screen by dragging its title bar.

To import the data from a file, you must specify its format and URL. The file, openings.htm, is stored in the recipes Web site as an HTML document. The other file types that you can import are XML and CSV. **XML (extensible markup language)** is a programming language that is similar to HTML but also permits the author to develop customized tags. **CSV (comma-separated values)** is another name for comma-delimited text, where commas separate data values in a text file.

2. Click the **Data type** list arrow, and then click **HTML**.

3. Click in the **URL** text box, and then type **http://localhost/recipes/openings.htm**

TROUBLE? If you are storing your Web site on a computer with a different name or on a different server, use the path for your server instead of the one provided in Step 3.

4. Click the **Refresh data from URL at run time** check box to select it. The data is imported into the spreadsheet component. See Figure 9-4.

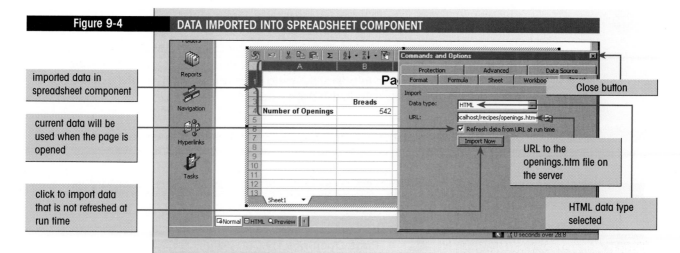

Figure 9-4 DATA IMPORTED INTO SPREADSHEET COMPONENT

Selecting the Refresh data from URL at run time check box ensures that the spreadsheet component will display the current data in the data source (openings.htm) whenever the Web page is opened or refreshed in the browser. However, the data source must be a file that exists in the Web site on the server. You cannot use this feature when you are importing data from an outside data source, because the browser will issue an error message. If you don't select the Refresh data from URL at run time check box, then you must click the Import Now button to import the data. If you use FrontPage to change the imported data, then those changes won't appear in the browser. Instead, the browser will use the original data source when loading the component.

Tyler decides that he doesn't want to link the spreadsheet component to the data source, so he asks you to disable this feature. When this feature is disabled, any changes that Tyler makes to the data in the spreadsheet component will be permanent because the data won't be refreshed from the data source at run time.

5. Click the **Refresh data from URL at run time** check box to clear it. The next time that you display the Import tab, the URL text box will be empty, because no run-time data source will be defined for the spreadsheet component.

6. Click the **Close** button ☒ on the Commands and Options dialog box to close it.

Resizing Worksheet Columns

Notice that the spreadsheet component contains vertical and horizontal scroll bars. Users can use these scroll bars to scroll the worksheet to view all of its columns. Tyler asks you to resize the columns so that users won't need to scroll the data in the spreadsheet component to view all of its columns.

To resize the worksheet columns:

1. Position the pointer on the right border of the column heading for column A. When the pointer changes to a ↔ shape, double-click the right border. Column A is resized to best fit the data it contains, which means that the column is slightly wider than the data it contains.

2. Repeat Step 1 to select and resize columns B though G to their best fit. See Figure 9-5. Now the data in the worksheet fits better in the spreadsheet component.

Figure 9-5	RESIZED WORKSHEET COLUMNS

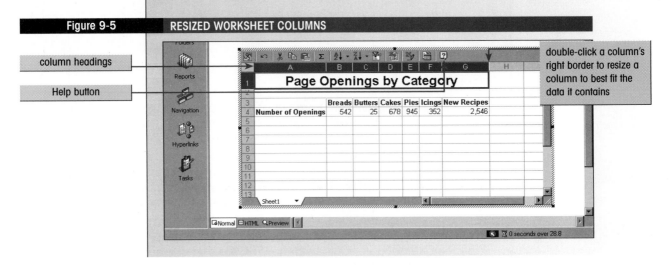

column headings

Help button

double-click a column's right border to resize a column to best fit the data it contains

Getting Help When Using the Spreadsheet Component

Regardless of your experience using Excel, you might need help using the commands in the Commands and Options dialog box. Fortunately, each Office component has its own Help system to assist you with these commands. Clicking the Help button on a component's toolbar (or right-clicking the component to open the shortcut menu and then clicking Help) opens the Help window for that component. Tyler asks you use the Help window to learn about formatting data in a spreadsheet component.

To get Help while using the spreadsheet component:

1. Click the **Help** button 🔲 on the spreadsheet component toolbar. The Microsoft Office Spreadsheet Component Help window opens.

2. If necessary, click the **Maximize** button 🔲 on the Microsoft Office Spreadsheet Component Help title bar to maximize the window, and then click the **Contents** tab (if necessary). See Figure 9-6.

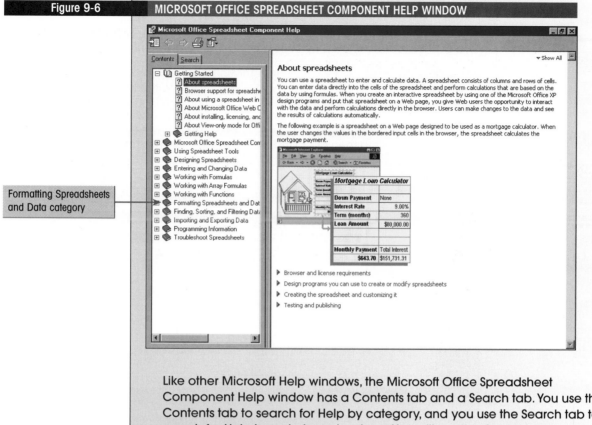

Figure 9-6   MICROSOFT OFFICE SPREADSHEET COMPONENT HELP WINDOW

Formatting Spreadsheets and Data category

Like other Microsoft Help windows, the Microsoft Office Spreadsheet Component Help window has a Contents tab and a Search tab. You use the Contents tab to search for Help by category, and you use the Search tab to search for Help by entering a key term. You will use the Contents tab to search for Help on formatting data.

3. Click the **plus box** to the left of the Formatting Spreadsheets and Data category.

4. Click **Format cells in a spreadsheet**. The pane on the right displays links to pages that describe how to change the format and alignment of data.

5. Click some of the links and read the Help pages that open to learn about formatting and aligning spreadsheet data.

6. After reading the information about formatting and aligning data, click the **Close** button ☒ on the Microsoft Office Spreadsheet Component Help window to close it.

When you need information about other formatting options, performing calculations, or other topics of interest, you can open the Help window to obtain information about your task.

Resizing a Spreadsheet Component in a Web Page

The spreadsheet component that you inserted in the Web page is an object, just like a picture or text. It is selected when a slashed border and sizing handles appear around the component. To resize the component, you drag a sizing handle.

Tyler thinks that the spreadsheet component might look better if you resized it to fit the data in the worksheet, thereby reducing the component's size.

To resize the spreadsheet component:

1. Make sure that the spreadsheet component is selected. Sizing handles and a slashed border should appear around the component.

2. Position the pointer on the middle-right sizing handle so the pointer changes to a ↔ shape, and then click and slowly drag it to the left until the right edge of the component is slightly to the right of column G in the worksheet.

3. Position the pointer on the middle-bottom sizing handle so the pointer changes to a ↕ shape, and then click and slowly drag it up until the bottom edge of the component is slightly below row 4 in the worksheet. See Figure 9-7.

| Figure 9-7 | RESIZED SPREADSHEET COMPONENT |

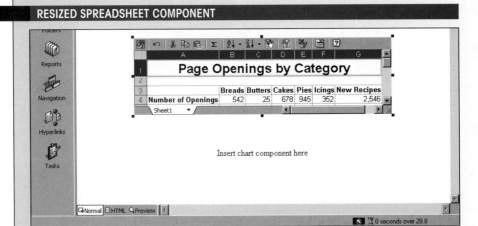

TROUBLE? If you cannot see all of the data in the worksheet, drag a sizing handle to make the spreadsheet component larger or smaller as necessary so that your component looks like the one shown in Figure 9-7.

4. Click the **Save** button 🖫 on the Standard toolbar to save the page.

Inserting a Chart Component in a Web Page

When you need to display data in a Web page graphically, you can insert an Office chart component, which lets you create many types of charts. The most commonly used data source for a chart is the data contained in a spreadsheet component. For a chart, the data source is an ActiveX control that links a chart component to its data. You use the Chart Wizard to connect to the data source and to specify the chart type, chart subtype, and data range to use for the chart. After inserting the chart component, you can change its properties by using the Commands and Options dialog box. This dialog box, which has the same name as the one used with a spreadsheet component, contains commands for creating and formatting charts.

The spreadsheet component that you added to the Activity Report Web page is a valid data source that you will use to create the chart. Tyler asks you to create a pie chart from this information. A **pie chart** displays data as pieces of a pie to show the relationship of each piece to the whole. Tyler feels that a pie chart will make it easy to determine which recipe categories are the most popular.

REFERENCE WINDOW   `RW`

Inserting a Chart Component in a Web Page That Contains a Data Source

- Open the Web page that contains the data source in Page view, and then position the insertion point in the desired location for the chart.
- Click the Web Component button on the Standard toolbar, click Spreadsheets and charts in the Component type list box, click Office Chart in the Choose a control list box, and then click the Finish button. A chart component is inserted in the page, and the Chart Wizard opens the Commands and Options dialog box and selects the Data Source tab.
- Click the Data from the following Web page item option button. If necessary, select the data source in the list box.
- Click the Data Range tab. In the Data range text box, type the range reference for the cells that contain the data you wish to include in the chart.
- Click the option button to identify the data series as appearing in rows or columns, and then click the OK button.
- If necessary, edit the series name and the ranges that represent the category labels and data values.
- Click the Type tab, and then click the desired chart type and chart subtype.
- Close the Commands and Options dialog box.

Tyler asks you to create a pie chart by using the data in the spreadsheet component. You will use a chart component to create the pie chart.

To create the chart component:

1. Scroll down the Web page as necessary so that you can see the "Insert chart component here" text. You will create the chart here.

2. Select the text **Insert chart component here**.

3. Click the **Web Component** button 🖉 on the Standard toolbar, click **Spreadsheets and charts** in the Component type list box, click **Office Chart** in the Choose a control list box, and then click the **Finish** button. The Chart Wizard inserts a chart component in the Web page and opens the Commands and Options dialog box. See Figure 9-8.

Figure 9-8   **CHART COMPONENT INSERTED IN THE WEB PAGE**

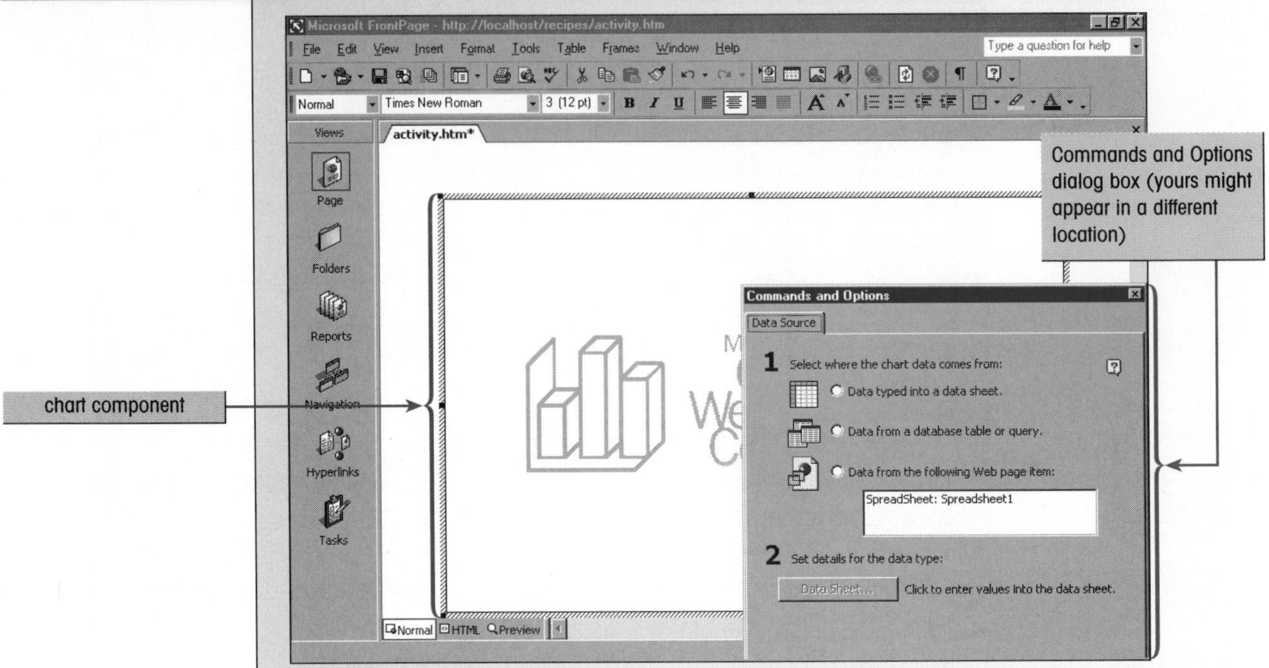

chart component

Commands and Options dialog box (yours might appear in a different location)

First, you must create or specify the data source for the chart. You can do so by typing data into a datasheet, by selecting a table or query object in a database, or by selecting an object in the existing Web page. Tyler wants you to use the spreadsheet component that you inserted in the Activity Report Web page, so you'll select the third option. After specifying the spreadsheet component as the data source, you must identify the data range that contains the data to be included in the chart. The data range that you select will vary based on the type of chart you are creating. Normally, you select the text that identifies your data (also called data labels) as well as the numeric data you are illustrating.

To specify the data source for the chart component:

1. On the Data Source tab, click the **Data from the following Web page item** option button. Because there is only one valid data source in the current Web page, the Spreadsheet: Spreadsheet1 item is selected automatically. The appearance of the chart component changes to show that you have selected a data source. See Figure 9-9.

Figure 9-9   DATA SOURCE DEFINED FOR THE CHART COMPONENT

spreadsheet component in this page selected as the data source for the chart component

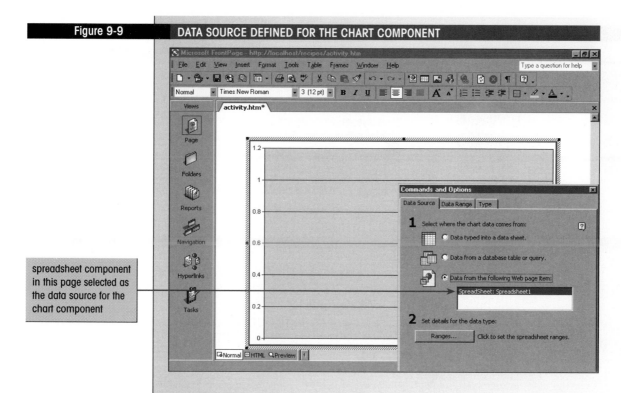

2. Click the **Data Range** tab. You use this tab to specify the data range for the data that you want to chart.

3. If necessary, drag the Commands and Options dialog box out of the way so that you can see the vertical scroll bar, and then drag the scroll box on the vertical scroll bar up so that you can see the spreadsheet component that you previously inserted. The spreadsheet data that you want to chart appears in the range A1:G4. For a chart, however, you need to provide only the data range containing the labels and their values, which in this case is B3:G4. See Figure 9-10.

Figure 9-10   EXAMINING THE DATA SOURCE

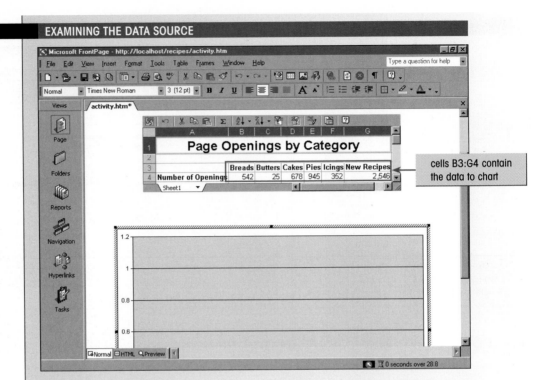

cells B3:G4 contain the data to chart

4. Scroll the page down so that the top of the chart component appears at the top of the Contents pane, and then click any white area in the chart component to select the chart component and redisplay the Commands and Options dialog box. See Figure 9-11. Several new tabs now appear in the Commands and Options dialog box. As you complete the chart component, tabs are added to the Commands and Options dialog box to provide tools for changing the chart's appearance. When the Commands and Options dialog box is displayed, clicking different places in the chart component changes the options in the dialog box so as to provide tools for formatting the area on the chart component that you clicked.

Figure 9-11   IDENTIFYING THE DATA RANGE

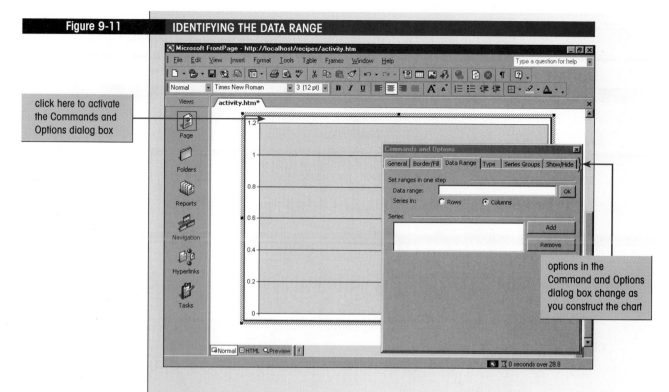

click here to activate the Commands and Options dialog box

options in the Command and Options dialog box change as you construct the chart

5. Click in the **Data range** text box, and then type **B3:G4**. This range contains the data to chart. The data appears in rows, with the label in the first row and the corresponding data value in the row below the label. You'll use the Rows option button to select this data series.

6. Click the **Rows** option button (if necessary), and then click the **OK** button to the right of the Data range text box. The chart component changes to show the labels and their values based on the information you just provided. See Figure 9-12.

Figure 9-12   DATA RANGE ADDED TO CHART COMPONENT

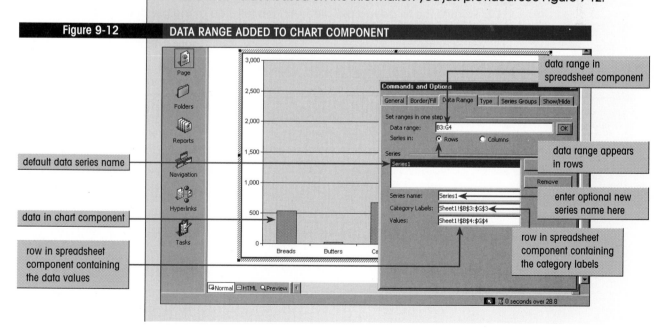

data range in spreadsheet component

data range appears in rows

default data series name

enter optional new series name here

data in chart component

row in spreadsheet component containing the category labels

row in spreadsheet component containing the data values

7. Click the **Type** tab. You use the Type tab to indicate the chart type and subtype. As you click the different chart subtypes on the right side of the Type tab, their names and descriptions appear at the bottom of the Type tab. See Figure 9-13.

Figure 9-13   TYPE TAB SELECTED

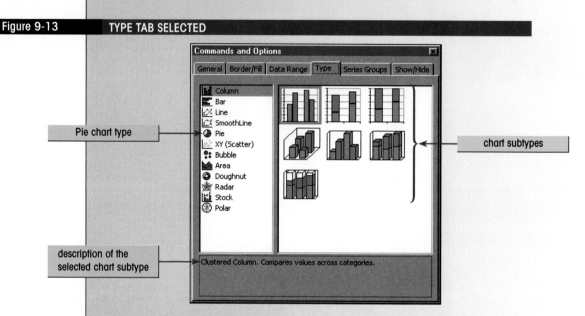

Pie chart type

chart subtypes

description of the
selected chart subtype

Tyler asks you to select a pie chart with the 3D Exploded Pie chart subtype.

8. In the pane on the left of the Type tab, click **Pie**, and then click the **3D Exploded Pie** chart subtype (the second pie chart in the second row). The chart component changes again to show an exploded pie chart.

9. Click the **Close** button ☒ on the Commands and Options dialog box. The dialog box closes and reveals the chart component that you created.

10. Point to the large red pie piece on the left side of the pie chart. A ScreenTip shows the category name (New Recipes) and its value in units and as a percent of the entire pie chart (2,546 or 50%). See Figure 9-14.

Figure 9-14   **3D EXPLODED PIE CHART**

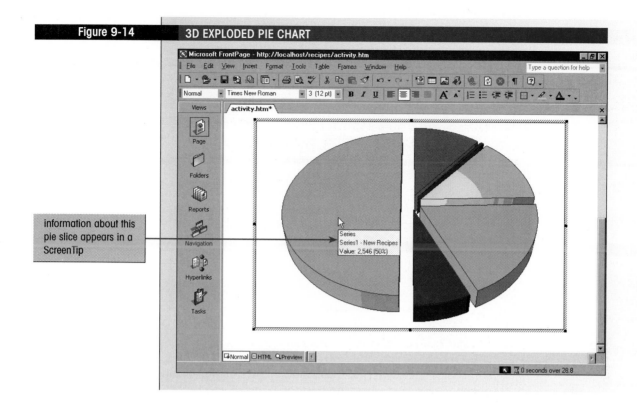

information about this pie slice appears in a ScreenTip

Adding a Title and Legend to a Chart Component

Tyler wants to make several changes to the chart component to make it easier to use. First, he wants you to display a legend with the chart and add a chart title. A **legend** is a box that relates the colors used in a chart to the values they represent.

To add a chart title and display the chart legend:

1. Right-click any white area in the chart component to display the shortcut menu, click **Commands and Options**, and then click the **General** tab (if necessary). The General tab contains options for changing the chart component's appearance. See Figure 9-15.

Figure 9-15   ADDING A TITLE TO THE CHART COMPONENT

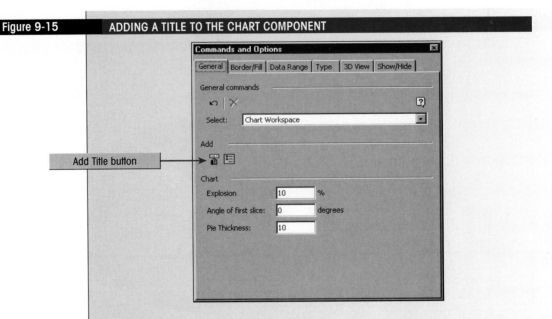

Add Title button

TROUBLE? Depending on where you right-click before opening the Commands and Options dialog box, you might see different options. If you do not see the same tabs as shown and described in the steps, click the area specified in the previous step to change the options in the dialog box.

2. Point to the **Add Title** button in the Add section of the dialog box. A ScreenTip identifies this button's name. You can use the ScreenTips to identify buttons in the Commands and Options dialog box.

3. Click . The text "Chart Workspace Title" is added at the top of the chart component. To create a title, select this placeholder text and then type a new title using the Format tab that appears.

4. Click the **Chart Workspace Title** placeholder in the chart component. A dark colored box appears around the title, and the tabs in the Commands and Options dialog box change to provide tools for working with titles.

5. Click the **Format** tab in the Commands and Options dialog box.

6. Select the text in the Caption text box, and then type **Activity by Category**. See Figure 9-16.

Figure 9-16   **FORMATTING THE CHART TITLE**

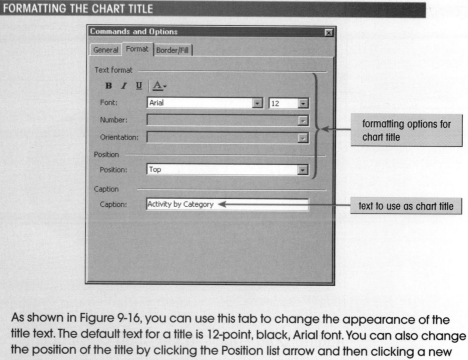

formatting options for chart title

text to use as chart title

As shown in Figure 9-16, you can use this tab to change the appearance of the title text. The default text for a title is 12-point, black, Arial font. You can also change the position of the title by clicking the Position list arrow and then clicking a new location in which to place the title.

7. Click any white area in the chart component, click the **General** tab in the Commands and Options dialog box, and then click the **Add Legend** button in the Add section.

8. Close the Commands and Options dialog box. The chart component now contains a title and a legend.

9. Save the page.

Resizing a Chart Component in a Web Page

You can resize the chart component by using the sizing handles, just as you resized the spreadsheet component. Tyler thinks that the chart component is larger than necessary, so he asks you to resize it.

To resize the chart component:

1. If necessary, click the chart component to select it. A slashed border and sizing handles should appear around the chart component.

2. Scroll up the Web page until you can see some of the spreadsheet component and some of the chart component.

3. Position the pointer on the top-right sizing handle on the chart component so that it changes to a ↗ shape, and then slowly drag it down and toward the pie chart until the chart is approximately the same width as the spreadsheet component. See Figure 9-17.

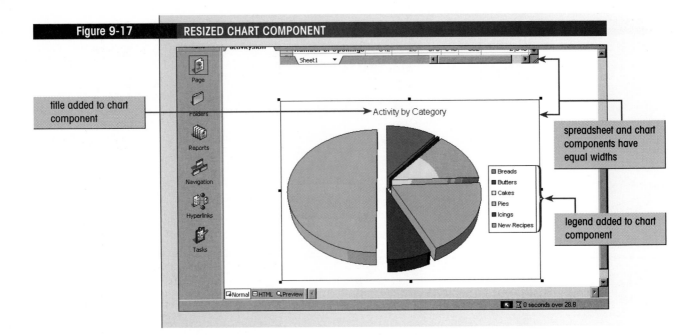

Figure 9-17   **RESIZED CHART COMPONENT**

title added to chart component

spreadsheet and chart components have equal widths

legend added to chart component

Adding Data Labels to the Chart Component

Although it is easy to point to a piece of the pie chart to view its details, Tyler thinks that the chart would be more effective if these values were permanently displayed. He asks you to add data labels to the pieces of the pie chart.

To add data labels to the pie chart pieces:

1. Click the chart component to select it (so that a slashed border and sizing handles appear around the component), right-click any piece of the pie chart to select it and open the shortcut menu, and then click **Commands and Options**. The Commands and Options dialog box opens and displays the options for Series1, which is the series that contains the chart's data.

2. In the Add section, click the **Add Data Label** button ⌊⌊⌋. Data labels are added to the pieces of the pie chart. See Figure 9-18.

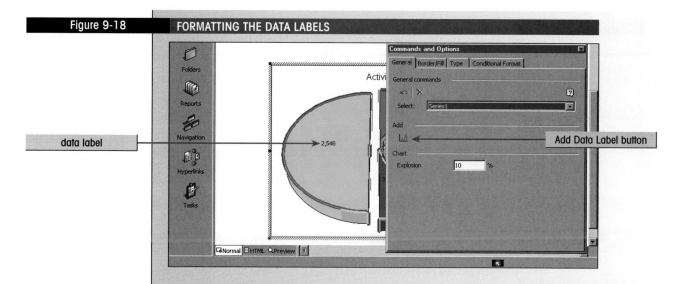

Figure 9-18 FORMATTING THE DATA LABELS

data label

Add Data Label button

The data labels include the values from the spreadsheet component for each category. These values would be easier to interpret if you also expressed them as a percentage of the entire amount and included the category names.

3. Click **2,546** in the red piece of the pie chart to select the data labels. The tabs in the Commands and Options dialog box change to display options for formatting data labels.

4. Click the **Data Labels** tab, and then click the **Category name** and **Percentage** check boxes to select them. As you select these check boxes, the category name and percentages are added to the data labels.

TROUBLE? If you cannot see the changes to the data labels, drag the Commands and Options dialog box to the lower-right corner of your screen.

The Separator list arrow lets you use a comma, space, or line break to separate the values that you selected for inclusion in the data labels. Tyler wants to separate the values with line breaks.

5. Click the **Separator** list arrow, and then click **(New Line)**.

6. Close the Commands and Options dialog box. The data labels are displayed in the chart with their category names, values, and percentage amounts. See Figure 9-19.

Figure 9-19   REVISED DATA LABELS

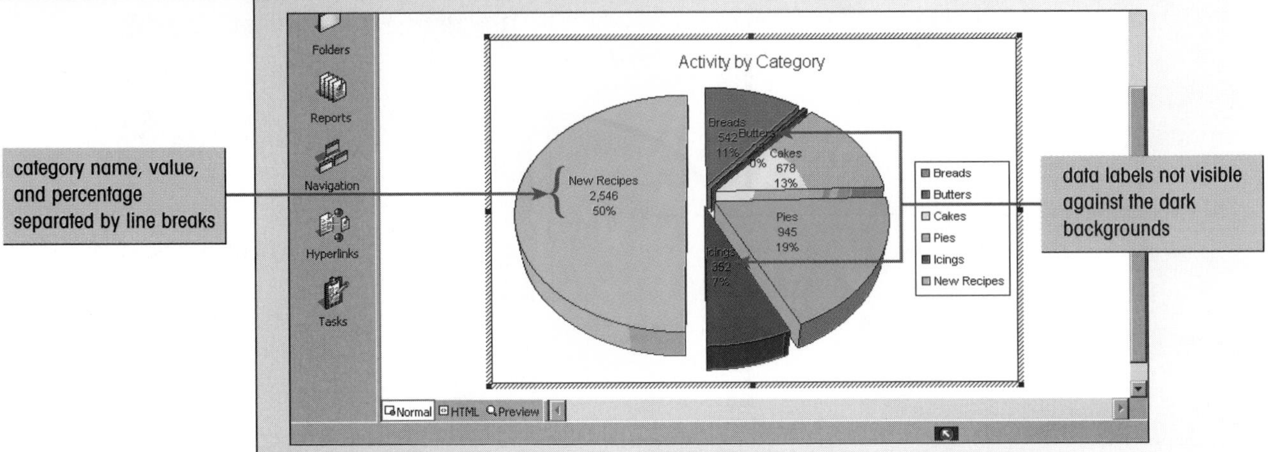

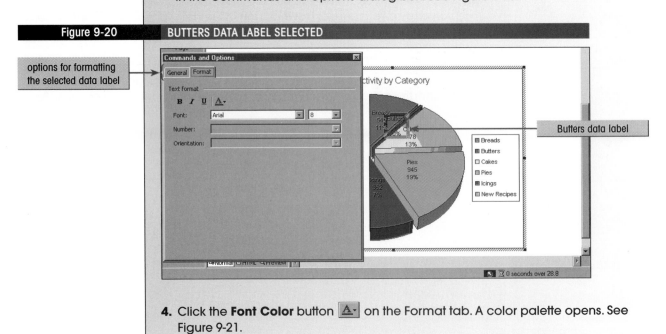

category name, value, and percentage separated by line breaks

data labels not visible against the dark backgrounds

As you examine the chart component, you notice that the labels for the Butters and Icings categories are not readable because they use black text on a dark background. Tyler asks you to change the text color for these labels to a lighter color so that they will be legible.

To change the text color of the data labels:

1. Right-click any data label to select all data labels and open the shortcut menu, and then click **Commands and Options**.

2. If necessary, drag the Commands and Options dialog box to the lower-left corner of the screen so that you can see the data labels for the Butters and Icings categories.

3. Click the data label for the Butters category, and then click the **Format** tab in the Commands and Options dialog box. See Figure 9-20.

Figure 9-20   BUTTERS DATA LABEL SELECTED

options for formatting the selected data label

Butters data label

4. Click the **Font Color** button ![A] on the Format tab. A color palette opens. See Figure 9-21.

Figure 9-21   **COLOR PALETTE FOR SELECTING A NEW DATA LABEL FONT COLOR**

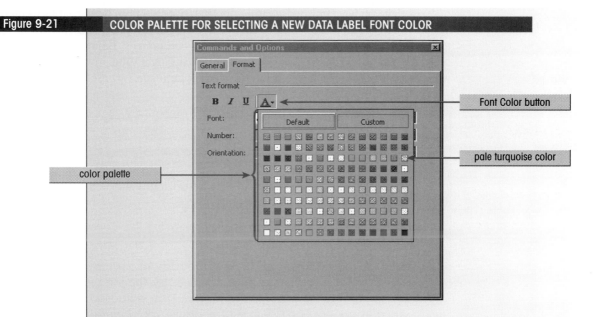

Font Color button

pale turquoise color

color palette

Because the background for the Butters piece of the pie is dark, you need to select a light color. Tyler recommends using a shade of blue to provide a good contrast with the black and gold pieces of the pie on which the data label appears.

5. Click the **pale turquoise** color (the last color in the third row) to select it. The color of the data label changes to light blue.

6. Click the data label for the Icings category, click **A**, and then click the **pale turquoise** color again. The color of the data label for the Icings category changes to light blue. See Figure 9-22.

Figure 9-22   **CHANGING THE FONT COLOR OF THE ICINGS DATA LABEL**

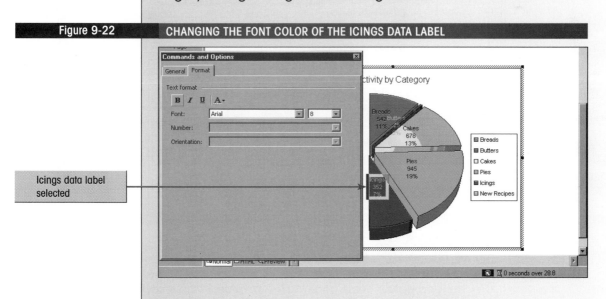

Icings data label selected

7. Close the Commands and Options dialog box, and then save the page.

Now that you have finished creating the Web page, you can preview it by using the browser. When you insert an Office component in a Web page, you provide users with the capability to temporarily change the data in the spreadsheet component. Because the chart component is based on data in the spreadsheet component, changing a value in the spreadsheet component will also change the data displayed in the chart component.

To preview a Web page that contains Office components and update data:

1. Click the **Preview in Browser** button 🔍 on the Standard toolbar.

2. If necessary, scroll down the Web page until you can see the chart component and the spreadsheet component.

3. Click the spreadsheet component to select it. If the Commands and Options dialog box opens, close it.

4. Select the value **25** in cell C4 in the spreadsheet component, and then type **850**. Watch the chart as you press the **Tab** key. The pie slice that represents the Butters category increases in size to reflect the increased value in the spreadsheet component. See Figure 9-23. Because you changed the font color of the data label for the Butters pie piece, its text is legible.

| Figure 9-23 | CHANGING A VALUE IN THE SPREADSHEET COMPONENT |

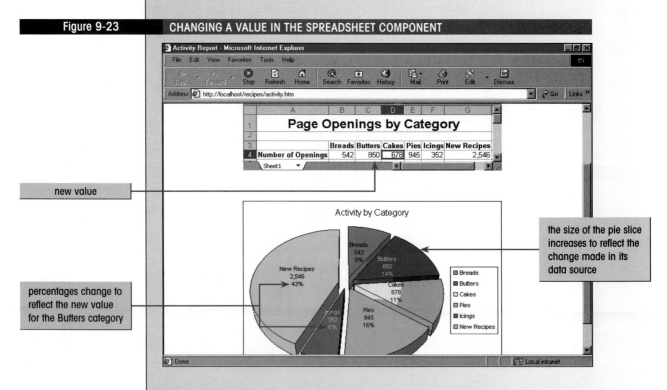

new value

the size of the pie slice increases to reflect the change made in its data source

percentages change to reflect the new value for the Butters category

You changed the value for the Butters category in the Web page that is displayed in the browser. If you refresh the page, your browser will display the changed data, not the original stored value, in the spreadsheet component and in the pie chart. The spreadsheet component in the Web page in FrontPage, however, still contains the *original* value, 25.

5. Click the **Refresh** button 🔄 on the toolbar. The Butters value is still 850 in the spreadsheet component.

TROUBLE? If the size of the spreadsheet component decreases, position the pointer on the lower-right corner of the component so that it changes to a ↘ shape, and then drag the corner down to increase its size until you can see the values in row 4.

6. Close the browser.

7. Click the **Refresh** button 🔳 on the Standard toolbar. The value 25 still appears in cell C4.

   When you use the browser to change data in an Office component, your changes are temporary. As a result, users of the page can analyze their own data without changing the original data in the page. To permanently change the data in the spreadsheet component, you must change it using FrontPage.

8. Select the value **25** in cell C4, type **900**, and then press the **Tab** key. The chart component changes to reflect the new value for the Butters category.

9. Save the page, and then preview it in the browser. The spreadsheet and chart components show the value 900 for the Butters category.

10. Close the browser, and then close the Activity Report page.

Inserting the spreadsheet and chart components has provided you with worksheet capabilities in the Web page, without requiring that you use Excel.

Using a PivotTable List Component in a Web Page

The last type of Office component—the PivotTable list—is an advanced tool that you can create by using data from a spreadsheet, database, or other source. You insert a PivotTable list component in a Web page just like any other component. Unlike with a spreadsheet component, into which you type or import data, and a chart component, which can use a spreadsheet component in the same Web page as a data source, you must create a connection to the data that you want to analyze with the PivotTable list component. This data source can be an Excel worksheet, an object in a database (such as a table or query), or another valid data source. For a PivotTable list component, the data source must be stored outside of the Web site.

In April and May, the orange groves at Sunny Morning Products were damaged by an unusually heavy infestation of black scale insects, which damaged a significant population of Valencia orange trees. Tyler wants to use a pivot table to analyze the order data for late April and May to calculate the financial impact of the damaged groves. He obtained data from the sales department in the form of an Excel worksheet, which includes the customer and invoice numbers, total order amounts, and order dates for Valencia orange shipments sent out during this time frame. Tyler can compare the number of orders placed and the number of orders actually shipped during this time frame with the same data from last year to assess the loss of revenue from the damaged crops.

REFERENCE WINDOW   RW

Using Spreadsheet Data in a PivotTable List Component in a Web Page

- In Page view, create a new page, or open the page in which you want to create the PivotTable list component, and position the insertion point in the correct location.
- Click the Web Component button on the Standard toolbar, click Spreadsheets and charts in the Component type list box, click Office PivotTable in the Choose a control list box, and then click the Finish button.
- Click the PivotTable list component to select it, and then click the Click here to connect to data link in the PivotTable list component.
- On the Data Source tab, click the Connection option button.
- Click the Edit button, browse to the drive and folder that contains the data source, click the data source file to select it, and then click the Open button.
- In the Select Table dialog box, select the worksheet that contains the data, and then click the OK button.
- Close the Commands and Options dialog box.
- Click the Field List button on the PivotTable list component toolbar.
- Drag the fields from the field list into the appropriate areas in the PivotTable list component.

Tyler stored the Excel workbook containing the order data in the Tutorial.09 folder on your Data Disk.

To create the PivotTable list component and a data connection:

1. Click the **Create a new normal page** button on the Standard toolbar. A new Web page opens in Page view.

2. Type **Black Scale Insect Damage**, click the **Center** button on the Formatting toolbar, click the **Style** list arrow on the Formatting toolbar, and then click **Heading 1**.

3. Press the **Enter** key. You will insert the PivotTable list component on this new centered line.

4. Click the **Web Component** button on the Standard toolbar. The Insert Web Component dialog box opens.

5. In the Component type list box, click **Spreadsheets and charts**, click **Office PivotTable** in the Choose a control list box, and then click the **Finish** button. A PivotTable list component is inserted in the Web page. See Figure 9-24.

Figure 9-24   PIVOTTABLE LIST COMPONENT ADDED TO WEB PAGE

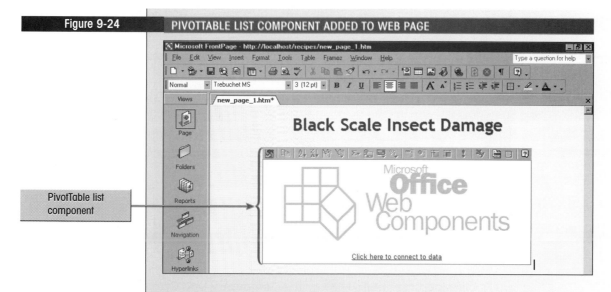

PivotTable list component

6. Click the component to select it. The component's border displays a slashed border and sizing handles.

7. Click the **Click here to connect to data** link. The Commands and Options dialog box opens. This dialog box contains options for connecting to the data that you want to analyze using the PivotTable list component. You will select the Excel workbook in the Tutorial.09 folder.

8. Click the **Connection** option button, and then click the **Edit** button. The Select Data Source dialog box opens. A list of any previously defined data connections appears in the list box. Because you are creating the data connection for the first time, you'll need to browse to the Tutorial.09 folder on your Data Disk.

9. Use the **Look in** list arrow and browse to your Data Disk, double-click the **Tutorial.09** folder, click **orders**, and then click the **Open** button. The Select Table dialog box opens. The worksheet data is stored on Sheet1, which is already selected because it is the only worksheet in the workbook. See Figure 9-25.

Figure 9-25   SELECT TABLE DIALOG BOX

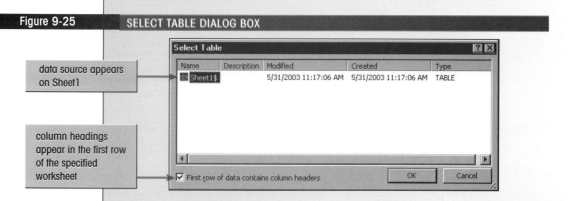

data source appears on Sheet1

column headings appear in the first row of the specified worksheet

10. Click the **OK** button. The connection string to the Excel workbook appears in the Connection text box and Sheet1$ appears in the Data member, table, view, or cube name text box. See Figure 9-26. This information identifies the file and object (in this case, a worksheet) containing the data.

Figure 9-26   COMPLETED DATA SOURCE CONNECTION

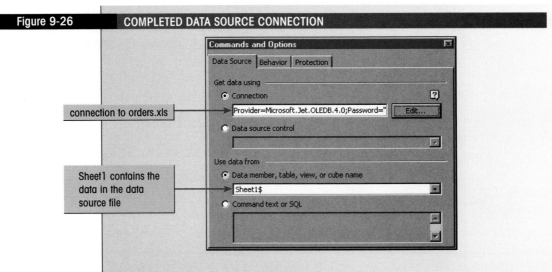

11. Click the **Close** button ☒ on the Commands and Options dialog box to close it. The PivotTable list component now includes four areas in which to insert fields from the worksheet. See Figure 9-27.

Figure 9-27   PIVOTTABLE LIST COMPONENT AFTER DEFINING THE DATA SOURCE

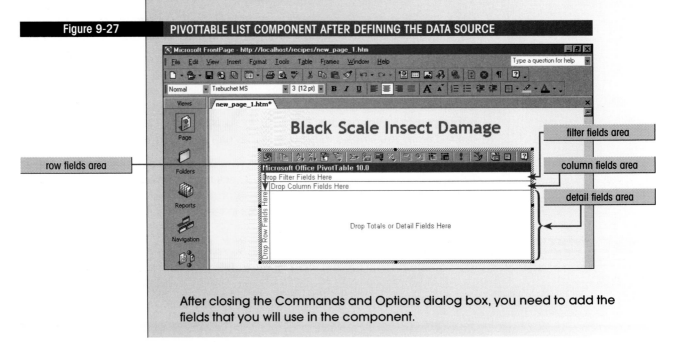

After closing the Commands and Options dialog box, you need to add the fields that you will use in the component.

Adding Fields to a PivotTable List Component

A PivotTable list component contains four field areas: filter, column, row, and detail. A **filter field** lets you restrict the data used in the component. For example, Tyler can limit the data to display only those orders occurring in a specific month, week, or day. A **column field** stores data that will become the column headings. A **row field** stores data that will become the row headings in the component. A **detail field** provides information about the data identified by the column and row headings. It might contain invoice totals or summary information about the fields, such as grand totals or average invoice amounts.

Tyler wants to set up the PivotTable list component to use a week number as a filter, the customer number as the row field, the invoice number as the column field, and the invoice amount as the detail field. To add these fields to the component, you must first display the field list. The **field list** displays the data fields from the data source. When you base a PivotTable list component on a worksheet, the column headings in the worksheet become the data fields in the field list. The Sheet1 worksheet in the orders workbook contains four column headings: InvoiceNum, OrderNum, Amount, and Date.

To display the field list and add fields to the component:

1. Click the **Field List** button 📧 on the PivotTable list component toolbar. The PivotTable Field List window (also known as the field list) opens. See Figure 9-28.

Figure 9-28	FIELD LIST FOR DATA SOURCE

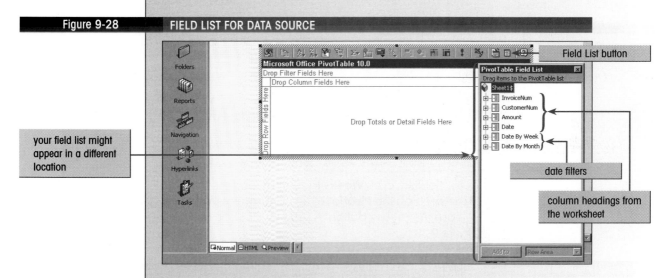

your field list might appear in a different location

The four fields from the worksheet appear in the field list, along with two new fields: Date By Week and Date By Month. You can use these new fields to filter date data.

2. In the field list, click **Amount**, and then drag it to the area of the component labeled "Drop Totals or Detail Fields Here." When this area has a blue border, release the mouse button. A new row which contains the column headings "Amount" is added to the component, along with the order amounts from each invoice. (See Figure 9-29.)

3. In the field list, click **CustomerNum**, and then drag it to the area of the component labeled "Drop Row Fields Here." When this area has a blue border, release the mouse button. A new column, which contains customer numbers from the worksheet, is added to the component. (See Figure 9-29.)

4. In the field list, click **InvoiceNum** to select it, and then drag it to the "Drop Column Fields Here" area on the PivotTable list component. When this area has a blue border, release the mouse button. A new row is added to the component. Each column contains an invoice number from the InvoiceNum column in the worksheet. See Figure 9-29.

Figure 9-29	FIELDS ADDED TO THE PIVOTTABLE LIST COMPONENT

invoice numbers from
the worksheet added
as column fields

customer numbers
from the worksheet
added as row fields

invoice amounts from
the worksheet added
as detail fields

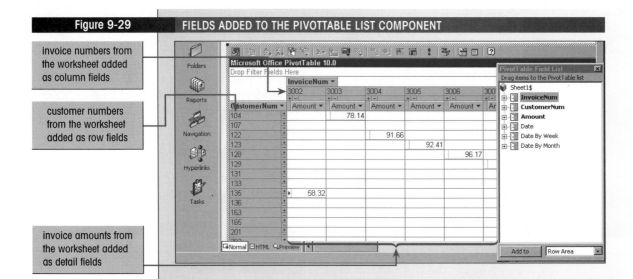

TROUBLE? If you drop a field in the wrong area in the PivotTable list component,
right-click the field name to open the shortcut menu, and then click Remove Field.

5. Click the **plus box** to the left of the Date By Week field in the field list. The field
   list expands to show several time periods by date.

6. In the field list, click **Weeks** to select it, and then drag it to the "Drop Filter Fields
   Here" area on the PivotTable list component. When this area has a blue border,
   release the mouse button. A Date By Week field is added as the filter field. See
   Figure 9-30.

Figure 9-30	COMPLETED PIVOTTABLE LIST COMPONENT

Date By Week added
as filter field

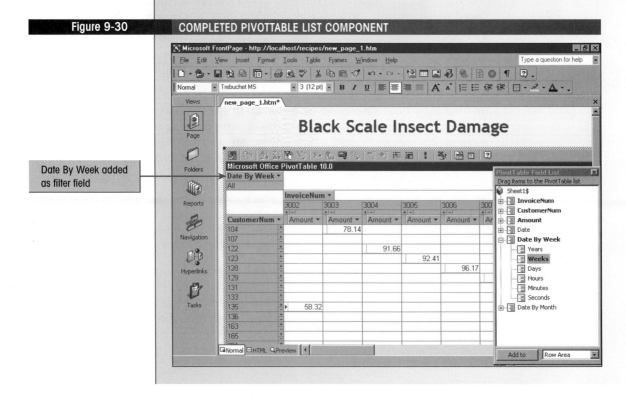

7. Click the **Close** button ☒ on the field list to close it.

8. Save the Web page using the filename **damage.htm** and the title **Black Scale Insect Damage** in the recipes Web site.

Using the Browser to Interact with a PivotTable List Component

Now that the PivotTable list component contains the appropriate data fields, you are ready to preview it using the browser.

To use a browser to view the PivotTable list component:

1. Click the **Preview in Browser** button 🔍 on the Standard toolbar. The Black Scale Insect Damage page opens in the browser.

TROUBLE? If a dialog box opens and asks whether you want to access data on another domain, click the Yes button.

TROUBLE? If you are using Internet Explorer 4.x for your browser, then you will be able to view the PivotTable list component but your ability to change its data might be limited. If you experience problems, ask your instructor or technical support person for help.

The first thing that Tyler wants to examine is the data for the last week of April, which is week 17.

2. Click the **list arrow** for the Date By Week field, click the **All** check box to clear it, click the **plus box** to the left of 2003, and then click the **check box** to the left of 17. You have set the filter to display fields from orders placed in the last week of April. See Figure 9-31.

| Figure 9-31 | CHANGING THE FILTER FIELD |

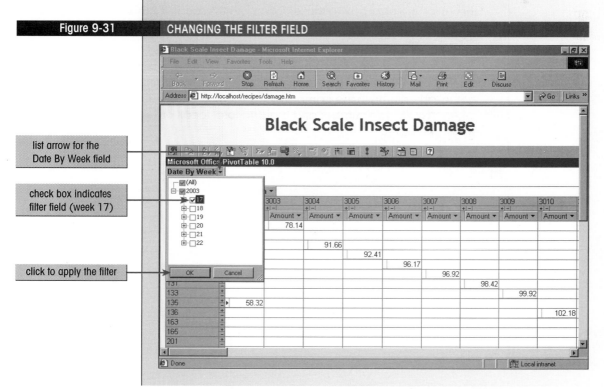

list arrow for the Date By Week field

check box indicates filter field (week 17)

click to apply the filter

3. Click the **OK** button. Only those invoice numbers, customer numbers, and amounts for orders placed during the time specified by the filter appear in the component. See Figure 9-32.

Figure 9-32	FILTER APPLIED TO THE PIVOTTABLE LIST COMPONENT

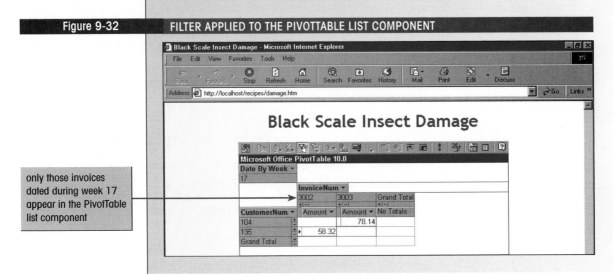

only those invoices dated during week 17 appear in the PivotTable list component

By examining the data provided, Tyler sees that only two orders of Valencia oranges were shipped during this week. During the same time last year, more than 65 orders were shipped, clearly summarizing the financial impact of the crop damage. Tyler now wants to view a total for the week's sales. To accomplish this goal, he asks you to add a summary field to the detail field.

To add a summary field to the PivotTable list component:

1. Click the **Field List** button 🔲 on the PivotTable list component toolbar, and then click the **plus box** to the left of Amount. A second Amount field appears in the field list.

2. Click the second **Amount** field to select it, and then drag it to the "No Totals" column in the component. When the No Totals column has a blue border, release the mouse button. A new Sum of Amount column heading is added as the last column in the component. The column calculates the invoice totals for each customer number and a grand total for all orders placed during this week. See Figure 9-33.

| Figure 9-33 | SUM OF AMOUNT COLUMN ADDED TO THE PIVOTTABLE LIST COMPONENT |

grand total (total sales during week 17)

sum detail field

sums the total for each customer (total sales by customer)

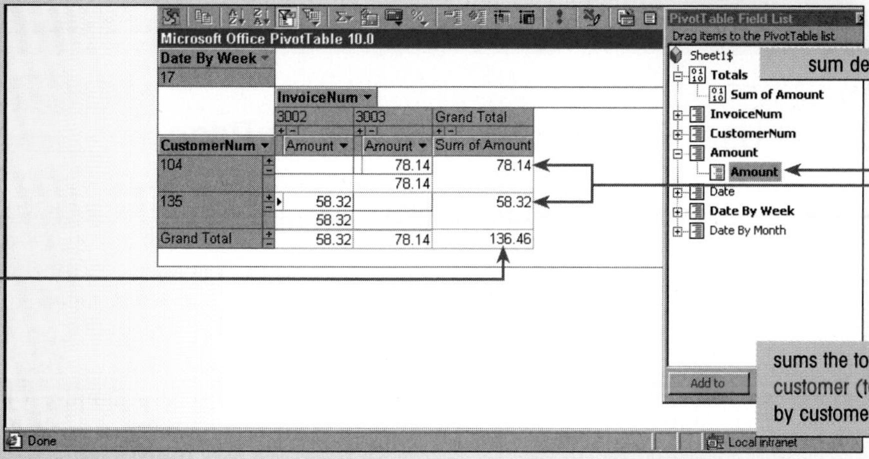

3. Close the browser, the recipes Web site, and FrontPage.

Tyler will use the data provided in the Web pages containing Office components in the next board meeting to begin the board's discussion of long-term planning, especially when discussing controlling insect infestations in the Valencia orange groves.

In the next session, you will create a style sheet that formats text, paragraphs, and hyperlinks in Web pages.

Session 9.1 QUICK CHECK

1. What are the three types of Office components that you can create in a Web page?

2. When should you use a spreadsheet component to display spreadsheet information in a Web page?

3. True or False: You cannot resize an Office component after inserting it in a Web page.

4. What is the data range for a chart component?

5. True or False: A data source for a PivotTable list component can reside in the Web site in which the component appears.

6. What are the four field areas in a PivotTable list component and what function does each field area serve?

SESSION 9.2

In this session, you will create a cascading style sheet that contains user-defined styles for HTML tags. You will link the cascading style sheet to a new Web page and use it to format headings, text, and hyperlinks in the new Web page.

Creating User-Defined Styles in a Web Page

Throughout this book, you have used the Style list box on the Formatting toolbar to create different styles of text in a Web page. For example, when you select text in a Web page that does not use a theme and then apply the Heading 1 style to it, FrontPage applies the default font and paragraph settings for that specific style to the text you selected. In this case, the default style for the Heading 1 style is 24-point, bold, Times New Roman, black, left-aligned text. When you apply a theme to the same Web page, the Heading 1 style changes to match the style defined for the theme for the Heading 1 style; for example, it might be 24-point, Trebuchet MS, blue, left-aligned text. In other words, you might apply the Heading 1 style to selected text in several Web pages, with the Heading 1 style having different characteristics in each page.

In any single Web page, the defined style for an HTML element will be the same throughout the page, unless you use the Formatting toolbar to apply different formats to specific elements. If your Heading 2 style is defined as 12 points, bold, and Times New Roman, then all text that uses the Heading 2 style in that Web page will be 12 points, bold, and Times New Roman.

Creating a Cascading Style Sheet

When you want to change the default style that is associated with an HTML tag in a Web page, you can use the Style dialog box to apply new characteristics to a specific HTML tag. For example, if you want the Heading 2 style to use 12-point, Arial font, then you would select the H2 tag in the Style dialog box and change its font specifications to 12 points and Arial. All text in the Web page that uses the Heading 2 style will then change to 12-point Arial. After you modify an HTML tag in the Style dialog box, the tag that you modified becomes a user-defined style. You can list user-defined styles separately to identify which ones have been customized.

Using styles is convenient when you want certain headings and other elements that appear within a Web page to have the same appearance. You could format each heading separately using the Formatting toolbar, but creating a user-defined style is much easier. It also ensures that all similar elements in the Web page have the same appearance.

To apply your user-defined styles to every page in a Web site, you can create those styles in a new Web page and then save the Web page as a cascading style sheet. A **cascading style sheet (CSS)** is a template that you use to link other Web pages to your user-defined styles. For example, you might create a cascading style sheet that uses a specific background picture and applies user-defined styles to the Heading 1, Heading 2, and Heading 3 styles. When you create a new Web page in a Web site, you can link the cascading style sheet to the new page, making these styles available immediately.

The only exception to this rule occurs when the Web page uses a theme. In this case, the theme provides the styles that define the various HTML tags in the Web page. To change the appearance of HTML tags in a Web page that uses a theme, click the Modify button in the Themes dialog box and then click the Color, Graphics, or Text button to change the style of a particular tag used in the theme. You can still use a cascading style sheet to make changes to a theme, but it is better to use the Themes dialog box to make most changes, as the theme's settings will override most user-defined styles.

During your meeting with the Web site development team, one team member suggested creating a new page in the recipes Web site that will promote special sales and events at Sunny Morning Products. For example, customers who order online from the Sunny Morning Products Web site during the first two weeks in November will receive a 10% discount on all sales as a bonus for ordering holiday gifts early. Tyler wants these "specials" pages to have a different appearance than do other pages in the Web site so as to distinguish them from the recipes and discussion group pages. He suggests that you create a cascading style sheet by defining a few of the styles that will be used in the specials pages.

REFERENCE   WINDOW   **RW**

Creating a Cascading Style Sheet

- Create a new Web page in Page view. If the Web page uses a theme or shared border, use the menu bar to remove these items.
- Click Format on the menu bar, and then click Style.
- In the Styles list box, click the HTML tag that you want to modify, and then click the Modify button.
- Click the Format button in the Modify Style dialog box, and then click the characteristic to be modified (Font, Paragraph, Border, Numbering, or Position).
- Make the desired changes in the dialog box that opens, and then click the OK button.
- Click the OK button twice to close the dialog boxes.

To create a cascading style sheet, you first define the styles in a Web page and then save the Web page as a HyperText Style Sheet in the Web site. After saving the cascading style sheet, you can link it to other Web pages by using the Style Sheet Links command on the Format menu. Note that a Web page saved as a cascading style sheet must not contain any content—it must be empty, except for the defined styles.

Tyler wants you to create a style sheet in which the Heading 1 style uses a centered, 24-point, maroon, Arial Black font. The Heading 2 style should use a left-aligned, 14-point, maroon, Arial Black font. Regular text in the Web page should use a 12-point, Arial Narrow font. Finally, hyperlinks should use a 12-point, navy, underlined, bold, Arial Narrow font. Tyler feels that these different settings, in addition to not using the Web site's theme, will make these pages stand out effectively.

To create a new Web page and open the Style dialog box:

1. Start FrontPage, open the **recipes** Web site from the server, and then, if necessary, change to Page view.

2. If necessary, click the **Create a new normal page** button [ ] on the Standard toolbar to create a new page. A new, blank page that uses the Web site's theme opens in Page view. You will change this page so that it will not use the theme.

3. Click **Format** on the menu bar, and then click **Theme**. The Themes dialog box opens.

4. Make sure that the **Selected page(s)** option button is selected.

5. Click **(No Theme)** in the list box, and then click the **OK** button. The page background changes to white, and the theme's elements are removed from this page.

6. Click **Format** on the menu bar, and then click **Style**. The Style dialog box opens. See Figure 9-34.

Figure 9-34 | **STYLE DIALOG BOX**

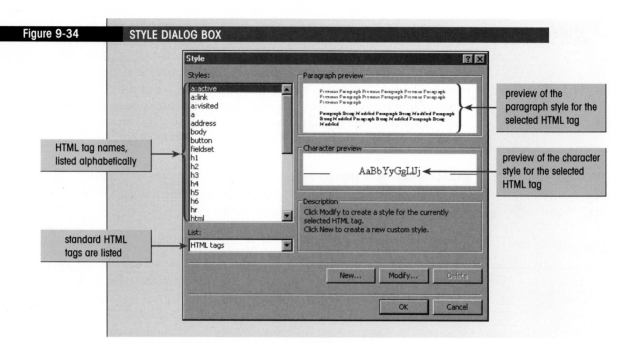

Modifying an HTML Tag's Default Style

The Styles list box includes all HTML tags available for use in your document. You might recognize some of the tags immediately—for example, the H1 tag defines a first-level heading in a Web page. Other tags, however, are not as easy to decipher. Unfortunately, FrontPage does not include a detailed resource to help you interpret the HTML tags listed in the Styles list box. If you need help in identifying which HTML tag to change in your Web pages, search the Internet for Web sites that describe HTML tags or consult an HTML reference book.

You will change the Heading 1 style first.

To modify the Heading 1 style:

1. In the Styles list box, click **h1**. H1 is the HTML tag equivalent for the Heading 1 style.

2. Click the **Modify** button. The Modify Style dialog box opens. The HTML tag name appears in the Name (selector) text box.

3. Click the **Format** button. See Figure 9-35. You will change the font first.

Figure 9-35   MODIFY STYLE DIALOG BOX

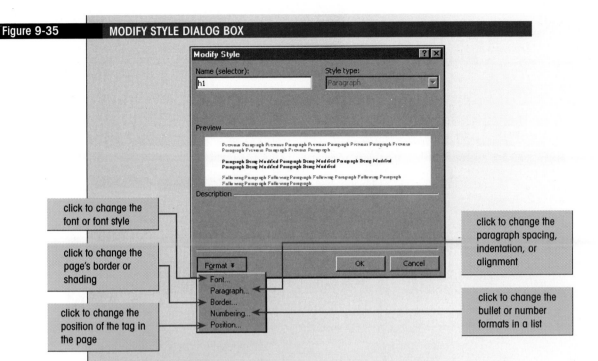

click to change the font or font style

click to change the page's border or shading

click to change the position of the tag in the page

click to change the paragraph spacing, indentation, or alignment

click to change the bullet or number formats in a list

4. Click **Font** in the Format button list. The Font dialog box opens. You need to change the font to 24 points, maroon, and Arial Black.

5. Scroll down the Font list as necessary, click **Arial Black** in the Font list box, scroll down the Size list and click **24pt**, click the **Color** list arrow, click the **maroon** color in the list, and then click the **OK** button. The Font dialog box closes, and the Modify Style dialog box now displays a preview and description of the new style. See Figure 9-36.

Figure 9-36   MODIFIED H1 TAG

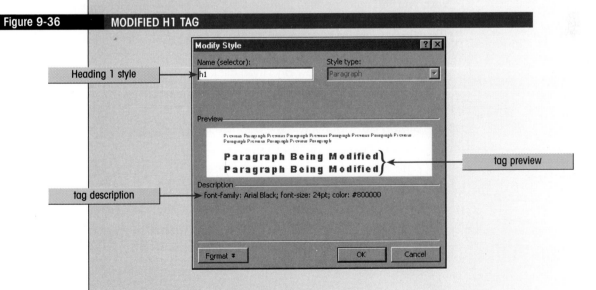

Heading 1 style

tag preview

tag description

You still need to change the paragraph alignment to centered, so you will not close the Modify Style dialog box yet.

6. Click the **Format** button, and then click **Paragraph**. The Paragraph dialog box opens.

7. Click the **Alignment** list arrow, and then click **Center**.

8. Click the **OK** button to close the Paragraph dialog box, and then click the **OK** button in the Modify Style dialog box to close it. The H1 style now appears in the Styles list box of the Styles dialog box as a user-defined style. See Figure 9-37.

Figure 9-37	USER-DEFINED STYLES IN THE WEB PAGE

H1 tag is now a user-defined style

preview of the selected style

description of the selected style

user-defined styles selected

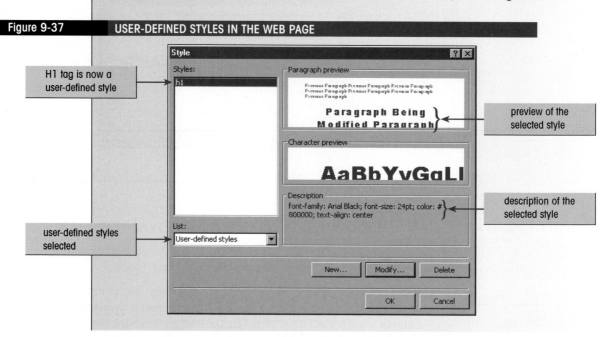

You can redefine other styles by changing the List list box to redisplay all HTML tags. Next, you will redefine the Heading 2 style according to Tyler's specifications.

To redefine the Heading 2 style:

1. Click the **List** list arrow, and then click **HTML tags**. The Styles list box now displays all HTML tags available for use in the document.

2. Click **h2** in the Styles list, and then click the **Modify** button. The Modify Style dialog box opens. You will change the font first.

3. Click the **Format** button, click **Font**, scroll down the Font list as necessary and click **Arial Black**, scroll down the Size list and click **14pt**, click the **Color** list arrow, click the **maroon** color, and then click the **OK** button. The Font dialog box closes. Next, you will change the alignment to left.

4. Click the **Format** button, click **Paragraph**, click the **Alignment** list arrow, click **Left**, and then click the **OK** button. The Paragraph dialog box closes. The Modify Style dialog box now displays the settings for the Heading 2 style. See Figure 9-38.

Figure 9-38	MODIFIED H2 TAG

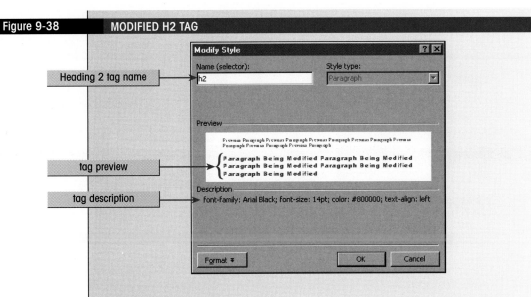

Heading 2 tag name

tag preview

tag description

5. Click the **OK** button. The Style dialog box displays all HTML tags in the Styles list box.

   TROUBLE? If necessary, click the List list arrow, and then click HTML tags to display that list.

Now you can customize the style used for hyperlinks. By default, hyperlinks appear as blue, underlined text. You will change the hyperlink style to match Tyler's specifications. The HTML equivalent for a hyperlink is the A tag.

To change the hyperlink style:

1. In the Styles list, click **a**, and then click the **Modify** button. To change the appearance of a hyperlink, you use the Font dialog box.

2. Click the **Format** button, and then click **Font**. The Font dialog box opens.

3. Scroll down the Font list and click **Arial Narrow**, click **Bold** in the Font style list, scroll down the Size list and click **12pt**, click the **Color** list arrow, click the **navy** color, click the **Underline** check box to select it, and then click the **OK** button. The Font dialog box closes, and the Modify Style dialog box displays the description for the A tag. See Figure 9-39.

Figure 9-39   MODIFIED TAG

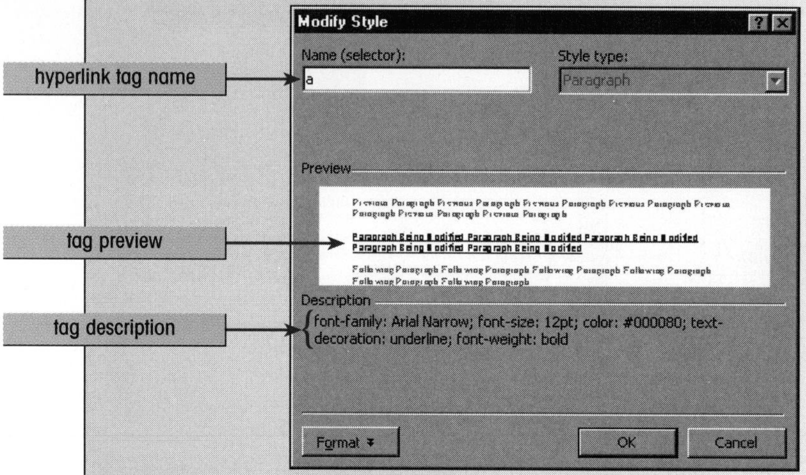

hyperlink tag name →

tag preview →

tag description →

4. Click the **OK** button to close the Modify Style dialog box.

Tyler also wants you to change the default font used with the Normal style to 12 points and Arial Narrow. The HTML tag for normal text in a Web page is the BODY tag.

To change the Normal text style:

1. Click **body** in the Styles list box, and then click the **Modify** button. The Modify Style dialog box opens.

2. Click the **Format** button, and then click **Font**. The Font dialog box opens.

3. Scroll down the Font list and click **Arial Narrow**, scroll down the Size list and click **12pt**, and then click the **OK** button.

4. Click the **OK** button in the Modify Style dialog box to close it. You can view the styles that you modified by changing the Styles list box to display user-defined styles.

5. Click the **List** list arrow, and then click **User-defined styles**. The Styles list box now includes the H1, H2, A, and BODY tags.

6. Click the **OK** button to close the Style dialog box. The Web page in which you have created these styles does not contain any content in Page view. The only "content" contained in the unsaved Web page is the styles. You can view these styles in HTML Page view.

7. Click the **HTML** button. The styles for the H1, H2, A, and BODY tags appear as gray text in the HTML document. See Figure 9-40.

Figure 9-40	HTML CODE FOR THE CASCADING STYLE SHEET

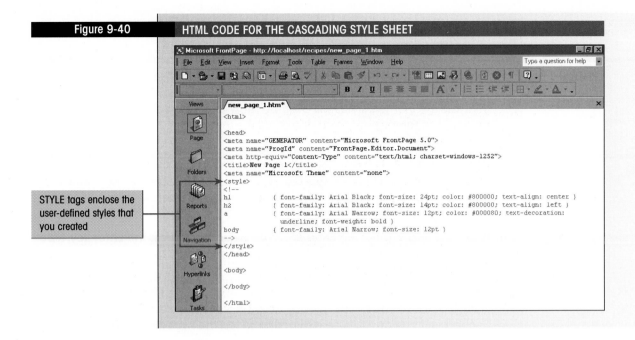

STYLE tags enclose the user-defined styles that you created

Saving a Web Page as a Cascading Style Sheet

The new Web page doesn't contain any content—it contains only the styles you created. If you entered and formatted content in this Web page, you could apply the new styles to text to use the Heading 1, Heading 2, Normal, and Hyperlink styles. In this case, however, you will save the Web page as a cascading style sheet to make it available for use with other pages. If you don't save a Web page that contains user-defined styles as a cascading style sheet, then the user-defined styles are available only within the Web page that contains them.

To save the Web page as a cascading style sheet:

1. Click the **Save** button 🖫 on the Standard toolbar. The Save As dialog box opens.

2. Click the **Change title** button to open the Set Page Title dialog box, type **Cascading Style Sheet** in the Page title text box, and then click the **OK** button.

3. Click the **Save as type** list arrow, and then click **HyperText Style Sheet**.

4. Select the text in the File name text box, and then type **specials**.

5. Click the **Save** button. The title bar for the Contents pane displays the page's filename, specials.css. The .css filename extension indicates that this page is a cascading style sheet.

Creating a New Web Page and Linking It to a Cascading Style Sheet

The cascading style sheet is now saved in the recipes Web site, and you can use the styles in this page by linking it to a Web page. You will close the specials.css style sheet, create a new Web page, remove the theme, and enter some sample text in the new page. Finally, you will link the cascading style sheet to the Web page. The new Web page will use the user-defined styles that you created in the cascading style sheet.

To create a new Web page that uses the cascading style sheet:

1. Click the **Close** button ⊠ on the Contents pane to close the specials.css page.

2. Click the **Create a new normal page** button 🗋 on the Standard toolbar to create a new Web page. The new Web page uses the Web site's theme. Because the theme's styles will override most user-defined styles (which you do not want to happen), you will turn off the theme for this page.

3. Click **Format** on the menu bar, click **Theme**, make sure that the **Selected page(s)** option button is selected, click **(No Theme)** in the list box, and then click the **OK** button. The Themes dialog box closes and the theme is removed. You will enter some sample text in the new Web page before linking it to the cascading style sheet.

4. Type **Heading 1**, press the **Enter** key, type **Heading 2**, press the **Enter** key, type **Normal**, press the **Enter** key, and then type **Hyperlink**.

5. Use the **Style** list box on the Formatting toolbar to format the Heading 1 text with the Heading 1 style and the Heading 2 text with the Heading 2 style. The Normal text that you typed already uses the Normal style, so you don't need to change it. You can create a hyperlink to test the hyperlink style.

6. Select the **Hyperlink** text, click the **Insert Hyperlink** button 🔗 on the Standard toolbar, and then scroll down the list and double-click **Default**. The Insert Hyperlink dialog box closes and the Hyperlink text changes to underlined and blue, indicating that it is now formatted as a hyperlink.

   Next, you will link the new Web page to the cascading style sheet.

7. Click **Format** on the menu bar, and then click **Style Sheet Links**. The Link Style Sheet dialog box opens. You can apply a cascading style sheet to all pages in the Web site or to only the selected page. You will apply the cascading style sheet named specials.css to the selected page.

8. Make sure that the **Selected page(s)** option button is selected, and then click the **Add** button. The Select Style Sheet dialog box opens.

9. Double-click **specials.css** in the list box. The Select Style Sheet dialog box closes, and the Link Style Sheet dialog box displays the specials.css file in the URL list box. See Figure 9-41.

Figure 9-41   **LINK STYLE SHEET DIALOG BOX**

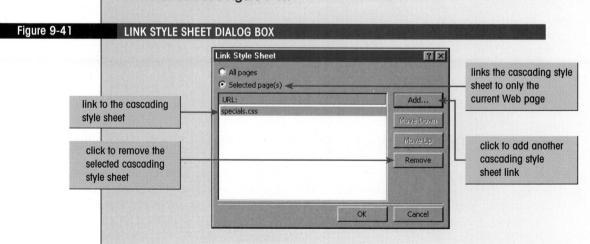

TROUBLE? If necessary, navigate to the recipes folder to select the specials.css file in the list box.

10. Click the **OK** button, and then click anywhere in the Web page to deselect any selected text. The text that you entered and formatted in the Web page now uses the styles that you defined in the cascading style sheet. See Figure 9-42. Any text that uses the Heading 1, Heading 2, Normal, or Hyperlink style in this Web page will be formatted using the specifications from the cascading style sheet.

Figure 9-42	WEB PAGE USES STYLES FROM THE CASCADING STYLE SHEET

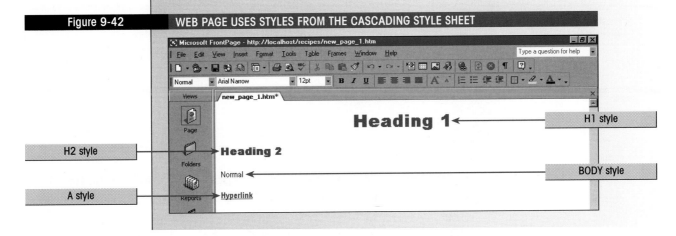

When you no longer want to use the cascading style sheet for a Web page, you can remove the link by clicking Format on the menu bar, clicking Style Sheet Links, selecting the cascading style sheet filename to be removed in the URL list box, and then clicking the Remove button. When you remove the link to the style sheet, the styles in the Web page return to the default settings.

Viewing the HTML Code for a Cascading Style Sheet

Tyler wants you to examine the HTML code that creates the styles in the cascading style sheet so that you will become more familiar with this type of document. You will also view the HTML code for the new Web page that you created to see how it is linked to the cascading style sheet. You will close this Web page without saving it, and then view the HTML code for the specials.css page.

To view the HTML code for a linked page and a cascading style sheet:

1. Click the **HTML** button. The HTML code for the unsaved Web page appears in Page view. See Figure 9-43. The Web page contains a LINK tag to the specials.css file. This link connects the Web page to the cascading style sheet, ensuring that the page uses the defined styles. If you changed the defined styles in the specials.css page, any pages that are linked to the cascading style sheet would be updated automatically.

Figure 9-43   HTML CODE FOR THE UNSAVED WEB PAGE

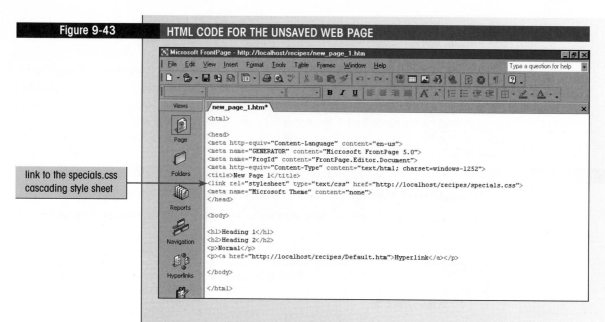

link to the specials.css cascading style sheet

2. Click the **Close** button ☒ on the Contents pane, and then click the **No** button to close the Web page without saving it.

3. Click the **Folders** button 📁 on the Views bar, and then scroll down and double-click **specials.css** in the Contents pane. The cascading style sheet opens in HTML Page view, and the Style toolbar opens in the window. Clicking the Style button on the Style toolbar opens the Style dialog box, in which you can change your user-defined styles, if necessary. A cascading style sheet contains only HTML code, so it is displayed only in HTML Page view. The cascading style sheet includes a comment section listing the names and definitions of the styles that it contains. Otherwise, the page contains only the standard HTML tags for a Web page. See Figure 9-44.

Figure 9-44   HTML CODE FOR THE SPECIALS CASCADING STYLE SHEET

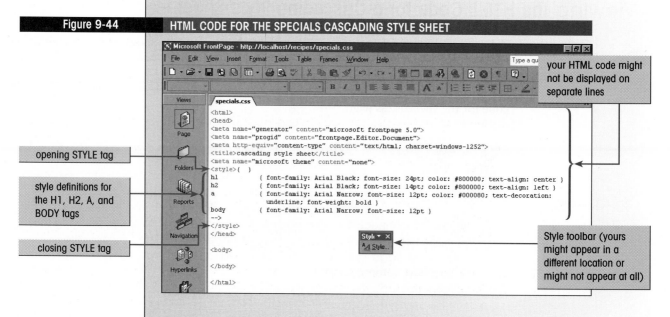

your HTML code might not be displayed on separate lines

opening STYLE tag

style definitions for the H1, H2, A, and BODY tags

closing STYLE tag

Style toolbar (yours might appear in a different location or might not appear at all)

4. Close the recipes Web site and then close FrontPage.

In the Review Assignments, you will complete your work on the recipes Web site. After carefully testing this site and ensuring that all pages have been added to it, Tyler will use the Publish Web command on the File menu to publish the recipes Web site from his computer's server to the Web server on which the site will be stored so it will be ready for Internet visitors.

Session 9.2 QUICK | CHECK

1. True or False: You can define more than one style for the same HTML tag in a single Web page.

2. True or False: A theme contains a set of styles that you might also find in a cascading style sheet.

3. To save a Web page as a cascading style sheet, choose the _____ option in the Save as type list box.

4. True or False: You can modify any HTML tag to create a user-defined style.

5. You use the _____ dialog box to link a Web page to a cascading style sheet.

6. A Web page that is saved as a cascading style sheet has a filename extension of _____.

7. True or False: You can open a cascading style sheet in Normal Page view.

REVIEW ASSIGNMENTS

Tyler wants you to customize the default components that you created in the Activity Report Web page. You will also apply the Web site's theme to the Activity Report Web page, and then set the properties for this page, the data source for the spreadsheet component, and the Black Scale Insect Damage page and its data source, so that they will not be published with the Web site.

If necessary, start FrontPage, insert your Data Disk in the appropriate disk drive, and then do the following:

1. Open the **recipes** Web site from the server in Folders view, and then open the Activity Report Web page (**activity.htm**) in Page view.

2. Apply the Web's default theme to the Activity Report Web page, and then save the page.

3. Add the **activity.htm** page to the Web site's navigation structure as a child page of the home page. Position the **activity.htm** page to the right of the Guest Book page. Insert a centered picture page banner at the top of the Activity Report Web page. Save the page.

Explore　　4. Click the spreadsheet component to select it, and then, if necessary, open the Commands and Options dialog box. Click cell A1 in the spreadsheet (this cell contains the text "Page Openings by Category"). Use the Format tab in the Commands and Options dialog box to change the text in cell A1 to 20-point, blue, italic, Trebuchet MS font.

Explore　　5. Select the chart component in the Activity Report Web page, and then open the Commands and Options dialog box for the chart title. (*Hint:* Right-click the chart title to open the shortcut menu, and then click Commands and Options.) On the General tab, make sure that the Select list box is set to "Title." Use the Format tab to change the font of the title to 20-point, bold, italic, blue, Trebuchet MS font.

6. Change the font of the data labels in the chart component to italic Trebuchet MS font.

Explore ▷ 7. Change the chart subtype to 3D Pie, and then save the page. (*Hint:* Click the pie chart and then use the Type tab to change the chart type.)

8. Change the value in cell C4 (the value for Butters) to 531. Save the Web page, and then preview it using the browser. Print the Web page, and then close the browser.

Explore ▷ 9. Open the Black Scale Insect Damage page (**damage.htm**) in Page view. Open the Commands and Options dialog box, and then use the Captions tab to change the caption for the report title bar in the PivotTable list component to "Sales Data for April and May." Change the title bar text font to Trebuchet MS.

Explore ▷ 10. Save the **damage.htm** page and then preview it in a browser. Use the browser to change the filter field to display only those invoices processed on Tuesday of week 18. Use the field list to add a "Sum of Amount" calculated field to the Grand Total column. Print the Web page and then close the browser.

11. Change the properties of the **activity.htm**, **damage.htm**, and **openings.htm** pages so that they will not be published with the Web site.

12. Close the **recipes** Web site and FrontPage.

CASE PROBLEMS

Case 1. Determining Appropriate Marketing Channels for Royal Hair Care Products

Valerie Suarez is planning to expand Royal Hair Care Products' ability to deliver products directly to its customers. In the next year, Valerie will change the Web site to accept online orders from customers and retailers. In the meantime, she wants the sales force to focus new styling gel product promotions in the places where customers most often purchase products. To help determine the most appropriate channels, she wants you to create a Web page using spreadsheet data, with the data being displayed in a stacked column chart. The data is collected from a form field in the Feedback Web page that asks users to specify where they purchase the product most frequently.

If necessary, start FrontPage, insert your Data Disk in the appropriate disk drive, and then do the following:

1. Read all the questions for this case problem, and then prepare a planning analysis sheet for the enhancements to the **royal** Web site.

2. Open the **royal** Web site from the server in Folders view. (If you did not create this Web site in Tutorial 7 and change it in Tutorial 8, ask your instructor for assistance.)

3. Create a new Web page in Page view, and then save it using the title "Sales Data" and the filename **sales**. On the first line of the Web page (but not in the top shared border), insert a centered spreadsheet component. Import the file named **rfb_data.htm** from the Tutorial.09 folder on your Data Disk into the **royal** Web site, and then import its data into the spreadsheet component. Do not select the option to refresh the data at run time.

4. Resize the columns in the spreadsheet component that contain data (columns A and B) to their best fit, and then resize the spreadsheet component so that only columns A and B and rows 1 through 8 are visible.

Explore ▷ 5. Add a new label in cell A8 with the value "Total." Change the label to 10-point, bold, blue, Arial font. (*Hint:* Use the spreadsheet component's shortcut menu to open the Commands and Options dialog box.)

Explore ▷ 6. Create a formula in cell B8 that calculates a sum of the values in cells B2 through B7. (*Hint:* Click in cell B8, click the AutoSum button on the spreadsheet component toolbar, make sure that the range B2:B7 is selected, and then press the Enter key.)

7. Insert a chart component on a new centered line below the spreadsheet component that you created in Step 3. Use the spreadsheet component as the data source for the chart component, the data range A1:B8, the series in columns, the Column chart type, and the Stacked Column subtype.

Explore 8. Change the value in cell A3 to "DiscStore," the value in cell A4 to "DeptStore," and the value in cell A6 to "Supermkt." What happens in the chart component?

Explore 9. Click one of the data labels in the chart component (such as DrugStore or DiscStore) to select all of the data labels, right-click the selected labels to open the shortcut menu, and then open the Commands and Options dialog box. Click the Axis tab, and then turn on the major gridlines. Use the Format tab to change the text format of the labels to bold. Use the General tab to add the title "Location" to the chart. (*Hint:* Click the white chart space, click the Add Title button on the General tab, click the title that appears in the chart component, and then change the caption using the Format tab.) Change the title to 14-point, bold, Arial font.

Explore 10. With the Commands and Options dialog box still open, click an axis label (such as 0, 250, or 500). Use the Format tab to change the axis labels to bold.

11. Turn off the shared border for the Sales Web page, and then insert the text "Purchase Locations" on a new line at the top of the Web page. Change the text to use the Heading 1 style. Insert a heading using the Heading 1 style on a new line between the spreadsheet and chart components using the text "Purchase Locations Column Chart."

12. Save the Web page, preview it using the browser, change the value for the Supermkt category to 286, and then print the page. Close the browser.

13. Change the properties of the Sales Web page and its data source so that it will not be published when the Web site is published to the Royal Hair Care Products Web server.

14. Close the **royal** Web site and FrontPage.

Case 2. Creating a Sales Data Web Page for Buffalo Trading Post Donna Vargas would like to use the Web site for Buffalo Trading Post to track sales in different retail categories. She wants to be able to use a Web page to analyze the data given to her by her accountant, Cody Susen. Cody doesn't have this data in an electronic format, so Donna will need to input it manually into a spreadsheet. Instead of using an Excel workbook to create the data, Donna wants to be able to use a Web page that you will create for her. She also wants to display a pie chart in the Web page that shows the relative amounts for each category.

If necessary, start FrontPage, insert your Data Disk in the appropriate disk drive, and then do the following:

1. Read all the questions for this case problem, and then prepare a planning analysis sheet for the enhancements to the **buffalo** Web site.

2. Open the **buffalo** Web site from the server in Folders view. (If you did not create this Web site in Tutorial 7 and change it in Tutorial 8, ask your instructor for assistance.)

3. Create a new Web page in Page view with the title "Sales Data" and the filename **salewkbk.htm**.

4. On the first line of the Web page (but not in the bottom shared border), create a heading using the Heading 1 style and the text "Sales Data by Category."

Explore 5. On the next line, insert a centered spreadsheet component. Enter the data shown in Figure 9-45 into the spreadsheet component. Format the column headings (cells B1 through D1) as 10-point, bold, centered, Arial text. Format the row headings (cells A2 through A7) as 10-point, bold, Arial text. Resize all columns to their best fit.

Figure 9-45

	Revenue ($)	Inventory Amount ($)	Sales Percentage
Women's	254,165	354,811	72%
Children's	25,644	84,511	30%
Accessories	10,264	11,265	91%
Men's	1,254	9,558	13%
Hats	157	865	18%
Shoes	2,955	6,988	42%

Explore   6. Insert a formula in cell B8 that computes the total of the values in cells B2 through B7, and then insert a formula in cell C8 that computes the total of the values in cells C2 through C7. In cell D8, enter a formula that computes the sales percentage, which is the revenue divided by the inventory amount. Use the Commands and Options dialog box to format the resulting value as a percentage (the percentage will be displayed automatically with two decimal places). In cell A8, enter the label "Totals." Format the values in cells A8 through D8 as 10-point, bold, red, Arial text. (*Hint:* Use the Help button on the spreadsheet component toolbar to get Help while completing Step 6.)

7. Resize the spreadsheet component so that only columns A through D and rows 1 through 8 are visible.

Explore   8. Insert a chart component on a new centered line below the spreadsheet component that you created in Step 5. Use the spreadsheet component as the data source, the data range A1:C7, the series in columns, the Bar chart type, and the Clustered Bar subtype.

Explore   9. Use the Commands and Options dialog box to add the minor gridlines to the chart. (*Hint:* With the Commands and Options dialog box open, click any axis label (such as 0 or 100,000) in the chart component to select all of the axis labels, and then click the Axis tab.)

Explore   10. Change the number format of the axis labels to currency.

11. Add the title "Inventory vs. Revenue" at the top of the chart component, and then add a legend to the chart component. (*Hint:* Click the white chart space to add a title.) Save the page.

Explore   12. Change the Heading 1 style for all pages in the Web site to center alignment without changing the Web site's theme. (*Hint:* Create and save a cascading style sheet, and then link it to all pages in the Web site. Use the title "Style Sheet" and the filename **styles.css**. Enter the title first.)

13. Change the properties of the Sales Data Web page and the cascading style sheet so that they will not be published when the Web site is published to the BTP Web server.

14. Preview the Sales Data Web page in the browser, print it, and then close the browser.

15. Use FrontPage to print the HTML code for the cascading style sheet that you created in Step 12.

16. Close the **buffalo** Web site and FrontPage.

Case 3. Displaying Salary Data in a Web Page for Garden Grill Garden Grill has always attracted the most qualified applicants for management and staff positions in its restaurants. One of the reasons that it has such a well-trained staff is that Garden Grill pays its employees higher salaries and rewards them with higher annual performance increases than do other national restaurant chains. To keep employee morale high, management conducts regular salary research to ensure that Garden Grill employees are enjoying higher rewards for their work.

Nolan Simmons just finished a study of starting salaries for three other national restaurant chains. He wants to include a Web page in the Garden Grill Web site that shows his study's results in a spreadsheet and chart. In addition, as part of the company's annual performance reviews, Nolan wants to use a Web page to view the last name, position, year hired, hourly wage, and potential wage after a 4% raise for all employees. This data will help him to plan the restaurant's operating budget for the next quarter. These new Web pages should be available only on the company's intranet, so Nolan asks you to set their properties so that they will not be published on the Internet Web site.

If necessary, start FrontPage, insert your Data Disk in the appropriate disk drive, and then do the following:

1. Read all the questions for this case problem, and then prepare a planning analysis sheet for the enhancements to the **garden** Web site.

2. Open the **garden** Web site from the server in Folders view. (If you did not create this Web site in Tutorial 7 and change it in Tutorial 8, ask your instructor for assistance.)

3. Create a new Web page in Page view with the title "Salary Data" and the filename **salary.htm**. Turn off the display of the top shared border for this page only. On the first line of the Web page, create a heading using the Heading 1 style and the text "Salary Data by Position."

4. On the next line, insert a centered spreadsheet component. Import the file **g_data.htm** from the Tutorial.09 folder on your Data Disk into the **garden** Web site, and then import the data from this file into the spreadsheet component. Do not select the option to refresh the data at run time.

Explore   5. Insert a formula in cell B8 that computes the average of the values in cells B2 through B7. Copy and paste this formula into cells C8, D8, and E8. Use the Format tab in the Commands and Options dialog box to change the number format of the values in cells B2 though E8 to currency. In cell A8, enter the label "Average." Use the Format tab to format the values in cells A8 through E8 as 10-point, bold, violet, Arial text. (*Hint:* Use the Help button on the spreadsheet component toolbar to get Help while completing Step 5. You'll need to learn how to use the AVERAGE function.)

6. Resize the spreadsheet component so that only columns A through E and rows 1 through 8 are visible.

Explore   7. On a new centered line below the spreadsheet component that you inserted in Step 4, insert a chart component. Chart the data cells A1 through E8 of the spreadsheet component, and use the series in columns, the Column chart type, and the Clustered Column subtype.

Explore   8. Use the Commands and Options dialog box to change the background color of the chart to white. (*Hint:* Use the Border/Fill tab to change the Plot Area fill color to white.)

9. Add a legend to the chart, and then add the title "Salary Comparisons."

10. Save the Salary Data Web page, preview it in the browser, print it, and then close the browser.

11. In Page view, create a new Web page using the filename **raise.htm** and the title "Raise Data." Turn off the display of the top shared border in this page only.

12. Create a user-defined style in this page only that centers text that uses the Heading 1 style. On the first line of the page, enter the title "Salary Data, 1999-2002" and apply the Heading 1 style to it.

13. On a new centered line below the heading that you created in Step 12, insert a PivotTable list component. Create a data connection to the file **g_raise.xls** in the Tutorial.09 folder on your Data Disk. The data you need to chart is stored on Sheet1, and the first row of data contains column headers.

Explore 14. Display the field list, and then add the fields from the field list to the PivotTable list component as follows:

a. The filter field is YearHired.

b. The row field is LastName.

c. The column field is Position.

d. The detail fields are HourlyWage and RaiseWage. (*Hint:* Drag the Hourly Wage field to the detail area first, and then drag the RaiseWage field to the right of the first HourlyWage column in the detail area. When a blue vertical line appears to the right of the HourlyWage column, release the mouse button to drop the field into the detail area.)

15. Save the Raise Data Web page, and then preview it in a browser. Use the PivotTable list component to display the data for those employees hired in the years 1999 and 2000 and for people employed as bartenders, cooks, and waitpersons. Print the Web page, and then close the browser.

16. Set the properties for the **salary.htm**, **g_data.htm**, and **raise.htm** pages so that they will not be published with the Web site.

17. Close the **garden** Web site and FrontPage.

Explore *Case 4. Using a Web Page to Analyze Sales Data for Replay Music Factory* Charlene Fields is pleased with the progress that you are making toward completing the Web site for Replay Music Factory. She anticipates that the online ordering system will be ready to go in a few weeks. While the company's music inventory is being entered into an Access database, Charlene asks you to create a PivotTable list component that she can use to analyze sales data of transactions of less than $100 for the Country & Western (C&W), Rock and Roll (RR), and Contemporary (Cont) music categories for the past year. She will use this information to analyze the buying habits of the company's customers and to make decisions about expanding Replay's stock of CDs in these categories. Because Charlene does not want this page to be accessible from the Internet, she asks you to set its properties so that it will not be published with the Web site.

If necessary, start FrontPage, insert your Data Disk in the appropriate disk drive, and then do the following:

1. Read all the questions for this case problem, and then prepare a planning analysis sheet for the enhancements to the **replay** Web site.

2. Open the **replay** Web site from the server in Folders view. (If you did not create this Web site in Tutorial 7 and change it in Tutorial 8, ask your instructor for assistance.)

3. In Page view, create a new Web page. Turn off the display of shared borders for this page only, and then set the page's properties so that it is not published with the Web site. Save the page using the filename **sls_data.htm** and the title "Sales Data."

4. In Navigation view, add the Sales Data page to the Web site's navigation structure as a child page of the Country & Western page (which is itself a child page of the Specials page). Turn off the display of the Sales Data page in the Web site's link bars by right-clicking it in the navigation structure, and then clicking Included in Navigation Bars on the shortcut menu.

5. Insert a PivotTable list component on a centered line at the top of the Sales Data page. Create a data connection to the file **replay.xls** in the Tutorial.09 folder on your Data Disk. The data you need to chart is stored on Sheet1, and the first row of data contains the column headings.

6. Display the field list, and then add the fields from the field list to the PivotTable list component as follows:

a. The filter field is empty.

b. The row field is Category.

c. The column field is Quarters. (*Hint:* The Quarters field appears below the "Date By Month" field.)

d. The detail field is Total.

e. Create a Sum of Total field to sum the values in each row field and also to create a grand total.

7. Click the title bar of the PivotTable list component, and then use the Commands and Options dialog box to make the following changes:
   a. Change the caption for the report title bar to "Transactions of Less Than $100."
   b. Change the fill color for the title bar to blue. (*Hint:* The Fill Color button appears on the Captions tab.)
   c. Change the font color of the text in the report title bar to yellow.
   d. Turn off the display of drop areas. (*Hint:* Right-click the component's title bar, and then click Drop Areas on the shortcut menu.)

8. Save the page, and then preview and print it in a browser. Use the PivotTable list component to answer the following questions about the data source on a separate piece of paper:
   a. What were total sales for the first quarter in each category?
   b. What were total sales for the first quarter overall?
   c. What were total sales in each category for the entire year?
   d. What were total sales for the entire year overall?
   e. What were total sales for September 16?

9. Close your browser, the **replay** Web site, and FrontPage.

LAB ASSIGNMENTS

Spreadsheets

These Lab Assignments are designed to accompany the interactive Course Lab called Spreadsheets. To start the Spreadsheets Lab, click the Start button on the Windows taskbar, point to Programs, point to Course Labs, point to New Perspectives Applications, and then click Spreadsheets. If you do not see Course Labs on your Programs menu, see your instructor or technical support person.

Spreadsheets Spreadsheet software is used extensively in business, education, science, and the humanities to simplify tasks that involve calculations. In this Lab you will learn how spreadsheet software works. You will use spreadsheet software to examine and modify worksheets and to create your own worksheets.

1. Click the Steps button to learn how spreadsheet software works. As you proceed through the Steps, answer all of the Quick Check questions that appear. After you complete the Steps, you will see a Quick Check Summary Report. Follow the instructions on the screen to print this report.

2. Click the Explore button to begin this assignment. Click the OK button to display a new worksheet. Click File on the menu bar, and then click Open to display the Open dialog box. Click the file Income.xls, and then press the Enter key to open the Income and Expense Summary worksheet. Notice that the worksheet contains labels and values for income from consulting and training. It also contains labels and values for expenses such as rent and salaries. The worksheet does not, however, contain formulas to calculate Total Income, Total Expenses, or Profit. Do the following:
   a. Calculate the Total Income by entering the formula =sum(C4:C5) in cell C6.
   b. Calculate the Total Expenses by entering the formula =sum(C9:C12) in C13.
   c. Calculate Profit by entering the formula =C6-C13 in cell C15.
   d. Manually check the results to make sure you entered the formulas correctly.
   e. Print your completed worksheet showing your results.

3. You can use a spreadsheet to keep track of your grade in a class. In Explore, click File on the menu bar, and then click Open to display the Open dialog box. Click the file Grades.xls to open the Grades worksheet. This worksheet contains all of the labels and formulas necessary to calculate your grade based on four test scores.

   Suppose you receive a score of 88 out of 100 on the first test. On the second test, you score 42 out of 48. On the third test, you score 92 out of 100. You have not taken the fourth test yet. Enter the appropriate data in the Grades.xls worksheet to determine your grade after taking three tests. Print your worksheet.

4. Worksheets are handy for answering "what if" questions. Suppose you decide to open a lemonade stand. You're interested in how much profit you can make each day. What if you sell 20 cups of lemonade? What if you sell 100? What if the cost of lemons increases?

In Explore, open the file Lemons.xls and use the worksheet to answer questions a through d, and then print the worksheet for question e.

   a. What is your profit if you sell 20 cups a day?
   b. What is your profit if you sell 100 cups a day?
   c. What is your profit if the price of lemons increases to $.07 and you sell 100 cups?
   d. What is your profit if you raise the price of a cup of lemonade to $.30? (Lemons still cost $.07; assume you sell 100 cups.)
   e. Suppose your competitor boasts that she sold 50 cups of lemonade in one day and made exactly $12.00. On your worksheet adjust the cost of cups, water, lemons, and sugar, and the price per cup to show a profit of exactly $12.00 for 50 cups sold. Print this worksheet.

5. It is important to make sure the formulas in your worksheet are accurate. An easy way to test this is to enter the value 1 for every value in your worksheet, and then check the calculations manually.

In Explore, open the worksheet Receipt.xls, which calculates sales receipts. Enter 1 as the value for Item 1, Item 2, Item 3, and Sales Tax %. Manually calculate what you would pay for three items that cost $1.00 each in a state where sales tax is one percent (.01). Do your manual calculations match those of the worksheet? If not, correct the formulas in the worksheet and print a formula report of your revised worksheet.

6. In Explore, create your own worksheet showing your household budget for one month. You can use real or fictitious data. Make sure that you put a title on the worksheet. Use formulas to calculate your total income and your total expenses for the month. Add another formula to calculate how much money you were able to save. Print a formula report of your worksheet. Then print your worksheet showing realistic values for one month.

QUICK | CHECK ANSWERS

Session 9.1

1. Spreadsheet, chart, and PivotTable list
2. You should use a spreadsheet component in a Web page when you (or other Web site developers and users) do not have Excel installed on your computer but you do have the Office XP components and a Web browser that supports them.
3. False
4. A cell or range of cells in a spreadsheet component that contains the data you want to chart
5. False
6. A filter field lets you restrict the data used in the component. A column field stores data that will become the column headings. A row field stores data that will become the row headings in the component. A detail field provides information about the data identified by the column and row headings.

Session 9.2

1. False
2. True
3. HyperText Style Sheet
4. True
5. Link Style Sheet
6. .css
7. False

CREATING
A WEB SITE FOR SECURITY SHREDDING, INC.

CASE

Security Shredding, Inc.

When Mary Schmidt retired from her career as a systems analyst, she still wanted to work. Her husband, Bob, was also retiring from his career as a computer programmer. With the help of their two sons, Jeff and Brad, Mary and Bob started a business that shreds documents and other materials. Security Shredding, Inc., began operations in 1990, at a time when many state agencies and public companies were beginning to realize the benefits of having their sensitive documents destroyed by independent specialists instead of using in-house resources. At first, Security Shredding primarily shredded documents, including personnel records, classified information, and financial information. The business quickly grew to include the destruction of non-salable materials such as unsold magazines and paperbacks, expired lottery scratch-off cards, and security videotapes.

Security Shredding soon outgrew its small storage area and relocated to a warehouse that houses several commercial shredders, paper bailers, and the company's offices. The firm also leases several unmarked trucks that are used to pick up materials from its clients. Security Shredding's warehouse is unmarked to guarantee the security and privacy of sensitive documents while they are being destroyed.

As business at Security Shredding has continued to expand, Mary has realized that the creation and management of a Web site might increase the efficiency of the company's operations and help market the company's services. Mary wants you to help her create a Web site with the following pages and features:

- A home page that describes the business and includes a picture and a hit counter

- An Experience page that describes the company's shredding experience and lists its professional affiliations

- A 3 S's of Shredding page that answers the question, "What should be shredded?"
- A Pickup Request Form page that lets clients use a form to request pickups
- A Pricing page that identifies the company's pricing policies
- A Size page that describes the company's equipment and facility
- A Services page that describes the company's pickup service, recycling efforts, and policies
- A Security page that describes the company's security measures and policies for ensuring the privacy and protection of materials it handles
- A Recycling Program page that includes information about how recycling efforts benefit the environment
- An E-Mail page that includes the e-mail addresses of the company's managers
- A protected discussion group of pages, which allows managers at Security Shredding to post information about the business or the industry in general to enhance interoffice communication

In addition to these Web pages, Mary wants to include pictures showing the company's operations. She wants the Web site to use a Web theme to ensure that pages in the site have a consistent appearance. She also wants the company's logo, name, mailing address, phone number, fax number, and e-mail address to appear at the top of each page.

If necessary, start FrontPage, insert your Data Disk in the appropriate disk drive, and then do the following:

1. Read all the questions for this case problem, and then prepare a planning analysis sheet for creating the Web site for Security Shredding.

2. Prepare a Web site plan that shows the desired Web pages and the expected hyperlinks from the home page.

3. Use the Import Web Wizard to import all of the files except for **shred.mdb** from the AddCase1 folder on your Data Disk into a new Web site named **shred**. Save the Web site on the server. After creating the Web site, make sure that it is enabled for Active Server Pages, ActiveX controls, and the FrontPage Server Extensions.

4. Use drag and drop to move all picture files into the Web site's images folder.

5. Use Navigation view to create the Web site's navigation structure. All pages in the Web site are child pages of the home page.

6. Open the home page in Page view. Add top and left shared borders to every page in the Web site. The left shared border should include navigation buttons. Select the comment component in the top shared border, insert the company's logo file (**logo.jpg**) from the Web site's images folder, resize the logo to approximately two inches high and wide, and then center it. Click the Resample button on the Pictures toolbar to make the logo's size in pixels match its current display size. Change the logo so that its background is transparent. One space to the right of the logo, enter the company's name (Security Shredding, Inc.), and then format it using the Heading 2 style. On a new line below the heading, insert the company's mailing address, phone number, fax number, and a mailto with the company's e-mail address using the following information: P.O. Box 20996, Austin, TX 78716-0996,

Phone 512-555-1104, Fax 512-555-0922, mail@securityshreddinginc.com. Format the company's information as centered, 10-point, Arial font. Finally, insert a horizontal line below the address information.

7. Edit the link bar in the left shared border so that all pages in the Web site include links to child pages and to the parent page. Format the links using the page's theme. Verify that the top shared border contains only the items that you added in Step 6, and then save the home page. Save the **logo.gif** file that you added to the top shared border in the _borders folder of the Web site.

8. Create appropriate META description and keywords tags for the home page, and then save the home page.

9. Insert the **paper.jpg** picture from the Web site's images folder between the first and second paragraphs of the home page. Center the picture, resize it to approximately 4 inches high and wide, resample the picture, and increase its brightness by clicking the appropriate toolbar button once. Add the alternative text "Paper Shredding" to the picture. Save the page, overwriting the existing picture in the images folder.

10. Create a cascading style sheet using the filename **styles** and the title "Styles." Create a user-defined style that changes the Heading 1 style to use a center alignment, then apply the cascading style sheet to all pages in the Web site. Set the properties of the Styles page so that it will not be published with the Web site.

11. Open the 3 S's of Shredding Web page (**what.htm**) in Page view. Change the "The Three S's of Shredding" text to the Heading 1 style, change the "Secure, Smart, Safe" text to the Heading 2 style, and then change the "What to Shred" text in the first column of the table to bold, navy, 12-point, Arial font.

12. Change the 3 S's of Shredding Web page so that the right column in the table uses a customized, light yellow background color. Change the left column in the table to use a customized, light blue background color. Make sure to select colors that maintain the readability of the table's data.

13. Change the heading "Secure, Smart, Safe" in the 3 S's of Shredding Web page to use an animation effect of your choice that draws attention to these three words when the page is loaded. Save the page and close the DHTML Effects toolbar.

14. Open each of the remaining pages in the Web site and review the contents. For each page, except for the 3 S's of Shredding Web page (**what.htm**), format lists using bullets and headings with the Heading 1 style. Insert at least one picture from the Web site's images folder in three different Web pages. Make sure that the pictures relate to the content of the pages in which you insert them. Use alternative text to describe each picture, and resize and resample the pictures as necessary to make them fit well in the pages. Save each page, overwriting the existing pictures in the Web site's images folder.

15. In the E-Mail Web page (**email.htm**), change the four names listed in the page to mailtos. The e-mail addresses are the person's name in all lowercase letters, with no spaces, followed by the domain securityshreddinginc.com. (*Hint:* In the Insert Hyperlink dialog box, click the E-mail Address button on the Link to bar to create the mailtos.) Save the page.

16. If necessary, save any Web pages, and then preview the entire Web site using the browser to confirm that the pictures, links, and lists are working as expected. Close the browser.

17. Apply an appropriate theme to the entire Web site.

18. In Navigation view, add a new Web page to the right of the 3 S's of Shredding Web page using the title "Search" and filename **search**. Next, open the Search Web page in Page view, and add a title with the Heading 1 style and a search component with the default settings. Make sure that the new page uses the Web site's shared borders and is linked to the cascading style sheet. Add text to the Search Web page that describes how to use the search component.

19. On a new line below the search component in the Search Web page, insert a search the Web component. Add instructions for using this component to the page, and then save it.

20. Open the Pickup Request Web page (**pickup.htm**) in Page view. Insert a form component in the page, and then cut and paste the information that appears below the first paragraph in the page into the form component. Choose the option to keep the source formatting. Use the existing labels in the page to create appropriate form fields to store the data that the form will collect. (Hint: The labels in the first part of the form component are stored in a table with invisible borders. Create the form field for each label in the same row and in the second column.) Change the default form field settings to use appropriately sized form fields and meaningful names. Set validation criteria for form fields that require it. Save the form's results as comma-delimited text in a file named **pickup.txt** in the _private folder of the Web site. In addition, save the date and time that the form was submitted to the server using a date and time format of your choice. Save the Pickup Request Web page, and then open the page in a browser and submit one form to the server. (Use your name as the client's name.) Print the confirmation page that appears, and then close the browser.

21. Add a hit counter to the home page with your choice of specifications, location, and style. Save the home page.

22. Change the filename of the Recycling Program Web page to **recycle.htm**.

23. Use the Discussion Web Wizard to add a discussion group to the current Web site. Construct the discussion group as follows:
    a. Include all of the main features (Submission Form, Table of Contents, Search Form, Threaded Replies, and a Confirmation Page).
    b. The title of the discussion group is Security Shredding Discussion. The discussion folder name is _disc.
    c. Choose the subject and comments input fields for the Submission Form.
    d. The discussion group is protected.
    e. Sort the messages in order from newest to oldest.
    f. Do not replace the existing home page in the Web site.
    g. The Search Form should report only the subject for matching documents.
    h. Use a dual interface frames page.

24. Add the Security Shredding Discussion Welcome page (**disc_welc.htm**) to Navigation view as a child page of the home page, positioning the **disc_welc.htm** page as the first page on the left. Change the title of this page to "Discussion Group."

25. Open the Discussion Group Web page in a browser, and then post a new article to the Web site and refresh the main page. All managers at Security Shredding will be authorized users, and they will use this discussion group for internal communications. (The Contents page will not display your name because your discussion group does not have any registered users. Registered names are automatically added to the Contents page when registered users post messages.) Close your browser.

26. Mary wants to store information from the pickup form in an Access database instead of storing it in a file on the server. Import the **shred** database from the AddCase1 folder into the **shred** Web site. Use the database connection name "Shred" and store all database files in the fpdb folder of the Web site. Change the Web site's settings to display hidden folders, and then verify the database connection.

27. Change the form component in the Pickup Web page (**pickup.htm**) to send its results to the **shred** database in the fpdb folder of the Web site. Set the form fields so that their data will be stored in the correct field in the **Results** table of the **shred** database. Do not save any additional fields.

28. Save the Pickup Request Web page, and then preview and refresh it in the browser. Submit a form to the server, using your name as the client name. Print the confirmation page that appears, and then close the browser.

29. Open the **shred** database from FrontPage, run the **Results Query**, and then confirm that the form handler correctly stored the record that you added in Step 28. Close Access.

30. Create a new page in Page view with the title "Pickup Information" and the filename **pickinfo.asp**. Change the setting for the Pickup Information page to exclude it when the Web site is published. Add a heading with the Heading 1 style at the top of the page using the text "Pickup Information." Link this page to the Styles cascading style sheet, and make sure that the page uses the Web site's shared borders. On a new line below the heading, create a Database Results region that displays the records from the **Results Query** in the **shred** database. Include all fields from the query, accept the default formatting options, and display all records together. After inserting the Database Results region in the Web page, change the column headings to more meaningful names, and then apply the Heading 5 style to these headings and center them. Save the page, and then preview it in the browser. Close the browser.

31. Recalculate the hyperlinks in the Web site, verify all hyperlinks in the Web site, and then run a Site Summary report. Correct any errors that are listed in Reports view. (*Note:* Ignore broken links to discussion group files and to the **disc_post.htm** page.)

32. Use the browser to thoroughly test the Web site. Print any pages as requested by your instructor.

33. Use Reports view to print a workflow report that shows only those pages with a "Don't Publish" status. (*Hint:* Choose the Publish Status report, click the list arrow for the Publish column, and then click Don't Publish.) Use WordPad to print the report; do not save the WordPad document.

34. Close the browser, the **shred** Web site, and FrontPage.

OBJECTIVES

In this case you will:

- Create a new Web site, import pages into it, and change the Web folder's settings

- Create a Web site's navigation structure using Navigation view

- Add and format shared borders in a Web site

- Add pictures to Web pages and create a Photo Gallery

- Apply a customized theme to a Web site

- Create a form component in a Web page

- Import a database into a Web site

- Create and format Active Server Pages

- Create spreadsheet and chart components in a Web page

CREATING
A WEB SITE FOR
PET ADOPTION
SERVICES, INC.

CASE

Pet Adoption Services, Inc.

Pet Adoption Services, Inc., is a not-for-profit organization that cares for lost, abandoned, and neglected dogs and cats in its shelters located throughout the United States. Pet Adoption Services finds caring homes for all healthy, nonaggressive pets brought to its shelters. The organization provides affordable veterinary services through its shelters, and all adopted pets must be neutered before leaving a shelter. To make its clinics more affordable for the entire community, Pet Adoption Services relies on time donations from local veterinarians.

Until recently, Pet Adoption Services has relied on radio advertising to communicate information about its pet adoption weekends across the country. Community reaction to these adoption events has been overwhelming. Madison Somero, president of Pet Adoption Services, has received feedback from many shelter directors indicating the need for a Web site. The center directors want to include a Web page for each pet offered for adoption in the weekend events. Madison wants the Web site to have a home page, a Dogs page, and a Cats page. Child pages of the Dogs and Cats pages will include brief descriptions of each pet available for adoption, along with each pet's photograph.

Because Pet Adoption Services is a not-for-profit organization, it relies heavily on the generosity of the community to ensure that each animal receives the proper care. Madison wants to include a Guest Book page in the Web site to collect information about potential donors of cash, food, and time. She hopes that the Web site will attract many donors, including veterinarians who will offer their services for free and provide inexpensive vaccines and medications. Because she hopes to collect a lot of information using the Guest Book page, Madison wants to use a form that sends its results to an Access database. She wants to view the data in the database using an Active Server Page and a data access page. In addition, she wants to create a Web page that shows the dollar amounts for donations received over the past four years by donation category.

Finally, Madison wants the Web site to have a consistent, professional appearance. She asks you to use the pages that she created and stored in the AddCase2 folder on your Data Disk to begin work on the new Web site.

If necessary, start FrontPage, insert your Data Disk in the appropriate disk drive, and then do the following:

1. Read all the questions for this case problem, and then prepare a planning analysis sheet for the Pet Adoption Services Web site.

2. Prepare a Web site plan that shows the desired Web pages and the expected hyperlinks from the home page.

3. Use the Import Web Wizard to import all of the files except for **pets.mdb** from the AddCase2 folder on your Data Disk into a new Web site named **pets**. Save the Web site on the server. After creating the Web site, make sure that it is enabled for Active Server Pages, ActiveX controls, and the FrontPage Server Extensions.

4. Use drag and drop to move all picture files into the Web site's images folder.

5. Use Navigation view to create the Web site's navigation structure. The **dogs.htm**, **cats.htm**, and **guest.htm** pages are child pages of the home page. The following are child pages of the **cats.htm** page: **buster.htm**, **phoebe.htm**, **razz.htm**, **tex.htm**, and **zoe.htm**. The following are child pages of the **dogs.htm** page: **chance.htm**, **maple.htm**, **rocky.htm**, **scout.htm**, and **spike.htm**.

6. Add a top shared border to all pages in the Web site that includes a centered page banner, and add a left shared border to all pages in the Web site that includes a link bar with links to child pages, the home page, and the parent page. Change the link bar style to use the page's theme.

7. In each of the 10 pet pages, insert the pet's picture on a new centered line below the pet's description. The filename of the picture is the same as the Web page's filename, except that it begins with "p_". (All picture files are saved in the Web site's images folder.) For each picture, add alternative text using the pet's name. Save and close each page.

8. Open the **dogs.htm** page in Page view. On a new line below the italicized text at the top of the page, insert a Photo Gallery. Choose the Montage layout. Insert each dog's picture (Chance, Maple, Rocky, Scout, and Spike) in the Photo Gallery, use the font formatting from the page, and enter the dog's name as the caption. Center the Photo Gallery component, and then save the page.

9. Open the **cats.htm** page in Page view. On a new line at the top of the page (but not in the top shared border), insert a Photo Gallery. Choose the Montage layout. Insert each cat's picture (Buster, Phoebe, Razz, Tex, and Zoe) in the Photo Gallery, use the font formatting from the page, and enter the cat's name as the caption. Center the Photo Gallery component, and then save the page.

10. Create META description and keywords tags for the home page, and then save the home page.

11. Apply a customized version of the Edge theme to the entire Web site. The theme should use vivid colors, active graphics, and a background picture. (If you do not have the Edge theme, select another theme.) Before applying the theme, change the body

font to MS Sans Serif, and then change the font for the page banner, vertical navigation buttons, and horizontal navigation buttons to Arial Narrow. Save the new theme using the name "Pets"; apply the Pets theme to all pages in the Web site.

12. Open the **guest.htm** page in Page view. Insert a form component in the page, and then cut and paste the existing form field labels from the page into the form component. Choose the option to keep the source formatting. (*Hint:* The labels for some of the form fields are stored in a table; make sure that you paste the entire table into the form component.) Create appropriate form fields; for those labels stored in the table, create the form field in the same row and in the second column. Rename the form fields to have meaningful names, and set each form field to store an appropriate number of characters. Define any necessary validation criteria to ensure that the user enters data correctly. Change the Submit and Reset buttons to have more meaningful form field names and the labels to "Submit Form" and "Clear Form," respectively. Save the Web page.

13. Import the **pets** database from the AddCase2 folder into the **pets** Web site. Use the database connection name "Pets," and store all database files in the fpdb folder of the Web site. Change the Web site's settings to display hidden folders, and then verify the database connection.

14. Change the form component in the Guest Book Web page (**guest.htm**) to send its results to the **Guest** table in the **pets** database that is stored in the fpdb folder of the Web site. Set the form fields so that their data is stored in the correct field in the **Guest** table. Do not save any additional fields. Save the page.

15. In Navigation view, create a new child page of the home page using the title "Guest Book Info." Open the Guest Book Info page in Page view. Change to Folders view, and then change the page's filename to **gst_info.asp**.

16. Enter the following description at the top of the Guest Book Info Web page: "This page displays data collected from the Guest Book Web page and stored in the Pets database." On the next line, insert a Database Results region that displays the records from the **Guest Book Query** in the **pets** database. Change the Database Results region so that it displays fields from the **Guest Book Query** in the following order: LastName, FirstName, EmailAddress, Address, City, State, Zip, HomePhone, WorkPhone, Extension, CashDonor, FoodDonor, TimeDonor, and ContactMe. Sort the fields in ascending order using the LastName field. Change the message that is displayed when no records are returned to "There are no records in the database matching your request." Use the default formatting options, and split records into groups containing 10 records each.

17. Change the column headings in the Database Results region in the Web page to more meaningful names, change the headings for the LastName, FirstName, EmailAddress, HomePhone, WorkPhone, CashDonor, FoodDonor, TimeDonor, and ContactMe columns to be displayed on two lines (use Shift + Enter to create the second line), and then change the Extension column heading to "Ext." Select the database fields (the row between the start and end of the Database Results region), and then change their font size to 10 points.

18. Change the Database Results region to use the Grid 3 Table AutoFormat style. (*Hint:* Click anywhere in the Database Results region, display the Tables toolbar, and then set the Table AutoFormat. When you're finished, close the Tables toolbar.)

19. Set the Guest Book Info Web page so that it does not use the Web site's left shared border and will not be published with the Web site. Save the page.

20. Open the Guest Book Web page (**guest.asp**) in the browser, and then complete the form using data that you make up and submit it to the server. Use the Home hyperlink

in the Guest Book Web page to open the home page, and then click the Guest Book Info link to open that page. Verify that the record you entered into the database is displayed in the Guest Book Info Web page. (*Note:* You might need to scroll the page to the right to see all of the columns.) Close the browser.

21. Open the **pets** database from FrontPage, and then use a Wizard to create a data access page based on the **Guest** table. Include all fields in the page, do not use a grouping level, sort the records in ascending order by LastName, and change the default title to "Guest Book Data Access Page."

22. Enter the title "Guest Book Data Access Page" at the top of the new data access page, and then save this page as **gst_dap** in the root folder of the **pets** Web site. Close Access.

23. Open the Guest Book Data Access Page (**gst_dap.htm**) in Page view. Apply the Blank theme to this page only, selecting the options to use vivid colors, active graphics, and a background picture. Change the settings to exclude the page when the Web site is published. Save the page, and then preview it in the browser. Use the data access page to add a new record to the database using real or fictitious data. (*Hint:* Enter the value "Yes" or "No" for the CashDonor, FoodDonor, TimeDonor, and ContactMe fields.) Print the new record, and then close the browser.

24. Create a new Web page in Page view with the title "Donation Data" and the filename **donation.htm**. Add the page to the Web site's navigation structure as a child page of the home page, positioning it to the right of the Guest Book Info page.

25. On the first line of the Web page, enter the following paragraph: "The following spreadsheet shows the total value of donations received by Pet Adoption Services, Inc. for food, cash, veterinary services, vaccinations, and medications. Veterinary services, vaccinations, and medications are valued at the market rate in the community in which they were donated."

26. On a new centered line, insert a spreadsheet component. Enter the data shown in the figure below into the spreadsheet component. Format the column headings (B1:F1) as centered, bold, 10-point, Arial font. Format the row headings (A2:A7) as left-aligned, bold, 10-point, Arial font. Format numeric data as currency. Change the color of the "Totals" and "Grand Totals" headings to red.

	1999	2000	2001	2002	Grand Totals
Food Donations	84,511	95,842	152,132	189,665	
Cash Donations	102,465	118,549	187,456	254,139	
Veterinary Services	167,995	145,884	159,643	162,513	
Vaccinations	94,123	89,569	88,641	87,035	
Medications	54,216	26,843	15,469	38,654	
Totals					

27. Use the AutoSum button on the spreadsheet component toolbar to create totals in the appropriate cells. (*Hint:* Enter the SUM function in cell F2, and then copy and paste cell F2 into cells F3:F7. Next, enter the SUM function in cell B7, and then copy and paste cell B7 into cells C7:E7.)

28. Resize the columns containing data to their best fit, and then resize the spreadsheet component to display only those rows and columns containing data.

29. On a new centered line below the spreadsheet component, insert a chart component. Use the data range A1:E6, the series in columns, the Column chart type, and the Clustered Column subtype. Add the title "Donation Data" to the chart component. Format the title using 24-point, bold, Arial font. Add a legend to the chart component, and then save the page.

30. Recalculate the hyperlinks in the Web site, verify all hyperlinks in the Web site, and then run a Site Summary report. Correct any errors that are listed in Reports view. (*Note:* Ignore any broken links to missing component files in the **gst_dap.htm** and **donation.htm** pages.)

31. If you have the necessary authorization to do so, set permissions for the **pets** Web site so that you are the administrator, and then add one other user to the Web site as an author. (*Note:* If you cannot change the permissions for a Web site, skip this step.)

32. Save all pages in the Web site as necessary, and then use the browser to thoroughly test the Web site. Print any pages as requested by your instructor.

33. Close the browser, the **pets** Web site, and FrontPage.

In this case you will:

- Use the Import Web Wizard to create a new Web site

- Add a shared border to all pages in a Web site

- Create a new frames page in a Web site and set it to open existing pages

- Animate text in a Web page

- Create hyperlinks to new and existing pages

- Add pictures to Web pages using absolute positioning

- Create META tags for a Web page

- Apply a theme to a Web site

- Create hover buttons in a Web page

- Search for information using a browser

- Create a form component and set it to send results to a database

- Create an Active Server Page in a Web site

- Create a site map

- Check the spelling in a Web site

CREATING
A WEB SITE FOR MARTY SHARIK, REALTOR

CASE

Marty Sharik, Realtor

Marty Sharik has been an independent realtor in West Lafayette, Indiana, for more than 25 years. In the past, he has relied on personal and professional referrals as his primary source of listings for residential properties. He has consistently been one of the top agents in West Lafayette.

Recently, Marty began worrying about competitors who were getting new listings from people who normally would work with him. He soon discovered that these agents had Web sites that promoted listings in West Lafayette. Each of these realtors used a Web site to promote his or her services to people moving to West Lafayette and its surrounding areas. When a potential homebuyer indicated an interest in a certain type of neighborhood, the agent could respond immediately with information about listings, the community, and relocation assistance.

Marty has decided to expand his business by creating a Web site that includes information about the community, his services, and his listings in West Lafayette. He wants to include a Web page for each property that he lists. Marty hopes that his new Web site will boost his listings, and that the service he provides will help him to establish relationships with the new residents of his hometown.

If necessary, start FrontPage, insert your Data Disk in the appropriate disk drive, and then do the following:

1. Read all the questions for this case problem, and then prepare a planning analysis sheet for Marty's Web site.

2. Prepare a Web site plan that shows the desired Web pages and the expected hyperlinks from the home page.

3. Use the Import Web Wizard to import all of the files that are saved in the AddCase3 folder on your Data Disk into a new Web site named **marty**. Save the Web site on the server. After creating the Web site, make sure that it is enabled for Active Server Pages, ActiveX controls, and the FrontPage Server Extensions.

4. Use drag and drop to move all picture files into the Web site's images folder.

5. Add a bottom shared border to all pages in the Web site. Replace the comment text with a left-aligned footer that consists of a copyright symbol and Marty's name on the first line. On the second line, add the text "Last updated" and a date field that indicates when the page was last edited. Format the date to display the day of the week and the full date, with the month spelled out. Format the footer using 10-point, bold, italic, Arial font.

6. Create a new page in the Web site using the Contents frames page template. The frames page should open initially with the **contents.htm** page in the contents frame and the **marty.htm** page in the main frame. Save the frames page using the filename **default.htm** and the title "Marty Sharik." Overwrite the existing file with the same name.

7. Create hyperlinks from the list in the Contents page to open the Marty Sharik page (**marty.htm**), Listings page (**listings.htm**), Relocation Services (**relocate.htm**), About Marty Sharik (**about.htm**), and Information Request (**info.htm**) pages in the main frame.

8. Turn off the display of the bottom shared border in the Contents page, and then save it.

9. Change the text "Over $100 million sold since 1974" in the Marty Sharik page (**marty.htm**) to use an animation effect of your choice. Change the "Marty Sharik" text to a WordArt style of your choice, and then center it. Save the page.

10. Open the Listings page in the frames page using the hyperlink that you created in Step 7. Change the listing number in each row of the table to a hyperlink that opens the Web page with the same title in the main frame. For example, create a hyperlink from the 51642 entry in the first row of the table to the **51642.htm** page in the Web site. Some listings do not have associated Web pages yet. In these cases, create a hyperlink from the listing number, and then use the Create New Document button in the Create Hyperlink dialog box to create the hyperlink and a new Web page at the same time. Choose the option to edit the new page later.

11. Insert each picture file that is stored in the Web site's images folder in the Web page with the same filename. For example, insert the picture file **p_57495.jpg** in the **57495.htm** Web page. Insert each picture on the first line of the Web page, resize the picture to approximately 3 inches wide and high, and then use absolute positioning to position the picture to the right of the first five lines in the Web page. After resizing each picture, click the Resample button on the Pictures toolbar to make its size in pixels match its current display size. If no picture file is available for a Web page that contains a property description, use absolute positioning to position text where the photograph will appear. The text box should tell the Web page user that a photograph is not available. For pages not containing a property description, enter the text "Coming Soon!" on the first line of the page (but not in the bottom shared border).

12. Create META description and keywords tags in the Marty Sharik page (**marty.htm**), and then save the page.

13. Apply a theme of your choice to the entire Web site. Make sure that the theme uses vivid colors, active graphics, and a background picture.

14. Open any Web page that includes a property description. Add a new, centered line below the property description. On the new line, create a hover button that includes the text "Request More Information" and contains a mailto to Marty's e-mail address (marty@martysharikinc.com). (*Hint:* Click the Browse button to the right of the Link to text box in the Hover Button Properties dialog box, and then click the E-mail Address button on the Link to bar.) Use 18-point, bold, yellow, Arial font on the hover button, and complementary colors and a mouse over effect of your choice. Save the page, and then test the hover button in the browser to make sure that you are satisfied with its appearance and to confirm that the mailto works correctly. Close the browser.

15. Copy the hover button that you created in Step 14 and paste it in the same location in the other Web pages that contain property descriptions. Center each hover button in the page. Save each page.

16. Open the Relocation Services Web page (**relocate.htm**) in Page view. Use your Web browser and your Internet connection to search for at least four Web sites that provide information about the community of West Lafayette, Indiana. When you locate an appropriate site, enter its URL in the Web page. Format the list of four hyperlinks as a bulleted list.

17. Open the Information Request Web page (**info.htm**) in Page view. Insert a form component, and then cut and paste the existing form field labels into the form component. Choose the option to keep the source formatting. Convert the form field labels (First Name, Last Name, E-mail Address, Home Phone, and Work Phone) into a table, insert a new column to the right of the existing column, insert the appropriate form fields for each label, change the form field properties as necessary, and create appropriate validation criteria. Format the table so that it has invisible borders and set its width at 100% of the browser window. (*Hint:* After setting the borders to invisible, you might still see the borders in Page view; they will not appear in the browser if you set them correctly.) Save the Web page.

18. Set the form component that you created in Step 17 to store its results in a new Access database. In the Options for Saving Results to Database dialog box, click the Create Database button so that FrontPage will create a database and a **Results** table for you. Do not include any additional fields. Follow the instructions to finish configuring the page, and then verify the database connection. Save the page.

19. Open the Information Request Web page in the browser, and then enter data for three different users. Close the browser.

20. Create a new Web page in Folders view using the filename **inforeq.asp** and the title "Information Request Data." Open the Information Request Data Web page in Page view. Insert a Database Results region in the Web page using the database connection that you created in Step 18. Remove the ID field and the additional fields from the Database Results region, and then sort the records in ascending order by last name. (*Note:* Even though you chose not to create additional fields in the form, FrontPage created a table with these additional fields in the database.) Create a search form in the Web page that lets Marty filter records using the "What can I help you with?" values. Use a formatting option of your choice, and display all records together. After creating the Database Results region and the search form, add instructions above the search form that tell Marty how to use the page. (*Hint:* List the values that Marty can use to filter the Database Results region records.)

21. Assign the Web pages in the Web site that include property descriptions to appropriate categories that you create, and then create a new page in the Web site to serve as a site map. Save this Web page using the filename **site_map.htm** and the title "Site Map." Include descriptive text in the Web page to inform Web site visitors how to use the page. Give an appropriate title to the page and format it using the Heading 1 style. After you save the Site Map page, add it to the frames page to open in the main frame. (*Hint:* Create a link to the Site Map page in the contents frame.)

22. Create a Search Web page in the Web site using a template. After creating the page, delete the placeholder footer text at the bottom of the page, and change the comment component at the top of the page to a "Search" heading. Save the page using the filename **search** and the title "Search."

23. Recalculate the hyperlinks in the Web site, verify all hyperlinks in the Web site, and then run a Site Summary report. Correct any errors that are listed in Reports view. (*Note:* Ignore broken hyperlinks to external URLs and to mailtos.)

24. Perform a spell check of all pages in the Web site and correct any errors that you discover.

25. Save all pages in the Web site as necessary, and then use the browser to thoroughly test the Web site. Print any pages as requested by your instructor.

26. Close the browser, the **marty** Web site, and FrontPage.

importing Web pages, FP 3.44–3.45

common backgrounds, FP 3.04–3.06

into frames pages, FP 4.41–4.42

importing from Web servers, FP 4.03–4.05

Import Web Wizard, FP 7.05–7.06

into Web sites, FP 3.02–3.06

Import Web Wizard, FP 2.08, FP 5.18–5.22, FP 7.04–7.06

Increase Font Size button, FP 2.16

Increase Indent button, FP 2.16

indexes, FP 2.42

indexing Web sites, FP 2.42

initial page(s), setting for frames, FP 4.42–4.43

Initial page option, Frame Properties dialog box, FP 4.47

input

forms for data input. *See* data input forms

Web site development, FP 2.03

Insert Columns button, FP 4.12

Insert Hyperlink dialog box, FP 3.21–3.22

inserting

background pictures, FP 2.29–2.32

Database Results regions in new Web pages, FP 8.13–8.15

data in tables, FP 4.20–4.22

files in Web pages, FP 3.06–3.08

form components in Web pages, FP 6.12–6.14

Office components in Web pages. *See* chart components; Office components; PivotTable list components

pictures in tables, FP 4.25–4.26

pictures in Web pages, FP 2.33–2.36

rows and columns in tables, FP 4.11–4.13

special characters, FP 2.20

table captions, FP 4.26–4.27

Web components into Web pages, FP 6.08–6.09

Insert Rows button, FP 4.12

Insert Table button grid, FP 4.06, FP 4.08

inside tags, FP 1.42

integers, FP 6.23

Internet, FP 1.04. *See also* **World Wide Web**

Internet Explorer, FP 1.05, FP 1.06–1.10

closing, FP 1.25

starting, FP 1.07–1.10

viewing HTML code, FP 1.43–1.44

Internet Information Services (IIS), FP 6.36, FP 6.37–6.38

Internet Protocol (IP) addresses, FP 1.10

Italic button, FP 2.16

J

Joint Photographic Experts Group (JPEG), FP 2.33

converting to GIF, FP 3.27–3.30

Justify button, FP 2.16

L

legends, chart components, FP 9.19

lines, horizontal, FP 2.36–2.37

link(s). *See* **hyperlinks**

link bar(s), FP 1.35, FP 2.12, FP 5.22–5.23

adding to Web pages, FP 2.12–2.13

adding to welcome page, FP 7.44–7.45

FrontPage, FP 2.12

home pages, FP 1.10

revising, FP 5.31–5.34

user-defined, FP 2.12

link bar components, FP 5.22

adding to pages, FP 5.37–5.38

Link Bar Properties dialog box, FP 5.31–5.34

linking. *See also* **hyperlinks**

Web pages to CSSs, FP 9.41–9.43

lists, FP 3.08–3.12

bulleted (unordered), FP 3.09–3.11

definitions, FP 3.08–3.09

TASK	PAGE #	RECOMMENDED METHOD
Access database, import into a FrontPage Web site	FP 8.07	See Reference Window: Importing an Access Database into a Web Site
Access query, open in Query Datasheet view	FP 8.05	Click the Queries object in the Database window, double-click the query name
Access table, open in Table Datasheet view	FP 8.04	Click the Tables object in the Database window, double-click the table name
Access, start and open an existing database	FP 8.03	See Reference Window: Starting Access and Opening an Existing Database
Action, undo previous in a data access page	FP 8.40	Click [icon]
Active Server Page, go to first page in the browser	FP 8.17	Click [icon]
Active Server Page, go to last page in the browser	FP 8.17	Click [icon]
Active Server Page, go to next page in the browser	FP 8.16	Click [icon]
Active Server Page, go to previous page in the browser	FP 8.17	Click [icon]
Active Server Page, save	FP 8.16	Click [icon], type the filename in the File name text box, click the Save as type list arrow, click Active Server Pages, click Save
Alternative text, add to a picture	FP 2.34	See Reference Window: Adding Alternative Text to a Picture
Background color, change for a table or table cell	FP 4.30	See Reference Window: Changing the Background Color or Picture in a Table or Cell
Background color, change for a Web page	FP 2.27	See Reference Window: Changing the Background Color of a Web Page
Background picture, insert in a Web Page	FP 2.30	See Reference Window: Inserting a Background Picture in a Web Page
Background sound, add to a Web Page	FP 2.38	See Reference Window: Adding a Background Sound to a Web page
Background, specify common	FP 3.05	In Page view, click Format, Background, click the Get background information from another page check box, click the Browse button, select the filename of the page to use, click OK
Banner ad, create in a Web page	FP 6.51	See Reference Window: Creating a Banner Ad
Bookmark, create hyperlink to	FP 3.16	See Reference Window: Creating a Hyperlink to a Bookmark

TASK	PAGE #	RECOMMENDED METHOD
Bookmark, create nontext-based	FP 3.19	Click the location to create the bookmark, click Insert, Bookmark, enter the bookmark's name in the Bookmark name text box, click OK
Bookmark, create text-based	FP 3.14	See Reference Window: Creating a Text-Based Bookmark in a Web Page
Border color, change for a table	FP 4.31	See Reference Window: Changing a Table's Border Color
Broken link, update for a picture	FP 3.46	Right-click ⌗, click Picture Properties, click the General tab, click Browse, browse for and double-click the file, click OK
Browser version, specify settings for	FP 7.08	Click Tools, Page Options; click the Compatibility tab; set the browser name, browser version, and server version; select the Internet technologies; click OK
Caption, add to a table	FP 4.26	See Reference Window: Adding a Table Caption
Cascading style sheet, create	FP 9.35	See Reference Window: Creating a Cascading Style Sheet
Categories, create for a Web site	FP 7.12	See Reference Window: Creating Categories and Assigning Pages to Them
Categories report, create	FP 7.10	Click ⌗, click the Report list arrow on the Reporting toolbar, point to Workflow, click Categories
Cell, copy contents into adjacent cells in a column in a table	FP 4.12	Select cell to be copied and cells to copy into, click ⌗
Cell, copy contents into adjacent cells in a row in a table	FP 4.21	Select cell to be copied and cells to copy into, click ⌗
Cell, split in a table	FP 4.15	See Reference Window: Splitting Table Cells
Cells, merge in a table	FP 4.16	See Reference Window: Merging Table Cells
Chart component, create in a Web page	FP 9.11	See Reference Window: Inserting a Chart Component in a Web Page That Contains a Data Source
Check box, add to a form	FP 6.25	Click the desired location, click Insert, Form, Checkbox
Column, delete from a table	FP 4.14	See Reference Window: Selecting and Deleting Rows or Columns in a Table
Column, insert in a table in a Web page	FP 4.13	See Reference Window: Inserting a Column in a Table
Column, resize in a table	FP 4.18	See Reference Window: Resizing a Row or Column in a Table
Column, select in a table	FP 4.14	See Reference Window: Selecting and Deleting Rows or Columns in a Table
Columns, distribute selected evenly in a table	FP 4.20	Click ⌗

TASK	PAGE #	RECOMMENDED METHOD
Columns, resize in a spreadsheet component	FP 9.08	Select the column(s), double-click ✛ on the right edge of a selected column
Data access page, create	FP 8.35	See Reference Window: Creating a Data Access Page
Data labels, add to a chart component	FP 9.20	Select the chart component, click the chart, click 🗎, click 📊
Data, import into a spreadsheet component	FP 9.06	Select the spreadsheet component, click 🗎, click the Import tab, click the Data type list arrow, click file type, click in the URL text box, type the path to the data, click Refresh data from URL at run time or click Import Now
Database connection, verify in a Web site	FP 8.09	See Reference Window: Verifying a Database Connection
Database Results region, insert in a Web page	FP 8.12	See Reference Window: Using the Database Results Wizard to Insert a Database Results Region in a Web Page
Discussion group, create	FP 7.27	See Reference Window: Using the Discussion Web Wizard to Create a Discussion Group
Drop-down box, add to a form	FP 6.17	Click the desired location, click Insert, Form, Drop-Down Box
Embedded file, save with a Web page	FP 2.31	See Reference Window: Saving a Web Page That Contains an Embedded File
File, insert in a Web page	FP 3.06	See Reference Window: Inserting a File in a Web Page
File, move in a Web site using drag and drop	FP 6.53	In Folders view, drag and drop the desired file in the Contents pane to the new folder in the Folder List
Filename, rename in Folders view for a disk-based Web	FP 5.21	See Reference Window: Renaming a Page's Filename and Title in Folders View
Filename, rename in Folders view for a server-based Web	FP 6.57	See Reference Window: Renaming a File in Folders View
Filter, remove in a data access page	FP 8.40	Click 🔽
Folder List, show or hide	FP 1.30	Click 📑
Folders view, change to	FP 1.33	Click 📁
Form component, add to a Web page	FP 6.13	See Reference Window: Creating a Form Component and Adding a Form Field to It
Form component, send results to a database	FP 8.31	See Reference Window: Configuring a Form to Send Results to a Database
Form field properties, change	FP 6.20	Double-click the form field
Form field, validate	FP 6.24	Double-click the form field, click Validate
Form results file, examine contents of	FP 6.48	Open the server-based Web in FrontPage, click the _private folder in the Folder List, double-click the form results file

TASK REFERENCE

TASK	PAGE #	RECOMMENDED METHOD
Form Web page, use	FP 1.22	See Reference Window: Using a Web Page That Contains a Form
Format Painter, use to copy and paste text formatting	FP 2.22	Click the text whose format you want to copy, click ⟨icon⟩, click the text to which to copy the format
Frame, add new to a frames page	FP 4.51	See Reference Window: Adding a New Frame to an Existing Frames Page
Frame, edit size of in a frames page	FP 4.43	Drag a border of the frame to new position
Frames page, create	FP 4.37	See Reference Window: Creating a Frames Page
Frames page, print in Internet Explorer	FP 4.53	Click File, Print, click desired option in the Print frames section, click OK
FrontPage link bar, add to a Web page	FP 5.38	Click in the desired location, click Insert, Navigation, select the link bar options, click OK
FrontPage link bar, revise	FP 5.31	Right-click the link bar component, click Link Bar Properties
FrontPage, start	FP 1.27	Click Start, point to Programs, click Microsoft FrontPage
Heading, create in a Web page	FP 2.17	See Reference Window: Creating a Heading in a Web Page
Help, get in FrontPage	FP 1.45	Type a question in the Ask a Question box, press Enter
Help, get while using a data access page	FP 8.40	Click ⟨icon⟩
Help, get while using an Office component	FP 9.08	Click ⟨icon⟩
Hit counter, create in a Web page	FP 6.49	See Reference Window: Creating a Hit Counter in a Web Page
Horizontal line, add to a Web page	FP 2.36	See Reference Window: Inserting a Horizontal Line and Changing Its Properties
Hotspot, create in a picture	FP 3.31	See Reference Window: Creating a Picture Hotspot (Image Map)
Hotspot, highlight in a picture	FP 3.33	See Reference Window: Highlighting Hotspots on a Picture
Hover button, change characteristics of	FP 5.13	In Page view, right-click the hover button, click Hover Button Properties
Hover button, create	FP 5.09	See Reference Window: Creating a Hover Button in a Web Page
HTML code, view for a frames page in FrontPage	FP 4.40	In Page view, click the Frames Page HTML button
HTML code, view for a No Frames page	FP 4.40	In Page view, click the No Frames button
HTML code, view for a Web page using FrontPage	FP 1.43	In Page view, click the HTML button

TASK REFERENCE

TASK	PAGE #	RECOMMENDED METHOD
HTML code, view for a Web page using Internet Explorer	FP 1.44	Click View, Source
HTML tag, modify style	FP 9.36	Click Format, Style, click the tag in the Styles list, click the Modify button, modify the desired characteristics, click OK
Hyperlink, create to another Web page	FP 3.21	See Reference Window: Creating a Hyperlink to an Existing Web Page
Hyperlink, create using drag and drop	FP 3.23	See Reference Window: Creating a Hyperlink Using Drag and Drop
Hyperlink, follow in Internet Explorer	FP 1.13	Click the hyperlink
Hyperlink, follow in Page view	FP 1.31	Press and hold down the Ctrl key, click the hyperlink
Hyperlinks view, change to	FP 1.36	Click 🔲
Hyperlinks view, print	FP 3.36	In Hyperlinks view, press the Print Screen key, start WordPad, click 🔲 , click 🔲
Hyperlinks, recalculate	FP 6.58	In Hyperlinks view, click Tools, Recalculate Hyperlinks, click the Yes button
Hyperlinks, show or hide to pictures	FP 3.34	In Hyperlinks view, right-click the Contents pane, click Hyperlinks to Pictures
Hyperlinks, verify	FP 6.59	In Reports view, click 🔲 on the Reporting toolbar, click the Start button
Initial page, set for a frame	FP 4.42	Click the Set Initial Page button, double-click the page to use
Internet Explorer, start	FP 1.08	Click 🔲 on the Quick Launch toolbar
Legend, add to a chart component	FP 9.19	Select the chart component, click the General tab, click 🔲
List, create bulleted	FP 3.10	See Reference Window: Creating a Bulleted List
List, create definition	FP 3.08	See Reference Window: Creating a Definition List
List, create nested	FP 3.11	See Reference Window: Creating a Nested List
List, create numbered	FP 3.11	See Reference Window: Creating a Numbered List
Mailto, create	FP 3.25	See Reference Window: Creating a Mailto
Marquee, create in a Web page	FP 2.40	See Reference Window: Creating a Marquee in a Web Page
Message, post to a discussion group	FP 7.32	See Reference Window: Posting a Message to a Discussion Group
Message, reply to in a discussion group	FP 7.36	See Reference Window: Replying to a Message

TASK	PAGE #	RECOMMENDED METHOD
Message, search for in a discussion group	FP 7.38	See Reference Window: Searching a Discussion Group
META tag, insert in a Web page	FP 2.43	See Reference Window: Inserting META Tags in a Web Page
Music, stop playing in Internet Explorer	FP 1.12	Click ⊗
Navigation structure, create	FP 5.23	In Navigation view, drag and drop filenames from the Folder List into the Navigation pane
Navigation view, change to	FP 1.34	Click ▨
Nonprinting characters, show or hide in a Web page	FP 4.10	Click ¶
Office component, resize in Page view	FP 9.09	Select the component, drag a sizing handle
Option button, add to a form	FP 6.15	Click the desired location, click Insert, Form, Option Button
Page banner, create	FP 5.38	See Reference Window: Creating a Page Banner
Page transition, create	FP 5.14	See Reference Window: Applying a Page Transition
Page view, change to	FP 1.29	Click ▤
Permissions, set for a Web site	FP 6.60	Click Tools, Server, Permissions
Photo Gallery, create	FP 5.46	See Reference Window: Creating a Photo Gallery in a Web Page
Photo Gallery, revise	FP 5.49	Right-click the Photo Gallery component, click Photo Gallery Properties
Picture, add to a Web page	FP 2.33	See Reference Window: Adding a Picture to a Web Page
Picture, animate in a Web page	FP 5.15	See Reference Window: Creating Animated Text or Pictures in a Web Page
Picture, bevel	FP 5.05	Click ▨ on the Pictures toolbar
Picture, change color characteristics	FP 5.05	Click ▨ on the Pictures toolbar, click desired option
Picture, change color to transparent	FP 3.30	See Reference Window: Changing a Color in a Picture to Transparent
Picture, convert to another format	FP 3.28	See Reference Window: Converting a Picture to Another Format
Picture, position absolutely in a Web page	FP 7.20	See Reference Window: Inserting Text or a Picture in a Web Page Using Absolute Positioning
Picture, restore all previously applied, unsaved effects	FP 5.05	Click ▨ on the Pictures toolbar

TASK	PAGE #	RECOMMENDED METHOD
Picture, rotate left	FP 5.05	Click ▨ on the Pictures toolbar
Picture, rotate right	FP 5.05	Click ▨ on the Pictures toolbar
PivotTable List component, insert in a Web Page	FP 9.26	See Reference Window: Using Spreadsheet Data in a PivotTable List Component in a Web Page
Program, close	FP 1.25	Click ☒ on the program's title bar
Program window, maximize	FP 1.09	Click ☐ on the program's title bar
Push button, change properties of	FP 6.27	Double-click the push button, change properties, click OK
Record, add to a database table	FP 8.24	Click the Tables object in the Database window, double-click the table name, click ▶✱ , enter the new record
Record, add to a database using a data access page	FP 8.41	See Reference Window: Adding a Record to a Database Table Using a Data Access Page
Record, delete from a table using a data access page	FP 8.40	Display the record, click ▶✕
Record, go to first in a data access page	FP 8.40	Click ◀◀
Record, go to last in a data access page	FP 8.40	Click ▶▶
Record, go to next in a data access page	FP 8.40	Click ▶
Record, go to previous in a data access page	FP 8.40	Click ◀
Record, save in a table using a data access page	FP 8.40	Click ▨
Records, filter by selection in a data access page	FP 8.40	Click in the field to filter, click ▨
Records, sort in ascending order in a data access page	FP 8.40	Click in the field to sort, click ↕↓
Records, sort in descending order in a data access page	FP 8.42	Click in the field to sort, click ↕↓
Repeated hyperlinks, show or hide in Hyperlinks view	FP 1.38	Right-click the Contents pane, click Repeated Hyperlinks
Reports view, change to	FP 1.33	Click ▨
Row, delete from a table	FP 4.14	See Reference Window: Selecting and Deleting Rows or Columns in a Table
Row, insert in a table in a Web page	FP 4.12	See Reference Window: Inserting a Row in a Table

TASK	PAGE #	RECOMMENDED METHOD
Row, resize in a table	FP 4.18	See Reference Window: Resizing a Row or Column in a Table
Row, select in a table	FP 4.14	See Reference Window: Selecting and Deleting Rows or Columns in a Table
Rows, distribute selected evenly in a table	FP 4.12	Click ▣
Save Results component, configure	FP 6.28	Right-click in the form component, click Form Properties
Search component properties, change	FP 6.06	Right-click in the search component, click Search Form Properties
Search form, add to an Active Server Page	FP 8.19	See Reference Window: Creating a Search Form in a Web Page That Queries a Database
Search Web page, use	FP 1.20	See Reference Window: Using a Search Web Page
Shared border, edit	FP 5.30	In Page view, click the shared border to select it, make changes
Shared border, turn off for a Web page	FP 5.37	See Reference Window: Turning Off Shared Borders for a Single Web Page
Shared borders, create for a Web site	FP 5.26	See Reference Window: Turning on Shared Borders for a Web Site
Shared template, save in a Web site	FP 7.22	See Reference Window: Saving a Shared Template
Site map, create	FP 7.13	See Reference Window: Creating a Site Map
Source control, disable	FP 7.18	Click Tools, Web Settings, click the General tab, click the Use document check-in and check-out check box to clear it, click OK, click Yes
Source control, enable for a Web site	FP 7.16	See Reference Window: Enabling and Using Source Control for a Web Site
Special character, insert in a Web page	FP 2.20	Click the desired location, click Insert, click Symbol, select the desired character, click the Insert button, click the Close button
Spreadsheet component, insert in a Web page	FP 9.04	See Reference Window: Inserting and Using a Spreadsheet Component in a Web Page
Subweb, create new and import pages into	FP 5.19	See Reference Window: Using the Import Web Wizard to Create a Subweb
Table, align in a Web page	FP 4.11	See Reference Window: Aligning a Table in a Web Page
Table, apply an AutoFormat to	FP 4.28	See Reference Window: Applying a Table AutoFormat
Table, create in a Web page	FP 4.08	See Reference Window: Creating a Table in a Web Page
Table, create nested	FP 4.22	See Reference Window: Creating a Nested Table

TASK	PAGE #	RECOMMENDED METHOD
Target frame, specify	FP 4.45	Click ⬛, click the Target Frame button, select the target frame, click OK, click OK
Task history, show or hide	FP 3.47	Right-click in the Tasks pane, click Show Task History
Task, add in Tasks view	FP 3.42	See Reference Window: Adding a Task in Tasks View
Task, change in Tasks view	FP 3.43	Double-click the task, change the settings, click OK
Task, delete from the Tasks list	FP 3.47	See Reference Window: Deleting a Task from the Tasks List
Task, mark as completed	FP 3.46	See Reference Window: Marking a Task as Completed
Tasks list, sort	FP 3.43	In Tasks view, click the column heading on which to sort
Tasks view, change to	FP 1.39	Click ⬛
Text area, add to a form	FP 6.21	Click the desired location, click Insert, Form, Text Area
Text box, add to a form	FP 6.20	Click the desired location, click Insert, Form, Textbox
Text, add over a picture	FP 5.06	See Reference Window: Adding Text Over a Picture
Text, align in a Web page	FP 2.18	See Reference Window: Aligning Text in a Web Page
Text, animate in a Web page	FP 5.15	See Reference Window: Creating Animated Text or Pictures in a Web Page
Text, change color of selected in a Web page	FP 2.21	Click the list arrow for ⬛, click desired color
Text, change font of selected in a Web page	FP 2.19	Click the Font list arrow, click new font name
Text, change selected to bold	FP 2.21	Click **B**
Text, change selected to italic	FP 2.19	Click *I*
Text, change selected to underlined	FP 2.16	Click U̲
Text, change size of for selected in a Web page	FP 2.20	Click the Font Size list arrow, click the desired font size
Text, find and replace in a Web site	FP 6.54	Click Edit, Replace, specify the text to find in the Find what text box, specify the text to replace it with in the Replace with text box, click the Find In Web button
Text, find in Web site	FP 6.54	Click Edit, Find, specify the text in the Find what text box, click the Find Next button
Text, position absolutely in a Web page	FP 7.20	See Reference Window: Inserting Text or a Picture in a Web Page Using Absolute Positioning
Theme, add to a Web site	FP 5.41	See Reference Window: Applying a Theme to a Web Site
Theme, change attributes of	FP 5.44	Click Format, Theme, change attributes, click OK

TASK	PAGE #	RECOMMENDED METHOD
Theme, customize	FP 5.45	Click Format, Theme, click the Modify button, change the desired settings, click OK, click OK
Thumbnail picture, create	FP 5.03	See Reference Window: Creating a Thumbnail Picture
Title, add to a chart component	FP 9.17	Select the chart component, click 🖼, click the General tab, click 🔳
Title, rename in Folders view	FP 5.21	See Reference Window: Renaming a Page's Filename and Title in Folders View
Title, rename in Navigation view	FP 5.25	See Reference Window: Renaming a Page's Title in Navigation View
Toolbar, show or hide	FP 1.34	Click View, Toolbars, click the name of toolbar to show or hide
Views bar, show or hide	FP 1.31	Click View, Views Bar
Web page, add to navigation structure	FP 5.35	See Reference Window: Adding a New Page in Navigation View
Web page, check in	FP 7.17	Close the Web page in Page view, right-click the Web page in Folders view, click Check In
Web page, check out	FP 7.17	Double-click the page name in Folders view, click Yes
Web page, check spelling in	FP 2.11	See Reference Window: Spell Checking a Web Page
Web page, close in Page view	FP 2.14	Click ✖ in the Contents pane
Web page, create new and add to the Tasks list	FP 3.38	See Reference Window: Creating a New Web Page and Adding It to the Tasks List
Web page, delete from navigation structure	FP 5.34	See Reference Window: Deleting a Page from the Navigation Structure
Web page, import from a Web server	FP 4.03	See Reference Window: Importing a Web Page from a Web Server
Web page, import into a Web site	FP 3.03	See Reference Window: Importing an Existing Web Page into a Web Site
Web page, link to a cascading style sheet	FP 9.42	Click Format, Style Sheet Links, click the Selected page(s) option button, click the Add button, double-click the style sheet's filename, click OK
Web page, preview in browser	FP 1.32	Click 🔍
Web page, preview using FrontPage	FP 1.31	In Page view, click the Preview button
Web page, print using FrontPage	FP 2.25	Click 🖨
Web page, print using Internet Explorer	FP 1.25	Click 🖨

TASK	PAGE #	RECOMMENDED METHOD
Web page, save as a cascading style sheet	FP 9.41	Click 🖫, click the Change title button, enter the page's title, click OK, click the Save as type list arrow, click HyperText Style Sheet, enter the page's filename in the File name text box, click Save
Web page, save in Page view	FP 2.14	See Reference Window: Saving a Web Page
Web page, scroll to bottom	FP 1.15	Press Ctrl + End
Web page, scroll to top	FP 2.21	Press Ctrl + Home
Web page, test	FP 2.23	See Reference Window: Testing a Web Page
Web site, close in FrontPage	FP 1.39	Click File, Close Web
Web site, create new	FP 2.07	Click Empty Web in the Task Pane, click the template or Wizard to use to create the Web site, enter the Web site's name in the Specify the location of the new web text box, click OK
Web site, display hidden folders	FP 7.39	See Reference Window: Displaying a Web Site's Hidden Folders and Files
Web site, open existing from server	FP 7.28	Click the list arrow for 📂, click Open Web, click the My Network Places button, double-click the Web server, click the Web site folder, click Open
Web site, open using FrontPage	FP 1.26	See Reference Window: Opening a Web Site
Web site, open using Internet Explorer	FP 1.11	See Reference Window: Opening a Web Site in Internet Explorer
Web site, publish	FP 6.39	See Reference Window: Publishing a Web Site to Your Computer's Server
Web site, publish changed pages	FP 6.43	See Reference Window: Publishing Changes to a Server-Based Web Site
Web site, set to run scripts	FP 8.11	See Reference Window: Setting a Web Site to Run Scripts
WordArt object, create	FP 5.51	See Reference Window: Creating a WordArt Object in a Web Page
WordArt object, revise selected	FP 5.53	Click 🖎 on the WordArt toolbar

Standardized Coding Number	Certification Skill Activity — Activity	Tutorial Pages	End-of-Tutorial Practice — Exercise	Step Number
FP2002-1	**Creating and Modifying Web Sites**			
FP2002-1-1	Create and manage a FrontPage web	2 (2.06–2.09)	Case Problem 1 Case Problem 2 Case Problem 3 Case Problem 4	1–3 1–3 1–3 1–3
FP2002-1-2	Create and Preview web pages	3 (3.38–3.42)	Case Problem 1 Case Problem 2 Case Problem 3 Case Problem 4	13 17 16 3
FP2002-1-3	Open, view, and rename web pages	1 (1.26–1.28, 1.30-1.31) 5 (5.21, 5.25, 5.35–5.36)	1: Review Assignment Case Problem 1 5: Review Assignment Case Problem 3	11, 13, 14 13 8 4
FP2002-1-4	Rename a web page	5 (5.21, 5.25, 5.35–5.36) 6 (6.56–6.57)	5: Review Assignment Case Problem 3 6: Case Problem 1	8 4 11
FP2002-1-5	Change the title for a web page on banners and buttons	5 (5.21, 5.25, 5.35– 5.36)	5: Review Assignment Case Problem 3	8 4
FP2002-2	**Importing Web Content**			
FP2002-2-1	Insert text and images	2 (2.09–2.11, 2.33–2.35) 3 (3.06–3.07)	2: Case Problem 1 Case Problem 2 Case Problem 3 Case Problem 4 3: Review Assignment Case Problem 1 Case Problem 2 Case Problem 3	4, 9 4, 11 4, 7 4, 12 3 6 7 6
FP2002-2-2	Insert Office Drawings, AutoShapes, and WordArt	5 (5.50–5.54)	Case Problem 4	6
FP2002-3	**Formatting Web Pages**			
FP2002-3-1	Apply text and paragraph formats	2 (2.15–2.23)	Review Assignment Case Problem 1 Case Problem 2 Case Problem 3 Case Problem 4	3, 4, 6 5–7 5–7, 9 5, 6, 8, 9 5–8
FP2002-3-2	Insert hyperlinks	3 (3.13–3.26)	Review Assignment Case Problem 1 Case Problem 2 Case Problem 3 Case Problem 4	2, 4, 6, 7, 13 7, 10–13, 16 9, 10, 12–17, 19 9-16, 20 3, 4, 9, 10
FP2002-3-3	Insert a date using shared borders	5 (5.31)	Case Problem 2	5

Standardized Coding Number	Certification Skill Activity		Tutorial Pages	End-of-Tutorial Practice	
	Activity			Exercise	Step Number
FP2002-3-4	Create and edit tables		4 (4.05–4.23)	Review Assignment	3, 5, 13
				Case Problem 1	4
				Case Problem 2	4, 8
				Case Problem 3	4, 6
				Case Problem 4	5, 6
FP2002-3-5	Apply web themes		5 (5.40–5.46)	Review Assignment	8
				Case Problem 1	8
				Case Problem 2	8
				Case Problem 4	3
FP2002-4	**Working with Graphic and Dynamic Elements**				
FP2002-4-1	Edit graphic elements		3 (3.27–3.31)	3: Case Problem 1	5
				Case Problem 2	5, 6
				Case Problem 4	7
			5 (5.05-5.07)	5: Review Assignment	3
				Case Problem 1	4
				Case Problem 3	3
FP2002-4-2	Create image maps		3 (3.31–3.33)	Case Problem 2	16
				Case Problem 3	14-17, 20
				Case Problem 4	10
FP2002-4-3	Add a FrontPage component to a web page		2 (2.39–2.42)	2: Case Problem 1	10
				Case Problem 2	12
				Case Problem 3	12
				Case Problem 4	9
			6 (6.08–6.09, 6.48–6.53)	6: Case Problem 1	10
				Case Problem 4	3
FP2002-4-4	Add a Photo Gallery		5 (5.46–5.50)	Case Problem 3	5, 6
FP2002-5	**Organizing and Viewing FrontPage Web Sites**				
FP2002-5-1	Use FrontPage views		1 (1.29–1.39)	1: Review Assignment	13, 14
				Case Problem 1	13
			3 (3.34–3.36)	3: Review Assignment	12
				Case Problem 1	18
				Case Problem 2	22
				Case Problem 3	19
				Case Problem 4	12
FP2002-5-2	Manage web structures		5 (5.22–5.36)	Review Assignment	8
				Case Problem 2	3, 10
				Case Problem 4	5, 7, 8

Standardized Coding Number	Certification Skill Activity Activity	Tutorial Pages	End-of-Tutorial Practice	
			Exercise	Step Number
FP2002-5-3	Organize web files	2 (2.31–2.32)	2: Case Problem 1	12
			Case Problem 2	15
			Case Problem 3	15
			Case Problem 4	15
		6 (6.27–6.30, 6.54–6.56)	6: Case Problem 1	5
			Case Problem 2	3
			Case Problem 3	9
			Case Problem 4	4
FP2002-5-4	Manage tasks	3 (3.37–3.48)	3: Review Assignment	9–11
			Case Problem 1	13, 14, 17
			Case Problem 2	20
			Case Problem 3	18
			Case Problem 4	3, 11
		6 (6.02)	6: Case Problem 1	9
FP2002-6	**Managing Web sites**			
FP2002-6-1	Publish a web page	6 (6.39–6.43)	Case Problem 1	7
			Case Problem 2	6
			Case Problem 3	7
			Case Problem 4	7
FP2002-6-2	Create Custom Reports	1 (1.33–1.34)	1: Review Assignment	13
		6 (6.58–6.59)	6: Review Assignment	7

Standardized Coding Number	Certification Skill Activity — Activity	Tutorial Pages	End-of-Tutorial Practice — Exercise	Step Number
FP2002e-1	**Creating and Customizing Web Sites**			
FP2002e-1-1	Modify web page layout	2 (2.15–2.23, 2.27–2.30, 2.33–2.37) 7 (7.20–7.22)	2: Review Assignment Case Problem 1 Case Problem 2 Case Problem 3 Case Problem 4 7: Review Assignment Case Problem 3	2–5 5–10, 13 5–13 5–12, 15 5–13, 15 2, 6 8
FP2002e-1-2	Create Sub webs	5 (5.18–5.21)	\<none\>	
FP2002e-1-3	Manage permissions for subwebs	6 (6.60)	\<none\>	
FP2002e-1-4	Create and apply custom themes	5 (5.40–5.46) 7 (7.45–7.47)	5: Review Assignment Case Problem 1 Case Problem 2 7: Review Assignment Case Problem 2 Case Problem 3	8 8 8 3 8 3
FP2002e-1-5	Customize shared borders	5 (5.22–5.23, 5.25–5.31, 5.37) 7 (7.43–7.44)	5: Review Assignment Case Problem 2 7: Case Problem 1	9 5, 6 8
FP2002e-1-6	Add and modify background images	2 (2.29–2.30) 7 (7.46–7.47)	2: Case Problem 3 Case Problem 4 7: Case Problem 2	10 11 8
FP2002e-2	**Using Navigational Features**			
FP2002e-2-1	Manage the structure of a web	5 (5.23–5.25, 5.34–5.36) 7 (7.13, 7.42)	2: Case Problem 2 Case Problem 4 7: Review Assignment Case Problem 1 Case Problem 2 Case Problem 3 Case Problem 4	3 5 4 5 5, 6 7, 8 5
FP2002e-2-2	Add navigation bars to page banners	5 (5.37–5.39) 7 (7.19, 7.43–7.45)	5: Case Problem 1 7: Review Assignment Case Problem 1 Case Problem 2 Case Problem 4	5 14 6 6 5
FP2002e-2-3	Add link bars	2 (2.12–2.13) 5 (5.37–5.38)	2: Case Problem 1 Case Problem 2 Case Problem 3 Case Problem 4 5: Case Problem 4	6 6 6 6 7, 8

Standardized Coding Number	Certification Skill Activity		End-of-Tutorial Practice	
	Activity	**Tutorial Pages**	**Exercise**	**Step Number**
FP2002e-3	**Customizing Tables**			
FP2002e-3-1	Format tables	4 (4.05–4.20, 4.24–4.27, 4.31–4.32)	Review Assignment Case Problem 1 Case Problem 2 Case Problem 3	3–8 4, 7 5 9
FP2002e-3-2	Split tables	4 (4.15–4.16)	Review Assignment Case Problem 1 Case Problem 4	5 4 3, 5, 6
FP2002e-3-3	Apply table AutoFormats	4 (4.28–4.30)	Case Problem 1 Case Problem 4	5 6
FP2002e-3-4	Nest tables	4 (4.22–4.23)	Case Problem 4	3, 5, 6
FP2002e-4	**Inserting and Modifying FrontPage Components**			
FP2002e-4-1	Add FrontPage components to web pages	2 (2.29–2.42) 5 (5.09–5.12) 6 (6.48–6.50) 7 (7.09–7.15) 9 (9.02–9.07, 9.10–9.16, 9.25–9.31)	2: Case Problem 1 Case Problem 2 Case Problem 3 Case Problem 4 5: Review Assignment Case Problem 1 Case Problem 3 Case Problem 4 6: Case Problem 1 7: Review Assignment Case Problem 3 9: Case Problem 1 Case Problem 2 Case Problem 3 Case Problem 4	10 13 12 9 2, 4, 9 5 7, 8 4 10 7 4–6, 9 3, 7 5, 8 4, 7, 13, 14 5, 6
FP2002e-4-2	Modify component properties	2 (2.29–2.42) 5 (5.12–5.13) 9 (9.07–9.10, 9.17–9.23, 9.31–9.33)	2: Case Problem 1 Case Problem 2 Case Problem 3 Case Problem 4 5: Review Assignment Case Problem 3 9: Review Assignment Case Problem 1 Case Problem 2 Case Problem 3 Case Problem 4	10 13 12 9 4 7, 8 4–11 4–6, 8–10, 13 5–7, 9–11, 13 5, 6, 8, 9, 15, 16 7, 8
FP2002e-5	**Creating Customer and User Feedback Web pages**			
FP2002e-5-1	Create forms for user input	6 (6.09–6.30) 8 (8.27–8.34)	6: Review Assignment Case Problem 1 Case Problem 2	4 4 3, 8

Standardized Coding Number	Certification Skill Activity — Activity	Tutorial Pages	End-of-Tutorial Practice — Exercise	Step Number
			Case Problem 3	4
			Case Problem 4	4
			8: Case Problem 1	4–10
			Case Problem 2	4–10
			Case Problem 3	4–10
FP2002e-5-2	Add search capabilities to web pages	6 (6.03–6.09)	6: Case Problem 1	3
		8 (8.18–8.23)	Case Problem 3	3
			Case Problem 4	3
			8: Review Assignment	3
			Case Problem 1	11, 12
			Case Problem 2	11, 12
			Case Problem 3	11, 12
FP2002e-6	**Integrating Databases**			
FP2002e-6-1	Connect a web site to a database	8 (8.07–8.15)	Case Problem 1	3
			Case Problem 2	3
			Case Problem 3	3
			Case Problem 4	3
FP2002e-6-2	Send form data to Access databases	8 (8.27–8.34)	Case Problem 1	4–10
			Case Problem 2	4–10
			Case Problem 3	4–10
FP2002e-6-3	Add query capabilities to web pages	8 (8.18–8.23)	Review Assignment	3
			Case Problem 1	11, 12
			Case Problem 2	11, 12
			Case Problem 3	11, 12
FP2002e-7	**Using Collaboration Features**			
FP2002e-7-1	Check HTML files in and out	7 (7.15–7.18, 7.28)	<none>	
FP2002e-7-2	Manage web folders	2 (2.40–2.42, 2.46–2.47, 2.51) 7 (7.29, 7.39–7.40, 7.48) 8 (8.07–8.09)	2: Case Problem 1	12
			Case Problem 2	15
			Case Problem 3	15
			Case Problem 4	15
			7: Case Problem 1	3
			Case Problem 2	3
			Case Problem 4	3
			8: Case Problem 1	3
			Case Problem 2	3
			Case Problem 3	3
			Case Problem 4	3
FP2002e-8	**Inserting Frames**			
FP2002e-8-1	Create frames	4 (4.34–4.40, 4.50–4.52) 7 (7.31)	4: Case Problem 1	3
			Case Problem 2	3
			Case Problem 3	3, 11
			Case Problem 4	4

Standardized Coding Number	Certification Skill Activity — Activity	Tutorial Pages	End-of-Tutorial Practice — Exercise	Step Number
			7: Case Problem 1	3
			Case Problem 2	3
			Case Problem 4	3
FP2002e-8-2	Specify target content in frames	4 (4.42, 4.45–4.46)	Case Problem 3	5, 8
			Case Problem 4	9
FP2002e-8-3	Create and customize banners	5 (5.38–5.39) 7 (7.19, 7.44–7.45)	5: Case Problem 2 7: Case Problem 1 Case Problem 2 Case Problem 4	10 6 6 5
FP2002e-9	**Generating Reports**			
FP2002e-9-1	Find broken hyperlinks	6 (6.57–6.59)	Review Assignment Case Problem 1 Case Problem 2 Case Problem 3 Case Problem 4	8 8 7 8 8
FP2002e-9-2	Locate most popular pages	1 (1.33–1.34) 9 (9.04)	<none>	
FP2002e-9-3	Locate problems	6 (6.57–6.59) 7 (7.12)	6: Review Assignment Case Problem 1 Case Problem 2 Case Problem 3 Case Problem 4 7: Case Problem 3	8 6, 8, 12 5, 7 6, 8 6, 8, 12 6
FP2002e-10	**Publishing Web Sites**			
FP2002e-10-1	Publish web sites from one server to another	6 (6.60–6.61)	<none>	
FP2002e-10-2	Use Personal Web Servers	6 (6.36–6.61)	Review Assignment Case Problem 1 Case Problem 2 Case Problem 3 Case Problem 4	1-6 7 6 7–9 7–12
FP2002e-10-3	Publish a site from one location to another	6 (6.60–6.61)	<none>	

FrontPage File Finder

Note: The Data Files supplied with this book and listed in the chart below are starting files for Tutorials 1 and 2. Starting in Tutorial 2, you will begin your work on each subsequent tutorial with the files you created in the previous tutorial. For example, after finishing Tutorial 2, you begin Tutorial 3 with your ending files from Tutorial 2. The Review Assignments and Case Problems also build on the starting Data Files in this way. You must complete each tutorial, Review Assignment, and Case Problem in order and finish them completely before continuing to the next tutorial, or your Data Files will not be correct for the next tutorial.

Note: Please read the "Read This Before You Begin" page on page FP 1.02 for important information about how to store your Data Files.

Tutorial	Location in Tutorial	Name and Location of Data File or Web Site	Files or Web Sites the Student Creates from Scratch
Tutorial 1	Session 1.1	A:\Disk1\MyWebs\SunnyMorningProducts	
	Session 1.2	A:\Disk1\My Webs\SunnyMorningProducts *(continued from Session 1.1)*	
	Session 1.3	A:\Disk1\My Webs\SunnyMorningProducts *(continued from Session 1.2)*	
	Review Assignments	A:\Disk1\My Webs\SunnyMorningProducts *(continued from Session 1.3)*	
	Case Problem 1	A:\Disk1\My Webs\Carpenter	
	Case Problem 2	No Data Files are used in the Case Problem.	
Tutorial 2	Session 2.1	A:\Disk2\Tutorial.02\Home.doc	A:\Disk2\My Webs\Sunny index.htm
	Session 2.2	A:\Disk2\My Webs\Sunny *(continued from Session 2.1)*	
	Session 2.3	A:\Disk2\My Webs\Sunny *(continued from Session 2.2)* A:\Disk2\Tutorial.02\WP53196.gif A:\Disk2\Tutorial.02\SMPLogo.gif A:\Disk2\Tutorial.02\Minuet.mid	
	Review Assignments	A:\Disk2\My Webs\Sunny *(continued from Session 2.3)*	
	Case Problem 1	A:\Disk3\Tutorial.02\Royal.doc A:\Disk3\Tutorial.02\Royal.gif A:\Disk3\Tutorial.02\Quantum.mid	A:\Disk3\My Webs\Royal index.htm
	Case Problem 2	A:\Disk4\Tutorial.02\Buffalo.doc A:\Disk4\Tutorial.02\Buffalo.gif A:\Disk4\Tutorial.02\Cheers.mid	A:\Disk4\My Webs\Buffalo index.htm
	Case Problem 3	A:\Disk5\Tutorial.02\Garden.doc A:\Disk5\Tutorial.02\Garden.gif A:\Disk5\Tutorial.02\WB02245.gif A:\Disk5\Tutorial.02\Casper.mid	A:\Disk5\My Webs\Garden index.htm
	Case Problem 4	A:\Disk6\Tutorial.02*.mid (Student either locates and selects a MIDI or WAV file on his or her own system or else selects a MIDI file from the Data Disk) A:\Disk6\Tutorial.02\WB61689.gif A:\Disk6\Tutorial.02\CD.gif	A:\Disk6\My Webs\Replay index.htm
Tutorial 3	Session 3.1	A:\Disk2\My Webs\Sunny *(continued from Tutorial 2 Review Assignments)* A:\Disk2\Tutorial.03\EmpPage.htm A:\Disk2\Tutorial.03\Customer.doc	
	Session 3.2	A:\Disk2\My Webs\Sunny *(continued from Session 3.1)* A:\Disk2\Tutorial.03\Employ.jpg	Employ.gif
	Session 3.3	A:\Disk2\My Webs\Sunny *(continued from Session 3.2)* A:\Disk2\Tutorial.03\Profile.gif A:\Disk2\Tutorial.03\Up.gif	Company.htm Products.htm Investor.htm
	Review Assignments	A:\Disk2\My Webs\Sunny *(continued from Session 3.3)* A:\Disk2\Tutorial.03\CustMgr.doc A:\Disk2\Tutorial.03\Up.gif A:\Disk2\Tutorial.03\WhatsNew.htm A:\Disk2\Tutorial.03\WhatLogo.gif	

FrontPage File Finder

Tutorial	Location in Tutorial	Name and Location of Data File or Web Site	Files or Web Sites the Student Creates from Scratch
	Case Problem 1	A:\Disk3\My Webs\Royal (continued from Tutorial 2) A:\Disk3\Tutorial.03\RCompany.htm A:\Disk3\Tutorial.03\RoyalHCP.gif A:\Disk3\Tutorial.03\Distrib.doc A:\Disk3\Tutorial.03\Up.gif A:\Disk3\Tutorial.03\RNews.htm A:\Disk3\Tutorial.03\RNewsLog.gif	RNews.htm RFeedbak.htm REmploy.htm
	Case Problem 2	A:\Disk4\My Webs\Buffalo (continued from Tutorial 2) A:\Disk4\Tutorial.03\BHow.htm A:\Disk4\Tutorial.03\BHowLogo.jpg A:\Disk4\Tutorial.03\BWMark.gif A:\Disk4\Tutorial.03\HowWorks.doc A:\Disk4\Tutorial.03\BWho.htm A:\Disk4\Tutorial.03\BWhoLogo.gif	BHowLogo.gif Up.gif BWhat.htm
	Case Problem 3	A:\Disk5\My Webs\Garden (continued from Tutorial 2) A:\Disk5\Tutorial.03\GEmploy.htm A:\Disk5\Tutorial.03\GNavBar.gif A:\Disk5\Tutorial.03\Manager.doc A:\Disk5\Tutorial.03\GBullet.gif A:\Disk5\Tutorial.03\Up.gif A:\Disk5\Tutorial.03\GAbout.htm	GAbout.htm GFeedbak.htm
	Case Problem 4	A:\Disk6\My Webs\Replay (continued from Tutorial 2) A:\Disk6\Tutorial.03\Replay.gif	Students create several new Web pages using filenames of their choice.
Tutorial 4	Session 4.1	A:\Disk2\My Webs\Sunny (continued from Tutorial 3 Review Assignments) http://www.course.com/downloads/newperspectives/fp2002/Investor.htm or A:\Disk2\Tutorial.04\Investor.htm A:\Disk2\Tutorial.04\Invest.gif A:\Disk2\Tutorial.04\FinPerf.gif	
	Session 4.2	A:\Disk2\My Webs\Sunny (continued from Session 4.1) A:\Disk2\Tutorial.04\Banner.htm A:\Disk2\Tutorial.04\Basket.htm A:\Disk2\Tutorial.04\Contents.htm A:\Disk2\Tutorial.04\Drink.htm A:\Disk2\Tutorial.04\Fruit.htm A:\Disk2\Tutorial.04\Ordrform.htm A:\Disk2\Tutorial.04\Ordrinfo.htm A:\Disk2\Tutorial.04\Catalog.gif A:\Disk2\Tutorial.04\Juice.gif	Products.htm
	Review Assignments	A:\Disk2\My Webs\Sunny (continued from Session 4.2) A:\Disk2\Tutorial.04\OrgBack.jpg	Shareholder.* Clothing.htm
	Case Problem 1	A:\Disk3\My Webs\Royal (continued from Tutorial 3) A:\Disk3\Tutorial.04\RStock.htm	RInvest.htm RFinInfo.htm Banner.htm Contents.htm
	Case Problem 2	A:\Disk4\My Webs\Buffalo (continued from Tutorial 3) A:\Disk4\Tutorial.04\BWhatLog.gif A:\Disk4\Tutorial.04\BNavWho.gif A:\Disk4\Tutorial.04\BNavHome.gif A:\Disk4\Tutorial.04\BNavHow.gif A:\Disk4\Tutorial.04\BNavWhre.gif A:\Disk4\Tutorial.04\BNavCon.gif	BWhat.htm Banner.htm Contents.htm Women.htm Children.htm Accessories.htm

FrontPage File Finder

Tutorial	Location in Tutorial	Name and Location of Data File or Web Site	Files or Web Sites the Student Creates from Scratch
	Case Problem 3	A:\Disk5\My Webs\Garden *(continued from Tutorial 3)*	GMenu.htm Contents.htm Appetizers.htm Sandwiches.htm Entrees.htm Desserts.htm Contact.htm
	Case Problem 4	A:\Disk6\My Webs\Replay *(continued from Tutorial 3)*	MSpecials.htm Students will create three new Web pages using filenames of their choice.
Tutorial 5	Session 5.1	A:\Disk2\My Webs\Sunny *(continued from Tutorial 4 Review Assignments)* A:\Disk2\Tutorial.05\Map.gif A:\Disk2\Tutorial.05\MapPage.htm	
	Session 5.2	A:\Disk2\My Webs\Sunny *(continued from Session 5.1)* A:\Disk2\Tutorial.05\Pie.htm A:\Disk2\Tutorial.05\Icing.htm A:\Disk2\Tutorial.05\Cake.htm A:\Disk2\Tutorial.05\Bread.htm A:\Disk2\Tutorial.05\P_Cake.jpg A:\Disk2\Tutorial.05\P_Bread.jpg A:\Disk2\Tutorial.05\P_Pie.jpg A:\Disk2\Tutorial.05\P_Icing.jpg A:\Disk2\Tutorial.05\Recipes.htm	A:\Disk2\My Webs\Sunny\ Recipes cranberry_bread.htm
	Session 5.3	A:\Disk2\My Webs\Sunny *(continued from Session 5.2)* A:\Disk2\My Webs\Sunny\Recipes *(continued from Session 5.2)* A:\Disk2\Tutorial.05\P_Cake.jpg A:\Disk2\Tutorial.05\P_Pie.jpg A:\Disk2\Tutorial.05\P_Bread.jpg A:\Disk2\Tutorial.05\P_Icing.jpg	
	Review Assignments	A:\Disk2\My Webs\Sunny *(continued from Session 5.3)* A:\Disk2\Tutorial.05\Beach.gif A:\Disk2\My Webs\Sunny\Recipes *(continued from Session 5.3)*	hard_candy.htm christmas_candy.htm
	Case Problem 1	A:\Disk3\My Webs\Royal *(continued from Tutorial 4)*	
	Case Problem 2	A:\Disk4\My Webs\Buffalo *(continued from Tutorial 4)* A:\Disk4\Tutorial.05\Bullet.gif	
	Case Problem 3	A:\Disk5\My Webs\Garden *(continued from Tutorial 4)* A:\Disk5\Tutorial.05\US.gif A:\Disk5\Tutorial.05\Italy.gif A:\Disk5\Tutorial.05\Mexico.gif	Specials.htm
	Case Problem 4	A:\Disk6\My Webs\Replay *(continued from Tutorial 4)*	
Tutorial 6	Session 6.1	A:\Disk2\My Webs\Sunny *(continued from Tutorial 5 Review Assignments)* A:\Disk2\Tutorial.06\Search.gif A:\Disk2\Tutorial.06\FormLogo.gif A:\Disk2\Tutorial.06\Feedback.htm	Search.htm
	Session 6.2	A:\Disk2\My Webs\Sunny *(continued from Session 6.1)* A:\Disk2\Tutorial.06\Form.doc	Feedback.txt
	Session 6.3	A:\Disk2\My Webs\Sunny *(continued from Session 6.2)* A:\Disk2\Tutorial.06\Banner1.gif A:\Disk2\Tutorial.06\Banner2.gif	http://localhost/Sunny

FrontPage File Finder

Tutorial	Location in Tutorial	Name and Location of Data File or Web Site	Files or Web Sites the Student Creates from Scratch
	Review Assignments	http://localhost/Sunny *(continued from Session 6.3)* A:\Disk2\Tutorial.06\Banner3.gif	
	Case Problem 1	A:\Disk3\My Webs\Royal *(continued from Tutorial 5)*	RSearch.htm RFeedbak.htm RFeedbak.txt http://localhost/Royal
	Case Problem 2	A:\Disk4\My Webs\Buffalo *(continued from Tutorial 5)* A:\Disk4\Tutorial.06\B_Contac.gif A:\Disk4\Tutorial.06\B_Where.gif	Contact.txt Contact.htm http://localhost/Buffalo Confirm.htm Where.htm
	Case Problem 3	A:\Disk5\My Webs\Garden *(continued from Tutorial 5)*	Search.htm GFeedbak.htm Feedback.txt http://localhost/Garden Feedback.htm FranInfo.htm
	Case Problem 4	A:\Disk6\My Webs\Replay *(continued from Tutorial 5)* A:\Disk6\Tutorial.06\Replay1.gif A:\Disk6\Tutorial.06\Replay2.gif A:\Disk6\Tutorial.06\Replay3.gif	Search.htm Feedback.txt private/Feedback.htm Feedback.htm http://localhost/Replay Confirm.htm FAQ.htm Students will create or import three image files into the Web site for use in a banner ad.

Note: *Please read the "Read This Before You Begin" page on page FP 7.02 for important information about how to store your Data Files and how to install the starting files for Case Problems 1 through 4.*

FrontPage File Finder

Tutorial	Location in Tutorial	Name and Location of Data File or Web Site	Files or Web Sites the Student Creates from Scratch
Tutorial 7	Session 7.1	Import the files b_icing.htm, chifcake.htm, chifpie.htm, default.htm, nut_brd.htm, and site_map.htm from the URL http://www.course.com/dow loads/newperspectives/fp2002 or import those same seven files from A:\Disk1\Tutorial.07 A:\Disk1\Tutorial.07\style.htm	http://localhost/recipes
	Session 7.2	http://localhost/recipes *(continued from Session 7.1)* A:\Disk1\Tutorial.07\netbkgnd.jpg	disc_cfrm.htm disc_frm.htm disc_post.htm disc_srch.htm disc_tocf.htm disc_welc.htm _disc folder with the files 00000001.htm, 00000002.htm, and tocproto.htm _borders folder with the files disc_aftr.htm, disc_ahdr.htm, disc_foot.htm, and disc_head.htm

FrontPage File Finder

Tutorial	Location in Tutorial	Name and Location of Data File or Web Site	Files or Web Sites the Student Creates from Scratch
	Review Assignments	http://localhost/recipes (*continued from Session 7.2*) A:\Disk1\Tutorial.07\c_cake.jpg A:\Disk1\Tutorial.07\pecan_br.htm A:\Disk1\Tutorial.07\org_cake.htm A:\Disk1\Tutorial.07\orgicing.htm A:\Disk1\Tutorial.07\org_pic.jpg	

	Case Problem 1	http://localhost/royal	disc_cfrm.htm
			disc_frm.htm
			disc_post.htm
			disc_srch.htm
			disc_tocf.htm
			disc_welc.htm
			_disc folder with the files
			  00000001.htm,
			  00000002.htm, and
			  tocproto.htm
			_borders folder with the files
			  disc_aftr.htm, disc_ahdr.htm,
			  disc_foot.htm, disc_head.htm,
			  and top.htm

	Case Problem 2	http://localhost/buffalo
		A:\Disk1\Tutorial.07\toptxtr.jpg
			disc_cfrm.htm
			disc_frm.htm
			disc_post.htm
			disc_srch.htm
			disc_tocf.htm
			disc_welc.htm
			_disc folder with the files
			  00000001.htm,
			  00000002.htm, and
			  tocproto.htm
			_borders folder with the files
			  disc_aftr.htm, disc_ahdr.htm,
			  disc_foot.htm, disc_head.htm,
			  and bottom.htm

	Case Problem 3	http://localhost/garden A:\Disk1\Tutorial.07\angel.htm A:\Disk1\Tutorial.07\pasta.htm A:\Disk1\Tutorial.07\pecan.htm A:\Disk1\Tutorial.07\pudding.htm A:\Disk1\Tutorial.07\p_pie.jpg A:\Disk1\Tutorial.07\p_angel.jpg A:\Disk1\Tutorial.07\p_puddng.jpg A:\Disk1\Tutorial.07\p_pasta.jpg	site_map.htm

	Case Problem 4	http://localhost/replay	disc_cfrm.htm
			disc_frm.htm
			disc_post.htm
			disc_srch.htm
			disc_tocf.htm
			disc_welc.htm
			_disc folder with the files
			  00000001.htm and
			  tocproto.htm
			_borders folder with the files
			  disc_aftr.htm, disc_ahdr.htm,
			  disc_foot.htm, disc_head.htm,
			  and top.htm

FrontPage File Finder

Tutorial	Location in Tutorial	Name and Location of Data File or Web Site	Files or Web Sites the Student Creates from Scratch
Tutorial 8	Session 8.1	A:\Disk1\Tutorial.08\recipes.mdb http://localhost/recipes (*continued from Tutorial 7 Review Assignments*)	cust_qry.asp custsrch.asp
	Session 8.2	A:\Disk1\Tutorial.08\guest.mdb http://localhost/recipes (*continued from Session 8.1*) A:\Disk1\Tutorial.08\guest_bk.asp	rslt_dap.htm
	Review Assignments	http://localhost/recipes (*continued from Session 8.2*)	
	Case Problem 1	http://localhost/royal (*continued from Tutorial 7*) A:\Disk1\Tutorial.08\royal.mdb	sendinfo.asp custinfo. asp cust_dap.htm
	Case Problem 2	http://localhost/buffalo (*continued from Tutorial 7*) A:\Disk1\Tutorial.08\buffalo.mdb	mailinfo.asp maillist.asp mail_dap.htm
	Case Problem 3	http://localhost/garden (*continued from Tutorial 7*) A:\Disk1\Tutorial.08\garden.mdb	comments.asp custinfo.asp cust_dap.htm
	Case Problem 4	http://localhost/replay (*continued from Tutorial 7*) A:\Disk1\Tutorial.08\replay.mdb	inv_dap.htm
Tutorial 9	Session 9.1	http://localhost/recipes (*continued from Tutorial 8 Review Assignments*) A:\Disk1\Tutorial.09\activity.htm A:\Disk1\Tutorial.09\openings.htm . A:\Disk1\Tutorial.09\orders.xls	
	Session 9.2	http://localhost/recipes (*continued from Session 9.1*)	specials.css
	Review Assignments	http://localhost/recipes (*continued from Session 9.2*)	
	Case Problem 1	http://localhost/royal (*continued from Tutorial 8*) A:\Disk1\Tutorial.09\rfb_data.htm	sales.htm
	Case Problem 2	http://localhost/buffalo (*continued from Tutorial 8*)	salewkbk.htm styles.css
	Case Problem 3	http://localhost/garden (*continued from Tutorial 8*) A:\Disk1\Tutorial.09\g_data.htm A:\Disk1\Tutorial.09\g_raise.xls	salary.htm raise.htm
	Case Problem 4	http://localhost/replay (*continued from Tutorial 8*) A:\Disk1\Tutorial.09\replay.xls	sls_data.htm

Additional Case 1		A:\Disk2\AddCase1\bales1.jpg
		A:\Disk2\AddCase1\bales2.jpg
		A:\Disk2\AddCase1\cans.jpg
		A:\Disk2\AddCase1\email.htm
		A:\Disk2\AddCase1\exp.htm
		A:\Disk2\AddCase1\index.htm
		A:\Disk2\AddCase1\logo.jpg
		A:\Disk2\AddCase1\paper.jpg
		A:\Disk2\AddCase1\pickup.htm
		A:\Disk2\AddCase1\pricing.htm
		A:\Disk2\AddCase1\secure.htm
		A:\Disk2\AddCase1\security.htm
		A:\Disk2\AddCase1\services.htm
		A:\Disk2\AddCase1\shred.mdb
		A:\Disk2\AddCase1\size.htm
		A:\Disk2\AddCase1\what.htm
			http://localhost/shred
			styles.css
			disc_cfrm.htm
			disc_frm.htm
			disc_post.htm
			disc_srch.htm
			disc_tocf.htm
			disc_welc.htm
			_disc folder with the files
			  00000001.htm and
			  tocproto.htm
			_borders folderwith the files disc_aftr.htm,
			  disc_ahdr.htm, disc_foot.htm,
			  disc_head.htm, top.htm, and left.htm
			pickinfo.asp
			_private\pickup.txt

FrontPage File Finder

Tutorial	Location in Tutorial	Name and Location of Data File or Web Site	Files or Web Sites the Student Creates from Scratch
Additional Case 2		A:\Disk2\AddCase2\buster.htm	http://localhost/pets
		A:\Disk2\AddCase2\cats.htm	donation.htm
		A:\Disk2\AddCase2\chance.htm	gst_dap.htm
		A:\Disk2\AddCase2\default.htm	gst_info.asp
		A:\Disk2\AddCase2\dogs.htm	
		A:\Disk2\AddCase2\guest.htm	
		A:\Disk2\AddCase2\maple.htm	
		A:\Disk2\AddCase2\p_buster.jpg	
		A:\Disk2\AddCase2\p_chance.jpg	
		A:\Disk2\AddCase2\p_maple.jpg	
		A:\Disk2\AddCase2\p_phoebe.jpg	
		A:\Disk2\AddCase2\p_razz.jpg	
		A:\Disk2\AddCase2\p_rocky.jpg	
		A:\Disk2\AddCase2\p_scout.jpg	
		A:\Disk2\AddCase2\p_spike.jpg	
		A:\Disk2\AddCase2\p_tex.jpg	
		A:\Disk2\AddCase2\p_zoe.jpg	
		A:\Disk2\AddCase2\pets.mdb	
		A:\Disk2\AddCase2\phoebe.htm	
		A:\Disk2\AddCase2\razz.htm	
		A:\Disk2\AddCase2\rocky.htm	
		A:\Disk2\AddCase2\scout.htm	
		A:\Disk2\AddCase2\spike.htm	
		A:\Disk2\AddCase2\tex.htm	
		A:\Disk2\AddCase2\zoe.htm	
Additional Case 3		A:\Disk3\AddCase3\51642.htm	http://localhost/marty
		A:\Disk3\AddCase3\57495.htm	default.htm
		A:\Disk3\AddCase3\74862.htm	info.mdb
		A:\Disk3\AddCase3\75436.htm	inforeq.asp
		A:\Disk3\AddCase3\78456.htm	site_map.htm
		A:\Disk3\AddCase3\87462.htm	search.htm
		A:\Disk3\AddCase3\88462.htm	84651.htm
		A:\Disk3\AddCase3\about.htm	87618.htm
		A:\Disk3\AddCase3\contents.htm	
		A:\Disk3\AddCase3\default.htm	
		A:\Disk3\AddCase3\info.htm	
		A:\Disk3\AddCase3\listings.htm	
		A:\Disk3\AddCase3\marty.htm	
		A:\Disk3\AddCase3\p_51642.jpg	
		A:\Disk3\AddCase3\p_57495.jpg	
		A:\Disk3\AddCase3\p_75436.jpg	
		A:\Disk3\AddCase3\p_78456.jpg	
		A:\Disk3\AddCase3\p_87462.jpg	
		A:\Disk3\AddCase3\p_88462.jpg	
		A:\Disk3\AddCase3\relocate.htm	